THE
[INSIDERS']®
→GUIDE←
TO
VIRGINIA'S
Blue Ridge

THE INSIDERS'® GUIDE TO

VIRGINIA'S Blue Ridge

by
Mary Alice Blackwell
and
Lin Chaff

The Insiders' Guide®
An imprint of Falcon® Publishing Inc.
A Landmark Communications company
P.O. Box 1718
Helena, MT 59624
(800) 582-2665
www.insiders.com

•

Sales and Marketing: Falcon Publishing, Inc.
P.O. Box 1718
Helena, MT 59624
(800) 582-2665
www.falcon.com

•

SEVENTH EDITION
1st printing

•

Publications from *The Insiders' Guide®* series are available at special discounts for bulk purchases for sales promotions, premiums or fundraisings. Special editions, including personalized covers, can be created in large quantities for special needs.
For more information, please contact Falcon Publishing.

ISBN 1-57380-127-5

Preface

Welcome to our favorite place.

Many Americans still long for a simpler way of life in smaller towns. This is where they find it, trading in business suits for blue jeans. It's a privilege to live in the Blue Ridge of Virginia, pure and simple. Every day is a feast for the senses. And at night, you can drift off to sleep knowing that if your environment can impact upon your sense of well-being, you are one of the luckiest — and happiest — people around.

This is the nostalgic land of Earl Hamner Jr.'s John Boy and the Walton family. You can still find a lot of general stores like Ike Godsey's. You can still find clucking, blue-haired ladies preparing banana pudding and fried chicken for Sunday School picnics in the country and small congregations worshipping in white, clapboard chapels. You can still find the strong family values that compel generations of extended families to all live down the same country lane. You'll find neighbors who mind their own business but are ever willing to lend a helping hand.

Welcome to a place where people still wave to strangers on back country roads, and children and the family dog still swim with patched innertubes in pristine creeks under covered bridges. Welcome to life in the slow lane, with many of the same benefits but few of the hassles of life in the fast lane.

For sheer beauty and tranquility, nothing equals the Blue Ridge of Virginia's mountains, flora, fauna, rivers and lakes. We're a rhapsody of riotous yellow fuchsia and redbud in the spring. We're a sonnet of sunny meadows with hovering hummingbirds and singing songbirds in the summer. We're a painter's palette of colors in the autumn. We're an aria to the simple setting of the first Christmas as we celebrate with handwrought wreaths and the tree we just cut out back on the snow-covered mountain.

We revere our environment, realizing a covenant with the land. We pull our cars off our highways to watch the sun go down, and we're filled with a sense of awe that a pinpoint of light bursting through a cloud can make a mountain appear to be wrapped in red velvet.

Ours is a land of great dynamics. We are inventors, like Cyrus McCormick, whose Shenandoah Valley mechanical reaper revolutionized the world. We are the land of Thomas Jefferson, the quintessential Renaissance man who invented not only the concept of democracy in America, but also the dumb waiter, the original mimeograph and the brave art of eating the "love tomatoe." We are the land of robots and fiber optics in Roanoke, smart road technology in the New River Valley and the High Flowing Community in Floyd County.

We are a land of great leaders. On our Natural Bridge, George Washington carved his initials and later bailed Washington and Lee University out of impending bankruptcy. Ours is a land where Robert E. Lee led troops to great valor and honor during a four-year Civil War that was supposed to last just a few weeks. Our Shenandoah Valley is where Stonewall Jackson exasperated his students at the Virginia Military Institute with his toughness and humorlessness and then went on to create a legend in military strategy still taught by U.S. military leaders.

We are a people who revere our history and honor our dead. We preserve our crumbling cemeteries and battlefields as hallowed ground. We build museums in the tiniest of communities as we welcome at least a half-million people a year to Monticello in Charlottesville and Montpelier near Orange. We build monuments to every Civil War battle ever fought and museums to honor our fallen soldiers.

We are a land of great scholarship and creativity, where the slave Booker T. Washington grew up in Franklin County to become one of the great African-American thinkers and leaders of all time. Born in Winchester, groundbreaking female author Willa Cather cultivated her sensitive descriptions of nature and immigrants and became a great journalist and novelist. In Lynchburg, the great Harlem Renaissance poet Anne Spencer entertained Martin Luther King, Congressman Adam Clayton Powell, Justice Thurgood Marshall and singers Paul Robeson and Marion Anderson at her garden home.

This is also a land of enormous, diverse culture. We flatfoot on Friday nights in the Alleghany Highlands. We go to drive-in movies and eat buttered popcorn in Rockbridge County while celebrities fly in from around the world to see our Virginia Film Festival in nearby Charlottesville. In Amherst County, near Lynchburg, we provide one of the largest residential colonies in the world for international artists and writers to stir their creative juices. At our colleges and cities, we display works of art and crafts equal to that of any metropolitan area in the country.

We're a big playground where you can camp, hike, bike, canoe, golf, boat, swim, horseback ride, hunt, fish, hang glide and soar until you drop!

We're a land of festivity looking for excuses to celebrate. We stage festivals to honor everything from apples, strawberries, garlic, dogwoods, wine and maple sugar to folklife and railroads.

This is also a land of superlatives. No matter which region of the Blue Ridge you visit, you'll find "the biggest," "the oldest," "the most important" or "nationally known" and "internationally acclaimed." Every region is a gem of multifaceted culture, like precious stones on a necklace, the common thread being the beauty of the Blue Ridge and our vast quality of life.

We are Charlottesville, land of Jeffersonian mystique and international chic. We are Staunton, heart of the Blue Ridge with our famous Fourth of July picnics in Gypsy Hill Park, begun by the world-famous Statler Brothers. We are Harrisonburg, with fields of golden, waving grain and hills white with turkeys and Roanoke, "Capital of the Blue Ridge," the largest metropolitan area off the Blue Ridge Parkway, voted by travel writers as the most beautiful road in the world. We are the intellectually stimulating New River Valley, home to gigantic Virginia Tech as well as a tie-dyed counterculture that came to Floyd County and never left the '60s. We're the staid German Baptists at Smith Mountain Lake, the playground of western Virginia, and we still hunt for the cryptic, elusive Beale Treasure in nearby Bedford County. We're Jerry Falwell and the Moral Majority in Lynchburg, the home of one of the largest churches in America. We're the residents of the pastoral Alleghany Highlands, where the sheep outnumber the human population and life is as slow and sweet as the maple sugar trickling down the trees in the spring.

Welcome to our favorite place. Everywhere you travel you'll find beauty that stops you in your tracks, people who are courteous, trusting and kind, and the opportunity to be transformed by the goodness of your environment.

Visit with us awhile. Rock on our wide front porches and sit a spell. Join us in our favorite pastime of watching the sun set over the Blue Ridge of Virginia. Have some peach cobbler and Virginia-made wine to settle you for the night. And when the stars blanket the Blue Ridge of Virginia, pack away your worries and tough times and mount a carousel horse (you can buy one in Newbern) to ride through your dreams.

The dream of the good life is all around you in the Blue Ridge. Whatever your dreams, chances are you'll have the opportunity to help make them come true in the Blue Ridge of Virginia — whether you decide to stay for a day or a lifetime.

About the Authors

Mary Alice Blackwell

Except for a couple of years in Canada, Mary Alice Blackwell has spent most of her life in the Blue Ridge. Born in Staunton, educated in Blacksburg, Mary Alice is now the features editor for *The Daily Progress* in Charlottesville.

Although she had planned on teaching history, journalism picked her instead. The underground newspaper she printed in high school should have been an early warning sign, but Mary Alice never considered putting fingers to the keyboard until the summer of 1973. That was when the sports editor for *The Staunton Leader* stopped by her softball game and asked the young catcher if she would like to be a stringer for the local paper. She had never met Hubert Grim Jr. before, but she has remained his grateful pupil since.

In less than two years, Mary Alice went from a part-time writer to assistant sports editor. During her 13-year stint in sports, she covered everything from college football to high school wrestling. Along the way she had the privilege of interviewing the likes of Lee Trevino, Ralph Sampson and a young athlete who came back from open-heart surgery to play tennis for his high school.

When Mary Alice went off to finish her communications degree at Virginia Tech, she continued to be a full-time writer, first as the sports editor of *The News Messenger* and later as the managing editor of the *Fayette Tribune*.

After backpacking across Europe, Mary Alice came back to the Blue Ridge. Hiking the scenic trails of the Skyline Drive proved more relaxing than toting a backpack through the streets of Paris. Her job at *The Progress* has given Mary Alice the added opportunity to encounter many more exciting people and places in the heart of Virginia's Blue Ridge. She hopes others will get the same opportunity after reading *The Insiders' Guide® to Virginia's Blue Ridge*.

Lin Chaff

Born in Slippery Rock, Pennsylvania, Lin D. Chaff arrived in Blacksburg in 1972 fresh out of West Virginia University as the editor of the *Blacksburg Sun*. While in Blacksburg, she fell in love with the Blue Ridge of Virginia and made it her life's mission to live and work there, taking time out to earn a graduate journalism degree at Northwestern University.

Before moving back in 1978 to become a reporter for the New River Valley Bureau of the *Roanoke Times*, she worked for Gannett newspapers, The Associated Press and on Capitol Hill and received a string of journalism awards.

In 1988, she started Lin Chaff Public Relations and Advertising of Roanoke, in part to promote tourism in western Virginia. The firm won a series of coveted awards for its work in public relations campaigns.

She co-wrote the first edition of the *Insiders' Guide® to Virginia's Blue Ridge*; this is her seventh Insiders' Guide.

Sadly, Lin passed away before editorial work on this edition was completed. Her influence is inescapable, however, and her words here stand as a tribute to her goal of sharing the unique beauty of the Blue Ridge with others.

Acknowledgments

This book is dedicated to the memory of Lin Chaff.

Lin was there to shape the very first *Insiders' Guide® to Virginia's Blue Ridge* and her dedication and skill enhanced the following five editions. Lin's talent could not be replaced with this volume, but her memory was with me during every tap on the keyboard. Lin, your words still live on in the following pages.

With more than 300 miles stretching from Leesburg to Pulaski, this is far from a one-person project. Without the assistance of writer Anne Patterson Causey — who helped track down, describe and photograph the sites — none of this would have been possible.

Thank you goes out to all the people who work at the chambers of commerce, visitor centers and tourism departments up and down both sides of the Blue Ridge. These folks are genuine fonts of information and kindness.

Special thanks goes out to Jenni Frangos, my editor at Insiders' Guides; Roanoke Valley Tourism Director Catherine Fox, Linda Holsinger at Mountain Lake, Paula J. Lilly at The Homestead, Barbara Payton at the Virginia Wine Marketing Office, Mitchell Bowman of Virginia Civil War Trails Inc., Anita Shelburne at *The Daily Progress* for her first-hand expertise of Virginia's horse country, and Connie Forsyth, Vicki Keyser and Sarah Keyser for their keen eyes and ears in the Shenandoah Valley.

For Seth, Linet, Nicolette and Rachel Blackwell, thank you for your constant support. And for the great suggestions and, no doubt, a large credit card bill when this book is published, thank you Janet Ross. I call her "Mom." You have always been my inspiration.

And, as Lin always said, to "the many others who firmly believe the Blue Ridge of Virginia is the most beautiful, special place on Earth."

— Mary Alice Blackwell

Table of Contents

Directory of Maps

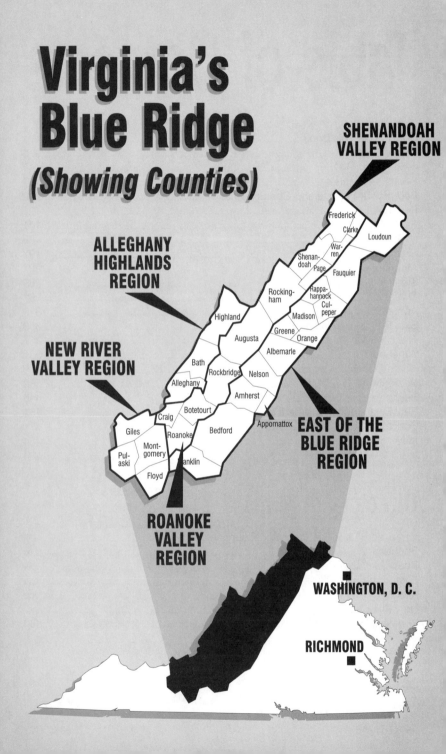

Shenandoah Valley Region

Roanoke Valley Region

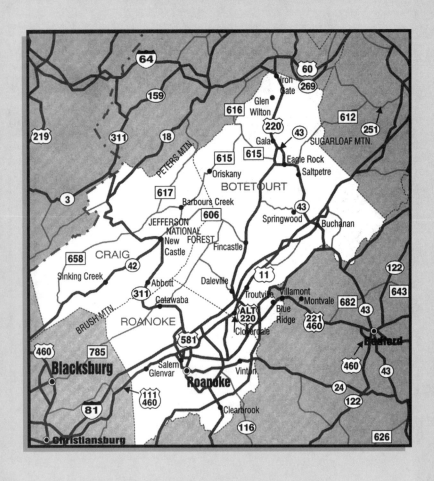

East of the
Blue Ridge Region

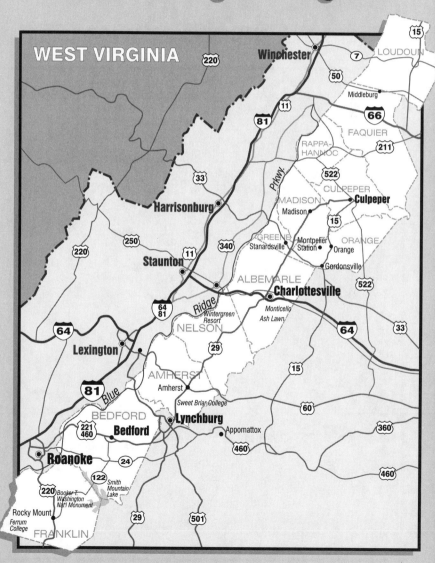

WEST VIRGINIA

220

Winchester

LOUDOUN

15

7

50

Middleburg

66

11

81

RAPPA-
HANNOC

FAQUIER

211

522

33

Pkwy

CULPEPER

MADISON

Culpeper

Madison

15

Harrisonburg

250

340

GREENE

Montpelier
Station

ORANGE

220

Stanardsville

Orange

11

Staunton

Gordonsville

522

64
81

ALBEMARLE

Charlottesville

Ridge

Wintergreen
Resort

Monticello
Ash Lawn

64

Lexington

NELSON

29

64

33

15

81

Blue

AMHERST

Amherst

Sweet Briar College

BEDFORD

221
460

Bedford

Lynchburg

Appomattox

60

360

460

Roanoke

24

220

122

Booker T.
Washington
Nat'l Monument

Smith
Mountain
Lake

Rocky Mount
Ferrum
College

FRANKLIN

29

501

460

Alleghany
Highlands
Region

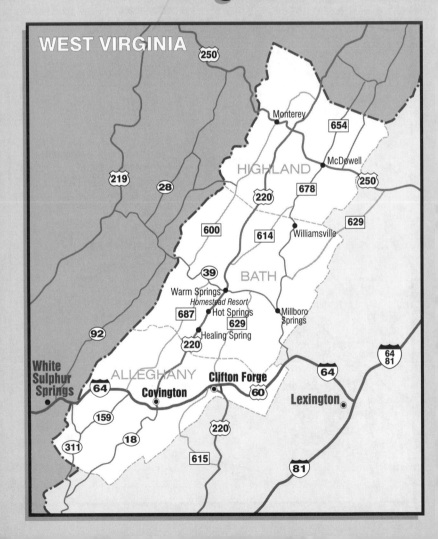

New River Valley Region

Presidents Thomas Jefferson, James Madison and James Monroe — whose homes are popular attractions in Albemarle and Orange counties — were part of what historians have called the Virginia Dynasty.

How to Use This Book

If you haven't been to the Blue Ridge region before, bring along your book and let us guide you to the best of the region — the best restaurants, accommodations, museums, shops, kids' activities and more. We live here, so we know about this area. We recommend the good spots, places we like to visit or that we recommend to our friends. If it's not good, we haven't included it in our book.

Of course, with a region as large as the Blue Ridge, we are bound to have left something out. If your favorite isn't included here, drop us a note. We are always interested in feedback.

The region covered in this book includes 30 counties from historic Winchester to rural Rocky Mount with scores of towns and cities in between. It was no easy task to gather and organize information on a territory of this size — more than a third of the state! If you are already familiar with this region, you will sympathize with us.

With so much ground to cover, we put a lot of thought into how to organize this book and present the material in a sensible and accessible way. We think we have produced a guide that is easy to use. Nearly every chapter is presented geographically, in regional segments, from north to south and east to west. We've defined five regions: the Shenandoah Valley, the Roanoke Valley, East of the Blue Ridge (also sometimes called the foothills), the New River Valley and the Alleghany Highlands.

Most chapters start with a regional header to orient you, followed by information about counties and cities in that region, with the overall geographic traffic pattern flowing south from the top of the Blue Ridge area, zigzagging back and forth from east to west.

We begin the book by introducing, in a general way, the five main regions of the Blue Ridge, as noted earlier, and their cities and towns. This is not meant to be the kind of guide that you must read from beginning to end to reap the benefit of buying it, but we do recommend that you start out by reading these overviews. They will give you an indication of what the areas have to offer, what makes our cities, towns and villages unique and worth visiting.

After the overviews comes the bulk of the book: sections on such topics as Civil War sites, restaurants and accommodations, each using the same geographical framework. In other words, if you're interested in visiting a winery in the Shenandoah Valley, look under that region's heading in the Wineries chapter. The same rule applies with nightspots, shopping, bed and breakfast inns and almost all the other topics we cover.

We alter our organization a bit in the Recreation chapter, which is arranged by type of activity, and in the Annual Events and Festivals chapter, which is chronological by months of the year. However, the geographic flow continues under those headings.

Another exception to this organization is the chapter on Skyline Drive and the Blue Ridge Parkway. Here, we let you know where you can eat and spend the night without departing from the two connecting mountaintop highways.

We've included maps to help you. It's a good idea, especially if you aren't familiar with the area, to spend some time studying them

before you dive into the book. They will help you understand visually how the regions are divided and what towns and cities belong in each one. You may also want to keep a more detailed road map handy to pinpoint some of the smaller highways and byways.

One important note to keep in mind as you use this guide: on July 15, 1995, the 703 area code that precedes many of the phone numbers in the Blue Ridge changed to 540. We've included this change in all our listings, but be aware that other brochures and pamphlets you may have may not have been updated.

We hope you have a good time exploring both this guide and the beautiful Blue Ridge area. Let us know what you think of the book, its organization and helpfulness. Write us at: Insiders' Guides, Falcon Publishing Inc., P.O. Box 1718, Helena, MT 59624. Or visit our website at www.insiders.com and make your comments there.

This state is overflowing
with interesting places
and people linked to our
nation's past.

Area Overviews

For many travelers, a vacation wouldn't be complete without an understanding of the history and local flavor of each destination. This state is overflowing with interesting places and people linked to our nation's past. Virginia is home to the first successful English settlement at Jamestown, the Colonial city of Williamsburg and countless Revolutionary and Civil War memorials all along the Blue Ridge Mountains.

Presidents Thomas Jefferson, James Madison and James Monroe — whose homes are popular attractions in Albemarle and Orange counties — were part of what historians have called the Virginia Dynasty. In fact, the Commonwealth has earned the nickname Mother of Presidents with four other native-born presidents: William Henry Harrison, John Tyler, Zachary Taylor and Staunton's own Woodrow Wilson.

What we hope to do is give you a brief understanding of the people and events that shaped our communities. Although we've narrowed our focus to the Blue Ridge, it's no easy task trying to give the local flavor of every town. In this chapter we've tried to highlight important historical facts about each area in the Blue Ridge and to provide descriptions of local attractions. These regional overviews are a great place to begin any Insider's vacation. So read on, and then turn to related chapters for more details. We hope our research will enrich your travels.

Shenandoah Valley

Shenandoah. The name conjures up images of rolling green farmland, beautiful old barns and the legendary Shenandoah River that winds north to Harpers Ferry, West Virginia. The American Indians called the river Shenandoah, meaning "daughter of the stars," for the sparkling points of light on its broad surface. The 200-mile-long valley that shares its path and its name stretches from Frederick and Clarke counties in the north almost to Roanoke in the south.

White explorers traveled through the valley as early as the mid-1600s, but it wasn't until the early 1700s that the first German and Scotch-Irish families began to put down roots here. They had migrated south from Maryland and Pennsylvania seeking fertile, cheap land and greater freedom for themselves and their children. Original barns and homesteads dot the landscape of the valley, and many museums along Interstate 81, including the Woodstock Museum in Shenandoah County, the Shenandoah Valley Folk Art Museum and Heritage Center in Dayton and the Frontier Culture Museum in Staunton, give visitors a closer look at the daily lives of these rugged pioneers.

Some of the heaviest fighting of the Civil War took place in the valley, and many of the war's hardiest soldiers hailed from here. According to Lt. Col. C.F.R. Henderson, author of the two-volume *Stonewall Jackson and the Civil War*, " . . . no better material for soldiers ever existed than the men of the valley. . . . All classes mingle in the ranks, and all ages. . . . They were a mountain people, nurtured in a wholesome climate, bred to manly sports, and hardened by the free life of the field and forest. To social distinctions they gave little heed. They were united for a common purpose."

The valley is also the burial place of many heroes of that terrible war. Robert E. Lee and Stonewall Jackson were laid to rest in Lexington. Lee was president of the city's Washington College (now Washington and Lee) after the war, and Jackson had taught natural philosophy at Virginia Military Institute for years. Jackson's horse, Little Sorrel, also is buried close to his master in Lexington. Jackson is memorialized in a rollicking musical called *Stonewall Country*, performed under the stars in summer at Lexington's Lime Kiln Theater.

The Shenandoah Valley was home to other great American leaders. Woodrow Wilson was born in Staunton, and a museum next to his birthplace tells all about his life and his vision for world peace. Also in Lexington is a museum honoring George C. Marshall, a VMI graduate who went on to lead the U.S. Army during World War II and later devised a plan to rebuild Europe after the war.

Visitors to the valley need not have a strong interest in history to enjoy the area's attractions. Majestic caverns filled with ancient and colorful calcite formations await the curious. The magnificence of Natural Bridge, once owned by Thomas Jefferson, is another destination. Rivers invite you to take a lazy canoe trip or an action-packed whitewater run.

Antiques lovers will delight in shops set in charming small towns. The northern stretch of U.S. Highway 11, between Winchester and Staunton, is known as Antiques Alley, with dozens of shops and antique centers interspersed between the two cities.

If you time your visit right, you'll catch some of the East's finest fairs and festivals, including Virginia's No. 1 agricultural fair at Harrisonburg, the Maple Festival in Highland County and the popular Apple Blossom Festival in Winchester.

Downtown districts beg for exploration on foot, offering a concentration of beautiful architecture, fine restaurants, boutiques and galleries. You can spend hours exploring Roanoke's city market area or historic downtown Lexington, Winchester or Staunton.

Modern accommodations are plentiful in the valley, and you'll discover quaint inns and bed and breakfasts in beautifully restored old homes. The Virginia Division of Tourism, (804) 786-4484, has information on many accommodations. For other services see our Bed and Breakfasts and Country Inns chapter.

The Shenandoah Valley has many more villages and towns than we can highlight, but the following introductions will give you a taste of what each area has to offer. A good way to get a flavor of the valley is to take a drive down U.S. 11 from Winchester to Staunton. There's less traffic so you can take your time enjoying the rolling hills and small towns filled with quaint shops and beautiful old homes.

Winchester

Once called Frederick Town after Frederick, father of King George III, Winchester and the surrounding area was settled by Pennsylvania Quakers in 1732. Soon after, Germans, Scots, Irish, English, Welsh and French Huguenots also followed the Great Wagon Road from Pennsylvania and put down roots here. Winchester was a thriving center of commerce during the settlement of our nation; pioneers obtained their wagons and provisions here for trips farther west and south.

Frederick County and Winchester saw much action during the Civil War. The armies of the North and South engaged in five battles and many skirmishes within or near Winchester, which changed hands more than 70 times. Stonewall Jackson used a home on Braddock Street for his headquarters during the war, and today his office remains much the way it was during his stay. The Kurtz Cultural Center downtown has a permanent exhibit, "Shenandoah — Crossroads of the Civil War," which provides details on the major battles fought here.

When he was 16, George Washington started his career in Winchester as a surveyor. Later, the father of our country saw to the protection of Virginia's frontier, overseeing the construction of Fort Loudoun, today a museum in Winchester. He also was elected to his first political office, as a member of the House of Burgesses, in Winchester.

Country-music fans know Winchester as the birthplace of Patsy Cline, that spunky, honey-voiced singer of the early '60s. In 1963 the 30-year-old Cline was killed in an airplane crash. She is buried in a simply marked grave at the Shenandoah Memorial Cemetery on U.S. Highway 522, also known as the Patsy Cline Memorial Highway.

On a literary note, the Winchester area was also the birthplace of another pioneering woman, novelist Willa Cather. Cather's family moved from Frederick County to Nebraska when she was 10.

Winchester is probably best-known for its annual Shenandoah Apple Blossom Festival. For four days every May, the town plays host to more than 250,000 visitors who gather to

Blue-hued mountain vistas are the rewards of a day's hike.

enjoy a parade, arts and crafts festivals, races, dances and a circus.

For more information about the Winchester area, call the Winchester-Frederick County Visitor Center/Chamber of Commerce at (800) 662-1360 or write to them at 1360 S. Pleasant Valley Road, Winchester 22601.

Stephens City

Chartered in 1758, Stephens City is second only to Winchester as the oldest town in the Shenandoah Valley. It was originally called Stephensburg after its founder, Lewis Stephens, who owned all of the town's 900 acres. As it expanded north, the town was called Newton and eventually was renamed Stephens City in the late 1900s. Rumor has it that Stephens City was almost picked as the county seat, but a bit of toddy swayed voters in favor of nearby Winchester.

Located just 8 miles south of Winchester,

Stephens City became a transportation hub thanks to its location along Va. Route 277 and U.S. 11. In fact, more than a dozen wagon makers and an equal number of blacksmiths set up shop on the busy corridor to Alexandria. The advent of the railroad nearly wiped out the need for these horse-drawn industries, but wagon rides are still a big part of the annual Newtown Heritage Festival in late May.

Although Stephens City has grown along with the times, part of Main Street (along U.S. 11) is much the way it was back in the early days when homes were built close to the road so families would have room for gardens out back. A walking tour of the city will take you past the home of wagon maker John Cryder and John Lemley's blacksmith shop. Dr. John Watkins Walls's house is still there. His son, William, assisted Dr. Hunter McGuire in amputating Stonewall Jackson's arm. While many places were vandalized during the Civil War, you can still see the site of the Lutheran and

Reform Church that dates back to 1786. Old Town Cemetery, too, still stands guard over many of the founding Stephens family.

Today, Stephens City has seen tremendous commercial and residential growth. The area is also home to many of the county's finest orchards, including Rinker Orchard on Marlboro Road. For more information about Stephens City, contact the Winchester-Frederick County Chamber of Commerce at 1360 S. Pleasant Valley Road, Winchester 22601, (800) 662-1360.

Middletown

This quaint town in southern Frederick County celebrated its bicentennial in 1996. Many of the old homes in town are said to have weathered bullets and cannonballs from the raging Civil War, and thanks to the vision of Peter Senseney, the blade of 20th-century bulldozers. When the town was chartered in 1896, Senseney required that all homes be built well back from the road. (When the Valley Pike was widened in the 1930s, none of the homes had to be torn down or moved.)

Middletown lies along U.S. 11, once the Great Wagon Road, the most important frontier highway in Colonial America. It has always been a favorite stopping place for valley travelers and has settled into an unhurried pace since I-81 siphoned off the faster traffic. A tavern built on the roadside in 1797 later became a stagecoach relay station and an inn; it's still in operation as the Wayside Inn and Restaurant, a beautifully restored watering hole in the center of town. The inn is a paradise for antique lovers with its Colonial furnishings, rare antiques and historic paintings. It's also noted for its hearty regional American cuisine.

Middletown is home to Belle Grove plantation house, a large grey stone mansion built between 1794 and 1797 by Isaac Hite, who married James Madison's sister. Every October the lush green fields of the plantation attract crowds for a major Civil War re-enactment hosted by the Cedar Creek Battlefield Foundation Inc. It's notable as one of the few re-enactments to take place on an original Civil War battlefield.

Wayside Theatre in downtown Middletown is the second-oldest theater in the state and hosts dramas, comedies and mysteries from May through December. Some famous faces got their start here, including Susan Sarandon, Jill Eikenberry and Peter Boyle.

For more information about Middletown attractions, contact the Winchester-Frederick County Chamber of Commerce at 1360 S. Pleasant Valley Road, Winchester 22601, (800) 662-1360.

Front Royal

This northern Blue Ridge town was once known as Helltown for all the shootings, brawls and hard drinking that went on here in the mid-1700s. Today Front Royal and surrounding Warren County, only 57 miles from the Beltway, are fast becoming a bedroom community of Washington, D.C. But Front Royal is also the northern gateway to the wilderness of the Shenandoah National Park. The north and south forks of the majestic Shenandoah River come together here, and campgrounds and canoe outfitters abound.

Front Royal has a revitalized downtown business district full of interesting boutiques and antique shops. An old-fashioned town clock sits in the village common, where a gazebo and picnic tables welcome tourists and downtown workers to sit for a spell.

The town has a Confederate museum that documents how this important rail and river junction withstood numerous clashes during the Civil War. History buffs can spend hours retracing the exploits of Mosby's Raiders or tracking Stonewall Jackson's famous Valley Campaign. Other attractions in the Front Royal area include Skyline Caverns, Skyline Drive

---

INSIDERS' TIP

October is the "peak" season to visit the Blue Ridge. It's a great time to catch the brilliant fall foliage while you tour a winery, take in a festival or watch a Civil War re-enactment.

and two wineries, Oasis Vineyard and Linden Vineyards and Orchards, offering tours and tastings.

For more information, write to the Chamber of Commerce of Front Royal and Warren County, 414 E. Main Street, Front Royal 22630. You can call them at (540) 635-3185 or (800) 338-2576.

Strasburg

Staufferstadt is the original name of Strasburg, a busy little town just south of Middletown in Shenandoah County. German Mennonites and Dunkards from York County, Pennsylvania, settled the village, which was renamed Strasburg in 1761.

Later the town was nicknamed Pottown for the high-quality pottery produced here during the antebellum period. The first potter came in 1761, and since then at least 17 potters have produced earthen and stoneware in Strasburg. You can see some of this pottery in the Strasburg Museum, which also displays Civil War relics, Native American artifacts and blacksmith collections.

History buffs will also enjoy the Museum of the American Presidents with its displays of presidential artifacts (a lock of George Washington's hair, for example) and biographical sketches of each of our 42 presidents. Those interested in the Civil War will want to stop by Hupp's Hill Battlefield Park.

Lovers of antiques will have a heyday in Strasburg. More than 110 dealers of high-quality antiques are housed under one roof in the downtown Strasburg Emporium. You'll find not only furniture representing every American era but also chandeliers, rugs, quilts, lace, pottery, baskets, iron beds and estate jewelry.

A great place to stay overnight in town is the Hotel Strasburg, a renovated Victorian hotel decorated with antiques that also are for sale. The hotel's restaurant has a popular following among folks from nearby valley towns and is by far one of the best places to dine for miles around.

For more information on Strasburg, Woodstock, New Market, Edinburg, Mt. Jackson, Basye and Orkney Springs, contact the Shenandoah County Travel Council at 125 S. Main Street, Woodstock 22664, (540) 459-2332.

Woodstock

This charming valley settlement was chartered in 1761 by an act of the Virginia Assembly, sponsored by George Washington, a representative from Frederick County. The Woodstock Museum on W. Court Street has artifacts such as portraits, quilts and a moonshine still recalling the valley's early settlement. The museum also sponsors a walking tour through town, where you can see examples of Federal, Greek Revival and Classic Revival architecture.

Woodstock, the county seat of Shenandoah, also is home to the oldest courthouse still in use west of the Blue Ridge. Another impressive structure in town is the massive Massanutten Military Academy, a coeducational school dating back to 1899.

Nearby Orkney Springs hosts the Shenandoah Valley Music Festival every spring and summer. Concerts are held in a covered, open-air pavilion and on the grounds of the historic Orkney Springs Hotel. This former hotel used to be a 19th-century mineral springs spa and resort.

Edinburg

If you can, try to stop by Edinburg about the third full weekend in September when the whole town turns out for the annual Edinburg Ole' Time Festival. It's like stepping back in time, especially when you are surrounded by the large white homes with wraparound porches dating back to the 1800s. You also won't want to miss the Edinburg Mill. Built in 1848, it survived a fiery threat from the Union soldiers during the Civil War.

Edinburg is also home to many wonderful shops along Main Street and the scenic Shenandoah Vineyards. The vineyard is open for tours and tastings.

Mount Jackson

Dating back to 1812, Mount Jackson was originally called Mount Pleasant, but the name was changed in honor of a frequent visitor, President Andrew Jackson. The small town is rich in history. Several of its buildings served as hospitals for both the Confederate and Union armies. Right on U.S. 11 is Soldiers Cemetery, the only cemetery in Virginia in which only Confederate soldiers are buried.

Just south of Mount Jackson on Va. Route 720 is Meem's Bottom Bridge, the longest covered bridge of the nine remaining in Virginia. The 200-foot single-span bridge was built by Franklin Hiser in 1892 so he could have easy access to his apple orchard. It is the last remaining covered bridge in the Shenandoah.

New Market

Here you will find caverns, museums, Shenvalee Golf Resort, a battlefield historical park and an excellent tourist information center for the whole Shenandoah Valley.

New Market was settled later than other valley towns. English settlers from the North and East named their village after a horse-racing town in England, and in the early days a racetrack actually operated near New Market. New Market is famous for the 1864 battle that involved 247 cadets fresh from the classrooms of Virginia Military Institute (see our Civil War chapter). You can view a stirring account of the battle on film at the Hall of Valor Museum at the New Market Battlefield Historical Park. The museum also presents a nonpartisan view of major Civil War events with its murals and life-size models. The Hall of Valor is just one of three museums that pay tribute to the battle. The Cavalry Museum and the New Market Battlefield Military Museum, which houses more than 2,500 original artifacts, are within a mile of each other on Va. Route 305. Each May the 220-acre battlefield hosts the state's longest running re-enactment: the Re-enactment of the Battle of New Market.

New Market is also at the epicenter of valley caverns: Shenandoah, Endless, Luray and Grand are accessible here.

While it sounds like a "sleeper" of an attraction, you shouldn't miss the Bedrooms of America Museum on Congress Street (U.S. 11). Eleven rooms of authentic furniture show every period of America's bedrooms from 1650 through 1930.

Luray

Luray is a central gateway to the 105-mile-long Skyline Drive. Page County is bordered by the Shenandoah National Park on the east and the George Washington National Forest on the west.

Luray, the county seat of Page, is the home of the internationally famed Luray Caverns, which can be explored in an hour-long guided tour. Housed in the same complex is the Historic Car and Carriage Caravan, an exhibit of antique cars, carriages, coaches and costumes.

Shenandoah River Outfitters in Luray and the Down River Canoe Company in nearby Bentonville offer canoe trips on the south fork of the Shenandoah River, which travels the entire length of Page County. Guilford Ridge Vineyard is just a few miles out of town and offers tours and tastings of its wines by appointment. And would you believe one of the state's largest reptile collections is in Luray? The Luray Reptile Center and Dinosaur Park on U.S. Highway 211 will keep your kids squealing for hours. Tame deer and llamas inhabit the petting zoo.

A good time to visit the area is Columbus Day weekend in October, when Page County throws its annual Heritage Festival. First held in 1969, it is one of the oldest arts and crafts shows in Virginia.

For more information on Page County, contact the Luray-Page County Chamber of Commerce at 46 E. Main Street, Luray 22835, (540) 743-3915.

Harrisonburg and Rockingham County

In the geographic center of the Shenandoah Valley sit Harrisonburg and Rockingham County. This area is known for panoramic vistas, abundant recreational opportunities and rich history. Harrisonburg is home to 16 major industries and serves as the financial and retail center for eight counties, including three in neighboring West Virginia. For travelers, it's a great place to settle in for a while and explore other attractions in the valley.

A thriving city, Harrisonburg is noted for its high quality of life. The downtown is currently undergoing a revitalization with an Agriculture and Transportation Museum in the works for the year 2000 and the new Virginia Quilt Museum (see our Attractions chapter for more information). A big addition to the city in the fall of 1997 was the downtown theater in the Rockingham Motor Company building, which features diverse entertainment such as live dramas, movies and an Opry-style variety show in the Nashville tradition. Some great restaurants are in Harrisonburg, too, including one of the state's best, The Joshua Wilton House on Main Street.

Opportunities for higher education abound in the area. Bridgewater College, Eastern Mennonite University and James Madison University are all here, so students and professors comprise a large part of the population. These schools also bring an abundance of educational and cultural opportunities to the community.

With more than 2,000 farms, Rockingham County is the state's leading producer of dairy, poultry and beef products. In fact, the county ranks second in the nation for the number of turkeys produced, according to a recent agricultural census. So valuable is poultry to the county's economy that a proud statue of a turkey stands alongside U.S. 11.

In nearby Dayton, visitors will enjoy a wonderful indoor Farmer's Market with more than 20 shops that sell fresh cheeses, baked goods, antiques, bulk grains and spices. It also has a fantastic country restaurant run by a former Mennonite missionary. It's not unusual to see a black carriage or two with horses parked out front — about 1,000 Old Order Mennonites, easily identified by their simple style of dress, live in the area.

More than 139,000 acres of George Washington and Jefferson National Forests lie in western Rockingham County. On the east, the county is bordered by the Shenandoah National Park. With so much forested land, it's no wonder that this county has such wonderful hunting and fishing opportunities (see our Recreation chapter). The Massanutten mountain range is just east of town and is home to Massanutten Resort, a year-round residential community known for its ski slopes, golf courses and impressive indoor sports complex.

Another recreational attraction just south of Harrisonburg (in Augusta County) is Natural Chimneys, a place where huge rocks tower to heights of 120 feet. From one perspective, these rocks resemble a foreboding medieval-style castle with turrets and towers, and this may have inspired the creation of the Natural Chimneys Jousting Tournament more than 175 years ago. The tournament is the oldest continuously held sporting event in America, having begun in 1821. Modern-day knights still match their skills in the ancient art of jousting here on the third Saturday in August every year. The Natural Chimneys Regional Park has 120 campsites, a swimming pool, picnic area, camp store, nature and bike trails and more.

For more information about attractions in the Harrisonburg and Rockingham County area, contact the Harrisonburg-Rockingham Convention and Visitors Bureau at 10 E. Gay Street, Harrisonburg 22802, (540) 434-2319.

Staunton

Called the Queen City on the Great Wagon Road, Staunton celebrated its 250th anniversary in 1997. A great city to explore on foot — if you don't mind a few hills — Staunton is full of Victorian, Greek Revival and Italianate architecture, unique shops, one-of-a-kind eateries and important historical sites. The city is the birthplace of President Woodrow Wilson, who was born in 1856 to a Presbyterian minister and his wife in a Greek Revival manse on Coalter Street. Today the manse is open for tours and sits next to a museum where you can learn all about Wilson's life, his political views and his vision for world peace. The Woodrow Wilson Museum also houses the president's 1919 Pierce Arrow limousine.

Another major attraction in Staunton is the Frontier Culture Museum, an indoor-outdoor living museum that features four authentic working farms and all kinds of domesticated critters. Staunton is an appropriate place for a museum that documents life in frontier America. It is the seat of Augusta County, which once stretched all the way to Mississippi. Most early settlers in the area were Scotch-Irish, including John Lewis, the first white man to build a homestead here in 1732. In 1749 Lewis' son, Thomas, laid out lots and streets for the new town of Staunton, named in honor of Lady Rebecca Staunton, Gov. William Gooch's wife.

Nineteenth-century Staunton grew by leaps and bounds following incorporation as a town in 1801. Education became a priority, with the establishment of the Virginia Institute for the Deaf and the Blind in 1839, Augusta Female Seminary in 1842 (now Mary Baldwin College), Virginia Female Institute in 1844 (now Stuart Hall School) and Staunton Military Academy in 1884.

The railroad came to Staunton in 1854, stimulating the city's growth as a center of commerce for the region. Today Amtrak serves the city, and the old C&O train station is a showcase of meticulous restoration work. There you'll find an authentic 1880s Victorian Ice Cream Parlor in the Pullman Restaurant serving dense, Italian-style ice cream in a room with antique-parlor and drugstore furnishings from ceiling to floor. Next door, the Depot Grille boasts a gorgeous, hand-carved antique walnut bar, and in the same building, Depot Antiques sells fine collectibles, Victorian and country furniture.

The wharf area has undergone restoration work; the old mill buildings and warehouses contain antiques shops, a pottery workshop and studio and a marvelous antique-car dealership. The Historic Staunton Foundation has a detailed brochure to guide visitors on a walking tour of the city.

Other attractions in Staunton include the beautiful Gypsy Hill Park and the Statler Brothers museum and office complex. Yes, these famous, down-home country music stars still live in their hometown.

For additional information about Staunton, contact the Staunton-Augusta Travel Information Center, 1250 Richmond Road, Staunton 24401. You can call them at (540) 332-3972 or (800) 332-5219.

Waynesboro, Stuarts Draft and Fishersville

Waynesboro, too, passed a milestone in 1997 with a weeklong bicentennial celebration. Named in honor of Revolutionary War hero Gen. Anthony Wayne, Waynesboro thrived as an industrial community during the late 1800s, a trend that continues today. Thanks in part to its convenient location just 8 miles east of I-81 and right off I-64, companies such as DuPont, Genicom and Hershey have plants near here.

Waynesboro extends to Afton Mountain, from which you can see all the way to Charlottesville and beyond. The Shenandoah National Park's southern tip ends on that mountain, and the Blue Ridge Parkway begins its southern trek there. One note of caution: beware crossing Afton Mountain during foggy weather; many fatal accidents have occurred here during thick fog so stay put if such conditions exist.

In Waynesboro, the P. Buckley Moss Museum is in a tall brick house surrounded by trees, a scene reminiscent of one of her famous watercolors. The museum is within easy walking distance of the Waynesboro Village Factory Outlet Mall, where you can find bargains in designer clothing, leather goods, imported china and more.

While in Waynesboro, you can also watch age-old techniques of brass molding at the Virginia Metalcrafters factory showroom. The Shenandoah Valley Art Center in downtown Waynesboro offers residents and visitors a place to enjoy the arts through exhibits, workshops, classes and performances.

Mennonites who live near Stuarts Draft have established some businesses such as The Cheese Shop that provide a refreshing alternative to standard grocery stores. And Milmont Greenhouses, on U.S. Highway 340,

---

INSIDERS' TIP

Virginia's largest industry is still agriculture, so if you're traveling by car, keep your eyes peeled for some of the roadside vegetable and fruit stands. If you have the time, you might even enjoy the pick-your-own orchards.

has grown from a Mennonite housewife's hobby nearly 20 years ago to a bustling business today. Speaking of green things, one of the leading perennial nurseries in the nation, Andre Viette Farm and Nursery, is based in Fishersville and is definitely worth visiting.

Recreational opportunities abound in the area. The Sherando Lake State Park is just outside Waynesboro, and Shenandoah Acres Resort, a fun family stop, is in Stuarts Draft.

For more information about attractions in the East Augusta County area, stop by the Staunton-Augusta Travel Information Center, 1250 Richmond Road, Staunton 24401, or call (540) 332-3972 or (800) 332-5219. For information on Waynesboro, call the Waynesboro-Augusta County Chamber of Commerce, 301 W. Main Street, Waynesboro 22980, (800) 471-3109.

Lexington and Rockbridge County

Perhaps more than any other place in the valley, downtown Lexington has retained the graceful beauty and genteel character of its prosperous past. And no other city or town in the Blue Ridge has a history that is so well-preserved and honored by its citizens. The town's heritage includes four of America's greatest generals. It seems that everywhere you go, you are walking on historic, hallowed ground.

Throughout Lexington's history, the presence of great military leaders has inspired its preservation efforts — George Washington, the great Confederate generals Robert E. Lee and Thomas J. "Stonewall" Jackson, and World War II hero Gen. George C. Marshall, the Nobel Peace Prize-winning creator of the Marshall Plan that rebuilt war-torn Europe — all contribute to Lexington's history.

Lexington is the historic and cultural heart of Rockbridge County (population 32,000), where most prosperous residents enjoy a genteel country-estate way of life. Many are early retirees who devote their considerable knowledge and energy to the community as volunteers and activists. Others are college professors at nearby Virginia Military Institute and Washington and Lee University.

The county boasts the breathtaking 3-mile-long Goshen Pass, a journey along the Maury River lined with rhododendron, laurel, ferns, mosses, magnificent pines, hemlocks, maples, dogwood and mountain ash. Goshen Pass, a popular place for swimming, tubing, canoeing and picnicking, is so beautiful that one prominent Lexington citizen, Matthew Fontaine Maury, asked that, after he died, his body be carried through the pass when the rhododendron were in bloom. Complying with his request in 1873, Virginia Military Institute cadets formed an honor guard and gave their professor his last wish.

The roles that Lexington's world-famous universities, VMI and Washington and Lee, have played in the area's historic culture cannot be underestimated. In 1796 George Washington saved W&L from bankruptcy with a gift of $50,000, which still receives dividends. For their role in the Civil War, VMI cadets are immortalized forever both on campus, with the statue Virginia Mourning Her Dead, and at the New Market Battlefield Museum and Hall of Valor (an hour north of the city). The Civil War Battle of New Market in 1864 was the first and only time in American history that an entire student body was recruited to fight a battle. When the smoke cleared, 10 cadets lay dead.

As a city that has had more than its share of encounters with famous presidents, it has had one rather unlikely encounter. Visitors can see the National Historic Landmark cadet barracks where actor Ronald Reagan's movie *Brother Rat* was filmed. The movie's premiere was held at Lexington's State Theatre.

VMI in 1997 lost one of its toughest battles ever — deciding whether to admit women, as ordered by the Supreme Court in 1996, or go private. Its board decided the costs of going private were not realistic, so women were admitted in the fall of 1997.

Many of Lexington's attractions focus on its famous former citizens. There's the Stonewall Jackson House, where the tough general lived while teaching natural philosophy at VMI, and the Stonewall Jackson Cemetery, his final resting place after he was mistakenly killed by his own soldiers. You can see his bullet-pierced raincoat at the VMI Museum. In a ceremony attended by hundreds and covered by *The Wall Street Journal* in 1997, the curious taxidermy display of his favorite war horse, Little Sorrel, was finally laid to rest after being on display for a century. Jackson's birthday is celebrated in Lexington every January 21 with a ceremony, cake and a free tour of the only home he ever owned.

Lee Chapel, still in use by W&L students, is another famous site. The famous striking white statue of the recumbent Lee by sculptor Edward Valentine is alone worth a visit to Lexington. The chapel also is the site of the famous Peale portrait of George Washington. You can see Lee's office as he left it in 1870 after assuming the presidency of W&L following his Civil War defeat. Lee's favorite mount, Traveler, also is buried on campus.

The third famous military landmark to see is the George C. Marshall Museum, where Marshall, VMI class of 1901, began a remarkable military career that led to his position as U.S. Army Chief of Staff and later recipient of the Nobel Prize in 1953. An electric map detailing the military march of World War II shows the breadth of what this military genius accomplished and why the United States earned a reputation world wide as a country with a heart in the aftermath of the war.

Lexington's historic sites are well-documented by its history-loving populace. You can even see the troughs where its famous equestrian residents, Little Sorrel and Traveler, refreshed themselves. A walking tour map will keep you exploring enough bridges and locks, churches, cemeteries, houses, mills, baths and springs to quench even the most avid history buff's thirst for knowledge, including a nearby museum dedicated to Cyrus McCormick, inventor of the mechanized reaper. The pamphlet is available at the Visitors Center at 106 E. Washington Street or by calling (540) 463-3777.

Every summer day, the Lexington Carriage Company leaves its hitching post at the Visitors Center and carries passengers from 9:30 AM to 5:30 PM. You can ride the same streets Jackson and Lee did on their famous horses.

Since the memory of two famous horses are awarded such places of honor in Lexington, it stands to reason the Commonwealth of Virginia saw fit to award Lexington its $12 million Horse Center, situated on 400 rolling acres. It is one of the top equine facilities in the United States with 4,000 spectator seats, 610 permanent stalls and a gigantic show arena. Its schedule of events includes everything from the Bonnie Blue Nationals to the Northeast Peruvian Horse Club Show.

Also bringing fame and visitors to the area is Lime Kiln Theatre, named by *Theatre Journal* as "the most unusual theater setting in the United States" because of its location in an abandoned kiln beside a craggy, wildflower-strewn hillside. Lime Kiln puts on an array of plays and musicals every summer that highlights the history and culture of the Southern mountains.

Going out into the countryside, there's the beautiful Chessie Nature Trail along the Maury River and numerous hiking paths in nearby mountains, among them the Appalachian Trail. If you'd like to see 100 years of nostalgia, stop by Olde Country Store on the way to Goshen Pass in Rockbridge Baths. If you like horseback riding, Virginia Mountain Outfitters, (540) 261-1910, will put together half-day or overnight trips that will take you along forest trails and trout-filled rivers to the tops of mountains.

If canoeing is your passion, the James River Basin Canoe Livery, (540) 261-7334, will outfit you with boats, supplies, maps and a shuttle service for a trip along with the mighty James River and the rushing Maury. Farther north, call Dick Pickle at Wilderness Canoe Company at Natural Bridge, (540) 291-2295, for outdoor fun and adventure.

The great outdoors should also include a visit to Hull's Drive-In, one of the premier mom-and-pop operations anywhere and one of the few surviving drive-in theaters in Virginia. It's open weekends mid-March through November.

In Buena Vista, 6 miles east of Lexington and the only other city in the county, you will find much of the county's manufacturing industry. You'll also find The General Store, a trip back in time for an unusual shopping experience. Every Labor Day, Buena Vista attracts huge crowds and state political leaders to a popular festival in Glen Maury Park.

Do not leave Rockbridge County without visiting Natural Bridge, one of the seven natural wonders of the world. The awesome limestone bridge is 215 feet high and 90 feet long (see our Attractions chapter).

Photo: The Roanoke Valley Convention and Visitors Bureau

A major Roanoke landmark, the Gothic-style St. Andrews Catholic Church looms over the downtown commercial landscape as a daily reminder of serene spirituality.

Whether visiting the Lexington area for its history, beauty or attractions, you'll be impressed with its sense of historical importance, its gracious old homes and its vibrant downtown district with fine restaurants and one-of-a-kind shops.

For more information on Rockbridge County or Lexington, contact the Lexington Visitor Center, 106 E. Washington Street, Lexington 24450. You can call them at (540) 463-3777.

Roanoke Valley

God lives here. You can tell from the scenery. So does Elvis, at least in miniature, at Miniature Graceland in Roanoke. The Roanoke Valley of Virginia, including Roanoke, Botetourt and Craig counties, the Town of Vinton and City of Salem, is home to about a quarter-million people who work and play in a cultured, historical place of incredible beauty.

Even I-81, which connects the Roanoke Valley, is beautiful. One of the first things visitors usually say is they can't get over the absence of potholes and rough pavement. Then they marvel at all the wildflowers, redbud, yellow forsythia and flowering orchards along western Virginia's main thoroughfare.

People usually don't set out to move to the Roanoke Valley. Instead, they are converted into relocating here. When you talk to people about how they came to live here, so many times the story starts out, "We were driving down the [fill in the blank with either a) Interstate or b) Blue Ridge Parkway], when we were so smitten that we moved here without even having jobs." Or else they discovered the Roanoke Valley while hiking on the Appalachian Trail, taking the Bikecentennial path coast to coast or vacationing at nearby Smith Mountain Lake. Inevitably, the conversation ends with, " . . . and we'd never go back home. We'll never leave this place."

Consider this: the Roanoke Valley of Virginia was the first in the state to have curbside recycling, mandatory comprehensive recycling and a downtown recycling program that also was a first on the North American continent. This should tell you something about Valley citizens' overwhelming sensitivity to their environment.

Parenting magazine calls the Roanoke Valley one of the 10 best places to raise a family in the United States. The U.S. Department of Education has recognized Roanoke Valley schools for being among the nation's best. *Inc.* magazine named the Roanoke Valley one of the country's top-100 hot spots for business development. The region is blessed with many community-minded businesses and industries.

Whether they live in historic Botetourt County, the lush, forested Catawba Valley of Craig County, the energetic cities of Roanoke or Salem, suburban Roanoke County or the quaint town of Vinton, Roanoke Valley residents are always glad to come home — and most of them never leave.

Botetourt County

If Virginia can be referred to as the "Mother of States," then Botetourt could be called the "Mother of Counties." With a population of 25,000, the county is home to an independent, history-loving people who are smug in the fact that their county, a land grant to Lord Botetourt, once stretched the whole way to the Mississippi River. Historic Fincastle has been the county seat since 1770. This vast tract of land once included the entire present state of Kentucky and much of what is now West Virginia, Ohio, Indiana and Illinois.

George Washington, Patrick Henry and Thomas Jefferson either appeared in Fincastle or sent their agents to lay claim to tracts of wilderness lands. Jefferson designed a county courthouse. After the Lewis and Clark expedition west, William Clark returned to Fincastle to marry resident Judith Hancock. Thousands of English, German and Scotch-Irish pioneers passed through on their way down the great Valley Road that traversed the famed Shenandoah Valley to settle the western frontier country.

Combining the talents of German craftsmen and Scotch-Irish merchants and lawyers, Fincastle's founding fathers built a town of well-proportioned houses and public buildings, a substantial number of which still survive. These include the Old Jail Building, the Court House Complex, the Presbyterian Church, the Botetourt Museum Building and the Botetourt

County Courthouse. Newer buildings, such as the historic Bank of Fincastle, a major force in the community, are designed to blend into the historic environment.

You can take a guided tour, by appointment, by contacting Historic Fincastle Inc. Write them at P.O. Box 19, Fincastle 24090 or call (540) 473-3077. On your tour you will see beautiful wrought-iron fences, balconies and gates, flagstone walks from the early 19th century, horse-mounting stones in front of the Presbyterian Church and early gravestones in church cemeteries, with the oldest dating to 1795. Steeples contain bells, the focal point of a much publicized and honored tradition of ringing out the old and ringing in the New Year.

It stands to reason that Botetourt County residents love antiques. The Chamber of Commerce will send you a brochure listing 25 different shops, most of them clustered in Troutville and Fincastle. The Troutville Antique Mart has a plethora of these shops. The town of Buchanan is also a blossoming area for antiques and other shopping, thanks to its Main Street program.

There are beautiful side trips from this area. For a striking view of orchards in bloom, take Laymantown Road left past Troutville Baptist, a cut-through road to U.S. Highway 220. Mounds of blooming apple trees against the setting sun are indeed a sight to behold. In fall the fruit of the harvest is available for the picking at seven orchards, most of them huge operations that also offer seasonal items, such as acres of pumpkins for Halloween.

Agriculture is still a big industry, but farmland is at a premium. There are bounties on Botetourt County real estate, with people desperate to buy the scenic farmland, which has often been in the same family for generations.

Two scenic landmarks tourists especially enjoy are the unusual, huge, jutting Eagle Rock boulders off U.S. 220 — they appear to be on the verge of falling at any moment into the gorge. Beyond on Route 220 is Eagle Rock's Roaring Run Furnace, part of the George Washington and Jefferson National Forests and typical of the scores of iron furnaces that were scattered throughout the hills and mountains of western Virginia. The single-stack, hot-blast charcoal furnace, built of large, squared

stones, was constructed in 1832, rebuilt in 1845 and rebuilt again early in the Civil War. Most of the pig iron produced was shipped to Richmond for the war effort.

A third landmark here on the National Register of Historic Places is Wilson Warehouse, built in 1839 at Washington and Lowe streets and now Buchanan's Community House. It is a relic of western Virginia's antebellum prosperity.

It stands to reason that Botetourt County's largest and most popular festival is Historic Fincastle Days in the autumn. Attending the festival, sponsored by Historic Fincastle Inc. and held in the charming, historic downtown, is serendipity to lovers of fine art and crafts, since Fincastle is home to several well-known Virginia artists including Mark Woodie and Harold Little.

Recreational opportunities abound, including hiking the Appalachian and Bikecentennial trails that pass by Blue Ridge Road in Troutville. Other major activities are canoeing or floating the James River and Craig's Creek and hunting, camping and fishing.

Although Botetourt County is a county with a past, it is definitely one with a bright future while it tries to hang on to its pastoral environment. For more information, contact the Botetourt County Chamber of Commerce at P.O. Box 92, Fincastle 24090, (540) 473-8280.

Craig County

Just as Botetourt residents are trying to protect their pristine environment, the rural residents of pastoral Craig (population 4,500) fiercely guard their stake in God's Country. Tourism is a major industry in this county, which is more than half-covered by the George Washington and Jefferson National Forests.

The county got its name from Robert Craig, delegate to the General Assembly from Roanoke County who was instrumental in legislation that formed Craig County in 1851. New Castle was designated the county seat, and the historic courthouse was erected the same year by slave labor. Its bell was cast at the same foundry as the Liberty Bell.

The county seat contains several charming old buildings that have been designated historical landmarks, including the courthouse (which was miraculously spared during the Civil War), a jail, Central Hotel and Star Saloon (now official headquarters of the Craig County Historical Society), First National Bank and the G.W. Layman office building. You'll see several lovely old homes in the area, including the Layman house (c. 1901), on the corner of Va. routes 311 and 42, and the big, brick castle-like Todd house at the top of the hill going out of town on Va. 42. In 1997, the town received a $16,000 state grant for more historic renovation. John Mulheren, a New York financier, has single-handedly taken it upon himself to help restore the town. So far, he's restored the old general store and plans to restore the old train depot, old hotel and mill. He's also raising buffalo and has started an annual Buffalo Auction in October at Paint Bank. Another civic-minded citizen, John Williams, has restored the old Paint Bank School building.

Also worth a visit is Tingler's Mill at Paint Bank. While this particular mill was built in 1873, grinding had been going on at the site since 1783. Henry Tingler was excused from military service in the Confederate Army because grinding meal was a higher war need. After 182 years of daily operation, the mill closed in 1965 but is now being restored. Here's an interesting, little-known fact: because of Civil War geographical boundary changes, the mill has been in two different states and five different counties without ever having been moved. In 1783 the land was part of Botetourt County, remaining so until 1792, when Monroe County, Virginia, was created. In 1851 Craig County was carved from parts of Botetourt, Monroe, Roanoke and Giles counties. In 1863 that portion of the county joined Monroe County when West Virginia was formed during the Civil War, but was returned to Craig County after the war.

The route of Gen. David Hunter's retreat in the summer of 1864 still has natives talking. The Union soldiers burned marriage records and Deed Book 1 and spilled ink on all the others. Then they chopped up parts of the courthouse for kindling. However, an order to burn the courthouse was somehow overlooked.

This gentle beauty of a county, rich in history, is noted as one of the most popular playgrounds in western Virginia. The scenery is spectacular. If you want to see the epitome of a quaint country road, travel Va. 42 from New Castle to Giles County. This delightful road, which crosses the eastern Continental Divide, passes old farms with rail fences, graveyards of Civil War veterans and late 19th-century houses.

Va. Route 658 in the John's Creek area takes you to the sites of two now-defunct summer resorts where people would come to "take the cure," as they called it, of the orange sulphur mineral waters. The 1987 movie, *In a Shallow Grave*, used the site of Blue Healing Springs resort's crumbling dance hall.

Another site to see is Hebron Church, built in 1830, which has a slave balcony. It's locked during the week, but arrangements may be made to visit through the Craig County Historical Society (see our Arts chapter).

The Appalachian Trail is one of the county's major attractions. Thirty miles of the Maine-to-Georgia footpath pass through this area, and several shelters and camping facilities are scattered along the way.

The Trout Branch to Dragon's Tooth section is 7 rugged miles, but the views are spectacular (park in the lot off Va. Route 311 in Roanoke County).

For mountain-bike enthusiasts, hikers and horseback riders, Craig County is peppered with trails that range from the easy to challenging, and all have scenic value. Some local favorites include Va. Route 179, the road over Bald Mountain, and Va. Route 177 over Potts Mountain. Va. Route 188, the road across the top of Brush Mountain, will take you past the monument where World War II hero Audie Murphy's plane crashed.

Camping enthusiasts can stay at Craig Creek Recreation Area, Steel Bridge and the Pines. Some of the best information on Craig County can be obtained from the New Castle Ranger District by calling (540) 864-5195 weekdays. It is located on Va. Route 615, 3 miles east of New Castle.

If you're looking for adventure, wildlife, blessed isolation and meditation, Craig County is the place to live or visit. For more information, contact the County of Craig, Corner of Court and Main streets, New Castle 24127, (540) 864-5010.

Roanoke

Capital of the Blue Ridge, Roanoke (population 96,400) has it all: history, culture, close-knit neighborhoods and a heady sense of environment. Its downtown was the first in North America to offer recycling, thanks to Downtown Roanoke Inc.

These happy environmental facts are the products of a cutting-edge grassroots environmental group, Clean Valley Council, gutsy government officials willing to take a stand, and Cycle Systems, an 80-year-old, fourth-generation recycling firm that has led Virginia in the recycling effort. Just like at Disneyland, you can count the moments before a piece of dropped litter is whisked out of sight . . . that is, if anybody has the gall to drop a piece in this earth-conscious area.

You'll probably do a double-take the first time you see Roanoke's Mill Mountain Star, visible for a radius of 60 miles. The 48-year-old, 100-foot-high star, newly refurbished in 1997, is a popular landmark for airplane pilots who frequently feel compelled to explain to passengers that what they think they're seeing below really is a gigantic, artificial star. The star has lured many people, including Elvis Presley, who donned a disguise to see it after a concert when his curiosity got the best of him. Beside the star are scores of contented, well-illuminated animals at Mill Mountain Zoological Park.

And, just in case you think Roanokers are the only ones who brag about their community, let's talk about awards. A University of Kentucky study calls Roanoke one of the nation's top-20 cities for quality of life. The *Zero Population Growth* newsletter says Roanoke is one of the 10 least stressful cities for quality of life. Downtown Roanoke's revitalization has been touted as one of America's 10 best by the National Trust for Historic Preservation. Its cultural center, Center in the Square, was named one of the best 25 attractions in the world in 1996 and received the prestigious Bruner Award for urban excellence in 1997. Roanoke's historic city market was named one of the nation's top destinations to visit in 1996. And three times in the past decade, including 1996, Roanoke has received the All-America City designation.

Always a crossroads for commerce, Roanoke's story began in the early 17th century. Native resistance to settlers was fierce. The city, formerly called Big Lick for its salt marshes, was later named Roanoke. "Rawrenock," meaning white beads, actually shells with holes worn on strings around the neck and arms and passed as currency among Native Americans, was described early on by Capt. John White, who attempted to settle Roanoke Island in North Carolina.

Little towns were the foundation for what is now the city of Roanoke. New Antwerp appeared in 1802 followed by Gainesborough in 1825 and Old Lick in 1834. Big Lick, chartered in 1874 with 500 citizens, became a railroad crossroads. After Norfolk and Western Railroad came to town in 1882, Roanoke grew quickly. Its historic city market still functions and is the anchor of the revitalized City Market square downtown.

Roanoke is the largest metropolitan city in Virginia west of Richmond and off the widely traveled Blue Ridge Parkway. It is the major center for transportation, served by the Norfolk Southern Railway, the Valley Metro bus system and a modern airport with a $25 million airport terminal built in 1990. The city is also the medical center of western Virginia, with more than 2,400 hospital beds and a gigantic medical center, Roanoke Memorial Hospitals.

The Roanoke Valley has a culture all its own. The Roanoke Symphony has been featured on the *Today Show* and in *The New York Times* and *The Wall Street Journal*. Cultural complements include Opera Roanoke and Center in the Square.

A national exhibition, "To the Rescue," puts Roanoke on the map as the birthplace of the volunteer rescue squad movement. The Explore Project — open, but a work in progress — is a re-creation of an 18th-century pioneer village on nearly 1,500 acres.

Perhaps the most curious of Roanoke's attractions is Miniature Graceland, a private collection of tiny scale-model buildings built by Kim Epperly, the Ultimate Elvis Fan (see our Attractions chapter). And a lighted fountain of recycled metal, which you can see off I-581, is a monument of sorts to Roanoke's devotion to recycling. It was a gift of Cycle Sys-

Photo: Wintergreen Resort

Climbing to higher elevations — whether by strenuous hike or an easy chairlift ride — is essential to get the best Blue Ridge views.

tems. Another curiosity is a Jupiter rocket seen beneath the Wasena Bridge. It belonged to the Transportation Museum, which abandoned the site after being flooded in 1985. Since then, the museum has been trying to get the funds to move it to its new Salem Avenue site.

There's family entertainment aplenty in Roanoke. Striving to live up to its nickname as Festival City of Virginia, Roanoke hosts the blockbuster, two-weekend-long Festival in the Park each May. Nearly 400,000 people attend this celebration of art, music and the human spirit that signals the start of summer in Roanoke. Other festivals include a celebration of African-American culture on Henry Street in the fall and the Chili Cook-off and Community School Strawberry Festival the first May weekend, when palates burning from flaming chili can get cooling ice cream and berries just down the block.

Roanoke is a great jumping-off point for side trips. The number of attractions within an hour's radius is unbelievable, and you'd need a good week's stay just to have time to see and do even half of what's available. Be sure to stop by the Roanoke Valley Convention & Visitors Bureau on the City Market, 114 Market Street, Roanoke 24011, (800) 635-5535.

Roanoke County

Roanoke County (population 80,000) is a mostly affluent suburban area surrounding the City of Roanoke. It includes the placid, comfortable town of Vinton. The county is noted for its superior school system, network of top-notch recreational centers and willingness to finance a superior quality of life for its citizens.

In 1838 mountainous Roanoke County was carved out of the huge county of Botetourt. Many of its communities are named for its peaks; one of the most unusual may be Twelve O'Clock Knob, so named because slaves west of Salem could look at the mountain and tell it was time for lunch when the sun was at a point just over the 2,707-foot peak. Underground springs, another of the area's natural resources, inspired other names, such as Virginia Etna Springs, site of a former water-bottling plant, and Big Cook Spring in Bonsack, an area heavily touched by the Civil War because of several blanket factories there. Legend has it that one factory was burned to the ground by the Yankees but the other was spared because its owner, with fingers crossed, promised not to sell blankets to the Confederate merchants down the road in

Roanoke City. Another spring, Botetourt Springs, became the site of Hollins College, one of the most prestigious undergraduate women's colleges in America (graduate programs are coeducational).

Bonsack, east of Vinton, was the home of Jim Bonsack, who quit Roanoke College to work on a competition to invent the first cigarette-rolling machine. Young Bonsack won the $75,000 competition, patented his machine in 1880 at the age of 22, made a fortune and spawned a national industry.

Roanoke County's pioneering spirit has extended to modern times. The county was the Roanoke Valley's pioneer in curbside recycling and has led the rest of the Valley in environmental concerns and issues. Unfortunately the recycling program was ended in 1997 due to cost. It also has been nationally recognized for governmental cooperation in a joint industrial park and library built with Botetourt County. In 1989 Roanoke was named an All-America City for its governmental cooperation, quality of life and support of the Explore Project.

Explore, a unique recreational and educational experience, is the county's tourism focus. It opened to the public in 1994. Many events are being held there now including astronomy field trips, bird watching, Sierra Club hikes and Scout projects. The restored Hofauger Farmhouse, the focus of the park, is complete and available for use with advance reservations. Explore's three main parts include a frontier settlement, a North American wilderness zoological park and an environmental education center. The park will be completed in various phases, with a major emphasis on environmental preservation.

Recreation and historical preservation have been a longtime focus for Roanoke Countians. Green Hill Equestrian Park is the site of the annual autumn polo match benefiting the Roanoke Symphony. It is one of 44 parks and recreational facilities in the Roanoke Valley.

Roanoke County is known for its family-oriented neighborhoods with styles ranging from urban townhouses to bucolic farmhouses and suburban subdivisions — prices averaging $150,000. Families also like the county for its superior school system, which offers remedial education and classes for the gifted.

Major employers include ITT, manufacturer of night vision goggles, Ingersoll Rand and Allstate Insurance. Tanglewood Mall is the county's busy shopping destination, and numerous family restaurants in the same area make this a magnet for the whole valley.

Most of all, however, Roanoke County is known as a desirable place to live because of the high quality and variety of suburban services it offers residents. For more information, contact the Salem-Roanoke County Chamber of Commerce at 9 N. College Avenue, Salem 24153, (540) 387-0267.

Salem

An old story has made its rounds in the *Roanoke Times* newspaper office about a cub reporter who, having just moved to Salem and feeling a sense of isolation, asked a veteran reporter just how long it would take to get accepted by her neighbors.

"Oh, about three," the old Salem native replied.

"Three years?" responded the incredulous cub.

"No, three generations, my dear!" was the reply.

To say the city of Salem (population 25,000) has a sense of its own history and self-sufficiency is an understatement. Salem, its name derived from "shalom," meaning peace, is the oldest and southernmost community in the Roanoke Valley. That historical fact pervades Salem's quaint, charming culture. Many of its historic downtown Victorian homes, with stained-glass windows, tin roofs and pointed towers, are on the National Historic Register.

Gen. Andrew Lewis started the settlement in 1768 when he acquired his estate, Richfield. In 1806 a charter to James Simpson created the town of Salem out of the Lewis estate, bounded by Union Street, Church Alley and Clay and Calhoun streets. Salem, chartered as a city in 1968, has a downtown museum operated by the local historical society.

Salem also has an excellent sense of community, especially when it comes to sports. The Salem Civic Center is the site of the fabulous Salem Fair and Exposition, the largest of its kind in Virginia.

You can do everything there from bungee jump to watch pigs race. The Civic Center seats 7,500 and offers a wide and varied program of community events.

For example, it's home to the Roanoke Valley Horse Show, one of the 10 largest in the country. Salemites' love for athletics borders on the fanatic and considerable emphasis is placed on recreation, with more opportunities available than in most other areas of similar size. Facilities include a 8,000-seat football stadium for the beloved Salem High Spartans. Salem also provides exciting Class A professional baseball through the Salem Avalanche, a farm team that plays at Salem Municipal Field. The city has three golf courses and is building a fourth.

Salemites also have a collective heart that never stops beating for their own. When high school football star Chance Crawford was paralyzed by a spinal injury during a football game in the early '80s, the townspeople rallied to pay his medical expenses. Beyond that, an annual ball tournament was arranged to assure the Crawfords would have no financial worries. As a final tribute, Crawford was overwhelmingly elected to public office.

Festivals are especially popular. Old Salem Days in September features one of the largest antique car shows on the East Coast as well as fine Salem art. One of the Roanoke Valley's best-known artists, Walter Biggs, lived here, and his legacy is carried on by Salem artists, such as Harriet Stokes.

Vigorous industries, such as General Electric and the regional Veterans Administration Hospital, are here. Salem is home to Roanoke College, a Lutheran-affiliated private liberal-arts school that lends enormous culture to the area's charm. Salem's downtown shopping district has numerous antique stores and mom-and-pop operations. Roanoke College students enjoy the local hangouts Mac & Bob's, Macados and Mill Mountain Coffee & Tea.

Many of Salem's citizens work, live and play within its boundaries and never feel the need to leave their beloved city, regardless of how long it really takes to become an Insider. For more information, contact the Salem-Roanoke County Chamber of Commerce at 9 N. College Avenue, Salem 24153, (540) 387-0267.

Vinton

Vinton, a small, unpretentious town (population 7,665) east of Roanoke, must be doing something right. Over the past several decades, in the midst of its homespun lifestyle, it has spawned and nurtured some of Virginia's most important modern leaders.

On any given day, Virginia House Majority Leader C. Richard Cranwell, called "the most powerful man in the Blue Ridge of Virginia," can be found having lunch downtown with his constituency, who call him "Dicky" and tell him how to run Virginia's Legislature. Fortune 500 Norfolk and Southern CEO David Goode still visits his wise dad, Ott, founder of Vinton's famous Dogwood Festival, at Ott's 50-year-old downtown real estate business to get advice.

Vinton also is an important leader in its own right. In 1990 it put other Virginia municipalities on notice when its forward-looking town council began the first mandatory comprehensive recycling program in the state, effectively reducing landfilled solid waste by 25 percent. Vinton is also proud of a school system ranked among the state's top 10, and its populace comes out in droves for the William Byrd High Terriors. Its school system has the highest average achievement scores in the Valley, and teachers' salaries rank ninth in the state.

Gish's Mill, built prior to 1838, provided a start for the town. David Gish sold his mill to Isaac White Vineyard in 1867, and by that time enough people had settled around the mill to form the basis of the town of Vinton. Although the mill burned, some of the brick walls still stand. The town was chartered in 1884 and relied on the railroad for employment. Moving into the future, the N&W Railway continued to be Vinton's most important industry. Today, Precision Weaving is Vinton's largest employer.

Vinton residents play as hard as they work, having easy access to recreation by the town's proximity to the Blue Ridge Parkway. Vinton's Folklife Festival and Farmer's Market are annual excuses to have a good time. And Vinton hosts the oldest festival in the Roanoke Valley, the Dogwood Festival, always a pageantry of queens, bands, floats and politicians that has attracted a number of celebrities over the past three decades. The first-class, all-American parade always ends at the Vinton War Memorial, Vinton's landmark building and cultural center.

Vinton serves its citizens well with plentiful recreational and spectator sports activities. Its municipal pool is beautiful and its recreation department program and special events are second to none. Vinton's untapped tourism potential is enormous as the center of the politically designated Blue Ridge Region of Virginia. In addition to being next to the well-traveled Parkway (9 million visitors a year travel the Virginia section), Vinton is the last commercial center before Smith Mountain Lake, Virginia's largest lake. It also is the gateway to Virginia's Explore Park.

In the meantime, it's the epitome of small-town living, and the best is yet to come. For more information, contact the town of Vinton at 311 S. Pollard Street, Vinton 24179, (540) 983-0613.

East of the Blue Ridge

This gorgeous stretch of land begins in Loudoun County, with its famous Hunt Country and landed gentry, and sweeps southward along the mountains all the way through Charlottesville and Lynchburg to Franklin County south of Roanoke.

For the most part we are talking about rural territory with few glaring billboards, convenience stores and shopping malls. It's an area rich in history that has little in common with the Shenandoah Valley across the mountains. In fact, the mountains had blocked early attempts at expansion from the east. Whereas the valley was settled primarily by Scotch-Irish and Germans who migrated south from Pennsylvania and Maryland, the foothills east of the Blue Ridge, especially Charlottesville and lands to the north, became home to families moving west from Richmond and the Tidewater area.

Though Interstate 66 cuts across the region, there is no north-south interstate paralleling the Shenandoah Valley's I-81. U.S. Highway 29 is the major artery from Culpeper to Lynchburg, along which you will find wineries, splendid antique shops and quaint country stores. The secondary roads winding through the region will also carry you through hunt country on your way to gorgeous bed and breakfasts and country inns, vineyards, pick-your-own apple orchards and historic mansions open for tours.

It takes a little more effort to tour this region and to do it right, but it's worth it.

Middleburg and Loudoun County

Middleburg, right on the line between Loudoun and Fauquier counties, is the acknowledged Hunt Country Capital and is surrounded by the estates of some of the country's wealthiest and most powerful people. Yet you'd be hard-pressed to identify some of them as they run errands in Middleburg dressed in jeans and gum boots. Until her death, Jackie Kennedy Onassis was a regular in Middleburg, foxhunting with the locals and browsing the town's elegant shops. Philanthropist Paul Mellon and the late ambassador Pamela Harriman had estates in the area, as does actor Robert Duvall. Before her divorce from Sen. John Warner (who owned a farm nearby), Elizabeth Taylor shopped in the local grocery stores. Paul Newman has been known to pop in for lunch at Red Fox Tavern when he has been racing cars at Summit Point in West Virginia.

Middleburg is a delightful anachronism because life follows a centuries-old rhythm as unchanged as its stone walls and pre-Civil War mansions. Horses are a part of daily life and a great equalizer. Your status in the real world

INSIDERS' TIP

Although there are no historical sites in her honor, Grandma Moses used to call the Shenandoah Valley home. Long before she began her painting career at the age of 70 in New York, she lived on her "Mount Airy" farm near Staunton with her husband and children.

matters a lot less than your horsemanship. You can rub elbows with celebrities and the horsey crowd during races and horse shows at Glenwood Park or at the Red Fox Tavern.

Most people are surprised Middleburg's town proper is so small and so uniformly historic. This is, of course, by design. If area property owners have anything to do with it, Middleburg will never see a 7-Eleven or McDonald's, nor will it give way to the wave of development working its way west from Washington, D.C. Very seldom does anything smaller than a 100-acre estate come on the market here. The locals opposed the Walt Disney Company when the entertainment giant planned to build a theme park in Haymarket, just east of Middleburg. Despite having the governor in its corner, Disney finally yielded to the powerful local forces and gave up the project.

There is plenty to see and do in Loudoun, especially in Leesburg and the postcard-perfect villages of Waterford and Hillsboro. Historical sites abound. Morven Park, built in 1780, was the home of two Virginia governors. There is also Oak Hill, the last home of President James Monroe, historic Oatlands Plantations, which schedules special events for the entire family throughout the year, and the Goose Creek Rural Historic District, about 10,000 acres that were once home to Quaker settlers. The village of Lincoln offers a wide variety of 18th-, 19th- and 20th-century rural architecture.

For more information on Loudoun County, contact the Loudoun Tourism Council, 108-D South Street S.E., Leesburg 20175, (800) 752-6118.

Warrenton and Fauquier County

Fauquier, which was named in honor of lieutenant governor Francis Fauquier, claims some of the most productive pastures in America, places where thoroughbreds thrive and the economy is still largely driven by a multimillion dollar equine industry. Paris and Upperville afford some of the most scenic and historic real estate in the Old Dominion. The historic district in Upperville includes many 19th-century buildings made of brick, wood and logs. This small community that formed in 1797 on the turnpike from Alexandria to Winchester got its name from its residential section, or "upper" end of the town.

Warrenton, the county seat, was originally known as Fauquier Court House. The moniker was changed to match an academy named in honor of Gen. Joseph Warren, a Revolutionary War hero. When Warrenton was occupied by Union troops during the Civil War, the town was the site of several raids by Col. John Mosby, also known as the Gray Ghost. He later made his home here after the war. In fact, he is buried in the Warrenton Cemetery, and a monument in his honor stands beside the courthouse.

A popular statue of Chief Justice John Marshall was erected in 1959 during the county's bicentennial celebration. His family home, Oak Hill, was built in 1773. Other favorite attractions in Fauquier County include Warrenton's Old Jail Museum, built in 1779, the Flying Circus Airshow in Bealeton and the Warrenton Hunt, which started in 1883.

For more information on Fauquier County, contact the Warrenton-Fauquier County Visitor Center, 183A Keith Street, Warrenton 20186, (540) 347-4414.

Rappahannock County

Rappahannock County to the south is home to one of the most charming, even Utopian, towns in America, "Little" Washington. It is the oldest of the 28 towns in the United States named for the Father of Our Country, who surveyed and laid out the town around 1749. Washington has its own internationally known restaurant and inn, a performing arts center, an artists' cooperative and several classy galleries, boutiques and antique shops.

Rappahannock's county seat, historic Sperryville, sits below the entrance to the Skyline Drive. It's a great little town to explore on foot, with antiques stores, galleries, arts and crafts studios and a shop where you can buy American Indian weavings, jewelry, quilts and crafts. Rappahannock, by the way, is one of the few counties along the Blue Ridge that derived its name from its earliest settlers. The county took its name from the river, which was named for the Rappahannock Indians, one of the five Powhatan tribes.

Among the northern foothills are two entries into Shenandoah National Park: Thornton Gap at U.S. 211 near Sperryville and Swift Run Gap at U.S. Highway 33, which passes through Greene County.

For more information, contact the Rappahannock County Administrator's Office at P.O. Box 519, Washington 22747. The phone number is (540) 675-3342.

Madison and Greene Counties

Madison County has no road into Shenandoah National Park, a source of longstanding frustration among many residents. The county lost more land to the national park than any other and was reportedly promised a gateway, but for some reason national leaders reneged. This history explains in large part the level of local outrage when park officials proposed expanding the national park's boundaries into the county. The officials eventually dropped the idea, realizing how ugly a battle it would be.

Ironically, Madison County has received national acclaim for one of its scenic roads, but not the Skyline Drive. The Va. Route 231 Scenic Byway, which runs through 50 miles of the Piedmont from Sperryville south to Shadwell, near Charlottesville, was named one of America's 10 Most Outstanding Scenic Byways in 1995. The recognition came from Scenic America of Washington, D.C., an organization that seeks to call attention to outstanding routes and preserve endangered ones.

Madison County's earliest settlers were German ironworkers. When they had completed the terms of their indentured servitude at Lord Spotswood's Germanna mines in Orange County, the Germans set out to build new lives for themselves as craftsmen and farmers. That tradition continues in Madison County. Many craftspeople, such as furniture makers, potters, wood carvers, quilters and jewelry artisans, make this area their home.

The same can be said for Greene County, where you can drop by the Blue Ridge Pottery on U.S. 33 leading to the Skyline Drive and chat with local potter Alan Ward as he works at his wheel. The store, which occupies the former Golden Horseshoe Inn built in 1827, is a kind of headquarters for arts and crafts made especially in Greene County (see our Shopping chapter).

For more information on Madison County, call the Madison County Chamber of Commerce at (540) 948-4455. The address is P.O. Box 373, Madison 22727. For more details on Greene County, contact the Greene County Chamber of Commerce, Main Street, Stanardsville 22973, (804) 985-6300.

Orange County

The beautiful, rolling hills of Orange County hold many historical attractions, including Montpelier, the 2,700-acre estate that was the lifelong home of James Madison and his equally famous and more popular wife, Dolley.

Orange County contains many reminders of the terrible war that nearly split our country in two. The Wilderness Battlefields in the eastern end of the county were the scene of the first clash between the troops of Robert E. Lee and Ulysses S. Grant in May 1864 in which 26,000 soldiers died. The battlefields are open for self-guided tours.

Nearby Gordonsville is home to the Exchange Hotel, a restored railroad hotel that served as a military hospital during the war. It served more than 23,000 soldiers within a year's time. It now houses an excellent Civil War museum.

Closer to Charlottesville are the Barboursville Ruins, what's left of a mansion designed by Thomas Jefferson for James Barbour, governor of Virginia, U.S. Senator, Secretary of War and minister to England.

Montpelier, settled by Madison's grandparents and now owned by the National Trust for Historic Preservation, is open for tours. The estate hosts a wine festival every May, featuring live music, crafts, food and local wines. Montpelier is also the scene of steeplechase races on the first Saturday of every November. Since 1928 this hallowed tradition has drawn huge crowds of horse-lovers.

The James Madison Museum is in nearby Orange, where you can visit the only surviving example of Thomas Jefferson's design for church architecture, St. Thomas Episcopal Church.

Orange County also boasts a thriving vineyard industry, harvesting a sizable amount of grapes each year. Along with the Barboursville Winery, which has been praised by *Wine Spectator* magazine, the county is home to the smaller Burnley Vineyards, one of the oldest vineyards in the region, and the newer Horton Cellars Winery (see our Wineries chapter).

For more information about these and other attractions and fine bed and breakfasts in Orange County, contact the Visitors Bureau, P.O. Box 133, Orange 22960, (540) 672-1653.

Charlottesville and Albemarle County

Charlottesville is a crown jewel of a city, with so much beauty, history, culture and lively commerce that it's no wonder it is growing by leaps and bounds. If he were alive, Thomas Jefferson, a native of the territory, would probably roll his eyes and sigh at the traffic congestion that now clogs such major arteries as U.S. Highway 250 and U.S. Highway 29. Such is the cost of the city's allure, though area residents are working hard to establish a plan for controlled growth.

Fortunately, Albemarle County, which surrounds Charlottesville on all sides, remains largely rural, with rolling pastures, elegant horse farms and lush forests that lead up to the wilderness of the Shenandoah National Park. And the city itself contains many enclaves of natural beauty, from the lovely gardens along the colonnade at the University of Virginia to fine old homes surrounded by mounds of azaleas, rhododendrons and camellias.

Monticello, the architectural wonder Jefferson designed and never stopped tinkering with, remains the area's leading attraction. The mountaintop estate opens its doors to visitors seven days a week, inviting all to glimpse Jefferson's genius through his architecture, gardens and innovations. Another fascinating exhibit about Jefferson's domestic life at Monticello lies down the hill and next to I-64 at the Monticello Visitors Center (see our Arts chapter).

Thanks to Jefferson's architectural abilities, the campus of the University of Virginia is considered one of the most beautiful in the nation. Jefferson designed the Rotunda of his academic village after the Roman Pantheon. The graceful Rotunda, the pavilions and their gardens and the whitewashed colonnade comprise the original university buildings. In 1976 the American Institute of Architects voted the original campus the most outstanding achievement in American architecture.

Not far from Monticello, on another mountain slope, is the home of James Monroe, Jefferson's friend and America's fifth president. Strutting, showy peacocks grace the lawn at Ash Lawn-Highland, where visitors can witness Monroe's cultured lifestyle and learn about a working farm of the 19th century. The boxwood-covered grounds come to life in the summer, when opera performances entertain guests under the stars (see our Arts chapter).

You'll find reminders of this rich history in the streets of downtown Charlottesville, especially around Court Square, where Jefferson and Monroe spent much of their leisure time. Here many buildings bear plaques dating to the early days of the city, making it easy to imagine what the city must have looked like when Jefferson practiced law here. Today several of Jefferson's descendants practice law in this history-rich section of town.

The Albemarle County Courthouse, built in 1762, served as the meeting place of the Virginia Legislature as the leaders fled Cornwallis' approaching army in 1781. State Legislator Daniel Boone was one of the seven men captured in a surprise raid on Charlottesville led by British Cavalry general Banastre Tarleton during that campaign. Tarleton failed at capturing then-governor Jefferson, but nabbed Boone at the corner of Jefferson and Park streets.

History buffs are not the only ones interested in the downtown historic district. Folks of all ages enjoy strolling along the pedestrian Downtown Mall, lined on both sides with boutiques, antique stores, restaurants, ice-cream shops, bookstores, movie theaters, art galleries and a new ice-skating rink. On Fridays, April through September, the Mall hosts a free concert series at its outdoor amphitheater. The series features some of the wonderful local bands from this music-rich town (the Dave

Matthews Band got its start in Charlottesville and has even played at this concert series). The culinary scene in Charlottesville has become rather lively and diverse as well. You'll be tempted by the Indian, Vietnamese, French, German, Italian, Brazilian and American nouvelle cuisine in the area.

Many famous figures of the film and literary world make their home in the Charlottesville area. Charlottesvillians are reportedly known for their ability to fake nonchalance at the sight of such individuals as Sissy Spacek, John Grisham, John Gardner, Rita Dove and Rita Mae Brown. It is considered gauche to gawk or ask for an autograph, and this must be one reason why these famous folks and their families seem to have found such a comfortable life here.

Of course, Charlottesville's association with the rich and famous is nothing new. The area was the setting for part of *Giant*, the Western film starring Elizabeth Taylor, Rock Hudson and James Dean. Randolph Scott, a leading star in *Ride the High Country*, one of the greatest Westerns ever made, lived at Montpelier for a couple of years when he was married to Marion duPont.

The affluence of Charlottesville has had a positive effect with the backing of such cultural resources as the Virginia Film Festival and the Virginia Festival of the Book. Patricia Kluge, ex-wife of the one of the richest men in America, provided the primary means to establish the film festival, held at UVA every October. Illustrious special guests have included Jason Robards, Jimmy Stewart, Gregory Peck, Ann Margret, Charlton Heston and a host of screenwriters, critics and academics.

A trip to Charlottesville isn't complete without at least one stop at a local winery for a sample, a bottle or a tour to learn how wine is made. At least a dozen wineries sit within easy driving distance of Charlottesville.

For more information about the Charlottesville area, you can pick up several free guides while in town. The complimentary *Charlottesville Guide*, available throughout the city, is a source of current events, including happenings in Orange and Madison counties, Waynesboro and Staunton. The *C'ville Weekly*, a free newspaper, will also fill you in on local activities.

You can also contact the Charlottesville/ Albemarle Convention & Visitors Bureau, 600 College Drive, Charlottesville 22902, (804) 977-1783. The University of Virginia also runs an information center at its police department at 2304 Ivy Road, Charlottesville 22903, (804) 924-7166.

Nelson County

Roughly a quarter of this rural, agricultural county lies in the George Washington and Jefferson National Forests. Wintergreen Resort, a four-season vacation paradise with a year-round residential community, hugs the mountains in the western part of the county. Crabtree Falls, a spectacular series of cascades, is one of the highlights of the forest along Va. Route 56, the scenic road that crosses the mountains and enters the Shenandoah Valley at Vesuvius. Apples are a mainstay of the local economy, and beef cattle is the second-leading industry.

Earl Hamner Jr., who wrote the hit family television show of the '70s, *The Waltons*, grew up in the tiny town of Schuyler (pronounced SKY-ler). For years fans have come to Schuyler searching for the old homeplace and other landmarks of the show. In 1992 the Walton's Mountain Museum opened in the very school attended by Hamner and his siblings. Actual sets from the show are set up in former classrooms, and all sorts of interesting memorabilia is displayed.

Another attraction in Nelson County is Oak Ridge, a 4,800-acre estate that belonged to Thomas Fortune Ryan, a leading financier at the turn of the century. A restored 50-room mansion, with its formal Italian gardens, greenhouse and 80 outbuildings, serves as a backdrop for a variety of festivals and cultural events, including a big Summer Festival in June.

Nelson County has four vineyards offering tours and wine tastings, enjoyable outings any time of year but especially in the autumn.

For more information on Nelson County, contact the Nelson County Division of Tourism at 8519 Thomas Nelson Highway, Lovingston 22949, (804) 263-5239 or (800) 282-8223.

Lynchburg and Amherst County

I consider it one of the most interesting spots in the state. — Thomas Jefferson

Democracy's founding father, who scandalized Lynchburg society by eating a "love apple" (tomatoes were thought to be poisonous), summed up best how Lynchburg's citizens feel about their city and its vast array of cultural, educational and recreational opportunities.

For the past 25 years, the national spotlight has shone on the politically active pastor of Lynchburg's internationally known Thomas Roads Baptist Church, the Rev. Jerry Falwell. Known as the City of Churches, Lynchburg (population 70,000) has 129 other houses of worship in addition to the church that launched the Moral Majority. Although the Quakers were the first religious group to settle here and strongly influenced Lynchburg's history, their opposition to slavery caused them to migrate to Ohio and Indiana.

Long before Falwell built his national church from a small Lynchburg congregation, Lynchburg's central location and role in transporting goods by river and railroad had already made it famous. Lynchburg's founder and namesake, John Lynch, was from hardworking Irish stock. His father, Irish runaway Charles Lynch, decided to learn a trade and, at the age of 15 apprenticed himself to a wealthy Quaker tobacco planter. The relationship worked out so well the Roman Catholic Lynch married the planter's daughter. Their equally enterprising son, reared as a Quaker, started a ferry service across the James River in 1757 — at the tender age of 17. In 1786 the Virginia General Assembly granted John Lynch a charter for a town, 45 acres of his own land. Lynchburg was incorporated as a town in 1805 and a city in 1852. Lynch also built the city's first bridge, replacing his ferry in 1812.

Historically known as the Hill City, Lynchburg attracted industrial magnates who dealt in tobacco and iron, the chief products of early Lynchburg. Their ornate, luxurious homes, bordered by enormous decorative wrought-iron fences, are alone worth a visit. Three of them have been made into sumptuous bed and breakfasts: Madison House, The Mansion and Langhorne Manor. Proprietors at all three will pamper you in the manner the original inhabitants were accustomed to.

The inns are in three of Lynchburg's seven original "hill" neighborhoods: College Hill, Daniel's Hill, Diamond Hill, Federal Hill, Franklin Hill, Garland Hill and White Rock Hill. Walking tour maps of the area are available from Lynchburg's Convention & Visitors Bureau at 216 12th Street, Lynchburg 24504. You can call them at (804) 847-1811 for a rundown on so many attractions it will take you a good week to see them all. There are many fine restaurants and great shopping here as well.

In the decade before the Civil War, Lynchburg was one of the two wealthiest cities per capita in the United States. As you would expect, its moneyed citizenry spawned a rich culture. Sarah Bernhardt and Anna Pavlova appeared at the Academy of Music, which opened in 1905. The old music hall has been purchased by Liberty University, which plans to restore it. Jones Memorial Library was completed in 1908 and is one of America's foremost genealogical research libraries. Lynchburg's Fine Arts Center, the city's cultural nucleus, houses two art galleries, a theater, two dance studios and the oldest continuous theater group in the country. Each year, 100,000 people — more than the city's population — take classes, hear concerts and see plays, ballet and art exhibits at the center.

Scores of famous authors sprang from Lynchburg's culture. Two of its most famous, curiously enough, gained their fame for their books on the opposite sides of democratic and racial issues. The great historian Dr. Douglas Southall Freeman, born in Lynchburg in 1886, received 24 honorary degrees and two Pulitzer Prizes, one in 1936 for his four-volume work, *The Life of Robert E. Lee.* The other, in 1948, was for a series on George Washington. Anne Spencer, an African American poet born in 1882, is the only Virginian whose works are included in the Norton Anthology of Modern American and British Poetry. She helped establish Lynchburg's first lending library for African Americans and started Lynchburg's first NAACP chapter. Frequent visitors to Spencer's restored home, garden and studio, Edankraal (open by appointment to visitors at

Photo: Bruce Roberts/Roanoke Valley Convention and Visitors Bureau

Roanoke sparkles when the sun goes down.

1313 Pierce Street), included Dr. Martin Luther King Jr., Dr. George Washington Carver, Jackie Robinson and Marion Anderson, the African-American singing star who was denied entrance to perform in Washington's Daughters of the American Revolution concert hall because of her race.

Interestingly enough, one of the founders of the DAR, Ellet Cabell, was born at Point of Honor, a beautifully restored Lynchburg mansion, now a museum, in the same area as Spencer's house. Point of Honor, so named for the gun duels fought there, was built by Dr. George Cabell Sr., whose most famous patient was Patrick Henry. East of Lynchburg, at Brookneal, is Red Hill Shrine, the last home and burial place of Henry, the great patriot and orator. Point of Honor is part of Lynchburg's city museum system, one which other cities would do well to emulate.

Any discussion of Lynchburg's history must also include the influence of Carter Glass, born in Lynchburg in 1858 and Secretary of the Treasury under President Woodrow Wilson. Glass served as a Virginia state senator from 1899 to 1902, in the U.S. House of Representatives from 1902 to 1918 and represented Virginia in the U.S. Senate from 1920 to 1946. He was the first living person to appear alone on a regular U.S. coin.

Lynchburg's quality of life is also greatly enhanced by its bustling community market at Bateau Landing, where shoppers can choose fresh produce and homemade goods. The annual Festival on the James and The Bateau Festival held in June celebrate the historic James River's contributions with entertainment, historic crafts exhibits and the start of the bateau race to Richmond. Kaleidoscope is an annual fall festival celebrating life in Central Virginia with an arts festival, bands, Riverfront Jamboree, craft show, pops picnic (dining on the lawn to some great music) and the Lynchburg Symphony.

Lynchburg has long been a leading industrial city. It has the highest per-capita manufacturing employment in Virginia. Today it is also home to 3,000 businesses and led the way in developing one of the state's first small business incubators. It is extraordinary how many early industries are still in business. The second-oldest funeral home in America, Diuguid's, has been comforting the bereaved since 1817. Lynchburg Gas Co., founded in 1851, was one of the first in the country to shed light on operating a gas utility. Wiley & Wilson Incorporated, started in 1901, is one of the oldest engineering firms in the United States. In 1901 John Craddock tried the first shoe company in the South on for size in Lynchburg, founding Craddock-Terry. It was a perfect fit; today Craddock-Terry's downtown outlet store offers a dazzling array of 300,000 pairs of shoes.

In 1889 the young pharmacist Charles Brown began selling his Chap-Stick lip balm. Since, his C.B. Fleet Company's product line has expanded to other national lines, including the first disposable enema and Summer's Eve douche. Babcock & Wilcox Co. and General Electric are other major employers.

As a major manufacturing center, Lynchburg played an important role in the Civil War. Perhaps none was more urgent than the advance of medicine for Civil War soldiers brought to the Pest House by Dr. John Jay Terrell. At the Pest House, in the historic Lynchburg Confederate Cemetery, you can view displays of Dr. Terrell's pace-setting work in establishing sanitary standards, including his 19th-century medical kit.

Lynchburg is home to nine diverse colleges. Randolph-Macon Woman's College was the first woman's college in the South to be accredited and the first to receive a Phi Beta Kappa chapter. The Maier Museum, an outstanding collection of American art, is also at the college. Sweet Briar is another well-known woman's college and is affiliated with the Virginia Center for the Creative Arts, an internationally recognized Amherst County working retreat for writers, artists and composers. Also here are Jerry Falwell's Liberty University, Lynchburg College, a liberal arts school, a community college, seminary and two business colleges.

Lynchburg's public schools also are outstanding. Both of its high schools and one of its middle schools have been designated as model schools by the Commonwealth of Virginia. The city also has 10 private schools, the most famous of which is The Virginia School of the Arts, a private boarding school for students grades 7 through 12. Talented young people from around the nation compete to enter the school, which encourages them to achieve the highest standards for performance in dance, drama, music or the visual arts.

High-school sports also are popular. Lynchburg is home to the Virginia High School Coaches Association All-Star Games, bringing the best in high school sports to the area. Colleges offer spectator sports, and when springtime comes, fans head for the diamond to see the area's only Double A professional sports team, the Lynchburg Red Sox.

Golf, tennis and swimming are other popular pastimes. The city operates 10 parks, 24 playgrounds, 34 tennis courts, 26 baseball diamonds and eight community centers. Miller Park is home to an Olympic-size pool. In the heart of Lynchburg is Blackwater Creek Natural Area with the Ruskin Freer Preserve, a 155-acre animal sanctuary.

Lynchburg's two hospitals, Virginia Baptist and Lynchburg General, have gained national attention by sharing staff and services to avoid duplication and keep down expenses. Lynchburg is served by an $8 million airport terminal, built in 1991.

A hub for daytrips, Lynchburg offers many nearby opportunities for sight-seeing. Visitors can go north to Schuyler, the restored home of Earl "John-Boy" Hamner Jr., author of the book on which *The Waltons* TV series was based. Just west of the city is Poplar Forest, Jefferson's summer retreat, now being restored but nevertheless open to the public. Twenty miles east is Appomattox, the site where our nation reunited after the Civil War. Monument Terrace, in the center of Lynchburg's downtown, honors the heroes of all wars.

Whatever you decide to see and do while in Lynchburg, you'll probably echo the words of Thomas Jefferson in deciding it is one of the most interesting spots in the state. For more information, contact the Greater Lynchburg Chamber of Commerce at P.O. Box

2027, 2015 Memorial Avenue, Lynchburg 24501, (804) 845-5966.

North of Lynchburg, Amherst County (population 29,000) was first inhabited by the Monocan Indians. It is named for Sir Jeffrey Amherst, the British commander of all forces in America from 1758 to 1763. Amherst led the British armies that successfully drove France from Canada and was the British hero of the Revolutionary War Battle of Ticonderoga against the upstart Colonists.

Amherst County was created in 1761 from a section of Albemarle County. In 1807 it was divided, and the northern part became Nelson County. Tobacco and apples were early cash crops.

Three-fourths of the county's rolling terrain is forests. The Blue Ridge Parkway offers dramatic views while providing the perfect spot for an afternoon picnic. The county is a popular recreation area boasting magnificent mountain views, clean air and thousands of acres of unspoiled forests, rivers and lakes. Numerous leisure and recreational activities can be found in the George Washington and Jefferson National Forests. The Appalachian Trail bisects Amherst County and affords the serious hiker the ultimate challenge. Winton Country Club, the 18th-century manor that was once the home of Patrick Henry's sister, opens its 18-hole championship golf course to the public here.

Twenty industries also are tucked away in the hills, including a German cuckoo clockmaker, Hermle-Black Forest Clocks.

The Amherst County Historical Museum, in the German Revival-style Kearfott-Wood House, built in 1907 by Dr. Kearfott, is being expanded to include four exhibit rooms and a gift shop. The upstairs is used for storing the museum's collection and office space. A reference library here is available to the public. You can reach the Amherst County Chamber of Commerce at (804) 929-1908.

Smith Mountain Lake

How do you spell relief?

L-A-K-E. Smith Mountain, that is, western Virginia's biggest playground and Virginia's largest lake. Smith Mountain Lake is 20,000 acres of placid waters, 40 miles long and surrounded by 500 miles of shoreline.

It touches Franklin, Bedford and Pittsylvania counties (combined population 142,000). The lake is a colorful place where people love to go and hate to leave. Purple sunsets, stunning blue water and a lot of wildlife, such as glossy green-headed mallard ducks and chubby, gray-striped bass, add to the local color.

As lakes go, Smith Mountain is relatively new. Like its older sister, Claytor Lake, south in Pulaski, Smith Mountain was formed when the Roanoke River was dammed to generate electrical power for Appalachian Power Company. It took six years and a crew of 200 to move 300,000 cubic yards of earth to make way for the 175,000 cubic feet of concrete used to build the Smith Mountain Dam. Full pond is 613 feet above sea level. The river started filling Smith Mountain Lake on September 24, 1963, and reached capacity on March 7, 1966. Archaeologists examining the excavation necessary to build the dam determined that Algonquins fished and hunted here long before anybody else did.

While Smith Mountain was a popular spot from day one, a real breakthrough for the lake was when developer Dave Wilson started Bernard's Landing Resort in the early '80s. Wilson, who later ran into financial problems, is widely credited with being the moving force behind opening the lake to everyone and making it a major western Virginia tourist attraction. Since, Bernard's Landing Resort and its gourmet restaurant, The Landing, have become the most important tourist attractions at the lake, bringing in people from around the country as condominium owners, many of whom offer public rentals. For people who enjoy bed and breakfast inns, the historic Manor at Taylor's Store on Va. Route 122 has been featured in *Southern Living* magazine (see our chapter on Bed and Breakfasts and Country Inns).

A second important addition to the lake's culture was the building of Bridgewater Plaza at Hales Ford Bridge on Va. Route 122. The center of Smith Mountain's social and nightlife, the Plaza has restaurants, a marina, small shops and Harbortown Miniature Golf Course, which is built out over the water. Bands play here on weekends during the summer. It's a fun place to take the kids to play arcade games or just pick up an ice-cream cone while listening to the band.

The year-round lake community, who live in the three counties that surround the lake, has only about 5,000 residents; its significant staid German Baptist population rarely mingles socially with outsiders. They dress similarly to Mennonites and can be identified by the women's mesh bonnets and the men's long beards. Widely known for their agricultural prowess, they live on some of the most beautiful farms you'll ever see and make or grow virtually everything they need.

The anchor of community events is the Smith Mountain Lake Chamber of Commerce and Visitor Center, whose members support the lake's goals and run a Welcome Center staffed entirely by volunteers. Many of them are retirees from the North. At the Chamber — located at Bridgewater Plaza, 16430 Booker T. Washington Highway 2, Moneta 24121 — you can pick up lots of brochures about marinas, Jet Ski and boat rentals, lake homes for rent, campgrounds, fishing guides and anything else you need to have a good time during your stay. The phone number is (800) 676-8203.

Annual events include a Fall Festival, the Wine Festival held at Bernard's Landing, various golf tournaments and dances and the Smith Mountain Tour of Homes to benefit the National Multiple Sclerosis Society and other local charities. The 1997 event was one of the most successful fund-raisers in the nation as people from all over came to see lake living at its best.

The lake offers plenty of things to do on weekdays and weekends. The major attraction is Booker T. Washington National Monument, the former home of the famous African-American statesman, 6 miles south of Hales Ford Bridge on Va. 122. Also stop by APCO's Visitor Center at the Dam off Va. Route 40 on Va. Route 908. It's full of hands-on exhibits for the kids and interesting audiovisuals about how the lake was formed. Smith Mountain Lake State Park, (540) 297-6066, has a full calendar of summertime activities including swimming, fishing and canoeing (see our Recreation chapter).

Golf is a major attraction for residents. However, unless you're a member of the Waterfront or Water's Edge residential communities, your game will be at Westlake's 18 beautiful holes or Mariner's Landing. Westlake's restaurant is also open to the public. As with the other planned communities, it sells villa homesites for those who want to live and play by a golf course.

Other pastimes are parasailing at Bridgewater Marina, (540) 721-1203; and riding Jet Skis (call the Chamber of Commerce for a list of rental places).

For the serious boater, of which there are many, there is the Smith Mountain Yacht Club and at least several dozen marinas offering services ranging from $100,000 houseboats to restaurants to dry-dock. Again, the Chamber of Commerce will give you a complete list. A word of caution: if you are interested in a quiet day on the water, Saturday probably is not the day to be out and about. That seems to be when weekenders, intent on an extra good time and sometimes bolstered by too much drink, take to the water. Sundays and weekdays, however, are relatively calm.

Now, let's talk about fishing, the original reason many people came to the lake. Smith Mountain has a well-deserved reputation as an angler's paradise, especially for striped bass. Some coves literally churn with stripers, especially in the autumn. Getting them to bite your bait is another matter. (See our Recreation chapter's "Fishing" section.)

Now that you've hooked your fish and are also hooked on the lake, let's turn our attention to buying your own vacation home here. Many a millionaire was made from lake real estate. People all over western Virginia are kicking themselves that they didn't buy when land was cheap. There are many tales of people recouping their original investment 10 times over within a decade. Those days, however, are long gone. A prime waterfront lot can easily sell at a starting point of $150,000. Still, lake property remains inexpensive to Northerners used to New Jersey-type real estate prices (see our Real Estate and Retirement chapter).

Regardless of whether you're just visiting or planning to buy real estate and stay, Smith Mountain will win your heart while you're here.

There's nothing more spectacular than a Smith Mountain sunset or more beautiful than the early morning mist blanketing the lake. You'll return many times to enjoy the view and have some fun. And that's no fish tale!

Bedford City and County

It's here Thomas Jefferson came to get away from it all at his summer home, Poplar Forest. That alone should tell you something about the quality of life in Bedford County. And some things never change. Even if nobody ever finds the famous Beale Treasure here, you can easily make a case that Bedford County and its charming county seat are a real "find" in themselves. Let's talk history.

The fastest-growing county outside Virginia's Urban Crescent of Northern Virginia, Bedford County (population 45,349) borders Smith Mountain Lake and is home to Smith Mountain Lake State Park. Bedford also is off the Blue Ridge Parkway, close to one of the Parkway's main attractions, the Peaks of Otter Lodge and Restaurant at Milepost 86, on a spectacular twin-peaked mountain that can be seen for miles.

Bedford is a Main Street Downtown Revitalization City with organizations devoted to its historic past. A wonderful museum and the Bedford County Public Library are downtown.

Bedford County was named for John Russell, fourth Duke of Bedford, who, as Secretary of State for the Southern Department of Great Britain, had supervision of Colonial affairs. The county was formed in 1754 from Lunenburg County and part of Albemarle County. The city was chartered in 1968; in the early '80s it renovated its historic downtown, where interesting shops and restaurants contribute to the ambiance.

Recreation abounds in Bedford County, with the Jefferson section of the National Forest on the north offering the many diversions of the Blue Ridge, including hunting, fishing, camping, picnicking and trails for both horseback riding and biking. Part of the Appalachian Trail passes through the area, with this section especially full of wildflowers and wildlife. The James River flows through in the northeast. City residents enjoy the 59-acre Liberty Lake Park, the heart of recreation. Bedford Lake and Park, 35 acres with a white-sand beach off Va. Route 639, offers swimming, boating, fishing and camping.

The county is largely rural, with half of its land devoted to farming, dairy and beef cattle and orchards. One of the oldest trees on record, definitely the oldest in Virginia, stands at Poplar Park in Bedford County. Bedford also is a manufacturing base for industries that make everything from pottery, clocks and golf carts to food flavoring and stew.

Bedford citizens have a rich small-town culture. There's The Little Town Players, a community theatre organization. The county's Sedalia Center offers classes in everything from classical music to back-to-the-land survival skills and is a tremendous asset to the community. Every Christmas, an estimated 100,000 visitors come to see the lighting display erected by the 200 retired Benevolent and Protective Order of Elks at that fraternal organization's national home.

Poplar Forest, just outside of Lynchburg, is one of the area's most popular destinations as history-lovers flock to see the ongoing excavation and renovation of Thomas Jefferson's beloved octagonal vacation home (see our Arts chapter).

The devout Christian with an imagination will enjoy seeing Holy Land USA, a 400-acre nature sanctuary whose aim is to be a replica of the Holy Land in Israel. Its owners invite study groups and individuals for a free walking tour. Primitive camping is allowed.

What will be Bedford County's major attraction scheduled for completion in 1999, a monument to D-Day of World War II, received sanction and major funding from Congress in 1996. Bedford was chosen because it lost a greater percentage of its men in that battle than any other town in the United States. A dedicated group of D-Day veterans fought for years to make the monument happen, and 51 years after the historic battle that changed the face of the war, they finally are seeing a well-deserved dream come true. National fund-raising chairman is Charles Schultz, creator of the comic strip *Peanuts*.

For more information, contact the Bedford Area Chamber of Commerce at 305 E. Main Street, Bedford 24523, (540) 586-9401.

Franklin County

Franklin County calls itself the Land Between the Lakes, Smith Mountain and Philpott. More miles of shoreline touch Franklin County than either of the other two border counties, Bedford or Pittsylvania. Excluding part-time residents who own lake vacation homes, Franklin County's population is 39,549.

For such a small, rural area, Franklin County has several national claims to fame. It has one of the proudest African-American cultures of any place in the Blue Ridge, evidenced by the Booker T. Washington National Monument. The famous former slave who became one of America's most important scholars and educators lived on a farm that is now the focus of the park near Hales Ford Bridge (see our Arts chapter).

Franklin County's other national claim to fame is a Blue Ridge researcher's dream, the acclaimed Blue Ridge Institute at Ferrum College, where the annual October Folklife Festival pays tribute to the treasured yet nearly forgotten skills of its Blue Ridge culture (see our Arts chapter). The Institute is a national treasure that promotes a culture. It greatly transcends what many Franklin Countians take for granted as everyday life. The Institute offers a museum, archives and records division and a re-created 1800s German-American farmstead to preserve the best of Blue Ridge culture. One of its finest creations, produced for Franklin County's Bicentennial in 1986, is a pictorial record of Franklin County life and culture.

The Blue Ridge Institute's Fall Festival brings many skilled, working craftspeople in for the delight of visitors. You will see demonstrations of spinning, quilt-making, shingle chopping and other homespun crafts. The Festival also offers unique spectator sports, such as Coon Dog Trials.

Another popular festival is the Boones Mill Apple Festival held each fall. Boones Mill is a great place for antiquing on the U.S. 220 corridor to Roanoke. One word of caution when driving through: slow down. The speed limit changes abruptly when you enter the town, and Boones Mill's town officer has had national write-ups for his official police car, a new blue Camaro, which sits on the curb and catches a lot of out-of-state speeders. It might be an important source of revenue to the town, but you'll probably want to make your donations to the county in another manner!

Ferrum College greatly enriches the quality of life for Franklin Countians. In 1997 it sponsored an Environmental Symposium that attracted nationally known speakers. Its fine arts program supports the Jack Tale Players, whose song and drama touring company brings to life the legends of the Upland South. Its Poetic Arts Company demonstrates through performance how poetry plays a vital role in everyday life. Both students and residents enjoy participating in the Blue Ridge Summer Dinner Theatre.

The culture of Franklin County is vastly different, from the early settlers in the county seat of Rocky Mount to the transplanted Northerners at Smith Mountain Lake. Yet a third culture, the German Baptist population, mostly keeps to itself. One exception is Boone's Country Store in Burnt Chimney. The best sticky buns on earth and other tempting edibles are prepared daily at this German Baptist store. People who live an hour's drive away admit to negotiating the winding road up Windy Gap Mountain just to stock their freezer with their "fix" of the sweet pastry.

Franklin County's history is as rich and varied as its people. Its first residents were German, French, English and Scotch-Irish settlers who moved from Pennsylvania in 1750. The county was formed in 1786 by the General Assembly. Munitions for Revolutionary War patriots were made from locally mined iron ore at an iron works on Furnace Creek, which is the county's oldest landmark.

One of the Civil War's most respected Confederate leaders, Lt. Gen. Jubal Early, second in command only to Gen. Stonewall Jackson, was born here. A foundation is restoring his birth home. Rocky Mount is full of many interesting historical buildings. One, the Claiborne House Bed and Breakfast, is open to the public. The Chamber of Commerce, in the courthouse downtown, can give you other pamphlets on historical tours and antique shopping opportunities.

Franklin County is also an outdoor paradise for hunting and fishing. Smith Mountain and Philpott lakes offer wonderful fishing if you have the patience and the right bait. Philpott, a 3,000-acre lake built by the U.S. Army Corps of Engineers, is more rustic than Smith Mountain and also offers boating, a beach and camping. For hunting, wild turkey proves to be the most popular game in the area.

The county's recreation department also offers a host of leisure-time sports and a county recreation program including the largest volleyball league in the state. Ferrum College also gives you a chance to root for championship teams in both men's and women's sports.

Another popular site in Franklin County is Whitey Taylor's Franklin County Speedway, with one of the best payoffs for a short-track 75-lap race in the country, a $5,000 fund.

Of all the counties surrounding the lake, Franklin's housing costs and taxes are generally the lowest, excluding its lakefront property. Farmland, scarce in so many areas of the Blue Ridge, is plentiful here. You're within easy commuting distance of either the Roanoke Valley or Martinsville, a furniture and knitting mill area with great furniture outlets (Stanleytown and Bassett) and the Tultex (sweatsuit) outlet stores. Franklin County's low taxes attract a lot of manufacturing industry. Cabinet makers, such as MW Company and Cooper Wood Products, call the county home.

When you're between stops, visit the land between the lakes. Whether you play, shop or visit one of its national attractions, you'll find plenty to fill up your time. For more information, contact the Franklin County Chamber of Commerce at 261 Franklin Street, Rocky Mount 24151 or P.O. Box 158, Rocky Mount 24151, (540) 483-9542.

New River Valley

The academically stimulating, scenic and mountainous New River Valley of Virginia is one of the most steadily growing areas of the Blue Ridge. It includes Montgomery County and the towns of Blacksburg and Christiansburg, the city of Radford, and Floyd, Giles and Pulaski counties. Although all are in the same area, you couldn't find a more diverse cultural group. The common thread again is the sheer beauty of the environment.

From the 1970s to 1990, the New River Valley's population grew by nearly a fourth to 152,720. People just keep on coming, and few ever leave. That's due to the presence of Virginia Tech, Virginia's largest university with 22,000 students, as well as Radford University's 8,000 students. Every year, scores of mountain-struck students are smitten by the New River Valley Flu, a curious mental illness that causes them to turn down lucrative jobs in the big city and vow to flip hamburgers or do whatever they have to in order to stay in the area.

Blacksburg was named by Rand McNally as one of the top-20 places to live in the United States. A publication for mature adults names it as one of the best retirement spots in the country. The reasons are diverse but mostly involve the winning combination of a scenic mountain vacation land and extraordinary cultural enrichment from its multinational university population.

An interesting historical fact is that the New River is actually old — really old! According to legend it's the second-oldest river in the world; only Egypt's historic Nile is older. The 300-million-year-old river is an anomaly because it flows from south to north and cuts through the Alleghenies from east to west. The New River is 320 miles long from its headwaters near Blowing Rock, North Carolina, to the point in West Virginia where it tumultuously joins the Gauley River to form some of the best whitewater rafting in the East. Outfitters at the Gauley River Gorge regularly host celebrities and nearby Washington politicians, such as Ted Kennedy, who are looking for a refreshing crash of water instead of a staggering crush of paper.

Unlike the populous Nile River area, the New River Valley was a vast, empty land with no permanent inhabitants when the first white explorers saw the area in 1654. Drapers Meadow near Blacksburg is regarded as the first New River settlement. Germans in Prices Fork and Dunkards in Radford established themselves about the same time. Native Americans ventured in only to hunt. For the first settlers, the natives were a threat greater than cold or starvation. Bands of Shawnees periodically would sweep in to kill settlers and destroy their homes. One such episode — a 1755 massacre of many Drapers Meadow residents — became the inspiration for a play. In the attack, Mary Draper Ingles and Betty Robinson Draper were taken hostage; Mary escaped and found her way home by following the New River. Her riveting saga, *The Long Way Home*, is re-created each summer on an outdoor stage in Radford. It is acted out at the homestead where Ingles and her husband eventually lived.

The New River Valley has an exciting textbook history that's matched by its history of research and development. Virginia Tech's IBM 3090 supercomputer was the first in the nation to be fully integrated with a university's computing network and made generally available to faculty and students. It's a fact there are more computers than telephones on campus. *The National Enquirer* once described Blacksburg as a village that had gone computer berserk. Blacksburg was featured as the lead story, "The Electronic Village," in *Reader's Digest* in 1996.

Virginia Tech's Corporate Research Center has 500 employees looking into everything from why illnesses can affect the immune system, very important to AIDS virus research, to robotics and fiber optics, all on the same 120-acre site. All total, $100 million is spent each year by Virginia Tech researchers, many of whom enjoy a national reputation. Business and industry are the largest users of the center and often bring their problems for analysis by some of the nation's greatest minds.

Here is a brief overview of the New River Valley's communities, with a short history and current attractions, many of which can be found outlined in detail in other chapters.

Blacksburg

The largest town in Virginia in both population and land, Blacksburg (population 35,000) sits majestically on a mountain plateau between two of nature's masterpieces, the Blue Ridge Mountains of Virginia and the great Alleghenies.

The growing town has a national recognition as an ideal community, charming, but with a constant flow of professors and students who lend to it most of its culture. Newcomers, students and others are easily and quickly as-

similated into the town's uniquely wonderful, abundant social life.

Touring Broadway shows, well-known speakers and popular musicians appear regularly on campus. Several university performing arts groups, the Audubon Quartet and Theatre Arts Program, are recognized nationally. Tech's NCAA Division I basketball and football teams often appear in postseason contests, and tailgating is the event every autumn. You've never seen anything until you see the enthusiasm when the Tech Hokies meet the University of Virginia Cavaliers.

These glowing quality-of-life reports can be attributed to the sprawling presence of Virginia Tech, its students and 5,000 employees and its innumerable cultural offerings, many of which are free to the Blacksburg community. It would be difficult to find another community in Virginia with as many professionals of every type, from educators to seafood industry experts. One of its most famous, Prof. James Robertson (see our Civil War chapter), was named the foremost Civil War historian in America by the United Daughters of the Confederacy.

Tech's outreach into the community through its Extension Service and other programs affects the quality of life across Virginia. While businesses are sending their problems to researchers, local veterinarians, for example, routinely send their toughest cases to Tech's Veterinary School.

However, Tech wasn't always the town's main focal point. Blacksburg's name comes from the William Black family, who contributed acreage after Blacksburg was granted a town charter in 1798. For 75 years the town was known as a quiet and pleasant place to live. Then, in 1872, Dr. Henry Black petitioned the General Assembly to establish a land-grant university in his town. The university opened with one building and 43 students.

Since then the town and college relationship has created a community that combines a small-town atmosphere with big-city sophistication. Shopping malls and Blacksburg's active downtown offer many things you usually see only in places like Washington, D.C. Yet the pace of life is relaxed. You won't see any smog to speak of, smell many fumes or be bothered by excessive noise. Blacksburg takes its quality of life seriously. Its town council is mostly made up, traditionally, of Tech educators who put their theories into practice.

Amidst all this heady academia, there's a universal love for recreation. You can immerse yourself in all kinds of outdoor fun within minutes. Floating down the New River with an innertube and cooler is a popular pastime. Swim in Blacksburg's municipal pool, which sits on a ledge overlooking the spectacular mountain range, or hike in the forest and sightsee along the Blue Ridge Parkway.

Transportation is efficient, with a terrific bicycle path reminiscent of big-city parks. The National Association of Public Transit ranks Blacksburg's municipal bus system as the best in the nation for its size. The heavily used and newly renovated Virginia Tech Airport sees many corporate jets.

As one of the fastest-growing, progressive communities in Virginia, many more people come to Blacksburg than leave. And, with all the area has to offer, that's liable to remain the trend for a long, long time. For more information, contact the Blacksburg Chamber of Commerce and Visitor Center at 1995 S. Main Street, Blacksburg 24060, (540) 552-4061. The Visitor Center is in Suite 901, while the Chamber is next door in Suite 902.

Christiansburg

Christiansburg, Montgomery County's seat and the fourth-largest town population in Virginia, is a charming, historic place anchoring a county population of 73,913. The county's rural villages of Shawsville and Riner are equally quaint. Va. Route 8 W. connects the county to the 469-mile-long Blue Ridge Parkway. A quiet river that flows under Main Street (the Wilderness Trail) marks the continental divide, where flowing groundwater changes its course toward the Ohio-Mississippi river system.

The last legal gun duel in this country, the Lewis-McHenry, was fought in Christiansburg's renovated Cambria historic district in 1808. Depot Street, location of the Christiansburg Depot Museum, was the site of the depot burned in 1864 by the Union Army. The Cambria Emporium, built in 1908, is now the site of a fabulous antique mall with its own antique General Store.

The town's skyline is dotted with history including the steeples of Old Methodist Church, built sometime in the early 19th century; Christiansburg Presbyterian, c. 1853; and Schaeffer Memorial Baptist, erected in 1884.

Christiansburg's founder was Col. William Christian, an Irish Colonial settler.

The town served as an outpost on the Wilderness Trail, opened by Daniel Boone as the gateway to the West for settlers such as Davy Crockett. In 1866 the legendary Booker T. Washington of nearby Franklin County supervised the Christiansburg Industrial School for black children.

The northern portion of Montgomery County contains nearly 20,000 acres of the Jefferson National Forest. The Bikecentennial and Appalachian trails pass through the county. Between Blacksburg and Christiansburg, on U.S. Highway 460, is the 90-acre Montgomery County Park, one of the area's many recreation spots. Facilities here include a swimming pool, bathhouse, fitness trail and picnic area. In all, the county has four 18-hole golf courses, 68 outdoor and five indoor tennis courts, 18 swimming pools, 37 ballfields and numerous playgrounds.

An added plus for Montgomery County is that real estate, both land and houses, costs significantly less than it does in Blacksburg. For the same money you can get so much more, with a fantastic quality of life as well.

For more information, contact the Montgomery County-Christiansburg Chamber of Commerce at 205 W. Main Street, Suite 4, Christiansburg 24073, (540) 382-4251.

INSIDERS' TIP

When considering trips to the Blue Ridge, think about a hub-and-spoke concept: stay in a metropolitan area and take side trips to smaller towns and attractions. After your first day, you'll get a feel for how long it takes to get places.

Giles County

If you love dramatic mountain scenery, don't miss Giles County, especially the autumn vista from U.S. 460 traveling south from Blacksburg. Giles County (population 16,500) is a mountain haven of forests, cliffs, cascading waterfalls, fast-flowing creeks and streams and, of course, the scenic New River. Its county seat, Pearisburg, is one of only two towns on the Maine-to-Georgia Appalachian Trail. Of the four covered bridges left in the Blue Ridge, two are in Giles County at Sinking Creek (see our Attractions chapter).

Giles County is a paradise for outdoors-lovers. Whether your preference is for golfing a challenging emerald-green course, fly-casting in an ice-cold mountain stream for trout, canoeing the New River's white water or hiking, Giles has it. Giles's most scenic attraction and one of the most-photographed in the Blue Ridge is the Cascades waterfall, which awaits you at the end of a rigorous, 3-mile hiking trail in Pembroke (see our Recreation chapter); the trek is not recommended for small children. After your uphill pull, which seems to last forever, your excellent reward for this adventure is bathing at the foot of the tumbling, 60-foot-high waterfall.

A tamer destination, and just as much fun for kids, is Castle Rock Recreation Area, for golf, tennis and swimming. Or rent a canoe and kayak (see our Recreation chapter). Giles County's most famous attraction is the fabulous Mountain Lake Hotel and Resort, set atop the second-highest mountain, Salt Pond Mountain, in Virginia and overlooking the town of Blacksburg, miles away (see our Resorts and Restaurants chapters). For years, it has been known for the beauty of its stone lodge and its gourmet cuisine. Of late, it is best known for the movie *Dirty Dancing*, filmed here as the epitome of early '60s-era great resorts

Another popular scenic destination is the attractive village of Newport, with its country store and steepled church. The quaint hamlet nestles at the foot of Gap Mountain at Sinking Creek.

Formed in 1806, the county was named for Gov. William Giles. In addition to tourism, Giles County's biggest employer is the Hoechst-Celanese Plant in Narrows. A bed-room community to many professionals, the county has a school system with one of Virginia's lowest student-to-teacher ratios — 16-to-1 — emphasizing a personal approach to instruction.

In addition to far-flung outdoor recreation Giles also offers the culture of its historic Andrew Johnston House, Giles Little Theatre and great antique shopping. A lot of Virginia Tech educators and professionals have discovered Giles, so you may have trouble finding available farmland. However, many gorgeous mountaintop chalets and homes are on the market at any given time. Contact the New River Valley Association of Realtors, (540) 953-0040. For more information on Giles County, contact the Chamber of Commerce at 101 S. Main Street, Pearisburg 24134, (540) 921-5000.

Radford

For quality of life, Radford (population 15,940) has the whole country beat — that is, if you want to stake it on longevity. The late Margaret Skeete, who died there in 1993 at the age of 114, was considered the oldest person in the United States and was listed in *The Guinness Book of Records*. Maybe living beside one of the oldest rivers in the world, the New River, had something to do with Skeete's remarkably long life. The river, which flows through this university city, adds something special to its quality of life.

Radford, the region's only independent city, was incorporated in 1892 and grew to be an important rail division point. It also became the home of Radford University, enrollment 8,000, and is the site of Virginia's only outdoor historical drama, *The Long Way Home*, depicting the famous story of Mary Draper Ingles's escape from the Shawnees.

Another of Radford's major attractions is 58-acre Bisset Park, with a walking trail beside nearly a mile of the tree-lined New River. This perfect park is capped off with a gazebo, swimming pool, several playgrounds and a tennis court. Colorful hot-air balloons also take off from the park. If you were to design the recreational area of your dreams, this would probably be it!

Radford's energetic downtown is a Main Street community and has seen numerous

Photo: Booker T. Washington National Monument

Noted scholar Booker T. Washington was born in this cabin in Franklin County.

unique small businesses start up, many serving the student population. To encourage small business development, Radford even publishes its own brochure, *New Business Start-up Guide*.

The impact of Radford University on the city is comparable to that of neighboring Virginia Tech's on the town of Blacksburg. The Dedmon Center, a $13 million athletic facility, is an unbelievable community gem featuring an air-supported fabric roof atop a gymnasium and natatorium. The adjacent grounds have several softball, soccer, field hockey and flag football fields. Radford is also fanatic about its high school Bobcats' sports teams.

Other noted Radford facilities include the 2,000-square-foot Flossie Martin Art Gallery, one of the Blue Ridge region's finest. A guest professor program has brought in entertainer Steve Allen, civil rights activist Jesse Jackson, Nobel Prize winner Elie Wiesel, Egypt's widowed Jihan Sadat (who displayed her own personal Egyptian art collection) and columnist Jack Anderson.

The city also has an outstanding academic tradition with its primary and secondary schools. Its school system, heavily influenced by college-educated parents, has been nominated by the Commonwealth of Virginia as one of the nation's best.

Radford's environment beside the sometimes placid, sometimes raging New River is symbolic of Radford's dynamic quality of life. For more information, contact the Radford Chamber of Commerce at 1126 Norwood Street, Radford 24141, (540) 639-2202.

Pulaski

The town of Pulaski and Pulaski County (population 34,496), named for Count Pulaski of Poland, a Revolutionary War hero, has attractions ranging from the historic sites to vast water recreation and sports, including a speedway and farm baseball team.

Old Newbern, Pulaski's first county seat and the only Virginia town totally encompassed in a historic district, is recognized by both the National Historic Register and the Virginia Landmarks Commission. You can tour the Wilderness Road Museum. Pulaski's renovated historic Main Street is also a fun stroll past 20 charming shops and quaint restaurants, mostly examples of Victorian architecture. Pulaski's downtown also is blessed with the New River Valley's cultural gem, its Fine Arts Center, which is housed in an 1898 Victorian commercial building (see our Arts chapter).

Outdoors enthusiasts will feel right at home at Claytor Lake. Like its younger counterpart, Smith Mountain Lake, Claytor was formed in 1939 to generate electricity for Appalachian Power Company (now American Electric Power). It is the centerpiece of a 472-acre state park that's a haven for boaters, anglers, horseback riders, campers and swimmers (its white-sand beach will make you think you're at the ocean). Nearby is a spectacular condominium development, Mallard Point. The county has another nice outdoor area, Gatewood Reservoir Park (see our Recreation chapter).

Sports fans will appreciate the New River Speedway, on U.S. 11. Open early April through late September, it is a NASCAR-Winston racing series track seating 10,000 fans. Pulaski County also is home to the highly respected New River Community College in Dublin.

Pulaski County workers also have an impressive mix of job opportunities. The Volvo GM Heavy Truck Corp. is one of the largest employers along with the Pulaski Furniture Company.

For more information, contact the Pulaski County Chamber of Commerce at P.O. Box 169, Pulaski 24301-0169, (540) 980-1991.

Floyd County

Follow Va. Route 8 south from Christiansburg and you'll find yourself in Floyd County (population 12,005). Just as movie stars are attracted to Charlottesville, '60s-era holdouts have been migrating to Floyd for the past 35 years. Their tie-dyed counterculture communes nestle quietly along with small farms in a county that promotes an employer of six people, Chateau Morrisette Winery, as one of its major industries. Many residents live quietly off the land.

Another employer makes gasohol, touted by some since the '70s gas crisis as the only way to fuel autos. A planned counterculture community has established a self-sufficient Ecovillage in Floyd County. High Flowing Community is an international community that focuses on sustainable agriculture, spiritual development and art with an emphasis on Mayan and shamanic influences.

Just don't go to Floyd actively looking for the counterculture. They have ingratiated themselves to the local farmers with their true sense of community spirit and are safely tucked away in the hills of Floyd, bothering no one and expecting the same treatment. The followers of this alternative lifestyle are most visible elsewhere, actually, at regional arts and crafts shows, where they sell their wares ranging from twisted grapevine baskets to tie-dyed and batik clothing and pottery. However, you don't have to leave Floyd to buy their wares.

One of the most prolific and amazing arts and crafts stores in the Blue Ridge, New Mountain Mercantile, 6 miles off the Blue Ridge Parkway on Locust Street, is the central location for area craftspeople to display and sell. You can spend hours investigating the building, art gallery and upstairs Byrd's Walden Pond Products, which offer self-help tapes and herbal body care, among other back-to-the-earth products.

Locals also can be found hanging out at the Blue Ridge Restaurant, in an early 1900s bank building, and Pine Tavern Restaurant and Lodge, a comfortable country inn where the fine food includes vegetarian fare.

The most famous regional landmark for both locals and tourists is the inimitable Cockram's General Store, where every Friday is a hoedown! During the day, the store sells the likes of corn cob jelly and local crafts. There's no admission for the Friday Night Jamboree with pure mountain music and dancing and a fun, friendly family atmosphere. Next door is the largest distributor of bluegrass and old-time music in the world. Other places that endear Floyd County to shoppers seeking the wild and wonderful are Schoolhouse Fabrics, housed in what was once an 1846 school, and Chateau Morrisette Winery and Le Chien Noir Restaurant in Meadows of Dan (see our Shopping and Arts chapters for the whole scoop).

The most famous national landmark here

is the picturesque Mabry Mill Blue Ridge Parkway Visitors Center, campground and recreation area. The restaurant here is quite good. The real feast, however, is one for the senses at the old-time, water-powered grist mill and interpretive historical buildings. This is usually the first place western Virginians take internationals for a true taste of American history and beauty.

The history of Floyd is actually rather sketchy, according to its Chamber of Commerce. Early land surveys showed an attempt to settle the area in 1740. The county was officially formed from Montgomery County in 1831. Floyd's original name was Jacksonville, named for Andrew Jackson, our nation's seventh president. Incorporated in 1858, the town changed its name to Floyd in 1896, although no one knows the official reason why.

When you visit the New River Valley, take a day to check out Floyd County, mingle with the locals, see some terrific arts and crafts and listen to some of the best bluegrass and gospel you'll ever hear. Floyd County truly is a sightseer's delight and photographer's paradise with the Blue Ridge Parkway's misty mountain views and miles of split-log fences. A map is smart when traveling Floyd's miles of rural, obscure back roads. You can receive this map and other information from the Floyd County Chamber of Commerce, P.O. Box 510, Floyd 24091, (540) 745-4407.

Alleghany Highlands

Alleghany County

Lovers of the outdoors, sports, antiques, railroads, history and good food can find their favorite things in Alleghany County (population 12,969). The county, situated on the Allegheny mountain range and half-covered by the George Washington and Jefferson National Forests, is the western gateway to Virginia. This vacation playground filled with gorgeous scenery is next door to wild, wonderful West Virginia's Greenbrier County, home of the world-famous Greenbrier Resort.

Before the formation of Alleghany County, property records were provided from Fincastle in Botetourt County, a two-day trip. So, in 1822, the County of Alleghany was formed, named after the mountains in which they lie, although the mountains are spelled differently than the county name.

Its county seat, Covington, was named in honor of Gen. Leonard Covington, hero of the War of 1812 and confidant to James Madison and Thomas Jefferson. Clifton Forge, the county's other populous area, was named for its iron production; it contributed cannons and cannonballs to the Civil War effort. During the Civil War, Alleghany County furnished more soldiers to the Confederacy than it had voters and suffered greatly in the war, since it was located next to West Virginia, which joined the Union.

After the war, Clifton Forge was selected by the Chesapeake and Ohio Railway as the site of its new depot. The coming of the railroad triggered economic growth, and in 1906 Clifton Forge received its city charter. Natural resources have always been Alleghany County's main industry; hemp, used in rope production, was an early product. The biggest boost to industrial progress came in 1899, when the West Virginia Pulp and Paper Co. decided to put a mill in Covington. The railroad and Westvaco Paper Mill continue to play important roles in the county's culture and economy.

Many of the counties attractions are tied to its history. In the charming historic city of Clifton Forge, the C&O Historical Society Archives preserves the railroad's artifacts and equipment. Also worth a visit is the Alleghany Highlands Arts and Crafts Center, displaying fine regional arts and crafts (see our Arts chapter).

Lucy Selina Furnace stacks, more than 100 feet tall, are reminders of the area's 19th-century iron industry. A stunning Victorian mansion built by the owner of the rich iron mines has been turned into the charming Longdale Bed & Breakfast. Local lore says a staff of eight was required just to maintain its gardens.

Nearby is the Longdale Recreation Area, which features miles of mountain trails, camping and sand-beach swimming. All are off I-64's Exit 10 on Va. Route 269 in Longdale. Roaring Run Recreation Area, the site of the ruins of an 1838 iron furnace, is another wonderful place to hike and picnic. It's off U.S. 220 S.

Photo: Wintergreen Resort

Many a discovery is made on a rocky mountaintop.

Other historic points of interest are Fort Young, a reconstruction of the original French and Indian War fort off I-64, Exit 4, near Covington. Lovers of architecture will enjoy seeing Oakland Grove Presbyterian Church, which served as a hospital during the Civil War. It can be seen in Selma off I-64 on Exit 7.

Water has also played a role in the history and life of the county. The unassuming, unmarked source of Quibell water, which rivals Perrier nationally, is next to a cattle grate crossing near to Sweet Chalybeate Springs. The water is trucked away daily for bottling in Roanoke.

Sweet Chalybeate (pronounced Ka-LEE-bee) Pools and gazebo, off Va. Route 311 near the West Virginia border, date back 150 years as a great pre-Civil War resort. It was renovated after lying in waste following the demise of the Civil War aristocracy. The pools now offer bathers the most highly carbonated mineral water in the world. Locals swear by the water's healing powers and many either take a dip or drink its water daily.

Outdoorsy fun awaits at several other Alleghany County sites. Twelve miles of water entice visitors to Lake Moomaw, a relatively new lake formed for power generation 19 miles

from Covington. Signs point the way. Residents and visitors have taken advantage of water-skiing, boating, fishing and swimming. Douthat State Park's 50-acre lake also offers a beach, bathhouse, boating and excellent trout fishing. Other facilities include a visitors center, restaurant and lodge as well as cabins, campgrounds and miles of hiking trails. And the world's largest pump storage facility in the world, Virginia Power's Back Creek Pump Storage Station, is also worth seeing.

For obvious reasons, anglers find Paint Bank State Trout Hatchery on Va. Route 311 an interesting place to visit. It is open daily from 7:30 AM until 4 PM. Rock lovers will want to visit Rainbow Gap or Iron Gate Gorge, which create a geologist's paradise a mile south of Clifton Forge on U.S. 220. For 12 million years, the Jackson River has been working on this masterpiece.

Across the border in West Virginia, the attractions are overwhelming. The big one, of course, is the world-famous Greenbrier Resort (see our Resorts chapter). The grounds alone are magnificent, and the resort welcomes visitors, even if you don't spend the night.

Also close to the West Virginia border, but

still in Virginia, is a great dining experience in a place called Crows. If you blink, you'll miss it, so keep a look out for the rustic sign with the eagle, indicating Eagle's Nest Restaurant (see our Restaurants chapter). Built beside a rolling waterfall, the restaurant has gourmet food so good that corporate officials flying into the area from around the world are some of its most loyal customers.

Several other West Virginia attractions within an hour's drive are north up W.Va. 92. Blue Bend swimming hole in Alvon, one of the best in the Blue Ridge, is one of them. Lake Sherwood, farther up W.Va. 92, is nice, too, and rents paddleboats. The Cass Scenic Railroad is close to Marlinton, as is Snowshoe Ski Resort. The town of Lewisburg, cultured and sophisticated, is also worth a visit for its charming downtown shops and Carnegie Hall, built by the same industrialist tycoon as its more famous counterpart.

The people are friendly and downright glad to see you in Alleghany County. Brochures of all the area's attractions can be picked up at the Jerry's Run Virginia Visitor's Center at 1 Welcome Center Drive, Covington 24426. Or, contact the Alleghany Highlands Chamber of Commerce at 501 Ridgeway Street, Clifton Forge 24422, (540) 962-2178. The chamber's main office is at 241 W. Main Street, Covington 24426.

Bath County

Nestled between Alleghany and Highland counties and bordering West Virginia, Bath County (population 4,799) doesn't even have a stoplight. What it does have attracts visitors, whether they're on a budget or staying at the world-famous Homestead Resort.

The bubbly mineral springs, or baths, that gave the county its name are a source of plea-sure for visitors. Bath County was founded in 1745 by pioneers of mostly Scotch-Irish descent, most notably John Lewis, who settled at Fort Lewis. One son, Charles, died in the historic Battle of Point Pleasant in 1774. The other son, John, built the first hotel on the site of the present Homestead Resort in 1766. His structure was destroyed by fire in 1901. In the meantime, M.E. Ingalls, president of the Chesa-peake and Ohio Railroad, bought the site, and the modern era of the resort was launched.

Some historic sites in the county are the Warwickton Mansion Bed & Breakfast at Hidden Valley, site of the movie *Sommersby*; the Anderson Cottage in Warm Springs; and Windy Cove Presbyterian Church at Millboro.

The real history of the county, however, lies in its springs, which have been drawing people for more than 200 years. Wrote one visitor in 1750, "The spring water is very clear and warmer than new milk." Thermal springs are found at Warm Springs, Hot Springs and Bolar Springs, at temperatures ranging from 77 to 106 degrees F. They flow at rates ranging from 2,500 to 5,000 gallons a minute. The water has a soft fizz of tickling bubbles, and taking of the baths is like lowering yourself into a warm vat of Quibell, whose source springs are in Alleghany County.

Public pools have been open at Warm Springs since 1761 and look today much as they did then. The covered pools were the cultural center of the rich and famous. Thomas Jefferson "took the waters" here for his health, as did the frail Mrs. Robert E. Lee (she had crippling arthritis), whose chair, used to lower her into the pool, is still on display at the ladies' pool.

Thus, the stage was set for the aristocracy to visit this scenic land, which is nearly 90 percent forest. That's how the internationally known Homestead Resort, detailed in our Re-

INSIDERS' TIP

The Roanoke Star atop Mill Mountain will turn 50 this year on the day before Thanksgiving. The Downtown Merchants Association and the Chamber of Commerce lit up the 10,000-pound neon structure as a Christmas season display in 1949. In fact, it was even listed as an unusual Christmas display in the December 19 issue of *Life* magazine. Today, it costs about $75 a month to light the local landmark that airplanes can see from 60 miles away.

sorts chapter, came into being. As Bath County celebrated its Bicentennial in 1991, the Ingalls family celebrated its 100th year of running the famous Homestead Resort. It was purchased in 1993 by Resorts International of Dallas, Texas, and is undergoing extensive renovation. The Homestead offers the superlatives of everything — recreation, dining, shopping — in a setting of style and grandeur equaled only by its neighbor, The Greenbrier, in nearby White Sulphur Springs, West Virginia.

The same crowd that goes to The Homestead are regulars at an absolutely serendipitous place, Garth Newel Music Center. The sound of critically acclaimed chamber music wafts through the mountains throughout the year, attracting cultured people from around the world. You never know which celebrity you'll see there taking in a concert while staying at The Homestead or visiting friends at a country estate. Locals leave them alone, though.

You don't need to be wealthy, however, to really enjoy your stay in Bath County. The county has many nice bed and breakfast inns and two outstanding ones, Meadow Lane Lodge and Fort Lewis Lodge. At Fort Lewis, hunting is the autumn and winter mainstay, and spring and summer offer lazy tubing down the placid Cowpasture River, hiking and camping and Caryn Cowden's wonderful cooking. It's a wholesome, airy retreat the whole family will enjoy (see our Bed and Breakfasts and County Inns chapter).

Dining is a pleasure here as well. The Inn at Gristmill Square, restored by the Hirsh family, is the center of Warm Springs, with its dining, shops and lodging. More great shopping awaits at the Bacova Outlet (see our Shopping chapter).

Spelunkers will find adventures in Burnsville's large caverns and sunken caves, while the forests and mountains beckon those who hike, hunt, fish or ride. The George Washington and Jefferson National Forests, Gathright Game Management Area and Douthat State Park are in the county.

The Bath County Chamber of Commerce has a visitors guide that will tell you everything you need to know about this natural, genteel land. Contact them at P.O. Box 718, Hot Springs 24445, (800) 628-8092.

Highland County

Nicknamed the Switzerland of Virginia, scenic Highland County (population 2,800) has more sheep than people, on land with a higher mean elevation than any county east of the Mississippi River.

Few places have preserved their surroundings and privacy so well. Even Highland County's official brochure invites businesses to locate here providing their "environment won't be endangered." One of the most influential conservation groups in America, the Ruffled Grouse Society, was founded here in 1961.

Highland County was established in 1847 from the counties of Bath and Pendleton, in what is now West Virginia. Its county seat, Monterey, sits 3,000 feet above sea level, while its western border in the Allegheny Mountains reaches elevations of 4,500.

Once the hunting grounds for the Shawnee, Highland was first entered by European settlers in the 1700s, when it was still a part of Augusta County, of which it remained until 1787. In the 10-year-long Indian War of 1754, the county was on the frontier. Highland men also made up the company that fought the Battle of Point Pleasant under the command of Col. Andrew Lewis.

An interesting note: German Gen. Erwin Rommel, the Desert Fox, visited Highland County prior to World War I so he could study Stonewall Jackson's military tactics at McDowell. Talk about biting the hand that feeds you! Later, Rommel used the same tactics against the United States and its allies.

To the visitor, Highland County is both beautiful and severe. Every March, this small population rallies to put on one of the top-20 festivals in America, the Highland County Maple Festival, which draws 70,000 over a two-weekend span. The festival takes you back to the time when tree sugar and tree 'lasses were found on every table, and when "opening" the trees and boiling down the sugar water were highland spring rituals. The tours and exhibits are both educational and enjoyable. Pancake (with maple syrup, of course) and trout suppers centered around the county seat of Monterey are unforgettable.

A Sugar Tour winds through some of the

loveliest spots in Virginia on Va. routes 637 and 640. Maple sugar camps throughout the county welcome visitors to view the actual process of syrup-making, from tapping the trees to collecting the colorless, almost tasteless sugar water. Gathered in plastic buckets or by plastic tubing, the water is then boiled in kettles, pans or evaporators until a barrel is finally reduced to a gallon of pure maple syrup. The campsites are Rexrode's Sugar Orchard, Puffenbarger's Sugar Orchard, Sugar Tree Country Store & Sugar House and Eagle's Sugar Camp. Tour maps are provided at the festival. One of the best things about the festival is tasting and shopping for all the pure maple syrup goodies — sugar candy, donuts glazed with maple syrup and funnel cakes — available at a cost vastly below retail. Highland's downtown antique stores also open for the occasion. Most are clustered around the classic Victorian Highland Inn, a downtown landmark, c. 1904, that has been restored and is now on the National Register of Historical Places. Its 20 rooms are furnished with antiques.

The Maple Museum on U.S. 220, a mile south of Monterey, is another fun stop depicting the traditional skills in sugaring (see our Arts chapter).

Summers are as cool here as any in the East. One word of warning: if you're driving in from another part of the Blue Ridge, expect to find snow on the ground as late as April, since Highland County gets about 65 inches of the white stuff a year. Bring jackets; the temperature will probably be at least 10 degrees colder than where you came from.

Outside of the maple culture, there are other interesting places to visit. If you want to see where many of those mouth-watering trout come from — and part of the reason behind this area's distinction as Trout Capital of the Eastern United States — visit the Virginia Trout Company on U.S. 220 north of Monterey. In business for nearly 40 years, the facility hatches rainbow trout from eggs and raises them to adulthood. You can fish for your own, buy them frozen or just watch them swim in the cold mountain water. The hatchery is open seven days a week, weekdays from 8 AM to 4 PM and weekends from 9 AM to 4 PM.

While you're in Highland County, you also can see the Confederate Breastworks (breast-high trenches) built in 1862 by 4,000 Confederate troops as a defense against Union soldiers. They are at the top of Shenandoah Mountain on U.S. 250 at the Highland-Augusta County line.

Also on U.S. 250 east of McDowell is the McDowell Battlefield, where 4,500 Confederate troops under Gen. Stonewall Jackson defeated 2,268 Union soldiers in a bloody conflict in 1862. This engagement was the first victory in Jackson's famous Valley Campaign. Nearby McDowell Presbyterian Church was used as a hospital, and soldiers are buried there.

People enjoy Highland as much for what is missing — traffic, pollution, noise and crowds — as for what is there. The pace is slow, and the scenery, beautiful. It's considered the best place in Virginia to bird watch, and fans say species that have flown the coop from other parts of the state can still be found here.

If you feel like flying the coop yourself, come to Highland and slow down like the maple sugar in January. Contact the Highland County Chamber of Commerce at P.O. Box 223, Monterey 24465, (540) 468-2550.

The Blue Ridge of Virginia is laced with world-renowned tourism routes such as the Skyline Drive and the Blue Ridge Parkway as well as scenic byways.

Getting Around

We've long been reminded by the travel industry that "getting there is half the fun." In Virginia's Blue Ridge, drive on the scenic roads, fly into mountain-ringed airports or take efficient metro bus systems to your favorite destinations. You'll find that the old axiom is true: getting here is a pleasure unto itself.

With its beautiful scenic mountains and interesting historical sites, Virginia is one of the most popular destinations in the Southeast. The Blue Ridge of Virginia is second only to Williamsburg among tourism destinations in the Old Dominion.

Travel experiences to the Blue Ridge are often among the most memorable and relaxing of times for visitors. But you've got to be armed with the right maps and travel information.

Highways and Byways

The Blue Ridge of Virginia is laced with world-renowned tourism routes such as the Skyline Drive, the Blue Ridge Parkway as well as scenic byways. All lead to their own wonderlands of hiking trails and magic mountain moments. (See our chapter on the Blue Ridge Parkway and Skyline Drive.) An interesting route in the works is the "Smart Highway" a 6-mile connector road from Blacksburg to Interstate 81.

Before you begin your trip, be sure to write the Commonwealth for two essential maps: the Virginia State Transportation Map and the Map of Scenic Roads in Virginia. You can order both from the Virginia Department of Transportation, 1401 E. Broad Street, Richmond 23219, (804) 786-0002.

Major Highways

For modern highway efficiency, the Blue Ridge offers Interstate 81 and Interstate 64, which intersect in the Shenandoah Valley. These are two of the busiest interstate roads in the Southeast. The Blue Ridge Parkway and Skyline Drive run parallel to I-81, which passes through the Shenandoah Valley's major cities of Harrisonburg, Staunton, Lexington, Winchester and Roanoke.

Intersecting I-81 is I-64, which runs from Charlottesville west to Greenbrier County in West Virginia and east to Richmond.

East of the Blue Ridge, U.S. Highway 29 running north and south connects smaller towns to the more metropolitan Lynchburg, while U.S. Highway 460 runs east and west, intersecting Bedford and Lynchburg before proceeding westward through the New River Valley. If you want rest stops with bathroom facilities, stick to I-81. Otherwise, you'll find the going mountainous and slow.

Byways

For beauty and adventure, the Blue Ridge byways have it all: more than 2,000 miles of special roads that offer something for everyone. A journey along the Blue Ridge of Virginia's scenic roads is one that is measured in memories instead of miles.

As an example, one of the most beautiful of these is Va. Route 39 to Goshen Pass, outside of Lexington. Point yourself west and head out of town. Before long, you'll come upon the Virginia Horse Center, a modern facility that operates year round and hosts horse shows, auctions, festivals and educational clinics (see our Horse Country chapter).

From this point on, the elevation increases to Goshen Pass. Here, you'll find easy access to roadside pulloffs from which you might see someone fishing or kayaking. These are perfect spots for a picnic, followed by some relaxation, as you daydream to the soothing sounds of the Maury River's rippling waters.

Continuing, you'll enter George Washington and Jefferson National Forests, surrounded by natural beauty and a world at peace with itself. Next will come Warm Springs, which got its name from the natural mineral springs that make places such as the Homestead Resort famous.

As you continue your journey toward the West Virginia border, you'll pass Hidden Valley Recreation Area and Blowing Springs Recreation Area, providing opportunities for camping, hiking and fishing.

At the end of Va. 39, we guarantee a refreshment of mind, spirit and body. Such are the miracles of the Blue Ridge byways. Many more are outlined on the special map provided by the Commonwealth.

Far southwestern Virginia is notorious for its rugged mountain roads that wind through coalfields, tunnels and mountain passes. These routes confounded even adventurous Daniel Boone, who steered clear of certain areas while leading settlers down the Wilderness Trail through the Cumberland Gap in 1775.

The Blue Ridge has come a long way since then. Daniel Boone and his entourage could never have imagined the well-placed private and major public airports which provide access to tourism and industry.

Airports

Both public and private airports, some convenient to major resorts, are an important means for out-of-state tourists to visit the area. More than 300 airports serve travelers in Virginia. These range from grass landing strips to large international facilities. Commercial air-

ports generate 35 percent of the air industry's economic impact in Virginia, while general aviation airports account for only 7 percent. Yet the importance of general aviation in the Blue Ridge is recognized by a constant upgrading of the existing air transportation system.

Of the existing system in the Blue Ridge, three large airports — Charlottesville, Roanoke and Lynchburg — receive varied commercial passenger service. They also provide a wide range of general aviation services for corporate and private aircraft. Others, such as the newly renovated Shenandoah Valley Regional at Weyers Cave and Ingalls Field, next to the Homestead Resort in Bath County, have limited scheduled flights. The majority of Blue Ridge airports are designed to accommodate single-engine and light twin-engine aircraft, which represent more than 90 percent of Virginia's aircraft.

In this chapter, we list the commercial airports, north to south, then the remaining scheduled service and general aviation airports.

Commercial Airports

Charlottesville-Albemarle Airport
201 Bowen Loop, Charlottesville
• **(804) 973-8341**

Charlottesville-Albemarle Airport is 8 miles north of Charlottesville in Albemarle County. It is accessible via U.S. 29 and Va. 649. The airport is served by four airlines that provide 32 daily departures to seven major hub airports, including Charlotte, Pittsburgh, Philadelphia, LaGuardia, Newark, Cincinnati and Washington/Dulles. From these points, connections are available to an additional 175 domestic and international destinations.

The terminal consists of a 60,000-square-foot building with four airline ticket counters and five airline gate areas, baggage claim space, a 500-space daily parking area, 61-space hourly parking lot and an on-site travel agency. A cafe/deli is also available as well as food and drink vending machines. The gift

Perched high on top of a mountain, you can see for miles and miles.

shop carries magazines, books and local novelties.

Car rental and on-call taxi service are available. Many of the local hotels provide courtesy shuttle service to and from the airport.

The Charlottesville-Albemarle Airport's market includes the cities of Charlottesville, Staunton, Harrisonburg and Culpeper and the counties of Albemarle, Greene, Madison, Culpeper, Orange, Louisa, Fluvanna, Nelson, Augusta and Rockingham.

General aviation services are provided by Corporate Jets Inc. of Pittsburgh, (804) 978-1474, and include aircraft fueling, hangaring and maneuvering. Flight instruction, air tours and aircraft rental are available through Blue Ridge Flight Center, (804) 978-2114, and Charlottesville Flight Center, (804) 964-1474. Auto rental service is provided at the general aviation terminal through Avis, and courtesy vehicles are also available.

Airlines: Colgan Airlines, (800) 272-5488; Comair, the Delta Connection, (800) 354-9822; United Express, (800) 241-6522; U.S. Airways Express, (800) 428-4322

Car Rentals: Avis, (804) 973-6000; Budget, (804) 973-5751; National, (804) 974-4664

Taxis: Nine taxi companies are available on a first-in, first-out basis and are typically waiting in front of the terminal. Nine area hotels offer courtesy shuttles.

Parking: (804) 973-5145

Lynchburg Regional Airport
4308 Wards Rd., Lynchburg
• **(804) 582-1150**

The Lynchburg Regional Airport is 6 miles south of Lynchburg in Campbell County and is accessible via U.S. 29. The airport is served by three airlines that provide 23 departures per day to six major hub airports, including Charlotte, Atlanta, Pittsburgh, Philadelphia, Washington National and Washington Dulles international airports. From these points, connections are available to more than 175 domestic and international destinations.

The Lynchburg Airport's west central Virginia market area includes the cities of Bedford and Lynchburg and the counties of Amherst, Appomattox, Bedford and Campbell.

Airport facilities consist of a 35,000-square-foot terminal building, built in 1992, with one airline ticket counter, six airline gate areas, second-level boarding capabilities, a 400-space daily parking area and an on-site travel agency.

Car rental and on-call taxi service also serve the airport. A number of hotels provide courtesy shuttle van service to and from their properties.

General aviation services are provided by Virginia Aviation, (800) 543-6845, for aircraft fueling, hangaring, maneuvering and flight instruction. This company also provides aircraft repair services, aircraft rentals and charter services, parking and tie-down.

Airlines: Atlantic Southeast Airlines, the Delta Connection, (800) 221-1212; United Express, (800) 241-6522; U.S. Airways Express, (800) 428-4322

Car Rentals: Avis, (804) 239-3622; Budget, (800) 527-0700; Hertz, (800) 654-3131

Taxi/Limousine: Airport Limo, (804) 239-1777

Parking: Republic Parking Systems, (804) 239-7574

Roanoke Regional Airport
5202 Aviation Dr. N.W., Roanoke
• (540) 362-1999

Roanoke Regional Airport is 3 miles northwest of Roanoke via I-581. It is served by five major airlines or their regional affiliates, which make 43 departures per day to 11 major hub airports, with nonstop or direct service to 17 cities. From these points, connections are available to any location all over the world. The Roanoke Regional Airport's market includes the cities of Roanoke and Radford and the counties of Alleghany, Bedford, Botetourt, Craig, Franklin, Floyd, Giles, Montgomery, Roanoke, Pulaski and Wythe.

The airport's dramatic glass-front, 96,000-square-foot building features four Jetway loading bridges, a modern baggage handling system and a panoramic view of the Blue Ridge Mountains. Parking is ample, with 1,038 daily and 227 hourly parking spaces. Other features are an on-site travel agency, a First Union Bank ATM, a snack bar, a restaurant and gift shop, a lounge and conference center and a telephone hotel reservation system.

Ground transportation is available from car rental companies and three on-call limousine services. A number of hotels provide courtesy shuttle van service to and from their properties. There are also taxis available.

Piedmont Aviation, (540) 563-4401, provides general aviation services including aircraft fueling, hangaring and maneuvering. In 1996 Piedmont announced its new Citation Jet, which seats up to five passengers with a two-pilot crew. Piedmont also offers aircraft maintenance, as does Executive Air Inc., (540) 362-9728; and Roanoke Aero Services, (540) 563-5212. Air charters are offered by Piedmont, (540) 563-4401; Executive Air Inc., (540) 362-9728; Hillman, (540) 366-5033; and Saker flying services, (540) 362-5331. Also available for charter flights is LC Flying Services, (540) 362-2501.

Airlines: U.S. Airways Express, (800) 428-4322; United Express, (800) 241-6522; Northwest Airlink, (800) 225-2525; Comair, the Delta Connection, (800) 354-9822; ASA, Delta Connection, (800) 282-3424

Car Rentals: Avis, (540) 366-2436; Budget, (540) 362-1654; Dollar, (540) 563-8055; Hertz, (540) 366-3421; National, (540) 563-5050

Ground Transportation: Blacksburg Limousine, (540) 951-3973; Cartier Limousine, (540) 982-5466; Roanoke Airport Limo, (540) 345-7710; Yellow Cab, (540) 345-7711; Liberty Cab (540) 344-1776

Parking: (540) 362-0630

General Aviation Airports

Winchester Regional Airport
491 Airport Rd. • (540) 662-5786

This airport at the northern end of the Shenandoah Valley is 2 miles south of Winchester and 42 miles northwest of Washington-Dulles International. Operated from 7 AM to 7 PM Monday through Friday and 8 AM to 8 PM on weekends, the airport has 24-hour U.S. Customs Service. After-hours service is available to pilots along with an all-weather access Localizer DME approach, automated weather observation system, Pan Am WeatherMation and a 5,500-foot runway with pilot-activated lighting. An executive meeting room with audiovisual equipment, fax and computer modem access makes business travel easier.

Available on field is on-demand air charter taxi service, overnight hangars, aircraft rentals, flight instruction and aircraft maintenance facilities. Transportation is available to nearby hotels, restaurants and golf courses. Car rentals are also available through prearranged reservations. Nightly tie-down fee is $5 for single-engine planes and $8 for larger craft.

Front Royal-Warren County Airport
Va. Rt. 4, Front Royal • (540) 635-3570

The airport is nestled in the beautiful Civil War Historic Shenandoah Valley, at the base of the Skyline Drive and Massanutten mountains. From dusk to dawn, accessible activities include bicycle trails, camping, bed and breakfasts and a variety of restaurants. A new facility includes a terminal building, 3,000 by 75-foot lighted runway with fuel, hangars and ramp space and overnight parking for $4. Also available are scenic flights, flight training, on demand charter and maintenance.

Sky Bryce Airport
County Rd. 836, off Va. Rt. 263, Basye • (540) 856-2121

This unattended private airport with a 2,240-foot asphalt runway is within walking distance of Bryce Resort, a large, recreational family resort offering year-round activities. No fuel or maintenance is available. The airport is open for daylight VFR operations only.

Luray Caverns Airport
County Rd. 652, Luray • (540) 743-6070

Luray Caverns Airport has a 3,300-foot paved, lighted runway, sells fuel and charges no fees for incoming craft. Between the world-famous Luray Caverns and the Caverns Country Club Resort, this facility offers free transportation from the airport to all Luray Caverns facilities.

New Market Airport
59 River Rd., New Market • (540) 740-3949

This airport 2 miles west of historic New Market and the Shenandoah Valley Travel Association Visitors Center has a flight training school, sightseeing rides, soaring, hot-air ballooning, aircraft rental, radio-operated lights and fuel sales with an after-hours fueling program. Hours of operation are 9 AM to 5 PM daily. Tie-down is $3.50 nightly, and cab service is available.

Bridgewater Air Park
Va. Rt. 727, Bridgewater • (540) 828-6070

Operated by K&K Aircraft and close to Bridgewater College, this airport sells fuel and has limited overnight tie-down sites at no fee. Hours of operation are 8 AM to 5 PM weekdays and 9 AM to 4 PM Saturday. Taxi service is available from Harrisonburg.

Shenandoah Valley Regional Airport
Va. Rt. 771 (Airport Rd.), Weyers Cave • (540) 234-8304

Shenandoah Valley Regional Airport is centrally located to serve the cities of Harrisonburg, Staunton and Waynesboro and the counties of Augusta and Rockingham. Renovations completed in 1996 have expanded the 10,000-square-foot General Aviation Terminal Building, which offers fixed base services, including fuel. Two terminals offer free use of PanAm WeatherMation and Automated Weather Observation System. An executive meeting room with audiovisual equipment and computer modem access make business travel easier.

Services available include air-charter service, corporate management services, aircraft rental, flight instruction, a restaurant, a testing facility and aircraft maintenance facilities. Airline service is provided by U.S. Airways, (540)

INSIDERS' TIP

The Dulles Toll Road (also known as Route 267) and the Dulles Toll Road Extension (DTRE) link Leesburg in Loudoun County and the Washington Dulles International Airport to the Capital Beltway (Interstate 495) and Washington, D.C.

Photo: Wintergreen Resort

Two wheels are sometimes the best way to get where you're going.

234-9257, with daily departures to Pittsburgh. Ground transportation is provided by local taxi services, which include Waynesboro City Taxi, (540) 949-8245; Harrisonburg City Cabs, (540) 434-2515; and Staunton City Taxi, (540) 886-3471. Also available is limo service from Luxury Limousine Limited, (540) 473-9740; Halterman's Limousine, (540) 432-3950; and Rodney's Limousine Service, (540) 885-4977. Rental cars are available from Avis, (540) 234-9961; and Hertz, (540) 234-9411.

Eagles Nest
Va. Rt. 5, Waynesboro • (540) 943-4447

Close to Wintergreen Resort, Eagles Nest offers fuel and mechanical service, with one mechanic on the field. The tie-down fee is $3 nightly. Aircraft rental and instruction are available.

Virginia Tech Airport
1600 Ramble Rd., Blacksburg
• (540) 231-4444

Adjacent to the Virginia Tech Corporate Research Center and a mile from the main 24,000-student campus, this busy airport is situated on the Eastern Continental Divide at 2,134 feet above sea level. A new terminal was finished in 1997 featuring a larger lounge, pilot lounge and unique architecture sporting the old beams of the original hangar. The runway is lighted and complemented by full-instrument approach capabilities. Along with refueling, flight instruction is offered and ground-school students can earn three academic credits from New River Community College. Hard-surface tie-downs cost $5 nightly. There is a waiting list for T-hangar space. Nearby car rental services include Holiday Ford, (540) 552-4331 or (540) 674-4141.

New River Valley Airport
Va. Rt. 100 N., Dublin • (540) 674-4141

Two miles north of Dublin, New River offers fuel, tie-down and hangar space. Flight training and aircraft rental is available. The runway is 6,200 feet long with ILS. Rental cars are available. The airport is within a short drive of Radford University and Virginia Tech and close to New River Community College.

Falwell Aviation Inc.
4332 Richmond Hwy., Lynchburg
• (804) 845-8769

Falwell, within the city limits of Lynchburg, offers fuel, maintenance, hangar space, flight instruction, aircraft rental and turbojet, turboprop and piston aircraft for charter. No landing or parking fees are charged, but it costs $2.50 for overnight tie-down.

New London Airport
Va. Rt. 1, Forest • (804) 525-2988

Between Lynchburg and Smith Mountain Lake, this airport offers fuel and minor maintenance. There is no tie-down fee. Skydiving is available. Auto drag races are held at the airport on Sunday.

Brookneal-Campbell County Airport Authority
Brookneal • (804) 376-2345

This unattended rural airport, six miles from Brookneal, has a pay phone on the field. Rental cars are available nearby, and there is no tie-down fee. Fuel is not available.

Smith Mountain Lake Airport
Va. Rt. 1, Moneta • (540) 297-4500

Adjacent to Virginia's largest lake, Smith Mountain Lake Airport offers fuel, sightseeing charters, limousine and car rental. Tie-down is $5 nightly. The airport received a grant from the Virginia Aviation Board in 1997 for removal of hazardous obstructions near the airport. Consultants also are looking at ways to bring the airport up to even higher standards due to an increase in use.

Ingalls Field
Va. Rt. 703, Hot Springs • (540) 839-5326

Gateway to the world-famous Homestead Resort, Ingalls Field might have no planes one day and look like O'Hare the next, depending on which conventions are meeting in the area. Because of the nature of its largest client, The Homestead Resort, catering became available during 1997, due to popular demand. It is the highest public airport in elevation east of the Mississippi River.

Rental cars and limo service are available to Hot Springs, Warm Springs and other Bath County points of interest. Overnight tie-down and landing fees depend on the size of incoming aircraft. Fuel prices are reasonable, and there's no parking fee.

Metro Bus Lines

Due to increased concern over energy consumption, ozone pollution and other critical issues facing the planet, public transportation is no longer just an alternative but an environmentally responsible way to travel. Major cities in the Blue Ridge offer bus transportation that is clean, accessible and inexpensive.

For a guide to public transportation in Virginia, call the Virginia Division of Tourism at (804) 786-4484. You'll receive an easy-to-read

INSIDERS' TIP

If you're tired of that Interstate blur, consider an alternative route. If you're not in a hurry, take one of our scenic routes for a real treat. Route 231 through Rappahannock or U.S. Highway 11 through the Shenandoah Valley will give you a real look at what the Blue Ridge has to offer.

map prepared by the Virginia Department of Transportation.

Roanoke

Greater Roanoke Transit Company
12th and Campbell aves. S.E.
• (540) 982-0305

Greater Roanoke Transit Company is Roanoke's regional transportation system, serving more than 5,500 passengers daily with its fleet of 46 buses. It has an extensive outreach program and tries hard to accommodate everyone from eager tourists to the disabled, who are given special consideration with STAR service.

The modern main terminal, Campbell Court, is in the heart of the thriving shopping district, across from First Union Bank on Campbell Avenue. Efficient and modern, the service is highly regarded by locals.

Riders may send for a bus guide in advance. Exact fare or your ticket should be ready, since bus drivers do not carry change. No smoking, eating or drinking is permitted on the vehicles. Signal the bus operator a block before you want to get off.

In days gone by, the primary mode of getting around was on horseback, as the area's many statues of Civil War leaders attest.

Charlottesville

Charlottesville Transit Service
315 Fourth St. N.W.
• (804) 296-RIDE
University Transit Service
1101 Millmont St. • (804) 924-7711

The City of Charlottesville's Transit Service and University Transit work together to provide dependable, efficient, convenient and safe transportation. Riders may send for a bus guide in advance. When riding, you should have exact fare or a ticket. The guide clearly marks designated transfer points and routes in various colors. Eating, drinking and smoking are not permitted. Two front seats may be reserved for senior citizens or those with disabilities.

Lynchburg

Greater Lynchburg Transit Company
Kemper St. • (804) 847-7771

Greater Lynchburg Transit serves both the City of Lynchburg and parts of Amherst County, carrying 3,500 to 4,000 passengers daily. Its fleet of 26 buses radiates from a main terminal at Plaza Shopping Center, the only transfer point, between Memorial Avenue and Lakeside Drive. You can write for a bus guide or pick one up on any bus or at the office on Kemper Street. Exact fare or a pass is required.

Trans-city Bus Lines

Greyhound cross-country buses serve major Blue Ridge cities, including Charlottesville, Lynchburg, Winchester and Roanoke. For more information, call (800) 231-2222.

Railroads

Many of the communities along the Blue Ridge sprang up along the railroad routes that crisscross the state. But with the advent of the automobile, trains began to fall out of favor. Today only a handful of cities have stops for passenger traffic.

A study by the Virginia Department of Rail and Public Transportation began in 1998 on proposed passenger rail service from Bristol to Washington, D.C., with more than a dozen stops in between. But for now, Amtrak runs two main routes through the Blue Ridge area.

The Cardinal route, from Union Station in D.C. to Chicago, has stops in Alexandria, Manassas, Culpeper, Charlottesville, Staunton and Clifton Forge.

The Crescent run, from Penn Station in New York to New Orleans, takes a more north-south route with in-state stops at Alexandria, Manassas, Culpeper, Charlottesville, Lynchburg and Danville.

Options range from sleeper cars, coach seating, Auto Train and services for travelers with disabilities. For schedules and reservations, call Amtrak at (800) 872-7245.

The Blue Ridge has
a wide selection
of comfortable
accommodations to
fit any budget.

Hotels and Motels

A key part to any vacation is finding a nice place to relax after a long day of sightseeing or shopping. The Blue Ridge has a wide selection of comfortable accommodations to fit any budget.

In this chapter, we provide a cross-section of the motel and hotel options in our area. Remember, this is a guide, not a directory. The region is so big we can't include every option available to travelers. But we can point you toward some of our favorites. See the Resorts and Bed and Breakfasts and Country Inns chapters for additional lodging choices. For those looking for something a little closer to the mountains, the Blue Ridge Parkway and Skyline Drive chapter also includes several cabins, lodges and campgrounds.

Price Code

Room rates vary according to location and degree of luxury, so we've categorized each property by using dollar signs based on the nightly rate for two people for a standard room.

$	less than $40
$$	$40 to $60
$$$	$61 to $85
$$$$	$86 and more

Unless we specify otherwise, major credit cards are accepted. Most hotels and motels do not allow pets, but we'll let you know the ones that do.

Shenandoah Valley
Frederick County

Holiday Inn
$$$ • 1017 Millwood Pike, Winchester • (540) 667-3300

This 174-room motel is a convenient base of operations for exploring historic Winchester and is close to shopping malls and movie theaters. Amenities include nonsmoking rooms, free and pay movies, convenient parking, a swimming pool, tennis courts, a fitness center, a restaurant and a lounge. No matter which direction you're traveling, it's easy to find — right at the intersection of Interstate 81, U.S. Highway 50, U.S. Highway 17 and U.S. Highway 522.

Hampton Inn
$$$ • 1655 Apple Blossom Dr., Winchester • (540) 667-8011, (800) 426-7866

One of Winchester's newest facilities, this 103-room inn is just a few miles from Shenandoah University. Amenities include a swimming pool, free continental breakfast, free local phone calls and free in-room movies. For the business-minded, ask about computer modem jacks or the multipurpose hospitality suite designed to accommodate small business meetings or private parties. Nonsmoking rooms also are available. The inn is near several restaurants, historic sites and a shopping mall. Children 18 and younger stay for free when accompanied by a parent.

Shoney's Inn

$$ • 1347 Berryville Ave., Winchester
• (540) 665-1700, (800) 222-2222

George Washington didn't sleep here, but this hotel is within miles of the first president's office. Other nearby historical attractions include Stonewall Jackson's Headquarters, Belle Grove Plantation and Patsy Cline's birthplace. The inn features 98 rooms, including 13 suites with microwaves and refrigerators. Amenities include an indoor pool, fitness room, sauna, free local calls and cable TV. Complimentary coffee and newspapers are available in the lobby. Fax service and meeting rooms are available. Shoney's Restaurant is adjacent to the inn. Children 18 and younger stay free in a parent's room. Discounts are available.

Baymont Inn

$$ • 800 Millwood Ave., Winchester
• (540) 678-0800, (800) 428-3438

You can have your free continental breakfast delivered to your room or walk across the parking lot to Bob Evans Restaurant. The Baymont Inn features cable TV, in-room coffee makers, VHS tape players and free local calls. The inn includes an executive conference center, and guests have use of a fax machine. Nonsmoking rooms and rooms with king-size beds are available. Children 18 and younger stay free in their parents' room.

Holiday Inn Express

$$$ • 165 Town Run Ln., Stephens City
• (540) 869-0909, (800) 785-7555

The newest hotel in Frederick County, the Express is within driving range of Olde Town, Belle Grove Plantation and Wayside Theater. The 70-room inn offers an outdoor swimming pool, exercise room, an on-premise laundry and valet service, remote control TV, a free breakfast bar, 24-hour coffee service and free local calls.

There are nine king whirlpool suites, and refrigerators and microwaves are available in some rooms. The inn also features fax and copying services and meeting rooms that seat up to 30. Ask about discounts.

Warren County

Quality Inn Skyline Drive

$$ • 10 Commerce Ave., Front Royal
• (540) 635-3161, (800) 821-4488

The three-floor 107-room Quality Inn, near the northern entrance to Skyline Drive, is a good overnight stop before going on the scenic highway. It's also convenient for exploring Front Royal or taking part in one of the town's excellent festivals. The motel rooms are comfortable and have cable TV. The motel restaurant is open for breakfast, lunch and dinner; several other restaurants also are nearby.

Shenandoah County

Hotel Strasburg

$$$ • 213 Holliday St., Strasburg
• (540) 465-9191

This white clapboard structure was built as a hospital after the Civil War. Decorated in antique Victorian furniture and folk and fine art (all of which is for sale), the hotel is decidedly charming, from the comfortable public rooms to the second-story balcony porch. The 29 cozy guest rooms have private baths, nine with Jacuzzis, and are individually decorated with period furniture, quilts, Victorian wall and floor coverings and classic window treatments. A new banquet room was added in 1997. Other special touches are toiletries, fresh flowers, baskets of greenery, telephones in each room and big, fluffy towels. Suites and staterooms also include a sitting area. Three beautifully appointed dining rooms and a lounge serve excellent continental meals with a country touch. On weekdays continental breakfast is included in the price of a room. This grand old hotel is within walking distance of the massive Strasburg Emporium (see our Shopping chapter), Stonewall Jackson Museum at Hupp's Hill, Wayside Theatre and Half Moon Beach. Golf packages with nearby courses are available.

Ramada Inn
$$ • 1130 Motel Dr., Woodstock
• (540) 459-5000

Rooms in this 126-unit motel have all the creature comforts, including free satellite TV. The Post Cards Restaurant serves three meals a day. Woodstock is a historic town, containing the oldest county courthouse (1792) in use west of the Blue Ridge Mountains. The town's lookout tower provides a spectacular view of the Seven Bends of the Shenandoah River.

New Market Battlefield Days Inn
$$ • 9360 George Collins Pkwy., New Market • (540) 740-4100, (800) 325-2525

On May 15, 1864, Union troops occupied Manor's Hill while the Confederates grouped to the south on Shirley's Ridge. The Confederate troops enlisted the help of young cadets from Virginia Military Institute and pushed the Yankees north. Ninety percent of the battle and casualties occurred on Manor's Hill, where the New Market Battlefield Days Inn now stands. The New Market Battlefield Park Hall of Valor and Military Museum, dedicated to the cadets of VMI, is adjacent to the hotel. Other attractions in the area include Shenandoah and Endless caverns and the New Market historic district. A short drive away are Shenandoah National Park, Skyline Drive, Luray Caverns and Bryce and Massanutten ski resorts. The 85 guest rooms feature king-size or double beds and cable TV. A restaurant serves breakfast and dinner. The motel has an outdoor pool.

Quality Inn Shenandoah Valley
$$ • 162 W. Old Crossroads St., New Market
• (540) 740-3141, (800) 228-5151

The Johnny Appleseed Restaurant and Apple Core Village Gift Shop are special attractions at this motel. Extra touches include in-room complimentary sunrise coffee and sunset cider. The 101 spacious rooms have free in-room movies, and the outdoor pool and sauna are good spots for relaxing afternoons. The inn also has a game room and miniature golf course and is near historic New Market, Luray Caverns and the New Market Battlefield.

The Shenvalee Golf Resort
$$ • 9660 Fairway Dr., New Market
• (540) 740-3181

This 42-room lodge has rooms overlooking the fairway or at poolside. The 27-hole PGA golf course has a practice driving range and a fully equipped pro shop. The resort also has regulation tennis courts, a large swimming pool and a fishing pond. You can take your meals in the dining room or visit the Sand Trap Tavern for a casual evening. To find the resort, take Exit 264 off I-81 and go 1 mile on U.S. Highway 11 S.

Page County

Budget Inn
$$ • 320 W. Main St., Luray
• (540) 743-5176, (800) 858-9800

Affordable, quiet and clean — that's what travelers will find at this small, no-frills motel. Cable TV and phones are in each of the 33 rooms. King-size beds and nonsmoking rooms are available. Several restaurants are two blocks away in downtown Luray.

The Cabins at Brookside
$$$ • 2978 U.S. Hwy. 211 E., Luray
• (540) 743-5698, (800) 299-2655

Your hosts, Bob and CeCe Castle, oversee a rare sort of accommodation — luxury cabins, with resident peacocks adding a royal touch. These charming cabins have modern baths, queen-size beds, elegant country decor, air-conditioning and heat year round. Front porches and private decks overlook a brook. Some cabins have fireplaces and indoor hot tubs. Room prices include a morning beverage tray. The cabins are adjacent to The Brookside Restaurant, where home-style cooking is served in a family-style setting (see our Restaurants chapter). An art gallery and gift shop feature limited-edition prints, unique items from local artists and artisans and other mementos of the Valley. The cabins are minutes from the Luray Caverns, Shenandoah National Park, Skyline Drive and New Market Battlefield.

Deerlane Cottages and Cabins
$$$$ • Off Va. Rt. 684, Luray
• (540) 743-3344, (800) 696-DEER

The views are outstanding from these quaint, private accommodations minutes from the Shenandoah River and nestled in the Massanutten Mountains. Choose one, two or three bedrooms with fireplaces, decks, kitchens, TVs, VCRs and other amenities. Some front the Shenandoah River; others have beautiful wooded settings. They're close to Skyline Drive and Luray Caverns. Horseback riding, hiking, fishing, golf and canoeing are nearby recreational possibilities. There is a minimum two-night stay. Dogs are permitted.

Ramada Inn Luray
$$$ • 131 Woodspringhill Rd., Luray
• (540) 743-4521, (800) 272-6232

Of the 101 guest rooms, 15 are furnished with antiques, and three rooms have Jacuzzis. Other amenities include cable TV, miniature golf, an outdoor pool, gift shop, bakery and a full-service restaurant. The Ramada is on U.S. Highway 211, just 3 miles from Luray Caverns. Skyline Drive is minutes away.

Rockingham County

Comfort Inn
$$ • 1440 E. Market St., Harrisonburg
• (540) 433-6066, (800) 228-5150

This chain motel has won awards for hospitality. Nonsmoking and wheelchair-accessible rooms are available, and the motel serves a complimentary continental breakfast every morning. The facility has an outdoor pool. Harrisonburg is in the heart of the valley, bordered by Shenandoah National Park on the east and George Washington and Jefferson National Forests on the west. Do as the locals do: head for the woods for fishing, hiking, biking and horseback riding. Discounts are available for AAA and AARP.

Four Points by Sheraton
$$$ • 1400 E. Market St., Harrisonburg
• (540) 433-2521

The Sheraton's a bit pricier than other area motels, but amenities include nonsmoking rooms, wheelchair-accessible rooms, indoor and outdoor pools, a Jacuzzi, a sauna, a restaurant and a lounge with entertainment most nights of the week.

The Village Inn
$$ • Va. Rt. 11 S., Harrisonburg
• (540) 434-7355, (800) 736-7355

Folks return again and again to this inn, where spacious, comfortable rooms and a variety of amenities, including a large outdoor pool, whirlpool baths and full-service restaurant keep guests happy. Single, double or queen-size beds are available, and some rooms even have decks overlooking the rolling hills of the Shenandoah Valley. All 37 rooms have cable TV with remotes, direct-dial telephones and individually controlled heat and air conditioning. A suite, an efficiency and nonsmoking rooms also are available.

Augusta County

Best Western Staunton Inn
$$$ • 260 Rowe Rd., Staunton
• (540) 885-1112

A popular place for business and vacation travelers in Staunton, Best Western Staunton Inn has the advantage of being beside one of Staunton's better restaurants, Rowe's Family Restaurant, at Exit 222 off I-81. It's just a few minutes driving time to downtown Staunton, Mary Baldwin College and the Museum of American Frontier Culture. The inn, with 80 guest rooms in a four-story building, serves a continental breakfast. An indoor heated swimming pool and protected corridors keep the weather from being a problem. Two double or king-size beds are available, along with nonsmoking rooms on request.

Comfort Inn Staunton
$$$ • 1302 Richmond Ave., Staunton
• (540) 886-5000, (800) 228-5150

This 98-room hotel is centrally located in the Shenandoah Valley just off I-81 on U.S. 250, making it an ideal home base from which to explore the area's attractions. It's also a convenient stop for travelers. Amenities include an outdoor pool, in-room coffee makers, clock radios and remote-control cable TV with free HBO. For a treat, stay in one of the hotel's whirlpool rooms. Rates include a complimentary continental breakfast and newspaper. Board games also are furnished at the front desk. Corporate and group discounts are available.

Hampton Inn
$$$ • 1490 Greenville Ave., Staunton
• (540) 886-7000, (800) HAMPTON

If you like to shop, this inn is right across the street from Staunton's shopping mall, plus it's just 2 miles from historic downtown and the Woodrow Wilson Birthplace. This new three-story hotel features a free continental breakfast, HBO, an outdoor pool, exercise room and free passes to the spa right next door. The inn also will provide alarm clocks for the hearing impaired or modem hookups for those who bring along work from the office. Sixty-five of the 75 rooms are nonsmoking. Ask about discounts for seniors.

Holiday Inn Staunton
$$$ • Va. Rt. 275 and I-81,
Exit 225, Staunton
• (540) 248-6020, (800) 932-9061

Historic downtown Staunton is less than five minutes from this 116-room hotel. Also nearby are the Woodrow Wilson Birthplace and the Museum of American Frontier Culture. Four suites are available, as are nonsmoking and wheelchair-accessible rooms. Other amenities include an indoor/outdoor heated pool and golf and tennis privileges at the adjacent Country Club of Staunton. Golf/

lodging packages also are available. A full-service restaurant in the hotel serves international cuisine, and the lounge features weekend entertainment.

Comfort Inn Waynesboro
$$ • 640 W. Broad St., Waynesboro
• (540) 942-1171, (800) 228-5150

Complimentary continental breakfast and *USA Today* newspapers are included in the price of rooms at this comfortable spot. You can also make free local calls, and all 75 rooms have remote-controlled cable TV with HBO. You can request room microwaves and refrigerators, and all rooms have coffee makers. During the warm months, guests can unwind in the spacious outdoor pool. The Comfort Inn is close to Wintergreen Resort, Waynesboro Factory Outlet Village, the Blue Ridge Parkway, Skyline Drive and the Museum of American Frontier Culture.

The Inn at Afton
$$ • U.S. Hwy. 250,
3 miles east of Waynesboro
• (540) 942-5201, (800) 860-8559

Enjoy fabulous views from atop Afton Mountain at this 118-room hotel. The Inn is convenient to I-64 and about 25 minutes west of Charlottesville. King-size beds and non-smoking rooms are available, and all rooms come with free local calling and cable TV with HBO. Be sure to request a view room, which is about $7 extra; you won't be disappointed by the breathtaking scenery. A heated pool is onsite, as is the hotel's restaurant, Dulaney's Steak and Seafood Restaurant, which offers room service to the hotel during breakfast, lunch and dinner.

Lexington

Hampton Inn
$$$ • 401 E. Nelson St., Lexington
• (540) 463-2223, (800) 426-7866

How can a hotel that opened in 1997 be

INSIDERS' TIP

Want to take Fido along on your Blue Ridge vacation? Some hotel chains will accommodate your pet, but they usually charge extra. Be sure to ask at the time you make reservations.

listed on the National Register of Historic Places? When Hampton Inn unveiled its new 86-room hotel, it managed to combine the old with the new. Just one block from historic downtown Lexington, the main hotel is attached to a 19th-century manor house. Ten of the rooms are located in the 1827 structure and are decorated with a bed-and-breakfast flair. Each room is named for historical people or places from Lexington — the Washington and Lee Room, the Stonewall Jackson Room — and each features fireplaces and period furniture. The rates for the manor house rooms run from $200 to $350. The remaining rooms on the hotel side start in the low $70s and include balconies, microwaves, minifridges and coffee makers. A continental breakfast is provided, along with free local calls, HBO and Disney channels. In the warmer months, you can use the outdoor pool and Jacuzzi, while a weight room offers year-round exercise opportunities.

Days Inn Keydet–General Motel
$$ • U.S. Hwy. 60 W., Lexington
• (540) 463-2143

Days Inn is 1.5 miles from the Lexington Visitors Center and is close to Virginia Military Institute. This hotel offers a few conveniences not always found at other hotels. For example, they will accept pets, and many rooms have refrigerators and wet bars. Each room is air-conditioned and has a TV. Senior citizen discounts are available.

Best Western Inn at Hunt Ridge
$$$ • I-81 and Va. Rt. 39, Lexington
• (540) 464-1500, (800) 464-1501

To match the beautiful Lexington countryside, this country-themed inn offers 100 guest rooms with a view of the Blue Ridge like no other in the area. You can relax in Hobbies lounge or take a dip in the indoor/outdoor pool. You'll be close to the Virginia Horse Center and historic downtown Lexington, and you can take advantage of G. Willaker's restaurant,

which serves all three meals and provides room service. Other extras include in-room coffee makers, electronic door locks, interior corridors and a guest laundry room.

Comfort Inn
$$ • Off I-81 Exit 191 and
I-64 Exit 55, Lexington
• (540) 463-7311, (800) 628-1958

Near the Virginia Horse Center and historic downtown Lexington , Comfort Inn is the perfect central location for daytrips. It offers a complimentary continental breakfast, in-room coffee makers, electronic door locks, interior corridors, a glass elevator, guest laundry, an indoor pool and free local calls. Children younger than 18 stay free. Several restaurants are next to the hotel. Pets are welcome.

Holiday Inn Express
$$ • I-64 and U.S. Hwy. 11 N., Lexington
• (540) 463-7351, (800) 480-3043

This beautifully renovated hotel offers Lexington's best complimentary deluxe continental breakfast. Each of the 72 rooms offers in-room coffee makers, electronic door locks, cable TV and free HBO. Holiday Inn Express is close to Historic downtown Lexington, Virginia Military Institute, Washington and Lee University and the Virginia Horse Center. It is a perfect location to start several daytrips. Senior citizen discounts are available.

Howard Johnson Inn and Restaurant
$$ • I-64 and I-81, Exit 195, Lexington
• (540) 463-9181, (800) 456-4656

This mountain view inn is directly off I-81 at Exit 195. Nearby you will find Historic Downtown Lexington, Natural Bridge, Virginia Horse Center and many other points of interest for all ages. The inn features 100 rooms with 50 mountain-view rooms and two wheelchair-accessible rooms. The facility also has an onsite restaurant that offers banquet and meeting facilities, a gift shop, outdoor pool, cable TV

INSIDERS' TIP

Several hotels in the region realize that travelers often combine business with sightseeing. If you have to take work along, ask if the hotel offers fax service or access to modems. Several do.

with free HBO and guest laundry. AARP, AAA and group discounts are available.

Ramada Inn
$$ • I-81 at U.S. Hwy. 11, Lexington
• (540) 463-6666, (800) 228-2828

The business traveler, families and tour groups will appreciate this hotel near Washington and Lee University, Virginia Military Institute and historic sites. The Inn has 80 guest rooms and three suites. The suites or double bedrooms are ideal for families with children. Two of the guest rooms are wheelchair-accessible, and 12 are nonsmoking. Amenities include an indoor swimming pool and cable TV. The banquet facilities can accommodate as many as 200 people. AARP discounts are available.

Natural Bridge

Fancy Hill Motel
$ • South Lee Hwy., Natural Bridge
• (540) 291-2143

In the heart of the Shenandoah Valley near Natural Bridge, the Blue Ridge Parkway and historic Lexington, this motel offers amenities for the traveler in a country setting. Travelers return time and again for its excellent rates, friendly staff and adjacent restaurant with wholesome home cooking. The rooms are extra clean, and smoking and nonsmoking rooms are available. It's the best of the small, charming places the Blue Ridge has become noted for.

Roanoke Valley
Roanoke,
Troutville and Salem

AmeriSuites Roanoke/ Valley View Mall
$$$ • 5040 Valley View Blvd.
Off I-581, Roanoke
• (540) 366-4700, (800) 833-1516

AmeriSuites makes the extra space, convenience and luxury of all-suite accommodations affordable. The hotel is close to attractions, shopping and restaurants. Features include an indoor heated pool, a fitness center and complimentary continental breakfast. All suites include a wet bar with microwave, refrigerator and coffee maker. Each suite also has a 26-inch TV with VCR and voice mail. Business travelers will appreciate the phone dataports in each suite and the business center that offers fax service, a copier and computer. Weekend and mid-week specials may be available.

Best Western Coachman
$ • I-81, Exit 503, Troutville
• (540) 992-1234

Just off I-81, a beautiful hilltop location with panoramic mountain views beckons travelers to this 98-room facility. Seven miles from Roanoke, Best Western has the advantage of being in beautiful Botetourt County, known for its flowering orchards with bountiful fruit and country scenery. In addition to being clean and offering a variety of accommodation options, the inn has one of the area's largest outdoor pools. Senior discounts are available.

Best Western Inn at Valley View
$$ • 5050 Valley View Blvd., Roanoke
• (540) 362-2400, (800) 362-2410

One mile from Roanoke Regional Airport, this new, three-story inn at Roanoke's largest shopping mall, Valley View, has 85 rooms with indoor corridors. The decor follows a country theme with Shaker-style furniture. Nonsmoking rooms and rooms with king-size beds are available. Amenities include cable TV, an indoor pool, in-room coffee makers and complimentary continental breakfast. Numerous nationally known restaurants are nearby. This hotel is the perfect location from which to take a daytrip.

To get here, take Exit 3E off Hershberger Road.

Clarion Hotel Roanoke Airport
$$$ • 2727 Ferndale Dr. N.W., Roanoke
• (540) 362-4500, (800) 252-7466

Indoor/outdoor pools, tennis courts, volleyball and golf are available at this outstanding hotel, which also has a piano bar and a club, Miami's. Oscar's Restaurant offers fine dining in the heart of this elegant hotel. Each of the 154 guest rooms is equipped with satellite TV, two phones, individual climate control, radio and two double beds or a king-size bed. Pets are allowed. Clarion Hotel, formerly the Sheraton, has more than 7,200 square feet in meeting and conference facilities. The main ballroom can accommodate events from a small dinner of 20 to a banquet of 350 people. A conference center and luxurious hospitality suites are ideal for business, meeting and social functions. AARP discounts are available. To get here, take the Hershberger Road Exit off I-581.

Colony House Motor Lodge
$$ • 3560 Franklin Rd., Roanoke
• (540) 345-0411, (800) 552-7026

Colony House is 2 miles north of the Roanoke entrance to the spectacular Blue Ridge Parkway. This small, quiet inn specializes in personal service. The 67 rooms are air-conditioned and carpeted and have direct-dial phones, cable TV and king-, queen- or double-size beds. A few suites are available, and the Lodge has an outdoor pool. You're close to great restaurants, terrific shopping, the interstate highway and downtown. Colony House is an ideal base for business travelers and tourists. Special discounts and rates also apply.

Comfort Inn–Roanoke/Troutville
$$ • Lee Hwy., Troutville
• (540) 992-5600, (800) 628-1957

Seventy-two guest rooms are available at this hotel, each equipped with cable TV. Other amenities include nonsmoking rooms, an outdoor pool, enclosed corridors and in-room coffee makers. Several restaurants are nearby. This a perfect location for daytrippers. Senior citizen and other discounts are offered.

Comfort Inn Airport
$$ • 3695 Thirlane Rd., Roanoke
• (540) 563-0229

Close to the airport, Valley View Mall and many major restaurants, Comfort Inn is a good choice for travelers who want cleanliness and ample amenities. Attractive rooms feature king-size or double beds and cable TV. Nonsmoking rooms are available. Free local calls and fax capabilities are available. Everyone can enjoy an indoor Jacuzzi and outdoor pool in summer, and the Inn offers a fitness center membership and complimentary continental breakfast. To get here, take the Exit 3E or Exit 2N off I-581 to Hershberger.

Comfort Suites at Ridgewood Farm
$$-$$$ • Off I-81, Exit 141,
Rt. 419 S., Roanoke
• (540) 375-4800, (800) 628-1922

Salem's all-new lodging facility, the Comfort Suites at Ridgewood Farm is nestled on a hilltop overlooking the beautiful Roanoke Valley with a spectacular mountain view. Conveniently located, the hotel offers interior corridors, an exercise room, electronic door locks, an elevator, an outdoor pool and whirlpool, complimentary breakfast and breakfast area with an outdoor balcony overlooking the mountains. Each double and king-bed suite features a guest living area with desks with a two-line telephone, special lighting, 25-inch TV with remote, in-room coffee maker, wet bar with refrigerator, microwave, large wardrobe closets and nightlights. Because of its convenient location, it is the perfect place for daytrips.

Hampton Inn Airport
$$ • 6621 Thirlane Rd., Roanoke
• (540) 265-2600, (800) 426-7866

Conveniently located a half-mile from I-81 and 2 miles from Roanoke Regional Airport, this Hampton Inn offers 79 spacious guest rooms, including two extended-stay king suites with a beautiful view of the Blue Ridge Mountains. Amenities include a free deluxe continental breakfast, *USA Today* newspaper, guest laundry, free shuttle service, microfridges, VCRs and dataport phones in all rooms. Available in the king suites are coffee makers. Activities available for guests are an outdoor pool and exercise room.

Hampton Inn Salem
$$ • 1886 Electric Rd., Salem
• (540) 776-6500, (800) HAMPTON

This conveniently located Hampton Inn recently opened in September 1997. It provides many amenities to its guests, including a free deluxe continental breakfast, free local phone calls, an exercise and fitness room, guest laundry and an outdoor pool. Each room is complete with a microfridge and TV with VCR. Also available are nonsmoking rooms and luxurious suites with whirlpools. Special extras for business executives are the business center, which is complete with appropriate business equipment, and six hospitality suite/meeting rooms.

Hampton Inn Tanglewood
**$$ • 3816 Franklin Rd. S.W. , Roanoke
• (540) 989-4000, (800) 426-7866**

Just 3 miles from downtown, close to Roanoke Memorial Hospital and across from Tanglewood Mall, the 59-room Hampton Inn on Franklin Road offers an expanded continental breakfast, cable TV, VCRs, direct-dial phones, copier and fax service, king executive rooms, continental breakfast, hair dryers, refrigerator/freezer and microwave and nonsmoking rooms. Hospital and commercial rates are offered.

Holiday Inn Airport
**$$$ • 6626 Thirlane Rd. N.W., Roanoke
• (540) 366-8861**

Only minutes from Valley View Mall and Roanoke Regional Airport, the Holiday Inn Airport offers complimentary transportation for busy travelers and executives. The hotel offers amenities to help you relax, including Sir Pete's Pub with several TVs, international beer and arcade games. Sir Pete's Grille serves exciting menu items. Sunday noon buffet is one of the longest-running in Roanoke, and this is also a popular place for business lunches. King leisure rooms, double rooms, parlor suites and executive suites are available. This property has recently undergone a complete remodeling process and can now offer the highest quality of service and comfort you can expect.

Holiday Inn Express Roanoke
**$$ • 815 Gainesboro Rd., Roanoke
• (540) 982-0100, (800) HOLIDAY**

The owners of the Holiday Inn Express know that it's the little touches that make a stay more pleasant. Guests are treated to a complimentary continental breakfast, coffee, newspaper and ice. The 98 rooms feature firm, extra-length beds, and each room has a clock radio, electronic fire alarm and a remote-controlled 25-inch TV with cable, including HBO, ESPN and Disney. Many rooms have sofas and desks, and some are equipped with whirlpool baths, microwaves and refrigerators. Nonsmoking rooms and facilities for the disabled are available, and guests may use the outdoor pool.

Holiday Inn Express
$$ • 2174 Lee Hwy., I-81 S. Exit 150-A, Troutville • (540) 966-4444

The Roanoke Valley's newest Holiday Inn sports all the amenities guests have been asking for at Holiday Inns. All 60 rooms have microwaves, refrigerators, remote control TVs with VCRs, movie rental and complimentary continental breakfast. Local calls are free, and valet service is available. Kids stay for free. Guests can use the outdoor pool, exercise room and sauna. Options are nonsmoking rooms, wheelchair-accessible rooms and Jacuzzi suites. Business guests can use the fax and copy service and meeting rooms. Golf and tennis are nearby, as are Hollins College, Natural Bridge and the Blue Ridge Parkway.

Holiday Inn Hotel Tanglewood
**$$ • 4468 Starkey Rd., Roanoke
• (540) 774-4400**

Close to Tanglewood Mall and just minutes from downtown Roanoke, this hotel's 196 guest rooms are traditionally furnished. Each comes with climate control, cable TV, a radio and two vanity dressing areas. Starkey's Bistro, in the hotel, serves continental breakfast or regional cuisine and also serves up a breathtaking view of the Blue Ridge Mountains. For some excitement, try the Elephant Walk lounge (see Nightlife) with its safari decor. The hotel offers outdoor swimming. Complimentary limousine service to the airport is available as well as rental cars, private limos and taxi service. A concierge level makes this an especially popular place with business travelers who like personal touches such as a complimentary newspaper and breakfast, hors

Photo: Roanoke Valley Convention and Visitors Bureau

Blue Ridge hotels range from the rustic to the elegant.

d'oeuvres and nightly turndown service. AARP rates are available. To get here off I-81, take the Franklin Road/Salem exit.

Holiday Inn Salem
$$ • 1671 Skyview Rd., Salem
• (540) 389-7061

Conveniently located off I-81 at Exit 137, Holiday Inn Salem offers a spectacular view of the Blue Ridge Mountains, brand-new accommodations, complimentary deluxe continental breakfast and a free daily paper. All guest rooms offer coffee maker, hairdryer, iron/board, dataport, large screen TV with cable and individual voice mail systems. Guests may choose executive king rooms or double bedrooms for families. There are wheelchair-accessible rooms available, and pets are allowed. Guests are encouraged to cool off in the beautiful outdoor pool/kiddie pool or relax in the Skyview Restaurant, where kids eat free. At Holiday Inn Salem, expect excellent service, lovely surroundings and comfortable accommodations.

Hotel Roanoke & Conference Center
$$$ • 110 Shenandoah Ave., Roanoke
• (540) 985-5900

The renovated landmark Hotel Roanoke & Conference Center has thrived in its several years of operation after being closed for five years. Built in 1882, this sleeping Tudor-style giant has been revitalized as a Doubletree hotel in partnership with Virginia Tech, an arrangement brought about when the hotel's previous owner, Norfolk Southern Railway, gave the grand dame of luxury hotels to the university in 1989. The reopening of the hotel, cherished by generations for its service, style and sophistication, has been embraced nationwide by those who remember Miss Virginia pageants and peanut soup. Visitors to any of the 332 rooms will be pleased to see the best was saved and the rest was modernized.

The 104-year-old hotel has been completely restored, from its Florentine marble floors to frescoes and vaulted ceilings. Visitors can stay in the same rooms where John D. Rockefeller, Amelia Earhart, Gen. Dwight Eisenhower and Elvis Presley stayed and looked out upon Mill Mountain. Both the hotel and conference center have been equipped with 21st-century technology including dual-line telephones, voice mail and computer hookups in every room.

The conference center can accommodate more than 4,500 people with 20 meeting rooms. A fitness facility and guest services are available. Visitors can have a drink in the Pine Room or dine in style in the Regency Room.

The Jefferson Lodge

$$ • 616 S. Jefferson St., Roanoke
• (540) 342-2951, (800) 950-2580

The Jefferson Lodge is in the heart of downtown Roanoke, just a few blocks from the main public library, city and federal government buildings, hospitals and shopping. It is only three blocks to the City Market and Center in the Square. One hundred newly decorated rooms await guests. Free parking, coin-operated laundry and color TV are all provided for your comfort. An outdoor swimming pool and family dining room are on the property. Special group rates are available.

Knight's Inn

$$ • 301 Wildwood Rd., Salem
• (540) 389-0280

Knight's Inn, 3.5 miles west of downtown Salem off I-81, is close to shopping, dining, attractions and major corporations. This clean, efficient accommodation has all ground-floor rooms, cable TV, kitchenettes, nonsmoking rooms, complimentary coffee service and free local calls. Senior discounts are available.

Quality Inn–Roanoke/Salem

$$ • 179 Sheraton Dr., Salem
• (540) 562-1912, (800) 459-4949

The Quality Inn is constantly renovating to offer you the most for your money. Ask about the new executive rooms with in-room coffee, dataport phones and 25-inch TVs. The restaurant and lounge are great for relaxing at the end of the day, or you can also take a swim in the large outdoor pool. Each morning you can also enjoy a free deluxe continental breakfast.

The Patrick Henry Hotel

$$ • 617 S. Jefferson St., Roanoke
• (540) 345-8811, (800) 303-0988

If you're staying in downtown Roanoke, this historic property is a fine choice. It's within walking distance to all the downtown attractions. When the Patrick Henry Hotel opened its doors for the first time in 1925, its 11-story exterior was already a wonder, but visitors and guests were astounded by the beauty of the interior. Today, the hotel, with its ornate decor, has been restored to its previous splendor, and it is one of two operating Virginia Historic Landmark hotels in Roanoke. To say the guest rooms are spacious is an understatement. Each has been modernized, but in a way that reflects the hotel's historic heritage. Rooms have kitchenettes. Complimentary continental breakfast, airport transportation, free parking, complimentary health club facilities nearby, smoking and nonsmoking floors and a first-rate restaurant, Hunter's Grille, are all a part of this hotel's list of amenities. As a bonus for travelers, some rooms are outfitted with amenities such as hair dryers, irons and toiletries.

Roanoke Airport Marriott

$$$ • 2801 Hershberger Rd. N.W.,
Roanoke • (540) 563-9300,
(800) 228-9290

The Roanoke Marriott has been ranked by its guests in the top 10 percent of all Marriott Hotels. Situated on 12 landscaped acres, the hotel welcomes its guests in an elegant lobby. The bar, Whispers, is just off the entrance. Nearby are the two hotel restaurants, Lily's and Remington's (see our Restaurants chapter). The hotel has 320 guest rooms and suites with numerous amenities, such as individual climate control, a radio, remote-controlled cable TV, two direct-dial telephones with message lights, video messages and complimentary personal-care products. Twenty-four hour room service, valet service, airport transportation and free parking are other services here.

The Marriott has indoor and outdoor pools, a fitness center, a sauna and whirlpool and two lighted tennis courts. For evening entertainment, guests can go to the hotel's lounge, Charades (see our Nightlife chapter). The grand ballroom, Shenandoah Ballroom, and six meeting rooms can accommodate groups of 20 to 900. Seventeen conference rooms are available, with more than 12,800 square feet of flexible space. Special rates include Two For Breakfast Weekends, Honeymoon Packages, Super Saver and long-term rates.

Rodeway Inn

$ • 526 Orange Ave., Roanoke
• (540) 981-9341, (800) 424-4777

Access to the Roanoke Civic Center is about as simple as it gets from this hotel, since the center is just across the street. The Rodeway Inn is also less than a mile away from Center in the Square, the historic Farmers Market and the Virginia Transportation Museum. Free coffee is offered each morning. The guest rooms have cable TV. Fax service and shuttle pick up are available. Ask about group, discount and seasonal rates.

Sleep Inn Tanglewood
$$ • 4045 Electric Rd., Roanoke
• (540) 772-1500, (800) 628-1929

The Sleep Inn, in the Tanglewood Mall area off I-581 at the Va. 419 Exit, is the area's new high-tech lodging for business and vacation travelers. The inn has 101 nicely decorated rooms with state-of-the-art security systems. Extras include a large desk in each room. The extra-large showers feature massaging shower heads. A complimentary *USA Today* newspaper and in-room coffee service are included with a complimentary breakfast. Nonsmoking rooms are available. Each room has a satellite TV with VCR. Also available is a golf package and fitness program. Business associates may charge meals to nearby restaurants including Texas Steak House, Ragazzi's and Mac & Maggies.

Travelodge–Roanoke North
$$ • 2444 Lee Hwy. S., Troutville
• (540) 992-6700, (800) 578-7878

Travelodge wants you to feel at home, so it provides a free continental breakfast, free coffee, tea and popcorn and free local calls. Rooms offer attractive furniture, cable TV, executive work areas and direct-dial telephones. Children younger than 18 stay free when sharing a room with their parents. Efficiency rooms are available for relocating personnel or long-term visitors. Pets are welcome, and rooms for the physically impaired and nonsmokers are available.

East of the Blue Ridge
Loudoun County

Holiday Inn
$$$ • 1500 E. Market St., Leesburg
• (703) 771-9200, (800) 272-6232

The former Carradoc Hall was grand as a historic mansion and is even grander as a full-service hotel. The 122 guest rooms and four mansion suites are elegantly decorated, as is the Black Orchid II Restaurant, which serves breakfast, lunch and dinner. The hotel has an outdoor pool, exercise room and free airport shuttle. Many sporting and historic attractions are nearby. Room rates include an extraordinary continental breakfast.

Days Inn
$$ • 721 E. Market St., Leesburg
• (703) 777-6622, (800) 329-7466

In the heart of downtown, you will be within a one-mile radius of several shopping centers and restaurants. Days Inn offers a free continental breakfast. The enclosed two-story building has 81 rooms — several are connecting rooms — plus two wheechair-acessible rooms. Guests may choose king or double beds. Nonsmoking rooms are available. Children younger than 17 may stay for free in a parent's room. Ask about other discounts.

Best Western Leesburg-Dulles
$$$ • 726 E. Market St., Leesburg
• (703) 777-9400, (800) 528-1234

Tired of looking like your clothes have been in a suitcase all week? This hotel has added a new feature: full-size ironing boards and irons in the king-size rooms. In all, the two-story inn includes 99 rooms with king or two double beds.

There is a seasonal heated outdoor pool and a restaurant, Canterbury Hall, that serves breakfast, lunch and dinner. Other amenities include in-room coffee makers, free local calls, TVs and, if you give them a day's notice, a free shuttle to Dulles Airport. Nonsmoking rooms are available. Ask about discounts.

Fauquier County

Comfort Inn
$$$ • 7379 Comfort Inn Dr., Warrenton
• (540) 349-8900

Of the 97 rooms in this upscale motel, 49 are king suites and four are whirlpool suites. Several units offer a kitchen, living area and bedroom. All rooms have a refrigerator and coffee maker, with microwaves available on request. Nonsmoking rooms also are available. A deluxe continental breakfast, newspaper and local calls are complimentary. Other amenities include a laundry, fitness room, basketball court, picnic tables, barbecue grill and an outdoor pool.

Howard Johnson Inn
$ • 6 Broadview Ave., Warrenton
• (540) 347-4141, (800) I-GO-HOJO

This newly remodeled 80-room facility has complimentary morning coffee and newspaper, cable TV and an outdoor pool. Nonsmoking rooms are available. Discounts include AARP. Bob's Big Boy Restaurant is next door.

Culpeper County

Comfort Inn
$$ • 890 Willis Ln., Culpeper
• (540) 825-4900, (800) 228-5150

In downtown Culpeper, this 49-room motel features an outdoor swimming pool, in-room coffee makers, free continental breakfast, cable TV and free newspapers. King-size beds and nonsmoking rooms are available. Although no room service is offered, several restaurants are nearby.

Holiday Inn Culpeper
$$ • U.S. Hwy. 29 S. Bus., Culpeper
• (540) 825-1253, (800) HOLIDAY

Easy access off U.S. Highway 29 makes this a convenient and affordable stop for travelers. The 159-room two-story motel has a restaurant and lounge, adult and children's outdoor pools and laundry services. Banquet facilities can accommodate up to 375. Babysitting services also are available.

Super 8 Motel
$$ • 889 Willis Ln., Culpeper
• (540) 825-8088, (800) 800-8000

Affordably priced, this 61-room motel provides free extended cable TV, free local calls and complimentary coffee and toast bar. Non-smoking rooms, microwave/refrigerator units and fax service also are available.

Albemarle County

Best Western Cavalier Inn
$$$ • 105 Emmet St., Charlottesville
• (804) 296-8111

The 118-room Cavalier is next to the University of Virginia in the center of Charlottesville. Suites, wheelchair-accessible rooms and nonsmoking rooms are available. The Inn has an outdoor swimming pool and serves a free continental breakfast to guests. Nearby attractions include Monticello, Ash Lawn, Michie Tavern and several wineries. Special packages are available for families, senior citizens, sporting events and business meetings. There is also a Getaway Plan, for those who are booking a two-night stay.

Residence Inn by Marriott
$$$$ • 1111 Millmont St., Charlottesville
• (804) 923-0300, (800) 331-3131

They call this the next best thing to being at home. For business travelers or those who want more of the comforts of home, this new 108 room all-suite hotel is one of the only places in town that offers fully equipped kitchens in every room. You can choose one bedroom, two bedrooms or even a studio that comes with more space than a traditional hotel room. Each suite has a work space; many feature multiple phone jacks for those who want to bring along their computers. If recreation is more your interest, there is an outdoor swimming pool and Sport Court for tennis, basketball or volleyball. If you want a break from preparing your own meals, stop by the lobby for a complimentary continental breakfast. The staff also hosts a weekly social hour and barbecue. To make your stay easier, Marriott will provide daily housekeeping, a va-

---

INSIDERS' TIP

If you are planning a spring break, don't forget about college graduations. Hundreds of parents and relatives will be looking for hotels around Charlottesville, Blacksburg and Harrisonburg, so make your reservations well in advance.

let, a guest laundry and will even do your grocery shopping for you. Pets can stay, too, for a non-refundable fee of $150.

Comfort Inn Charlottesville
$$$ • 1807 Emmet St., Charlottesville
• (804) 293-6188, (800) 228-5150

The Comfort Inn in Charlottesville offers double and king rooms. Easy access to the U.S. 250 Bypass puts the University of Virginia and historic sites such as Monticello within minutes of the hotel. Amenities include free continental breakfast, cable TV, morning newspapers, in-room coffee makers and an outdoor pool. Nearly three-fourths of the 64 rooms are nonsmoking rooms. Be sure to book early during college football season and graduation when the town fills up.

Courtyard by Marriott
$$$ • 638 Hillside Dr., Charlottesville
• (804) 973-7100, (800) 321-2211

Shopping, historic sites and the University of Virginia are all close to Courtyard by Marriott.

Of the 150 rooms, 120 are nonsmoking. All have cable TV and free in-room coffee makers. Two wheelchair-accessible rooms and 12 suites are available. Guests may use the indoor pool, whirlpool and exercise room. The inn has a restaurant and lounge. Evening room service is available. Discounts are available for AAA and AARP.

Holiday Inn & Conference Center Charlottesville
$$$ • 1901 Emmet St., Charlottesville
• (804) 977-7700, (800) 242-5973

This pleasant hotel is on U.S. 29 just north of Charlottesville, with easy access to the University of Virginia, Michie Tavern, Ash Lawn and Monticello. The 172 rooms and two suites are modern and comfortably decorated; each offers cable TV.

The indoor heated pool has a patio area for relaxing or sunning outdoors in season. A free airport shuttle is available to guests. The recently opened restaurant, Damon's, The Place for Ribs, is open for breakfast, lunch and dinner and provides room service for the hotel.

The English Inn
$$$ • 2000 Morton Dr., Charlottesville
• (804) 971-9900, (800) 338-9900

Following the centuries-old British tradition, your breakfast is complimentary at this well-appointed chain hotel. Guests are served a continental morning meal in the Windsor Room, amid comfortable furnishings, a fireplace and fine art. Other amenities include an indoor pool, a sauna and an exercise room with a Universal weight system. Guests also receive free passes to a nearby health club. The inn has 21 king suites, designed with a Queen Anne flair with a sitting room and wet bar. The other 67 rooms are contemporary in style and have two double beds.

All rooms have cable TV, AM/FM clock radio, shower massage and automatic wake-up service. Banquet and meeting facilities are available. A courtesy limousine serves airport travelers.

Hampton Inn
$$$ • 2035 India Rd., Charlottesville
• (804) 978-7888, (800) HAMPTON

Guests in the Hampton's 123 rooms enjoy free airport shuttles, free local calls and a complimentary continental breakfast. The spacious and comfortable rooms have cable TV and air conditioning. Nonsmoking rooms are available. The Inn has an outdoor pool, and numerous restaurants are nearby. Charlottesville's major attractions, such as UVA, Monticello, Ash Lawn and Michie Tavern, are within easy reach of the inn, which is on U.S. 29 north of the city at the Seminole Square Shopping Center.

Days Inn
Charlottesville–University
$$$ • 1600 Emmet St., Charlottesville
• (804) 293-9111

All 129 rooms and two suites at this hotel are handsomely decorated and equipped with cable TV. The exercise room has a treadmill, Universal gym and sauna; outside is a large pool and a landscaped courtyard. The hotel has its own restaurant, Red Lobster. Ask about discounted rates.

Holiday Inn–Monticello
$$$ • 1200 Fifth St., Charlottesville
• (804) 977-5100, (800) HOLIDAY

You'll be close to downtown Charlottesville and just 4 miles from historic attractions at this 130-room high-rise hotel. Amenities include in-room coffee makers, free local calls, extended cable TV packages and free passes to a local exercise club. Meeting and banquet facilities are available for up to 150 people. The hotel's restaurant, Charlotte's, is open for breakfast and dinner.

Red Roof Inn
$$$ • 1309 W. Main St., Charlottesville
• (804) 295-4333

Within walking distance of the University of Virginia, this renovated hotel is a perfect location for sightseeing or for families who are visiting relatives in the nearby UVA Hospital. In fact, Red Roof Inn offers hospital discounts. The five-story hotel serves coffee in the lobby, and each room has cable TV with access to movies and video games. Of the 135 rooms, more than 90 are nonsmoking with several larger wheelchair-accessible rooms. Two restaurants are located within the Inn, Chesapeake Bagel and Hard Times Cafe, which specializes in burgers, chili and microbrews. The Inn offers a discount for Sam's Club members.

Hampton Inn and Suites
$$$ • 900 W. Main St., Charlottesville
• (804) 923-8600, (800) HAMPTON

Opened in the summer of 1997, this new hotel is designed with the business traveler in mind. There is a board room that seats 12 and a conference room that can seat up to 35. Of the 100 rooms, 25 are suites and eight are equipped with fireplaces. The executive suites also offer microwaves and mini-refrigerators. Amenities include deluxe continental breakfast, a complementary shuttle, plus free local calls, HBO and Cinemax. Several nearby restaurants are within walking distance. The Inn is one block from the University of Virginia.

Knights Inn
$$ • 1300 Seminole Tr., Charlottesville
• (804) 973-8133

Just off U.S. 29 near shopping malls, restaurants and shops and within a five-minute drive of the University of Virginia, this member of the clean and comfortable national motel chain has 116 rooms, all on one floor. The motel caters to a largely tourist crowd, along with UVA alums who flock to Charlottesville in the fall for football games and special events at the university. It's an affordable option, but book early for weekends any time of the year. The Inn features an outdoor pool, free cable and coffee. Some rooms come with a kitchenette.

Omni Charlottesville Hotel

$$$$ • 235 W. Main St., Charlottesville • (804) 971-5500, (800) THE-OMNI

You can't beat this spectacular hotel's convenient downtown mall location, which puts guests within easy walking distance of many good restaurants, shops and galleries. The hotel's facilities can accommodate all sorts of events, from a cocktail party for 30 to a conference for 600. Indoor/outdoor pools, a whirlpool, sauna, health club and restaurant are on site. The 208 rooms and six suites are elegantly decorated; three are wheelchair-accessible, and more than half the rooms are designated nonsmoking.

Quality Inn–University

$$$ • 1600 Emmet St., Charlottesville • (804) 971-3746

All 69 rooms at this conveniently located hotel are handsomely decorated and equipped with cable TV. A deluxe continental breakfast is included in the price of the rooms. The exercise room has a treadmill, Universal gym and sauna; outside is a large pool and a landscaped courtyard. Ask about discounted rates for AAA and AARP.

Ramada Inn–Monticello

$$ • U.S. Hwy. 250 E. and I-64, Charlottesville • (804) 977-3300

This inn has 101 comfortable rooms with nice features and options, such as Jacuzzis, king- and queen-size beds, nonsmoking units and free cable TV. A restaurant is on the premises, and the meeting and banquet space can accommodate up to 250. An exercise room, sauna and outdoor pool are available

to guests. The Ramada offers senior citizen and other discounts.

Doubletree

$$$$ • 2350 Seminole Tr., Charlottesville • (804) 973-2121

Surrounded by 20 acres in the northernmost portion of Charlottesville, this 234-room hotel offers all the creature comforts in a palatial setting. Amenities include two restaurants, heated indoor and heated outdoor pools, whirlpools, an exercise room, tennis courts and jogging trails. Charlottesville's largest conference facility, Doubletree has added a new gift shop and a banquet room that can accommodate large receptions and parties. Discounts are available for AAA and AARP.

Lynchburg

Comfort Inn

$$ • U.S. Hwy. 29 Expwy. at Odd Fellows Rd., Lynchburg • (804) 847-9041, (800) 228-5150

Comfort Inn Lynchburg offers guests a clean, comfortable and affordable room in the heart of the city. A free shuttle service is available to guests from the airport, bus station and train station. All guests receive a free full breakfast buffet or continental breakfast, the use of the exercise room and a large outdoor pool. The meeting rooms are available for business meetings, family reunions or wedding receptions. AAA or AARP discounts are welcome.

Days Inn Lynchburg

$$ • 3320 Candler's Mountain Rd., Lynchburg • (804) 847-8655, (800) 787-DAYS

Days Inn Lynchburg is an award-winner among the Days Inn chain. It is centrally located in Lynchburg and is easily accessible from Routes 29, 501 and 460. The hotel is directly across the street from the mall and within a mile of more than 20 restaurants. Electronic-card locks give an added feature of security. More than 75 percent of the 131 guest rooms are nonsmoking, and half are equipped with microwaves, refrigerators, coffee makers,

25-inch stereo TVs, iron/ironing boards, hair dryers, alarm clocks and snack packs.

The hotel has a large pool and play area. Business travelers will appreciate the hotel's complimentary airport shuttle service. The hotel's DayBreak Family Restaurant provides a free hot breakfast for all guests. The restaurant's hours are 6 AM to 2 PM and 5 PM to midnight daily, and breakfast food is served all day.

Hilton–Lynchburg
$$$$ • 2900 Candler's Mountain Rd., Lynchburg • (804) 237-6333, (800) HILTONS

Families with children should consider the Lynchburg Hilton. In addition to adequate amenities and prompt service, children of any age stay for free when they occupy the same room as their parents. The 168 attractive guest rooms and suites are furnished with large, comfortable beds, cable TV and direct-dial telephones. Suites also feature wet bars, refrigerators and double, full-length, bi-fold mirrored doors. Wake-up service, a gift shop, a newsstand and a courtesy van are other conveniences. The Hilton has an exercise room, a heated indoor pool, spa and sauna. Johnny Bull's Restaurant serves some of the finest cuisine in Lynchburg, focusing on American, continental and regional dishes. The Imbibery is the hotel's bar.

Howard Johnson Lodge
$ • U.S. Hwy. 29 N., Lynchburg • (804) 845-7041, (800) 446-4656

The 72 rooms here have oversized beds, plush lounge chairs, a writing desk and an extra vanity. Guests receive free local phone calls and cable TV, and views of the Blue Ridge Mountains are great from the private patios and balconies. Next door is Aunt Sarah's Pancake House.

Innkeeper Lynchburg
$$ • 2901 Candler's Mountain Rd., Lynchburg • (804) 237-7771, (800) 822-9899

The Innkeeper offers a free continental breakfast and comfortable, clean accommodations. The guest rooms have extra-length

beds, remote-controlled cable TV, desks, sofas and direct-dial touch-tone phones. Non-smoking rooms and facilities for the disabled are available, as are whirlpool baths or shower massages and swimming pools.

Children younger than 16 stay free, and roll-away beds are complimentary. Corporate, senior citizen and tour/group rates are available.

Ramada Inn & Conference Center
$$ • U.S. Hwy. 29 and Odd Fellows Rd., Lynchburg • (804) 847-4424, (800) 2-RAMADA

Ramada Inn & Conference Center is the newest full-service hotel in the Greater Lynchburg area. The property, located just off U.S. 29 Expressway at Exit 7, features 216 guest rooms, a restaurant, lounge and meeting/banquet rooms. When staying at the inn, you'll enjoy great services in a convenient central location. Wake up to a free hot breakfast buffet (with corporate rate rooms or higher) and complimentary coffee. Other amenities include courtesy van transportation to and from Lynchburg Regional Airport. Guest rooms have 20-inch remote-control cable TV and free HBO and dataport phones. There's also an outdoor pool. The Ramada Inn also has the Seasons Restaurant and Lounge as well as convenient access to River Ridge Mall, Cattle Annie's and other area attractions. AAA, AARP, corporate, government and group discounts are available.

Smith Mountain Lake

Lake Inn Westlake Corner
$$ • 45 Enterprise Ln., Hardy • (540) 721-3383, (888) 446-LAKE

The Lake Inn, popular with bass anglers, opened in 1996 with its new extension now totaling 60 rooms and one large conference room. Lake Inn is the only motel on Smith Mountain Lake. It offers a variety of accommodations, including rechargeable outlets for boats, king- and queen-size beds, one suite, two wheelchair-accessible rooms, air-conditioning, free local calls, cable TV and a recliner and coffee maker in each room. The

Photo: Richmond Times Dispatch

Crabtree Falls provides a picturesque setting for contemplation.

location makes it convenient to the heartbeat of the lake.

Bedford County

Peaks of Otter Lodge
$$$ • Mile 86, Blue Ridge Pkwy., Bedford • (540) 586-1081

This popular lodge is like no hotel you've ever seen and is an autumn tradition for fall foliage fans around the world. Peaks of Otter is surrounded by the beauty of the Blue Ridge Mountains and lush green countryside, with a gorgeous lake nearly at its doorstep. The lodge's interior reflects the natural setting, with wood and subtly blended textures, tones and colors.

The 59 rooms offer double beds and private baths. Three large suites also are available. Each room opens onto a private balcony. The lodge has no telephones, so you

can truly unwind and relax away from the rat race. The lodge has a cocktail lounge and dining room. Call ahead for seasonal rates. (Also see our Blue Ridge Parkway and Skyline Drive chapter.)

Rocky Mount

Comfort Inn
$$ • 1730 N. Main St., Rocky Mount • (540) 489-4000

Beautiful Smith Mountain Lake is just 20 miles away from this hotel. Ferrum College also is nearby. The 60 rooms have cable TV and AM/FM radios. A continental breakfast and sunrise coffee are complimentary to all guests. An outdoor pool is on the property. New to the inn is Ippy's Restaurant, which offers lunch and full dinner menu plus a lounge. Also adjacent to the Inn is a new batting cage and putt-putt golf course.

New River Valley

Montgomery County

Best Western Red Lion
$$ • 900 Plantation Rd., Blacksburg
• (540) 552-7770, (800) 528-1234

This hotel on 13 wooded acres is an ideal site for a meeting or banquet, since the facilities can accommodate as many as 400. The 104 guest rooms include two suites and one wheelchair-accessible room. Hearty meals are served in the dining room, and the hotel has a lounge with nightly entertainment. The grounds include three tennis courts.

Blacksburg Inn
$$$ • 3503 Holiday Ln., Blacksburg
• (540) 951-1330

Nostalgics will love this hotel for its railroad-theme restaurant, Vicker's Switch. The hotel's 98 nicely decorated rooms have numerous conveniences. The inn has a honeymoon suite with sauna and Jacuzzi. Banquet and meeting rooms are also available. A lounge, coin-operated laundry and Showtime TV are available for guests.

Hampton Inn
$$$ • 50 Hampton Blvd., Christiansburg
• (540) 382-2055, (800) 426-7866

This 124-room hotel is right off I-81 at Exit 118, making it a convenient stop for travelers who want to visit downtown Christiansburg or nearby Virginia Tech. Be prepared: since the hotel is so close to Blacksburg, it is difficult to get reservations on those weekends when the Hokies have a home football game. Rates also may run a little higher for weekends and special events. There are rooms for all sizes, including singles, doubles, kings and king studies. The studies feature a king-size bed and a sleeper sofa. All the rooms are equipped with coffee makers, irons and ironing boards and offer HBO and free local calls. A continental breakfast is provided each morning, but several restaurants are nearby, including Shoney's and local favorites, the Huckleberry and the Farmhouse. Don't forget a bathing suit for the outdoor pool. Children younger than 18 stay free.

Radford

Best Western Radford Inn
$$ • 1501 Tyler Ave., Radford
• (540) 639-3000, (800) 528-1234, (800) 628-1955

Nestled in the heart of the New River Valley, the Best Western Radford Inn offers Colonial-style, deluxe rooms featuring cable TV, in-room coffee makers, wall-mounted hair dryers and two touch-tone phones. King, double, smoking and nonsmoking rooms are available. A gazebo-style indoor swimming area with whirlpool, sauna and exercise facilities is provided for guests year-round. Complimentary *USA Today* newspapers are also one of the many amenities. Damon's, The Place for Ribs, located inside the Best Western, is a full-service restaurant, offering breakfast, lunch and dinner. Banquet rooms and meeting facilities that can accommodate up to 250 people are also available.

Comfort Inn Radford
$$ • 1501 Tyler Ave., Radford
• (540) 639-4800

The Comfort Inn Radford is the ideal place for the family, tourists and corporate clients alike. This 100 percent smoke-free facility offers a peaceful and relaxing atmosphere. King and double rooms are available. This hotel offers its guests a two-room suite, complete with hot tub and refrigerator. An indoor, gazebo-style pool area complete with sauna, whirlpool and exercise facility is provided adjacent to the hotel. The rooms are fully equipped with cable TV, touch-tone phones, in-room coffee makers and wall-mounted hair dryers. Wake up to a complimentary continental breakfast before heading out for a day of touring the area or meeting with business partners. Damon's, The Place for Ribs, is located on a sister property. Banquet rooms and meeting facilities are available and accommodate up to 250 people.

Executive Motel
$ • Lee Hwy., Radford • (540) 639-1664

This small motel is clean and comfortable — and very affordable. Its location near St. Alban's Hospital and Radford Shopping Plaza

provides added convenience. Each of the 26 rooms has two double beds, a refrigerator, air conditioning, direct-dial telephones and color TVs with cable TV. Many restaurants, including fast food, are nearby.

Super 8 Motel
$ • 1600 Tyler Ave., Radford
• (540) 731-9355, (800) 848-8888

Super 8 provides a lot of amenities, including cable TV, waterbeds upon request, a 24-hour desk, wake-up calls and free coffee each morning. And the rates are famously affordable. Nonsmoking rooms and business singles are available upon request.

Pulaski County

Comfort Inn
$$ • 4424 Cleburn Blvd., Dublin
• (540) 674-1100, (800) 221-2222

A special feature of this hotel is Emily Virginia's Restaurant. Motor coach groups get a special red carpet greeting, apple cider reception and fresh apple farewell. Each of the 100 rooms has individual temperature control, satellite TV, AM/FM clock radio and direct-dial touch-tone phones. Some rooms have Jacuzzis. The conference room has a wet bar, and a private banquet room is also available. AARP and other discounts are offered.

Alleghany Highlands

Alleghany County

Knights Court
$$ • Valley Ridge Rd., Covington
• (540) 962-7600, (800) 843-5644

This motel is within a two-block radius of shopping and fine restaurants. The 74 rooms, including nonsmoking rooms, have air conditioning, cable TV, direct-dial phones for free local calls, coffee makers and kitchenettes. Also enjoy a free continental breakfast daily. A small conference room is available with advance notice. Truck parking is available.

Comfort Inn
$$ • Mallow Rd., Covington
• (540) 962-2141, (800) 221-2222

Guests receive a free continental breakfast, and all 99 rooms are equipped with air conditioning, coffee makers, cable TV (VCR available) and direct-dial phones with free local calling.

Also available are king-size beds, nonsmoking rooms and two-room suites. Laundry service is available. The hotel has an outdoor pool and indoor whirlpool. A full-service restaurant, The Painted Elephant Restaurant & Lounge, is adjacent to the hotel, and great shopping is within a two-block radius of the hotel.

Best Western Mountain View
$$ • Madison Ave., Covington
• (540) 962-4951, (800) HOLIDAY

The restaurant, the Brass Lantern, is especially nice here. The rooms are equipped with air conditioning, cable TV and direct-dial phones. Nonsmoking rooms are available. The outdoor pool and nearby shopping facilities are other amenities. Banquet/meeting rooms for as many as 250 people also are available.

Bath County

Wilderness Ranch in Bluegrass Hollow
$$ • Va. Rt. 683, Millboro
• (540) 997-9225

If you're looking for a hunter's paradise, writer's haven or artist's delight, travel through Douthat State Park to this private locked and gated 100-acre enclave of rustic log homes by the George Washington and Jefferson National Forests in Bluegrass Hollow. Three modern log homes have baths, kitchens, large porches and picnic tables. The cabins accommodate up to 22 people. Dining is "bring your own." A country wilderness adventure, Wilderness Ranch is close to numerous seasonal attractions year-round including Douthat State Park and The Homestead Resort. Pets are allowed at additional charge.

Highland County

Highland Inn
$$ • Main St., Monterey
• (540) 468-2143, (888) 466-4682

Paul Smith is innkeeper of this cozy spot in Monterey, fondly referred to as "Virginia's Switzerland." This Victorian home was built in 1904 to serve the lodging needs of tourists escaping from the summer heat of nearby cities. Eastlake porches with gingerbread trim and rocking chairs are so inviting you will want to stay indefinitely. Each of the 17 guest rooms has a private bath and is decorated with antiques and collectibles. Choose a standard room (double bed), deluxe room (king-size bed or two beds) or a suite (two rooms). A complimentary continental breakfast is provided each morning, with dinner served in the Monterey Room. The Black Sheep Tavern offers beer and wine every day except Sunday.

You'll find Blue Ridge
innkeepers to be among
the most cordial hosts
in the world and
genuinely concerned
about your well-being
and comfort.

Bed and Breakfasts and Country Inns

If the attractions aren't enough to draw you to the Blue Ridge, there's enough history and mystery at our inns to make it difficult for you to leave these cozy retreats. Slip into the tranquility of country life at an old stagecoach inn on the Valley Turnpike in Woodstock, sharpen your acting skills in an entertaining role-playing weekend at The River House or get closer to heaven at the Bent Mountain Lodge that sits high in the Blue Ridge. No matter what your interests, you can find the perfect place to relax.

Each of these grand old bed and breakfast inns and country inns has its own distinct charm, with histories as varied as the decor. How many of us dream of spending the night in a mansion? Experience just that at Lynchburg's Mansion Inn. You can stay on the former site of an ancient Native American village at Silver Thatch Inn in Charlottesville. Or you may be swept away by the beauty of bubbling springs at Meadow Lane in Warm Springs.

A significant number of the inns are in restored, historic properties. Historic and other attractions of exceptional interest plus skiing, fishing, boating, swimming and horseback riding are all within reasonable reach of a bed and breakfast inn. Many can accommodate special dinners, weddings, receptions and other social and meeting functions.

You'll find Blue Ridge innkeepers to be among the most cordial hosts in the world and genuinely concerned about your well-being and comfort. Virginia is internationally known for Southern hospitality, and these antique country manors can convey to you a sense of tranquility that's hard to find anywhere else.

Many inns do not allow children and pets. We have indicated those that do accept them. Be sure to verify this before making a reservation.

Price Code

As in our Hotels and Motels chapter, we provide a dollar key to assist you in determining the cost of a one-night stay for two at the inns we've listed in this chapter. Note the rate indicated is for the standard accommodation; rates may vary according to additional amenities and special requests. Most inns require a deposit of one night's price to confirm reservations. Several of the lodgings list prices under the Modified American Plan, meaning prices reflect a night's stay as well as two meals (breakfast and dinner). The rates indicated here are for the high season, April through October; some inns reduce rates in the off-season, except those in ski areas.

$	**$45 to $65**
$$	**$66 to $85**
$$$	**$86 to $105**
$$$$	**$106 and higher**

Note that if an inn has rooms that fall within two price categories, it will be listed in the lower range. For example, if the rooms cost between $80 and $95, we will feature it in the $$ category because you can find accommodations within the lower price bracket.

Reservation Services

The following services are available to assist you in selecting a bed and breakfast or country inn.

Every January the **Bed & Breakfast Association of Virginia,** P.O. Box 791, Orange 22960, puts out a descriptive booklet of unique lodging across the state called *Guide To Virginia's Inns and Bed & Breakfasts.* It's free if you don't mind waiting for their bulk mailing every three weeks, or for $3 you can have a guide mailed right away. Their phone numbers are (540) 672-0870 or (800) 296-1246. For reservations, call the **Virginia Tourism Corporation** at (800) 934-9184.

Blue Ridge Bed & Breakfast also publishes a free brochure featuring more than 50 inns, farms and historic houses in four states. Write them at Route 2, Box 3895, Berryville 22611; reach them by phone at (540) 955-1246 or (800) 296-1246.

Guest House Bed & Breakfast is a reservation service for the Charlottesville and Albemarle County area. For a descriptive brochure, write P.O. Box 5737, Charlottesville 22905, or call (804) 979-7264.

Shenandoah Valley

Frederick County

Brownstone Cottage
$$ • 161 McCarty Ln., Winchester • (540) 662-1962

If you are looking for a little pampering, start your visit at Brownstone Cottage. It's small: there are only two suites, but that's what owners Chuck and Sheila Brown say makes this inn special. "We get a lot of people from Washington who just want to get away from the rat race," Chuck Brown said. "We're not very big, so we kind of spoil them. They love the special attention."

The Browns will put you up in their new home, a French-Armenian cottage that is more reminiscent of an English Tudor bed and breakfast. You can take in the scenic countryside from the deck or cozy up amid Victorian antiques in the sitting room. One suite has its own private whirlpool, while the other is more for families. It includes a king-size bed, a day bed that converts into another king, a sitting area and private bath. Children older than 12 are welcome.

Every morning, freshly brewed coffee will be waiting to start off a full country breakfast with Chuck's homemade pancakes or bread. The candlelit breakfast is served in the formal dining room on fine china.

The Inn at Vaucluse Spring
$$$$ • 140 Vaucluse Spring Ln., Stephens City • (540) 869-0200

This classic Virginia inn offers eight rooms, two suites and two guest houses on the 100-acre estate built by Shenandoah Valley artist John Chumley.

The new owners call their newly renovated Manor House their crown jewel. Built by Capt. Strother Jones in 1785, the Manor House is nestled among 200-year-old boxwoods and stately trees with massive canopies. Inside it's an antique lover's dream. Each of the three upstairs bedrooms includes fireplaces with the original mantels, ancient heart-pine floors and private baths with Jacuzzis. The stone-walled lower level features three more bedrooms and a common room filled with overstuffed chairs and the original cooking fireplace. The downstairs rooms all feature queen-size beds, private baths and fireplaces.

Four accommodations are in the Chumley Homeplace, including the Chumley Suite and the Hite Suite. The two guest houses, The Gallery and Mill House Studio, feature king-size beds and Jacuzzis. Mill House, a two-level suite that overlooks Vaucluse Pond, used to serve as the artist's studio.

A full country breakfast is served in the airy Chumley Homeplace dining rooms, a stone-floored terrace that is just off the kitchen. If you prefer, your breakfast will be brought to your room. They also have picnic lunches available for anyone taking a walking or cycling tour.

The Cottage, at left, is the oldest building at Sharp Rock Farm Bed and Breakfast. In the background is Old Rag Mountain.

For an additional charge, a four-course gourmet dinner is available on Saturday nights by reservation only. Before dinner, guests may gather in the Keeping Room, a comfy common area in the Homeplace with hardwood floors, exposed wooden beams in the ceiling and a large stone fireplace.

Fort Valley and the Skyline Drive are minutes away. Vaucluse is a nonsmoking inn, but guests may smoke on the grounds. Children older than 10 are welcome.

Wayside Inn
$$$ • 7783 Main St., Middletown
• (540) 869-1797, (877) 869-1797

Since 1797 this old stagecoach stop has been coddling travelers along U.S. Highway 11, once a major north-south thoroughfare. Two-hundred years ago it served as the Wilkinson Tavern, later changing its name to Larrick's Hotel after the Civil War. A third floor was added in the 1900s, along with a new name, Wayside Inn.

This restored 18th-century country inn has maintained its flair for Southern hospitality. Each of its 24 guest rooms is furnished in period antiques, including four-poster beds with canopies, cannonball and acorn-carved details, plus French, Provincial and Greek Revival period pieces. Allow yourself a couple of hours to examine the inn's artwork and curios.

For an additional charge you can savor a hearty breakfast, lunch or dinner. The restaurant serves excellent Southern-style meals in seven private dining rooms and a large main dining area. The Wayside Theater (see our chapter on The Arts) is just down the street, and many historical attractions are nearby.

Clarke County

The River House
$$$ • U.S. Hwy. 50 E., Boyce
• (540) 837-1476

Cornelia and Donald Niemann will make your stay on this historic property near the Shenandoah River a memorable one. The site, known in 1780 as Ferry Farm and part of the huge Carter Hall estate, was surveyed by a young George Washington for Lord Fairfax. It served as a field hospital in the Civil War and in the 1940s was a popular restaurant and tavern.

Renovations and expansions have created an imposing Virginia fieldstone residence with five air-conditioned guest rooms, each with a private bath and working fireplace. Each room is elegantly appointed, spacious and has its own personality. Snacks and an early continental breakfast in the two kitchenettes may precede a hearty brunch in the dining room. Rooms are accessible to the disabled. Cribs, playpens and high chairs are available for small children. Corporate rates are available. Each room has a telephone, and a fax machine, copier and modem are on site.

The surrounding 17 acres of open woodlands and river frontage, just an hour from Washington, D.C., give the inn a distinctively rural ambiance. Numerous historic sites, horseback riding, biking, strolling, golf, tennis, antiques and other shopping options and award-winning dining are all within easy travel distance.

Special theme weekends are available at house parties. Three-day Country House parties are tailored for groups — families, couples, friends — and may include wine-and-cheese gatherings, candlelight dinners, picnics, planned activities and a gourmet brunch. There are 11 different programs, from antique seminars to wine tastings. One of the most popular is "Enter Laughing — A Weekend in the Country," with role-playing and other hijinks wrapped around a peaceful retreat.

Warren County

Killahevlin
$$$$ • 1401 N. Royal Ave., Front Royal
• (540) 636-7335, (800) 847-6132

Irish immigrant and limestone baron William Carson built his home on the highest spot in Front Royal, calling it "Killyhevlin" for the place in Northern Ireland he cherished as a child. The house was designed by the architectural firm that created Washington's grand Old Executive Office Building. It is said that during the Civil War two of maverick Confederate Colonel John Singleton Mosby's men were hanged here, and Union troops often camped in this strategic spot.

Owners Susan and John Lang, both with Irish roots, were captivated by the brick Edwardian mansion and instructed their interior designers to make sure the taste of Ireland remained at the forefront of the house's decor. Each of the six accommodations has a queen-size bed, working fireplace, private bath with whirlpool tub and shower, and a wonderful view. Four of the six rooms have porches.

Breakfast, a sumptuous repast of fresh fruits, breads and a variety of entrees, is elegantly served. The Langs have recently added an Irish pub with complimentary Irish beer and wine for their guests. Killahevlin is listed in both the National Register of Historic Places and the Virginia Landmarks Register.

Chester House Bed and Breakfast
$$ • 43 Chester St., Front Royal
• (800) 621-0441, (540) 635-3937

This charming Georgian-style home was built in 1905 by international lawyer Charles Samuels, who was intent on creating an architectural treasure. Chester House is still noted for its elaborate terraced gardens with wisteria arbors and boxwood gardens. Inside, local artisans designed the intricate woodwork and dentil molding. Marble mantels, fountains and statuary were imported from Europe. The main house has six air-conditioned rooms, four with private baths. The Royal Oak Suite has a four-poster queen-size bed, fireplace, sitting room, private bath and views of the garden. The Blue Ridge Room features a wrought iron king-size bed, private bath and also overlooks the garden. The Skyline Room offers a four-poster queen-size bed and a fireplace.

Innkeepers Ann and Bill Wilson are excited about their new Carriage House. Built in 1905, they had it restored in 1996. This premiere accommodation, which they call the "honeymoon cottage," is a two-story bungalow with 5-foot arched windows, a spiral staircase, a living room, full kitchen and a tiled bath with a whirlpool for two under a skylight. A king-size bed is in the loft plus lots of extras, including a stone fireplace, a CD player, TV and phone. The cottage runs about $190 per night, $165 if you stay more than one night.

Chester House serves freshly squeezed orange juice, homemade pastries, cereals and fruit every morning for breakfast. Entrees could include Bill's famous "mile high popovers," Ann's orange French toast or buttermilk waffles with blackberries and maple syrup. Don't forget the select teas and brewed coffee. Later you can enjoy refreshments on the portico or sip sherry by the fireplace in one of three sitting rooms. Terry robes, fluffy towels, fresh flowers and homemade cookies will be waiting to pamper you back in your room. Smoking is limited to the television room. Children 12 and older are welcome.

Shenandoah County

The Inn at Narrow Passage
**$$$ • U.S. Hwy. 11 at
Chapman Landing Rd., Woodstock
• (540) 459-8000, (800) 458-8002**

This log inn overlooking the Shenandoah River has been welcoming and protecting travelers since the 1740s. Back then, it was a haven for settlers seeking refuge from Indian attacks along the "narrow passage," where only one wagon could pass one at a time, and travel was dangerous. It also served as Stonewall Jackson's headquarters during the Valley Campaign of 1862.

Ed and Ellen Markel have taken great care in restoring this landmark to its 18th-century look and maintaining the warm ambiance of the original inn. The inn is furnished in antiques and Colonial reproductions. Each bedroom has comfortable amenities; many have working fireplaces. The inn is centrally heated and air-conditioned. Breakfast is served in the Colonial dining room, often before a cheery fire. Guests can relax by the massive limestone fireplace in the living room or enjoy the

views of the sloping lawns and river from the porch.

Hiking and fishing are recreational options at the inn. Nearby you'll find historic battlefields, wineries, caverns and skiing at Bryce Resort. The inn is 2 miles from I-81; take Exit 283 just south of Woodstock. A conference room is available for executive retreats.

River'd Inn
**$$$$ • 1972 Artz Rd., Woodstock
• (540) 459-5369, (800) 637-4561**

Cross over a low-water bridge on the north fork of the Shenandoah River and, if the river rises, the locals say you are "rivered in." This Victorian inn, at the base of Massanutten Mountain off U.S. 11, sits on one of the famous seven bends of the Shenandoah. Host Diana Lurey oversees the 25 acres of secluded natural areas offering picnicking, hiking and relaxing. A wraparound veranda and swimming pool are other leisure options.

The inn is centrally heated and air-conditioned, and the eight guest rooms are furnished with fine antiques. All rooms have fireplaces and private baths with whirlpool tubs.

The inn offers quiet dining in three elegant dining rooms, each with a distinctive fireplace and intimate seating. Meals are elegant, candlelight affairs with fresh-cut flowers, linen, china and gourmet cuisine. Highlights of a typical brunch might be chilled peach champagne soup with fresh strawberries, eggs Benedict, local pan-fried trout and a pecan tartlett with fresh whipped cream. Dinners feature such gourmet mainstays as lobster tail, filet mignon and chicken cordon bleu.

Country auctions, antique and craft shops, horseback riding, fishing and other river-oriented activities beckon. Nearby attractions include the New Market Battlefields and Civil War Museum, Massanutten and Bryce ski resorts, Skyline Drive, caverns, Wayside Theatre and numerous other historic and cultural sites.

INSIDERS' TIP

Many inns and bed and breakfasts offer greatly reduced rates in the off-season (November through March, except in ski areas). You'll save money, and you can fully enjoy amenities such as fireplaces, hot cider and snow-covered meadows.

Page County

Locust Grove Inn
$$$$ • 1456 N. Egypt Bend Rd., Luray • (540) 743-1804

With almost a mile of frontage on the Shenandoah River, this inn is an angler's paradise. But others, too, will enjoy its mountain views, 53 acres of pastures and unique log farm that dates back to the 1760s. Built on an American Indian campsite, the home was owned by a German immigrant who fought in the Revolutionary War. His grandsons later fought for the Confederacy.

The large house has been refurbished, but pieces of the old house are evident throughout with exposed logs, working stone fireplaces and original colors and woodwork. Since Locust Grove is owned by an artist and antique collector, most of the inn has been furnished with pre-Civil War antiques.

The five spacious guest rooms all have central air conditioning, private baths and mountain or river views (some have both!). Rates include breakfast as well as refreshments in the afternoon or evening. Children, pets and smoking are not allowed.

The Ruffner House Inn
$$$ • 440 Ruffner Rd., Luray • (540) 743-7855

This inn is actually two houses with six guest rooms with private baths that can accommodate as many as 16 people for reunions and retreats. But couples, too, will enjoy the inn's 20 park-like acres just outside Luray. A garden spa makes relaxing that much easier.

The c. 1840 brick manor house has grandly scaled rooms restored by a leading Virginia conservator with antique Victorian decor and fine art. Built in the early 1900s, the farmhouse boasts a marble and glass solarium. Breakfast is served between 9 and 10 AM, though you may request early coffee.

MayneView
$$$ • 439 Mechanic St., Luray • (540) 743-7921

This bed and breakfast inn in the heart of Virginia's lush Shenandoah Valley offers fine accommodations and breathtaking mountain views from its position between the Shenandoah National Park and the George Washington and Jefferson National Forests. Guest rooms are well-appointed with feather beds, fireplaces and private baths.

Gourmet cuisine is another attraction here. The Shenandoah sunrise is a great backdrop for the morning meal, which includes gourmet coffees, teas, homemade muffins, pastries and jams. If you want to sleep in, a bountiful breakfast buffet and cooked-to-order breakfasts are also available. For the ultimate indulgence, plan ahead for breakfast in bed. Innkeeper Shar Mayne also offers packages that include dinner.

Enjoy sweeping mountain views from the inn's newly added outdoor spa. A relaxing grape arbor and fountain offer another way to spend a lazy afternoon or evening.

Spring Farm Inn
$$$$ • 13 Wallace Ave., off U.S. Hwy. 211, Luray • (540) 743-4701

This 200-year-old historic brick Colonial sits on 10 acres of grounds with mountain panoramas visible from nearly every vantage point. A gazebo, hammocks and a patio bring guests outdoors to enjoy the secluded, natural setting, which is part of a bird sanctuary. A veranda running the full length of the house commands views of the Blue Ridge Mountains, while a porch on the other side of the house frames a view of Massanutten Mountain.

Guests may choose from three large bedrooms with a shared bath, a suite with a private bath and a glass-enclosed sitting area (the better to see those gorgeous mountains!) or the cottage, which also has a private bath. Innkeeper Thelma Mayes provides a full breakfast each morning and refreshments every hour of the day.

This serene retreat is near numerous natural and historic sites and lots of recreational opportunities. It is 2.5 miles from Luray Caverns (see our Attractions chapter) and 8 miles from the entrance to Skyline Drive.

Woodruff House Inn
$$$ • 330 Mechanic St., Luray • (540) 743-1494

This highly rated inn is described by the Woodruffs as an "1882 fairytale Victorian," and it delivers on that promise with its antiques, Oriental rugs and hallmark silver catching the firelight in cozy Victorian parlors. Expanded to include the c. 1890 Victorian house next door, the inn now has six guest rooms, each with its own private bath. Three rooms in the main house come equipped with Jacuzzis built for two, including the rooftop, fireside Jacuzzi suite.

An elegant afternoon tea, an evening high tea buffet dinner, morning gourmet coffee service in your room and a fireside candlelight breakfast are included in the room price. Innkeeper Lucas Woodruff is a chef, so fantastic food is de rigueur. Private label wines from Virginia's Barboursville Vineyard are available.

In the garden (which is romantically lit by little white lights after dusk) are gazebos and two hot tubs that set the tone for a romantic, relaxing evening. By day, visitors can take advantage of nearby attractions such as Luray Caverns, New Market Battlefields or Skyline Drive.

Jordan Hollow Farm Inn
$$$$ • 326 Hawksbill Park Rd., Stanley
• (540) 778-2209, (888) 418-7000

This 145-acre horse farm is nestled in a secluded hollow surrounded by the Shenandoah National Park and the George Washington and Jefferson National Forests. Though activities abound here, Jordan Hollow is about taking it easy. Innkeepers Gail Kyle and Betsy Anderson invite guests to relax on the enormous wraparound porch and walk through the lush meadows and fragrant woods. It's a farm environment with a steady, quiet pace.

A stable on the property can accommodate riding for the beginner as well as pony rides for children younger than 8. Guests can bring and board their own horses if they choose. There also are plenty of walking paths and trails for those who prefer to rely on two legs.

The inn is quite large, with 21 guest rooms, all with private baths and some with fireplaces and Jacuzzis. The buildings, except for Arbor View Lodge and Mare Meadow Lodge, are the original farm buildings. The decor is country antique.

The Farmhouse Restaurant serves a full breakfast and dinner for guests (dinner is not included in the price of a room) in three dining rooms. The American regional cuisine takes advantage of seasonal ingredients, so menus change every few months.

For indoor entertainment, the Carriage House offers a large common area with games, books and cable television. Other nearby activities include swimming, hiking, canoeing, fishing, skiing, museums, antiques and craft shops. The farm is a short drive from Lake Arrowhead, Luray Caverns, Shenandoah National Park and George Washington and Jefferson National Forests. Children are allowed, but be sure to notify the reservationist when you book your stay.

Milton House Bed & Breakfast
$$$ • 113 W. Main St., Stanley
• (540) 778-2495, (800) 816-3731

Innkeepers John and Karin Tipton pamper guests with Southern hospitality in their beautifully refurbished 1915 Southern Colonial home ordered from Sears, Roebuck and Co.'s Big Book Catalog. The inn, 7 miles south of Luray, is filled with antiques, Karin's handmade quilts, floral arrangements and dried-flower wreaths. A collection of Steiff bears and rabbits along with June McKenna limited-edition Santa Clauses are charming distractions.

The inn is rich in detail — long, sweeping porches cooled by stately fir trees, leaded-glass windows that create a kaleidoscope of sunbeams in the morning, detailed stenciling and other architectural attractions. Rates can include a memorable candlelight fireside dinner, a soak in the outdoor garden Jacuzzi, early morning coffee and a special breakfast of Belgian waffles with fresh fruit or stuffed French toast with orange-apricot sauce.

All rooms have private baths, and a suite with a double shower is available. Several rooms have fireplaces. The property also includes a log cabin, built in 1991, with two deluxe accommodations that include living/sitting areas, queen- or king-size beds, private baths, hot tubs, gas log fireplaces and decks with mountain views. One unit also has a kitchen.

The inn also offers a mountain cottage nestled at the foot of Massanutten Mountain, with panoramic views of the Blue Ridge Mountains, and the Shenandoah River and a 15-acre lake five minutes away. The retreat has two bedrooms, a living room with a hot tub by the stone fireplace, cathedral ceilings, a fully equipped kitchen, bath, screened porch and stone barbecue. Smoking is permitted in designated areas. Weekly rates are available.

The Ruby Rose Inn Bed and Breakfast
$$$ • 275 Chapel Rd., Stanley
• (540) 778-4680

This lovely Victorian home, c. 1890, is the ideal setting for a peaceful retreat — just ask members of the British Parliament, who are the inn's most famous guests. Comfortably furnished and newly remodeled, The Ruby Rose has a private cottage with a king-size canopied bed; the Mayhew Suite; and two guest rooms with private baths. All rooms have fireplaces and Jacuzzis.

Guests awaken to a full homemade breakfast, which may include Belgian waffles with preserves, apple pancakes or an omelette. Beverages and homemade goodies are always available.

Surrounded by mountains, tall oaks and colorful flower beds, the inn sits in the valley between Shenandoah National Park and George Washington and Jefferson National Forests — scenic areas for hiking and biking. If you place your order a day in advance, the inn will provide a box lunch for your outdoor excursion. They also can supply a cooler and ice.

Other "neighborhood" activities include horseback riding, golfing, fishing at Lake Arrowhead, canoeing, rafting, antique shopping and tracing historic Civil War battles and skirmishes by the markers that dot the area. The famous New Market Battlefields, a few miles away, hosts a spring re-enactment. Luray, Shenandoah and Endless caverns are just a few minutes' drive.

Pets are not allowed. Guests must refrain from smoking inside buildings, but a flagstone patio is available for guests who wish to smoke.

Rockingham County

Joshua Wilton House, Inn and Restaurant
$$$ • 412 S. Main St., Harrisonburg
• (540) 434-4464

Roberta and Craig Moore welcome guests to their elegantly restored Victorian home, which lies in the heart of the Shenandoah Valley. Restoration efforts have preserved much of the original architecture.

The Moores will spoil you with a complimentary glass of wine or beer in the evening, and their gourmet breakfast, including homemade pastries, fresh fruits and a delicious pot of coffee, is enough to summon anyone out of bed. On site is one of the state's most acclaimed restaurants with both cafe dining and fine dining available. The innovative menus feature a variety of locally grown foods (see our Restaurants chapter).

The inn's bedrooms are furnished with period antiques to give them the charm of the 1880s. All five bedrooms have private baths, reading areas and telephones.

The Wilton House is within walking distance of James Madison University and downtown Harrisonburg. A variety of athletic activities, such as golfing, biking, hiking, swimming and skiing, are accessible from the inn. This old mansion is an oasis of quiet charm and gracious living surrounded by the Blue Ridge Mountains.

Hearth N' Holly Inn
$$ • 46 Songbird Ln., Penn Laird
• (540) 434-6766, (800) 209-1379

Doris and Dennis Brown's pleasant bed and breakfast inn is 5 miles from I-81 and 10 minutes from Massanutten Resort and James Madison University. Situated on 15 acres, the Colonial and Victorian inn has four guest rooms with queen-size brass beds, private baths and fireplaces.

A full country breakfast, with a choice of two entrees, is served from 8 to 11 AM. Dinners are also available on request, and the innkeepers love pulling out all the stops to host weddings and other special events.

Diversions within easy reach include the theater, arts and sports events at the university; skiing at Massanutten Resort; Skyline Drive and the Blue Ridge Parkway; Civil War battlefields; and Endless, Grand and Luray caverns. Be warned: it will be hard to leave this inn, with its sunroom, picnic pavilion, hot tub, queen-size hammock and wooded walking trails. In late 1997 the Browns added a full wraparound porch for those who would like to sit outside and enjoy the swings.

Augusta County

The Inn at Keezletown Road
$$ • 1224 Keezletown Rd., Weyers Cave • (540) 234-0644, (800) 465-0100

This elegant, 100-year-old Victorian in the quaint village of Weyers Cave has spectacular views of the Blue Ridge Mountains. The four large guest rooms are furnished with antiques, comfortable beds and Oriental rugs. Each has a private bath, sitting area, air conditioning and cable TV. All have queen-size beds, except for one, which affords either two twins or a king.

The innkeepers, Sandy and Alan Inabinet, provide a full country breakfast that includes fresh eggs from the inn's own chickens. Dinner reservations may be made, though advance notice is required. The grounds have wonderful gardens including a formal herb garden and a goldfish pond, and guests may walk on the adjacent trail through the town's park or sit and rock on the inn's porch.

The inn, just 10 minutes from Harrisonburg, is near historic sites. Other attractions are within easy driving distance, as are the Shenandoah Valley Regional Airport in Weyers Cave and several colleges. Children ages 14 and older are welcome. Smoking is limited to the garden and porch. Pets are not permitted.

Ashton Country House
$$ • 1205 Middlebrook Ave., Staunton • (540) 885-7819, (800) 296-7819

With 25 beautiful acres surrounding this country retreat, it's hard to believe the center of town is a mere mile away. A c.1860 Greek Revival brick manor house, Ashton has been owned by Dorie and Vince DiStefano since 1994. The 40-foot center hall with an 11-foot ceiling hints at the manor house stylings you'll find throughout. Ashton is filled with a combination of Victorian antiques and reproductions. Fully renovated in 1995, the inn's elegant hardwood pine and maple floors are decorated with exquisite Oriental rugs.

No detail is overlooked in providing for guests' comfort. Four double guest rooms and one suite are available, each with a private bathroom with shower. Four of the rooms have fireplaces.

Every morning the DiStefanos offer a hearty full breakfast, including omelettes made to order and homemade muffins. You can even sample a few homemade desserts with beverages in the morning or afternoon.

Three verandas overlook the expansive grounds, which include barns, outbuildings and pastures to explore. Children are accepted with notice. Wheelchair access and a specially equipped bathroom are available.

Belle Grae Inn
$$$$ • 515 W. Frederick St., Staunton • (540) 886-5151, (888) 541-5151

This authentically restored inn, built in 1870, will please you with its 15 luxurious guest rooms and appetizing menu. It is named for two of the surrounding mountains, Betsy Belle and Mary Grae. The Scotch-Irish settlers in the area, reminded of their homeland, named the mountains for Scottish landmarks. Belle Grae sits atop a hill in historic Staunton. Wicker rockers invite relaxation on the veranda, and white gingerbread stylings decorate the porch of the main, original building.

One of the first things a guest sees is the double-entrance door with four stained-glass panels and a crystal oval in which the inn's name is engraved. Period reproductions and antiques, which are for sale, are found throughout the dining rooms, bistro, lounge and other lovely rooms. The bedrooms each are furnished a little differently, but all are appropriate to the period. You can sit in front of your cozy fireplace (most rooms have them) and sip complimentary brandy from long-stemmed glasses. Most rooms also have telephones,

Photo: Clifton — The Country Inn

Touches of home — fireplaces, home-cooked breakfasts and maybe a library — are part of what makes a bed and breakfast inn so special.

and all have private baths and such amenities as English herb soaps and bath oils. Joined by pathways and walks are five restored 1870s to 1890s vintage houses. These are available to families or for executive retreats.

The popular chef prepares meals using fresh breads, fruits and vegetables and the best meats. Breakfast festivities begin at 7 AM in the garden room, where early risers may enjoy coffee, juice, poppy-seed bread (a house specialty) and complimentary newspapers. A full hot breakfast is also served from 7:30 to 9 AM.

Activities in the area include walking tours through gorgeous historic Staunton, shopping at a gigantic antique warehouse or chess and backgammon in the quiet of the inn's sitting room.

Frederick House
$$$ • 28 N. New St., Staunton
• (540) 885-4220, (800) 334-5575

Six stately houses were rescued from demolition and transformed into Frederick House. These Greek Revival buildings have been restored and the rooms inside graciously appointed with antiques and paintings by Virginia artists. The oversize beds add an extra touch of comfort. Each of the 10 rooms and six suites has its own private bath, cable TV,

telephone, radio and air conditioning. A full, delicious, home-cooked breakfast is served each morning in two dining rooms.

One activity we recommend is a relaxing stroll through the town to photograph Staunton's gorgeous architecture and to visit the town's antique and specialty shops. Woodrow Wilson's birthplace is only two blocks away (see our Attractions chapter), and Mary Baldwin College is next door. Cycling, hiking and touring are perfect activities in the surrounding Blue Ridge and Allegheny mountains. Hosts Joe and Evy Harman will point out places of interest and provide a bit of history as well.

Fine dining is available at McCormick's Restaurant, adjacent to the Frederick House, and at several other restaurants within walking distance.

The Sampson Eagon Inn
$$$ • 238 E. Beverley St., Staunton
• (540) 886-8200, (800) 597-9722

This elegant inn, which has won preservation awards, is in the historic Gospel Hill section of Staunton, adjacent to the Woodrow Wilson Birthplace and Mary Baldwin College. The property's original owner, Sampson Eagon, was a Methodist preacher who held services on the grounds here during the 1790s.

Don't expect any preaching today, however: the inn is tailor-made for privacy, with three distinctive guest rooms and two suites, each furnished with beautiful period pieces, a queen-size canopied bed, cozy sitting area and modern bath. Telephones, air conditioning and private TVs with VCRs are standard in the rooms. The inn even has a fax machine, in case you can't get away from the office completely.

The day begins with a full gourmet breakfast in the formal dining room (although the accent is on casual). Entrees include such dishes as pecan Belgian waffles, Grand Marnier souffle, pancakes and an array of egg choices. Refreshments are available throughout the day, with beverages and gourmet chocolates brought right to your room.

The inn was selected in 1993 by *Country Inns Magazine* as one of America's Best Inn Buys, and *Gourmet* magazine writes that proprietors Frank and Laura Mattingly "take the second 'B' in B&B seriously." This antebellum home also has been included in *Southern Living* and *Travel and Leisure* magazines. This is indeed the place for a memorable retreat. The inn is not appropriate for children younger than 12 and does not accept pets. No smoking is allowed at the inn.

Thornrose House at Gypsy Hill

$ • 531 Thornrose Ave., Staunton
• (540) 885-7026, (800) 861-4338

Otis and Suzanne Huston are the innkeepers at this beautiful bed and breakfast inn in Staunton's Gypsy Hill area. The moment you step into the grand entranceway, you begin to discover the charm of this Georgian Revival brick home and its five comfortable guest rooms. Named for English localities, each room is decorated accordingly and includes a private bath.

You'll awaken to the aroma of a heart-healthy breakfast, with entrees ranging from banana-pecan pancakes and waffles to egg souffles and French toast. Afterwards, you'll want to venture out and see the sites that make Staunton so special. Nearby attractions include the P. Buckley Moss Museum, Grand Caverns and the Museum of American Frontier Culture. Across the street is 300-acre Gypsy Hill Park, where you can play golf, tennis (rackets and balls provided) or swim. The Statler Complex, owned by country music's award-winning Statler Brothers, is right down the street.

Thornrose House has lovely gardens gracing its acre of grounds. The wraparound veranda with rocking chairs is perfect for an afternoon tea. The sitting room has a fireplace and grand piano. School-age children are welcome.

The Iris Inn

$$ • 191 Chinquapin Dr., Waynesboro
• (540) 943-1991

The charm and grace of Southern living in a totally modern facility surrounded by woods — that's The Iris Inn. The brick-and-cedar inn was built on 20 acres in 1991 and is ideal as a weekend retreat, business accommodation or tranquil spot for the tourist. Its focus is on comfort, with seven spacious guest rooms decorated in nature and wildlife motifs, each with private bath. The inn recently added two suites in a separate building.

The main building has six guest rooms, each furnished with 18th-century reproductions, family pieces and antiques, and each has a specific theme — the Deer Room, Wildflower Room, Pine Room, Bird Room and Duck Pond. The bright, airy rooms all have king- or queen-size beds (some have a day bed for a third person). One room is equipped for the disabled. The seventh guest room, the Hawk's Nest, is an efficiency unit, complete with kitchenette and sitting area; it's ideal for longer stays and a favorite of honeymooners.

The Great Room, in addition to being the breakfast room, provides a gathering place around the high, stone fireplace where guests may relax and enjoy the woodland views. Beverages are available at the check-in area, and a bottomless cookie jar is on the sideboard. A balcony library overlooks this beautiful room, providing panoramic views of the Shenandoah Valley. Wraparound porches on both floors and a three-story lookout tower — a hot tub is on its first floor! — are popular with guests.

In 1996 a new building was added to include two luxury suites, one of which connects to a meeting room. About 50 yards from the main house, this traditional, contemporary building has gas log fireplaces, treadmills, TVs, VCRs and private balconies.

The full two-course breakfast includes home-baked breads, juice and fruit, fresh-brewed coffee and an entree that changes daily. Nearby attractions are Waynesboro's Virginia Metalcrafters and P. Buckley Moss Museum, historic Monticello and Ash Lawn-Highland near Charlottesville, Skyline Drive, the Blue Ridge Parkway and the Appalachian Trail.

The Lodge at Penmerryl Farm
$$ • Greenville School Rd.
(Va. Rt. 662), Greenville
• (540) 337-0622, (800) 808-6617

The Lodge at Penmerryl Farm is a welcoming retreat in an elegant country setting for vacationers and equestrians. Adjacent to the lodge is the Equestrian Centre at Penmerryl Farm, a year-round horse training complex and breeding facility that stands two champion Irish draught stallions. You can bring your own horse or ride one of the centre's thoroughbreds.

Originally the summer home of the Pittkin family, the lodge includes 10 comfortable guest rooms with private baths. Each adjoins a central great room, which has a full kitchen and a dining and lounge area ideal for groups. A hot tub off the great room provides a relaxing end to a day of riding or tennis. A continental breakfast and lunch are served each day.

Penmerryl also rents two three-bedroom log cabins. Although the continental breakfast and lunch is not included in the $159.95 daily rate, each cabin is equipped with a full kitchen. (You can, however, join in the meals for an additional charge.)

Other leisure activities include swimming in one of two pools, or sailing and fishing on the 22-acre lake. Golfing, skiing and biking are within a short distance of the farm.

Lexington and Rockbridge County

A Bed & Breakfast at Llewellyn Lodge in Lexington
$$ • 603 S. Main St., Lexington
• (540) 463-3235, (800) 882-1145

This charming 1940s brick Colonial home is in the heart of Lexington, within walking distance of all the city's historic sights. Ellen and John Roberts are your hosts. Ellen's a gourmet cook who has been a part of the airline, travel, hotel and restaurant industries. John Roberts is a native Lexingtonian, born in the Stonewall Jackson House, once a hospital, now a museum.

The friendly atmosphere is noticeable from the start as you are met at the front door with refreshments. The comfortable living room, which has a large fireplace, is a perfect setting for good conversation. The Lodge has a separate television and telephone room and is air conditioned. Each of the bedrooms is distinct, designed to meet the needs of a variety of guests. Each room has extra-firm bedding, a ceiling fan and private bathroom. Highlights include a pencil-post bed, wicker furniture, an oak spindle bed, brass beds and four-poster beds. A first-floor room can accommodate disabled persons who do not require a wheelchair.

A gourmet breakfast awaits you each morning — fantastic omelettes, Belgian waffles, French toast, Virginia maple syrup, homemade muffins and breads, bacon, sausage, ham, juice, coffee and teas.

After breakfast, take on the great outdoors. John has compiled an extensive *Trail & Outdoor Guide*, packed full of great advice on hiking, fishing and other outdoor activities. The Lodge offers fly-fishing, golf, canoeing, horseback riding and outdoor theater packages. The Robertses are happy to help you design a memorable outdoor adventure.

Smoking is not permitted in the guest rooms or dining room, and pets are not allowed. The Blue Ridge Animal Clinic, (540) 463-7799, a vet-attended pet kennel, is nearby. The Lodge is designed with adults in mind, although children ages 10 and older are welcome. Super winter rates and midweek discounts are available.

Brierley Hill
$$ • 985 Borden Rd., Lexington
• (540) 464-8421, (800) 422-4925

Guests at this bed and breakfast inn rave about the wonderful food and beautiful accommodations, not to mention the breathtaking views from the large veranda. Situated on

8 acres of hillside farmland, the inn is quiet and romantic, and the hospitality is second to none. Owners Barry and Carole Speton enjoy the finer things in life and want to share them with their guests. Barry is a former lawyer and is interested in antique books, prints and furniture. Carole is the former director of the Canadian Figure Skating Association; she enjoys gardening, quilting and cooking.

The inn is decorated throughout with Laura Ashley wall coverings, fabrics and linens. Each of the five guest rooms has an elegant bed (four are canopy beds, and one is an antique brass bed), a private bathroom and sitting area. The Deluxe King Room has an additional day bed, fireplace and TV. A two-room suite has a fireplace, Jacuzzi and private patio looking out to spectacular views. The inn is fully air conditioned, and fireplaces in the dining and living rooms warm the winter chill.

Guests feast on a full country breakfast of Grand Marnier French toast, buckwheat banana pancakes, French scrambled eggs with cream cheese and herbs, eggs Benedict or Belgian waffles with strawberries and sour cream, in addition to juice, fresh fruit and ham, bacon or sausage. Afternoon tea, served during the cooler months, includes homemade cakes, breads, scones and cookies. Advance notice is required for dinner — and it is worth it! The evening meal features fresh herbs and vegetables from the garden as well as entrees such as boneless salmon steak with red wine and mushroom sauce, rib-eye roast with herbs and red wine sauce and spicy stuffed chicken breast with sun-dried tomatoes.

You can relax in the serenity at Brierley Hill by lounging on the veranda or strolling down a country road. If you're up for a little more adventure, you can go sightseeing in historic Lexington or take advantage of special packages for theater, horseback riding, winter getaways and specials for midweek stays. Children older than 14 are welcome. Smoking is restricted to the veranda or garden. No pets are allowed.

Fassifern

$$ • 27 Gallery Ln., Lexington • (540) 463-1013, (800) 782-1587

Visitors to the Virginia Horse Center pass right by Fassifern, a place of striking beauty — tall weeping willows surround a small pond, and bright flowers abound when the weather is warm. Fassifern is on 3 acres just across the road from the Art Farm, a gallery with summer workshops that teach the traditional methods of Chinese painting (see our chapter on The Arts). On the other side of the Art Farm is the Horse Center (see our Horse Country chapter).

This bed and breakfast inn's main building is a beautiful old home, built in 1867. There's also the Dependency, formerly an ice house and servants' living quarters, which now houses two guest rooms. Owner Francis Smith lives on the property, but guests need not feel they must tiptoe around someone's private home — this house is set up for guests and their needs. The guest living room is elegant but cozy, furnished with an old pump organ and piano, a stuffed leather chair and sofa and lots of magazines and books. Or you may choose to relax in one of the other two private sitting areas.

Each of the four guest rooms is air conditioned and has a private bath. The Austrian Room is furnished with gorgeous European antiques, while the Country Room is more casual, with golden oak furniture and bright reddish print wallpaper. The two other rooms, known as the Virginia Room and the Colonel's Quarters, are also beautifully furnished and very comfortable.

The dining room is the setting for a full, hearty breakfast that includes freshly squeezed orange juice, homemade granola, fresh fruit, croissants and other breads, country ham spread and hot chocolate, coffee and tea.

Children ages 12 and older are welcome. The owner recommends calling as far in advance as possible to make reservations.

The Hummingbird Inn

$$$ • 30 Wood Ln., off Va. Alt. Rt. 39, Goshen • (540) 997-9065, (800) 397-3214

This unique Victorian Carpenter Gothic, "born" in 1780 and completed in 1853, has been nationally recognized for its country charm and elegance. Owners Jeremy and Diana Robinson have done a beautiful job redesigning the interior. Its five guest rooms, furnished with antiques, are colorful and spacious, and each has a private bath (two have

Steeles Tavern Manor dates back to 1781.

double Jacuzzis). The Eleanor room, with an antique queen-size bird's-eye maple bed, fireplace and claw-foot tub, was named to commemorate Eleanor Roosevelt's stay here in 1935.

Full country breakfasts include bacon or sausage, homemade bread and foods unique to the area. A four-course dinner, served on Saturday only, is available with 48-hour notice and $35 per person. Typical entrees include lavender- and herb-roasted Cornish game hen, fillet of salmon en croute or medallions of pork tenderloin in a pink peppercorn-mustard sauce. Dinner includes a bottle of wine.

The house features wraparound verandas on the first and second levels, original pine plank floors and a rustic den, solarium and music room. Lovely perennial and rose gardens line the property.

During Goshen's boom days in the late 1800s and early 1900s, the inn was directly across from the town's railroad station, and the steps from the tracks to the inn's private road are still in place. Trains still roll through several times a week, but never at night to disturb guests' sleep.

A wide trout stream defines one of the property lines, and only five minutes away is the gorgeous Goshen Pass, a popular spot for

kayaking, picnicking and sunbathing in warm weather. This place is not to be missed when the rhododendron are in bloom! Guests can also enjoy a relaxing float in inner tubes along Mill Creek, which flows behind the inn. Just 20 minutes away is historic Lexington, with its fine restaurants and shops, the Virginia Horse Center, George Marshall Museum, Stonewall Jackson House and other historic sites.

The Inn at Union Run
$$ • 325 Union Run Rd.
(Va. Rt. 674), Lexington
• (540) 463-9715, (800) 528-6466

A friendly, down-to-earth couple, Roger and Jeanette Serens have won rave reviews for the service and enticing cuisine they offer at The Inn at Union Run. The c. 1883 federal manor and carriage house is on 11 picturesque acres with views of the Allegheny and Blue Ridge mountains. The property, just 3 miles from historic Lexington, is on a mountainside along a creek and is bordered by a bird sanctuary. Civil War history abounds, starting with Union Run Creek, named for the Union army that camped on the grounds in June 1864. The inn is decorated throughout with numerous Civil War paintings and antique pieces.

Downstairs the manor house has a parlor, common room and a small, intimate dining area for guests. Upstairs are three guest rooms with private porches overlooking the creek and pond. The guest rooms feature Jacuzzis, fireplaces, overhead fans and air conditioning. An adjacent carriage house has five guest rooms, all with private baths and three with Jacuzzis. A covered porch offers a view of the spectacular mountainside.

The common areas and guest rooms are filled with authentic period American and Victorian antiques, including Meissen porcelain, Venetian glass and furniture collections. Many of these antiques are from the estates of S.S. Kresege, Helena Rubenstein, Henry Wadsworth Longfellow and Winston Churchill. The Serens have acquired their antiques over a period of 30 years and welcome the opportunity to provide guests a tour of the collection.

Roger and Jeanette serve welcome drinks and afternoon tea to guests upon arrival. A full country breakfast features such specialties as French toast made with English muffins or croissants topped with fresh strawberries and whipped cream, gingerbread or corn bread pancakes, specialty souffles and eggs Benedict — Union Run style with spinach, artichokes and hollandaise sauce. The inn also offers gourmet meals to guests and to the public in a romantic dining room. Discriminating gourmands from around the Shenandoah return repeatedly for the cuisine (see our Restaurants chapter).

The Inn at Union Run offers special packages to guests who want to combine their stay with horseback riding, murder mystery dinners, wine tastings, plays or concerts at Lime Kiln Theatre or W&L's Lenfest Center (see our Arts chapter), aromatherapy/massages and special holidays.

The Keep Bed and Breakfast
$$ • 116 Lee Ave., Lexington
• (540) 463-3560

This bed and breakfast inn in a gorgeous Victorian home sits on a quiet corner in the heart of Lexington's historic residential district. Owners Bea and John Stuart offer guests two suites and a double-bed room, each with a private bath. Don't expect a lot of froufrou here — the decor is elegant and understated. The Stuarts put on a lavish breakfast, complete with linens on the table, and also serve dinner upon request. At tea time, the owners are always happy to share tea, coffee or sherry with their guests. "We like to spoil nice people," says Bea.

Summertime travelers to Lexington will be grateful for the central air conditioning at The Keep, which is a short walk from museums and shops in downtown Lexington. The inn does not allow children younger than 12 but does welcome small, well-behaved pets on request.

Lavender Hill Farm
$ • 1374 Big Spring Dr., Lexington
• (540) 464-5877, (800) 446-4240

Sarah and John Burleson's 200-year-old farmhouse sits on the banks of Kerrs Creek and has three light, airy guest rooms with private baths. One of the queen-size rooms can be rented as a suite; it connects to a second room with a double bed. The inn is decorated throughout with art from local artists.

Horseback trips led by Virginia Mountain Outfitters are a unique aspect of a stay here. Trail rides and riding workshops are geared to all levels of riding experience. The inn was designed with animal lovers in mind. Visit the Burleson's sheep roaming the pastures or play fetch with their dogs. The farm is also conducive to birding, fishing and hiking and is a great starting point for a biking trek. Horse (or other livestock) boarding is available for guests in the farm's new barn, built in spring 1997.

John is a great chef who loves to cook with herbs and vegetables grown on the farm. Four-course dinners, $19.50 per person, are optional and require reservations.

A Horse Lovers Holiday package is available, including a two-night stay, breakfast, dinner and picnic lunches both days, along with the use of horses, tours and all instruction. Guests can get special theater packages during the summer months, when the local Lime Kiln Theatre puts on its outdoor evening plays and Sunday night concerts. The Burlesons will purchase tickets and pack a gourmet picnic dinner to take along to Lime Kiln, where the bucolic grounds are conducive to sipping wine and feasting. They are also willing to create packages according to guests' interests.

The Burlesons don't allow pets or smoking inside the house. But they do welcome children accompanied by "well-behaved adults."

Oak Spring Farm

$$$ • 5895 Borden Grant Tr., Raphine
• (540) 377-2398, (800) 841-8813

Some of Oak Spring Farm's most unique aspects are often found grazing in the pasture — exotic animals from Natural Bridge Zoo share these 10 pastoral acres north of Lexington. You'll also find an abundance of birds around the perennial garden, wildflowers and orchard.

The beautifully restored 1826 plantation manor house is a Virginia Historic Landmark and is listed on the National Historic Register. The living area is furnished with family antiques, and one of the guest rooms, the Vineyard Room, has a 200-year-old mantle headboard on the queen-size bed. This room shares views of the vineyard and countryside with the private bath, complete with claw-foot tub and ceramic shower. The Willow Room overlooks the huge weeping willow tree and pond. The largest room, the Orchard, has a pretty four-poster bed, antique dresser and sitting area with views of the Blue Ridge and the orchard. All guest rooms have private baths. The Vineyard Room can be combined with a separate double bedroom and sitting area to create a suite.

After an elegant, full country breakfast you can tour the grounds. A spring house is still in use along with the woodshed, smokehouse, chicken coop and granary. The bank barn was rebuilt just after the Civil War. An archeological dig site is recovering the blacksmith forge that help to shod horses for the Confederacy. Within 15 minutes of Oak Spring Farm are the sites of historic Lexington, McCormick's Farm, Wade's Mill, Buffalo Springs Herb Farm, the Virginia Horse Center, VMI and Washington & Lee University.

A four-course dinner is available with advance notice. Pets and smoking are not allowed. Well-behaved children older than 12 are welcome.

The Orchard House at Boxerwood Garden

$$$$ • 963 Ross Rd., Lexington
• (540) 463-2697

The Orchard House is a charming one-bedroom cottage in the midst of uniquely beautiful Boxerwood Garden (see our Attractions chapter), where internationally acclaimed photographer Sally Mann grew up. The screened porch and ceiling-to-floor windows in the living room provide an enchanting view of the garden and mountains year round. The tastefully decorated double-bed cottage almost blends in with the scenery. A spacious white kitchen and large bathroom are part of the arrangement. The large, airy sitting room overlooks the garden on one side and an herb garden on the other. A continental breakfast is delivered the night before, or guests can make use of the full kitchen. Weekly rates are available. A minimum two-day stay is required on weekends from March through May and September through November. The Orchard House does not allow children.

Steeles Tavern Manor

$$$ • Va. Rt. 606 and U.S. Hwy. 11,
Steeles Tavern • (540) 377-6444,
(800) 743-8666

Leave the kids home and prepare to be pampered. Let innkeepers Eileen and Bill Hoernlein worry about the details while you enjoy a romantic getaway. Try breakfast in bed or an intimate candlelight dinner. Robes, extra towels and a stocked refrigerator are just a few of the extras here, all designed so couples need not ask for anything. Guests have all the privacy they want.

The inn has five guest rooms, each with a

private bath, double-size Jacuzzi and TV/VCR. Each room is named for a flower — dahlia, buttercup, wisteria, hyacinth and rose — and has a king- or queen-size bed and a sitting area. The house and guest rooms are tastefully decorated in antique furniture, quilts and lace.

The Hoernleins bring out their fine china, light the candles and put on classical music, creating a special atmosphere for a sumptuous country breakfast. If you're an early riser, Eileen will have hot coffee waiting at your door each morning. Afternoon tea is served between 4 and 5 PM. Guests can also arrange to share a romantic Saturday night dinner ($90 per couple) at the manor. The five-course meal includes a choice of three entrees — filet mignon, chicken or seafood — and a bottle of Virginia wine.

Hospitality in the small town of Steeles Tavern on Lee Highway (U.S. 11) dates back to 1781, when David Steele provided lodging to travelers between Staunton and Lexington. The home Steele's descendants built in 1916 underwent extensive restoration in 1994. In 1995 the Hoernleins opened its doors as a highly rated inn, completing the circle. The inn sits on 55 acres, has a stocked fishing pond and views of the Blue Ridge. Children younger than 14, pets and smoking are not permitted. Weekend packages are available.

Stoneridge Bed & Breakfast
$$$$ • Stoneridge Ln., Lexington
• (540) 463-4090, (800) 491-2930

When Norm and Barbara Rollenhagen decided to leave northern New Jersey after Norm's quarter-century in the service station business, the couple launched a search for a bed and breakfast inn to call home and share with guests. After several years they came upon this stately antebellum mansion, once the center of a small plantation. Previous owners made additions to the house, but the original structure, built in 1829, still stands. Stoneridge sits in secluded bliss on 36 acres of fields, streams and woodland, yet it's just minutes from downtown Lexington.

The house is rumored to have been a stagecoach stop for the weary traveler between Staunton and Roanoke. The Rollenhagens are continuing this history of hospitality. The inn's spacious front porch beckons to guests as they arrive. Through the original Adams-style double doors are rooms with high ceilings, intricate mouldings, elaborate mantels and heart-pine floors. Barbara, an interior designer, has added her special touch to every room, including curtains she made herself, refinished furniture and antiques. The library contains an extensive collection, so you can enjoy a good book by the cozy fire. Satellite television is available, and antique car buffs will appreciate an invitation to view Norm's collection.

The inn has five lovely guest rooms, all with central air conditioning, ceiling fans and private baths. The Ms. Wilma Evans Matthews Room, named for the former owner of Stoneridge, has a queen-size mahogany bed with rice carvings, marble-faced fireplace and grand mountain views. The Kathryn Cross Room, in the older section of the house, features a queen-size brass-and-white porcelain bed. The Sweet Alice Suite has a large bedroom and a small second bedroom, perfect for a third person. A separate seating area and private balcony create the balance of this spacious suite. The Kingsley Newman Room, the inn's largest, has two entrances, the outside one leading to a private porch; an in-room Jacuzzi for two is opposite the fireplace. The John Howland Room has a private balcony, Jacuzzi for two and views of the mountains.

Breakfast is served in the dining room or on the patio in pleasant weather. Savor fresh fruit; homemade blueberry, banana or raisin-bran muffins; varieties of scrambled eggs with fennel, cheddar cheese or other goodies; and a number of special dishes such as quiche Lorraine, French toast from homemade French bread and buttermilk banana pancakes. Stoneridge offers a large selection of Virginia wines at moderate prices. Norm will gladly help you select a bottle from the inn's wine cellar.

Explore the grounds or visit nearby historic Lexington, Lime Kiln Theatre, Stonewall Jackson House or Lee Chapel. Stoneridge is convenient to Virginia Military Institute and Washington & Lee University.

Reservations are required. A two-night

minimum applies to university-related activities, holidays and weekends from May through November.

Pets cannot be accommodated, and smoking is allowed only on the porch, patio and grounds. A romantic getaway, the inn is designed with adults in mind; however, well-behaved children older than 12 are permitted with prior arrangement.

Sugar Tree Inn
$$$ • Va. Rt. 56, Steeles Tavern
• (540) 377-2197, (800) 377-2197

Innkeepers Sarah and Hal Davis maintain a unique inn less than a mile off the Blue Ridge Parkway near Steeles Tavern. The narrow, winding driveway takes you back to a scenic mortise-and-peg timber and stone lodge, from which you can see 40 miles across the mountaintops and watch wildlife as close as 100 feet or less. At an elevation of 2,800 feet and nestled securely along the mountainside, this inn actually feels a part of the surrounding landscape. In spring, the woods are a riot of trillium, rhododendron, laurel and dogwood blossoms, and in autumn you don't just look at the fall colors, you walk among them.

Sugar Tree Inn opened to national acclaim in 1983, changing hands to the Davises in 1993. The couple renovated and added all sorts of amenities, including private baths. Eleven spacious rooms and suites occupy three buildings. In the main lodge, the Sugar Tree Country Room has a king-size bed, vaulted ceiling and oversize whirlpool bath with a mountain view. Each room has a wood-burning fireplace and private bath; some have whirlpool baths, ceiling fans and VCRs.

The main building is quite spectacular, with a two-story stone fireplace at the heart of the large common room. The renovated dining room is airy and overlooks a pretty rock garden. Dinners are served nightly — romantic, candlelight affairs featuring such entrees as stuffed quail or beef tenderloin medallions with mushroom sauce — and sumptuous breakfasts are served in a glass-walled dining room.

The historic and cultural attractions of Lexington and Staunton are a short drive away. If you are arriving via I-81, take Exit 205 to reach the lodge.

Roanoke Valley

Roanoke and Salem

The Inn at Burwell Place
$$ • 601 W. Main St., Salem
• (540) 387-0250, (800) 891-0250

Upon completing graduate school at Virginia Tech, Cindy MacMackin left the area for a career in hospitality in the nation's capital. Twenty years later she has fulfilled her wish to return to the Roanoke Valley. She's putting her years of experience to work as owner of this turn-of-the-century mansion at the southern end of the Shenandoah Valley. Since acquiring the inn, the MacMackins, along with their general manager Rebecca Martin, have been remodeling and redecorating to create a rich, elegant atmosphere.

The home is decorated throughout with late 19th-century period antiques in walnut and cherry. Six hundred yards of silk fabric and antique handmade Oriental rugs adorn the rooms. There are two bedrooms and two suites available, all with a telephone and most with cable TV. Each of the bedrooms' private bathrooms still has its original fixtures and tub. The suites have Jacuzzis.

The Inn at Burwell Place endeavors to accommodate the business traveler, a need Cindy felt was going unanswered. A fax machine on the premises is part of that quest. Professional tanning beds are also available.

After a continental breakfast of cereals, fresh fruit, croissants and other favorites, visit the sights of Salem. The historic downtown area is full of antique shops. Roanoke College and Salem's Farmers' Market are within walking distance, and a short drive will take you to Dixie Caverns, the Blue Ridge Parkway, Mabry Mill, Peaks of Otter, Natural Bridge and historic downtown Roanoke. Return after a day's exploring to afternoon tea on the porch, or spend your day relaxing out back in the gorgeous formal English gardens.

The inn hosts weddings, corporate holiday parties and similar occasions. However, they will only book two major events per month, so be sure to call well in advance for

Photo: Mayhurst Inn

Splendid historic inns are a Blue Ridge tradition.

this type of reservation. Pets are not permitted, and smoking is not allowed inside the inn. The request is for well-supervised children. Roanoke College events such as parents' weekends or commencement require a minimum two-night stay.

Walnuthill Bed & Breakfast
$$ • 436 Walnut Ave. S.E., Roanoke • (540) 427-3312

Innkeeper Mark C. Brown has traveled extensively and brings a knowledge of both old and new world hospitality to Walnuthill. The house, built in 1916, was obviously meant to last, as it was reinforced with steel beams. The front entrance has windows of leaded glass with beveled panes. The foyer and the "gathering room" are elegantly decorated. The charming interior of this home was personally decorated by the innkeeper's late wife, Ute S. Brown, a professional design consultant.

The three guest rooms feature queen-size beds, air conditioning, ceiling fans, cable TV and private baths. One of the bathrooms is a converted sun porch with a wall of windows and a Jacuzzi tub. Each of the rooms (The West Room, The Executive Room and The East Room) has its own style — all are bright and spacious and offer comfort and serenity.

The foyer and the Gathering Room inspire a feeling of welcome, warmth and friendly atmosphere. The dining room is decorated with simple elegance. A full gourmet breakfast is served each morning. Mark creates his menu fresh daily, always to the satisfaction and delight of his guests.

After breakfast the large veranda is a great place to relax, especially in the hammock. A stroll through the flower gardens surrounding Walnuthill is always a favorite pastime. Or head for adventure in historic downtown Roanoke. Walnuthill is just minutes from the Civic Center, the Downtown Farmers' Market, Center in the Square, Mill Mountain Theater and Mill Mountain Zoo. Walnuthill is designed with adults in mind. Children may be accommodated with special arrangements. Small pets may also be accepted occasionally. It's best to call ahead to discuss either arrangement.

East of the Blue Ridge

Loudoun County

The Colonial Inn
$$$ • 19 S. King St., Leesburg
• (703) 478-8503, (800) 392-1332

The Colonial Inn is set in the heart of historic downtown Leesburg, just 30 minutes from Washington, D.C., and 15 minutes from Dulles International Airport. Parts of the building, including the beautiful stone-framed entrance, date to the late 1700s.

The decor has been selected to pay tribute to the inn's Colonial past; each of the 10 guest rooms have 18th-century-style American furniture, wood floors, fine rugs and impressive period pieces such as rustic farm dressers. All the rooms have queen-size poster beds, private baths, telephones, cable television and individual heat and air conditioning. Some rooms have fireplaces, whirlpool baths and adjoining rooms.

Rates include a breakfast at the nearby Georgetown Cafe and Bakery. The inn serves lunch and dinner in its four dining rooms.

Cornerstone Bed and Breakfast
$$$ • 16882 Clarks Gap Rd., Paeonian Springs • (540) 882-3722

Molly and Dick Cunningham preside over this historic gem in the Catoctin Mountains, just five minutes from Leesburg's historic district. Two guest rooms with private baths are comfortably furnished with antiques, in the tradition of Victorian railstop guest homes. Guests awake to a sumptuous full breakfast.

This 1750s home is a favorite stop for bicyclists. It's right off the Washington and Old Dominion Railroad Trail, a 45-mile linear park from Purcellville to Washington. On the grounds at Cornerstone are exquisite gardens

and a pool. Nearby attractions include historic Harpers Ferry, battlefields, vineyards and hunt country events.

The Red Fox Inn
$$$$ • 2 E. Washington St., Middleburg
• (540) 687-6301, (800) 223-1728

This c. 1728 inn began as a tavern, serving as a stopping point for traveling colonists including a young surveyor named George Washington, who was known to stop in around 1748. During the Civil War, the house became both a Confederate headquarters and a hospital for soldiers. The pine service bar still used today was constructed from the field operating table used by an Army surgeon. In 1887, the building once again became a tavern and has since been offering food and lodging. Today, however, visitors are more likely to be city-weary travelers looking for a country hideaway.

The Red Fox Inn's lodging options include the original building as well as three nearby historic properties — The Stray Fox Inn, The McConnell House Inn and The Middleburg Inn. In all, the inns offer 23 rooms and suites decorated in beautiful period furniture such as canopy and poster beds. Most rooms have private baths, and some have sitting areas. Fresh flowers, cotton robes, bedside sweets and a morning paper are among the extras. Breakfast is continental style, served in the Red Fox Restaurant, which also serves lunch and dinner (see our Restaurants chapter).

The Norris House Inn
$$ • 108 Loudoun St. S.W., Leesburg
• (800) 644-1806, (703) 777-1806

A federal-style home built in 1760, this inn in the city's historic district has been voted the best inn in Leesburg for four years in a row by the *Leesburg Today* reader's survey.

The Inn has six rooms and three shared baths. Guests have access to the common rooms, including the stately dining room, parlor, library, sunroom and veranda overlooking the award-winning gardens. Rooms are appointed with antiques and a variety of canopy, brass and feather beds. Three bedrooms have working fireplaces, as do the library and dining room.

The Norris House has been operating as a

bed and breakfast since 1981 with Pam and Don McMurray serving as proprietors and innkeepers for the past eight years. The rooms are air conditioned, and guests are treated to a full country breakfast. A fax, computer center and four meeting rooms are available for those who want to combine business with comfort. Children older than 12 are welcome. Smoking is restricted. Nearby sites include Oatlands Plantation and Balls Bluff National Battlefield.

Fauquier County

The Ashby Inn
$$$ • 692 Federal St., off U.S. Hwy. 50, Paris • (540) 592-3900

Yes, Virginia, there is a Paris in the Piedmont. Adding to the charm of this Fauquier County village is The Ashby Inn and Restaurant, which occupies a home dating back to the 1820s and serves some of the best food west of the Washington Beltway.

Six guest rooms in the main building are decorated with studied, elegant simplicity to let the magnificent view of the mountains reign. Of these, the Fan Room with its two skylights, fan window and private balcony is among the most coveted. Four delightful larger rooms occupy this former one-room schoolhouse, each with its own private porch facing the Blue Ridge. Quilts and blanket chests impart a country feel in all rooms, but you won't find creaky floors or clanking pipes. Everything at The Ashby Inn is first-class. Oriental rugs have even been added to each room.

Hosts Roma and John Sherman are busy during dinner hours at the restaurant, but you may get to know them over breakfast — a feast reserved for guests. Roma is an avid horsewoman who also takes humanitarian trips to Bosnia, and John is a former House Ways and Means Committee staffer and former speechwriter.

1763 Inn and Restaurant
$$$ • 10087 John Mosby Hwy., Upperville • (540) 592-3848, (800) 669-1763

Uta and Don Kirchner have turned a complex of six old farm buildings on 50 acres into a heavenly getaway steeped in history and comfort. The stone house restaurant dates to 1763 and was once owned by George Washington. This cozy restaurant in the main farmhouse overlooks a pond with swans and is decorated with items the Kirchners have gathered on their travels. The restaurant menu is German-American and a credit to Uta's homeland (see our Restaurants chapter).

Sixteen bedrooms are dispersed among the main house, log cabin cottages and a stone barn atop a hill. Each room is distinctively decorated. Naturally, there is a George Washington room, but you also will find a German and a French room, each furnished in the style of those countries. Another room includes a museum-size portrait of FDR that once hung in the Mexican Embassy. Most have hot tubs and fireplaces.

Other amenities include a swimming pool, tennis courts and a fishing pond. Nearby activities include horse country events such as horse shows, steeplechases and fox hunts as well as hiking and shopping in Middleburg.

Rappahannock County

Belle Meade Bed & Breakfast
$$$ • 353 F.T. Valley Rd., Sperryville • (540) 987-9748

You can expect understated luxury and comfortable elegance at this turn-of-the-century Victorian inn. Renovated in 1994, the inn has four guest rooms, each with a scenic view and a private bath. There's also a cottage with a private bath, deck and porch.

A hearty breakfast starts a busy day here. The 137 acres are gorgeous in any season — fall foliage and winter cross-country skiing are especially enticing — and hiking and birding are popular pastimes. The inn has a 60-foot swimming pool and hot tub. If you plan ahead, owners Susan Hoffman and Mike Biniek will serve you a four-course candlelight vegetarian dinner for $30 a person. Massages by a licensed massage therapist can be arranged.

Attractions in the area include Old Rag Mountain, a popular hiking destination (see our Recreation chapter). Skyline Drive and Luray Caverns are nearby, as are many fine restaurants and wineries. On weekends, parents can leave their children at the inn's summer day camp while they explore the area.

Bleu Rock Inn

$$$$ • 12567 Lee Hwy. (U.S. Hwy. 211), Washington • (540) 987-3190

Situated on 80 acres in Rappahannock County, this cozy country inn is in a renovated farmhouse with five guest rooms, each with a private bath. It overlooks lush meadows, a pond and tall shade trees with a vista of the mountains beyond. Several acres are carefully tended vineyards that supply wines for the inn. After a glass of wine in the lounge, you can dine fireside in one of three dining rooms. An open-air terrace overlooks the vineyards of Cabernet Sauvignon, Chardonnay and Seyval grapes.

You can stroll through pastures where horses graze, or try your hand at catching bass, catfish and bluegill from the pond. Rappahannock County offers ample opportunities for skiing, bicycling, canoeing, golfing, hiking and spelunking. Historical sites and wineries are not far from the inn.

Bernard and Jean Campagne are the owners and operators of Bleu Rock Farm and Inn. Jean has been honored with the medals of Merite Agricole de France, Academie Culinaire de France, Cordon Bleu and Maitre Cuisinier de France. But you won't need his credentials to know the food here is delicious. Breakfast, which is only served to overnight guests, is spectacular. It begins with fresh orange juice and coffee served with hot biscuits, croissants and muffins. Next is a fruit plate from the inn's orchards. The main course could be an omelette or Santa Fe French toast served with maple syrup and creme fraiche. Either may be accompanied by a spicy homemade pork sausage and sauteed apples. This breakfast will really knock your socks off, and the dinners are equally superb.

Well-behaved children older than 8 are welcome. You may even bring your pets if you give the Campagnes prior notice. The inn is closed Monday and Tuesday.

Foster-Harris House

$$$$ • 189 Main St., Washington • (540) 675-3757, (800) 666-0153

Phyllis Marriott's turn-of-the century frame home is right on Main Street in this popular little tourist town. The house offers four air-conditioned guest rooms, each with a private bath, queen-size bed and a wonderful view of either the mountains or the perennial gardens. The Mountain View Suite has a whirlpool tub big enough for two and a wood-burning stove for winter evenings. The Garden Room has mountain views and overlooks the inn's herb and flower gardens.

Phyllis, a former Washington, D.C., caterer and delicatessen owner, prepares a full breakfast every morning and serves afternoon refreshments in the parlor, on the porch or beneath a grand old plum tree. Smoking and pets are not allowed.

Area attractions include orchards, vineyards, fairs, antique shops and local theater. Hiking, biking and horseback riding are available too.

The Gay Street Inn

$$$ • 160 Gay St., Washington • (540) 675-3288

At the end of a quiet, dead-end street sits this 150-year-old stucco home, a restored farmhouse with three spacious guest rooms and a suite, resident dog and cat and lovely gardens out back. All rooms have views of the mountains, private baths and Colonial wallpaper from the Shelbourne Museum Collection.

One room has a canopy bed and a working fireplace. The suite has a full kitchen and is a great option for families; it is also available for short-term rental for those who want an extended stay. Children and pets are welcome here. A portable crib is available on request.

Innkeepers Donna and Robin Kevis prepare a marvelous morning feast, which sometimes includes frittata, smoked turkey sausage, home fries and homemade corn muffins served in the inn's new breakfast room.

The Gay Street Inn is charming, homey and convenient to Washington's shops and restaurants. The Shenandoah National Park is nearby, as are caverns and other natural attractions.

Heritage House

$$$$ • 291 Main St., Washington • (540) 675-3207, (888) 819-8280

Jean and Frank Scott's elegant inn dates back to 1837 and is said to have been used by Confederate Gen. Jubal Early as a command center during the Civil War. It's in the heart of "little" Washington, a minute's stroll from shops, historic landmarks and the famous Inn at Little Washington. The great outdoors are at your back door here, including Shenandoah National Park and Skyline Drive. Not far away are the Rapidan, Rose and Thornton rivers and other well-known trout streams.

The four gracious guest rooms have air conditioning and private baths. Each has its own theme: the suite has a sitting room/sun porch with a view of the Blue Ridge; the Lace Room has blue-flocked wall coverings, crystal lamps and antiques; the Amish Room is decorated with a simple antique double bed, rag dolls and an original Thomas Palmerton landscape. Charles Dickens' Old Curiosity Shop and the city of London create the theme of the British Room, featuring David Winter cottages and castles.

At 9 AM, guests are served a sit-down gourmet breakfast of hot entrees, fruit, home-baked fruit breads, juice and a variety of coffees and teas. Freshly baked treats and hot beverages are available to guests all day.

The Inn at Little Washington
$$$$ • Middle and Main sts., Washington
• (540) 675-3800

If you want to be pampered beyond your wildest dreams and eat food more delicious than you thought possible, then The Inn at Little Washington should certainly be No. 1 on your list. Situated in a quiet Rappahannock County town, it is one of the top-rated inns in the United States. Praise has come from far and wide, including *USA Today*, *People* magazine, *The New York Times* and the *San Francisco Chronicle*.

Reinhardt Lynch and Patrick O'Connell are the owners. Lynch takes care of the day-to-day operations at the Inn — little stuff such as making sure the 3,000 requests for Saturday night dinner are narrowed down to 65 diners. O'Connell causes all the commotion with his culinary masterpieces. The prix fixe dinners include five to six courses. (The price does not include alcohol, tax or gratuity.) Diners select from 11 entrees and 15 desserts. (See our Restaurants chapter.)

The Inn's 12 guest rooms are furnished with antiques, overstuffed reading chairs and canopied beds and elegantly decorated with faux bois woodwork and draped fabrics. The scent of fresh-cut flowers mingles with that of potpourri. Old-fashioned silhouettes hang on the wall. Colorful pillows form a mountain of comfort on the bed, but don't succumb before soaking in a tub of pine-scented bubbles in the marble-and-brass bathroom. Swathed in a plush white robe, you can watch the fountain from your balcony and pinch yourself to see if you're still awake. The Inn is very popular, so advance reservations are a must.

The Middleton Inn
$$$$ • 176 Main St., Washington
• (540) 675-2020, (800) 816-8157

The Middleton Inn is an elegant historic country estate in a rural setting with mountain views. The house, which has an impressive center hall and high ceilings throughout, was built in 1850 by Middleton Miller, who designed and manufactured the uniform worn by Confederate soldiers. The house has eight working fireplaces, including one in every bedroom, and each of the four guest rooms has a private marble bath.

Sharing a 5-acre knoll with the house are three other original buildings — the summer kitchen, the smokehouse and the slave quarters. The latter is now a two-story guest cottage with a working fireplace and Jacuzzi.

Owner Mary Ann Kuhn, a former CBS producer and *Washington Post* reporter, serves a full gourmet breakfast with fresh fruit, homemade breads and a hot entree, which might be eggs Benedict or raspberry pancakes.

The inn combines the best of town and country, with cattle grazing in an adjoining pasture and shops just two blocks away. Washington and the surrounding area are rich in antique and craft shops, natural wonders such as the Skyline Drive and small-town festivals that pull visitors into the spirit of the place.

Sharp Rock Farm Bed and Breakfast
$$$$ • 5 Sharp Rock Rd., Sperryville
• (540) 987-8020

This serene bed and breakfast sits on a 23-acre farm right across from one of the most popular hiking spots in Virginia, Old Rag Mountain. Surrounded by hills, pristine farmland and jagged Old Rag just across the field, this peaceful site, with the Hughes River meandering by, is a perfect retreat from the hectic life in the city. Innkeepers David and Marilyn Armor, who bought the property two weeks after a visit to Rappahannock County from their home in California, have restored the main house and other buildings on the farm, most of which were built in 1792 and 1864.

Accommodations include The Cottage, the oldest building on the farm. Dating to 1790, the cozy two-story home still has its original plank flooring. It has an eat-in kitchen, two bedrooms, one bath, a living room plus a wide deck with a breathtaking view of Old Rag. The Carriage House is another private dwelling with great views of the mountain and Hughes River. The bedroom/sitting room is light and cheery and opens onto a deck shaded by an ancient cherry tree. The Carriage House has 150-year-old pine flooring, a mini refrigerator, hot plate and modern bath.

All accommodations are air conditioned, but there are no televisions or telephones, because Marilyn Armor feels that her peaceful retreat should be an opportunity for guests to communicate with each other and grow closer. Guests are welcome to use the phone in the main house. The rooms are stocked with games and books. The Armors call it their lending library, allowing guests to borrow a book if they leave before they're finished. Guests also can fish year round for fresh trout in the river or take a dip in the mountain-fed water of Sharp Rock swimming hole.

Of course, Sharp Rock Winery is right on the premises. This five-acre winery, a hand-selected grape operation, just bottled its first vintage in 1997. The winery is open for public tours and tastings on Saturdays from March to November, but overnight guests are welcome to tour the winery and taste the wines, made on site by David Armor (see our Wineries chapter).

A large gourmet breakfast can include Marilyn's specialty of salmon quiche or an egg-and-sausage strada, Belgian waffles, blueberry pancakes or a variety of omelets. Guests may choose freshly squeezed orange juice or a smoothie. Guests also receive an afternoon snack of a dessert and beverage. She enjoys making homemade desserts and may provide any number of treats, including lemon bread, plum bread, banana bread (all cakes made in loaf pans) or chocolate chip, peanut butter, molasses or oatmeal cookies.

Culpeper County

Fountain Hall Bed & Breakfast
$$$ • 609 S. East St., Culpeper
• (540) 825-8200, (800) 29-VISIT

George Washington, the first county surveyor of Culpeper, referred to the town as "a high and pleasant situation." It still is, and Fountain Hall enjoys an enviable location in this charming village, once part of a large tract owned by Virginia's royal governor, Sir Alexander Spotswood. Hosts Steve and Kathi Walker have decorated the six large, sunlit guest rooms with antiques but provided the modern conveniences of a telephone and private bath in each. Some rooms have whirlpool tubs and outdoor porches.

Breakfast in the sunny morning room is a leisurely affair of fresh croissants topped with country preserves, plus cereals and juices.

Games are set up on the lawn, and formal gardens are perfect for strolling. The streets of Culpeper beckon history and antique buffs. You can hike, fish and ride horseback nearby. Golf and canoeing packages are available.

Madison County

Graves' Mountain Lodge
$$$$ • Off Va. Rt. 670, Syria
• (540) 923-4231

This inn is known far and wide for its delicious, homemade family-style meals, served in a large dining hall on long wooden tables. Room prices include three meals, which is a blessing because you wouldn't want to miss one of these country spreads (see our Restaurants chapter for more information). The atmosphere at meals sets the tone for the entire Graves' Mountain experience — informal family fun in the midst of friendly and easygoing folks. Relax in one of the inn's rocking chairs or take a long hike on one of the many easily accessible trails. Whatever your activity choice, you will find lots of country hospitality here.

Graves' Mountain is family-owned, and its perch on the edge of Shenandoah National Park puts it close to a host of outdoor activities. Fishing, hiking and hunting are popular pastimes. The inn also offers swimming in a junior Olympic-size pool, horseback riding on more than 100 miles of scenic trails, tennis on one of six courts, volleyball, softball and horseshoes. The recreation center has books, magazines, games, a piano and a television for rainy days. Tours of the cannery, where Graves makes dozens of specialty preserves, relishes, jams and spreads, is another rainy-day option. The gift shop sells mountain crafts, Native American and folk carvings and jewelry.

The lodge has several accommodation styles. The Ridgecrest Motel has 22 rooms and two conference rooms, and Hilltop Motel has 16 rooms, some with televisions. Ridgecrest and Hilltop are modern accommodations. The Old Farm House, built in the early 1800s, has seven rooms with half-baths and a portico to the shower house. You can still see the original handhewn logs and mud chinking in The Old Farm House, though it has been renovated. Eleven cottages are in the vicinity of the lodge. The cabins include the lower cabin built in the 1920s and used as a Boy Scout camp. The upper cabin is in a secluded area. Wildwind, originally a one-room schoolhouse, overlooks the Robinson River. Blackwood and Greenwood are newer cabins. The lodge closes the Sunday after Thanksgiving and reopens the third weekend in March. Reservations are required for overnight stays.

The Inn at Meander Plantation
$$$ • U.S. Hwy. 15, Locust Dale
• (540) 672-4912, (800) 385-4936

In the heart of Jefferson's Virginia, The Inn at Meander Plantation offers the charm and elegance of Colonial living. The stately mansion, built in 1766 by Joshua Fry, is the centerpiece of an 80-acre estate. Converted to a bed and breakfast inn in 1993, the house contains five sun-drenched bedrooms, each with a private bath. Four-poster queen-size beds are piled high with plump pillows atop down comforters.

Throughout the house are private nooks for reading, and guests gather in the parlor,

once often visited by Thomas Jefferson and the Marquis de Lafayette. A baby grand piano awaits for impromptu concerts.

A full plantation-style gourmet breakfast is served daily in the formal dining room or under the arched breezeway. Full dinners and picnic lunches can be arranged. Outside, white rockers line both levels of the expansive back porches, providing peaceful respites for sipping afternoon tea. The boxwood gardens are dotted with secluded benches and a hammock. Croquet, volleyball, badminton and horseshoes are set up on the lawns, and the woods are made for strolling. Overnight boarding for horses is available at the stables.

The innkeepers are Suzanne Thomas and Suzie and Bob Blanchard. Suzanne, a former newspaper publisher, finds time now for freelance writing. Suzie continues her career as a food writer, and Bob has a training and consulting company.

The inn is in a bend of the Robinson River, 9 miles south of Culpeper. The best of the countryside is close at hand including wineries, antique shops and historic sites.

Greene County

Edgewood Farm Bed & Breakfast
$$ • 1186 Middle River Rd., Stanardsville
• (804) 985-3782, (800) 985-3782

A 130-acre farm with rushing streams and deep woods surrounds this beautifully restored farmhouse, which was built in 1790 and expanded in the 1860s. Each of the three period-decorated bedrooms has a fireplace. Private or shared baths are available (with special touches such as pleasantly scented goat's milk soap, lotion and shampoo made in nearby Charlottesville).

Hosts Norman and Eleanor Schwartz greet guests with refreshments and smiles, and that's just the beginning of the pampering. When you open your door to the aroma of coffee and fresh muffins wafting up to your room, you'll find a silver service of hot coffee and fresh flowers and the morning paper. Breakfast is a generous array of home-baked muffins, coffee cakes and other breads, plus fresh fruit. Picnic lunches are available by special arrangement.

Within a 30-mile radius of the farm are historic and natural attractions such as Skyline Drive, Monticello, Montpelier, Ash Lawn-Highland and the University of Virginia. Vineyards and antique and craft shops are also close by.

The Lafayette Hotel
$$ • 146 Main St., Stanardsville
• (804) 985-6345

This 1840 historic landmark is a full service bed and breakfast and a delightful restaurant. The Georgian-style building has three levels with 11-foot ceilings and sweeping colonnaded porches. The frame is of hand-hewn mortise and tenon beams with 15-inch thick walls made of local red brick. Large windows provide a view of the Blue Ridge Mountains and the quaint town of Stanardsville.

The Lafayette was built as a stagecoach line hotel and served as a hospital for the Confederacy during the Civil War. In the 20th century it has been a private residence, a boarding house, apartment building and home to several businesses, including the area's first telephone exchange, newspaper and post office. Innkeepers Whitt Leford, Nick Spencer and Daniel Huff began renovations in 1996 and continue to carefully restore this special Virginia landmark.

Accommodations include a wheelchair-accessible guest room on the first level along with the restaurant. The second floor has four guest rooms decorated in 19th-century furnishings and warm country house decor. The rooms have queen-size beds and comfortable sitting areas, as well as their original fireplaces and individually controlled heating and air-conditioning systems. Rates for rooms with shared baths are $80, while rooms with private baths rent for $100. A full breakfast is included for two people. Dinner packages are available.

The Lafayette is on Route 33, just 10 minutes from the entryway to the Skyline Drive and Shenandoah National Park.

Orange County

Mayhurst Inn
$$$$ • 12460 Mayhurst Ln., Orange
• (540) 672-2243, (888) 672-5597

Robert E. Lee was a frequent visitor. He was here on that May morning when Gen. A.P. Hill christened his daughter Lucy "Lee" Hill. Stonewall Jackson and the Army of the Northern Virginia camped out here for six months. In fact, he reviewed his troops from the rooftop tower on Hill's home.

It's no wonder this 1859 mansion is listed on the National Registry of Historic Places. Today, Peg and Bob Harmon have restored the Italianate Victorian plantation home to the grandeur of its past. You can wander Mayhurst Inn's 37 acres, passing by several 200-year-old trees. Explore the summer kitchen and smokehouse or stop by the pond.

Inside, an oval spiral staircase will lead you to all four floors. Take refreshments on the porch or in the library or parlor, or take in the view from the rooftop tower. There are six newly renovated accommodations to choose from. Each has a private bath and fireplace and is decorated with antiques, but each has its own distinct personality. The teal, olive and tan Generals' Room pays homage to the three Confederate generals who stayed here. The Madison Room, decorated in Dolley Madison's favorite shade of scarlet, is named in honor of the man who built Mayhurst, the great-grandson of President James Madison. Other rooms include the Magnolia, the Garden, Southern and the Italian Suite, complete with a bust of David overlooking a black granite whirlpool. The suite also features a four-columned custom-made queen-size bed, a sofa bed, a sitting room and its own balcony.

The Harmons serve a three-course breakfast each morning with freshly baked bread and muffins, juices, fruit and a rotating entree, including waffles smothered in fresh fruit or a veggie omelette. You have a choice of dining on the porch, by the fireplace in the dining room or in the privacy of your own room.

The Shadows
$$ • 14291 Constitution Hwy., Orange
• (540) 672-5057

This restored 1913 stone inn is surrounded by old cedars on 44 acres in Orange County. Innkeepers Barbara and Pat Loffredo invite you to forget about the hassles of the modern world and enjoy a relaxing stay in their Craftsman-style house. Curl up in front of the large stone fireplace with a cup of cider or select a good book from the library. Hold hands on the porch swing or chat with other guests during afternoon tea. Whatever your choice, the pace is slow and quiet.

Four artfully decorated guest rooms are individually named and creatively appointed. The Blue Room has a queen-size pre-Civil War walnut bed and a day bed, and its natural cedar bathroom features a vanity, claw-foot tub and pedestal sink. The Rose Room is full of frills and lace, with a full-size high-back oak bed and a private upper deck. The Peach Room is an Edwardian delight with a king-size burled walnut bed and a private hall shower. The Victorian Room, with a full-size iron and brass bed, has a private hall bathroom with a tub/shower.

In addition, the Loffredos have lovingly restored two cabins, just a few steps away from the house. The two-room Rocking Horse Cabin is decked in country crafts, has a gas log fireplace, a queen-size bed and private deck. The other two-room cottage, a former cook's quarters, sports its own deck.

A memorable country gourmet breakfast is served each morning. Entrees have included French toast, souffles and poached pears. Reservations are accepted and require one night's deposit. Older children are welcome to stay at the inn.

Sleepy Hollow Farm
$$ • 16280 Blue Ridge Tnpk., Gordonsville • (540) 832-5555, (800) 215-4804

This cozy 18th-century house is filled with nooks and crannies; bedrooms feel like private hideaways. Flower and herb gardens surround the house, and the broader surroundings include woods and rolling fields where cattle graze. Beverley Allison and her daughter, Dorsey Allison-Comer, run the inn, which has been the Allison family home for decades.

The atmosphere here is casual and comfortable, with a dog and cats serving as the palace guards. In their rooms, guests find a welcome basket stocked with Virginia peanuts, fruit and homemade chocolate-chip cookies. If this isn't enough to snack on, a freshly baked cake is always available in the sitting area. The formal dining room is very pretty and overlooks the herb garden and distant rolling hills.

In the main house, three guest rooms and a suite all have private baths. The cottage has two suites, one with a Jacuzzi room, kitchen and wood stove, the other with a fireplace and refrigerator. A beautiful pond on the grounds can be used for swimming or fishing, and ducks and their ducklings glide around the pond each spring. Speaking of babies, Sleepy Hollow is one of the few bed and breakfast inns in the area catering to children. A crib and playpen are available, and the suites are popular with families.

Rates include a sumptuous full country breakfast and afternoon tea, if requested. Private dinners are also offered by prior arrangement, and the owners like to hold wine tastings when several guests stay more than one night. They also host small weddings. Skyline Drive, Monticello and Montpelier are nearby.

Tivoli
$$$ • 9171 Tivoli Dr., Gordonsville • (540) 832-2225, (800) 840-2225

Tivoli is a three-story, 24-room Victorian mansion atop a hill. Framed by 14 massive Corinthian columns, the house commands views of the Blue Ridge Mountains and its own 235-acre working cattle farm. Four carefully restored bedrooms — each with private bath and working fireplace — are available for guests. Owners Phil and Susie Audibert pride themselves on their don't-leave-hungry breakfasts, featuring dishes made from big, fresh brown eggs.

With its ballroom (complete with a Steinway grand piano), 12-foot-high ceilings, state-of-the-art kitchen and antique-filled living and dining rooms, Tivoli also offers ample space for wedding receptions, private parties, small conferences and seminars. Wineries, Civil War battlefields, Monticello, Montpelier, gourmet restaurants, amateur theater and Shenandoah National Park are all within easy driving distance. Guests are encouraged to walk the farm's rolling pastures and miles of wooded trails.

Willow Grove Inn
$$$$ • 14079 Plantation Way, Orange • (540) 672-5982, (800) 949-1778

If you want to live and breathe history, consider this antebellum mansion with formal gardens and sloping lawns. Willow Grove Inn, listed on the National Register of Historic Places and designated a Virginia Historic Landmark, was built by Joseph Clark in 1778. A brick addition was added in 1820 by the same craftsmen who had just completed work on Thomas Jefferson's University of Virginia. The mansion, the exterior of which is a prime example of Jefferson's Classical Revival style, fell under siege during the Civil War. You can still see trenches near the manor house, and a cannonball was recently removed from its eaves. Generals Wayne and Muhlenberg also camped here during the Revolutionary War.

Tucked into 37 secluded acres, this 18th-century plantation retains its original Colonial atmosphere. Fine American and English antiques decorate the manor house, and English boxwood, magnolias and willows grace the lawns.

Owner Angela Mulloy has figured out how to help her guests unwind. A newspaper and pot of fresh coffee will be at your door in the morning, along with freshly baked muffins if you want something before the hearty breakfast.

Rates include breakfast and dinner, which is served in distinctive dining rooms offering varying atmospheres — Clark's Tavern is dark, cozy and casual, while the Dolley Madison Room is formal and resplendent in delicate china and crystal. (See our Restaurants chapter for more information on the restaurant.)

Antique furnishings, wide pine flooring and original fireplace mantels preserve the traditional character of each of the inn's four rooms and six suites. Named for Virginia-born presidents, each room is furnished with antique beds and heirloom quilts. You'll also find fresh flowers, down pillows and comforters and coconut milk baths in your private bathroom.

Albemarle County

Clifton — The Country Inn
$$$$ • 1296 Clifton Inn Dr., Charlottesville • (804) 971-1800, (888) 971-1800

Clifton wins rave reviews around the country for its elegance, comfort and gourmet dining. *Country Inns* magazine calls it one of the top 12 inns in the nation. Clifton is an imposing 18th-century manor house with a pillared veranda and a clear view to Monticello (when the trees are not in leaf).

Clifton was built by Thomas Mann Randolph, husband of Thomas Jefferson's daughter, Martha, on land that once adjoined the Shadwell Plantation, Jefferson's birthplace. It is believed to have been built as an office for Randolph, but it became his home in his later years. Clifton offers overnight guests a slower pace, where the only important decisions are whether to play a few wickets of croquet, read a book by the fire, float around the lake on an inner tube or practice a Chopin prelude on the grand piano.

Tea is served at 4 PM, complete with gourmet teas, fresh fruits and freshly baked treats. Every room has its own fireplace, freshly stocked with wood and ready for the strike of a match. Guests are also warmed by down comforters on antique beds. All of the 14 rooms and suites have private baths that are as individual and unusual as the rooms themselves.

One of the most popular rooms, the Martha Jefferson, has wall and bed hangings and a rug the color of rich vanilla ice cream. The carriage house is a spectacular guest suite featuring a stair railing and other architectural artifacts from the dismantled Meriwether Lewis home. This seems especially fitting because Martha and Thomas Randolph's affection for Lewis was such that they named their fourth son after him.

Outside, flower beds surround a manicured croquet court. Down the lawn from the enclosed veranda is a spacious gazebo, a tennis court and a swimming pool with waterfall and heated spa. All this is surrounded by 40 acres of dense forest; a short walk brings you to a dock on the 22-acre private lake. This is the perfect point to begin a swim or a lazy float in an oversized inner tube.

Full breakfasts include fresh fruit, sausage or bacon, a lavish entree, juice and coffee or tea. Clifton also operates a restaurant that serves gourmet dinners to the public nightly. (See our Restaurants chapter). Exquisite meals consist of five or six courses. Light refreshments — freshly baked cookies and a self-serve refrigerator stocked with sodas — are always available for guests. The Clifton staff will prepare luncheons and private dinners to order. The Inn is just 4 miles from Monticello.

The 1817 Historic Inn

$$$ • 1211 W. Main St., Charlottesville • (804) 979-7353, (800) 730-7443

If you suspect this inn in a historic townhouse might be too stiff and formal for your fancy, consider the friendly black lab sitting quietly in the hallway, so happy for a scratch behind the ears, and owner Candace DeLoach, who encourages her guests to sit back and relax in the living room and munch on the M&Ms she keeps in a big bowl.

Eclectic decor makes this place unique in tradition-bound Charlottesville. For instance, the living room is decorated with Biedermeier chairs, American Empire chests, Venetian tables and a big zebra-skin rug. The total effect is exciting but comfortable. This is precisely the aim of Candace, who grew up in Savannah, graduated from college in South Carolina and then moved to New York, where she worked as an interior designer for 10 years.

In spring 1993, Candace opened DeLoach Antiques in a townhouse that adjoins the inn. All the antiques and furnishings in the inn are for sale, at reasonable prices for the Charlottesville area. Both buildings were built in 1817 by one of Thomas Jefferson's master craftsmen, James Dinsmore of Northern Ireland. Dinsmore was the principal carpenter at Monticello and at several original dormitories at the University of Virginia. With another master builder, Dinsmore was Jefferson's principal carpenter for the Rotunda, which is only a few blocks from The 1817. Candace named her two-bedroom suite in his honor.

Breakfast includes hearty muffins, granola, yogurt, piles of fresh fruit, juice and coffee. The Tea Room Cafe is a delightful addition to The 1817 (see our Restaurants chapter).

All the bedrooms evoke a romantic mood, whether it be the spacious Mattie Carrington room, with French antiques and a glass chandelier, or the exotic Lewis and Clark room, with an African cowhide rug, fur pillows and English hunt pictures. The Sleeping Porch is also enchanting, furnished with two double beds draped with mosquito netting canopies and made up entirely in cream linens. Our favorite is Mrs. Olive's Room in the back, with

its many white-shuttered windows hung with silk balloon valances and its loveseat, chair and tufted ottoman that make for a comfortable place to read and write letters.

The inn's convenient location makes it a popular destination for parents of UVA students. Within easy walking distance is The Corner, a block or two of restaurants, clothing stores and other shops across from campus. Some of Charlottesville's most appealing restaurants are along Elliewood Avenue in this neighborhood.

The Inn at Sugar Hollow Farm

$$$ • Va. Rt. 614, 3 miles off Va. Rt. 810, White Hall • (804) 823-7086

Dick and Hayden Cabell are the innkeepers at this 70-acre wooded farm in the Moorman River Valley at the edge of the Shenandoah National Park. The site served as a trading post originally, and its history goes back to the days of Thomas Jefferson.

The new inn was custom-built in 1995 and has five distinctive bedrooms with cozy corners for reading and relaxing as well as several comfortable common areas. Each bedroom has a different theme, ranging from woodland to Colonial, and has a connecting private bath. Two rooms have whirlpool baths. Wood-burning fireplaces warm you in four of the bedrooms, and one guest room meets the needs of the physically disabled.

The oak-beamed country-style family and dining rooms open to a broad, bluestone terrace offering a grand view across the gardens and fields to Pasture Fence Mountain and the Blue Ridge. A library and sunroom are other relaxing options.

A full country breakfast features egg specialties, homemade granola, fresh fruit from the inn's gardens and freshly baked muffins or pastries. Freshly prepared refreshments are always on hand. A family-style dinner is available on Saturday nights for an additional charge.

Exploring the outdoors tops the list of activities here; the nearby national forest offers hiking and biking trails. Equestrian events at Foxfield and Montpelier and Charlottesville's numerous historic attractions are nearby; Wintergreen Resort is within an hour's drive. Children older than 12 are welcome.

Inn at the Crossroads
$$ • 5010 Plank Rd., North Garden
• (804) 979-6452

Surrounded by beautiful countryside 9 miles south of Charlottesville, the Inn at the Crossroads commands spectacular vistas of the foothills of the Blue Ridge. It is near many of the region's finest natural attractions, including Crabtree Falls, Devil's Knob Mountain and the James River.

The aptly named inn and one-time tavern, built in 1820, sits at the crossing of two Colonial roads: a north-south route linking Charlottesville with Lynchburg (now U.S. 29) and an east-west pike connecting the James River with the Shenandoah Valley (now Va. 692). The four-story Federal-style home is on the National Register of Historic Places and a Virginia Historic Landmark. Through the years, the "ordinary" served as a meeting place, polling center, post office and trading post. The location makes for easy access to Charlottesville as well as many of the surrounding attractions.

New owners Maureen and John Deis have added private baths in all five guest rooms in the main house as well as a two-room cottage, ideal for families. The cottage sleeps four and has a refrigerator and bar-sink. The inn's two common rooms are replete with books, antiques and curios. A full breakfast is included in the room price. Children of all ages are welcome here.

Inn at Monticello
$$$$ • 1188 Scottsville Rd.,
Charlottesville • (804) 979-3593

Norman and Rebecca Lindway invite guests to "spend the day at Thomas Jefferson's beloved Monticello. Spend the night with us." This country manor house was built in the mid-1800s in the valley of Jefferson's Monticello Mountain. On the grounds of the house are dogwoods, boxwoods, azaleas and beautiful Willow Lake. Sit back and enjoy the view from one of the rockers on the porch or join in a game of boccie ball on the manicured lawn.

Inside are five elegant bedrooms, each furnished with period antiques and reproductions. The beds are made with crisp cotton linens and down comforters. Some rooms have special features, such as a working fireplace, four-poster canopy bed or private porch. Each room is air-conditioned and has a private bath.

The aroma of freshly ground coffee will lure you from your warm bed. The ever-changing, large gourmet breakfast menu includes such delicious entrees as fresh blueberry stuffed French toast, nutmeg buttermilk pancakes with fresh fruit or homemade scones.

The inn is convenient to Monticello, Michie Tavern, Ash Lawn-Highland (the home of James Monroe), Montpelier (the home of James and Dolley Madison) and many vineyards. Children 12 and older are welcome. A two-night minimum stay is required on weekends and holidays.

Silver Thatch Inn
$$$$ • 3001 Hollymead Dr.
at U.S. Hwy. 29 N, Charlottesville
• (804) 978-4686

Built in 1780 by Hessian soldiers, the Silver Thatch Inn's central house brings to mind the architecture of Colonial Williamsburg. The house is an immaculately restored white clapboard building surrounded by dogwoods, magnolias and pines.

The Hessian Room of the inn is named for Hessian soldiers captured in New York during the Revolutionary War and marched south to Charlottesville. They built a two-story log cabin on the site of a former Native American settlement, where the Silver Thatch Inn now stands. In the 19th century, the inn served as a boys' school, then a tobacco plantation and, after the Civil War, a melon farm. A wing was added in 1937, and a cottage was built in 1984 to complement the main building.

Owners Vince and Rita Scoffone have decorated the inn with early American folk art, quilts, reproduction furniture and antiques. The seven guest rooms are named for Virginia-born presidents. The Thomas Jefferson Room has a pencil-post, queen-size canopy bed and fireplace. All rooms have private baths and several have fireplaces. Guests will find fresh, homemade cookies waiting for them in their rooms.

The Silver Thatch Inn has a restaurant with three dining rooms, a sunroom and a bar where guests can have a complimentary glass of wine or beer before dinner. Dinner is served

Tuesday through Saturday. The menu changes frequently but always includes a vegetarian special and entrees such as grilled filet mignon to satisfy conventional tastes. Two of the more exotic items on one winter menu included roasted quail Sonoran (served with a Southwestern sauce of tomatoes, onions, olives, bacon and garlic) and lamb chops Fez (grilled with Merguez sausage, Moroccan tomato sauce and couscous). Among the desserts were a hazelnut-brown sugar tart with Frangelica cream and a flourless chocolate cake with pecans. (See our Restaurants chapter.)

Silver Thatch is a short drive from the University of Virginia, Monticello, Montpelier and Ash Lawn-Highland. Skyline Drive and the Blue Ridge Parkway are a half hour away. Guests have access to an outdoor swimming pool.

The Downtown Inn

$$$$ • 213 E. Water St., Charlottesville • (804) 977-1601

This quiet old building on Charlottesville's historic Downtown Mall was converted into a lavish bed and breakfast just a couple of years ago. The bed and breakfast is upstairs above the charming restaurant, which serves dinner Tuesday through Saturday. Be sure to make reservations for High Tea, held between 3 and 6 PM. This elegant affair includes hot scones, tea sandwiches, fresh strawberries and cream and English loose teas.

The building was originally constructed in 1902 as the C.H. Williams Department Store. Fourteen-foot high ceilings, marble floors, Palladian windows, Palladian bathrooms and six-foot stained glass panels are some of the decorative features. There are two rooms that share a bath. They can be rented separately or combined with the suite. One has a queen-size bed, the other has two twin beds.

The *piece de resistance*, however, is the master suite. A hallway leads through the kitchen and dining room to an open atrium with vaulted ceiling, skylights and a six-person Jacuzzi. The suite has hardwood floors with decorative rugs and a working fireplace. The large kitchen, fully appointed with a range, dishwasher, refrigerator, freezer and marble counter, is handy for those who want to eat in. The walls are original brick and the open arches in the kitchen allow conversation with a guest while the meal is prepared.

The mirrored dining room is formal, decorated with *objets d'art*, chandelier and candelabra and features seating for eight. There is a large master bedroom off the atrium with a queen-size four-poster bed, working marble-tiled fireplace, marble bath and shower stall. The sitting area in the front of the suite overlooks the historic downtown mall and is equipped with a TV, VCR, CD player and overstuffed sofas. The suite is also decorated with original artwork by Cheret, a teacher of Toulouse-Lautrec. The master suite has been a favorite of honeymoon couples, while families have rented the entire upstairs. The Inn is centrally located in the heart of downtown Charlottesville with Monticello and Ash Lawn-Highland within easy driving distance.

200 South Street

$$$$ • 200 South St., Charlottesville • (804) 979-0200, (800) 964-7008

This inn is actually two restored houses in downtown Charlottesville. The restoration was completed in 1986, and every detail of 200 South Street was meticulously re-created or renewed, including the classical veranda and a two-story walnut serpentine handrail. The larger of the two buildings was built in 1856 for Thomas Jefferson Wertenbaker, son of Thomas Jefferson's first librarian and close friend, and remained a residence until the 20th century. In the following years, the building was believed to have housed a finishing school for girls, a brothel and then a boarding house before it was transformed into the inn.

Innkeepers Brendan and Jenny Clancy have decorated the 20 rooms with lovely English and Belgian antiques. You can choose a room with a whirlpool bath, a fireplace, a canopy bed or a private living room suite. Every room has a private bath.

The inn's main gallery houses an ongoing exhibition of Virginia artists and part of the private collection of Holsinger photos of historic Charlottesville. A complimentary continental breakfast, afternoon tea and wine are available to guests. The inn is only steps from the finest restaurants, shops and entertainment in the area and 4 miles from UVA and Monticello. It's hard to leave the comforts of

200 South Street, though; the library, sitting room, upstairs study, veranda and garden terrace beckon.

Fluvanna County

Palmer Country Manor
$$$$ • Va. Rt. 640, Palmyra
• (804) 589-1300, (800) 253-4306

This estate of 180 acres was once part of a 2,500-acre plantation known as Solitude. Palmer Country Manor was built by Richard McCary, a mason who also built the Palmyra Stone Jail and Carysbrook Plantation. McCary prospered, and within 20 years he and his wife owned 583 acres. However, in 1858 he was arrested for murder, put in the jail he built and found it necessary to sell the entire plantation.

Owners Kathy and Greg Palmer opened the estate as a bed and breakfast in 1989, with the furnishings and ambiance of an 1834 plantation house. You can stay in three rooms in the historic plantation house, with its library, parlor and screened porch, or in one of the 10 suites in private cottages. Each air-conditioned cottage has a fireplace, king- or queen-size bed, color television, full bath and large private deck. Six cottages have Jacuzzi baths. Each can accommodate as many as four people. Guests are served a complimentary breakfast every morning, and a lavish five-course candlelight dinner is available every night.

Adventurous types may want to raft the whitewater on the James River or hike, picnic, fish or relax in the nearby woods. Romantics can opt for a champagne hot-air balloon ride at sunset.

Louisa County

Ginger Hill Bed & Breakfast
$$ • 47 Holly Springs Dr., Louisa
• (540) 967-3260

Ginger Hill, a country cottage on 14.5 secluded, wooded acres not far from Charlottesville, is surrounded by natural diversions — a fishing pond with a canoe, two beaver ponds and a variety of birds and animals

to watch. The inn is also a good base for daytrips to historic, recreational and cultural sites.

The home was built in 1992 with the generous features (10-foot ceilings, a fireplace and porches) found in older homes, but with the modern amenities of air conditioning, bathrooms and ample parking for cars, trailers and boats. The inn has two sunny guest rooms, each with a private bath and sitting area.

Innkeepers Ron and Ginger Ellis provide a full Southern breakfast in the formal dining room, on the porch or even at the picnic table by the pond. Afternoon and evening refreshments are available, and a light supper can be arranged at an additional cost.

The inn can accommodate pets with prior notice. Special occasion packages are available, as are corporate rates and special activities such as a fishing trip or cruise on Lake Anna or a tour of Civil War sites. Fishing and boating packages are especially nice, as the Ellises have a 20-foot motorboat to ferry guests around the lake.

Prospect Hill Plantation Inn
$$$$ • 2887 Poindexter Rd., Trevilians
• (540) 967-2574, (800) 277-0844

A graceful English tree garden shades the manor house, and a boxwood hedge lines the entranceway to this 1732 mansion. A few steps away are the slave quarters, the overseer's house, slave kitchen, smokehouse and carriage house. A large open lawn unfolds for a quarter-mile. This is Prospect Hill, a plantation that is more than two centuries old. Michael and Laura Sheehan are the innkeepers today, but the tradition of hospitality began long before their time.

After the Civil War, the son of the plantation owner returned to find Prospect Hill overgrown and run down. In order to make ends meet, he was forced to take in guests from the city. In 1880 he built an addition to Prospect Hill and remodeled the old slave quarters for guest bedrooms. This renovation created an interior as beautiful as the extraordinary magnolias, tulip poplars and giant beeches in the yard. The slave quarters have beamed ceilings and warm, crackling fireplaces. The rooms in the manor house are adorned with antique furnishings and lovely quilts, and all have fireplaces. A private veranda offers a view over the hillside. The inn has 13 guest rooms, each with a modern bathroom, some with Jacuzzis. There are also three private dwellings on the grounds.

A full country breakfast is served to you in bed or at a table in your room. Dinner is served as well; a bell will ring to summon you to one of three candlelight dining rooms for your five-course feast. Dishes are traditional French with Provençal and American accents. Tea time is a ritual at Prospect Hill, and you can also sip a glass of Virginia wine before dinner.

On the grounds or nearby you can go hiking, picnicking, fishing, biking or swimming. Sunset champagne hot-air balloon rides are easily arranged. The inn is in the Green Springs Historic District of Louisa County, near Skyline Drive, Blue Ridge Parkway, Monticello, Ash Lawn-Highland, the University of Virginia, Montpelier, the Barboursville Vineyards and Oakencroft Vineyard and Winery.

Nelson County

Acorn Inn
$ • 2256 Adial Rd., Nellysford
• (804) 361-9357

This cozy, art-filled bed and breakfast provides a creative and inexpensive home base for exploration of the area's many offerings. Skiing and golf at Wintergreen Resort, winery tours, cycling, hiking, fishing and a host of mountain sports are all close to Acorn Inn. And with rates from $39 to $55 in the inn and $95 for two in the cottage, Acorn Inn is a great value.

Three different lodging styles are available: The Inn, Acorn Cottage and the Farmhouse. The Inn, once a horse barn, offers 10 comfortable rooms, each with a double bed and original stall doors. A recently added 880-square-foot meeting room with kitchenette is ideal for corporate retreats, weddings and reunions. Guests are charmed by the colorful folk art

and a relaxed Scandinavian atmosphere. The common room features a beautiful Finnish soapstone bake oven. Ladies' and gentlemen's bathrooms are shared in the inn.

Acorn Cottage, with its own kitchen and bath, is perfect for honeymooners or families with small children who want more privacy. Two guest rooms in the Farmhouse — which also is the home of the innkeepers, Kathy Plunket Versluys and Martin Versluys — are available during the busiest seasons. These two rooms share a bath.

A continental breakfast each morning features a delicious variety of homemade breads, muffins and fruit cobbler along with fresh fruit, juice, coffee and tea.

Looking Glass House
$$ • 10273 Rockfish Valley Hwy., Afton
• (540) 456-6844, (800) 769-6844

This 1848 pre-Victorian farmhouse near the Blue Ridge Parkway is an English country-style inn that takes its name from a Lewis Carroll tale. The inn, within a half-hour's drive of Charlottesville, Monticello and Wintergreen Resort, used to be the county's tax preservation office.

Today, innkeepers Janet and Earl Hampton have decorated their four guest rooms with antiques. Each room is air-conditioned and has a fireplace and private bath. Vintage linens are used on all guest beds. Two wicker-furnished porches offer views of the countryside, while the library and formal drawing room are comfortable settings for reading, parlor games and television. Refreshments are served each afternoon.

Breakfast in the formal dining room starts with freshly baked muffins or breads and juice, followed by a second course of seasonal fruits and then the main course, which could include stuffed cinnamon French toast with apricot cheese filling or rosemary-almond croissants. The broiled grapefruit is the house specialty. Fourth-generation antique china, silver and crystal dating back to the 1800s make the

---

INSIDERS' TIP

Several inns have added dinner to their list of options. These can be wonderfully romantic candlelight affairs. Just remember to give innkeepers advance notice if you would like to dine in.

meal even more special. Coffee and tea are available to early risers on the antique buffet outside the rooms.

Fresh-cut flowers from the garden grace the inn's interior, and guests may stroll through the rose garden or the plantings along the two stream banks or take a dip in the inn's pool. Last year, the Hamptons planted more than 20 more rose bushes along the fragrant path.

The Mark Addy
$$$ • 56 Rodes Farm Dr., Nellysford • (804) 361-1101, (800) 278-2154

Beautifully restored, The Mark Addy offers the richness and romance of a bygone era. The inn is a former estate house, Upland, that was begun as a four-room farmhouse in 1884 and expanded to its current size by 1910.

Guest rooms are decorated in individual themes: Oriental, English, Victorian or the military-style Colonel's Room. Each has a private bathroom with either a double whirlpool bath, double shower or an antique claw-foot tub with shower. Five porches and a hammock are available for lounging. Public rooms include a dining room, a parlor, a library and a sitting room with cable TV, VCR, games and phones.

Each room has a decanter of liqueur, and breakfast is a hearty meal. Innkeepers John Maddox and Saverio Anselmo take pride in their cuisine de grandmere. Dinner is served on Saturday nights for an additional charge.

Nearby attractions include Skyline Drive, Monticello, wineries, Wintergreen Resort and all the shops, museums, restaurants and social activities of the university city of Charlottesville. For those who are happiest when browsing through curiosity shops, Tuckahoe Antique Mall and Jordan's are just a few miles away. But antique lovers won't have to travel far: the inn opened its own antique and gift shop in one of the outbuildings. For the more adventurous, canoeing, hiking and rafting are minutes away.

The Meander Inn at Penny Lane Farm
$$ • 3100 Berry Hill Rd., Nellysford • (804) 361-1121

The Rockfish Valley of Nelson County is the setting for this country farmhouse on 50 acres of horse-grazed pasture and woods. Rick and Kathy Cornelius are the innkeepers of the Meander Inn, an 80-year-old Victorian home just 100 yards from the Rockfish River. The five guest rooms are decorated with Victorian or country antiques and four-poster beds. Each has a private bath.

If you rise early enough, you can help fetch the morning eggs from the hen house and give the horses their breakfast grain. Or you can wake just in time to savor a tasty country breakfast.

Leisurely afternoons can be spent sipping tea or lemonade on the porch (served with warm chocolate-chip cookies) or watching the guinea hens play in the brush. As the inn's name suggests, you can meander along Skyline Drive and behold the spectacular scenery. Among the activities within easy reach are skiing, canoeing, horseback riding, tennis, golf, fishing, hiking, swimming and biking.

After a day's activity, it's fun to enjoy a glass of Virginia wine and sit around the woodstove listening to the antique player piano or soak in the outdoor hot tub by starlight.

Trillium House
$$$ • 3421 Wintergreen Dr., Nellysford • (804) 325-9126, (800) 325-9126

Betty and Ed Dinwiddie's Trillium House is in the middle of the posh Wintergreen Four Seasons Resort, overlooking the 17th fairway of the Devil's Knob Golf Course. Guests have the use of the resort's 11,000 acres, with its tennis, golf, swimming and skiing facilities and several restaurants. However, you may want to dine at the Trillium House; breakfast is served daily to guests, and dinner is offered Friday and Saturday by appointment.

Trillium was built in traditional country inn style in 1983 and has 10 individually decorated, soundproofed rooms and two suites, all with private baths and controlled temperature. The cedar-sided inn has a great room with a 22-foot-high ceiling, a large family library, a TV area, a garden room and a spacious dining room.

If you can tear yourself away from the resort, the glories of Charlottesville, with its historic sites and excellent shopping, as well as the Skyline Drive and Blue Ridge Parkway, await.

Amherst, Monroe and Lynchburg

Dulwich Manor

$$ • 550 Richmond Hwy., Amherst • (804) 946-7207, (800) 571-9011

You will know your journey is over when you turn onto the winding country lane and see the inviting porch of this estate, set on five secluded acres in Amherst County. Flemish bond brickwork and fluted columns decorate the outside of this late-1880s English-style manor house. Nestled in the countryside and surrounded by the Blue Ridge Mountains, Dulwich Manor abounds with beauty and country appeal.

Hosts Bob and Judy Reilly have created a serene getaway. Period antiques decorate the rooms, and the living room and study each have a large fireplace to set a cozy, relaxed mood. The six bedrooms are reminiscent of an English country home — beds are canopied brass or antiques — and you can choose a room with a fireplace or window seat for relaxing afternoons or evenings. The Scarborough Room also offers a whirlpool tub and a canopied queen-size bed.

Each day begins with a full country breakfast, including fresh fruits and juices, inn-baked muffins and breads, country sausage, herb teas and hot coffee. Take a stroll after breakfast and see the natural beauty of the Washington and Jefferson National Forests. The Blue Ridge Parkway is nearby for hiking, picnicking or photographing the view. Natural Bridge and Caverns, Peaks of Otter and Crabtree Falls are scenic spots for a lunch. This area of the country is also full of history: Washington, Jefferson and Patrick Henry were all born near here. The Appomattox Courthouse, Monticello, Ash Lawn and Poplar Forest are all within a short distance of Dulwich. In the evening you can return to watch the gorgeous sunset over the mountains or relax in the outdoor hot tub.

Well-behaved children are welcome. Pets are not allowed. Smoking is allowed in designated areas only.

Fair View Bed and Breakfast

$$ • 2416 Lowesville Rd., Amherst • (804) 277-8500

"I used to feel somewhat apologetic because there's not more activity in our area, but I discovered that most people come here because it's quiet and beautiful and restful," says innkeeper Judy Noon. "When you look out the window, all you see is mountains. 'Fair View' is an understatement. Even the stars seem brighter than they do other places, so our guests tell us."

Tootsie, an enthusiastic Labrador, takes her welcoming duties quite seriously, and it's OK if you bring your pet as long as you clear it beforehand with Judy and husband, Jim.

Fair View was built by a Yankee doctor two years after the Civil War, as is indicated by the inscription on a dining room window pane: "This house was built in 1867. Fair View July 22 in 87." Local legend says the doctor fell in love with a local girl. The home he built for her is most unusual, in that its Italianate style is more common in New York's Hudson River area. "It's a toned-down Italianate," says Judy. "They can be very grand with fountains, terraza and marble floors — but this is just a big, comfortable farmhouse."

The three guest rooms, each with a private bath, are furnished with antiques "which are meant to be used," says Judy. A fourth room, the Duck Room, is available for children or a third person. The house is fully air conditioned. A modest teddy bear collection started by Judy some years ago has grown to

---

INSIDERS' TIP

Bed and breakfasts are a good change of pace. But if you are looking for an active nightlife with a smorgasbord of entertainment, be aware that quite a number of these delightful getaways are in small towns or out in country settings. If you prefer nightclubs to picturesque scenery, some of these may be quieter than your taste.

a delightful hodgepodge of more than 50 bears, thanks to donations from her guests. Another guest sent a small tea set, which the bears, of course, enjoy immensely!

Breakfast is customized to the dietary needs of guests, but Judy loves to whip up a hearty country eye-opener featuring her specialty, grits quiche.

Lynchburg Mansion Inn Bed and Breakfast

$$$$ • 405 Madison St., Lynchburg
• (804) 528-5400, (800) 352-1199

Built in 1914 for James R. Gilliam Sr., this 9,000-square-foot Spanish Georgian mansion sits on a half-acre in the Garland Hill Historic District. A 6-foot-high iron fence surrounds the main house and carriage house. Three separate entrance gates are anchored in massive piers, and upon arrival guests drive under the columned porte-cochere to the six-column entry portico. The front door opens onto the 50-foot grand hall with restored cherry columns and wainscoting. The cherry and oak staircase has 219 spindles. Just inches from the back door is a hot tub, and a lovely garden gazebo overlooks the herb and perennial gardens.

The inn offers three rooms and two suites, all with little extras (like an iron and ironing board in each room) to help make you feel right at home. All rooms have a full, private bathroom and their own special touches — including hair dryers, lotion, shampoo and conditioner.

Decor varies from the Victorian-style Gilliam Room (with mahogany four-poster bed with steps, a rose-patterned comforter, plump pillows and billowing lace) to the light and airy Country French Room that's done in crisp Laura Ashley prints, a bleached four-poster bed and armoire. One garden suite is actually an apartment-size set-up perfect for families, with both a queen-size bed in the bedroom and a queen-size sleeper sofa in the living room. In fact, the suite is large enough that it warrants two TVs and two telephones.

The morning newspaper is delivered to your door along with a freshly brewed pot of coffee and a pitcher of juice, and a full breakfast is served in the dining room with fine china, crystal and silver. You can plan your outings at an information center in the back hall. After a day of sightseeing and shopping, retire to the elegant living room and sink into an overstuffed fireside chair. Smoking is permitted only on the veranda. The innkeepers request well-behaved children and no pets.

1880s Madison House Bed & Breakfast

$$ • 413 Madison St., Lynchburg
• (804) 528-1503, (800) 828-6422

Robert C. Burkeholder built 1880s Madison House for wealthy tobacconist George Fleming. This example of Italianate and Eastlake Victorian architecture, notable for its elaborate New Orleans-style cast-iron porch, sits in the historic Garland Hill District of Lynchburg. The "painted lady" exterior testifies to something wonderful within.

Innkeeper Jaene Haske has maintained the original floor plan, which has remained untouched for more than a century. Distinctive features include crystal chandeliers, an intricate peacock stained-glass window, numerous fireplaces and original woodwork. The 1880s Madison House library has books from as far back as the late 1700s as well as many Civil War books and artifacts. The inn is filled with an extensive collection of antiques, one of the best in Lynchburg.

Each bedroom includes a mix of antiques and modern conveniences, such as private telephone lines and televisions with cable. Your comfort is considered in such details as soft robes provided in your room, 100 percent cotton linens and bath towels and air conditioning. The Gold Room has a bay window, king-size canopy bed, sitting area, antique vanity and working fireplace. The Madison Suite has a private sitting room with a TV and writing desk and a bed chamber with a queen-size canopy bed. The Rose Room has a queen-size brass bed with a dresser and armoire and a working fireplace, and the Veranda Room has a screened-in sitting porch with Victorian-style white wicker. Each room has a private bath, two featuring original fixtures from the turn of the century.

A leisurely breakfast in the dining room consists of freshly perked coffee, fresh fruit, homemade coffee cakes, oven-baked omelettes and English drop pudding. Eggs

Benedict may also be served. Return for afternoon English tea at 4 PM every day.

After breakfast, you can visit some of the historic sites in and around Lynchburg, such as Poplar Forest, the Old Court House Museum and Appomattox Court House. The Blue Ridge Parkway, Skyline Drive and underground caverns are also close by. Ask about walking-tour brochures and points of interest. Lynchburg has five historic districts rife with heritage.

Smoking and pets are prohibited. Bringing children is discouraged, although some exceptions may be made. The inn is available for special events such as business meetings with breakfast, lunch or dinner; bridal and baby showers; and various types of holiday parties. Reservations are strongly recommended.

Once Upon a Time Bed and Breakfast

$$ • 1102 Harrison St., Lynchburg • (804) 845-3561

Families will delight in a stay at this Second Empire Victorian home. While many bed and breakfasts do not accommodate young guests, this inn's owners, Lori Ann and Tom Hughes, warmly invite your children to visit with theirs — they have four daughters! In fact most visitors say that from the moment they arrive they feel just like part of the family, and that's just the sentiment the owners want to proffer. Antiques decorate the guest areas of the home, including the parlor, music room and dining room.

The most whimsical and wonderful rooms are the themed guest rooms. The Frog Prince room, in greens and blues, is reminiscent of that classic tale, and the innkeepers have even left a copy of the book there for you to share. The headboard of the queen-size bed is adorned with a water lily, and a golden ball completes the details. The Three Bears Suite is perfect for families. One of its rooms has a queen-size bed, and the other has a daybed with trundle, easily accommodating a family of four. Teddy bears await your arrival on a bench in the hall. The suite is furnished in browns, greens and pinks. Both the single room and the suite have private baths with claw-foot tubs and showers.

The day starts with a full breakfast. The menu changes daily, but everything is always homemade and fresh. You can expect things like blueberry pancakes, omelets or even chocolate waffles with fresh strawberries and whipped cream. You will probably find some of Lori Ann's homemade jam along with fresh baked biscuits. After breakfast you can step out back and see Tom's progress with the property's 80-plus antique rose bushes. To keep the kids busy, there's a swingset, playhouse and the family's two dogs.

Once Upon a Time is in the heart of Lynchburg, with plenty of historic, cultural and recreational activities nearby. At day's end, return to the inn for dessert with the Hughes family. It's always available, from 7 to 10 PM each night (special reservations are not necessary), and Tom and Lori Ann love to visit with their guests during this relaxing time. As with all old and historic homes, Once Upon a Time is constantly undergoing some renovations. But the owners invite you to come and see the progress they are making as they return this mansion to the glory of its earlier years. The inn cannot accommodate pets. Children younger than 6 stay for free, children ages 6 to 12 stay for $10 per night, and children 12 and older stay for $20 per night.

Winridge Bed & Breakfast

$$ • 116 Winridge Dr., Madison Heights • (804) 384-7220

Winridge Bed and Breakfast, 14 miles off the Blue Ridge Parkway, offers a panoramic view of the Blue Ridge Mountains and the simple elegance of country living. The Colonial Southern home sits on a 14-acre country estate built in 1910 by Wallace A. Taylor, president of the American National Life Insurance Company of Richmond. LoisAnn and Ed Pfister are the hosts now, and the landmark has been restored to its original grandeur. Four massive columns adorn the entry portico, and grand windows allow views of the surrounding countryside from anywhere in the home.

The inn has three guest rooms. The Habecker Room has a queen-size, four-poster bed and private bath with ceramic-tiled shower. The Walker Room has a queen-size cannonball bed, and the Brubaker Room has two twin beds. The Walker and Brubaker rooms share a hallway bath with footed tub and brass and porcelain shower.

Breakfast is served every morning in the lovely old dining room. The estate offers plenty of entertainment: explore the meadows, swing under the big shade trees or relax on the porches. The library and living room are full of books, magazines and games. If you prefer to venture off the grounds, the Blue Ridge Parkway, National Historical Park at Appomattox Courthouse, Poplar Forest (Thomas Jefferson's summer home) and several colleges are all within a short drive. Nearby natural sites include Crabtree Falls, Peaks of Otter and Natural Bridge and Caverns.

Smoking is permitted outside only. Children are welcome and are invited to play with the Pfister children.

Goodview

Stone Manor Bed & Breakfast
$$ • 1135 Stone Manor Pl., off Va. Rt. 653, Goodview • (540) 297-1414

Don and Mary Davis purchased this former golf clubhouse on Smith Mountain Lake at auction not long ago. After about a year of renovations, cleaning and hard work, the couple opened Stone Manor in 1996 to rave reviews. They have already enjoyed repeat visits from guests who claim that each stay is unforgettable.

The three bedrooms are each decorated to reflect a different theme of recreation on the lake: boating, fishing and golfing. The Captain's Quarters is the most popular because of its gorgeous views of Smith Mountain Lake and the whirlpool tub under a skylight. All the rooms have private baths.

Start the morning with coffee or tea on the patio or by the pool. A delicious full breakfast is then served in the dining room. Each day you'll find fresh fruit, juice, a muffin or bread and a main dish, such as Mary's special Captain's Choice orange French toast. Vegetarian or other special diets can be accommodated as well.

For recreation try one of the manor's theme sports. Golf courses are within a few minutes drive, or you can try your luck at fishing off the inn's dock. Facilities also are available for guests who wish to bring their own boat. Although there is no boat ramp at the inn, the Davises will provide transportation to and from the nearest boat launch. Of course you can relax and sunbathe by the deck or swim in the pool.

Several points of interest are within moderate travel distances, including the Blue Ridge Parkway, which is just 15 minutes away. Also nearby are Bridgewater Plaza (with restaurants, shops, games and minigolf), Booker T. Washington National Monument, Explore Park and Peaks of Otter. A little farther away is historic downtown Roanoke, with its Farmers' Market, numerous shops and restaurants. Like most guests, however, you'll want to make it back in time to see the extraordinary sight of the sun setting over the mountains and across the lake.

Smoking is not permitted in the manor, nor are pets. Children older than 12 are welcome.

Rocky Mount and Smith Mountain Lake

The Claiborne House Bed and Breakfast
$$ • 185 Claiborne Ave., Rocky Mount • (540) 483-4616

English-style gardens surround the 1895 Victorian Claiborne House, an elegant turn-of-the-century home in Franklin County. This tranquil getaway is nestled between the Blue Ridge Parkway and Smith Mountain Lake. The best place to enjoy the scenery is from the 130-foot wraparound porch furnished with white wicker furniture.

Victorian-era furnishings add charm to the interior. Each room has a king-, queen- or twin-size bed and private bath. Breakfast is a gourmet meal that may include fresh berries or other homegrown fruits in season or homemade bread. Specialties are eggs Benedict, blueberry crepes, spinach souffles and sourdough pecan waffles. Guests awaken to fresh coffee placed outside their doors.

You can spend your day reading a book from the lending library, strolling through the lovely English gardens or sitting by the goldfish pond. Margaret and Jim Young are your hosts and can help you plan a day in the area.

Smith Mountain Lake offers year-round activities — fishing, golf, tennis and biking — on its 500 miles of shoreline. Booker T. Washington National Monument is just minutes away. Ferrum College and its Blue Ridge Farm Museum, Mabry Mill, Peaks of Otter, Mill Mountain Zoo and Roanoke's historic Farmer's Market are all within a short drive.

Well-behaved children are welcome. Sorry, no pets are allowed. Smoking is restricted to the outside areas only, and advance reservations are requested.

The Manor at Taylor's Store
$$ • 8812 Washington Hwy., Smith Mtn. Lake • (540) 721-3951, (800) 248-6267

The Manor at Taylor's Store offers both a charming historic main house and a fabulous new lodge featuring antique quilts and a main room large enough for meetings of 25. This was an important place when, in 1799, Skelton Taylor first established Taylor's Store as a general merchandise trading post at this site in Franklin County. It served the community and travelers alike for many years. Later, the building functioned as an ordinary and a post office. The original manor house was built in the early 1800s as the focus of a prosperous tobacco plantation. The present-day home, once featured in *Southern Living*, has emerged as a lovely blend of the periods in which it has been restored.

Lee and Mary Tucker are your hosts at this 120-acre estate. The manor itself features several common areas, a formal parlor with a grand piano, a sunroom full of plants and a great room with a large fireplace. You may also enjoy the billiard room, guest kitchen or the fully equipped exercise room. You can commission a hot-air balloon ride for breakfast if you book in advance, getting a bird's-eye view of Smith Mountain Lake.

The home is furnished with period antiques. Each guest room has a unique decor and ambiance. You can stay in the Castle, Plantation, Victorian, Colonial or English Garden suites. The Toy Room is decorated with antique toys, quilts and an extra-high queen-size canopied bed with steps. The Christmas Cottage is ideal for families with children; it has three bedrooms, two baths, a fully equipped kitchen, den with stone fireplace and

a large deck with gorgeous views of the six ponds and wilderness area. Each guest room has a private bath, and some have a private balcony. There are two guest kitchens.

After a fresh gourmet breakfast — Mary specializes in heart-healthy cooking and published a cookbook in 1995 — you can go hiking, picnicking, canoeing and fishing in one of the spring-fed ponds on the estate. There are also swimming docks, a gazebo and even a resident flock of geese! You can soak in the hot tub or lounge on the sundecks. Nearby are Smith Mountain Lake, Booker T. Washington National Monument, the Blue Ridge Parkway and all of Roanoke's sights.

Smoking and pets are not allowed. Children are welcome in the cottage. Advance reservations are important.

New River Valley

Blacksburg

L'Arche
$$ • 301 Wall St., Blacksburg • (540) 951-1808

An elegant 1907 Federal Revival-style home takes you away from it all — right in the heart of downtown Blacksburg. Vera Good opened this renovated landmark, just a block from Virginia Tech, in 1993. Six comfortable guest rooms are decorated with fluffy comforters and handmade quilts. Each features a private bath, queen-size bed and fresh flowers. One room is accessible to the physically challenged. The Country Room will accommodate a family with two children.

Guests may read, chat and relax in the drawing room, and the two cavernous dining rooms overlook the gardens. Share a table for two on the wide porch or sit under the Jeffersonian gazebo, which is sometimes the setting for weddings. Recreation is close at hand: whitewater rafting on the New River, boating at Claytor Lake State Park or picnicking by Cascades Waterfall. You'll find horseback riding, horse shows and carriage rides at Dori-Del Equine Center. Nearby Virginia Tech and Radford University provide cultural and athletic events.

Breakfast at L'Arche is an event. The inn serves fresh fruit, home-baked breads, muffins and cakes, homemade granola and spiced teas. The morning repast may also include French toast, fluffy omelettes or pancakes and waffles. Special dietary needs can be accommodated. Dinner may be served upon request.

Reservations are strongly encouraged. A two-night minimum stay is necessary on football weekends, commencement, parents' weekend or other special events at Tech. Smoking is permitted outside on the grounds. Gift certificates are available.

Christiansburg

The Oaks Victorian Inn
$$$$ • 311 E. Main St., Christianburg
• (540) 381-1500

Massive oak trees, believed to be more than 300 years old, surround this estate in Christiansburg, which has been widely recognized for lodging excellence. A green lawn stretches for what seems like miles, and the home itself stands like a fairytale castle. Major W.L. Pierce built the buttercup-yellow Queen Anne Victorian for his family, completing it in 1893. The home remained in the Pierce family for almost 90 years.

Margaret and Tom Ray converted The Oaks into a country inn. The luxurious manor is well suited for both leisure and business travelers. Guest rooms have queen- or king-size canopy beds with Posturepedic mattresses, fireplaces and window nooks. Other amenities include telephones with private lines and dataports, mini-refrigerators stocked with complimentary refreshments, decanters of sherry and valet service on request. The private baths in each room are stocked with plush towels, fluffy terry robes and English toiletries. The garden gazebo houses a Hydrojet hot tub.

In 1997 The Oaks was selected by the National Trust for Historic Preservation for the cover of its guidebook and was one of 52 properties chosen for the 1998 engagement calendar. The inn has been a member since 1993 of the Independent Innkeepers Association, an international organization where membership is by invitation only. Guests from 49 states and 30 countries have visited.

Each morning, guests wake to freshly ground coffee and a newspaper. The breakfast menu is varied and features such specialties as spinach or asparagus quiche Provençal; Belgian waffles served with butter-pecan ice cream, blackberries, a homemade sauce made with grapefruit and Grand Marnier and topped with toasted almonds and coconut; fresh fruit in honey and Amaretto; and a variety of fresh breads. A bounty of fresh fruits and juices are available as well.

Take some time after breakfast to lounge on the wraparound porch with its Kennedy rockers and wicker chairs. Investigate the books and games in the parlor or study or have a nice chat in the sunroom. Cable television is provided. Nearby, you can hike on the Appalachian Trail and boat or fish on Claytor Lake. The historic Newbern Museum, *Long Way Home* outdoor drama, Mill Mountain Theatre, Center in the Square, Smithfield Plantation and Chateau Morrisette Winery are a short drive away. The Oaks' Victorian Christmas each December is a special event.

Gift certificates are available. Advance payment and a two-night minimum are required for special-event weekends at local universities. Corporate rates are available Sunday through Thursday.

Pulaski County

The Count Pulaski
Bed & Breakfast and Gardens
$$ • 821 N. Jefferson Ave., Pulaski
• (540) 980-1163, (800) 980-1163

The move to 821 N. Jefferson Avenue was Florence Byrd Stevenson's 63rd — and last! She and her husband, William H. Struhs, established the first bed and breakfast inn in

Pulaski in this house that is more than eight decades old. The four-story brick home has three stairways and three upper guest rooms. The American Room has a canopied four-poster bed so high off the floor you have to climb into it using a step-stool. A crested plate on the door to the Polish Room represents the royalty of the Polish count for whom Pulaski is named. Twin beds come together to make a king-size bed. Hand-decorated wooden pieces around the writing desk show fairy stories. James Michener's *Poland* lies on the desk, a gift given to Stevenson as a child. The French room is decorated with lithographs of Parisienne scenes. The seats of its two rose-wood chairs were done in needlepoint by Stevenson's mother.

All the rooms have private baths. The rest of the house is decorated with furnishings from Florence's times in Europe and Asia, along with family antiques. A 1912 Steinway baby grand sits in the living room, and a Vietnamese temple bell sits on the mantel along with a Byrd clock that has been in the family for more than 100 years. Ceiling fans, air conditioning and fireplaces add comfort throughout the house.

Start the day with an elegant gourmet breakfast served on a 100-year-old table with china, crystal and silver. Then explore Pulaski's revitalized Main Street, famous for its antique shops. Nearby are museums and national and state parks.

Reservations are suggested. Children and pets can't be accommodated. The Count Pulaski is a smoke-free establishment.

Claytor Lake Homestead Inn
$$ • off I-81, Exit 92, Draper
• (540) 980-6777, (800) 676-LAKE

This historic inn is the only bed and breakfast on beautiful Claytor Lake. Innkeepers Douglas and Linda Eads have redecorated and revitalized this lakeside home, which they opened to guests in 1996. Little extras and special touches make the Homestead Inn unique. From the beginning of your stay, when the Eads greet you at the door with a specially created nonalcoholic drink, you will see how intent they are on pampering their guests.

The home is decorated throughout with antiques, reproductions and collector's pieces.

The lovely living room, with fireplace, is a wonderful place to gather with friends or family to relax, read, play cards or chat. Most rooms in the cozy old house have a spectacular view of the lake. The brick and stone wraparound porch provides rocking chairs and a magnificent view.

Each of the five guest rooms has all the comforts of home including color television, a VCR and a private phone. Beds vary in size from king-size to two twin-size beds. Private and shared baths are available. Breakfast is served in the dining room, and you may join others at the main table or dine at a small table for two. Southern hospitality accompanies Southern and country-style cooking: each day you'll find special dishes such as homemade muffins, fruit pancakes and homemade biscuits. Guests of the inn may also request dinner; the dining room is open to non-guests only on weekends.

Numerous recreational opportunities are available at the inn. Spend your afternoon on the 550 feet of private white sand beach along the lake. The marina building is perfect for picnics and parties. You can rent small paddleboats; full boat-launch facilities are available. Nearby is an 18-hole PGA golf course and the New River Trail. A short drive will take you to historic downtown Pulaski, Wilderness Road Regional Museum in Newbern or the Blue Ridge Parkway.

The Inn is open year round. Advance reservations are suggested. Special rates for corporate reservations and weekend package rates are available.

Floyd County

Bent Mountain Lodge
$$ • off U.S. Hwy. 221 (Bent Mountain Rd.), Copper Hill • (540) 929-4979

The views are heavenly, in beauty and proximity, from this lodge overlooking the Blue Ridge Parkway from 3,200 feet. Mornings are made for sitting in a big rocking chair on your deck and gazing at the mountains and rolling countryside, a scene that innkeepers David Wood and Michael Maiolo get to see every day! Wood has been a teacher, a textbook salesman, director of food services for the

Texas Rangers baseball club and a real estate agent who writes literature for young people. Maiolo is a former high school English teacher with a passion for Faulkner.

There are no planned activities, just areas for you to explore. The beauty of nature is emphasized here. The owners have cut back the trees so the wildflowers — black-eyed Susans, daisies, fire pinks, sundrops and many more — can grow in abundance. They are developing the meadows through a wildflower program to ensure a maximum variety of flowers. Almost anytime during the spring and summer you will find a riot of blooming flora. Nature trails wind through the woods. This beauty and tranquility is part of the reason Bent Mountain Lodge is becoming a retreat for many — a place to relax and relieve the stresses of city life.

The lodge is decorated with country elegance and has five guest rooms and one two-room suite. Each has a private bath with Jacuzzi and plush carpet. Quilts cover some beds, and some of the rooms have high ceilings. The large dining room is oak-paneled and constructed with hand-hewn timbers; bookshelves run from the floor almost to the 20-foot-high ceiling. A glass wall of French doors opens onto the 3,000-square-foot deck. A huge fireplace rounds out the room. The entire lodge is air conditioned.

The lodge serves guests three meals a day. The specialty is a country dinner with pot roast, chicken or country ham and fresh vegetables, bought from local farms when available. Virginia wines are also featured. While the restaurant is reserved for guests of the lodge, it will occasionally serve dinner to non-guests with advanced reservations. Group meals may be arranged as well, but Wood emphasizes these additional meals will only be served as long as they are not an inconvenience to guests.

Many weddings and conferences have been held here. Bent Mountain Lodge is also a great place for small weekday business meetings. These are generally held in the lounge, which has a fireplace and a bar from the former Floyd Mercantile store. Whatever the reason for your stay, Wood and Maiolo want you to feel at home. For that reason, they place few restrictions on guests. Children

and pets are welcome, smoking is OK, and there is no minimum stay. So relax and enjoy the view.

The lodge is closed from January 2 through April 15 each year. Individual lodging is also unavailable in November or December due to the frequency of inclement weather. However, group reservations in November receive special consideration.

Alleghany Highlands

Clifton Forge
and Covington

Longdale Inn Bed & Breakfast
$$ • 6209 Longdale Furnace Rd., Clifton Forge • (540) 862-0892, (800) 862-0386

Stone gates welcome you to Longdale Inn, formerly known as Firmstone Manor. Driving up the arched drive lined with flowering plum trees offers you a view of Longdale Inn's dusty-rose mansion and the Allegheny Mountains. A myriad of flowers and exotic shrubbery enhance the charm of this 1873 Victorian inn set near the southern tip of Virginia's beautiful and historic Shenandoah Valley.

Kate and Bob Cormier greet guests in the magnificent entrance hall, which takes you back in time to when Ulysses S. Grant was president and Virginia's first hot-blast iron furnace was established at Longdale. You can explore Longdale Inn's 23 rooms, each superbly restored and decorated with many original items from the Firmstone-Johnson mansion, owners and iron masters of the Longdale Iron Works. Architectural details abound, and floor-to-ceiling windows bring in mountain breezes and soothing sounds of the surrounding Allegheny Mountains.

The Inn has 10 bedrooms and suites, furnished in Victorian or Southwestern decor. One suite furnished in white wicker with muted peach and gray tones is especially popular with honeymooners. A country breakfast, served in the dining room, includes freshly brewed Allegheny Star coffee, fruit, juices and cereals, followed by the chef's entree. You can request a picnic lunch for your outing, and afternoon refreshments are served. Relaxing activities here include croquet on the side lawn beneath century-old shade trees or strolling the 12 acres of grounds rich with the wildflowers and songbirds that surround Longdale Inn.

Shopping and recreation sites are plentiful in the area. One mile west of the Inn, Longdale National Recreation Area has a variety of trails and a mountain lake for swimming. Outdoor enthusiasts and photographers will want to see the North Mountain Trail. Nearby national forest roads and trails are ideal for cross-country skiing and mountain biking. You can soak in the fabled mineral waters of the Hot and Warm Springs or the Sweet Chalybeate Springs, or go to Douthat State Park and Lake Moomaw for swimming, boating, fishing and hiking. Highland has many antique shops and auctions, and Lexington offers the Virginia Horse Center and outdoor theater, concerts and several museums. Several challenging golf courses are nearby.

Longdale Inn also hosts gatherings, such as family reunions, meetings, seminars, retreats and weddings. Children of all ages are welcome and so are pets, with advanced arrangements.

Milton Hall Bed & Breakfast Inn
$$ • 207 Thorny Ln., Covington
• (540) 965-0196

The Hon. Laura Marie Theresa Fitzwilliam, Viscountess Milton, built this manor in 1874. Lord Milton was ill and Lady Milton hoped the peace and tranquility of the countryside and beautiful mountain scenery would help return him to health. Today, Milton Hall still stands on 44 acres just west of Covington, in the community of Callaghan. Surrounded by the Allegheny Mountains, the house, with its gables, buttressed porch towers and Gothic trimmings, is a contrast to its rustic surroundings. The inside is not as ornate, and, while it is spacious, it is more of a large country home than a mansion.

A roomy living area and equally large dining room each have two sets of French doors opening to the gardens in the south lawn. Each guest bedroom has a private bath, except for the center bedroom with the oriel window that has become the Milton Hall logo. (Addition of

a bathroom would require a drastic change in the original floor plan, and no one advocates that.) Some rooms feature queen-size beds and fireplaces. The second-floor master bedroom suite has a sitting area. One of the original bedrooms in the servants' quarters has been converted into a bath suite with whirlpool and fireplace. Some rooms have telephones; a central hall phone is available to all guests.

A full breakfast is served in the dining room. Picnics or elegant basket lunches are available to sightseeing guests, and dinner may be served by special arrangement. Plenty of attractions are nearby — Lake Moomaw, national forests and state wildlife management areas are just a few. There is also the famous Humpback Bridge, Virginia's oldest standing covered bridge, within walking distance. The bridge is the nation's only surviving curved-span covered bridge.

Children are welcome, with proper supervision. Pets accustomed to an environment such as Milton Hall are also welcome.

Millboro
and Warm Springs

Fort Lewis Lodge
$$$$ • River Rd., Millboro
• (540) 925-2314

In 1754, Col. Charles Lewis built a stockade to protect the southern pass of Shenandoah Mountain from Indian raids. This frontier outpost became a vast 3,200-acre farm, situated deep within the Allegheny Mountains. For more than 200 years, this area has remained virtually unchanged. The spectacular scenery and rushing mountain streams are enough to take your breath away. About 18 years ago, John and Caryl Cowden moved from Ohio to manage and operate the farm. Today they are your hosts at this mountain retreat. They have restored the old red-brick manor house and the Lewis grist mill, dating back to 1850, adding a guest lodge.

The large gathering room is framed with massive beams of oak and walnut. The observation tower, which is actually an enclosed stairway leading to the top of an adjoining silo, provides 360-degree views of the grounds; the silo also has three bedrooms. The lodge's 12 bedrooms are decorated with wildlife art and handcrafted walnut, cherry, red oak and butternut furniture, much of it made by local craftsmen from wood cut right on the property. Each guest room has a private bath. Historic hand-hewn log cabins are also available to guests. These romantic hideaways feature queen-size beds, sleeper sofas, large stone fireplaces and rocking chair porches. There are also little extras such as refrigerators and coffee makers. All the cabins have private baths.

Meals are served in the 19th-century grist mill. Two meals are included in the room rate under the Modified American Plan, and all dishes are homemade and scrumptious. A full country breakfast includes freshly baked breads, eggs, sausage, bacon, fruits and French toast with locally made maple syrup. The buffet dinners include fresh vegetables from the farm's garden. You may also have a box lunch prepared to take along with you.

Outdoor activities are abundant here, with more than 2 miles of the meandering Cowpasture River flowing through the valley for swimming, tubing and sport fishing (it's catch-and-release) for smallmouth bass and trout. Several state-stocked trout streams are nearby. Miles of marked trails and old logging roads allow you to stroll along or explore.

Meadow Lane Lodge
$$ • Va. Rt. 39, Warm Springs
• (540) 839-5959

Meadow Lane Lodge is the keystone jewel in the crown of heritage tourism country inns. The estate cannot be seen from the road. You must wind your way up a narrow lane, between meadows and woods, finally emerging at a large clearing — and there it is: a white frame house with green and yellow trim. The stone dairy house and the old icehouse are right out of the days before refrigeration. The deck behind the 1920s barn is an overlook where guests can see a nature preserve home to almost any plant or animal native to Virginia. Two miles of the Jackson River flow through the property; 1.5 miles up the river is a limestone spring, the origin of Meadow Lane's water supply. Peacocks, a pet duck and Japanese silkies (a type of chicken with black skin and white feathers) roam the grounds.

The history of Meadow Lane goes back to Colonial days, when the land was part of the original grant given to Charles Lewis, an early Virginia settler, by King George III. An old log cabin, built in 1750, is visible from the west side of the Jackson River, and a stockade built around the cabin during the French and Indian War eventually became known as Fort Dinwiddie. Today, Philip and Catherine Hirsh are the third generation of Hirshes to own Meadow Lane. In 1995, the inn was featured in a nationally broadcast Tide detergent commercial.

The guest rooms are designed to combine modern comfort and antique grandeur. Choices include double rooms, suites with fireplaces and private cottages. Some rooms have surprising little extras, such as a 19th-century walnut dropleaf table, engravings or a private porch. The Common Room has a fireplace at each end. The Breakfast Room's 1710 oak sideboard is set with a full Southern breakfast each morning.

The Bacova Guild showroom is nearby, as are the Garth Newel Music Center, The Homestead and Lake Moomaw. But many guests just like to stay put and play croquet on the lawn — it's the house specialty. The 1,600-acre expanse allows for hiking, fishing, canoeing and creative loafing. Children older than 6 are welcome. No pets are allowed without prior approval.

Monterey

Highland Inn
$$ • Main St., Monterey
• (540) 468-2143, (888) INN-INVA

Paul Smith is the innkeeper at this cozy spot, nestled in the valley of the land fondly known as "Virginia's Switzerland." This Victorian three-story building, heralded as "The Pride of the Mountains," was built in 1904 to serve the lodging needs of tourists escaping the summer heat of nearby cities. Today it still caters to those looking to escape the hectic life, and upon arrival, its antique charm and surrounding ambiance immediately take guests a step back in time. Eastlake porches with gingerbread trim and rocking chairs for every guest — even a comfy hammock — are so inviting you will want to stay indefinitely.

All 17 guest rooms have private baths and are individually decorated with antiques and collectibles. Guests may choose a standard room (double bed), deluxe room (king-size bed or two beds — one even boasts a private entrance to the second-story porch), a suite (two rooms) or the honeymoon suite (two rooms with a canopy bed and lace trim). Guests may enjoy a game of checkers in the game room or search for the perfect souvenir in the Monterey Treasures gift shop.

A complimentary continental breakfast of fresh breads and muffins (made by Paul), as well as cereal, fresh fruit and hot coffee, is served every morning. Candlelight dining is offered in the Monterey Room on Friday and Saturday nights, while diners looking for a more casual atmosphere may enjoy a drink in the Black Sheep Tavern (every day except Sunday), where Virginia wines are the specialty. Menu items change nightly to ensure freshness, but generally include baked mountain trout, grilled lamb loin chops with a garlic-spearmint demi-glaze, pecan-coated chicken breast and grilled porterhouse steak. Bring your own favorite recipes to be included in the "Highland Inn Guests Cookbook."

Guests flock here in March for the Maple Festival (see our Annual Events and Festivals chapter) and again in October to view the gorgeous fall foliage. George Washington section of the National Forest (see our Recreation chapter) surrounds the county and offers hiking, fishing, birdwatching and unmatched hunting. Antiquing, shopping, golf, swimming and skiing are all nearby.

Mile-high Mountain Lake Resort was made famous by the movie *Dirty Dancing*, **and Bernard's Landing on Smith Mountain Lake was the site of Bill Murray's zany flick** *What About Bob?*

Resorts

The Blue Ridge has an enviable concentration of resorts, the most famous of which are The Homestead and The Greenbrier, an embarrassment of riches within a half-hour's drive of each other. Charlottesville's Boar's Head Inn is legendary for its Old World decor, extensive sports facilities and special events such as its Wine Festival and Merrie Olde England Christmas.

The Blue Ridge resorts have lured visitors from all over the world, including Hollywood. Mile-high Mountain Lake Resort was made famous by the movie *Dirty Dancing*, and Bernard's Landing on Smith Mountain Lake was the site of Bill Murray's zany flick *What About Bob?* Many of the stars of Jodie Foster and Richard Gere's *Sommersby* stayed at The Homestead while filming nearby in Bath County. Of course, you will find other resorts with great amenities that Hollywood has not discovered yet, and you can even see one of the seven natural wonders of the world.

The listing that follows, from north to south and east to west, tells you about the resorts' histories, amenities and what sets each apart. Unless otherwise noted, major credit cards are accepted.

Shenandoah Valley

Bryce Resort
1982 Fairway Dr., Basye
• **(540) 856-2121, (800) 821-1444**

Bryce Resort offers an intimate, family-centered experience. This small resort sits on the western lip of the Shenandoah Valley in the Shenandoah Mountains. On a map you will find it in Shenandoah County near the West Virginia border.

Bryce is especially attractive to golfers and outdoor enthusiasts. Popular as a winter skiing recreation getaway (see our Skiing chapter), it is also unique for its grass skiing. Yes, we said "grass," in which participants glide down the resort's hills on short, tread-like skates during the summer months. Grass skiing requires considerable physical strength and agility and is offered to those 12 and older ($25 gets you a lift ticket, ski rental and instruction).

Bryce's 18-hole golf course is a par 71, 6261-yard mountain layout. Facilities offer a driving range, putting green, club and cart rentals, professional instruction, individual club storage and a fully stocked golf shop. Cart and greens fees range from $30 to $45 depending on the day of the week and the time of day. Adjacent to the entrance of Bryce, a miniature golf course is open daily in the summer and weekends in spring and fall. Admission is $3.50 for adults and $2.50 for kids 12 and younger.

The whole family can enjoy Lake Laura, a 45-acre man-made private lake with its own grassy beach, offering swimming, boating, windsurfing and fishing. Beach admission is $3, free for children younger than 5. Windsurfing instruction is certified and begins on a land-based simulator before you head for the water. The novice package costs $40; board rental alone is $20 an hour. Canoes and paddleboats are also available to rent.

From Memorial Day to Labor Day, the resort's T.J. Stables provides daily one-hour guided trail rides for $20 and pony rides for kids ages 3 to 6 for $5 (closed Wednesdays). The rest of the year, the stables are open on weekends only as weather permits.

Mountain biking and in-line skating are growing sports at Bryce. You can rent Diamond Back mountain bikes and Rollerblades at the ski rental shop for $15 for three hours.

Tennis is another favorite activity at Bryce Resort, which has lighted outdoor courts and a well-stocked pro shop. Court time is $10 an hour; light tokens for night play cost $3 per hour.

Lodging options include studio condominiums, townhouses and chalets, all privately owned and rented through the resort's real estate agencies. The decor can be quite interesting, often reflecting the history of this colorful and friendly valley. Many units are furnished with kitchenettes.

Lodging prices vary according to seasons and accommodations. Condos on the ski slopes, each with a great fireplace, bedroom and bath, rent for $95 nightly (there's a three-night minimum during ski season). During the summer, you can stay all week for $390. Two-bedroom townhouses on the golf course rent for $115 nightly or $700 per week, or you can stay in one of the scattered chalets ranging from $250 to $730.

The resort is on Va. 263, 11 miles west of Interstate 81 off Exit 273. Sky Bryce Airport is a five-minute walk from the resort.

Natural Bridge Resort
U.S. Hwy. 11 S., Natural Bridge
• **(540) 291-2121, (800) 533-1410**

Natural Bridge is a Virginia Historic Landmark and is listed on the National Register of Historic Places. Built in the shadow of one of the seven wonders of the natural world, Natural Bridge Resort isn't posh in the same sense as some of the other great resorts of the Blue Ridge, but it's definitely worth seeing and staying at overnight because of its unique character. Many make the trip just for the unique Easter Sunrise Services as well as for the nightly Dramas of Creation, a spectacular light and sound show. Both are held under the 23-story-high, 90-foot-long limestone arch that gives this resort its name.

The story of Natural Bridge, a 36,000-ton structure carved by Mother Nature millions of years ago, is a historian's delight. Early on, the bridge was worshipped by the Monocan Indians. Thomas Jefferson was the first American to own the bridge, which he purchased from King George III in 1774. George Washington surveyed the bridge as a lad. In fact, you can still see the spot where he carved his initials. Colonists made bullets by dropping molten lead off the bridge into the cold creek water below. During the War of 1812, soldiers mined the nearby saltpeter cave to make explosives.

Additional attractions here are the massive caverns — some folks say they're haunted, with ghostly voices still heard as late as 1988 — and the Natural Bridge Wax Museum, which houses life-like figures including a gallery of American presidents. A huge gift shop sells such tasty fare as homemade fudge and candy made to look like rocks; it also carries typical souvenirs and fine gifts. For lunch or a snack, a deli in the gift shop has several fast-food stations and is open during fall and summer.

For recreation, the tennis courts, indoor heated swimming pool and 18-hole Mini-link Indoor Golf Course are popular features. Each attraction costs $8 per adult and $4 per child (ages 6 to 15); special combination rates are $7.50 per adult and $3.50 per child to visit the wax museum and caverns.

Accommodations feature 180 rooms in the refurbished Natural Bridge Inn and Conference Center and cozy Stonewall Inn, where the food is both delicious and plentiful, and the service is first-class. Nightly room rates are $29 to $69 weekdays and $39 to $89 Saturday and Sunday, depending on the season. A three-room suite is $125 weekdays and $150 Saturday and Sunday. Personal checks are accepted for advance deposits only.

Natural Bridge is 13 miles from the Blue Ridge Parkway, minutes off I-81 (Exits 175 and 180), 12 miles from Interstate 64, 39 miles north of Roanoke and just minutes from Downtown Historic Lexington. Traveling in either direction on I-81, you can't miss it.

East of the Blue Ridge

The Boar's Head Inn, A Country Resort
U.S. Hwy. 250 W., Charlottesville
• **(804) 296-2181, (800) 476-1988**

The Boar's Head Inn, on a 53-acre country

Photo: Wintergreen Resort

Large resorts offer many extra amenities, including pools, golf courses and recreational activities.

estate, has 173 guest rooms and suites, 12 meeting rooms (including a grand ballroom), two dining rooms, three outdoor swimming pools, specialty shops and a modern sports club. Amenities include massages, facials, aerobics, a complete fitness center and 20 tennis courts, two platform tennis and four squash courts. The 18-hole championship Birdwood golf course is adjacent to the resort. Hiking, fishing, horseback riding and sightseeing are available nearby.

The resort hosts an October Virginia wine festival that includes a grand six-course dinner with live entertainment. At Christmas, staff drapes the inn in pine boughs, ribbons and sparkling lights and serves hot cider by the fireside. The winter holiday season is busy with horse-drawn carriage rides, crafts and food demonstrations, puppet and magic shows, Virginia cloggers, wine tastings, lectures and concerts, including one on Christmas Eve.

The inn's architectural style recalls an earlier era, but its facilities offer all the modern amenities. A major renovation project has added a sense of luxury to the already elegant rooms. The new look will include four poster beds, oak and walnut accents, opulent window treatments and Italian Anichini linens. In giving the old and new feel, the antique reproduction desks will be modernized with data port outlets. Even the bathroom sinks are being replaced with washstand cabinets to give guests more storage space.

The Boar's Head has a top-ranked tennis program, and the hot-air balloon flights over the breathtaking countryside are not to be missed.

The history of the inn, which takes its name from the Old English symbol for festive hospitality, is a colorful one. Three decades ago the inn's founder, John B. Rogan, moved an 1834 mill to its present spot from near Thomas Jefferson's historic Monticello. The mill, with its massive hand-hewn beams, is the heart of the resort and home to The Old Mill Room, one of Virginia's highest-rated restaurants. Regional delicacies and gracious service are the hallmarks here (see our Restaurants chapter).

Casual family dining is the specialty at Racquets Restaurant in the Sports Club. The menu focuses on heart-healthy entrees and light fare.

Public rooms are furnished with English antiques, and guest rooms feature custom-designed period reproductions. The manicured grounds are showcases for traditional Southern flowers and greenery.

Daily rates run from $159 to $199, but Boar's Head also offers seasonal packages, ranging from the traditional bed and breakfast to the whimsical bed, breakfast and ballooning. Other packages feature golf and tennis and historic sites such as Monticello and tours of local wineries.

From I-64, take Exit 118B to U.S. 250 W. The inn is 1.5 miles on the left.

Keswick Hall
701 Club Dr., Keswick
• **(804) 979-3440, (800) ASHLEY-1**

For the ultimate in pampered living, Keswick lives up to its promise of "a fine estate drawing on the best traditions of English County Life." Owner Sir Bernard Ashley, cofounder of the internationally known Laura Ashley fashion company and founder of Ashley House Inc., has added a wonderful new chapter to the long and fascinating history of Keswick. Broad Oak, a pre-Civil War mansion, once stood here, replaced by Villa Crawford in 1912. Twice the location of the Virginia State Open Golf Tournament, it became a country club in the 1940s. Now it is the 600-acre Keswick Estate, a magnificent backdrop for Keswick Hall, a country house hotel, Keswick Club, an exclusive golf and leisure club, and attractive residences (see our chapter on Real Estate and Retirement).

At Keswick Hall, Sir Bernard wants visitors to feel as if they were house guests in an old English house with a butler and a maid. Phyllis Koch, the Ashley House interior designer, has made each of the 48 rooms so distinctive that no two are alike. They are decorated with antiques from Ashley's collection and, of course, Laura Ashley fabrics in the familiar flowery prints and more sophisticated styles. All the suites have themes, and the inn emphasizes details such as pure cotton sheets, fluffy bathrobes and other creature comforts.

Public rooms include a drawing room, the Crawford Lounge for English afternoon tea with scones and jam, the inviting morning room with fireplace and piano and the snooker room for an after-dinner game. Informal meetings or functions are often held in these comfortable,

naturally lighted rooms. The Keswick Board Room is perfect for private meetings.

Dining is a special aspect of the Keswick Hall experience. Dishes combine classic European recipes and the best of modern cooking methods, using fresh produce from the community and the estate's own herb garden. Complementing the fine food are wines from an extensive cellar and the view of vine-covered terraces and lovely gardens. Dinner is $58 per person.

The Keswick Club, the centerpiece of which is an 18-hole Arnold Palmer-designed golf course, is a private club. However, guests at Keswick Hall are granted temporary house memberships that enable them to use the golf course, tennis courts and clubhouse facilities at an extra charge. Within the clubhouse is an indoor/outdoor pool, exercise room, Jacuzzi, steam room and sauna. A new Olympic-size outdoor pool with children's facilities was recently added. The dining room and clubhouse, an Old English tavern, serves authentic ale, and light meals are served à la carte in the European-style Bistro overlooking gardens and the course.

Lodging rates range from $195 for a room to $645 for a master suite, which includes a full country house breakfast and traditional afternoon tea. Weekly rates vary depending on the season. Call and ask about their golf, tennis and "Jazz Under the Stars" packages.

From Charlottesville, go east on Bypass U.S. 250, east on Va. 22 and right onto Va. 744 until you reach a stop sign. Keswick is directly ahead.

Wintergreen
Va. Rt. 664, Wintergreen
• **(804) 325-2200, (800) 325-2200**

Wintergreen, an 11,000-acre resort along the spine of the Blue Ridge, enjoys a reputation as one of the most environmentally conscious facilities in the Blue Ridge and has won awards for its conservation efforts.

Wintergreen consistently ranks among the Top 50 Favorite Family Resorts named by *Better Homes and Gardens* and the Top 10 Family Mountain Resorts chosen by *Family Circle* magazine. In 1998, the Society of American Travel Writers gave the resort and the Winter-

Photo: Wintergreen Resort

Four Blue Ridge resorts offer skiing and other winter activities,
in addition to warm-weather pursuits.

green Nature Foundation its Phoenix Award for environmental achievement.

Tennis magazine has named Wintergreen one of its Top 50 Tennis Resorts for the past 12 years, and in 1996 *Golf Digest* rated the resort's Stoney Creek course the second-best in Virginia and the 34th-best resort course in the country. While Stoney Creek occupies the valley, giving guests the unique opportunity to play golf and ski on the same day (see our Skiing chapter), the resort's mountaintop Devils Knob Course has the highest elevation in the state.

Tennis buffs have their pick of 20 composition clay and five all-weather hard-surface courts. Court rates range from $10 to $16 for singles, and tennis clinics, workouts and ball-machine rentals are available. Registered guests can play for free midweek, and reduced rates are available on weekends.

Swimmers can take advantage of an indoor pool at the Wintergarden Spa and five outdoor pools. Water enthusiasts also have 20-acre Lake Monocan for swimming and canoeing. Mountain bikes can be rented by the hour for $9 ($30 daily), and a 30-mile network of marked hiking/biking trails offer spectacular views of the Blue Ridge and the Shenandoah Valley. The resort puts out a handy trail map (which can be purchased at the Outdoor Center for $5) that details information about each trail, including intensity levels.

Wintergreen offers seasonal horseback riding, pony rides and wagon rides. (See our Recreation chapter.) After all the activity, you might want to relax in a hot tub at the Wintergarden, which has indoor and outdoor pools, exercise room and saunas. Admission is free for resort guests.

Special events, such as the Spring Wildflower Symposium, are featured throughout the year and include holiday celebrations such as an Appalachian Mountain Christmas, with horse-drawn carriage rides and candlelight dinners.

In summer, Camp Wintergreen offers a variety of children's programs for toddlers to teens. The program introduces youngsters to the beauty and wildlife of the Blue Ridge. Babysitting services are also available.

Wintergreen has been undergoing $15 million in capital improvements, including a new golf clubhouse. The already nationally ranked Stoney Creek golf course opened nine more holes designed by Rees Jones, while the Wintergreen Golf Academy added new facilities and equipment. A new putting green, chipping green and expanded practice tee are just a few of the changes at the Academy. Ask about the portable computerized digital video, designed to help golfers improve their strokes right on the practice tee.

The Stoney Creek clubhouse was also expanded to include a larger pro shop, a fitness facility and a new look for the Cafe Verandah.

The new Tennis Pavilion at Devils Knob has turned tennis into a year-round sport at Wintergreen. The complex features three indoor Deco-Turf courts, locker room facilities, a larger clubhouse and pro shop, and indoor viewing deck, stadium seating and a lounge for the Wintergreen Tennis Academy. The new changes could be among the reasons *Tennis Week* placed Wintergreen in its Gold List of the Top 100 tennis resorts in the world.

Six restaurants provide varied dining choices, from a cappuccino bar in the Gristmill lobby of the recently renovated Mountain Inn to gourmet fare in the elegant Copper Mine. Seasonal restaurants are open according to golf and skiing schedules, and the resort has three lounges, one with live entertainment. (See the Wintergreen listing in our Restaurants chapter.)

Wintergreen has 300 rental homes and condominiums, ranging from studio-size to seven-bedroom. Most have fireplaces and fully equipped kitchens, and many have spectacular views. Daily rates range from $115 to $655 depending on size and season. Weekly rates run $89 to $506 per night. Various packages are available, including golf, tennis, family, sports and romantic getaways.

The resort is 32 miles southwest of Charlottesville, bordering the Blue Ridge Parkway. From I-81 take U.S. 250 E. to Va. 151 S. to Va. 664. Then just follow the signs to Wintergreen.

Bernard's Landing
775 Ashmeade Rd., Moneta
• **(540) 721-8870, (800) 572-2048**

The word "tranquility" springs to mind when describing Bernard's Landing. This serene place is the only resort on the Blue Ridge's most popular lake, Smith Mountain Lake, although a rash of motels are planned. The largest lake in Virginia with 500 miles of shoreline, it has become a watery playground for people from all over the East Coast. This resort's majestic view of Smith Mountain and magnificent fiery orange sunsets sinking into the crystal clear water have drawn artists and photographers from around the world.

Bernard's Landing was built in 1981 on what was once a prosperous farm worked by slaves of the Parker family. The family home, an original brick plantation house, still stands at the center of Bernard's activity, as a clubhouse. Appalachian Power (now American Electric Power) filled the lake in 1966, submersing 22,000 acres and making many Franklin, Bedford and Pittsylvania county farmers instantly wealthy. Bernard's was built on the widest part of the lake and is one of few places where you can view the full expanse of the 7-mile-long Smith Mountain Lake.

For its 1990 production of *What About Bob?*, Walt Disney Productions searched the entire United States for a lake resort with just the right combination of qualities to portray

INSIDERS' TIP

In 1992 the Pentagon confirmed that a secret, 112,000-square-foot, bombproof underground bunker large enough to house the president, his cabinet and Congress, was constructed beneath The Greenbrier resort during the Cold War. In July 1995, the lease between the government and the resort was terminated, and The Greenbrier was given control of the bunker. Currently, the 30-ton doors of the bomb shelter are open and guests can see it during regularly scheduled tours.

the fictitious Lake Winnipesaukee, New Hampshire, an out-of-the-way vacation spot that still had luxurious amenities. A staff of 100, including actors Bill Murray and Richard Dreyfus, stayed nearly six months for the filming of the popular comedy. Many of the guests were so impressed with the lake's pristine beauty they stayed even longer. That's because Bernard's has become known as the place where people come to get away from it all. Although friendly, Franklin County residents grant you privacy, whether you're sailing, swimming or just absorbing the silence.

The well-planned waterfront community sits on its own peninsula and is designed to take advantage of its natural surroundings, mainly mountains reflected in the sparkling lake. As you drive up, the resort impresses you with its huge expanse of lawn that separates the buildings. There are sandy beaches for swimming and sunbathing and an Olympic-size swimming pool. The clubhouse features a health club with exercise equipment, indoor handball courts and six tennis courts. Clearly, the draw is the water. But if you want more than a splendid view, there's plenty to keep you entertained.

Smith Mountain is an angler's paradise. Nationally known for its striped bass fishing, the lake boasts the state's record striper, weighing 45 pounds (this record seems to get broken every year). If you're into fishing (see the Fishing section in our Recreation chapter), Bernard's operates a marina and rents fishing, pontoon and ski boats right at the dock. The Virginia Commission of Games and Inland Fisheries manages an adjoining 5,000 acres for hunting enthusiasts.

The resort's restaurant, The Landing, serves gourmet meals and is the most popular spot on the lake for fine dining. The Landing, with its nautical theme, packs many a picnic lunch for boaters and consistently earns *Roanoker* magazine's "Best Restaurant on the Lake" award. Probably every resident at the lake has enjoyed Bernard's sumptuous Sunday brunch, truly worth a tasting trip. The savory omelets are the most requested item. Prices are reasonable for great sandwiches or evening entrees at the dockside restaurant.

Bernard's rental facilities include one- to three-level townhouses, single-level homes and one- to three-bedroom condos. They feature fireplaces, decks, skylights and cathedral ceilings. Nightly rentals in peak season range from $120 for a one-bedroom condo to $260 for a three-bedroom town house.

It is a 45-minute drive from either Roanoke or Lynchburg to Bernard's Landing. From Roanoke, drive south on U.S. Highway 220 to a left on Va. Route 697 at Wirtz. Follow this road to its intersection with Va. Route 122, and turn left. Continue for approximately 7 miles, then turn right on Va. Route 616 at Central Fidelity Bank. Drive 7 miles, then turn left on Va. Route 940, which will dead-end at Bernard's. From Lynchburg, take U.S. Highway 460 W. to Va. Route 122 and drive about 25 miles to Va. Route 616. Turn left and follow above directions to Bernard's.

Alleghany Highlands

The Homestead Resort
U.S. Hwy. 220, Hot Springs
• (540) 839-7785, (800) 838-1766

The Homestead, one of the South's major resorts, is grandly situated on 15,000 acres in the Allegheny Mountains. It has been one of America's highest-rated resorts for more than 30 years, yet it's as homey as its name suggests and famous for its afternoon teas in its long, wide lobby. Washington and Jefferson strolled these grounds, and Lord and Lady Astor honeymooned here. The most unusual "guests" of all began their visit December 29, 1941, three weeks after the attack on Pearl Harbor, when 363 Japanese diplomats, along with many Japanese citizens in the United States, were placed at The Homestead for a three-month internment.

The Homestead has been pampering guests since the late 1700s, when the aristocracy of Virginia went to the mountains instead of enduring the lowland heat with the common folk. In those days, it was fashionable in high society to move from one mountain spring to another en masse. Originally valued for medicinal purposes by Native Americans, the springs around The Homestead became centers of social activity.

Hot Springs, where The Homestead has stood for more than a century, was one of the

Photo: Wintergreen Resort

Staying at a resort makes it easier to get on some of
the best golf courses in the Blue Ridge.

most prominent springs in Virginia. The lineage of The Homestead as a resort and its tradition as a place to "take the waters" can be traced back to 1766. The spa of today was built in 1892, the dream of M.E. Ingalls, great-great-grandfather of the previous owner, who sold it in 1993 to Club Resorts Inc. of Dallas, Texas. Throughout 1994 to 1998, vast improvements were made to the infrastructure, physical structure and grounds. Previous years' renovations have concentrated on restoring and modernizing the infrastructure while the recent changes are more visible. You will immediately notice a new brick paved front drive and extensive resort-wide landscaping. The emphasis on guest service has increased. The most visible improvements include the addition of an exterior grand staircase connecting the Great Hall to the renovated casino and surrounding expansive lawns. New is the Jefferson Parlor, featuring an octagonal floor plan, custom furniture and a series of specially commissioned murals depicting the history of Hot Springs. It also houses the Homestead's first-rate Business Center and Travel Agency and serves as a dramatic entrance to the resort's most historic and elegant meeting rooms. The Tower Library renovation showcases more than two centuries of American resort history, including a fascinating photo exhibit of famous resort visitors. The library is impressive, complemented by an awesome bay window as well as mahogany paneling. Equally impressive is the Wine Room. With its 11-foot ceilings, the room's redwood walls and racks can hold 3,900 bottles. A highlight is the 400-piece, 35-square-foot stained-glass window, reflecting Italian-tile floors.

Restoration of The Homestead's 106-year-old European-style spa features a state-of-the-art beauty salon, offering facials, manicures, pedicures and traditional salon services. Many spa and beauty products are now Homestead signature items available for purchase. A new fitness center, weight room and aerobics rooms also have been added to the spa. Even the reception area is new, featuring vaulted ceilings, hardwood floors and beautifully detailed woodwork. The Homestead's spring-fed indoor pool, constructed in 1903, has also undergone extensive restoration. The two covered pools at Warm Springs and the sheltered

The Sport of Kings

Some may argue that golf has been the crown jewel at The Homestead for more than 75 years, but in 1998 the real "sport of kings" arrived at the Bath County resort.

That's when Duane Zobrist Jr. brought his falcons, hawks and owls to The Homestead, making it one of the first resorts in Virginia and only the third on the East Coast to offer falconry.

Close-up

"There is one resort in Vermont, the Equinox, and one in West Virginia, The Greenbrier, that has such falconry programs," said Zobrist, founder of the Falconry and Raptor Education Foundation. Zobrist's West Virginia-based non-profit foundation also runs the program at the Greenbrier.

"Right now we are offering beginner lessons," he said. "We take out small groups and show them our hawks, owls and falcons and explain all about them. We talk for about 30 minutes, then we do flying demonstrations, where the birds fly free and *usually* return to the falconer," he added with a good natured laugh.

"Then we put a glove on each of the students, put a falcon on their fist and take their picture. People have just been enthralled."

And educated, too.

Falconry traces its beginning to China nearly 4,000 years ago. Back then, hunting game with trained birds was an effective way to put meat on the table. But as the centuries passed by — and the gun arrived — falconry became much less widespread.

— continued on next page

Photo: The Homestead

Duane Zobrist Jr. and Mike O'Dell offer classes in the ancient and revered sport of falconry.

Although sportsmen marveled at watching their winged companions take flight, hunting was no longer the primary goal. Training falcons to respond to command became known as sport for noblemen. It was, indeed, called the "sport of kings," most likely because only royalty was allowed to own many of the rare birds.

Even in modern times just finding information on the sport can be hard to come by.

"I became interested in falconry when I was 9 years old," Zobrist said. "That was because my dad always wanted to do it, but he could never find any books on falconry here. Whenever he would travel abroad, he would bring back a book. That's why he always wanted to go to England."

Like father like son. The young Zobrist even trained in England.

"I was going to be a lawyer," he said. "I had finished up my undergraduate work in Utah at BYU, but I really had a desire to work with falcons. I wanted to find out if there was some way to turn my avocation into a vocation."

He will be the first to tell you that he opened his foundation on "a wing and a prayer."

"I had no clue how it would do," the Homestead's director of falconry said. "But now through small groups — of five to six people in a group — we are educating 6,000 people a year, plus we also go into schools, too."

Homestead guests may sign up to get the royal treatment. Classes are available from April 1 through Dec. 31. Call (800) 838-1766 for more information.

---

drinking spring have been preserved in their natural condition. Eleanor Roosevelt's special chair is still at the women's pool.

Legions of visitors swear by the springs' curative properties. The magnificent, ornate indoor pool is fed continuously by waters of the Octagon Pool, which can be viewed in front of the spa. The most popular spot of the architectural award-winning pool renovation is the point at which the natural mineral waters come rushing out. With a new striped cabana and restored interior, the new pool decor could be a scene from *Casablanca*. The spa has two outdoor pools as well.

Since 1994, golf, which is king at this resort, also has received attention. The Homestead course has undergone more than $1 million in improvements, overseen by architect Rees Jones, and The Golf Advantage School also opened. Throughout the renovation, championship golf play continues to be available on three 18-hole courses, one of which has been the site of the U.S. Amateur and boasts the oldest first tee in continuous use in the United States. *Golf Digest* and *Golf* magazine rank the Cascades Course among the top in the nation. John D. Rockefeller used to spread his wealth here by tossing shiny dimes into the pool of water in back of the first tee for the caddies to fight over. President William Taft nearly created a scandal by playing the "frivolous" game of golf on the Fourth of July holiday here at the turn of the century. Golf carts are included in the rates, which range from $88 to $118 for the champion course. A nice touch after the game is a visit to Sam Snead's, where the food is presented in a casual atmosphere amidst Snead's memorabilia (including 35 framed golf balls that are among Snead's holes in one).

Additional undertakings include the addition of three new specialty shops and renovations of corridors and foyers in the South Wing and 86 guest rooms in the famed "Tower." The children's playground and clubhouse, KidsClub on Cottage Row, also have been updated. Tennis is also superb at The Homestead, with eight courts, including all-weather ones. Singles are $10 per person, and doubles are $7.50 per person, per hour.

Fishing is another favorite sport (permits cost $20), as are skeet, trap and sporting clays at The Shooting Club, where a round of 25 birds costs $22. Hiking and horseback riding are other popular activities, and a carriage ride along scenic trails in a fringe-topped surrey is a pleasant option. Indoor entertainment includes bowling and movies.

Winter brings a whole new round of sports with skiing (see our Skiing chapter) and ice-skating. Half-day skating sessions cost $5.50 weekends and holidays. Some winter weekends are priced for the budget-minded pocketbook. Bring the kids!

Accommodations at The Homestead are classic. Nearly 200 guest rooms in the East Wing and 100 rooms in the Main Building have been renovated. Five hundred and twenty-one spacious guest rooms fill the sweeping Colonial-style building topped by a modern highrise clock tower. Inside are white Corinthian columns, high-ceiling rooms and turn-of-the-century crystal chandeliers. Daily room rates in high season, April through October, are $314 to $388 for double occupancy; in value seasons, $240 to $338. Children's rates are available. Prices include breakfast and dinner in one of 10 dining outlets.

From I-81, take Mt. Crawford/Va. 257 Exit W. to Va. Route 42, then go south to Millboro Springs. Take Va. Route 39 W. to Warm Springs and U.S. 220 S. to Hot Springs. Ground service is available from Roanoke Regional Airport. Ingalls Field, Hot Springs, is nearby, serving private and corporate aircraft.

The Greenbrier
300 W. Main St. (U.S. Hwy. 60),
White Sulphur Springs, W.Va.
• (304) 536-1110, (800) 624-6070

This monumental top-rated National Historic Landmark is set in 6,500 acres of breathtaking mountain scenery. In 1995, NBC's *Today Show* chose The Greenbrier as the showcase for a host of ultra-special gifts. A visit to the Christmas shops at the resort is worth a trip in itself during the holiday season.

The Greenbrier's history, its charm and its star-studded guest list have enchanted people for two centuries. The resort has hosted world summits and celebrities in the midst of the little town of White Sulphur Springs. You never know what famous person you'll see strolling the resort's grounds. In 1981, when the U.S. government wanted the ultimate in rest and recreation for the former Iranian hostages, it chose The Greenbrier.

The resort's history has been nothing short of incredible, beginning in the 18th century when aristocratic Southerners came to drink the mineral waters, stroll and chat while avoiding the summer sun. Twice during wartime, the U.S. government took over the resort as a hospital. The first occupancy was in 1861, when the Confederacy claimed it as its military headquarters. The Greenbrier came perilously close to total destruction during the 1864 occupation by Union troops, when it was ordered burned. Only a plea from a U.S. senator saved the resort. Later Gen. Robert E. Lee used it as his summer home. During World War II, former guest Gen. George Marshall (for whom the museum in nearby Lexington, Virginia, is named) turned The Greenbrier into a 2,200-bed hospital and called it Ashford General. According to locals, many a wounded soldier, upon awakening, thought he had died and gone to heaven.

After the war, again a resort, The Greenbrier was refurbished and redecorated. Its interior designer used more than 30 miles of carpeting, 45,000 yards of fabric, 40,000 gallons of paint, 15,000 rolls of wallpaper and 34,567 individual decorative and furniture items on the job. The outstanding results stand today.

Staff outnumber the guests, with 1,600 employees and a 1,200-guest capacity. Accommodations and facilities include 518 guest rooms, 121 cottages, 33 suites, 30 meeting rooms, three championship golf courses, 20 tennis courts and a $7 million spa. To ensure you are adequately fed, 110 chefs (no kidding — 110!) serve you elegant dinners in The Greenbrier's acclaimed combination of classical, continental and American cuisine, in five settings. The list of culinary awards is seemingly endless. The Greenbrier's own cooking school, La Varenne, is highly praised.

Next door is the world-famous Greenbrier Clinic, a diagnostic center with a team of 10 physicians where CEOs can have a checkup in the morning and play golf in the afternoon on a course designed by Jack Nicklaus. A 1996 article in *The Wall Street Journal* stated that 5,000 people each year spend time at the health clinic — at $600 a night.

Golf gets a lot of attention at this resort. *Condé Nast Traveler* readers rate Greenbrier golf best in the continental United States. Sam Snead, The Greenbrier's golf pro emeritus, played his best game ever here. The Sam Snead Festival held its 24th annual event during 1999. You might see him motoring around

Photo: Wintergreen Resort

Suites provide an extra room for entertaining friends.

the course in his golf cart, which is specially fitted with a platform for his dog. Bob Hope, Bing Crosby, Arnold Palmer, former president Dwight Eisenhower and the Prince of Wales have played here. The Greenbrier was the 1997 site of the First Annual Bimbo Coles Celebrity Charity Golf Invitational. Bimbo was a star athlete at Greenbrier East High School and Virginia Tech. He now plays for the NBA Golden State Warriors. Golf is complimentary for guests during December, January and February; fees range from $45 in the off-season to $95 in peak season. The golf cart is extra at $36.

For the tennis set, 15 outdoor Har-Tru courts and five indoor Dynaturf courts await play. The fee for doubles is $42 per hour indoors. Other recreational possibilities are croquet, indoor and outdoor swimming, bowling, billiards, trout fishing, hiking, horseback riding, carriage rides, mountain biking, falconry, whitewater rafting, cross-country skiing, trap and skeet shooting and shopping in a large gallery of wonderful stores. For a touch of heaven, give yourself a gift of one (or more) of the 18 treatments at the new spa and have your own nutritionist and exercise trainer design an individual program for you. A five-day spa package costs $2,500.

Rates are based on a Modified American Plan, which includes breakfast and dinner in the main dining room. Nowhere else is The Greenbrier's Southern heritage more apparent than at the breakfast table, with fresh brook trout, hominy grits, Virginia ham and bacon, corn bread and biscuits. Dinner is truly an event. A string ensemble provides music, and dinner is served amid candlelight and chandeliers. The vichyssoise is a favorite of Greenbrier regulars, as is its famous peaches and cream for dessert. In 1989 The Greenbrier delivered 10,000 of its famous handmade chocolate truffles for former president George Bush's inaugural dinner.

The Greenbrier's accommodations are available in a variety of packages, including golf, tennis and family. Its tariff schedule ranges from $154 to $245 per person nightly November through March on the Modified American plan to $194 to $313 per person April to October. Special weekends include the La Varenne Signature Series of cooking (tuition: $2,000). Easter features a morning service atop Kate's Mountain, a favorite of the locals for its breathtaking beauty. The resort offers other weekend packages for Mother's Day and Fourth of July ($463 a couple).

You don't have to stay overnight to enjoy The Greenbrier. You can have dessert and beverage for two for about $25. Have a snack and then tour the Presidents' Cottage Museum or visit the Miniature Shop, a little dollhouse that sells only miniatures. You also may want to tour The Creative Arts Colony, more than a dozen arts and crafts shops featuring original work and unique handcrafted gifts. The Carleton Varney Gift Gallery, new in 1997, is a wonderland of distinctive gifts from Baccarat, Nardi of Venice and Tiffany & Co. You can snack and shop and then save your dollars for the total experience!

In 1995 The Greenbrier was named West Virginia Corporation of the Year in recognition of the resort's long tradition of leadership in educational and other programs to benefit West Virginians.

To get there, take the White Sulphur Springs exit off I-64. Turn right onto W.V. Route 60 and travel 2 miles; the entrance is on the left. The Amtrak Station is across the street. Accessible by air from Greenbrier Valley Airport and Roanoke Regional Airport, the resort is 1½ hours away by limousine.

New River Valley

Mountain Lake Resort
Mountain Lake • (540) 951-1819, (800) 346-3334

Let Mountain Lake Resort "Put You On Top of the World," as the slogan goes. And they mean it! If you saw the majestic sandstone lodge at the top of the mountains in the movie, *Dirty Dancing*, you saw Mountain Lake Resort. The beauty of this grand old hotel was forever

captured in 1986 after Vestron Pictures, searching for a gentle, romantic 1960s-era resort, saw an ad for Mountain Lake in an airline magazine. The rest is history. Everyone wants to know where Patrick Swayze slept when he stayed here, and the room stays booked.

But there's far more history than that to Mountain Lake, one of only two natural freshwater lakes in Virginia and one of the highest natural lakes in the East. It was formed when a rock slide dammed the north end of the valley, creating a 100-foot-deep lake fed by underground streams that rarely allow the water temperature to rise above 72 degrees.

The first report of a pleasure resort here was in 1857, and the first hotel was wooden. In the early 1930s William Lewis Moody of Galveston, Texas, purchased the property and built the present huge hotel from native stone. His elder daughter, Mary, who died in 1986, loved to sit under the great stone fireplace in the lobby, which is still inscribed with "House of Moody." Mary ensured her beloved Mountain Lake, where she stayed each summer, would keep its 2,600 acres of natural paradise in perpetuity by establishing a foundation in her name.

When you sit in a rocking chair on the great stone front porch overlooking the lake, you can't help but feel refreshed and renewed at this haven for body and spirit. Summer offers the opportunity to relax in cool mountain air, and in the autumn, few fall foliage vistas can compare to Mountain Lake's. The air is rare, and so is the experience!

Open May 1 to November 28 only, the resort offers a variety of boating, fishing (guests must furnish own equipment), hiking, biking, tennis, swimming and lawn games. A health club is equipped with a whirlpool and sauna. And the Recreation Barn offers games, snacks and several shops featuring Appalachian arts

and gifts. Mountain Lake celebrates the fall season with an Oktoberfest every weekend from mid-September through October.

In 1997, Mountain Lake opened its 20 miles of hiking trails to mountain bikes. Adult and children's bikes, helmets and child seats are available to rent.

Two national cycling events took place at the resort in 1998. The eight-mile Misty Mountain Hop in late September was the highest mountain bike race on the East Coast and the largest sanctioned in Virginia, while the two-day Mountains of Misery Challenge drew more than 200 cyclists from around the country in late May.

Also new to Mountain Lake are guided deer hunts. The area has been closed to hunting for more than a half a century, but the Wilderness Conservancy at Mountain Lake developed this program in 1998 with the cooperation of the Virginia Department of Game & Inland Fisheries as a part of an effort to manage Virginia's growing deer population.

Three-day guided hunts offer resort guests packages patterned after traditional deer-hunting lodges in the Southeast. Overnight accommodations in the Chestnut Lodge, meals, two guided hunts a day and deer processing are included in the packages, which start at $875. The hunts will be offered through November

28 and space is limited to 15 participants. Call (540) 626-5139 for reservations.

Fishing in the spring-fed lake for bass, trout and sunfish is available for guests through November 1.

The food is consistently superb in the dining room, where guests lucky enough to get window tables will see a panorama of bluebirds, snowbirds and redbirds scolding spoiled squirrels, who are awaiting handouts from guests. Neat attire is requested for evening meals, which are a gourmet's delight. Brunch is $14.95, and dinner is $19.95 per person. Many Virginia Tech parents make the 17-mile trip just for the meal, which can be booked with a reservation.

Accommodations include the 50-room hotel in which room amenities may include a fireplace and a whirlpool, the 16-room Chestnut Lodge nestled among the trees, and, in the summer, 13 wooden cottages with fireplaces. Prices for couples range from $115 nightly to $195 in the lodge, with a small additional charge for each child. Most guests stay on the Modified American Plan, which includes lodging, breakfast, dinner and use of all facilities and equipment. Personal checks are accepted.

To get there, take the U.S. 460 Bypass around Blacksburg to Va. Route 700. Follow this road for 7 steep, winding, scenic country miles straight up to Mountain Lake.

Southwest Virginia

Doe Run Lodge Resort and Conference Center
Mile 189, Blue Ridge Pkwy., Fancy Gap
• **(540) 398-2212, (800) 325-6189**

Just across the border of Floyd County, in Patrick County, Doe Run Lodge Resort and Conference Center and its High Country Restaurant are nestled in the most beautiful part of the Blue Ridge Parkway. With Groundhog Mountain as the midpoint on this road of pastoral beauty, your senses will be overwhelmed by what this year-round resort has to offer. If the scenery just isn't enough for you, live entertainment is held weekends April through October, and outdoor festivals are frequent.

Doe Run Lodge Resort and Conference Center was built to fit the beauty of the environment. The chalets are constructed of wood beams and stone, and floor-to-ceiling windows allow magnificent views. Each large suite has a fireplace, two bedrooms, two full baths and a living/dining area. The chalets and villas are furnished and have complete kitchens. Millpond Hideaway, designed for executives and honeymooners, has a whirlpool tub, a luxury shower and steam cabinet, a full-suite stereo and TV, a fireplace and an enclosed garage.

The historic Log Cabin dates back to 1865 and was moved to the lodge from another site. The exterior remains primitive, but the interior features a queen-size bed, a whirlpool tub, a shower, a natural stone fireplace and a TV/VCR. The Executive Suite is a modern chalet with a whirlpool tub, a luxury shower and steam cabinet and full-suite stereo and a TV. The area also boasts personal homes and building sites available for sale.

High Country Restaurant offers regional fare such as country ham steak and fresh rainbow trout from its own stocked pond. Continental cuisine features fresh seafood, aged beef and pasta dishes. The restaurant will pack picnic lunches too.

Nearby attractions include Groundhog Mountain Overlook, a championship 18-hole golf course, Mabry Mill, Pucketts Cabin, Chateau Morrisette Winery, Lover's Leap Park, Nancy's Fudge and Old Mayberry Store and Mineral Shop.

In-season rates range from $109 to $224 per night. Call for off-season rate specials, which are a real bargain. Group, corporate and government rates also are discounted.

The most exciting happenings in regional dining have involved innovative chefs preparing Virginia-grown food in wonderful and surprising new ways.

Restaurants

It's not a question of "Where can I eat?" It's more along the lines of "What type of food do I feel like eating today?" Blue Ridge dining has come a long way since the days of country ham, fried chicken, peanut soup and apple pie. Sure, plenty of old-fashioned restaurants still offer hearty, conventional Southern fare. But the most exciting happenings in regional dining have involved innovative chefs preparing Virginia-grown food in wonderful and surprising new ways.

It's fusion food we're seeing on the plates at upscale restaurants. This cuisine combines local ingredients with international influences to create an array of gastronomical treats. Of course, not everything works, but when the experiments of our regional chefs do succeed, it's pure eating pleasure.

Many of these cutting-edge restaurants tend to be concentrated in the Charlottesville area and the northern foothills region of the Blue Ridge. Others are in remote rural areas such as Eagle's Nest in Crows or Chateau Morrisette in Floyd County. Highly acclaimed dining spots include the internationally renowned Inn at Little Washington and the Bleu Rock Inn, both just an hour from the "big" Washington beltway; Prince Michel Restaurant in Leon; Clifton — The Country Inn and Memory and Company in Charlottesville; and the Joshua Wilton House in Harrisonburg. These just scratch the surface, though.

A large number of chefs rely primarily on local products for their dishes. Virginia farm-raised trout is commonly pan-fried or smoked; Chesapeake Bay blue crab, both hard-shell and soft-shell, is served in season; and locally raised rabbit, veal, venison and poultry are prepared in a variety of ways. Virginia-grown fruits and vegetables are too numerous to name, but most notable are the region's peaches and apples. And, of course, one of the fastest growing areas of Virginia's agriculture is grapes, which are made into dozens of varieties of wines at the state's 52 wineries.

Many restaurants have taken advantage of the gorgeous countryside and the historic buildings to create beautiful and unique settings for their diners. Peaks of Otter Lodge in Bedford, Chateau Morrisette in Floyd County and the historic restaurants inside Shenandoah National Park offer magnificent tableside views.

Some of the region's finest restaurants are tucked away inside beautifully renovated country inns, including L'Auberge Provencale in White Post and Prospect Hill in Trevilians. Others sit smack in the middle of quaint downtown districts such as Charlottesville's downtown mall, Roanoke's downtown district and Lexington's historic streets.

Because of the vastness of the region we have attempted to cover in this guide, we were unable to list every good restaurant in every city, town and village. We hope your favorite is included. But if it is not, drop us a line with your suggestions. We update this book every year and may add your favorite to this list.

Most restaurants accept major credit cards for payment; we indicate those that do not.

Price Code

Readers may be able to challenge our pricing guidelines for the restaurants listed below. Personal choices and menu changes will prove us wrong in some cases. Still, we created this code to provide you with a basic idea of the cost of entrees for two not including desserts, alcoholic beverages, sales tax or gratuity.

$	Less than $20
$$	$21 to $35
$$$	$36 to $50
$$$$	More than $51

You'll notice this chapter does not include restaurants in the Shenandoah National Park; those are listed in our chapter on the Blue

Ridge Parkway and Skyline Drive. However, you'll find just about every kind of national chain represented throughout the Blue Ridge.

The restaurants profiled in this guide are listed alphabetically under regional sections, then by counties. As in other chapters of the book, we begin with the northern stretch of the Blue Ridge and work our way south, zigzagging east and west over the mountains and Shenandoah Valley.

Bon appetit!

www.insiders.com

See this and many other **Insiders' Guide®** destinations online.

Visit us today!

Shenandoah Valley

Frederick County

Cafe Sofia
$$$ • 2900 Valley Ave., Winchester • (540) 667-2950

This lovely restaurant serves the only Bulgarian food in the Shenandoah Valley and some terrific seafood dishes as well. One of its most popular dishes is pierogies — seafood or chicken sauteed with vegetables, wrapped in a puff pastry with cheese and baked. Of course, you'll also find staples such as homemade moussaka, goulash, baklava and homemade Bulgarian yogurt. The restaurant is filled with old world touches. An antique woodstove heats the entrance in the winter months, while family needlework decorates the walls. Special decorating touches include handmade tablecloths, hand-embroidered menus, framed embroidery pieces and an extensive doll collection. It is open for lunch and dinner Tuesday through Friday and dinner only on Saturday. You will need reservations on Fridays and Saturdays.

Cork Street Tavern
$$ • 8 W. Cork St., Winchester • (540) 667-3777

This historic building, dating back to the 1830s, sits on one of the oldest streets in Winchester. In fact, Lord Fairfax and his agent gave the street its name in 1759. The building itself survived heavy shelling from three battles during the Civil War. As you might expect, the original tavern still has that rustic atmosphere. However, you can take a quick leap into modern day in the new section that was added in 1995. It's a sports lover's dream with six televisions. Be warned: you might want to wear your Washington Redskins jersey. Cork Street Tavern is extremely popular with the locals for its barbecued ribs, but you can also choose broiled trout, swordfish steak and venison pot pie. Beverages range from Virginia wines to microbrews. The Tavern is open daily for lunch and dinner.

Tucano's Restaurant
$$ • 12 Braddock St., Winchester • (540) 722-4557

Once you step through the door at Tucano's, you leave behind the historic district of Old Town Winchester and enter a little corner of Brazil. This is cozy fine dining with a "neat casual" dress code. Candlelight adds a romantic atmosphere for what the family-run business calls Brazilian international cuisine. Among the favorites on the varied menu is the Mouqueca Baina, white fish, shrimp, clams and mussels in a special Brazilian sauce. Veal Bellaboca, the Italian favorite, includes stuffed veal served with potatoes and fresh vegetables. The locals keep coming back because the staff makes an effort to remember the customers and their favorite meals. It's open for lunch and dinner Monday through Friday with dinner only on Saturday. Reservations are accepted.

Violino Ristorante Italiano
$$ • 181 N. Loudoun St., Winchester • (540) 667-8006

Marcella and Chef Franco Stocco serve classical dishes of Northern Italy in this romantic restaurant in downtown Winchester. Choose a traditional favorite or sample some of the chef's creations. The lasagna with fresh smoked salmon is a favorite. The menu offers about 15 to 20 homemade pastas, plus there are more than 20 vegetarian items on the menu. On Fridays and Saturdays, musicians from Shenandoah University add to the romantic atmosphere with a little classical music. You also may eat outside on the patio. Violino serves lunch and dinner Monday through Saturday. Reservations are strongly suggested.

Wayside Inn
$$ • 7783 Main St., Middletown
• (540) 869-1797

Opened in 1797, this elegantly restored 18th-century inn has been in operation for more than 200 years. Excellent regional American cuisine is served in seven antique-filled dining rooms, one of which is the old slave kitchen. Special features on the menu are peanut soup, spoon bread and country ham, a variety of game and seafood dishes and homemade desserts. Unless you have a reservation, expect to wait on weekends for a table, as this is a favorite with locals. Wayside Inn is open daily for all meals and serves a hearty country breakfast.

Clarke County

L'Auberge Provencale
$$$$ • U.S. Hwy. 340, 1 mile south of U.S. Hwy. 50, White Post
• (540) 837-1375

Perhaps Virginia's most celebrated French restaurant, L'Auberge is but an hour's drive west of Washington, D.C., in the gentle hill country of the northern Shenandoah Valley. Expect superb authentic cuisine fashioned from the Provence region of France. The five-course prix fixe menu costs $57 a person and has plenty of options for each course. An excellent wine selection, including vintages from local vineyards, adds to the upscale experience. The restaurant serves breakfast to inn guests daily and dinner Wednesday through Sunday. Reservations are needed for weekends.

Shenandoah County

Hotel Strasburg
$$ • 213 S. Holliday St., Strasburg
• (540) 465-9191

Victoriana abounds in this wonderfully restored and converted 1895 hotel. The tables, chairs and paintings are supplied through the nearby Strasburg Emporium; every item is for sale so the furnishings are always changing. The restaurant has a strong following in the northern Shenandoah Valley and is known for its generous portions, courteous service and delicious meals. Dinner specialties include a mixed grill, Veal Guisseppe, filet mignon, various pasta dishes plus one of the favorites, a Cajun grilled swordfish. Attire ranges from casual to coat and tie. (One recent evening, a bride still wearing her gown was seated near a couple dressed in shorts.) Reservations are recommended on the weekends. The restaurant is open for lunch and dinner on weekdays, breakfast buffet, lunch and dinner on Saturday and breakfast buffet and brunch on Sunday. (See our Hotels and Motels chapter.)

The Spring House
$$ • 325 S. Main St., Woodstock
• (540) 459-4755

Word has it that an underground spring used to be on this property, and town folk came to fetch spring water from the lady who lived here. Folks still come here for refreshment, though the spring is now closed. Breakfast, lunch and dinner are served daily. Specialty entrees include Eleanor's Delight, a creamy seafood mixture on an open kaiser roll, with tomato and cheese. Dinners come with homemade walnut rolls and honey butter and a trip to a huge salad bar.

Southern Kitchen
$ • Congress St. on U.S. Hwy. 11, New Market • (540) 740-3514

If you're hungry for traditional Southern food, nothing fancy, this is the place. Established in 1955, Southern Kitchen is known for its peanut soup, fried chicken and barbecued ribs of beef. It's open daily for breakfast, lunch and dinner.

Warren County

Main Street Mill
$ • 500 E. Main St., Front Royal
• (540) 636-3123

You can't miss the barn-like building just across from the visitor center, but what's inside will surprise you. Artist Patricia Windrow's trompe l'oeil murals of farm animals and Civil War scenes are disturbingly realistic. The simple lunch and dinner meals, ranging from chicken to blackened hamburger, are well-prepared and nicely presented. Main Street Mill is open for lunch and dinner daily. Dress is casual.

Page County

The Brookside Restaurant
$ • 2978 U.S. Hwy. 211 E., Luray
• (540) 743-5698, (800) 299-2655

The fresh air and natural setting in Luray will give you a hearty appetite, which will serve you well for the daily all-you-can-eat homestyle lunch and dinner buffets at The Brookside. On the weekend and holiday Mondays, you can get the breakfast buffet. The salad bar includes goodies you might remember from Grandma's kitchen, and the melt-in-your-mouth breads, pastries and desserts are made fresh daily. The Brookside is open daily for breakfast, lunch and dinner from mid-January through mid-December. See our Hotels and Motels chapter for information on Brookside's luxury cabins.

Parkhurst Restaurant
$$$ • 2547 U.S. Hwy. 211 W., Luray
• (540) 743-6009

This place is popular with golfers who play Luray's courses in spring, summer and fall. The atmosphere is casual, although tables are set with cloth napkins, crystal, china and candles. The menu has considerable variety with items such as escargot, tomato-shrimp bisque, fettuccine with shellfish, Veal Oscar and a curry dish. Every meal comes with a wonderful relish tray, served with a fresh, light garden dip, homemade breads and more. The Parkhurst is open daily for dinner. Reservations are recommended.

Rockingham County

Blue Stone Inn
$$ • U.S. Hwy. 11, Lacey Spring
• (540) 434-0535

The professors from James Madison University love this place and are willing to stand in long lines for a table, so plan your visit early or late. Specialties are tender steaks and fresh farm-raised fish such as Lacey Spring trout. The atmosphere is rustic tavern-style with deer heads mounted on the wall — some credited to owner Mike Olschofka, whose grandfather bought the restaurant in 1949. It's open Tuesday through Saturday for dinner.

El Charro
$$ • 1570 E. Market St., Harrisonburg
• (540) 564-0386

This is a good Mexican restaurant with locations also in Dale City and Fredericksburg. The menu is standard Mexican fare: burritos, enchiladas and tacos. Be sure to try the delicious homemade chips and salsa, available in three degrees of heat. Service is fast, and the staff is courteous. El Charro is open every day for lunch and dinner.

Joshua Wilton House
$ (cafe), $$$$ (fine dining)
• 412 S. Main St., Harrisonburg
• (540) 434-4464

Pricey but worth it, the restaurant inside this beautifully restored Victorian home serves the most exquisite food in town and is easily one of the state's finest dining spots. It's hard to believe the place was once a fraternity house for James Madison University students. Craig and Roberta Moore gutted the whole building and started over, creating a beautiful, romantic place to have dinner — and spend the night.

The wine list of more than 240 selections includes a variety of American and imported wines at very reasonable prices. The food is

Photo: Clifton — The Country Inn

Many of the Blue Ridge's most highly acclaimed dining spots are found in country inns.

eclectic regional with emphasis on fresh produce and local products. In the fine dining section, the fixed-price, five-course dinner costs $36 a person. Menus change regularly, but specialties include a smoked salmon appetizer on apple potato cake topped with dill crème fraîche and salmon roe and a tasty crème brûlée. Reservations are required for fine dining and are accepted in the cafe for parties of six or more. While the same chef prepares meals for both fine dining and the cafe, prices are lower in the cafe because meals are served à la carte. Dinner is served Tuesday through Saturday. (See our Bed and Breakfasts and Country Inns chapter for information on an overnight stay here.)

L'Italia Restaurant and Lounge
$$ • 815 E. Market St., Harrisonburg
• (540) 433-0961

Brothers Emilio and Gervasio Amato own these restaurants right off Interstate 81 in Harrisonburg and Staunton. The pasta and sauces are all homemade, and many of the entrees are prepared with a light touch for fat- and cholesterol-watchers. One of the outstand-ing offerings is gnocci, tiny dumplings filled with ricotta cheese and topped with a tomato and meat sauce. L'Italia's Staunton restaurant is at 23 E. Beverley Street. Lunch and dinner are served Tuesday through Sunday.

Pano's
$ • 3190 S. Main St., Harrisonburg
• (540) 434-2367

Within the French provincial exterior is a casual, wood-paneled family restaurant offer-ing 60 entrees at lunch and 78 at dinner. Meals are nicely done, and the prices are right too. Pano's is open daily for breakfast, lunch and dinner. It has breakfast and lunch buffets on Sunday. Choose from pasta, seafood, poul-try, beef and salads, prepared in simple Ameri-can style. Seniors receive a 10 percent dis-count.

The Village Inn
$ • Va. Rt. 1, Box 76, 1.5 miles south of Harrisonburg • (540) 434-7355

The dining room at this small, family-owned motel serves simple, delicious American-style meals prepared by Mennonite cooks. The Inn has a gorgeous view of the mountains and is one of the highest rated restaurants in the area. The Inn serves breakfast and dinner every day except Sunday, and buffets are offered most meals. Alcohol is not sold, but you may bring your own.

Huyard's Country Kitchen
$, no credit cards • Va. Rt. 42, Dayton • (540) 879-2613

Owner David Huyard and his cooks serve up ham, beef, chicken and vegetables buffet-style. The food is homemade and very tasty. The "kitchen" is in the Dayton Farmer's Market, where you can shop for kitchen items, lace, fudge, antiques, fresh cheese, homemade breads and much more. Huyard's opens at 9 AM Thursday, Friday and Saturday and closes in the early evening, except Fridays when it stays open until 8 PM.

Augusta County

Capt'n Sam's Landing
$$ • 2323 W. Main St., Waynesboro • (540) 943-3416

If you love seafood, come dine with the captain. Surrounded by a nautical decor, you can indulge in fish, crab, oysters, lobster, scallops and clams prepared in a variety of ways. The steak and chicken dishes are good too. All entrees are served with a trip to the salad bar (or one hot vegetable) and a choice of french fries, baked potato or rice. Don't miss the weeklong Shrimp Feast that's held one week every month — all the shrimp you can eat is prepared nine ways. The adjacent pub serves fresh popcorn and a special menu. Capt'n Sam's is open for dinner every day except Sunday. Reservations are accepted for parties of six or more.

Scotto's Italian Restaurant and Pizzeria
$ • 1412 W. Broad St., Waynesboro • (540) 942-8715

Join in the casual family atmosphere at Scotto's, where the owners take great pride in their Italian heritage and in the art of true Southern Italian cooking. The homemade dishes, including chicken and veal Parmesan and

gourmet pizzas, are all reasonably priced and available for takeout or delivery. Lunch and dinner are served every day.

South River, An American Grill
$$ • 2910 W. Main St., Waynesboro • (540) 942-5567

Open seven days a week for lunch and dinner, South River offers 20 feet of vegetarian salad bar (with homemade salads and fresh fruit) and a varied menu. Favorites include prime rib and shrimp, St. Louis-style barbecued ribs, hand-patted burgers, homemade soups and an inexpensive children's menu. South River's atmosphere is pure Blue Ridge, with large picture windows, lots of plants, a fireplace and a full-size hang glider suspended from the ceiling. The restaurant also offers banquet facilities for as many as 100 and off-premises catering.

Weasie's Kitchen
$, no credit cards • 130 E. Broad St., Waynesboro • (540) 943-0500

The down-home cooking and laid-back setting draw many regulars and tourists to this former Dairy Queen. Opened by Mary Eloise Roberts — known as Weasie — more than a decade ago, this dining spot finds success in Weasie's basic Southern recipes. Weasie passed away, and the restaurant is now owned by Joyce and Blair Campbell. Breakfast is the big draw, with homemade biscuits and gravy the most requested items. Desserts, all homemade, are also popular. Breakfast, lunch and dinner are served daily, and Friday and Saturday it's open 24 hours.

The Beverley
$ • 12 E. Beverley St., Staunton • (540) 886-4317

This restaurant has been around for 27 years and is known for its luscious homemade pies and generous afternoon teas. It's a small, family-owned place where you can also get real whipped potatoes and country ham on homemade bread. Traditional English tea is served from 3 to 5 PM on Wednesday and Friday and includes sandwiches, cake, cheese, fruit, scones and other pastries. The Beverley is open Monday through Friday from 7 AM to 7 PM and Saturday from 7 AM to 5 PM.

The Depot Grille
$$ • Train Station, 42 Middlebrook Ave., Staunton • (540) 885-7332

This popular dining spot in the old freight depot portion of the restored C & O train station has a 50-foot antique oak bar. On the menu are fresh fish, crab cakes, seafood combination platters, salads and a "lite bites" selection. Daily specials, tasty desserts and a children's menu round out the choices. The Depot Grille has a full bar, including a selection of beers and wines from around the world. The restaurant is open for lunch and dinner daily.

Edelweiss German Restaurant
$ • U.S. Hwys. 11 and 340 N., Staunton • (540) 337-1203

Edelweiss offers authentic German cuisine in the rustic setting of a log cabin. German-born owner and chef Ingrid Moore uses many of her mother's recipes to prepare specialties such as sauerbraten, roast beef that is brine-marinated for up to five days and schnitzel, thinly cut, tender breaded pork. If you are new to German food, ask for the sampler. You can try five different items to see what you really like. Fresh vegetables are served family style. For dessert the house specialty is *schwarzwalder kirschtorte* (Black Forest cake). If you enjoy beer with your meal, you'll find a nice selection of imported light and dark beers. Attire is casual, and a half-price children's menu is available. The restaurant is open daily for lunch and dinner.

McCormick's Pub and Restaurant
$$ • 41 N. Augusta St., Staunton • (540) 885-3111

This historic building on the corner of North Augusta and Frederick streets is at the crossroads of downtown Staunton, so it's not unusual to find a mixture of families, business types and young couples. Once used as the town's YMCA, the building has housed this popular eatery since 1981. The name pays homage to Cyrus McCormick, the 22-year-old inventor who revolutionized agriculture with his mechanical reaper. In fact, the chestnut wood found throughout the restaurant is from his family's estate, just 30 miles south of Staunton. You may dress casually for the American fare in one of two fine dining rooms or come prepared to watch the day's big game on one of two televisions in the more contemporary full-service bar. A second floor is reserved for catered affairs. ShenanArts, a local theatrical company, has hosted several dinner-theater productions here.

Angus beef and steaks are among the menu favorites with the local crowd, while McCormick's also serves up seafood and chicken dishes. Everything is made from scratch and specials are offered daily. Dinner is served every day from 5 PM to midnight. Reservations are recommended for the dining rooms, while it's first come, first served in the pub. With many of the downtown businesses closing in the early evening, it's not difficult to find nearby parking.

Pampered Palate Cafe
$ • 28 E. Beverley St., Staunton • (540) 886-9463

This is another great watering hole smack in the middle of the most interesting shopping area downtown. Here you'll find gourmet deli sandwiches such as roast beef and Brie on French bread, bagels, stuffed potatoes, quiche, iced strawberry tea and cappuccino served with luscious Italian desserts. You can get a continental breakfast too. The place sells a lot of wines, including the best Virginia ones, as well as gourmet coffees, gift baskets and imported candies. Wine tastings are offered too. The cafe is open Monday through Saturday from 9 AM to 5:30 PM.

The Pullman Restaurant
$$ • Train Station, 36 Middlebrook Ave., Staunton • (540) 885-6612

Step back in time as you enter this authentically restored turn-of-the-century train station that includes a Victorian ice-cream parlor. The

---

INSIDERS' TIP

If atmosphere is as important to you as cuisine, the Blue Ridge has many historic inns that serve meals.

building is furnished with antique fixtures and advertising signs. The menu features updated versions of old-time railroad dining car fare, including a variety of steaks, seafood, sandwiches and lighter meals. A lunch soup-and-salad bar is offered six days a week, along with an elegant Sunday brunch buffet. You can sit along the train station concourse and watch the trains pass (Amtrak stops Wednesday, Friday and Sunday), and be sure to visit the elegantly appointed bar room. The Pullman is open for lunch and dinner daily.

Rowe's Family Restaurant and Bakery

$ • Richmond Ave., Staunton
• (540) 886-1833

They opt for fresh cut flowers instead of linen tablecloths. Oh, it may not be fancy, but if you're in the mood for some down-home country cooking, Rowe's is the place to be. Locals are willing to wait in line — sometimes as long as 45 minutes — to savor the hospitality, homemade food and bargain prices. Baked pork tenderloin with homemade mashed potatoes has been a local favorite since the Rowes opened the restaurant 53 years ago. Williard Rowe came up with the idea in 1947, but the customers really started lining up after his wife, Mildred, came down to show him how to cook. Mildred Rowe, 86, still comes down to greet hungry travelers for a couple of hours each day. It's a friendly atmosphere and most of the people who work there have been there for years. Of course, all the food is homemade: ham, cubed steak, chicken, even the pies are made from scratch, including everything from apple pie to coconut cream. There is not a full bar, but beer and wine are available. Located right off I-81 at Exit 222, Rowe's draws a lot of business from tourists following the New York to Florida corridor, but there is ample parking close by. Rowe's is open daily from 7 AM to 8 PM. Reservations are allowed if you have a party of six or more.

Wright's Dairy Rite

$ • 346 Greenville Ave., Staunton
• (540) 886-0435

This is the place where world-famous musicians the Statler Brothers hung out while they were growing up. The country quartet even mention the restaurant in "Carry Me Back," although some might not know that "Hamburger Dan's" is a reference to this still popular local eatery. Just drive up to the curbside speakers, place your order and a server brings your meal out to your car. You can also eat indoors or call for take out, but the unique curbside service will carry you back to the 1950s. The Wright family opened Dairy Rite 42 years ago with two ice cream machines. Today you can satisfy that craving for a juicy burger and fries with fresh, homemade food that's quick and tasty. Dairy Rite makes its own onion rings everyday, as well as barbecue and slaw. With their homemade vegetable soup, "nothing comes out of a can"; they make just enough chicken, egg and tuna salad to serve for the day. Also popular for 35 years now. Or, try chicken, shrimp or a foot-long hotdog. Dessert is the hardest part — you have to choose from a plethora of ice cream treats including sundaes, cones and floats. An Insider favorite is the milkshakes, which come in nine flavors, including raspberry, cherry, butterscotch and banana. (The fruit shakes have bits of real fruit.) And — shades of the '50s — you can even get a malted shake. This is a place you can drop in for lunch, dinner or a late snack. Dairy Rite is open from 10 AM to 10 PM Sunday through Thursday and 10 AM to 11 PM on Fridays and Saturdays. Who knows, you might even see one of the Statler Brothers. They still drop in from time to time.

Lexington and Rockbridge County

Harbs' Bistro

$ • 19 W. Washington St., Lexington
• (540) 464-1900

The sophisticated atmosphere, excellent food and fine service at this bistro and gallery make it a popular lunch spot and evening watering hole for students and other locals (see our Nightlife chapter). Harbs' is the quintessential bistro with an intimate, unpretentious club atmosphere. The walls are covered with art, and the restroom signs are modeled after a bull and the Statue of Liberty. During the

Photo: Lexington Visitors Bureau

Buffalo Springs Herb Farm in Rockbridge County is an extraordinary 18th-century stone house and garden open for herbal teas, luncheons and tours.

day, choose from the menu of hearty sandwiches, salads, desserts and other specials. The hero sandwiches are served on freshly baked loaves. The dinner menu changes frequently, but you can count on fresh, delicious bistro fare. Reservations aren't necessary, but you may wish to call ahead for prompt lunchtime service. It is open for breakfast, lunch and dinner Tuesday through Saturday and breakfast and lunch on Sunday and Monday.

The Inn at Union Run
$-$$ • 325 Union Run Rd.,
Va. Rt. 674, Lexington
• (540) 463-9715, (800) 528-6466

The Inn at Union Run sits on 11 beautiful acres outside of Lexington, and dining here is a real treat. The romantic dining room seats 22 to 25 guests at antique tables with candlelight. The ambiance is truly memorable, enhanced by gorgeous furniture and such interesting items as Toby mugs dating back to 1755 and 16th-century wine glasses.

The restaurant serves American regional cuisine created with local herbs and vegetables when available. The chef has a flair for Italian, Greek and American regional dishes. The Union Run Bourbon Street Steak was selected for third place honors recently in the B&B Country Inn Beef Cook-off sponsored by the Virginia Cattleman's Association.

The inn is famous for its breakfasts, highlighted by such specialties as gingerbread pancakes and eggs Benedict Union Run style. The dinner menu, just as desirable, begins with the inn's own country pâté — unique because it is made with pork. Chicken Oscar, Black Angus strips and filet mignon with a zesty sauce or blackened are all superb choices. There are numerous seafood dishes available as well, prepared northern Italian–style. Desserts include homemade sorbets, Bailey's Irish Cream mousse and a mystery chocolate/pecan pie that has guests calling weeks in advance to make reservations with it in mind. A full wine list is available; the Inn has been awarded the Three-Cluster Governor's award for Outstanding Sales and Promotion of Virginia wines.

The inn serves guests and the public Tuesday through Saturday throughout the year. Special functions, such as group luncheons, weddings, wine tastings and murder mystery dinners are available by special arrangement. (Also see our chapter on Bed and Breakfasts and Country Inns.)

Southern Inn
$$ • 37 S. Main St., Lexington
• (540) 463-3612

This charming historical restaurant has been a tradition in Lexington since the 1930s.

The Inn, in the heart of downtown, specializes in Virginia wines. Visit this family restaurant for traditional Southern-style cooking, sandwiches or Greek and Italian dishes. Southern Inn is open seven days a week for lunch and dinner.

Willson-Walker House
$$$ • 30 N. Main St., Lexington
• (540) 463-3020

The beautiful architecture of this 176-year-old Greek-Revival townhouse sets the scene for an elegant dinner or brunch. But you are welcome whether you're wearing coat and tie or shorts and loafers. The interior, recently remodeled, has period antique furniture and artwork. Opening off of the foyer are the two main dining rooms, each with a fireplace with a faux-marble mantel and two portraits, c.1840. The menu of creative American cuisine affirms why the Willson-Walker House was named "One of the Best in Virginia" by *Travel & Leisure* magazine in 1997. It lists such tempting dishes as Virginia Lacey Springs' sauteed trout paired with local Rockbridge Chardonnay, veal medallions, poultry, pasta, pork and beef. Desserts are scrumptious and include homemade Bailey's Irish Cream cheesecake and frozen chocolate-and-peanut butter mousse. There's also a children's menu. Second-floor banquet rooms are available for private parties. You can also dine outdoors on the veranda from May to October. The restaurant serves lunch and dinner Tuesday through Saturday. Lunch is not served on Saturday from January to March. Reservations are recommended for lunch and dinner.

Maple Hall
$$$$ • U.S. Hwy. 11 N., off I-81 at Exit 195, 6 miles outside of Lexington
• (540) 463-4666

Fine dining in an elegant atmosphere describes the Maple Hall experience. This antebellum mansion is full of gorgeous antiques and restorations. The seasonal menu allows for the freshest and most delicious cuisine

imaginable. Some favorites include filet mignon, sesame chicken and pasta à la carbonara. It's open seven days a week for dinner only. Reservations are requested.

Natural Bridge Restaurants
The Colonial Dining Room
$$ • U.S. Hwy. 11 S., Natural Bridge
• (540) 291-2121

An oasis of good family food, the Natural Bridge Village restaurants are as popular with the locals as they are with visitors at this gigantic tourist attraction. Known for its Friday night seafood buffet and Sunday brunch, The Colonial Dining Room serves quality food daily, including breakfast seven days a week. The menu offers a variety of Virginia fare (since this is a major tourism spot) such as red-eye gravy and grits, and there are other all-American favorites such as banana pudding and fried chicken. You'll feel comfortable dressed in after-church garb or Bermuda shorts. Waitresses, some with more than 30 years' experience, offer service that is second to none. (See our Resorts chapter.)

Roanoke Valley

Roanoke

Alexander's
$$$ • 105 S. Jefferson St., Roanoke
• (540) 982-6983

Excellent food and renowned service make this restaurant well worth the trip into downtown Roanoke. It always has been considered one of Roanoke's finest throughout its evolutions of location and hours. The menu goes through several revisions each year, and you are always sure to find a delicious selection. Bread and desserts are freshly made. Don't miss the chocolate amaretto cake or the chocolate fudge walnut pie. Alexander's beef dishes are especially popular, as is its seasonal mixed grill of pork, lamb and chicken. Grilled tuna, pan-seared salmon and veal Alexander are other favorites. Whatever you find on the menu will be gourmet, made of only the finest, freshest ingredients and served with flair. Dinner reservations are recommended. Lunch is served Wednesday only; dinner is served Tuesday through Saturday. The restaurant is also open for private parties seven days a week.

Awful Arthur's Seafood Company
$$ • 108 Campbell Ave., Roanoke
• (540) 344-2997

Seafood lovers, cast your anchor at Awful Arthur's on the historic Roanoke City Market. The decor is nautical and basic, just like the food. The main attraction is the large raw bar serving an assortment of items you'd expect on a real visit to the ocean. The Captain's Sampler offers a bit of it all, with oysters, shrimp, clams, crab legs, crawfish and mussels. Fresh is the only language spoken by the chef, and you can expect everything to taste like it just arrived from the dock. Appetizers include the standard oysters Rockefeller and fried calamari. Also expect surprises such as seafood pizza. In addition to the array of seafood, you'll find other dinner favorites such as New York sirloin steak. If dinner isn't on your agenda, at lunch you can get a terrific sandwich or fresh fish of the day. A full wine list specializes in Virginia varieties with California and Oregon and pricey French vintages represented too. A nice selection of microbrews is available at Awful Arthur's as well. Awful Arthur's is open for lunch and dinner daily. Reservations are welcome.

Billy's Ritz
$$ • 102 Salem Ave. S.E., Roanoke
• (540) 342-3937

Housed in a century-old hotel building with a screen door that slams when you enter, this traditional American grill is just one block from Roanoke's historic Farmer's Market. You can join the happy-hour crowd at an oak bar and dine in casual elegance in any one of four unique rooms amid a collection of art and antiques — or have your meal in the open-air courtyard. Although known for its great steaks, variety of salads, grilled fish and teriyaki dishes,

Billy's Ritz excels at a variety of other cuisine as well. The Pasta Raphael is sure to please, and don't miss the prime rib on weekends. Billy's Western chili is probably the most popular in the area. Wine is available by the bottle or glass from an extensive list. The star of the dessert list is ice cream cake. Dinner is served every night. Reservations are recommended for large groups.

Carlos Brazilian International Cuisine
$$ • 312 Market St., Roanoke
• (540) 345-7661

Hundreds of faithful feijao preto (black bean) lovers come from all over the Shenandoah Valley to partake of the magic that is Carlos Amaral's international cuisine. When you ask the Roanoke Valley's leading gourmands to list their favorite restaurants, Carlos will always make the list. Carlos's time spent working in 28 different restaurants has manifested itself in a menu quite unlike anything even lovers of Brazilian food have seen. What Carlos does with simple fare, such as black beans and angel hair pasta spiced with international flavor, packs the place for both lunch and dinner on Roanoke's bustling City Market. Carlos is open for lunch and dinner Monday through Saturday.

Charcoal Steak House
$$$ • 5225 Williamson Rd., Roanoke
• (540) 366-3710

Voted Roanoke's Best Restaurant Overall and Best Steak by *Roanoker Magazine* readers, Charcoal Steak House has been a Roanoke institution for fine dining since 1957. The taste-tempting menu lists more than 50 savory entrees including prime rib, charcoaled choice steaks, poultry, veal, fresh seafood, rock lobster tail and authentic Greek dishes. In addition to individual dining, the restaurant is popular for large family and business gatherings since many consider the Charcoal Steak House staff part of the family. In the evening, live entertainment is offered in the main dining room. Lunch and dinner are served Monday through Friday, and dinner only is served on Saturday. Reservations are definitely recommended on weekends at this Roanoke institution.

Corned Beef & Co.

$$ • 107 S. Jefferson St., Roanoke
• (540) 342-3354

Probably the most successful deli operation in town, Corned Beef & Co.'s hearty fare, served up by three former fraternity brothers who graduated from Roanoke College, is known both for its great food and downtown atmosphere. Now it's also known as the only restaurant in town with a brick pizza oven in its new expansion. A sports bar also has been added. The name says it all — don't look for anything pretentious here. What you will find is good, basic deli sandwiches (Jazzbo, All-American Combo) served quickly in a first-class atmosphere of marble and mahogany. It's open for lunch and dinner Monday through Saturday, 'til 2 AM Thursday through Saturday for the wee-small-hours crowd. (See our Nightlife chapter.)

El Rodeo Mexican Restaurant

$ • 4301 Brambleton Ave., Roanoke
• (540) 772-2927
$ • 4017 Williamson Rd., Roanoke
• (540) 362-7919
$ • 260 Wildwood Rd., Salem
• (540) 387-4045

This popular family restaurant will whisk you away to Mexico with its south-of-the-border decor and ethnic foods. Ingredients are printed on the menu for those unfamiliar with Mexican food. Expect the cuisine — fajitas, taquitos Mexicanos, La Chicana, enchiladas de polo (chicken enchiladas) and more — to be on the mild side. Select from vegetarian, children's and lunch-only menus as well. The chef is always willing to accommodate your substitutions. El Rodeo is open for lunch and dinner every day.

The Library

$$$$ • 3117 Franklin Rd., Roanoke
• (540) 985-0811

The Library, one of the most elegant and exclusive dining establishments in the Roanoke Valley, is rated among the top seven restaurants in Virginia. It also is a recipient of the Dirona designation, one of 568 restaurants in North America to bear this distinction of quality. The decor is that of a well-stocked library, adding to the memorable dining experience. French cuisine, served by candlelight, includes such classics as veal Princess, veal with shrimp and crab and a Bearnaise sauce; and English Dover sole with spaghetti squash, beurre blanc and almonds. Desserts include mousse for traditional tastes and fresh fruit Romanoff for something a bit different to close an exquisite meal. A full wine cellar features French, Virginia and California wines. Dinner is served Tuesday through Saturday. Reservations are recommended.

Lily's

$$ • At the Roanoke Airport Marriott, 2801 Hershberger Rd., Roanoke
• (540) 563-9300

This casual restaurant in the Roanoke Marriott features an array of steaks, seafood and pasta dishes as well as popular buffets and children's menus. On Sunday, Lily's offers a Bountiful Brunch with sumptuous items too numerous to mention. It's open every day, and reservations are suggested.

Luigi's

$$$ • 3301 Brambleton Ave., Roanoke
• (540) 989-6277

This Italian gourmet restaurant was established after the tradition of Mama Leone's restaurant in New York City. Naturally, the spaghetti is wonderful; coupled with the other pasta selections, it's an Italian gourmet's delight. Some of the special treats include veal Luigi's, shrimp scampi and the popular Cappuccino L'Amore, a blend of gin, brandy, rum, creme de cacao and Galliano liquors topped with a cinnamon stick, clove and whipped cream. Homesick Northerners can get real Italian desserts such as cannoli and spumoni. Luigi's is definitely a cut above any other Italian restaurant in town, both for food and service. Each dish is prepared by your

---

INSIDERS' TIP

If you like a dish, ask for a recipe or list of ingredients. Many chefs are happy to share their secrets.

special order, so count on a leisurely dinner with a lot of attentive service. Dinner is served daily. Luigi's is open until midnight Friday and Saturday.

Macado's

$ • 120 Church Ave., Roanoke
• (540) 342-7231
$ • 3247 Electric Rd., Roanoke
• (540) 776-9884
$ • 209 E. Main St., Salem
• (540) 387-2686

At Macado's the decor is as interesting as the food, and both keep the restaurant packed with a younger crowd. A big hot-air balloon hangs from the ceiling, and pictures and keepsakes from local or nationally known bands decorate the walls. You'll see the Three Stooges riding in an airplane, a section of a real classic car on the wall, old toys, posters, nostalgic collectibles and antiques. The extensive menu could take your entire lunch hour to read. It specializes in a delicious array of hot and cold deli sandwiches; the salads and chili are exceptional too. Macado's has several locations in the Roanoke and New River valleys including Blacksburg, Radford, Salem and two in Roanoke. Macado's is open daily for breakfast, lunch and dinner and stays open until the wee hours.

Mediterranean Italian & Continental Cuisine

$$ • 127 Campbell Ave. S.E., Roanoke
• (540) 345-5668

A Turkish touch by owner Ihsan Demirci has turned this out-of-the-way place on the Roanoke City Market into one of the busiest restaurants on the block. Pasta is the main attraction — it's delicious, plentiful and inexpensive. Lovers of fettuccine Alfredo and stuffed shells will be delighted to see their favorite Italian dishes prepared just right. Health-food lovers also are treated to an array of pasta dishes with fresh vegetables, seafood and chicken. The chicken Saltimboca, a tender breast of chicken with proscuitto and mozzarella cheese smothered in a light sauce of Marsala wine and onions, makes watching your weight bearable in this den of delights. Veal dishes are another attraction, especially the veal Frances, tempting filets of veal dipped in a light egg batter and pan-browned in white wine and lemon sauce. Spaghetti is the side dish, of course. The Mediterranean is open Monday through Friday for lunch and dinner; dinner only is served on Saturday.

Mill Mountain Coffee and Tea

$ • 112 Campbell Ave. S.E., Roanoke
• (540) 342-9404
$ • 4710 Starkey Rd., S.E., Roanoke
• (540) 989-5282
$ • 17 E. Main St., Salem
• (540) 389-7549

Success breeds success, and nowhere is this more true than with restaurants. Although Mill Mountain Coffee and Tea really isn't a full-service restaurant, it is one of the most popular hangouts in the Roanoke Valley (see our Nightlife chapter). All locations offer a delicious variety of baked goods, and the Salem and Starkey Road locations offer lunch menus that include soups, salads and sandwiches. They copy the famous Seattle coffeehouse concept — a laid-back atmosphere for mingling — which Roanoke Valley restaurant patrons have enthusiastically embraced. The draw, of course, is the multitude of coffee, tea and Italian soda flavors readily available for refill. Another appealing aspect is having a quiet place to go to talk or conduct business. All you have to do is place your order, sit down and enjoy the company. All coffees are freshly roasted on the premises.

Nawab Indian Cuisine

$$ • 118-A Campbell Ave., Roanoke
• (540) 345-5150

Nawab, in the heart of Roanoke's downtown historic district, offers a richly varied Indian menu of fresh, natural ingredients, wholesome sauces and flavorful spices. Choose from a versatile selection of natural foods — all can be prepared mild, medium, hot or Indian hot with freshly-ground herbs and spices. Try one of the tandoori specialties, such as tandoori chicken tikka or boti kebab. The tandoor is a special pit oven made from clay and fueled with charcoal. All meats, poultry and seafood marinade overnight then are skewered and broiled in the tandoor, giving them a delicious and unique flavor. Vegetarians will be in heaven here with numerous meatless dishes to choose from. The vegetable dorma will make your mouth water with its nine fresh vegetables cooked in a blend of spices and cream and sprinkled with nuts. The palak paneer is made of spinach with Indian cheese cubes cooked in mild spices and herbs. For dessert try kheer, traditional Indian rice pudding with nuts, flavored with cardamom and rose water. Nawab is open daily for lunch and dinner. There is a lunch buffet Monday through Friday and lunch specials are served within 10 minutes. Children's portions are available on some items at half-price.

The Roanoker Restaurant

$$ • Colonial Ave. at I-581
and Wonju St., Roanoke
• (540) 344-7746

This restaurant has held high standards for 56 years, and it shows. It's busy day and night, every day of the week, filled with loyal customers whose parents and grandparents ate here. Run by the Warren family all these years, The Roanoker is frequented by customers who have come to expect quick service and farm-fresh quality food. On July 1, 1996, owner E.C. Warren celebrated his 50th birthday and the restaurant's 55th anniversary by printing a special menu with the July 1, 1941, cover of the Roanoke Times on the front. Then E.C. picked up the tab for every customer's meal! Several thousand Roanokers whose food was free celebrated both events along with the Roanoker. The Roanoker has been voted Best Place to Eat With Your Mother, and it is! Breakfast is a crowd pleaser; menu favorites include red-eye gravy and ham with biscuits and grits. The restaurant serves breakfast, lunch and dinner daily.

Roanoke Weiner Stand

$, no credit cards • 25 Campbell Ave.,
Roanoke • (540) 342-6932

In 1916, when Prohibition caused the decline of Salem Avenue by forcing its saloons to close their doors, brick-paved Campbell Avenue took over as Roanoke's main thoroughfare. The road was exciting and new, with streetcars and electric street lights. And the Roanoke Hot Weiner Stand opened for business at the location where it would remain for more than 75 years. Harry Chacknes opened

the stand with a six-burner stove, a kitchen that measured 13 by 7 feet (including counter space) and six stools. And, right in the heart of the Magic City, you could get a steaming, plump hot dog for just a nickel. Almost eight decades later, times have changed. What once cost you five pennies now runs you $1.05. The original six stools increased to 19 in 1988 when the Weiner Stand became a part of Center in the Square. The place even traded up for a more modern stove after using the old one for 72 years. But some things haven't changed a bit. The stand is still in the Chacknes family. Harry's wife, Elsie, ran it in the 1960s. Now his nephew, Gus Pappas, is the owner. Elsie's nephew, Mike Brookman, works in the kitchen. And, while John Liakos is not actually a blood relative, he is certainly a part of the family after working here for more than 30 years. You can still get that delicious, plump hot dog. And we don't think the friendly conversation and warm, honest smiles will ever leave the kitchen of the Roanoke Weiner Stand. It's open for breakfast, lunch and dinner Monday through Saturday.

Sunnybrook Inn Restaurant

$ • 7342 Plantation Rd., Roanoke
• (540) 366-4555

In 1983 Howard and Janet Schlosser found the perfect place that created the right atmosphere for their home-style cooking. Sunnybrook Inn, a large farmhouse built in 1912, was the homestead of a 150-acre dairy farm. Each day, the Schlossers bake homemade pies, cakes and rolls in their kitchen. Their menu is a compilation of recipes — some 100 years old — from all over western Virginia. The peanut butter pie here is legendary. Diners also love the oysters, fresh from the Chesapeake Bay and served year round. Every Friday and Saturday Sunnybrook Inn serves a spectacular seafood buffet with crab legs and fried oysters. There are separate children's prices. The restaurant is open for breakfast, lunch and dinner daily. Reservations are required for large groups.

Texas Tavern

$, no credit cards • 114 W. Church Ave.,
Roanoke • (540) 342-4825

As soon as you open the door to this 64-

Photo: The Roanoke Valley Convention and Visitors Bureau

Fresh produce is readily available in this area, and local restaurants
take advantage of the opportunities to use it.

year-old white brick Roanoke landmark, you can smell the hamburgers and hot dogs sizzling on the grill. You will notice that the countertop is dented and dull, and some of the stools are long overdue for attention. Men in industrial-white T-shirts, work pants and aprons shout "hello" over the bubbling chili and chattering customers. The staff is neighborly and will shoot the breeze with you — that is, if they have the time. A sign reads, "We serve 1,000 people 10 at a time." Never mind. You didn't come here for pamperin' — you came for some of the best chili this side of Texas. The Tavern is a great place for a quick, hot lunch or a midnight snack. It serves all the standards — hot dogs, hamburgers and, of course, chili. And if you order a nice cool drink, you won't get a Styrofoam cup or even an aluminum can. Only glass soda bottles and straws are found here. Texas Tavern is near three (pay) parking lots, which is a bonus, since they have little parking space of their own. It is also just a few blocks away from the Farmer's Market and Center in the Square. The restaurant is open 24 hours a day, seven days a week. (See our Nightlife chapter.)

309 First Street
$$ • 309 Market St., Roanoke
• (540) 343-0179

Dining at 309 First Street is like having your favorite meal with an old friend. If there's one thing that stands out about this place, it's the repeat business it enjoys as a downtown Roanoke favorite on the historic City Market. It's especially popular as a lunch spot for urban professionals. It serves lunch and dinner in a sunny, contemporary dining room under a skylight filled with green plants. Menu specials include seafood salad and chicken fingers. Burgers are popular choices — the Burgundy Burger has a hint of fine wine, the Tex-Mex Burger is well-seasoned with jalapeños, hot sauce and cheese, and the First Street Favorite is a top-of-the-line gourmet burger with bacon and Swiss. Dinner selections include traditional favorites such as filet mignon, chicken teriyaki and sauteed seafood supreme (a combination of fish, crab, scallops and shrimp sauteed in herbs and butter). Also available to please the vegetarian taste is grilled vegetables and polenta. All dinner selections

include a salad, hot bread and butter, fresh steamed vegetables or seasoned rice, and baked potato, onion rings or fries. It's open for lunch Monday through Saturday. Dinner is served Tuesday through Saturday.

Wildflour Cafe and Catering
$$ • Towers Mall, Roanoke
• (540) 344-1514
Wildflour II Market and Bakery
$$ • 1212 Fourth St. S.W., Roanoke
• (540) 343-4543

If you're going to eat lunch at either of the Wildflour restaurants, be sure and get there before 11:30 AM. The small Towers Mall operation's healthy and homemade food was so popular in Roanoke that the owners expanded to a new location in Old Southwest with Wildflour II Market and Bakery. But it's still tough to get a seat because the food is so fabulous. The folks here cook from scratch early, so the smell of fresh baking bread lures people who've been thinking about eating there since morning. The breads du jour, of the European-style hearth variety, are arranged in a flower pot at the cash register for all to smell and admire. The best red beans and rice we've ever eaten comes out of this place — we could eat it every day and not tire of it. The salads are varied and gourmet. As a nice touch, the young owners take the time to chat and get to know everybody, yet run extremely efficient operations. Wildflour is open Monday through Saturday for lunch and dinner.

Salem

Mac 'N' Bob's
$ • 316 E. Main St., Salem
• (540) 389-5999

If you want to go to *the* hangout in Salem, this is it! Directly across from Roanoke College, Mac 'N' Bob's (see our Nightlife chapter) is without a doubt the place for both locals and college kids to eat in Salem. Voted Best Neighborhood Restaurant by readers of *Roanoker Magazine* in 1996, it offers casual dining with good service. You can get your basic burger and sandwiches fixed the way you want. Along with wholesome salads and terrific desserts that appeal to everyone, there is also a full menu of pasta, fresh fish, steak, ribs and chicken.

Catawba

The Homeplace
$$ • 4968 Catawba Valley Rd., Catawba • (540) 384-7252

"Down-home cooking that makes you want to eat all your veggies" is the slogan of this grand old farmhouse and family restaurant just outside Roanoke. The home-style food is served family-style in bowls placed right at your table. Fried chicken, mashed potatoes and gravy, pinto beans, baked apples and hot biscuits are menu staples here. A neighborly and courteous staff will make you feel right at home. Thursday is Barbecue Night, but you can still order the regular fare. Always plan on a wait of at least 20 minutes, since Roanokers pack the place on weekends. You won't mind waiting on the big front porch, where you can pet the farm felines. Dinner is served Thursday through Sunday. If you're dieting or watching your cholesterol, don't go near this place! They all eat the way Grandma and Grandpa used to, before we knew everything that was bad for our arteries.

East of the Blue Ridge

Loudoun County

The Green Tree
$$$ • 15 S. King St., Leesburg • (703) 777-7246

This famous watering hole, surrounded by the enchanting homes, historic buildings, shops and museums of Leesburg, specializes in authentic 18th-century recipes and does its own baking. The original building was constructed in 1768, when it was opened as an inn and tavern. Try a house specialty, such as Robert's Delight (choice beef rolled in sweet herbs and spices) or Jefferson's Delight (liver presoaked in milk, sauteed with onions on top), while listening to 18th-century music. It's open daily for lunch and dinner. Reservations are preferred on the weekends.

Tuscarora Mill Restaurant
$$ • 203 Harrison St. S.E., Leesburg • (703) 771-9300

In a restored grain mill in Leesburg's historic Market Station complex, this restaurant serves regional American cuisine with international influences. The Japanese-style tuna is served on a bed of jasmine rice with a cucumber salad. In season, try the roasted salmon with stir-fry veggies. It's open for lunch and dinner daily.

Back Street Cafe
$$ • 4 E. Federal St., Middleburg • (540) 687-3122

Tutti Perricone reigns over this tiny eatery a block off Main Street and makes sure that her patrons are well-fed and undisturbed, no matter how famous they are. Actor Robert Duvall has been known to frequent the place, as do many political notables from Washington. The mostly Italian menu contains some wonderful fish and pasta dishes, and the daily specials are innovative and tasty. The outside deck is great for people-watching in good weather. On Friday and Saturday nights, Tutti engages one or two jazz musicians and can sometimes be persuaded to sing with them. Back Street Cafe serves lunch and then opens again for dinner Monday through Saturday. It also operates a sizable catering business.

The Coach Stop
$$ • 9 E. Washington St., Middleburg • (540) 687-5515

This casual dining restaurant features regional cooking with dishes such as cream of

---

INSIDERS' TIP

Some of your best meals in the Blue Ridge may be in the least formal settings. Browse the local newspaper for small-town fundraisers or celebrations. The locals whip up their finest recipes for these occasions and love to feed visitors.

peanut soup, Virginia ham, locally grown trout and fresh prime rib. The Coach Stop is known for its homemade onion rings, which come thinly sliced and piled high. Nightly specials often take advantage of in-season regional seafood — shad roe, soft-shell crab and the like. A children's menu is available, and reservations are strongly suggested for weekend nights. It's open daily for breakfast, lunch and dinner.

Red Fox Tavern
$$$ • 2 E. Washington St., Middleburg • (540) 687-6301, (800) 223-1728

The Red Fox serves delicious traditional Virginia fare such as peanut soup and crab cakes, along with continental seafood, beef and game dishes. Built in 1728, the tavern, believed to be the oldest continuously operating dining establishment in the Old Dominion, sits in a lovely 18th-century stone building in the middle of Middleburg, Hunt Country's premier antiquing and equine center. The restaurant serves breakfast, lunch and dinner daily. Reservations are recommended.

Fauquier County

Ashby Inn & Restaurant
$$$ • 692 Federal St., off U.S. Hwy. 50, Paris • (540) 592-3900

Paris, Virginia, (population 47) was not as exotic as it sounds until Roma and John Sherman abandoned the metropolitan fast lane in 1984 and bought the c. 1829 house across the street from the original Ashby Tavern. They turned the place into one of the finest restaurants in Virginia and, with the acquisition of several other buildings, created a bed and breakfast inn that has finicky Washingtonians swooning in luxury and comfort (see our Bed and Breakfasts and Country Inns chapter).

More than 100 diners turn out for each of the Shermans' delightful Sunday brunches, which are held hunt breakfast–style on the back patio overlooking the foothills of the Blue Ridge. The dinner menu undergoes a complete change weekly to make room for the Shermans' ingenuity, and the specialties of the house are legend. Ashby Inn crab cakes are world-famous but barely outshine a

plethora of winter game dishes, gravlaks of Atlantic salmon, gumbo with duck and oysters, and more. You can count on the vegetables being local, and the tomatoes, herbs and peppers being fresh from John's garden. The rustic restaurant serves sumptuous breakfasts to its guests and is open for dinner Wednesday through Saturday. Reservations are necessary.

The Depot
$$ • 65 S. Third St., Warrenton • (540) 347-1212

Inside this historic restored train station you will find both American and Mediterranean cuisine, including salads, seafood, a Middle Eastern eggplant dish, veal piccata, rack of lamb and more. The airy dining room has 14 French doors that overlook a garden and restored caboose. Train memorabilia, such as lanterns and crossing signs, hang from the walls. The Depot is open Tuesday though Saturday for lunch and Tuesday through Sunday for dinner.

Fantastico-Ristorante Italiano Cafe & Bakery
$$ • 640 Warrenton Ctr., Warrenton • (540) 349-2575

The Italian food here attracts plenty of locals who come for fresh seafood, veal, lamb chops and homemade pasta — served in the Northern Italy tradition that emphasizes light wine sauces, capers, rosemary, olives and the like. The separate bakery and cafe serve fabulous desserts and pastries; it's a great spot to hang out and enjoy cappuccino, espresso and dessert. Fantastico-Ristorante is open Monday through Friday for lunch and dinner and Saturday for dinner only. Reservations are recommended.

Napoleon's
$$ • 67 Waterloo St., Warrenton • (540) 347-4300

Napoleon's regional American cuisine has French influences because the chef is French born. A regular menu is complemented by eight to 12 daily specials that take advantage of whatever is fresh and good. Specialties include seafood croustade, a variety of seafood served in a puff pastry with cream sauce, and filet en croûte, a filet wrapped in puff pastry, baked, sliced and served with a Madeira sauce. You can dine outside on the terrace during warm weather or inside by the fireplace during cold months. It's open for lunch and dinner Monday through Saturday and for brunch on Sunday. Reservations are suggested.

1763 Inn
$$ • 10087 John Mosby Hwy., Upperville • (540) 592-3848, (800) 669-1763

Uta and Don Kirchner have decorated their historic inn (which is as old as the name implies) with treasures found in their travels, including a Czechoslovakian chandelier and Meissen china from Uta's native Germany. The restaurant is divided into small, intimate dining rooms, one overlooking a lake where swans reside. The cuisine, naturally, is German-American and nicely done, right down to the freshly made breads and desserts. It's a delightful place to stay as well as dine (see our Bed and Breakfasts and Country Inns chapter), and history buffs can browse through the Civil War memorabilia in the sitting room next to the bar. It's not a restaurant for small children; in fact, children are not allowed Saturdays after 6 PM. The dining room serves breakfast to inn guests every day. It's open Wednesday through Sunday for dinner and on weekends for lunch and dinner. Reservations are requested.

Rappahannock County

Bleu Rock Inn
$$$$ • 12567 Lee Hwy. (U.S. Hwy. 211), Washington • (540) 987-3190

Owned by brothers Jean and Bernard Campagne, who also operate La Bergerie in Alexandria, the Bleu Rock Inn is situated on 80 acres about an hour from the Washington, D.C., beltway. The Inn's three dining rooms have fireplaces, and in warm weather, the terrace is a wonderful place to have dinner, drinks or dessert. The food is French-American with an international flair; menus change weekly but husband-and-wife team Richard and Lynn Mahan (formerly of the Inn at Little Washington) always serve a wonderful Key lime cake. It's open Wednesday through Sunday for din-

ner as well as brunch on Sunday. Reservations are suggested. (For more information about an overnight stay at the Inn, see our Bed and Breakfasts and Country Inns chapter.)

Four & Twenty Blackbirds
$$$$ • U.S. Hwy. 522 S. and Va. Rt. 647, Flint Hill • (540) 675-1111

This wonderful restaurant is on the border of the Shenandoah Valley region, a short drive from Front Royal. Owners Heidi Morf and Vinnie DeLuise prepare creative American cuisine. The menu changes completely every three weeks so that the cooks can take advantage of the best available seafood and local produce. The first-floor dining room is small but offers privacy for romantics; the tables are in nooks with screens of lace or floral prints. For dinner, guests can select from four appetizers, eight entrees and three desserts. The same dish is never served twice, but appetizers have included baked mussels stuffed with Mexican apple-smoked bacon and served with corn relish. Entrees have included beef filet kebabs in a red wine sauce sparked with blue cheese and walnuts and served with lemony sauteed potatoes and snow peas. Desserts are homemade and fabulous. The restaurant serves brunch on Sunday and dinner Wednesday through Saturday beginning at 5:30 PM. Reservations are suggested.

The Inn at Little Washington
$$$$ • Middle and Main sts., Washington • (540) 675-3800

A little more than an hour's drive from the city, this highly acclaimed country inn is a favorite of Washington, D.C., media stars and politicians. Celebs can be spotted here several times a week; Paul Newman even spent his 64th birthday here.

Be prepared to spend big money for exquisite regional American cuisine complemented by a 12,000-bottle wine cellar. The restaurant has been praised worldwide. The menu changes daily, and guests are served a seven-course meal for a fixed price. Co-owner and chef Patrick O'Connell says he's not satisfied if a dinner is "good" or "fine" — he wants his meals to be among the best his diners have ever experienced. People worldwide who visit The Inn say it serves some of the best food in the world — no small claim. The menu varies with the seasons, venison in the fall, lamb in the spring.

On Saturday, dinner costs $108 per person, not including tax, tip or wine. Sunday through Thursday the price is $88; Friday, it's $98. The restaurant is open for dinner every day except Tuesday, but during the busy months of May and October, dinner is served every day. Reservations are required and, in fact, can be hard to come by. (See our Bed and Breakfasts and Country Inns chapter for information on the inn.)

Madison County

The Bavarian Chef
$$$ • U.S. Hwy. 29, 5 miles south of Madison • (540) 948-6505

This restaurant a few miles north of Charlottesville serves huge portions of family-style German cuisine. The food is extraordinary, especially the sauerbraten and homemade desserts, which include a Bavarian nutball and Tiroler apfelstrudel with vanilla sauce. You can also order conventional American seafood dishes. Reservations are suggested. The restaurant serves dinner Wednesday through Sunday.

Bertines North
$$ • 206 S. Main St., Madison • (540) 948-3463

It looks like a stately old Virginia home with a wraparound porch and towering shade trees, but step inside and you'll feel like you've landed in the Caribbean: the inviting aroma of chef Bernard Poticha's special gumbo fills the air as you take in the colorful walls, a deep-sea blue in one dining room, salmon pink in the other. Steel band reggae plays lightly in the background. Bernard's wife, Christine, is happy to discuss the colorful art they use to decorate their seven-year-old restaurant. Sea fans adorn the walls, large shells surround the fireplace, original paintings by a Caribbean artist, still others by the artist's two sons, a mantel filled with Haitian work carvings and more brought back from the Potichas' 10-year

stay in the Caribbean. The couple, who met and married in Chicago, settled in St. Martin, where they ran a popular restaurant and guest house. When their son was born, they decided to move back to the States, so they brought their combination of Creole, Cajun, Italian and French recipes to the foothills of the Blue Ridge.

Their crab cakes and "steak on a hot rock" are local favorites and they've added Jamaican-style Jerk Chicken by request. But those in search of a real Caribbean treat might be enticed to sample the Conch Stew or Blackened Swordfish. Bernard goes light on the spices on most of the Creole selections, but he also offers a dish of his homemade hot sauce if you prefer to pep things up a bit. Beer and wine compliment the meals, or you can have Key lime soda or non-alcoholic ginger beer. Save room for dessert: Bertines offers homemade pecan pie, coconut pie, rhubarb cake (in season) and a delightful chocolate mousse. In the warmer months, dining is also available on the front porch. Dinner is served beginning at 6 PM Friday through Monday or by reservation Tuesday through Thursday. The couple say the restaurant will be "open until closing," but the last service is usually around 9 PM.

Graves Mountain Lodge
$$ • Off Va. Rt. 670, Syria • (540) 923-4231

Folks come from miles around for this abundant Southern fare. Long pine tables seat locals and travelers, many of whom stay in the lodge's overnight accommodations (see our Bed and Breakfasts and Country Inns chapter). Using foods fresh from the Graves garden, chefs prepare country-style favorites such as Southern fried chicken, pan-fried trout and tasty Virginia ham. Meal prices include the whole spread, beverage to dessert (which you will want to be sure to save room for). You can count on getting plenty to eat — too much, if you're not careful. These meals are popular, so call well in advance for reservations.

The Lodge welcomes families and has plenty to do for everyone. After dinner, if you're not too full to leave your chair, take a hike on one of the trails that crisscross the Lodge grounds or drop a pole in a nearby fishing spot. Or just sit back on one of the many porch rockers while the kids play games in the recreation room.

Prince Michel Restaurant
$$$$ • U.S. Hwy. 29, between Culpeper and Madison
• (540) 547-9720, (800) 800-WINE

The owners of Prince Michel Vineyards operate this exquisite French restaurant. Its prix fixe menu emphasizes contemporary versions of traditional French cuisine and includes a choice of several imaginatively presented dishes for each course. The restaurant offers the extraordinary cuisine of Alain Lecomte, a Frenchman who took first place in the prestigious Concours National de France des Chefs de Cuisine in 1990. He re-creates his highly acclaimed French specialties using local products and pairs these dishes with Prince Michel and Rapidan River wines.

Guests enter through Prince Michel's wine shop, where they may taste wine at the attractive wine bar and browse the wine museum. (Also see our chapter on Wineries.) Styled by Parisian designer Ariane Pilliard in collaboration with local artist Marie Taylor, the decor focuses on trompe l'oeil effects, including floor-to-ceiling murals that transport guests to the Bordeaux region of France. Opulent table settings with French linen add to the atmosphere of elegance.

The restaurant is open for lunch and dinner Thursday through Saturday with a gourmet lunch served on Sunday afternoons. Reservations are required for dinner.

Greene County

Blue Ridge Cafe
$$ • 8315 Seminole Trail, Ruckersville
• (804) 985-3633

If you are looking for good American cuisine in a relaxed atmosphere, drop by Blue Ridge Cafe right off U.S. 29. Shawn Hayes, owner of the cafe, serves a mixture of American grill with an international flair. Besides burgers, you can order barbecue ribs, steaks, prime rib, crab cakes, seafood, Mediterranean

salads and pan-seared flounder. Past specialties have included lobster scampi and steak imperial. The Blue Ridge also has a full bar. The cafe is casual with black carpet and white walls in high gloss and black crown molding. Decor also includes oak tabletops and lots of mirrors and plants, which gives it a fresh, open feeling. Visitors include tourists as well as business people meeting over power lunches, so you'll feel comfortable in jeans or a suit. The cafe is open for lunch and dinners seven days a week. Sunday brunch, a local favorite, is served from 10 AM to 2 PM. Reservations are requested for parties of seven or more.

The Lafayette
$$ • 146 Main St., Stanardsville
• (804) 985-6345

Daniel Huff, Whitt Ledford and Nick Spencer decided to give the folks in Greene County a place where they can go and feel special, so the trio from Charlottesville began remodeling the stately 1840 building on Main Street. During the Civil War, it was used as an office for the Confederate army during the Battle of Stanardsville. The new owners tried to make the interior look as it might have appeared in 1840. While the dining room has a formal feel, you will be comfortable whether you are decked out in coat and tie or wearing khakis and a polo shirt. The menu features a variety of regional American dishes including mountain trout almondine, braised duckling and lamb chops. Save room for the homemade desserts, especially the Kahlua cake and amaretto cake. Wine and beer are available. Lunch and dinner are served Tuesday through Saturday with a popular brunch and dinner on Sunday.

Vinny's New York Pizza & Pasta
$$ • U.S. Hwy. 29 in Countryside Square Shopping Center, Ruckersville
• (804) 985-4731

In 1988 Vinny decided to leave Long Island and set up shop in Greene County, and for the past 11 years, customers have been willing to make the drive from Albemarle and Madison counties to savor the authentic Italian dishes and gourmet pizzas. One of their trademarks is the 18-inch pizza, one of the largest made in town. The family-owned restaurant caters to a family crowd, and includes special selections for children younger than 12. Adults may choose from a wide variety of pizzas, pastas, salads and heroes. Dinners also range from eggplant parmigiana to a veal cutlet. Beer and wine are available. Vinny's has been so popular with the local crowds that they have added a takeout spot in northern Albemarle County and a full dinner restaurant in Charlottesville. The restaurants are open daily for lunch and dinner.

Orange County

Willow Grove Inn
$$$$ • 14079 Plantation Wy., Orange
• (540) 672-5982, (800) 949-1778

Limoges china, crystal chandeliers, Chippendale chairs . . . you get the picture. This elegant plantation home, built in 1778, is now a full-service inn with a sensational restaurant. The regional American cuisine is the most contemporary thing about this magnificent place. The menu changes frequently depending upon the season, but four-course meals have included such items as bourbon molasses-glazed quail with herbed sweet potato cakes or smoked Rag Mountain trout with horseradish cream. Desserts are homemade and truly scrumptious. The friendly bartender will help guests select an appropriate wine for dinner. The menu also sometimes suggests a particular wine for each entree and offers a full range of dessert wines, after-dinner liqueurs and dessert coffees. Reservations are recommended. Dinner is served Thursday through Sunday, with brunch also offered on Sunday.

Albemarle County

Aberdeen Barn
$$$ • 2018 Holiday Dr., Charlottesville
• (804) 296-4630

This is a well-established restaurant known for its roast prime rib and charcoal-grilled steak. But you can also have lamb chops, Australian lobster tail, crab cakes, shrimp scampi and other seafood delights here. The atmosphere

is candlelit and intimate, and the Sportsman's Lounge has live entertainment several nights a week. Reservations are suggested. Dinner is served Monday through Saturday, while lunch and dinner are served on Sunday.

Awful Arthur's Seafood Company
$$ • 333 W. Main St., Charlottesville
• (804) 296-0969

This casual seafood restaurant housed in a historic 1700s building specializes in fresh seafood and has an awesome raw bar. The menu includes steaks, chicken, salads, pasta and sandwiches. Dining options vary. Upstairs is a quiet, candlelit atmosphere, downstairs is a lively raw bar, and in the basement is a comfortable sports bar with billiards and darts. Awful Arthur's serves lunch and dinner daily, and catering is available. Reservations are accepted.

Baja Bean Co.
$ • 1327 W. Main St., Charlottesville
• (804) 293-4507

On The Corner near the Rotunda, this California-style Mexican restaurant serves up lighter meals than the typical Tex-Mex fare. When owner Ron Morse moved here from San Diego, he brought the healthier California sensibility with him. The vegetarian specialties for lunch and dinner are especially popular. A full bar offers 11 Mexican beers and 12 brands of tequila. All dishes are freshly made, including hot and mild salsas. The festive restaurant is decorated with banners and T-shirts from Puerto Vallarta, Cancun, Cozumel and other Mexican hot spots. Baja Bean Co. is open daily for lunch and dinner; expect to wait for a table on weekends. Reservations are not accepted. (Also see our Nightlife chapter.)

Biltmore Grill
$$ • 16 Elliewood Ave., Charlottesville
• (804) 293-6700

One of the most attractive things about this restaurant is the wisteria-covered arbor that shades an outdoor dining area. A popular restaurant for UVA students, the place serves pasta dishes, unusual and hearty salads and much more. You'll find a wide selection of imported and domestic beer. The dessert menu includes such yummy items as a Tollhouse Cookie Pie, grasshopper pie and peanut butter surprise. The Biltmore is open daily for lunch and dinner. (Also see our Nightlife chapter.)

Blue Ridge Brewing Company
$$ • 709 W. Main St., Charlottesville
• (804) 977-0017

If this friendly, casual place smells like a brewery, that's because it is one. In fact, it's Virginia's first brewery restaurant, which opened in 1988 (see our Nightlife chapter). The home brews are named for Blue Ridge mountain peaks, such as Humpback stout, Hawksbill golden lager and Afton red ale. The eclectic menu includes such dishes as filet mignon, bourbon steak, pesto lasagna, Thai pork chops and blackberry cobbler. The smoked-trout wonton appetizer is out of this world. The bar is open every night until 2 AM. Lunch and dinner are served Wednesday through Sunday, and dinner is served on Monday and Tuesday.

Blue Bird Cafe
$$ • 625 W. Main St., Charlottesville
• (804) 295-1166

Enjoy innovative cuisine in a casual, eclectic atmosphere at this cafe in the historic downtown area. Whether you choose to dine outdoors on the patio or inside, you'll find the experience enjoyable. A diverse menu includes fresh seafood, hand-cut prime beef, poultry and pasta dishes. This is the home of what the menu touts as "World Famous Blue Bird Crab Cakes." Fine French, American and Virginia wines are served, as are domestic, imported and microbrewery beers. Full bar service and cappuccino and espresso complement your meal, which simply must include one of the delicious, homemade desserts. The Blue Bird is open for lunch and dinner daily. Brunch is served on Sunday. Dinner reservations are accepted. Ample parking is available.

The Boar's Head Inn and Sports Club
$$$$ (Old Mill Room), $$ (Racquets)
• U.S. Hwy. 250 W., Charlottesville
• (804) 296-2181, (800) 476-1988

The Boar's Head Inn's Old Mill Room is a restored 1834 grist mill serving regional fare accompanied by a nationally recognized wine list. The menu changes about four times each year, but some of the chef's specialties have included cider-marinated pork loin and seared Outer Banks tuna steak. Sunday brunches here are impressive: omelettes and Belgian waffles made to order, pastries, breads, cheeses, smoked fish, breakfast meats and egg dishes, among other dishes. Reservations are required in the Old Mill Room for dinner and are suggested for lunch and breakfast. It's open daily. The less formal Racquets Restaurant and Lounge offers inn guests elegant dining in a casual atmosphere. There is a healthy, all-American menu for lunch and dinner Monday through Saturday, plus a weekday evening light-fare lounge menu. (See our Resorts chapter for more information on the inn.)

Bodo's Bagel Bakery and New York Sandwich Shop
$ • Preston Ave. and Harris St., Charlottesville • (804) 293-5224
$ • Emmet St. and U.S. Hwy. 25 Bypass, Charlottesville • (804) 977-9598
$ • 1609 University Ave., Charlottesville • (804) 293-6021

Some of the best bagels in town. Sandwiches emphasize fresh, simple ingredients with some unusual twists such as a hummus and sprouts sandwich. Most everything is good but take note of the Caesar salad, "everything" bagel and delicious soups. Atmosphere is lively and loud, with great music playing all day long. Both kids and adults love this place because of its easy rhythms and wonderful food. All three locations are open daily for breakfast, lunch and dinner.

C & O Restaurant
$$ • 515 E. Water St., Charlottesville
• (804) 971-7044

For more than 20 years, this celebrated establishment was two restaurants in one, an upscale and expensive dining room upstairs and a more casual and pocketbook-friendly bistro downstairs. In either place, the dining was noteworthy. In fact, William Rice, editor-in-chief of *Food and Wine Magazine* said, "I can confidently assure you that not since Jefferson was serving imported vegetables and the first ice cream at Monticello has there been more innovative cooking in these parts than at the C & O Restaurant." Well, in 1997, owner Dave Simpson changed the setup to what has been called a marriage of both worlds. It's a little less formal and a lot less expensive. Plus a new menu, including favorite dishes from both upstairs and downstairs, is now served throughout. Although it changes frequently, the menu has featured such French cuisine as duck breast with a blueberry ginger sauce. The C & O has maintained its extensive wine list, including some very old wines. The restaurant is open daily for lunch and dinner. There is also a late-night menu with soups, salads, desserts and coffee served until 2 AM. Reservations are accepted.

Carmello's
$$ • 400 Emmet St., Charlottesville • (804) 977-5200

It's no wonder that a variety of professionals found Carmello's. It's right across the street from University Hall, the site that hundreds of UVA alumni visit regularly to watch their alma mater play basketball. But it's a combination of quality Northern Italian cuisine, reasonable prices and an atmosphere of comfortable elegance that keeps Carmello's alumni coming back for more. Along with daily specials, there are between 40 and 50 items on the menu, including veal, fish and chicken, all served with pasta. Carmello's also offers an extensive wine list. It's open daily for dinner. Reservations are accepted.

Clifton — The Country Inn
$$$$ • 1296 Clifton Inn Dr., Charlottesville • (804) 971-1800, (888) 971-1800

This elegant, historic inn was home to Thomas Mann Randolph, governor of Virginia and Thomas Jefferson's son-in-law (see our Bed and Breakfasts and Country Inns chapter). The restaurant serves a prix fixe dinner daily — five courses on weekdays, six on weekends. Luncheons are available by private arrangement. A typical winter dinner might start with smoked duck, move on to a soup of pureed

winter vegetables and salad of organic greens, continue with a passion-fruit ice and a choice of either rack of veal with wild mushrooms or grilled swordfish, ending with a chocolate terrine. Clifton also recently built a 5,000-bottle wine cellar and added outdoor dining. Reservations are required.

College Inn
$ • 1511 University Ave., Charlottesville • (804) 977-2710

This University Corner landmark serves a wide assortment of Greek, Italian and American dishes. As the name suggests, it's a popular dining spot and watering hole among the university set but also caters to a loyal following of Charlottesville natives and tourists. The restaurant is open daily for breakfast, lunch and dinner.

Court Square Tavern
$, no credit cards • Fifth and Jefferson sts., Charlottesville • (804) 296-6111

This bar on historic Court Square is a watering hole for lawyers and other professionals in town. No wonder. It has between 135 and 150 imported bottled beers and a huge array of beers on tap as well as hard apple cider. The tavern-style menu includes, among others, homemade soups, sandwiches, grilled bratwurst and cheesecake.

The British pub atmosphere features antique mirrors and engravings, a stained-glass window and copper-topped bar. The tavern is open from lunchtime until midnight Monday through Saturday and for dinner (until 11:30 PM) on Sundays.

Coupe deVille's
$ • 9 Elliewood Ave., Charlottesville • (804) 977-3966

This is a busy place that attracts scores of UVA students. The food is inexpensive but sophisticated. You can get fresh pasta that's made locally, along with sandwiches, seafood and homemade soups. A rotisserie cooks Peruvian-style chickens. You can dine indoors or outdoors on the garden terrace (even in the rain, since there's an awning). Coupe deVille's is open weekdays for lunch and Monday through Saturday for dinner.

Eastern Standard Restaurant and ES Cafe

$$ (upstairs restaurant); $ (cafe)
- **102 Old Preston Ave., Charlottesville**
- **(804) 295-8668**

This popular restaurant, next to the Omni Hotel, serves American cuisine with Asian accents. The menu, which changes seasonally with daily specials, includes vegetarian dishes, fine aged meats and seafood complemented by an extensive wine list. The restaurant is on two levels and operates as two different establishments. The main level is a bistro, ES Cafe, where most entrees are priced at less than $10. Co-owner and chef Sean Concannon is a graduate of the Johnson and Wales Culinary Arts School. ES Cafe is open Tuesday through Sunday. Upstairs is a warm, comfortable dining area overlooking the historic downtown mall. Its new chef, Janet Henry Jospe, brings experience from Japan. Dinner is served here Wednesday through Saturday at a steeper price. Parking validation is available for the nearby Omni Hotel parking lot.

Greenskeeper Restaurant

$ • 1517 University Ave., Charlottesville
- **(804) 984-4653**

A popular college and townie hangout (it's open until 2 AM every night), the Greenskeeper defies categorization. The menu is all over the map, from pita-pocket sandwiches and grilled eggplant to pastas and burgers on whole-grain buns. The restaurant is open for lunch and dinner daily. Validation is available for both Corner parking lots.

Hamiltons'

$$$ • 101 W. Main St., Charlottesville
- **(804) 295-6649**

The husband-and-wife team of Kate and Bill Hamilton each had spent nearly a decade working in the food industry when they decided it was time to go into business for themselves. Three years ago, they opened their own stylish contemporary American restaurant on the historic Downtown Mall, and Hamiltons' quickly won raves as one of the best new restaurants in town. The decor is striking. It's light, some would say hip. But Bill Hamilton says their goal was to create a cross-cultural atmosphere with their decor and food. The menu changes every two weeks or so, but always includes fresh seafood, meats and pasta, complemented by an eclectic wine list. If Nasi Goreng is on the menu, try it. The spicy Indonesian-style stir fry includes shrimp, grilled chicken and smoked pork. All desserts and breads are made in-house, and there is a full service bar. Patio dining is available when the weather permits. Hamiltons' is open for lunch and dinner Monday through Saturday. Reservations are recommended. Tables book well in advance on the weekends, and the lunches are very popular too.

The Hardware Store Restaurant

$ • 316 E. Main St., Charlottesville
- **(804) 977-1518**

The Grand Old Hardware Store Building, a city landmark since 1895, houses this restaurant that offers a huge variety of food. Inside the central dining area, you'll see the same ladders and shelves that belonged to the old hardware store, which operated continuously from 1895 to 1976. This was the original sales area. On the Water Street end of the restaurant, the hardware store's offices have been transformed into dining rooms, and you can see the original typewriters and adding machines used by the store's clerical workers decades ago. The restaurant, open for lunch and dinner Monday through Saturday, is known for its generous portions in beverages, sandwiches and salads. Ribs, pasta, mesquite-grilled chicken and crepes are also on the menu. If you simply want to satisfy your sweet tooth, choose from pastries or order a treat from the old-fashioned soda fountain. You'll find plenty of free parking at the Water Street door.

HotCakes

$$ • 1137-A Emmet St., Charlottesville
- **(804) 295-6037**

No, it's not a pancake house. HotCakes, in the Barracks Road Shopping Center, has a bakery, gourmet take-out counter and an eat-in lunch menu. The prices are high, but the food is worth it. Homemade pastries, pies and cakes are fabulous. Many wealthy local residents buy take-home meals or use the popular catering service. HotCakes is open daily for lunch and dinner. It stays open until 11 PM on Friday and Saturday to allow for late-night noshing.

The Ivy Inn
$$$ • 2244 Old Ivy Rd., Charlottesville • (804) 977-1222

Transport yourself back to Jefferson's time at The Ivy Inn. Fine china, tablecloths and candlelight set the stage for wonderfully elegant regional food with international influences. In cold weather, cozy up by one of the two fireplaces in this 210-year-old manor house, with its high ceilings and Virginia Colonial-style decor. Dine in one of several inviting rooms either upstairs or downstairs; whatever your choice, you'll want to linger over these relaxing meals. Warm-weather days will take you outside for romantic patio dining.

The menu features modern American cuisine with European flair. A specialty of the house is rack of lamb, served a variety of ways, depending on the season and the mood of the chef. It's tender and savory, with delicate flavors you will enjoy. Desserts are, of course, homemade, so save room. The Inn is open for dinner every day; brunch is served on Sunday. With advance notice, lunch is available for parties of 15 or more. You'll find The Inn just off the U.S. 250 Bypass, 1 mile west of the University of Virginia.

Little John's
$ • 1427 University Ave., Charlottesville • (804) 977-0588

Be it lunchtime or the middle of the night, Little John's is the place to go if you've got a hankering for a New York-style deli sandwich. Open 24-hours a day, Little John's is on The Corner, a short walk from the Rotunda at UVA. Specialties are the Nuclear Sub (a combo of coleslaw, turkey, barbecue and mozzarella) and the Baby Zonker (a bagel with cream cheese, bacon, tomatoes and onions).

Maharaja
$$ • U.S. Hwy. 29 at Seminole Square Shopping Ctr., Charlottesville • (804) 973-1110, 983-0440

If spicy, rich Indian cuisine is your desire, this is the place to dine. The restaurant has a cozy but Spartan atmosphere. You'll find a variety of curries and chicken, shrimp and fish tandoori (which means it's marinated in herbs and spices and grilled in a clay oven) and more. Ginger, tamarind, cumin, cashews, almonds and yogurt are some of the ingredients blended together and served with meats, fish or vegetables, making this cuisine exciting to the palate. You can ask for your food to be chili hot, medium or mild. There also are many vegetarian dishes on the menu, and the Indian beers are quite popular. Maharaja is open daily for dinner and serves lunch every day except Monday. Reservations are suggested for dinner. The restaurant also offers catering services, patio dining and take-out.

Martha's Cafe
$ • 11 Elliewood Ave., Charlottesville • (804) 971-7530

This is a popular place on The Corner, and it's no wonder. The food is freshly made, interesting and reasonably priced, and the atmosphere is casual. Martha's has been around since 1976 and served cappuccino long before it was in vogue in this city. The menu emphasizes chicken and fish, and nothing is deep fried. It's known for its crab cakes, but another popular item is the sesame-chicken salad with peanut-garlic dressing. The cafe is situated in an old house with an enormous elm tree out front. You can dine indoors or, in spring or summer, outside on a cobblestone patio under the elm tree. As with most of the restaurants on crowded Elliewood Avenue, you need to park in the centrally located parking garage. Martha's is open daily for lunch and dinner.

Memory and Company
$$$ • 213 Second St. S.W., Charlottesville • (804) 296-3539

Founded as a cooking school in the early 1980s, Memory and Company continues as one of the finest restaurant traditions in the city. The restaurant is situated in a historic landmark, c. 1840, adjacent to 200 South St. Inn and within walking distance of downtown Charlottesville. Executive chef and owner John Corbett trained at the California Culinary Academy in San Francisco and has catered to the likes of Robert Mondavi, Silver Oak Cellars and Iron Horse Vineyards in California wine country. Corbett still gives cooking classes, which are quite popular.

A choice of dining rooms is available, including an exhibition cooking/dining area, a quaint and quiet dining room with wine racks and art displayed by local artists and, when weather permits, outside seating in the herb garden or patio area. The 300-plus wine list emphasizes California wines, though Corbett carries French, Virginia and Italian varieties also. The menu changes seasonally and features country French and classical Italian food with accents of California cuisine. The four-course prix fixe meal includes a selection of appetizers, entrees and desserts, all created daily from fresh ingredients. Dinner is served Wednesday through Saturday. The restaurant is nonsmoking, and reservations are requested.

Metropolitain
$$$$ • 1214 W. Water St., Charlottesville • (804) 977-1043

If you are in the mood for a little French chic, drop by the Metropolitain. Robert Strini's large objets d'art, suspended from the painted brick wall, are sure to catch your eye, but it's the artistically presented dishes that will command your full attention. The menu, featuring French dishes with a Southern influence, changes every month. Black sea bass and trout are popular entrees, and bison is offered periodically. The Metropolitain also serves dishes with Asian and Italian accents. Be sure to start your meal off with the roasted red pepper soup with calamari and aioli. And what better way to end an evening than with a perfect souffle or even Chocolate, Chocolate, Chocolate, a diet-killing dessert with four kinds of chocolate. If you would like to sample a mix of the Metropolitain's finest offerings, the owners offer a six-course tasting menu. There is a full bar, where you can order anything from a mixed drink to a $450 bottle of California Bordeaux. The restaurant serves dinner daily. Business is brisk, so reservations are highly recommended. A public parking lot and two parking garages are nearby.

Michie Tavern
$ • 683 Thomas Jefferson Pkwy., Charlottesville • (804) 977-1234

At Michie Tavern, a 200-year-old converted log house called The Ordinary serves a sumptuous lunch buffet of fried chicken, black-eyed peas, stewed tomatoes, coleslaw, potato salad, green bean salad, beets, homemade biscuits, cornbread and apple cobbler every day of the year. It's a taste of early America with recipes dating back to the 1700s. Even the servers are dressed in attire from the 18th century. Lunch costs $10.54, not including beverage, dessert or tax.

Monsoon
$$ • 113 W. Market St., Charlottesville • (804) 971-1515

Born in Taiwan and raised in South East Asia, owner and chef Lu-Mei Chang fuses the strong, direct flavors of the Orient to create startlingly delicious cuisine. The flavors are simple, and the ingredients fresh — lemon grass and basil are staples. A personal favorite is Paht Thai, rice noodles and vegetables seasoned with tamarind juice and fish sauce and served with either seafood, chicken, beef or vegetables — you won't be disappointed with this choice. Squid is tenderly cooked and expertly seasoned in all the dishes — a great seafood choice. The drinks list is extensive, with lots of exotic teas, Asian sodas and beers. And a note about the decor: it's one of a kind, with smoky-colored graffiti art by artist Steven Keene from floor to ceiling. Some tables and chairs are even covered with his work, which creates an artsy, yet intimate atmosphere. It's open for lunch Monday through Friday and dinner every night.

Moondance Cafe
$$$ • 201 E. Main St., Charlottesville • (804) 984-3933

This place is one of the well-kept secrets in Charlottesville. The owners don't spend a lot of money on advertising, but word-of-mouth recommendations keep business booming at Moondance Cafe. It bridges the gap between elegance and fine dining. The walnut paneling, piano music and fireplace creates a relaxed atmosphere for the cigar-and-martini set.

Photo: Wintergreen Resort

You'll find everything from upscale bistros to down-home barbecue joints in the Blue Ridge area.

It's a place that young Frank Sinatra would have frequented. Open since October 1994, it was named one of the best new restaurants in Charlottesville in 1995 by the local press. The cuisine is definitely French, but the crab cakes rival the best from Maryland. The owners say they want customers to feel welcome. In fact, one of the two owners will always be on hand. Moondance is open for lunch and dinner Monday through Saturday. Brunch is served on Sunday. Patio dining is available. Reservations are recommended on the weekends.

Northern Exposure

$$ • 1202 W. Main St., Charlottesville • (804) 977-6002

You'll find wholesome American food, or "big" food as the managers call it, at this spot, a short walk from University of Virginia and a few minutes drive from the Downtown Mall area. They also pride themselves as having the only rooftop dining in town. The menu is diverse, with dishes ranging from homemade

pizza to New York strips. Pasta dishes include ravioli, lasagna and linguine. The restaurant's biggest seller is Broiled Bistro Steak sauteed in red wine with garlic and served with fresh mushrooms. The atmosphere is casual, but cloth napkins and tablecloths add a touch of elegance. A large patio is great for outdoor dining when weather permits. The restaurant's theme is New York, with photos of the city and famous New York baseball players on the walls and items such as Bronx Cheesecake (it's actually made in the Bronx) on the menu. Homemade desserts include strawberry shortcake and Key lime pie. A children's menu is also available. Northern Exposure is open daily for lunch and dinner and for Sunday brunch.

Oregano Joe's

$$ • 1252 Emmet St., Charlottesville • (804) 971-9308

This is a popular, informal Italian restaurant one block north of Barracks Road Shopping Center. In fact, it was featured in the 1996 book *Where the Locals Eat: A Guide to the Best Restaurants in America.* Owners Carl and Victoria Tremaglio use fresh local ingredients and imported Italian products, making all sauces, soups and dressings from scratch. Daily specials often include such seafood as salmon, swordfish, tuna and red snapper. You can have cappuccino, espresso and international coffees and Virginian and Italian wines from the full bar. Children are welcome and so are take-out orders. Oregano Joe's serves lunch on weekdays and dinner daily. Reservations are advised for groups of eight or more for lunch or dinner. A new private dining room can accommodate parties of 20 to 50.

Random Row
$$ • 247 Ridge-McIntire Rd., Charlottesville • (804) 296-8758

This family restaurant has been a hometown gathering spot for three decades. The menu is loaded with classic and down-home favorites served in generous portions and followed by heavenly desserts. Specialties include Albuquerque nachos, the black bean tortilla stack and lime chicken salad. The restaurant is open daily for lunch and dinner.

Rococo's
$$ • Hydraulic Rd. and Commonwealth Dr. in the Village Green, Charlottesville • (804) 971-7371

The quest to find the restaurant most favored by locals would bring many a visitor to Rococo's, an elegant but casual Italian restaurant featuring homemade ravioli, fettuccine, free-range veal, mesquite grilled seafood and meats, gourmet pizza and more. The restaurant was featured recently in *Bon Appetit*. Since 1988 Rococo's has emphasized the freshest ingredients and creative interpretations of traditional Italian dishes. Some of its specialties are wild mushroom pizza, mesquite-grilled half-chicken marinated in balsamic vinegar and rosemary, and house specialty tortellini bellisima. Desserts, such as peanut butter swirl cheesecake and chocolate toffee ice-cream pie, are homemade and fabulous.

The restaurant has an award-winning wine list and a full-service bar. It's open for lunch Monday through Friday, brunch on Sundays

and dinner every night. The restaurant accepts reservations for parties of five or more and welcomes families.

Saigon Cafe
$ • 1703 Allied Ln., Charlottesville • (804) 296-8661

The atmosphere is relaxed and comfortable at Charlottesville's first Vietnamese restaurant. Some of the specialties of the house are Vietnamese egg rolls served with fish sauce and grilled lemon chicken. The soups are especially noteworthy. Chinese lunch specials are amazingly inexpensive. Saigon Cafe is open daily for lunch and dinner.

Silver Thatch Inn
$$$$ • 3001 Hollymead Dr. at U.S. Hwy. 29 N., Charlottesville • (804) 978-4686

The menu changes every six weeks or so at this exquisite, candlelit restaurant in a beautiful c. 1780 inn (see our Bed and Breakfasts and Country Inns chapter). The Silver Thatch serves upscale regional American cuisine, with an emphasis on fresh produce. Two typical entrees are grilled breast of duck and grilled breast of chicken. The wine list is all-American, with an emphasis on those from California and Virginia, and recent additions of vintages from Washington and Oregon. Desserts are homemade, beautifully presented and mouth-watering, such as passion fruit cheesecake and tiramisu. Reservations are recommended. Dinner is served Tuesday through Saturday.

Southern Culture
$$ • 633 W. Main St., Charlottesville • (804) 979-1990

This hip cafe and restaurant serves Southern coastal cuisine. A favorite dish is Louisiana Short Stack, a crab, shrimp and scallop cake topped with jalapeño tartar sauce. Or try the seafood-okra gumbo and sweet potato fries. The bright and lively atmosphere creates an exciting place for dining and chatting with friends or a loved one. The bar is a lively gathering place for intellectuals and artists of all sorts. The restaurant and bar are open daily for dinner and drinks and Sunday for brunch. Free parking is available.

Spudnut Coffee Shop
$ • 309 Avon St., Charlottesville
• (804) 296-0590

You can't say you've had a true taste of Charlottesville until you've stopped by this popular doughnut shop. For 30 years, Richard F. Wingfield has been up before dawn, kneading, shaping and baking his unique breakfast treats. Oh, Spudnut serves a few sandwiches — your basic tuna salad, egg salad and BLT — but what keeps customers coming back to this well-worn shop are Wingfield's spudnuts. "They're made with potato flour," says Wingfield's daughter Lori Fitzgerald. "Potato flour is more difficult to work with than wheat flour, and it takes a little longer, but my dad is quite a baker." Every morning except Sunday, he creates nine different kinds of spudnuts, including glazed, cinnamon, chocolate and coconut, plus a few honeybuns, too. While the shop can seat 15 to 20 people, most customers stop by on their way to work. "I'd say 95 percent of what we do is take-out," Fitzgerald says. "But we do have a group of people who come in regularly . . . some have been coming in for 30 years." Lori and her sister Glenda, a nurse, have been helping out in the shop most of their lives. "I have gone off to school," Lori says, "but I came back. I like to work with my dad." Spudnut is open from 6 AM to 2 PM Monday through Friday and 6 AM to noon Saturdays. A dozen spudnuts will run you about $4.25, tax included. You can also quench your thirst with coffee, hot chocolate, soft drinks or whole milk.

St. Maarten Cafe
$ • 1400 Wertland St., Charlottesville
• (804) 293-2233

This is a favorite of UVA students — a place to forget your troubles and imagine you're far away on a tropical island. It has a late-night menu from 11 PM to 1 AM. The cafe serves a lot of fresh seafood and burgers, and all the soups are made from scratch. St. Maarten Cafe, on The Corner near the college campus and hospital, is open every day until the wee hours; Sunday brunch is also served. It gets crowded on Friday, Saturday and Tuesday, when a double-wing special brings in crowds of UVA students.

Tastings
$$$ • 502 E. Market St., Charlottesville
• (804) 293-3663

This restaurant, wine bar and wine shop combo is run by William Curtis, who also owns the popular Court Square Tavern nearby. You can stop first at the bar and sample a wine to order with your dinner or simply drink and munch on a few crackers. Foods are straightforward, fresh and deeply satisfying. The wood grill adds a delicate flavor to meats and fish. Year-round entrees include crabmeat casserole and grilled salmon with Béarnaise sauce, and in the summertime, strawberry rhubarb pie is the seasonal favorite. Most times the menu will incorporate an array of Pacific Northwest-grown wild mushrooms. You can select your dinner wine from more than 2,000 in the shop or order a half or full glass from a list of about 125 wines. Better yet, Curtis will prepare a flight of three wines to sample during dinner. The wine list has received the Best of Excellence award from *Wine Spectator* magazine. Lunch is served Monday through Friday with dinner available Tuesday through Saturday. Reservations are appreciated.

The Tea Room Cafe at the 1817
$, no credit cards • 1211 W. Main St., Charlottesville • (804) 979-7353

For a sunny setting, try lunch at The Tea Room Cafe. Open weekdays, it's in the solarium, overflowing onto the gallery-style back porch of the beautifully appointed 1817 historic bed and breakfast (see our Bed and Breakfasts and Country Inns chapter). You'll choose from gourmet soups, salads and sandwiches at reasonable prices. The Tea Room specializes in tea, of course, and lemon desserts.

The Virginian
$$ • 1521 University Ave., Charlottesville
• (804) 984-4667

A University of Virginia tradition for generations, The Virginian closed briefly in 1995 and reopened under new management. The food, atmosphere and service have remained distinctly the same over the years, despite the change in ownership. You still feel like you have stepped into a timeless college restaurant where professors discuss department politics at one table while students quaff beer in another. Large wooden booths are the only way to dine here, so don't plan on sitting together if you come with a big crowd. The food is good with an ambitious menu offering everything from burgers and pasta to quiche and grilled dishes. A late-night menu is mostly burgers and chili, and the Sunday brunch choices include eggs Benedict, omelettes, French toast and huevos rancheros. The Virginian is open daily for lunch and dinner.

Nelson County

The Blue Ridge Pig
$ • Va. Rt. 151, Nellysford
• (804) 361-1170

Some claim this is the best barbecue in the Blue Ridge. Local carpenters and farmers line up next to golfers and skiers from nearby Wintergreen Resort for these tasty meats and sandwiches. The offerings are just as diverse as the clientele — choose from pulled pork or sliced beef barbecue, ribs and smoked turkey, all fired in a large hickory-burning smokehouse that sits behind the restaurant. Side dishes garner their share of praise as well — oniony potato salad laden with a delicate dill sauce and spicy baked beans are made on site. With a gas station on one side and a car wash on the other, the Blue Ridge Pig is not lacking for atmosphere. Actually, the small dining area is quite pleasant, with rustic chairs, benches and tables. You'll have to decide whether to eat inside or out, but the hardest decision you will have to make is what to eat. For that reason, many travelers make this a regular stop. About 40 minutes from Charlottesville and Waynesboro and 15 minutes from Wintergreen Resort, the Blue Ridge Pig is certainly worth a detour from U.S. 250 or U.S. 29. The Pig is open daily for lunch and dinner.

Lovingston Cafe
$ • 165 Front St., off Va. Rt. 29,
Lovingston • (804) 263-8000

This unpretentious cafe in the heart of Lovingston serves an array of good, old-fash-

ioned American eats, including great burgers, grilled chicken breast sandwiches, pizza, pasta, fish and soup. It's a nice place to unwind on your way to or from Charlottesville, which is just a few miles to the north. The restaurant is open daily for breakfast, lunch and dinner.

Wintergreen
$-$$$$ • Va. Rt. 664, Wintergreen
• (804) 325-2200, (800) 325-2200

Wintergreen, an 11,000-acre resort, has six restaurants offering varied dining choices, from sandwiches and burgers at Cooper's Vantage to fantastic, gourmet fare in the elegant Coppermine. Also on the mountaintop are the Garden Terrace, offering casual family dining with emphasis on health-wise dishes, and the Devil's Knob Golf Clubhouse. In the valley, the Rodes Farm Inn is famous for its hearty, though pricey, Southern fare, and the Verandah serves delightful American and French cuisine with Cajun influences. See our Bed and Breakfasts and Country Inns chapter for more information on the privately owned Trillium House, which is also at Wintergreen. (Also see our Resorts and Skiing chapters.)

Fluvanna County

Prospect Hill
$$$$ • 2887 Poindexter Rd., Trevilians
• (540) 967-0844, (800) 277-0844

This historic plantation inn, 15 miles east of Charlottesville, houses a beautifully decorated, candlelit restaurant that serves classic French cuisine with Provencale and American accents. Menus change nightly to take advantage of the best and freshest ingredients available, but a recent spring menu included fire-roasted, maple-glazed rack of veal served with a Merlot wine sauce and wild spring mushrooms. Desserts, often pastries, are fabulously elaborate. The fixed-price, five-course dinners cost $45 a person, not including wine, taxes or gratuities. Epicurean Nights feature a seven-course meal with seven wines. Innkeepers Michael and Laura Sheehan invite dinner guests to arrive early for a Virginia wine tasting and to stroll the grounds or sit by the crackling fire. Dinner is served daily, and breakfast is offered to guests of the inn. Reservations are required.

Lynchburg

Bateau Landing
$, no credit cards • Main at 12th St., Lynchburg • (804) 847-1499

Lynchburg's historic community market, Bateau Landing, offers an array of country fare — fresh eggs, country ham and homemade jams and jellies — with breakfast and lunch. Produce changes seasonally. After having a piece of homemade cake, pie or a cookie, you can browse the market and whet your appetite for shopping. This is a fun place for the whole family, with ever-changing vendors and seasonal goods.

Cafe France
$$$ • 3225 Old Forest Rd., Lynchburg • (804) 385-8989

Jazz helps create an upbeat atmosphere in the fresh and original setting marked by an art deco decor and a wine bar. Lunch and dinner menus are extensive. Lunch calls for sandwiches, soups and burgers. An additional menu is available with the day's specials, which could include a French dip, soft-shell crab sandwich or seafood au gratin. There is also a soup, dessert and coffee du jour. The dinner menu is even more varied — Jamaican prime rib and Cornish game hen are standards, and other favorites include rack of lamb with Pommery mustard and seasoned bread crumbs and Virginia jumbo lump and backfin crabmeat served with buerre blanc sauce. A menu of dinner specials offers alternatives. A deli take-out menu is available as well. Lunch and dinner are served Tuesday through Saturday. Deli take-out is available Monday through Saturday. Reservations are suggested for dinner.

Charleys
$ • 707 Graves Mill Rd., Lynchburg • (804) 237-5988

There is always something special going on at Charleys that will appeal to business people as well as families. The menu is as varied as the atmosphere and includes fajitas, fresh seafood, chicken cordon bleu and prime rib as well as soups, salads and sandwiches. The restaurant is open for lunch, dinner and late-night dining daily. Reservations are suggested for parties of six or more.

Clayton's
$ • 3311 Old Forest Rd., Lynchburg • (804) 385-7900

Clayton's is a casual restaurant with table service by a friendly staff. You can have breakfast and lunch daily and dinner twice a week. Choose from chicken Tina (boneless chicken breast wrapped in bacon with mushroom sauce), grilled marinated shrimp, a grilled vegetable sandwich plus two hot specials daily. The restaurant is open for breakfast and lunch daily. Dinner is served Wednesday and Friday.

The Farm Basket
$, no credit cards • 2008 Langhorne Rd., Lynchburg • (804) 528-1107

Don't miss The Farm Basket while you're in Lynchburg! Regardless of your age or nature, it's the kind of place that will fascinate you for hours with its shopping opportunities. Then it will amaze you once again with its tiny restaurant that's always packed with locals and others who keep coming back for the homemade food prepared by cooks who are creative in both new and old recipes. The white meat chicken salad with grapes on a homemade yeast roll will melt in your mouth. Have dessert — the chocolate tarts are delicious — on the deck overlooking Blackwater Creek. They will also prepare a box lunch. It's open daily except Sunday.

The Landmark Steakhouse and Lounge
$$ • 6113 Fort Ave., Lynchburg • (804) 237-1884

The Landmark allows you to have an elegant dinner in a casual atmosphere. The rustic decor will make you feel at home, while special touches such as linen tablecloths make dining here an occasion. The steak has a hickory charcoal flavor. You can also choose from chicken and seafood dishes. The restaurant has a full bar and an extensive wine list. A nonsmoking section is also available. The Landmark is open for lunch Tuesday through Friday. Dinner is served nightly. Reservations are suggested on weekends and during busy seasons, such as Christmas and prom time.

Meriwether's
$$ • Boonsboro Shopping Ctr., Lynchburg • (804) 384-3311

At the site formerly occupied by Emil's Swiss Restaurant, Meriwether's has taken the casual dining crowd by storm with its California fern bar style. The restaurant was started by the husband-and-wife team who ran the much-lauded food service at Randolph-Macon College, Marie Meriwether-Godsey and her husband, Ed Godsey. They have offered upscale catering to the Lynchburg crowd for years, most recently serving Mikhail Gorbachev and Lech Walesa at Popular Forest. A typical Virginia fare meal includes real Southern ingredients such as grits and pork tenderloin with an onion and bourbon sauce. Signature dishes include produce from as many local farmers as possible. Also look for exotica such as couscous, sundried tomatoes, portobello mushrooms, bruschetta and hamburger on focaccia. The Market Shop offers packaged gourmet treats, fine wines, T-shirts, cups, jockey caps and flower arrangements. Meriwether's is open Monday through Saturday for lunch and dinner.

Texas Steak House
$ • 4001 Murray Pl., Lynchburg • (804) 528-1134

A real Texas dinner awaits you at this steakhouse, where a casual setting and a Lone Star State theme set the stage. The choices are vast, but steaks dominate the menu with 7- and 9-ounce fillets. Try a Yellow Rose of Texas or a Hershey Brownie for dessert. It's open for lunch and dinner Monday through

Friday and dinner only Saturday and Sunday. Reservations are not accepted, but call-ahead seating is offered.

Smith Mountain Lake Area

The Anchor House
$$ • Va. Rt. 122, Bridgewater Plaza • (540) 721-6540

When you hear the music, you'll know you're near The Anchor House. You'll be in the middle of all the action, day and night, at this lively place on the lower level of Bridgewater Plaza, the hub of activity at Smith Mountain Lake. This is a great place to dine, relax and meet people. It has an outdoor cafe, a salad bar, weekend entertainment and cocktails in the evening. The food is good — your basic burgers, salads and snacks plus an extensive list of spirits.

The Landing Restaurant at Bernard's Landing
$$ • Va. Rt. 940, Moneta • (540) 721-3028

If you want the finest dining and best view on the lake, this premier restaurant at Bernard's Landing's has them. It's truly a special place, worth the 45-minute drive from Roanoke or Lynchburg. Everything on the menu is a delight. Whether you want a sandwich (try the chicken salad) or a seafood platter of shrimp, scallops, flounder and deviled crab, you can expect a gourmet twist to your order. Friday and Saturday nights offer wonderful seafood and prime rib buffets. There probably isn't a soul on the lake who hasn't been to Sunday brunch, with waffles and fluffy omelettes served to your precise instructions. If you're going to the lake to experience it the way Insiders do each weekend, don't miss this dining opportunity. Nothing can match the gentle lake

---

INSIDERS' TIP

So what exactly is Blue Ridge cuisine? Insiders claim it's everything made in, intended for and consumed by Virginians. Virginia country ham is a good place to start, but you can also get Virginia peanut soup, Virginia applewood smoked turkey, chicken, pheasant and trout and, of course, succulent pork barbecue.

breezes and nautical decor as a pleasant distraction from the everyday world. Bernard's Landing is open for lunch and dinner Monday through Thursday; breakfast, lunch and dinner are served Friday and Saturday; and brunch and dinner are served on Sunday.

Paddle Wheel Cruises
$$$ • Va. Rt. 853, Moneta
• (540) 297-7100, (800) 721-3273

Glide across gorgeous Smith Mountain Lake while enjoying some of the best food around. You can ride on the luxurious *Virginia Dare*, a 19th-century sidewheeler, or on the *Blue Moon*, a 51-foot motor yacht perfect for smaller groups. Bask in the sun on an afternoon cruise or relax with a cocktail while watching the sun set across the lake on your way to the Smith Mountain Lake Dam. A substantial plated buffet features chicken, beef and seafood. Many trips feature live entertainment. The cruises run year round, but times vary. Call for reservations and specific information on specialty cruises, charters and sight-seeing tours. Located near the Smith Mountain Lake State Park, Paddle Wheel Cruises is accessible by land and water. This is a wonderful experience for lake lovers of all ages. Reservations are required.

White House Restaurant
$$ • Va. Rts. 608 and 626, Huddleston
• (540) 297-7104

A pleasant restaurant specializing in family fare, White House has a complete salad bar and a special Friday seafood buffet. Lunch features deli sandwiches, including German hot dogs. For dinner, try the great charbroiled steaks, pasta dishes and fresh seafood such as grilled tuna steaks and shrimp scampi. Desserts are freshly made and include such temptations as rice pudding, cheesecake and coconut pies. White House Restaurant is open daily for breakfast, lunch and dinner.

Dudley Mart & Restaurant
$, no credit cards • Va. Rts. 670 and 668, Wirtz • (540) 721-1635

Frequented by locals and close to the Smith Mountain 4-H Center, this revamped country school built in 1931 is now home to one of Smith Mountain Lake's most delightful dining surprises with an old-fashioned flair. The homemade barbecue and roasted chicken are worth the trip, and it's a great place for a quick meal while you're touring the lake. You'll find the kinds of odds and ends and groceries you would in old-timey country stores, and takeout is available. Stop by daily for breakfast, lunch and dinner.

Sal's Pizza Restaurant
$ • Fairway Village Shopping Ctr.
• (540) 721-8904

Homesick Northerners will feel right at home at one of the most established and best restaurants on the lake. Sal's is a family place that folks keep coming back to for the spaghetti and pasta specialties and fantastic salad bar. The pizza is everything you'd hope for in authentic Italian cuisine, and an adequate wine list complements your meal. Kids have a separate menu and can choose their favorite pasta dishes at a reduced price. When you visit on weekends, don't miss the $5 breakfast buffet for a tasty value. Sal's is open seven days a week, breakfast through dinner.

Bedford County

The Bedford Restaurant
$ • U.S. Hwy. 460 W., Bedford
• (540) 586-6575

For delicious down-home cooking, try The Bedford Restaurant. Have a real country-style breakfast with eggs, tenderloin, toast and chipped beef gravy over homemade biscuits. The lunch menu offers a variety of sandwiches. For dinner, try the honey-dipped chicken, cooked to order, or pork barbecue. The restaurant is open daily.

Franklin County

Jerry's Steak House
$ • U.S. Hwy. 200, 1 mile north of Rocky Mount • (540) 483-2070

Jerry's is a family restaurant featuring charcoal steaks, fresh seafood, Italian specialties and more. Sirloin and rib-eye steaks are cooked to your preference and served with sauteed mushrooms. Fresh shrimp scampi or frog legs (for the more adventurous diner) are offered along with a surf 'n' turf special for those who can't decide. Jerry's is open Monday through Friday for lunch and dinner and Saturday for dinner.

Leppo's Country Inn

$ • 10692 W. Gretna Rd., Sandy Level
• (804) 927-4444

Owners Joe and Ida Leppo fell in love with Smith Mountain Lake nearly 10 years ago. That's why the couple decided to leave their established business in Maryland and start over again in Franklin County. They offer big portions at reasonable prices. Folks come from all over to sample the fresh fried chicken, homemade chili, fried shrimp, crab cakes and other favorites. Pies, cakes and cookies are baked fresh on the premises, and baked goods or birthday cakes can be made to order. Another special feature of this restaurant is Ida's mail-order cookie business, Aunt Ida's Cookies. Leppo's Country Inn is open for lunch and dinner Tuesday through Friday and breakfast, lunch and dinner on Saturday and Sunday.

Olde Virginia Barbecue

$ • 108 Meadowview St., Rocky Mount
• (540) 489-1788

Come discover the most succulent pork, beef ribs and chicken barbecue in the county. This restaurant, a local landmark, has created its own Olde Virginia Barbecue Sauce and is a favorite hangout for the Franklin County crowd. You've just never tasted better barbecued chicken and ribs anywhere else, and people who don't even like coleslaw can't believe how great the Olde Virginia's real Southern variety tastes. Children have their own menu. The restaurant's open seven days a week for lunch and dinner.

New River Valley

Blacksburg

Anchy's

$ • 1600 N. Main St., Blacksburg
• (540) 951-2828

A relaxing family atmosphere surrounds you as you dine in this college-town favorite. The menu consists of Euro-Asian favorites and treats such as fresh seafood and steaks. Anchy's is open for lunch and dinner Tuesday through Friday and Sunday; dinner only is served on Saturday. Reservations are suggested.

Bogen's

$ • 622 N. Main St., Blacksburg
• (540) 953-2233

Probably the most popular local restaurant with the college crowd and business people, Bogen's slogan is "Casual with Class." The food is inexpensive, and the atmosphere is great. The menu features gourmet sandwiches, deluxe burgers, charbroiled steaks, spicy barbecued ribs and chicken and tempting seafood. To top it off, get cappuccino and one of the outrageous ice cream desserts — sky high and wonderful! Owner Bill Ellenbogen is keeping in pace with the Blacksburg Electronic Village as well. In 1995, he christened his cyberbar, an Internet-connected computer in the bar, and has received nationwide press coverage, most recently in *Reader's Digest*. Bogen's opens for dinner and the lounge is open until late night (see our Nightlife chapter).

Sunrise House Chinese Restaurant

$ • 1602 S. Main St., Blacksburg
• (540) 552-1191

Another top-notch Chinese restaurant in Blacksburg, the Sunrise has a relaxing atmosphere and a varied menu. You can feast on Crabmeat Lagoon, General Tso's chicken, Triple Delight and Hawaii Five "O." Prices are very reasonable. Sunrise House is open seven days a week for dinner. Reservations are accepted but not necessary.

Vicker's Switch

$ • At the Holiday Inn Blacksburg,
3503 Holiday Ln., Blacksburg
• (540) 951-1330

Vicker's Switch, the Holiday Inn Blacksburg's comfortable restaurant with a friendly staff, has a varied menu that includes blackened swordfish, country ham and grilled chicken salad. Friday nights feature a seafood buffet, and on Saturday it's prime rib. It opens

Many Blue Ridge restaurants, such as the Mountain Lake Resort Restaurant, offer fine dining in breathtaking scenic settings.

for breakfast, lunch and again for dinner Monday through Saturday. On Sunday, brunch and dinner are served. Reservations are suggested on special-occasion dates.

Christiansburg

The Farmhouse

$$$ • Cambria St., off U.S. Hwy. 460 • (540) 382-4253, (540) 382-3965

Exceptional service is a trademark of this authentic farmhouse-turned-restaurant. The farmhouse was part of an estate built in the 1800s and opened as a restaurant in 1963; an old train caboose was added in the early 1970s. The staff extends Southern hospitality to its diners, who include families, corporate executives and college students. The rustic setting, decorated with both antiques and country furnishings, adds to the ambiance. The menu is full of such favorites as prime rib, jumbo ocean shrimp cocktail, steak and the famous Farmhouse onion rings. A separate children's menu is available. The Farmhouse is open seven days a week for dinner. It also serves lunch on Sunday.

The Huckleberry

$$$ • 2790 Roanoke St. • (540) 381-2382

Convenient and luxurious, this restaurant is near I-81 and several hotels in the Christiansburg area. Two lounges, Whispers and Sundance, offer Top-40 and country-and-western entertainment in beautiful decor (see our Nightlife chapter). Your hosts, the VanDykes, offer homey settings, some next to fireplaces that roar on cool nights. The succulent barbecued items are slow-cooked in "the finest hickory-smoking oven money can buy." The restaurant also guarantees the high quality and freshness of its beef. You can choose from baby back ribs, Dijon chicken, filet mignon and broiled lobster tail. A varied wine list includes several Virginia vintages. The Huckleberry dessert specialties are ice cream fantasies — drinks made with real ice cream, cream, fresh fruits, nuts, candies and fine liqueurs. Kids have their own menu here too. It's open daily for dinner.

Stone's Cafeteria

$, no credit cards • 1290 Roanoke St. • (540) 382-8970

A longtime favorite with locals and tourists alike, Stone's gives you real country food as fast as you can go through the cafeteria line to get it. Lovers of dishes such as fried chicken, greens, mashed potatoes and pinto beans will be in their glory, both when they taste and when they pay. Stone's is open for breakfast, lunch and dinner Monday through Saturday.

Radford

Macado's Restaurant and Delicatessen

$$ • 510 Norwood St. • (540) 731-4879

One of a chain of family-owned restaurants throughout the Blue Ridge, including locations in Roanoke and Blacksburg, Radford's Macado's offers a fun dining alternative in the New River Valley. Macado's is popular both with students and professionals for its overstuffed sandwiches and unique, antiques- and collectibles-filled decor. The deli has a wonderful wine selection, including Virginia labels. Macado's is open from mid-morning to the wee hours daily.

Giles County

Mountain Lake Resort Restaurant

$$$ • Va. Rt. 700, Mountain Lake
• (540) 626-7121, (800) 346-3334

If dining in absolutely gorgeous surroundings is your idea of a great evening, as it is for many from nearby Virginia Tech, then you should drive the 7 winding miles up the mountain — the second-highest in Virginia — to Mountain Lake. This 2,600-acre paradise was the setting for the movie *Dirty Dancing*, and that glorious scenery wasn't designed in the prop room. For miles all you see are tall trees, rolling hills, beautiful wildflowers and a clear mountain lake. And as if that weren't enough, the dining is out of this world. (See our Resorts chapter.)

The elegant atmosphere matches the outstanding cuisine. It may include chilled blackberry soup, sauteed shiitake mushrooms, London broil Madeira or red snapper with pecan butter, if the chef is in a gourmet mood, or you may get Swiss onion soup, top round with horseradish and Chicken Polynesian. Breakfast is a buffet of Giles County country favorites such as Appalachian buttermilk pancakes, biscuits and gravy or local produce. Sunday brunch is popular for special events from May to October, when Mountain Lake is open. The prices are low for the high quality of the food. Reservations are important, since guests of the resort dine there as part of their stay.

Pulaski County

MimiAnne's Gourmet Coffee & Pastries

$ • 93 W. Main St., off Va. Rt. 99 W.,
Pulaski • (540) 980-6464

Pulaski's only espresso bar can be found at MimiAnne's, where you can get everything from gourmet coffee to chicken chili. Special menu items, like Broken Hearts French Toast (raspberry sauce ladled over French toast), are included for Saturday morning diners. MimiAnne's is open Monday through Saturday and is wheelchair-accessible.

New River Cruise Company

$$$ • Howe House Visitors Center Dock,
Claytor Lake • (540) 674-9344

Take a ride on the *Pioneer Maid* across stunning Claytor Lake and enjoy authentic foods made with recipes from our Colonial past. Due to its size — 60 feet long by 18 feet wide — this vessel can provide a fully enclosed deck and an open starlit one. Each day, the boat departs from the visitor center dock and cruises down the New River at approximately 5 miles per hour. A narrative of historical points along the world's second-oldest river enhances your trip. Lunch cruises feature deli sandwiches and fresh salads. The moonlight dinner/dance cruise is called Virginia is for Lovers, with local talent providing the music for dancing under the stars. On the dinner menu are George Washington Ham, Thomas Jefferson Fried Chicken, cooked greens with garlic and tomato and Virginia spoon bread. The cruises are two hours of drifting through the fantastic Blue Ridge Mountains. Office hours are 9 AM to 5:30 PM Tuesday through Sunday. Reservations are required.

Floyd County

Blue Ridge Restaurant Inc.

$, no credit cards • 113 E. Main St.,
Floyd • (540) 745-2147

Lunchtime regulars and those just passing through will find plenty of friendly faces here. The generous servings and honest-to-goodness real food — real mashed potatoes, not instant, and pinto beans that are always soaked dried beans, not canned — are well known in the area. Choose from such delicious country-style favorites as hot cakes, country ham, grilled tenderloin and fried squash. Children have their own dinner menu at a reduced price. The restaurant is open daily for breakfast, lunch and dinner May to November and shorter hours through the winter.

Le Chien Noir
$$ • At Chateau Morrisette, Meadows of Dan • (540) 593-2865

Built to resemble a French castle, Chateau Morrisette, a family-owned winery in the Rocky Knob growing district, produces world-class Virginia wines and also has a charming restaurant. Founded in 1978, the winery is small enough to remain in the family and yet large enough to produce several varieties of award-winning wines. The winery's restaurant serves both American and international cuisine in an elegant old world atmosphere. Although the fabulous wines are the highlight of Chateau Morrisette, luscious menu items such as grilled honey-soy chicken on an organic green salad with raspberry vinaigrette and fresh fruit will please your palate as well. The Jazz on the Lawn events are reminiscent of a Monet painting of a French picnic, and the price is right at $7 a plate. Visitors are welcome to tour the facilities, sample the wines and enjoy a light meal surrounded by the magnificent Blue Ridge Mountains. Le Chien Noir is open for lunch Wednesday through Sunday. Dinner is served on Friday and Saturday evenings. Reservations are requested.

Pine Tavern
$$, no credit cards • U.S. Hwy. 221 N., Floyd • (540) 745-4482

Live music and theater are reasons enough to lure you to Pine Tavern, where dinner theater is performed on Tuesday evenings for an additional $4 on the price of your meal. Dinner is served before the show, and dessert and coffee are available during intermission or after the show. Special nonsmoking evenings are set aside for those who would not be able to attend otherwise. Area bands play in the

dining room on Saturday evenings, and the Dave Figg Quartet plays jazz here several times a month (see our Nightlife chapter).

The menu sparkles with delectable dishes such as lasagna, eggplant parmigiana, Szechuan tofu and baba ghanoush. The chef uses organic and locally grown vegetables in season. Vegetarians may select from a special meatless menu that includes vegetable stir-fry, black bean chili and French onion soup. The chef even uses separate cutting boards for vegetables and a separate deep fryer with vegetable oil for veggies only. Pine Tavern is open Wednesday through Sunday for dinner and Saturday for lunch and dinner. Reservations are suggested on Friday, Saturday and holidays.

Alleghany Highlands

Alleghany County

The Cat & Owl Steak and Seafood House
$$ • Off I-64 at Low Moor Exit • (540) 862-5808

Rail memorabilia and antiques create a timeless atmosphere as you dine in this beautiful home remodeled by owner-operator Bruce Proffitt, whose father and uncle opened the Cat & Owl 25 years ago. A concourse covers the walkway, giving it the appearance of a railroad passenger depot. This steak and seafood restaurant has a Victorian atmosphere that will please the eye and a wide selection of tasty dishes that will delight the palate. Steaks are FDA Choice and prepared on an open charcoal broiler. The Cat & Owl was opened a quarter of a century ago to serve railroad workers in nearby Clifton Forge. There already was a C&O Restaurant in Clifton Forge, so the restaurant was named Cat & Owl to symbolize the first letters of the railway's name. You'll enjoy the decor including a barber chair, player piano and a machine once used to crank out personalized pencils. Selections such as charbroiled shrimp, filet mignon and fresh tuna steak have kept the Cat & Owl popular. Finish off your meal with delicious banana fritters. The restaurant is open Monday through Saturday for dinner. Reservations are suggested.

Lakeview Restaurant at Douthat State Park

$, no credit cards • Va. Rt. 629, Clifton Forge • (540) 862-8111

This historic landmark is a vision of rustic beauty. The casual dining area has high-beamed ceilings and a large gorgeous fireplace. The porch overlooks a 50-acre lake stocked weekly with trout. Try the sandwich menu for lunch, the buffet on Friday, Saturday and Sunday evenings and the pleasing à la carte Monday through Thursday. Lakeview Restaurant is open daily for lunch and dinner.

Eagle's Nest Restaurant

$$$ • 4100 Kanawha Tr., Covington • (540) 559-9738

At Eagle's Nest, established in 1930, you can have a gourmet meal on a deck overlooking a waterfall, somewhat like dining in Frank Lloyd Wright's private home. The nature lover and adventurous tourist will love this place that's in the middle of practically nowhere (about 1½ hours west of Roanoke and 20 minutes from White Sulphur Springs, West Virginia). It's one of the most intriguing places in the entire Blue Ridge. In an ancient log cabin decorated with antiques, beside that breathtaking waterfall outlined in purple irises and a pool filled with trout and ducks, you'll see chubby felines (the restaurant's charity cases) roaming the mountain crags 70 feet straight up. The scenery alone makes this place one you won't forget. But nothing about the food is forgettable either.

Served on country-blue speckled metal plates, dinners may be international in flavor one day, with a cucumber and mint salad, or traditional, with fresh brook trout, the next. Salads may be mandarin orange with pecan, and the soup may be cream of leek. Select from a full complement of house wines, including their own Virginia table wine under the Eagle Nest Label with Horton Wineries. The Horton Vineyards received gold ratings for two wines in the 1994 and 1995 Governor's Cup Wine Competition. Eagle's Nest is also among an elite group of award-winning Virginia wine retailers and restaurants. They are Covington's only honoree as a Three Cluster top award winner in the Virginia State and Wine Marketing Program. The waitstaff provides impeccable service. This is an experience anyone in love with the Blue Ridge shouldn't miss. Fidgety children might not do well here, since the pace is leisurely. The restaurant is open for dinner seven days a week. Reservations are requested.

Best Western, Brass Lantern

$$ • U.S. Hwys. 60 and 220, Covington • (540) 962-4951

A relaxing atmosphere and top-notch service accompany your meal here. An all-new menu includes T-bone, New York strip and blackened rib-eye steaks. You can also choose Alleghany trout and shrimp prepared three ways. Chicken dishes include chicken Eugene, consisting of ham and provolone topped with mushroom sauce. For dessert, look to all-American pies such as apple and pecan. It's open seven days a week, breakfast through dinner.

Imperial Wok

$ • 348 W. Main St., Covington • (540) 962-3330

A Chinese restaurant of high caliber, Imperial Wok is a favorite of Covington residents and is known miles around for its quality. The more popular dishes include the Seafood Delight, chicken and shrimp combo and mixed vegetables with shrimp. Another favorite is the Happy Family meal, which is made with chicken, beef, pork, shrimp and fresh vegetables. It's open daily for dinner.

James Burke House Eatery

$ • 232 Riverside St., Covington • (540) 965-0040

Stop at this restaurant in a historic home (c. 1817) for breakfast or lunch. The menu includes soups, sandwiches, salads and desserts, all homemade and delicious. Especially popular are the quiche, Greek salad and homemade chicken- and tuna-salad sandwiches. The restaurant is open Monday through Friday.

Bath County

Cafe Albert
$$ • The Homestead, Hot Springs
• (540) 839-7777

Come discover this small, intimate cafe in Hot Springs, outside the looming Homestead. It used to be a guest cottage in the Homestead's earlier days and is one of the few structures that survived a 1901 fire there. Here is an opportunity to dine in a bistro setting. Continental breakfasts and light lunches are on the menu, as are an assortment of freshly baked breads, pastries and cookies from The Homestead kitchens. You can start off your day indoors or on the patio with fresh berries, sliced banana with cream or melon. Then try the scrambled eggs Western style with cheddar cheese served with toast and fresh fruit. Or sample the Cafe's Crepe Albert, paper-thin crepes with fluffy scrambled eggs and tomato butter sauce served with smoked, sugar-cured ham.

Cafe Albert's lunch menu is just as tasty. While waiting for your lunch, the cafe offers you its own strawberry spritzer or Virginia apple cider cooler. You have a choice of sandwiches, such as hot corned beef or chicken salad, all served on rye, white, whole wheat, brioche or croissant. You will also receive your choice of macaroni, potato, fruit or tortellini salad, coleslaw or cottage cheese. Lunch entrees include Spinach Salad Supreme; Virginia's Highland County smoked beef frank with chili, sauerkraut and relish; and the Cafe's Shenandoah Croissant, a thinly sliced breast of turkey with spinach leaves on a Homestead croissant, with watercress spread, pepper jelly and potato salad. Peanuts, cheeses and marmalades are featured in Cafe Albert's "Made in Virginia" section. The cafe is open year round on Saturday and Sunday for breakfast, lunch or early dinner; outdoor service is available in warm weather.

The Casino Club
$$ • The Homestead, Hot Springs
• (540) 839-7894

Adjacent to the first tee of The Old Course, The Casino Club offers a casual menu of mostly light fare, specialty drinks and desserts. You can dine out on the lawn in view of the beautiful tennis courts or indoors. The Casino is open daily April through October.

The Grille
$$$$ • The Homestead, Hot Springs
• (540) 839-7552

If you want to get all dressed up — coat and tie for men are required here — you'll appreciate the fabulous setting and gourmet dining at The Homestead, which offers a delightful menu for lunch, dinner or late supper daily from April through October. Your taste buds will be tempted by treats like poached Maine lobster Americaine, grilled yellowfin tuna steak and Chateaubriand for two. Reservations are required.

The Homestead Dining Room
$$$$ • The Homestead, Hot Springs
• (540) 839-7563

The world-renowned Homestead (see our Resorts chapter) offers exquisite dining and dancing with a decidedly sophisticated ambiance. The menu changes nightly and is always exquisite. Start with dishes like Virginia applewood smoked trout with horseradish and wasabi sauces. Entrees include fresh Maryland soft-shell crab, roast peppered Virginia coast wild striped bass or roast prime sirloin of beef. Ladies and gents are expected to dress for dinner, which is served daily. Reservations are required. You can also have breakfast here.

Sam Snead's Tavern
$$ • The Homestead, Hot Springs
• (540) 839-7666

Sam Snead's Tavern is housed in a historic old bank building complete with the original vault that houses the tavern's wine collection. The restaurant is named after native and lifetime Hot Springs resident Sam Snead, a heralded professional golfer who has won more golf tournaments than any golfer living or dead. The Tavern serves the very best in American and Continental cuisine in a convivial atmosphere. Entrees include The Hole in One, jumbo (22 ounce) beef rib chop; The Nineteenth Hole, a 12-ounce rib-eye steak; and Sam's Cheeseburger with fries, with cheddar, Monterey Jack and American cheeses. Other favorites are the grilled petit filet mignon with

Cajun spiced shrimp and the pan-seared Allegheny Mountain rainbow trout. For a real treat, have a slice of their fresh baked pie du jour. Homemade meals are served daily.

The Waterwheel Restaurant
$$$ • The Inn at Gristmill Square, Warm Springs • (540) 839-2231

Continental cuisine is served in the setting of an old mill here. This area, composed of restored 19th-century buildings, is full of rustic beauty. The restaurant's fresh smoked trout is a favorite. Appetizers may include bourbon shrimp or a pâté Maison country loaf of sausage, chicken livers and pork tenderloin blended with brandy and spices and served with house chutney. Entrees range from an all-American grilled rib-eye to swordfish and pasta of the day. Guests are invited to descend past the grinding water wheel to the well-stocked wine cellar. Dinner is served daily; there's also a Sunday brunch.

Highland County

Highland Inn
$$ • Main St., Monterey • (888) 466-4682

This historic inn is a memorable setting for dinner. Formerly the Hotel Monterey, this three-story landmark is one of the few mountain resorts of its size still in operation in Virginia. Lace curtains, candlelight and classical music set the mood. Local fresh mountain trout and grilled Brace of Quail are just two of the creative choices. Be sure to leave room for the maple pecan pie, made rich with Highland County maple syrup — simply delicious. The Inn is open for dinner Monday through Saturday and for brunch on Sunday.

The Dave Matthews
Band had a regular
weekly gig at Trax in
Charlottesville before
they signed with RCA.

Nightlife

The Blue Ridge may be known more for its scenic beauty than its sound of music — but that trend is slowly changing, thanks in part to The Dave Matthews Band. There has always been a marvelous collection of musicians performing in and around the Blue Ridge, but the quintet from Charlottesville put a national spotlight on the area's nightlife scene.

It used to be you could drop by Trax in Charlottesville and see the local band for less than five bucks. Today, the Grammy-winning stars are playing in sold out arenas around the world. Their success has brought other acts to the region who want to play in Dave Matthews's back yard, and it is not unusual to see representatives from record companies scouting the local clubs for the "next Dave Matthews Band." In fact, September 67, from Charlottesville, and Everything, a band from James Madison University, recently signed recording contracts.

Now, it's true, most visitors to the Blue Ridge don't come for late nights or the bar scene. Daytime activities are so plentiful and enjoyable that most folks don't miss the lack of night-prowling opportunities that are more common in metropolitan areas.

However, clubs in the college towns of Charlottesville and Roanoke are sure remedies for the in-bed-at-a-reasonable-hour syndrome. You just need to know where to look, and we can point you toward some of the hot spots.

There is something to match almost any taste. Big resorts such as The Homestead, The Greenbrier, Wintergreen and the Boar's Head Inn also offer a range of nightlife activities. The Homestead has a DJ on weekend nights, The Greenbrier likes to entertain with live Big Band sounds, while the Boar's Head has a comfortable piano lounge. Or you can try the Floyd County General Store, where everybody from miles around comes on Friday nights for a real hoedown.

Shenandoah Valley

Frederick County

The Daily Grind
3 S. Loudoun St., Winchester
• **(540) 662-2115**

This shop on the walking mall serves lunch in its outdoor cafe as well as hosts a variety of bands in the evening. Local jazz, rock and folk musicians perform on Friday and Saturday, while Wednesday is open-mike night.

The Satisfied Mind Bookstore and Coffeehouse
11 S. Loudoun St., Winchester
• **(540) 665-0855**

For a relaxed experience, try the Satisfied Mind. You can buy new and used books, sample a selection of specialty coffees or hear a mix of acoustic, jazz and folk music on Friday and Saturday nights.

Rockingham County

Encounters Lounge
Va. Rt. 644, Harrisonburg
• **(540) 289-9441**

After a cool night on the slopes, you can warm up to a little dance music at Encounters Lounge at Massanutten Resort. This glass-walled club serves light meals throughout the day. During ski season, you can sit back and sip a hot toddy while listening to live regional bands on Friday and Saturday nights. There's a pretty good size dance floor here, too, if you are so inclined. Call for a schedule of performers and cover charge.

Froggies Lounge
1 Pleasant Valley Rd., Harrisonburg
• **(540) 434-9981**

The sports-oriented lounge in the Ramada Inn offers a comfortable setting to sit back, enjoy a few beverages and listen to local musicians. The weekends are pretty full with karaoke night on Friday, live bands on Saturday and comedians taking center stage on Sunday. The cover charge runs about $5.

JM's Bar & Grill
1007 S. Main St., Harrisonburg
• **(540) 433-8537**

JM's is designed with the college student in mind, and its location couldn't be better — right across the street from the JMU campus. This sports bar caters to the sandwich lover and serves up a pretty nice mix of music too. Local and regional bands play here on the weekends, and the cover charge will vary with each band. The lounge offers comedy on some Sundays. Bring your pool stick.

Main Street Bar and Grill
153 S. Main St., Harrisonburg
• **(540) 432-9963**

Here's where the college students hang out. Just a couple of blocks from the James Madison University campus, Main Street bills itself as the "Valley's cleanest restaurant, dance club and concert hall." There is usually something going on every evening from Wednesday through Saturday. Musicians, ranging from Northern Virginia's emmitt swimming to the AC/DC tribute band Hells Bells, keep the rock rolling, usually until 2 AM. The cover charge varies with each group. The space is available for parties or special events on Mondays, Tuesdays and Sundays.

Scruples
1400 E. Market St., Harrisonburg
• **(540) 433-2521**

In the Sheraton Four Points Hotel (see our Hotels and Motels chapter), the action is at Scruples, a lounge offering disc jockey-guided music every night except Thursday, when it hosts a popular comedy club, and Sunday, which is karaoke night. Local bands play some Saturdays. There is a small cover charge.

Augusta County

Bistro Bar
515 W. Frederick St., Staunton
• **(540) 886-5151**

In Staunton, evening entertainment takes on a more refined and relaxed tone at the Belle Grae Inn, a restored Victorian mansion on Frederick Street that has received the Historic Staunton Preservation Award and is consistently ranked as one of America's top inns (see our Bed and Breakfasts and Country Inns chapter). The Bistro Bar in this historic downtown inn and restaurant has classical and jazz music on Friday and Saturday nights during dinner. The decor is sophisticated and so is the service. In this classy atmosphere, surrounded by period antiques, you can relax to the sounds of regional classical and jazz musicians. You'll want to experience this gem for yourself.

Blue Mountain Coffees
18A Byers St., Staunton
• **(540) 886-4506**

If you would rather not wait up for a late-night concert, you can sample a little of Staunton's jazz scene in the afternoon at Blue Mountain Cafe. A jazz guitarist plays at this four-year-old restaurant every Wednesday from noon to 1:30 PM, and there's no cover charge. While you're here, try the bagel sandwiches.

Chubby's Sports Bar
1300 Greenville Ave., Staunton
• **(540) 887-8392**

It's easy to see that this new nightspot in Armand's Steak House caters to the visual crowd. The back wall is filled by a giant TV screen that stands nearly 6-feet tall. There's another screen to the side and TVs are tucked away in every nook and cranny so avid sports fans won't miss a second of the action. The

Though Blue Ridge nightlife tends toward the serene, there are still places where you can kick up your heels.

Photo: Wintergreen Resort

weekends, however, belong to those who love their entertainment live. Friday night is comedy night. Rock bands perform almost every Saturday. Cover charge is around five bucks. If you work up an appetite, the restaurant serves everything from nachos and chicken wings to steaks and homemade lasagna.

Dulaney's Lounge
U.S. Hwy. 250, Afton • (540) 943-7167

Local bands play every Friday and Saturday night at this lounge at the Inn at Afton (see our Hotels and Motels chapter). There maybe a few oldies or beach music sets, but you usually will hear Top-40 sounds. The cover charge varies. The inn is 3 miles east of Waynesboro just off Interstate 64 at Exit 99.

McCormick's Pub and Restaurant
41 N. Augusta St., Staunton
• (540) 885-3111

For more action, McCormick's Pub and Restaurant, on Augusta and Frederick streets, has occasional live music. The selections on

Thursday and Saturday nights range from classical to alternative, with some jazz thrown in as well. Wednesday's open-mike night is popular with the locals.

L'Italia
23 E. Beverley St., Staunton
• (540) 885-0102

Staunton has developed quite a jazz following. During the summer, there are free weekly jazz concerts in Gypsy Hill Park, and many of the regional acts who perform there are also frequent performers at L'Italia. Dress up or come as you are to this Italian restaurant and listen to free performances during dinner on Friday and Saturday nights.

Luigi's
111 N. Augusta St., Staunton
• (540) 886-5016

This is a popular spot with the Staunton crowd. Pizza and subs are on the menu, while a live local band comes in to play alternative or acoustic sets every other Tuesday.

Mulligan's Pub & Eatery
Va. Rt. 275, Staunton • (540) 248-6020

Mulligan's Pub & Eatery in the Holiday Inn right off Interstate 81 offers live bands playing rock, pop or oldies every Friday and Saturday nights and karaoke on Thursday. There is a cover charge. On Tuesday you can listen to acoustic acts for free.

Mill Street Grill
1 Mill St., Staunton
• (540) 885-5887

This cozy restaurant is in the enchanting old converted grist mill in the historic White Star Mill Building. Although the owners closed the upstairs Tavern, where DJs used to rule, you can still tap your toes once a week. On Wednesdays the downtown eatery serves up a night of jazz.

Lexington and Rockbridge County

The Drama of Creation
Natural Bridge of Virginia
• (800) 533-1410

For a truly breathtaking and religious experience, attend Natural Bridge of Virginia's Drama of Creation (see our Attractions chapter), held nightly throughout the year. This 45-minute program combines classical music and special lighting under Natural Bridge to tell the Biblical story of creation.

Harbs' Bistro
19 W. Washington St., Lexington
• (540) 464-1900

A quiet, sophisticated alternative, Harbs' Bistro serves wine, beer, cappuccino, extraordinary desserts and a full menu (see our Restaurants chapter). The patio is a perfect place to sip a cool drink on a hot summer night.

Lenfest Center
Washington & Lee University, Lexington
• (540) 463-8000

Washington & Lee's Lenfest Center (see our Arts chapter) hosts concerts and other events throughout the year. Call for a schedule.

Lime Kiln Theater
Lime Kiln Rd. • Box Office,
14 S. Randolph St., Lexington
• (540) 463-3074

Without question, the most exciting nightlife in Lexington in the summer happens at the outdoor Lime Kiln Theater (see our Arts chapter). The Sunday Night Concert Series draws huge crowds to hear reggae, bluegrass or folk music. Nearly every other night, Lime Kiln Theatre stages a play with a theme that relates in some way to the culture of the Southern mountains.

Lime Kiln has great picnic spots for dining before the performances.

The Palms
101 W. Nelson St., Lexington
• (540) 463-7911

The Palms is a downtown restaurant and bar with a big-screen TV. This is a popular college hangout, but locals also feel at home here.

Roanoke Valley

Things definitely start getting livelier if you drive an hour south of Lexington to the Roanoke Valley. If you're looking for nightlife, skip the bedroom communities of Botetourt and Craig counties, though. Everybody's home with their families, sleeping. However, you can rub shoulders with fellow insomniacs, dating couples or the newly single seeking to be double at a variety of nightspots in the rest of this area.

Most clubs offering live entertainment or

INSIDERS' TIP

If you are making a trip to Charlottesville in the summer, you can hear top bands from across the region playing every Friday from 5:30 to 8 PM at the outdoor amphitheater on the historic downtown mall. Fridays After Five starts in mid-April and runs through September. The shows are free.

Photo: Wintergreen Resort

Many restaurants in this area double as local nighttime hangouts.

dance music charge an admission price, but it is usually less than $5.

Charades
2801 Hershberger Rd. N.W., Roanoke
• (540) 563-9300

Charades, at the Marriott off I-581 on Hershberger Road, is a great place for DJ-inspired dancing. Come early for the hungry-hour buffet and stay for the fun. The club runs frequent promotions and theme nights.

Cheers
Va. Rt. 419 and Braeburn Dr., Salem
• (540) 389-4600

Cheers is a lively, classy bar with a raised dance floor that stays full every weekend night. Every Wednesday night the stage is packed with wanna-be stars singing and dancing to karaoke music. Live entertainment on weekends includes both local and regional bands.

Chico & Billy's Prestigious Pizza & Pasta Palace
32 Market Sq., Roanoke • (540) 342-1197

Where else can you find a fresh, hot pepperoni pizza at 2 AM . . . for $5? Chico & Billy's started its late-night weekend business by walking through the downtown Market, hot pizza in hand, selling to the hordes of downtown bar hoppers being sent home for the night. Now crowds line up around the block to buy two, three or more pizzas to feed their hunger. Standing in line becomes a social event itself.

The Coffee Pot
2902 Brambleton Ave., Roanoke
• (540)774-8256

Established in 1936, The Coffee Pot is "Roanoke's Oldest Roadhouse." Events ranging from birthday parties to weddings and everything in between have been held here. The

Coffee Pot offers live music five or more nights a week. "The Grand Ol' Uproar" is an open-mike night for folk and bluegrass musicians. Blues, jazz and rock 'n' roll lovers alike will enjoy the variety and talent of the musicians that frequent this club.

Confeddy's
24 Campbell Ave., Roanoke
• **(540) 343-9746**

Confeddy's is one of a number of great places on Roanoke's City Market to catch live entertainment. Show off your talent on Wednesday nights at open-mike night, hosted by a local band who will back up your vocal or musical performance. Upstairs you'll find a popular place to shoot a game of pool, although some don't like the long wait for the single table. Downstairs on weekend nights you can dance the night away to local and regional bands like Stone Groove and Key West.

Corned Beef & Co.
107 S. Jefferson St., Roanoke
• **(540) 342-3354**

Corned Beef & Co. is known as Roanoke's best nightspot, and the crowds on Friday and Saturday nights are definitely an indication of this distinction. You will usually find a DJ pumping out the music and keeping the dance floor packed. Bands play here on occasion as well. If you need a break from dancing, you can head upstairs to the rooftop deck where many of Roanoke's VIPs have been spotted lounging and sipping drinks.

Downstairs, large brick ovens turn out wood-fired pizzas that are absolutely delicious. (See our Restaurants chapter.) Corned Beef & Co. partners with a local radio station to host special events (like pre-concert parties and St. Patrick's Day celebrations) almost monthly.

The Elephant Walk
4468 Starkey Rd., Roanoke
• **(540) 774-4400**

The Elephant Walk is an upscale dance club located in the Holiday Inn near Tanglewood Mall. The club is known for Roanoke's best bar food, usually found at their happy hour buffets. The young, rich and beautiful of Roanoke can often be found here dancing the night away.

Full Moon Cafe
107 Market Sq., Roanoke
• **(540) 342-4593**

Full Moon is the only place on the market with yard-high beer steins. Few ever make it to bottoms up, and when they do, it's a real splash! Local recording artists Radar Rose host an open-mike night on Wednesday that brings incredible talent from miles around. Live entertainment is featured throughout the weekend as well.

Mac 'N' Bob's
316 E. Main St., Salem • **(540) 389-5999**

Mac 'N' Bob's (see our Restaurants chapter) has been a favorite of Salem residents and Roanoke College students alike for nearly 20 years. The 48-foot bar and three TVs are great for getting together with friends and watching the big game. On Thursday nights during the school year, the restaurant has live entertainment. If you're looking for a college crowd, this is the place to go!

Mill Mountain Coffee & Tea
112 Campbell Ave., Roanoke
• **(540) 342-9404**

A more sedate place to congregate is Mill Mountain Coffee & Tea, in the heart of the downtown City Market. You can sip cappuccino or Italian iced tea while you people-watch from the tables outside on the sidewalk or tables in the two alcoves by the huge windows at the front of the shop. They've got some of the best coffee and tea du jour in the Blue Ridge, along with yummy desserts. Everybody who's anybody meets here for both business meetings and fun.

The same goes for the other Mill Mountain locations at 4710 Starkey Road in Roanoke and 17 E. Main Street in Salem. (See our Restaurants chapter.)

Mill Mountain Star
Off Blue Ridge Pkwy., Roanoke
• **no phone**

Many dates end, or begin, at this incredible illuminated landmark overlooking Roanoke near Mill Mountain Zoo (see our Attractions chapter). The star, a 100-foot-high metal structure, is magnificent itself, but the nighttime view of Roanoke is breathtaking. *Roanoker Magazine* readers called it the "Best Place to Propose Marriage," and you often hear about newlyweds returning on their anniversary to this special spot. Don't miss this truly unique experience.

O'Dells On The Market
19 Salem Ave., Roanoke
• **(540) 342-9340**

With the exception of the gorgeous antique mirrored bar that lines one wall, O'Dells is far from ostentatious. The real charm and charisma here come from the incredible jazz and blues acts the club features on weekend nights. Many nights may be standing room only, but it's worth it to experience a caliber of musicians you won't find elsewhere.

The Park
615 Salem Ave., Roanoke
• **(540) 342-0946**

For an alternative experience, do The Park and mingle with Roanokers both gay and straight. Many consider it the best place in town to dance because of its all-night Saturday hours (5 AM closing time) and spacious dance floor. You'll find people from your office right alongside the drag queens and teenagers with yellow, red or purple hair and black nail polish. (Good luck telling who's who!)

The Pine Room at Hotel Roanoke
110 Shenandoah Ave., Roanoke
• **(540) 985-5900**

If you're looking for an elegant evening away from the throngs of 20-somethings you typically find in the Downtown Market area, try the Pine Room in posh Hotel Roanoke & Conference Center (see our Hotels and Motels chapter). A gorgeous setting and marvelous service are indicative of facilities at this five-star hotel. The Pine Room offers live weekend entertainment (acoustic musicians), billiards and atmosphere.

Spurs Restaurant & Lounge
1502 Williamson Rd., Roanoke
• **(540) 344-0500**

If line-dancing is more your style, try Spurs. A roomy dance floor and free early evening dance lessons will have your feet tapping in no time. The club offers live music on weekend nights, including some top acts from around the country. A recent expansion made way for an additional dance floor in a room where the DJ plays Top-40 dance music.

Star City Diner
118 S. Jefferson St., Roanoke
• **(540) 343-9301**

A fun downtown attraction is Star City Diner, which you can't miss. Its skyline includes a new wave version of the old-fashioned Big Boy Restaurant statue — complete with earring and tattoo. The interior is as outrageous as its exterior. Every inch of the walls (and ceiling) is covered with off-the-wall memorabilia. The restaurant serves a variety of late-night fare and is open 24-hours.

Texas Tavern
114 W. Church Ave., Roanoke
• **(540) 342-4825**

This no-frills lunchtime landmark in downtown Roanoke is also a favorite spot for a midnight snack. Voted "Best Late Night Food" by Roanokers, Texas Tavern will satisfy the heartiest late-night appetite. (See our Restaurants chapter.)

INSIDERS' TIP

If you're looking for big-time entertainers, the Nissan Pavilion at Stone Ridge is just a few miles east of Fauquier County in Bristow. This outdoor amphitheater hosts the biggest names in the business from late spring to early fall. Among those on 1999's schedule are Lenny Kravitz, The Black Crowes, Shania Twain, 'NSync, Jimmy Buffett, Tom Petty, Paul Simon and Bob Dylan. Call (800) 551-SEAT for tickets.

East of the Blue Ridge

Orange County

Firehouse Cafe
137 W. Main St., Orange
• **(540) 672-9001**

This cafe in downtown Orange offers live music on weekends, mostly rhythm and blues. There is usually no cover charge, but call first to find out schedules and prices.

Albemarle County

Baja Bean Company
1327 W. Main St., Charlottesville
• **(804) 293-4507**

You can be the star at this Mexican restaurant (see our Restaurants chapter). Every Monday night, Gretchen Casler hosts an open-mike night. You'll find plenty of seating on the patio to listen to live music on some Friday and Saturday nights. There is no cover.

Biltmore Grill
16 Elliewood Ave., Charlottesville
• **(804) 293-6700**

This popular eatery was listed as one of the Top-100 college bars in the country in the October 1997 issue of *Playboy* magazine. When the nearby University of Virginia is in session, you may hear everything from acoustic guitar acts to rock bands. The Biltmore serves interesting salads, desserts and pasta dishes too. Also see our Restaurants chapter.

Blue Ridge Brewing Company
709 W. Main St., Charlottesville
• **(804) 977-0017**

The Blue Ridge Brewing Company, Virginia's first restaurant/brewery, is a popular hangout for UVA students. It serves wonderful homemade meals and beers (see our Restau-

rants chapter), and live acoustic music on Saturdays. Some events are free, some charge.

Bomb Shelter
946 Grady Ave., Charlottesville
• **(804) 296-8045**

When John Ross Cann decided to open a new nightclub in downtown Charlottesville, he already had a name picked out. He was pleasantly surprised to find out that his building did, indeed, contain an old bomb shelter. Drop by and you can hear a variety of regional hip-hop and rock bands every weekend. The cover charge is usually in the $5 range. The sandwiches with deli-meat and fresh baked bread are a blast, too.

Durty Nelly's
2200 Jefferson Park Ave., Charlottesville
• **(804) 295-1278**

Durty Nelly's is a gritty little joint that serves sandwiches and has live music, usually local rock 'n' roll, folk or country bands, Tuesday, Thursday, Friday and Saturday nights. Schedules often change with the seasons, so call ahead if you're headed their way. There is usually a cover charge, around $3.

Katie's Country Club
U.S. Hwy. 29 N., Charlottesville
• **(804) 974-6969**

This nightspot in the Shoppers World Shopping Center is a popular spot for those who like to listen and dance to country music. Live regional bands play every Friday and Saturday night. On Thursdays a DJ drops by to spin Top-40 dance tunes. In 1997, the club started a summer teen dance night on Tuesdays that was chaperoned by area teachers. There will be an admission fee at the door, usually $5 or $6.

Max
120 11th St. S.W., Charlottesville
• **(804) 295-6299**

Max boasts having the largest dance floor

INSIDERS' TIP

If big dance floors are a plus in your nightlife expectations, the New River Valley has the largest in the region at Huckleberry's in Christiansburg.

in central Virginia. It has DJs on Thursday nights and live country music on the weekends. Students pour in on Wednesdays for country line-dance classes. Call for the cover charge.

Michael's Bistro
1427 University Ave., Charlottesville
• (804) 977-3697

You might catch a lot of University of Virginia students at this restaurant. It's right across the street from the campus, plus there's no cover charge when bands perform. Michael's Bistro is going for themed nights, usually acoustic or bluegrass on Sunday, funk and rock on Monday and jazz on Tuesday.

Miller's
109 W. Main St., Charlottesville
• (804) 971-8511

Miller's on the Downtown Mall, an excellent jazz club and restaurant, offers live music Monday through Saturday. Trumpet player John D'earth, who toured with Bruce Hornsby, plays here regularly. You'll also hear blues and acoustic. A big outdoor patio is great in the summer if the heat isn't too withering. Cover charge is usually less than $5. (Oh yes, Dave Matthews used to tend bar here.)

Montereys
2162 Barracks Rd., Charlottesville
• (804) 977-0166

There's music nightly at this local favorite in the north wing of the Barracks Road Shopping Center. You can hear blues, jazz and country by local and regional bands or some nights a DJ will be on hand to spin your favorite dance tunes. Wednesday, however, you're on your own. It's karaoke night. The cover charge runs about $3.

Orbit Billiards & Cafe
Corner of University Ave. and 14th St., Charlottesville • (804) 984-5707

It may be tough to find a table here even when live music isn't on the schedule. This popular local hangout is upstairs above Espresso Corner near UVA. Aside from pool and sandwiches, Orbits tries to book weekly local shows ranging from hard fusion to Delta blues. You may even catch an Irish act or two. Call to check for listings and cover charges.

Outback Lodge
917 Preston Ave., Charlottesville
• (804) 979-7211

This small club in Preston Plaza packs a wide mix of local, regional and national acts throughout the year. While most of the music leans to the blues side, Outback also has been known to bring in funk, rock and alternative music on Tuesday through Saturday nights. (There is usually a billiard tournament underway on Sunday.) The cover charge varies, but it's usually around five bucks.

Prism Coffeehouse
214 Rugby Rd., Charlottesville
• (804) 97-PRISM

We talked about the Prism Coffeehouse in our Arts chapter but mention it again here because it is such a great place to hear live bluegrass, folk and other acoustic music. The coffeehouse occasionally brings in nationally (and sometimes internationally) known musicians such as John Hartford and Tony Rice. The Prism also provides a forum in which the area's top folk, acoustic and bluegrass musicians can perform. There is an admission fee, and it is closed during the summer months.

Terrace Lounge
U.S. Hwy. 250 W., Charlottesville
• (804) 296-2181

The Terrace Lounge at the Boar's Head Inn (see our Resorts chapter) is a piano lounge with live music Tuesday through Saturday. George Melvin, who has recorded a live CD of his concerts at the Boar's Head, provides the entertainment. There is no cover charge. When the weather's nice, you can sit outside on an open porch overlooking the inn's pond.

Tokyo Rose
13 University Shopping Center, Charlottesville • (804) 296-3366

During the day, Tokyo Rose is a popular sushi bar, but at night, this small club has rocked Charlottesville with some of the cutting-edge stars on the national independent music scene. The Rose has hosted everyone from Juliana Hatfield to punk rock bands whose names we can't print in a family-oriented book. Even John Lennon's son, Sean, dropped in to play with his pals from Cibo Matto. Someone's on stage most weekends, and you might catch a couple of acts during the week as well. Call for cover charges.

Trax
122 11th St. S.W., Charlottesville • (804) 295-8729

If you are looking for what's hot in modern rock, Trax marks the spot. It's the hot place in town to listen to some nationally known and popular regional and local artists. In the past couple of years, artists such as Jewel, 311, Wilco, Son Volt, Cracker, Matchbox 20, Shawn Colvin and George Clinton and the P-Funk Allstars have packed the house. There is something going on almost every night, and you never know who might just be the big stars of tomorrow. (The Dave Matthews Band had a regular weekly gig here before they signed with RCA.) Price of admission will vary with each band.

Nelson County

Bistro 151
Va. Rt. 151, Nellysford • (804) 361-1463

At this Nelson Country restaurant you can listen to a little free piano music during dinner on most Saturday evenings and also to blues, rock and country music on several weekends. The Bistro is easy to find, right in the Valley Green Shopping Center. Call for schedule and cover charges.

Cooper's Vantage
Va. Rt. 151, Wintergreen Resort • (804) 352-8090

Wintergreen Resort near Nellysford can be a lively place, particularly during ski season, when skiers pack the bar and dance floor at Cooper's Vantage, a slopeside nightspot and restaurant. Its lounge regularly has live entertainment, running the gamut of Top-40, country and rock 'n' roll bands, on the weekends in summer and fall, nightly during ski season. There's usually no cover.

Lynchburg

While Lynchburg is typically a quiet city, there are a few nightspots that will provide you with some late-night excitement.

Badlanders
4007 Wards Rd., Lynchburg • (804) 237-7114

Badlanders is a country-western bar in the heart of Lynchburg. It has live bands Wednesday through Saturday night. There is a cover charge, but if you arrive before the entertainment starts (usually before 8:30 PM), they'll admit you for free.

Cattle Annie's
4009 Murray Pl., Lynchburg • (804) 846-2668

Cattle Annie's, next to the Holiday Inn, is a country-western entertainment complex. The place features a 4,500-square-foot dance floor and offers dance lessons and live entertainment throughout the week, Tuesday through Saturday. Top-name country bands, like the Kentucky Headhunters, are featured every month, and fans of '70s Southern rock will occasionally find their icons performing in concert at Cattle Annie's as well. Wednesday is family night; all ages are welcome. Women are admitted for free on "Feelin' Frisky Friday."

Jazz Street Grill
3225 Old Forest Rd., Lynchburg • (804) 385-0100

For unique atmosphere and some hot live jazz, try Jazz Street Grill, located in the Winn-

---

INSIDERS' TIP

Those little-known bands you hear today could be the next big stars of tomorrow. Trax in Charlottesville has a reputation for bringing in the hot young acts on the rise. One of its recent acts, Jewel, was a 1997 Grammy nominee for best new artist of the year.

Photo: Roanoke Valley Convention and Visitors Bureau

The Roanoke City Market is the focal point of many after-dark activities.

Dixie Shopping Center. This New Orleans Cajun-style restaurant hosts talented jazz musicians every Friday and Saturday night.

T.C. Trotters
2496 Rivermont Ave., Lynchburg
• **(804) 846-3545**

If you are searching for the college crowd in Lynchburg, look no further than T.C. Trotters. Wednesday night is College Night, and the bar serves up nickel drafts to those bearing a college I.D. Live entertainment hits the stage every night from Tuesday through Sunday and varies from Top-40 to blues. For a more tranquil evening come on Sunday night for folk music.

New River Valley

One hour south, you'll hit College Town, USA: the New River Valley. If you feel self-conscious around The Young and The Tanned, stay in Roanoke, where the crowd is older. If you don't, head for Blacksburg pronto! There you'll find two major universities, Virginia Tech and Radford, within cruising distance of each other. Where to start? How about Blacksburg, home to 23,000 college students.

Blacksburg

Bogen's
622 N. Main St., Blacksburg
• **(540) 953-2233**

Bogen's (see our Restaurants chapter) has become well-known in recent years for its cyberbar. Although the restaurant is popular with college students, you can rub elbows with Blacksburg's young professionals as well.

Hokie House Restaurant
322 N. Main St., Blacksburg
• **(540) 552-0280**

Hokie House, located right across from the Virginia Tech campus, is a local favorite. The restaurant has a sports bar upstairs and a casual bar and dining downstairs. It also has seven pool tables, air hockey and other video games to occupy those late-night hours. Thursday and Friday nights you can order late-night breakfast from midnight to 3 AM.

Preston and Company
218 N. Main St., Blacksburg
• **(540) 552-7471**

This club used to be Arnolds; it has a new name, but they are still serving up a mix of "hot stuff" food and music for the college crowd. You can find a DJ serving up entertainment most weekend nights, but the bar occasionally features live bands. It's also known to be a hangout for several of the bands who have come to town to perform at Virginia Tech. Ladies, gather your girlfriends and head here for karaoke on Wednesday night. It's also Ladies' Night, and you'll get in for free.

Sharkey's Grill
216 N. Main St., Blacksburg
• **(540) 552-2030**

Sharkey's is home of the Super Mug (a 34-ounce beer mug) and is known for the "best wings and ribs in town." Happy Hour lasts nearly all afternoon here — from 2 to 9 PM! The restaurant has two bars, five pool tables, a pinball machine and a juke box. There are also five TVs so you don't have to miss a minute of the game!

South Main Cafe
117 S. Main St., Blacksburg
• **(540) 961-6316**

This restaurant is an entertainment hub in Blacksburg. The entertainment, provided live six nights a week, is as diverse as the crowds who congregate here. Monday you'll find jazz music floating from the doorway. The "Old Time Jam" on Tuesday nights features local musicians who play to the delight of cloggers and square dancers. Wednesday night is a long-standing party, where a Grateful Dead cover band called The Kind gets everyone dancing. Thursday through Saturday other local or regional acts perform to a mostly college-age audience. The atrium has pool tables, foosball and video games.

Christiansburg

Huckleberry's Restaurant
2790 Roanoke St., Christiansburg
• **(540) 381-2382**

Huckleberry's (see our Restaurants chapter), on U.S. Highway 11 off the I-81–Virginia Tech Exit, has two lounges that offer Top-40 and country entertainment. Country-music lovers should definitely stop here to boot-scoot on the largest dance floor around.

Radford

Whiners Sports Bar & Grill
612 E. Norwood St., Radford
• (540) 633-5315

Whiners' casual atmosphere and six TVs (two are big-screens) make it the perfect hangout for sports nuts. The bar runs food and drink specials throughout the week. Friday and Saturday nights you can catch local and regional bands playing just about every genre of popular music.

Floyd County

Floyd County General Store
206 S. Locust St., Floyd
• (540) 745-4563

In Floyd County, you'll do your rocking and rolling country style at the legendary General Store's Friday night live hoedowns (see our Attractions chapter). Here bluegrass and old-time musicians entertain crowds for free every Friday night.

Pine Tavern
U.S. Hwy. 221 N., Floyd
• (540) 745-4482

Head for the Pine Tavern in Floyd, where anybody who's anybody, including local musicians, hangs out on Saturday night to be entertained! Come on Sunday night to watch, or participate in, open-mike night. The Pine Tavern also has dinner theater every Tuesday in June and offers nonsmoking performances part of the time. (See our Restaurants chapter.)

Alleghany Highlands

The western limits of the Blue Ridge limits its nightlife to the great Homestead and Greenbrier resorts. Also see our Skiing chapter for information on night skiing in this winter wonderland.

The Presidents Lounge
The Homestead Resort, Hot Springs
• (800) 838-1766

The Presidents Lounge at The Homestead (see our Resorts chapter) is an elegant place to gather before and after dinner. Adorning the walls are portraits of the 13 presidents who have visited the resort. Downstairs in The Sports Bar you will find big-screen and other TVs for viewing sporting events; you can also play billiards and Foosball here. There is also a DJ after 10 PM on weekends.

Old White Club
The Greenbrier, White Sulphur Springs, W.Va. • (800) 624-6070

Elegance awaits you at The Greenbrier (see our Resorts chapter), where you can dance under sparkling chandeliers to live bands of the contemporary or Big Band variety. Visiting the Old White Club will make it a night to remember.

Most towns in the Blue Ridge have at least one quaint antique shop and a place featuring the work of local crafters.

Shopping

Whether you're looking for antiques, handcrafts or outlet malls for bargains in clothing and housewares, the Blue Ridge region has a wonderful variety of choices. Of course, we have the usual shopping malls, Wal-Marts and Kmarts. But most towns in the Blue Ridge have at least one quaint antiques shop and a place featuring the work of local crafters.

Some fine furniture makers in the region, such as E.A. Clore in Madison or Suter's in Harrisonburg, sell directly to the consumer. You must visit their showrooms to see what they make because you won't find their beautiful furniture elsewhere.

This is also true for the shops selling fine handcrafts. Places such as the Blue Ridge Pottery on U.S. Highway 33 near Skyline Drive and Limeton Pottery in Front Royal specialize in ceramics that are crafted literally right next door. Other shops, such as Forever Country in New Market and the Handcraft House in Madison, represent dozens of artisans whose creations also cannot be found in department stores.

Charlottesville is known for its fine downtown shops that sell crafts and other objets d'art from around the globe. In this Blue Ridge city you can just as easily find an African mask or Indian totem as a bar of American soap.

If you're visiting from out of state and want a made-in-Virginia souvenir, plenty of shops specialize in such products. Virginia Born and Bred in Lexington is one fine example, selling beautiful brass and silver items as well as folk art, woven goods, peanuts, jams and jellies. Virginia Made in Staunton and The Virginia Shop in Charlottesville are others.

The following is a description of some of our favorite shops in the cities, towns and rural areas we've covered in this guide. This is in no way a comprehensive listing, and we may have inadvertently missed your favorite shop. Drop us a line and give us your Insider's perspective if you know of a top-notch place we've missed.

Also, in the retail world shops come and go, so call ahead if you have your heart set on a particular store. This seems especially true in the antique trade. We've given you the businesses' phone numbers to save you possible disappointment at the end of a long drive.

Shenandoah Valley

Winchester and Frederick County

An eclectic mix of antiques, galleries, furniture stores, fine clothing plus sidewalk cafes and indoor dining can be found in historic Old Town Winchester. More than 200 shops and services are in the 45 block National Historic District, including **Kimberly's**, (540) 662-2195, at 135 N. Braddock Street. Housed in Civil War general Sheridan's headquarters, Kimberly's sells fine European linens, stationery and home furnishings.

One of the finest places in the region to find handcrafted jewelry, pottery, basketry and textiles is **Winchester's Handworks Gallery**, (540) 662-3927, in the Loudoun Street Mall (for pedestrians only). Call ahead, as this gallery at 150 Loudoun Street operates on seasonal hours. Around the corner at 25 W. Piccadilly Street is the beautiful **Colonial Art and Craft Shop**, (540) 662-6513, which sells fine china, crystal, silver, elegant lamps and picture frames. You can also pick up one-of-a-kind gifts at **Hands on Pottery**, (540) 722-2610. The shop at 15 E. Boscawen Street includes a gallery and studio with work by potter Alicia White Daily.

Claire's at Creekside, (540) 662-0344, is one of several shops in Creekside Village, a

Williamsburg-style shopping development on U.S. Highway 11 south of Winchester. Claire's, at 100 Creekside Lane, carries women's clothing and accessories.

Antique collectors will enjoy a stop at **Millwood Crossing**, (540) 662-5157. There's approximately 10,000 square feet of antiques and specialty shops in this old apple-packing warehouse at 381 Millwood Avenue. Wooden floors and hand-hewn beams add to its comfortable charm. Inside is a collection of antique shops featuring American country pieces in pine, walnut, cherry and oak. Specialty shops include Flags Unlimited, Victorian Accents, Civil War Dressmaker and Apple Shop with local jams and jellies. Millwood is a half-mile off I-81 on U.S. 50 West.

Winchester is also home to the **Apple Blossom Mall**, (540) 665-0201. More than 70 stores, including many specialty shops, can be found at this indoor facility at 1850 Apple Blossom Drive.

A fun stop on a shopping excursion is Winchester's **Everything Rubbermaid**, (540) 678-4695. This retail store at 2238 Valley Avenue, on U.S. 11, features more than 2,500 Rubbermaid products that are made in Winchester's Rubbermaid factory.

The Cedar Creek Relic Shop, (540) 869-5207, a couple of miles away at 7841 Main Street in downtown Middletown, claims to have the largest collection of authentic Civil War relics for sale in the Shenandoah Valley. If you're looking for a sword, bayonet or musket from that bloody war, this shop has it. Be sure to call ahead to check on hours.

Shenandoah County

Strasburg considers itself the antique capital of Virginia. We don't necessarily endorse this claim, but we do agree that very fine antiques can be found here at fair prices.

Whether you're a serious collector or someone who just likes to drool over beautiful things, you must visit the **Strasburg Emporium**, (540) 465-3711, a 65,000-square-foot downtown building that houses more than 110 antiques and art dealers. The building, at 150 N. Massanutten Street, used to be a silk mill. Along with high-quality formal and country furniture, you'll find a lot of unusual items at the Emporium, such as iron beds and estate jewelry. The Strasburg Emporium is open daily and has plenty of free parking.

Every Friday, Saturday and Sunday, a huge flea market takes place between Woodstock and Edinburg, offering antiques and collectibles both inside and outdoors. To get to **The Flea Market**, (540) 984-8771, take Exit 283 from I-81. It's at 164 Landfill Road just off U.S. 11.

Richard's Antiques, at 14211 Old Valley Pike, (540) 984-4502, specializes in fine country and formal antiques and paintings. It's a mile south of Edinburg on U.S. 11.

New Market's downtown **Paper Treasures**, at 9595 Congress Street, (540) 740-3135, is a fascinating place to browse through old books, magazines and prints. The store sells old copies of *Collier's Weekly*, *The Saturday Evening Post*, *Ebony*, *Life*, *McCalls*, *Ladies Home Journal* and hundreds of other titles from the early the 1800s to the 1990s. Paper Treasures also carries old Civil War maps and books and a good selection of children's literature.

Shenandoah Valley Crafts and Gifts, at 9365 Congress Street (U.S. 11), (540) 740-3899, has a great mix of country furniture, fireworks, handloomed rugs, white oak baskets, quilts and Virginia hams — and don't miss the Rock Shop. At 9373 Congress Street is the **Christmas Gallery**, (540) 740-3000, which sells handmade crafts, wreaths, Snow Babies, Dept. 56 villages and hundreds of ornaments.

Warren County

If you follow U.S. 522 S. from Winchester toward Front Royal on a weekend, you'll find that traffic slows to a crawl on Commerce Avenue at a big outdoor flea market, **Front Royal Antique and Flea Market**, (540) 636-9729, where you can find almost anything your heart desires. On Va. Route 522 just outside Front Royal, a smaller weekend flea market, **Shen-Valley Flea Market**, (540) 869-1561, is a fun place to browse, and you can make some good finds among the array of books, T-shirts, tools, used furniture and glassware. Both flea markets stay open according to the weather. Rain and severe cold will keep most venders away.

If you want to shop indoors year round, visit the **Warren County Fairgrounds**, (540) 635-5827, where a flea market is held 9 AM to 5 PM on weekends. The fairgrounds are on Va. 522, 5 miles north of Front Royal at 26 Fairgrounds Road.

Simonpietri's Gift and Pawn Shop, at 528 S. Royal Avenue, (540) 635-3558, at the edge of town has a kitschy mixture of tourist items, plus crafts, guns and musical instruments. **The Royal Oak Bookshop**, 207 S. Royal Avenue, (540) 635-7070, has a wonderful selection of new, used and publishers' remainder books. It's open daily, but if you stop by after hours, you can sort through a selection of paperbacks and hardback books on the front porch to get you through the night. They only cost 10¢ each. Across the street at 206 S. Royal Avenue is **J's Gourmet**, (540) 636-9293, where you can purchase an assortment of wines from right here in Virginia to South Africa, Bulgaria and Greece. The shop also carries exotic coffees, spices, breads, meats and cheeses, and you can sample whatever assortment of goodies that the staff is preparing for the day.

Page County

In downtown Luray, **Mama's Treasures**, (540) 743-1352, has an extensive collection of colorful glassware and old costume jewelry. You can also find antique furniture and quilts at the shop at 22 E. Main Street. At 24 E. Main Street, is **Bren's**, (540)743-9001, which sells a variety of home-decor items such as antiques, estate jewelry, gift books and Victorian accents and angels.

Five miles east of Luray on Va. 211, at the entrance to the Shenandoah National Park, sits the **Pine Knoll Gift Shop**, (540) 743-5805. This old-time store is crammed with Elvis and Hank Williams souvenirs, knives, quilts, baskets, coonskin caps, Native-American moccasins and jewelry, jams and jellies, fireworks, great fudge and peanut brittle plus Blue Ridge pottery, rocks and minerals. The **Page Cooperative Farm Bureau**, 139 Virginia Avenue, (540) 743-5194, has an enormous selection of farm, garden and home items; you'll find a lot of everything at this unique store, from a full line of pet and livestock food to work clothes and Weedeaters. At **Gulliver's**, 55 Main Street, (540) 743-4460, you can browse through the bookstore then enjoy your selection in the store's coffeehouse/sandwich shop. An art gallery opened upstairs in 1997.

Rockingham County

Antiques

Nearly two dozen antique shops can be found throughout this area, which includes not just the thriving university city of Harrisonburg but also the little towns of Mt. Crawford, McGaheysville, Dayton and Elkton.

Chalot's Antiques, (540) 433-0872, is a mecca for lovers of fine old furniture. At 445 Main Street in tiny Mt. Crawford, in a building nearly 200 years old, the shop has six showrooms of high-quality 18th- and 19th-century antiques. The shop has hundreds of pieces of flow blue China, Victorian bric-a-brac, primitive accessories and old glassware.

Farther east, in Elkton, is one of the area's finer antiques shops, the **Curiosity Shop**, 306 W. Spotswood Trail, (540) 298-1404, where you'll find antique furniture, folk art, primitives, quilts and old tools for the most discriminating buyer. The shop has been open since 1973.

Jeff's Antiques, 90 Main Street in Dayton, (540) 879-9961, specializes in oak and walnut furniture and also carries pottery, primitives, toys and oil lamps.

Downtown Harrisonburg has several shops selling antiques and collectibles, most notably **James McHone Antique Jewelry**, (540) 433-1833. Here, at 75 S. Court Square, you'll find exquisite estate and antique jewelry, sterling flatware and oil paintings. **Villager Antiques**, 673 N. Main Street, (540) 433-7226, sells stained-glass windows and pottery along with oak and walnut formal furniture. At 779 E. Market Street, **Rolling Hills Antique Mall**, (540) 433-8988, has more than 50 dealers selling a variety of antiques and collectibles.

Farmers Markets

Just south of Harrisonburg on U.S. 11, **Shenandoah Heritage Farmer's Market**, (540) 433-3929, features an antiques mall, a produce market and a collection of specialty shops that sell just about everything, including crafts, bulk foods, local souvenirs, local artwork and home decorating items. You can also buy ice cream and pretzels. A new restaurant, Dinner Bell Cafe, offers home-cooked country meals. To find the market, take Exit 243 off I-81. It's right at the Harrisonburg city limits.

It's definitely worth driving to the little town of Dayton, just south of Harrisonburg, for the **Dayton Farmer's Market**, (540) 879-9885, a place where the merchants are incredibly friendly. Inside the indoor market on Warm Springs Road, peddlers sell fresh poultry, seafood, beef, home-baked goods, fresh fruits and vegetables, cheeses, nuts and dried goods. Specialty shops carry Early American tin lighting, pottery, quality antiques and handcrafts, clothes and even grandfather clocks.

Among the array of shops at Dayton Farmer's Market you'll find Swiss Valley Lace, The Cheese Place and Reflections of Yesteryear, which sells handcrafted furniture and Amish collectibles. You can have a hearty, delicious lunch at Huyard's Country Kitchen inside the market. Dave Huyard also runs an art shop, and you can see a sample of his work above the restaurant. The Dayton Farmer's Marker is south of Harrisonburg on Va. 42.

Handcrafts

Nearby on Va. 42 in Dayton is the **Clothes Line**, (540) 879-2505, a fabric shop that also sells brilliantly colored hand-woven rugs and quilts. Look for the hitching post out front where buggy-riding Mennonites tie their horses while they shop.

The Mennonite-operated **Gift and Thrift Shop** at 227 N. Main Street in downtown Harrisonburg, (540) 433-8844, takes you around the globe with its selection of gorgeous weavings, ceramics, clothing and other crafts made in about 35 developing nations. Many of the artisans are refugees, disadvantaged minorities or people with physical disabilities. The proceeds go to the Mennonite Central Committee, the relief and development wing of the church. The prices are great, and spending money here helps people in need.

Suter's Handcrafted Furniture at 2610 S. Main Street, (540) 434-2131, has been around since the early 1800s, when Daniel Suter, a skilled Mennonite cabinetmaker and carpenter, settled in the Harrisonburg area and began making furniture. Today, William Suter and his daughter, Carol, carry on the family tradition of quality craftsmanship. The company makes gorgeous Colonial reproductions in cherry, mahogany and walnut, using the finest techniques. They have showrooms here and in Richmond, or you can call for a free brochure.

The Bay Pottery on 142 Main Street in nearby Broadway, (540) 896-2417, sells unique handcrafted porcelain jewelry, pottery, wooden items, rugs and other crafts.

East of Harrisonburg in McGaheysville is the **Country Goose Gift and Craft Shop**, (540) 289-9626, that sells fine crafts made in the Shenandoah Valley. On McGaheysville Road, it's a short drive from Massanutten Resort on Va. 996. Here you will find salt-glazed pottery, handmade country furniture, folk art, baskets, benches, pillows, quilt racks, weavings and much more.

Other Unusual Shopping Spots

Harrisonburg's central business district has some specialty shops worth a visit, such as **A Touch of the Earth**, (540) 432-1894. This shop at 163 S. Main Street features Native American jewelry, women's clothing, pottery, drums and an extensive selection of beads. **Shotsie's Christmas & Collectibles**, 4090 Evelyn Byrd Avenue, (540) 433-9627, sells all-season collectibles and unusual Christmas items.

North of Harrisonburg near Timberville is a great place to partake of the region's sweetest crop of all — apples. **Showalter's Orchard and Greenhouse** on Va. 881, (540) 896-7582, has its own cider mill and sells freshly pressed cider and many varieties of apples from late September through December 1. The year-round greenhouse operation also sells just about anything that grows, from herbs to poinsettias. **Ryan's Fruit Market** on North Mountain Road northwest of Timberville, (540) 896-1233, sells apples, peaches and pumpkins from the first of September to mid-November. It's on Va. 613.

Locals flock to the **Green Valley Book Fair**, (540) 434-0309, held several weekends in the spring, summer, fall and winter at a warehouse off Va. 682 near Mt. Crawford. Every spring and fall there is also a record fair, lasting only a single weekend. New books and records are sold at cut-rate prices.

For those who prefer their shopping all under one roof, **Valley Mall** at 1925 E. Market Street, (540) 433-1875, has 80 department and specialty stores.

Augusta County

Antiques

You'll find more than 50 stores under one roof at the **Colonial Mall** at 1331 Greenville Avenue, (540) 885-0315, but historic downtown Staunton is full of interesting boutiques, including many antique shops. The city has a treasure trove of architectural delights packed into five National Historic Districts, offering numerous places to hunt for antiques, many of which are within easy walking distance of one another.

Near the renovated Wharf Area, you can easily get lost in the **Jolly Roger Haggle Shop**, (540) 886-9527. The shop at 27 Middlebrook Avenue is a treasure chest of coins, jewelry, china, old money, weapons, Civil War and Native American artifacts and much more. **Rose Street Interiors**, 2209 N. Augusta Street, (540) 886-0578, sells, crafts, collectibles, gifts and custom frames.

Depot Antiques, (540) 885-8326, has moved to a new location on U.S. 250 east of Staunton. The lovely shop (once featured in

Southern Living) features an array of country formal furniture pre-1860s folk art and gifts. Depot Antiques is open by appointment only.

Just north of Staunton on Va. 11 in Mt. Sydney, **Dusty's Antique Market**, (540) 248-2018, houses more than a dozen dealers of oak and walnut furniture, tools, quilts, primitives and other old things. **Rocky and Brenda's Gold and Silver** on U.S. 11 in Weyers Cave, (540) 234-8676, is a jewelrymakers delight. They sell gold and silver jewelry plus flatware and coins.

Also north of Staunton on Va. 11 in Verona is the **Verona Antiques and Flea Market**, (540) 248-3532, which is open Thursday through Sunday. Thirty dealers sell a large variety of oak, pine, cherry, walnut and other antique furniture along with quilts and linens, old books, china and more. The market is right across from the firehouse.

Handcrafts

The **Virginia Made Shop** at 286 Rowe Road, (540) 886-7180, has an extensive collection of foods, wines, handcrafts and other souvenirs from the commonwealth. It's just off I-81 at Exit 222 right next to the **Bacova Guild Company Store**, (800) 544-6118. Also at 286 Rowe Road, Bacova is famous for silkscreened handcrafts such as rugs and mailboxes.

Silver Linings, (540) 885-7808, in the downtown area at 16 W. Beverley, is a popular shop with tourists and locals. You'll find jewelry, including exotic and hard-to-find beads, and folk art from around the world along with clothes, pocketbooks and funky bric-a-brac. Across the street is the fascinating **Once Upon a Time** at 25 W. Beverley, (540) 885-6064, that sells antique clocks and modern watches of every variety. They also do repair work. It's "open by chance or by appointment."

Elder's Antique and Classic Automobiles, 114 S. New Street, (540) 885-0500, has

INSIDERS' TIP

The early bird gets the bargain. Remember that many of the mom-and-pop shops in the smaller towns along the Blue Ridge close early, many by 5 or 6 PM. So if you want to do some heavy-duty shopping, do it earlier in the day or call ahead to see how long the store will be open.

a big window through which you can see sleek old Rolls Royces and other beauties. You can see between 40 and 60 antique automobiles from 9:30 AM to 6 PM Saturdays or by appointment.

Specialty Shops

Rockfish Gap Outfitters, (800) 851-6027, is a fabulous place to pick up equipment for all your outdoor adventures, be they on a biking trail, camping trip or a paddle down the river. Located just a few miles off the Appalachian Trail on U.S. 250 in Waynesboro, the shop is a favorite restocking place for backpackers. Open Monday through Saturday, the store carries the best in tents and bags, including North Face and Sierra Designs, and a plethora of backpacks, daypacks and fanny packs. They also stock Gary Fisher, Trek and Cannondale Bikes, kayaks and canoes by Old Town Perception and Blue Hole, as well as Gramicci and Patagonia clothing. You can even pick up cooking utensils and some freeze-dried pizza or beef stroganoff to rustle up a hearty feast on the trail. This place truly is a smorgasbord for the outdoor adventure fanatic.

A number of Mennonite-operated businesses make shopping a real pleasure in the Stuarts Draft area. **The Cheese Shop**, (540) 337-4224, three-fourths of a mile north of Stuarts Draft on Tinkling Springs Road, has been an Amish-Mennonite family business since 1960. The store sells more than 30 varieties of cheese at great prices, along with nuts, dried fruits and other dry foods in bulk at the shop on Va. 608. The Cheese Shop is closed on Sundays.

Also on Va. 608 near U.S. 340, **The Candy Shop**, (540) 337-0298, sells a complete line of Hershey products, including reproductions of early tins and glass. Tours of the nearby Hershey plant in Stuarts Draft are not given,

but some of the items made there include Reese's Pieces, Whatchmacallits and Bar None. The Candy Shop also carries quilts, which they will custom make, along with handmade outdoor furniture. The shop is closed Sundays.

Other Unusual Shopping Spots

The first block of E. Beverley Street in downtown Staunton is a fun place to browse through shops and have lunch. **The Pampered Palate**, 26 and 28 E. Beverley Street, (540) 886-9463, sells gourmet sandwiches and also has an unusually good selection of Virginian, French and Italian wines. They do gift baskets too. Next door at 24 E. Beverley Street, **Grandma's Bait**, (540) 886-2222, carries fine clothing for infants and children, and the **Golden Tub Bath Shop** at 20 E. Beverley Street, (540) 885-8470, sells everything for the bath including elegant soaps, towels and accessories. **Holt's China and Gifts**, 16 E. Beverley, (540) 885-0217, specializes in beautiful china, fine glassware and special occasion gifts, including Lefton's Colonial Village and the Margaret Furlong Collection. **The Emporium**, 101 E. Beverley, (540) 885-1673, features a large selection of toys and gifts. **Arthur's**, 13 E. Beverley, (540) 885-8609, has a dazzling collection of lamps, Colonial Williamsburg reproductions and brass, pewter and silver items and accessories for the home.

Fanciers of the unique will want to browse through **Collector's Choice**, 18 W. Beverley, (540) 885-8572. The downtown shop has a wonderful selection of sculptures, dolls, toys, collector's plates and figurines among other curios. There is even a huge selection of gifts for the dog in your life. **Honeysuckle Hill**, 100 E. Beverley, (540) 885-8261, sells antiques, collectibles and gifts. The store's star attractions are handpainted birdhouses, made by a

Shenandoah Valley couple. The birdhouses come in 50 different designs and can be personalized. Just down the road is the **White Swan Gallery**, 107 E. Beverley Street, (540) 886-0522, where you can see and buy the work of regional artists, including the work of gallery owner/wildlife artist Laura Gilliland. Laura's art is as eclectic as her shop, which also sells American antiques and folk art.

Book lovers can get their fill of best-sellers and all types of new books at **The Bookstack**, 1 E. Beverley Street, (540) 885-2665. The shop also carries gift items, T-shirts and stationery.

In downtown Waynesboro at 328 W. Main Street is the **Valley Framing Studio and Gallery**, (540) 943-7529, which claims it has the Shenandoah Valley's largest inventory of frame supplies, limited-edition prints and other gifts.

Another special find in Waynesboro is **The Christmas Store**, 326 W. Main Street, (540) 943-6246. It carries Christmas collectibles, Snow Village, Heritage Village, Christopher Radko, Dept. 56, ornaments, antique Santa reproductions and American Christmas folk art along with other interesting curios. The shop is open from July to December. There is a second The Christmas Store at 286 Rowe Road in Staunton, (540) 885-8174. This larger shop is open year round.

Outlet Shopping

Waynesboro Village, (540) 949-500, is a factory outlet mall right off I-64 at Exit 94 in Waynesboro. This attractively designed outdoor mall at 601 Shenandoah Village Drive houses dozens of specialty shops carrying discounted brand-name clothing, shoes, luggage, home furnishings, lingerie and more. Liz Claiborne, Corning/Revere, Bass Shoes, Barbizon, Capacities Inc., Bacova Guild, Leather Loft, L'Eggs/Hanes/Bali and Bugle Boy are but a few of the stores here. Arts and crafts vendors often sell quality merchandise in the center area of the mall.

The Virginia Metalcrafters, (540) 949-9432, outlet in the mall will probably stir your curiosity enough to make you fight for a parking place at their foundry, showroom and retail store in downtown Waynesboro at 1010 E. Main Street. Through an observation window, you can watch craftsmen use the age-old technique of pouring molten brass into sand molds;

the brass objects are later ground, sanded and polished into faithful reproductions of 17th- and 18th-century pieces. The foundry reproduces candlesticks, lighting fixtures, fireplace tools and other pieces from historic places such as Colonial Williamsburg, Charleston, Newport, Monticello, Winterthur and Old Sturbridge Village. Their number at the outlet mall is (540) 949-8190.

Lexington

Antiques

For the largest display of antiques, go to **Lexington Antique & Craft Mall**, U.S. 11 N., (540) 463-9511, 40,000 square feet of quality arts and crafts with 250 dealers.

The **Lexington Historical Shop** in College Square Shopping Center off U.S. 11 N., (540) 463-2615, is the only shop of its kind in Virginia. It specializes in Confederate, horse and transportation-related original materials — autographs, documents, books, prints, soldiers' letters, flags, belt buckles, uniforms and more — to awe any Civil War buff. Owner Bob Lurate also offers Virginia-related histories, rare, out-of-print books and first-edition books, maps and other documents along with antique quilts and other collectibles. A catalog is available.

One of the finest antique stores in the Rockbridge County region is **Old South Antiques Ltd.**, (540) 348-5360, in the charming village of Brownsburg, 15 minutes north of Lexington via U.S. 11/ 710 or Va. 39/252. Old South specializes in New England, Pennsylvania and Southern antiques in original paint and refinished cherry, walnut and pine. The shop is recommended by American Country South for its country-style wares and known for its large selection of American Country furniture and accessories.

Braford Antiques on Va. 130, (540) 291-2217, is another exquisite shop down the road from Natural Bridge. The Brafords have a fine collection of 19th-century American furniture and pieces from Asia.

General Stores

Enjoy a step back in time with the Lexington area's real general store, **The General**

Store, 2522 Beech Avenue in Buena Vista, (540) 261-3860. Open since 1891, it has been in continuous business for more than 100 years and in many ways is actually a working museum. Don't miss the made-in-Virginia items and country crafts. This store even offers you the once-in-a-lifetime opportunity to visit an old-fashioned working outhouse! And next door is a swinging bridge across the river — a rare find these days. Visitors love The General Store with its early farm and transportation exhibit and century-old display cases. Aromas waft through the old building, where you can find a bit of everything including blue jeans, bulk seeds, fabric and kitchenware.

Handcrafts

Artists in Cahoots, (540) 464-1147, is a cooperative gallery of local artists and crafters downtown at 1 W. Washington Street. You'll find oil and watercolors, pottery, metalwork, handblown glass, photography, sculpture, handpainted silk scarves, porcelain jewelry, stained glass and decoys.

Other Unusual Shopping Spots

Downtown shopping is a panorama of boutique-type shops that will keep you browsing all day. **Virginia Born and Bred** at 16 W. Washington Street, (800) 437-2452, is a sophisticated shop chock-full of Old Dominion handcrafts, wine, fine brass work, linens and more. For sleek or funky dresses and exotic jewelry and accessories, don't miss **Pappagallo** at 23 N. Main, (540) 463-5988.

If new and used books are your idea of a perfect afternoon of browsing, go to **The Best Seller** on 29 W. Nelson Street, (540) 463-4647. Try the **Second Story**, (540) 463-6264, located with The Lexington Historical Shop in College Square Shopping Center. Both stores carry new and used, out of print and first editions on horse-related, Confederate-related and transportation material.

If you're hankering for chocolate, head down to **Cocoa Mill Chocolates** at 115 W. Nelson Street, (540) 464-8400. Hand-dipped, scrumptious confections are sold individually or by the box, and the owners also have a mail-order service.

In Rockbridge County on Va. 606 at Racine, Don Haynie and Tom Hamlin welcome you to the wonderful world of herbs in a big way. They are the darlings of the local garden club set for the way they have renovated **Buffalo Springs Herb Farm**, (540) 348-1083, an extraordinary 18th-century stone house and garden open for herbal teas, luncheons and tours. These two perfectionists have a huge following for their herb workshops that always feature flawless food (such as handpressed herbal cookies) and decor. A gorgeous gift shop in a big red barn sells herbal products, dried flowers and garden books. The display gardens look like something out of Colonial Williamsburg. You'll see a culinary garden, springhouse tea garden and foursquare heirloom vegetable and herb garden.

To make a wonderful trip even better, add historic **Wades Mill**, (540) 348-1400, to your itinerary. Next to Buffalo Springs Herb Farm, this working water-powered flourmill is listed on the National Register of Historic Places. The mill is open from April to mid-December and produces and sells all kinds of bread flours, cornmeal, cereal and bran. It also sells gift boxes.

Botetourt County, Troutville and Fincastle

Antiques

Many a Roanoker loves to take a trip out to the cool, crisp countryside in autumn, buy apples from the county orchards and go antiquing. The opportunities are numerous on U.S. 11 heading into Troutville and U.S. 220 on the way to historic Fincastle. Both towns have more than their fair share of terrific little antique shops. In Troutville, the **Troutville Antique Mart**, 102 Sunset, (540) 992-4249, beside the Troutville Fire Station, provides the best opportunity for browsing under one roof. Here, a dozen dealers display fine antiques and collectibles, and the prices are some of the lowest you'll find. How about a first-class 1890s leather and wooden trunk for $100? You may find it here.

Handcrafts

A real unexpected gem in a rural area, in the same building as a swimming pool store and monument designer, **Amerind Gallery**, 885 Roanoke Road off U.S. 220 N., Daleville, (540) 992-1066, specializes in artwork of Native American and Western artists. It is a member of the Indian Arts and Crafts Association and guarantees the authenticity of every Native American handmade item in the gallery. A visit here is a veritable education in American art forms and cultures, expressed in superb original works, including a wide selection of the same beautiful silver jewelry you would find in New Mexico.

In Troutville on U.S. 11 you'll find the **Apple Barn Orchard** and **Apple Barn Country Store**, (540) 992-3636, owned by Al and Rachael Nichols. The orchard is a working apple farm. Pick your own apples before you leave the picturesque orchard setting or select prepackaged ones. On cold days and special occasions, you can enjoy hot, spiced or slushy cider. The country store also sells bacon, butter, jellies and various other food products, as well as Amish-made furniture, Beanie Babies and Boyds Bears. It is also a Gold Paw Dealer.

You also can visit their **Apple Barn II–Gifts & Collectibles**, (540) 992-3551, at 50 Boone Drive, right on the corner of Boone and U.S. 11. This store is an exclusive outlet for Cat's Meow collectibles and is its No. 2 national dealer. But don't forget to check out their **Old Country Store** on Main Street in Buchanan, (540) 254-6677, which also sells country collectibles, Beanie Babies, Amish-made furniture, Boyds Bears and is a Gold Paw dealer. A walkway joins the Old Country Store with the Apple Barn Gallery, a P. Buckley Moss dealership. All the latest Roanoke Valley collectibles, including Cat's Meow Roanoke collection of local landmarks, can be found in these shops.

Orchards

Botetourt County is apple orchard country. Nothing is more beautiful than the acres of delicate apple blossoms that signal the coming of spring in the Blue Ridge. The county has quite a few orchards, large and small. Probably the biggest and best-known are **Ikenberry**, 1265 Roanoke Road, (540) 992-2448, and **Layman's**, 1075 Roanoke Road, (540) 992-2687, both on U.S. 220 in Daleville. In addition to apples of every kind, you can buy such seasonal specials as pumpkins, sweet corn and peaches. As each year goes by, more and more orchardists are selling off their vast spreads to meet the demand for developable land. How long this area will be known for its orchards is questionable.

Roanoke Valley

Roanoke

Antiques

The Roanoke Valley is a treasure chest of top-notch, low-cost antiques. **Roanoke Antique Mall**, (540) 344-0264, is Roanoke's largest antique mall with more than 100 quality dealers and 25,000 square feet of timeless collectibles at 2302 Orange Avenue N.E. on U.S. 460.

You'll find a tremendous variety downtown. **Sandra's Cellar**, 109 Campbell Avenue S.E., (540) 342-8123, is a nostalgic trip through antiques, vintage clothing, furniture and toys. **Bob Beard Antiques**, (540) 981-1757, is open "by chance or appointment" at 105 Market Street, and it's a source of unexpected finds. The slogan at **Russell's Yesteryear**, 117 E. Campbell Avenue, (540) 342-1750, is "When you visit the Market, stop in and see us. If you don't we both lose money." For a complete list of antiques shops in the valley, call (540) 342-6025.

Handcrafts

If fine handcrafts are what you're seeking, look no farther than the historic City Market. You will find the perfect gift and probably end up buying something for yourself as well. **Gallery 3**, 213 Market Street, (540) 343-9698, offers the epitome of art for the kitchen, wood, glass, gifts and clothing. Gallery 3 is a favorite shopping spot for corporate art collectors, who will find works by both local and nationally known artists. On the first Friday of each month, Gallery 3 offers Art By Night, featuring local artists and their work. Custom framing also is available.

Also located on the Market, at 206 Market Square, is **Studios on the Square Gallery**, (540) 345-4076, a second-floor studio where 18 working artists have studios and demonstrate and sell wares that include pottery, paper, fiber, wood, textiles, jewelry, baskets, stained glass, photography and fine paintings. Not only does this gallery have works from working artists, but you can also find exquisite fine arts here. The climb upstairs to this treasure house of arts and crafts stores is well worth it. You'll think you're in a loft in New York City, and chances are you won't leave empty handed.

Outlets

On U.S. 220 S., hunters and those who like the camouflage look can track down bargains at **Trebark Outfitters**, 3434 Buck Mountain Road, (540) 774-9007. Jim Crumley, the inventor of Trebark camouflage, lives in Roanoke and offers good deals at his store. Hunting and fishing lovers and fans of the sporting life will also enjoy the **Orvis Factory Outlet**, downtown at 21-B Campbell Avenue, (540) 344-4520, and the outlet at West Salem Plaza Shopping Center in Salem, (540) 389-8190. Summers are an especially good time to shop, since you can get discounts of up to 80 percent on winter items offered in their national catalog and in the **Orvis Retail Store**, 31-B Campbell Avenue, (540) 344-4310, just a block away. For household items, go to Crossroads Mall on Williamson Road to **Waccamaw Pottery**, (540) 563-4948.

Specialty Stores

Specialty stores and boutiques abound throughout the Roanoke City Market. The Market Building and surrounding streets anchor the popular shopping area. You can buy uniforms, working clothes and casual sportswear at **Sam's On the Market**, 304 Market Street, (540) 342-7300, undergoing remodeling. Sometimes, you may find canteens and other types of army gear there.

La De Da, 102 Church Avenue, (540) 345-6131, a whimsical boutique for women's clothing, caters to the young and young-in-spirit with flowing clothing. **Printer's Ink**, (540) 774-3445, a full-service bookstore at 4917 Grandin Road Extension, carries all kinds of books, magazines, Hallmark cards, gift items and Dept. 56 items. Another good place to buy books and magazines is **Ram's Head**

Bookshop in the Tower Shopping Mall on Colonial Avenue, (540) 344-1237. **Books-a-Million** at Crossroads Mall, 1515 Hershberger Road, (540) 366-6682, offers sinful desserts and flavorful coffees and teas to entice you to stay awhile and browse through their amazing selection of books.

For fun, contemporary clothing, jewelry and gifts "for mother and daughter alike," try **Gone Coco** at 32 Market Square, (540) 345-2604. This intimate downtown shop carries clothing in natural fabrics, including cotton and linen. The fashion is fun but not too funky, so you can wear your new outfit to work. **Greenfields**, at 32 Market Square, (540) 345-5139, specializes in authentic lines of sports jerseys and caps. Here you can find just about any sport represented, including major and minor leagues and college teams, on jerseys and caps.

From grand cru to jug wine, **Lee & Edwards Wine Merchants**, 309 S. Jefferson, (540) 343-3900, will certainly provide temptation for your taste buds. In addition to a wide array of wines, including Virginia specialties, you will also find a good selection of gourmet items, such as fine olive oils, mustards, salsas and terrific cheeses. And speaking of temptation, it can also be discovered at **The Peanut Store**, 304A First Street, (540) 342-4477. Upon opening the door, you can smell the delicious roasted nuts, from Virginia peanuts to a special party mix. The shop also offers terrific chocolate- and caramel-covered nuts made by a Virginia candy company. Christmastime brings out the gift tins, and the store will even ship burlap bags of peanuts across the country.

Scribner Screen Printing, 907 Fourth Street, (540) 345-8337, offers name brands at outlet prices. You will find neat stuff for the whole family, including a selection of collegiate prints. A gift shop specializes in engraving, T-shirts and even glass etching. **The Gift Niche**, 101 Market Square, (540) 345-9900, specializes in collectibles and gifts. The shop is an authorized Paw Dealer for Boyds Bear and Friends collectibles. The Gift Niche also carries the Seraphim Classics Angels.

Check out **Beginner's Luck**, 314 Market Street, (540) 343-6144, for some unique gift ideas. From the left-handed merchandise (found in the left side of the store, of course) to home accessories, you'll find a little of everything here. Other popular items include an extensive Sheila collection and music boxes that sell out as quickly as they arrive in the store.

For unique children's gifts, **Imagination Station**, (540) 343-5205, is the place to visit either at 305 Market Street or at Towers Shopping Center, (540) 343-7646. Not just an ordinary toy store, Imagination Station offers European-style toys and supplies for science experiments with an emphasis on education. Wooden dollhouses and furniture and collectible dolls by Madame Alexander, Gotz and Corolle are featured items here.

Musicians, guitar enthusiasts and anyone who appreciates fine stringed instruments should visit **Fret Mill Music**, (540) 982-6686. A wide selection of new and vintage guitars, mandolins, banjos and fiddles is available. The store also sells amplifiers, hand percussion and drum equipment. Often you can walk in and find a seasoned musician trying out a new instrument, which is another compelling reason to stop by!

The major malls in the area — Crossroads, Tanglewood and Valley View — also have some specialty stores.

Salem

Antiques

Salem has set out to become famous for its antiques and is aggressively recruiting dealers to make it so. Main Street is a sheer delight for antique lovers with **Green Market Antique Mall**, 8 E. Main, (540) 387-3879; **Wright Place Antique Mall**, 27 W. Main, (540) 389-8507; **Elite Antiques & Consignments**, 17 W. Main, (540) 389-9222; **Olde Salem Stained Glass Art & Antiques**, 115 E. Main, (540) 389-9968; **Salem Market Antiques**, 1 W. Main, (540) 389-8920; and **Virginia Showcase Antiques**, 4 E. Main, (540) 387-5842, for starters. Other antique stores are scattered throughout the city. For a complete list, call the Salem-Roanoke County Chamber of Commerce at (540) 387-0267.

East of the Blue Ridge

Loudoun County

Grab your wallet and head for historic downtown Leesburg (at the intersection of U.S. 7 and U.S. 15) where more than 100 specialty retailers do business along Market and King streets.

The city's colorful **Market Station**, at 180-D South Street S.E., offers 20 shops and a delightful setting amidst renovated historic old buildings that in the 1800s made up an area known as "the Wharf." The Wharf was home to grain and farm supply merchants, a blacksmith, livery stable, an ice house, McKimmey's Mill and the W&OD Railroad Depot. Today, five of the seven Market Station buildings are original structures from that two-block area.

Some of the many diverse shops that now do business in the new Market Station include **Leesburg Emporium and Smoke Shop** at 205 Harrison Street S.E., (703) 777-5557, which has been selling pipes, tobacco, premium cigars and other smoking accessories for 19 years. It's located in what had been the stationmaster's house that dates from 1915. Or stop by **My Friends and Me**, 118 South Street S.E., (703) 777-8222, a shop housed in an 1840s log house built of American chestnut. This toy shop has an exquisite collection of bears and dolls for all ages. Don't forget to fulfill your jewelry needs with a visit to **Designer Goldsmiths**, 203-A Harrison Street S.E., (703) 777-7661. This delightful shop is owned by Les Thompson and Stephanie DeLage who specialize in goldsmithing, silversmithing, designing, setting precious and non-precious stones as well as reproductions and repairs.

If you still haven't had enough, more than 250 stores stretch along the U.S. 7 corridor up to the Fairfax County line. This route will take you through the communities of Ashburn, Sterling and Sterling Park.

West of Leesburg on U.S. 7 in Round Hill is **Hill High's Country Store**, (540) 338-7173, where you can shop for handmade crafts and

The Leesburg Corner Premium Outlets opened in November, 1998.

rest from your shopping labors with a deli sandwich or their specialty, a wedge of hot fruit pie. There is even a picnic site with free fishing.

At the southern edge of Loudoun County is Middleburg, the capital of Virginia's Hunt Country. Washington Street (U.S. 50), the town's main artery, is lined with antique, clothing, saddle, book and jewelry shops — more than 60 stores in the historic district alone. Wander down the cobbled side streets to find more antiques, riding clothes, home furnishings, handcrafted gifts, clothing and art.

The Old Lucketts Store Antiques, (703) 779-0268, is just seven miles north of Leesburg on U.S. 15 in Lucketts. The landmark building dating back to 1910 was once the town's post office, general store and Lucketts family home. Today the restored facility houses 20 antique dealers, carrying a mix of items ranging from country primitive and garden accents to quilts, kitchenware and art deco.

Specialty Shops

The Finicky Filly at 100 W. Washington Street, (540) 687-6841, carries very upscale women's clothing, accessories and gifts. **Es-** tates of Middleburg on W. Washington Street, (540) 687-8027, has a selection of period antiques, rugs, silver and estate items on consignment. Be sure to check out the **White Elephant** at 103 Federal Street, (540) 687-8800, another consignment shop that handles everything from antiques to clothing. It's not unusual to find treasures such as a pair of barely used Gucci shoes — and even more fun to speculate as to what Middleburg celeb might have worn them. **Dominion Saddlery** at 8 E. Washington Street, (540) 687-6720, and the **Tack Box** at 7 W. Federal Street, (540) 687-3231, cater to the equestrian crowd and have delightful Hunt Country gifts. **The Fun Shop** on Washington Street, (540) 687-6590, has an interesting array of gifts. It's actually a mini department store with everything from linens to toys.

Several exceptional art galleries include **Red Fox Fine Art**, behind the Red Fox Tavern at 2 E. Washington Street, (540) 687-6301; and **The Sporting Gallery** at 11 W. Washington Street, (540) 687-6447, the town's oldest gallery. Both have paintings and bronzes of the caliber you'd expect in a major city.

Outlets

More than 1 million shoppers visited the new **Leesburg Corner Premium Outlets**, (703) 737-3071, less than four months after it opened in November 1998. This new center, at the intersection of Leesburg Turnpike and the U.S. 15 bypass, brings upscale outlet shopping to the northern edge of Virginia's Blue Ridge. The center's first of three phases features 60 stores, including Polo Ralph Lauren Factory Store, Off 5th Saks Fifth Avenue Outlet, Banana Republic, Britches Great Outdoors Factory Store, Tommy Hilfiger, Nautica, Gap Outlet, Liz Claiborne, Nike, Reebok, London Fog, Jockey, Kenneth Cole, Coldwater Creek, Waterford, Wedgwood and Mikasa, in an outdoor village setting. The center is being built in three phases and will have 100 outlet stores when complete, offering everyday savings of 25 to 65 percent.

Fauquier County

Like Leesburg, Warrenton's exterior is lined with malls and fast food places, but the historic center of town is still a fun place to shop.

Among the many antique stores is **Courthouse Antiques** at 52 Main Street, (540) 349-9275. This 2,700-foot building is filled with furniture, silver and quilts. Down the road at 81-B Main Street is **Antiques and Accents**, (540) 349-8021, which specializes in general decorative accents for the home, including handpainted furniture. **Sarah Belle's** at 110 Main Street, (540) 349-4549, offers vintage linens and textiles plus American art pottery and jewelry.

Loveladies Antiques at 53 E. Lee Street, (540) 349-8786, has a wide array of jewelry. Also ask about their flatware and textiles. It's a porcelain paradise at **Nitty Gritty Antiques** at 26 Ashby Street (540) 347-3000. More than 100 Christmas plates cover one wall of the shop. **Fox Den Antique Mall** at 39 W. Lee Street, (540) 347-1162, is a multi-dealer shop that offers a diverse collection of antiques and collectibles. You'll also find gift shops, specialty stores and saddleries in the historic old town; it's definitely worth a visit.

Rappahannock County

The tiny community of Little Washington has fewer than 200 residents, but boasts a number of sophisticated galleries, antique shops and places to buy fine handcrafted gifts.

Peter Kramer, 311 Gay Street, (540) 675-3625, has been making beautiful furniture for 27 years in this lovely old town. Each of his creations is one-of-a-kind, a handcrafted creation made from native American wood. Some of the furniture is rather whimsical, while other pieces are more classical and austere. Conveniently located in the same building, **Talk of the Town**, (540) 675-1690, is operated by Kramer's wife. This 5-year-old shop on Gay Street carries crafts and decorative accessories.

Another eclectic shop on Main Street is **Rare Finds**, (540) 675-1400, with collectibles and decorating items ranging from bridal gifts to Oriental carpets. **The Gay Street Mercantile**, 337 Gay Street, (540) 675-1410, features supplies from eight dealers, ranging from primitive to formal antiques. Geneva Welsh, who specializes in watercolor portraits of animals, is the resident artist. The shop itself is a showplace. The building was constructed in the 1700s.

Just south of Washington in Sperryville, you'll find scores of antique and craft shops, including the **Sperryville Emporium**, 12018 Lee Highway off Va. 211, (540) 987-8235, a series of connecting buildings where you can find everything from antiques and apples to country hams and honey.

INSIDERS' TIP

If you have your heart set on a unique shop or store, always call ahead to be sure there will be someone there when you plan to go. Many shop owners are escapees from the big city or natives whose first priority is quality of life and second priority is running a retail establishment. Farming and other obligations might get in the way of their regular hours.

Faith Mountain Company on Main Street in Sperryville, (540) 987-8547, sells flowers, herbs, crafts and fashions for women, with many items priced well below retail. A few miles down Va. 211 on Va. 651 is **Elmer's Antiques**, (540) 987-8355, which handles walnut, cherry and oak antiques. **Country Manor** at 11576 Lee Highway, (540) 987-8761, is the last shop on Va. 211 W. before you get to the Skyline Drive. Here you can browse for hours among carvings, baskets and women's fashions. Country Manor also sells gasoline.

Culpeper County

Heading south to Rapidan on U.S. 15 is **Carousel Antiques**, 9607 James Madison Highway, (540) 825-1558. This shop carries a nice variety of old treasures including glassware and china. It's closed Wednesday and Thursday.

Madison County

Madison is headquarters for **E.A. Clore Sons Inc.**, (540) 948-5821, makers of simple but handsome furniture since 1830. Nestled in a hollow three-tenths of a mile from Va. 637, E.A. Clore specializes in handmade Early American furniture from walnut, cherry, oak and mahogany. E.A. Clore sells directly from its factory to the consumer, and its showrooms are right next door.

The Little Shop of Madison at 320 S. Main Street, (540) 948-4147, is a quilt-making supply shop and a decorating business specializing in window treatments.

Just to the north, in the tiny mountain town of Criglersville, sits the **Mountain Store**, (540) 923-4349, open Thursday through Sunday. It's a truly wonderful place that offers pottery, candles, books, handmade crafts and an interesting selection of children's toys and jigsaw puzzles.

Two miles south of Madison on U.S. 29, called the "antique corridor" by locals, are several shops worth visiting. **Eunice & Fester Antiques**, (540) 948-4647, is a humorous landmark with sophisticated items for the serious collector. It has a fine selection of American furniture from Colonial to art deco. Accessories with design merit are emphasized. Reup-holstered vintage furniture is a specialty. **Handcraft House** on U.S. 29, (540) 948-6323, sells very fine crafts made by more than 300 artisans from across the nation. It features the largest selection of Cat's Meow houses, rubber stamps and accessories in central Virginia, Byers' Choice Carolers and Yankee candles.

About 7 miles south of Madison on U.S. 29 is **Country Garden Antiques**, (540) 948-3240, a unique antiques shop that also specializes in garden ornaments imported directly from England and antique period mantles. Items in this eclectic collection include American and English antique furniture, old silver and pewter, Chinese imports, prints and paintings, primitives, folk art, handpainted imported tiles and French medieval-style tapestries.

Orange County

At one time, Orange County was one of the largest Virginia counties ever formed, stretching to the Mississippi River on the west and the Great Lakes to the north. Today, its territory is more modest, but it's packed with historic landmarks and shops with period pieces.

The **Somerset Shop** at 110 E. Main Street in Orange, (540) 672-2511, features high-quality handcrafted gifts and accessories, from place mats and shells to candles and baskets. **The Country Mouse** at 1143 E. Church Street in Orange, (540) 672-5336, carries gifts, primitive jewelry, soaps, herbs, teas and herb books, some of which are by Virginia writers.

Across from the post office in Barboursville on U.S. 33 is **Elsie's Antique Shop**, (804) 985-2778. Elsie's, which offers an ever-changing array of items, is only open Saturday and Sunday until 4 PM.

Greene County

When U.S. 29 arrives in Ruckersville, it intersects with U.S. 33 and forms a crossroads that bustles with activity for antique lovers. The three-story **Greene House Shops**, (804) 985-2438, at the intersection of these two major highways houses at least 50 dealers of antiques, crafts, quilts and all kinds of gifts. It's open every day and even accepts credit cards. Across the road is the **Country Store Antique**

Photo: Richard T. Nowitz/The Roanoke Valley Convention and Visitors Bureau

Plan a holiday shopping trip through the Blue Ridge to
collect traditional, festive crafts for your tree.

Mall, (804) 985-3649, which houses 14 different dealers with a variety of antiques and collectibles. Next door to the mall is **Antique Collectors**, (804) 985-8966, which offers Victorian furniture, china, crystal and sterling.

Early Time Antiques and Fine Art, (804) 985-3602, also in Ruckersville on the north bound lane of U.S. 29, has a good reputation for its 18th- and 19th-century furniture, oil paintings and accessories.

Whether you're in the market for English or Western tack, **Crawford Saddlery** on U.S. 29 in Ruckersville, (804) 985-4262, offers a fine selection of new and used saddles. In fact, there's just about everything in store for horse lovers, including blankets, riding apparel, Ariat English boots, western jewelry, buckles, watches and horse care products. The store is owned by Joe Crawford, a rider who owns a dozen horses on his own farm in nearby Madison County.

Heading west on U.S. 33 to 9 Golden Horse Road is a popular stop called the **Blue Ridge Pottery**, (804) 985-6080, housed in what was once the Golden Horseshoe Inn, c.1827. The inn, which sits along the old Spotswood Trail, used to serve travelers making the difficult climb over the mountains. Gen. Stonewall Jackson reportedly stayed here during the war, using the inn as his temporary headquarters only a few weeks before he was killed. Alan Ward and his family throw their stoneware pottery in a little studio right next door to Blue Ridge Pottery and welcome visitors. Ward's pottery, which is modeled after traditional Valley styles but painted with modern, vibrant glazes, is sold in the shop along with gourmet coffee, apple butter and jams. Treat yourself to the ice cream parlor too.

Albemarle County

Antiques

The Charlottesville area has more than two dozen antique stores, not counting the dozens of mini-shops that share a single roof.

West on U.S. 250 at 3449 Ivy Road is an exclusive shop, **1740 House Antiques**, (804) 977-1740. The historic setting — a national landmark — houses a choice collection of period American and English furniture and fine

art. **DeLoach Antiques** at 1211 W. Main Street, (804) 979-7209, is a charming place to find stylish and unusual decorative objects and antiques at very good prices. An eclectic selection of Neoclassical, French, English and American pieces are displayed throughout an elegantly decorated townhouse that was built by one of Thomas Jefferson's master craftsmen in 1817. It's really three shops in one. There's a place to stay, the 1817 Historic Bed and Breakfast, and a lunch cafe.

If you're interested in either antique or 20th-century rugs from the villages of the Middle East, stop by the **Sun Bow Trading Company** at 108 Fourth Street N.E., (804) 293-8821. Saul, the owner, has many a tale to tell about these tribal textiles and nomadic Oriental rugs and his journeys to find them.

Jordan, 7581 Rockfish Gap Turnpike in Greenwood, (540) 456-8465, is about 15 miles west of Charlottesville on U.S. 250. This upscale shop sells elegant fine home furnishings, unique accessories and distinctive gifts. While you will find antiques here, you will also find a full range of furniture and art. From decorative oil paintings to American and English Colonial-style furniture, you'll enjoy browsing through this one-of-a-kind store. Travelers don't worry: Jordan will ship anything anywhere. Jordan recently opened a second shop, (804) 295-0030, on Charlottesville's Historic Downtown Mall at 506 E. Main Street.

Also on Charlottesville's Downtown Mall, you'll find several interesting antique spots. **20th Century Art & Antiques** at 201-D E. Main Street, (804) 296-6818, offers an eclectic mix of furniture, lamps, art and collectibles. The shop's collection of art deco and arts and crafts are especially interesting and plentiful. **Ming-Quing Antiques** at 111 W. Main Street, (804) 979-8426, sells Chinese antique furniture shipped directly from mainland China. Look for the red lanterns.

While not actually an antique shop, **Consignment House Unlimited** at 121 W. Main Street, (804) 977-5527, has loads of great finds, especially in the jewelry department. Finally, at 216 Fourth Street N.E., just a few blocks off the Downtown Mall, **Court Square Antiques**, (804) 295-6244, has several dealers with a large selection of furniture, jewelry, quilts, dolls, glassware, books and more. Court Square is

Photo: Anne P. Causey

Market Station is home to several shops and the Tuscarora Mill Restaurant in Leesburg.

open 10 AM to 5 PM Wednesday through Saturday or by appointment.

Bookstores

Charlottesville has a reputation as a book-lover's paradise. Countless writers call the area home, including best-selling author John Grisham and former U.S. Poet Laureate Rita Dove. There are also plenty of folks who just like to read. A 1994 survey by *U.S. News & World Report* ranked Charlottesville third in the nation behind Seattle, Washington, and Austin, Texas, in book readers per capita. Judging by the number of bookstores in the area, they weren't exaggerating.

There are nearly 20 bookstores in the area, including **New Dominion Bookshop** on the historic Downtown Mall at 404 E. Main Street, (804) 295-2552, which is one of the oldest booksellers in town and caters to the hometown crowd.

Quest Bookshop Inc. at 619 W. Main Street, (804) 295-3377, specializes in books on spiritual, religious and New Age topics.

Something is always going on at **Barnes & Noble Bookstore**, (804) 984-0461, the area's largest bookshop. Aside from carrying more than 100,000 books, this store at 1035 Barracks Road in the Barracks Road Shopping Center hosts readings, book signings, seminars, music in the cafe plus two weekly story times for children.

Charlottesville has many good second-hand book shops. **Blue Whale Books**, (804) 296-4646, is a little gem on the Historic Downtown Mall at 115 W. Main Street. Here, you will find used, rare and out-of-print books, as well as maps and a few prints.

If you're looking for out-of-print books, the **Daedalus Bookshop** on 121 Fourth Street N.E., (804) 293-7595, has 80,000 books on three floors. The **Heartwood Bookshop**, (804) 295-7083, has two locations at 5 and 9 Elliewood Avenue. At No. 5 is a large used book collection including secondhand scholarly and popular books both in hardback and paperback, while No. 9 has an impressive rare book collection, with an emphasis on Americana and literature.

After spending five years in Lovingston, **Read It Again, Sam**, (804) 977-9844, joined the growing list of bookstores on the Downtown Mall in Charlottesville in June 1997. Its new location at 214 E. Main Street, which includes a whole wall of mysteries, has thousands of used and rare books.

Handcrafts

Charlottesville is known for having an abundance of shops that sell exquisite crafts from around the world. Many of the shops seem more like galleries, and some function as both. The historic Downtown Mall is a good place to start exploring such stores.

The New York Times called Penny Bosworth's **Signet Gallery** a place "where craft . . . becomes art." The shop, at 212 Fifth Street N.E. in Charlottesville, (804) 296-6463, carries handmade work by more than 300 artists and craftspeople from around the country. The two-room shop is filled with jewelry, clothing, ceramics, glass, leather goods, toys and garden ornamentals. It's not unusual to find an 8-foot totem pole, a full-length lamb-skin coat or handpainted frames. Sterling jewelry by David Yuman also can be found here. Jackson, probably the city's most well-known Basset hound, is always around to greet visitors. Signet Gallery is one of the few stores in the historic district to have its own parking lot.

O'Suzannah, (804) 979-2888, centrally located on the mall at 201-A E. Main Street, is a gallery of contemporary crafts that sells jewelry, pottery, art pieces and hand-printed clothing. **Cha Cha's**, (804) 293-8553, just next door at 201-B E. Main Street, sells eccentric, eclectic items for the home. Here you can buy leopard-print switch plates and retro-style fabrics. If you are looking for funky, look here.

The McGuffey Art Center, (804) 295-7973, is a renovated elementary school within walking distance of the downtown mall housing a contemporary gallery (see our chapter on The Arts). A number of the gifted artists at work here are represented by galleries in New York and other major cities. A small gift shop sells some of their creations. You'll find pottery, photography, prints, stained glass, sculpture, jewelry and much more.

Specialty Shops

"On the Corner" is the local term for a tight little neighborhood of shops, cafes and restaurants only a half-block from the Rotunda and the original UVA campus. A number of specialty shops make the corner an interesting place to browse. Many of these shops validate parking for both local lots and the 14th Street parking garage.

At 103 14th Street is **Innovations**, (804) 971-8088, a hair salon catering to the university and professional crowd. Some say you have to be a magician to get through four rigorous years at the demanding University of Virginia — no wonder **Magic Tricks** at 101 14th Street, (804) 293-5788, is nearby, selling a wide assortment of amusing tricks, gags, games and novelties.

Barr-ee Station at 1501 W. Main Street, (804) 979-7981, is a great outlet store that sells brand-name, high-quality clothing for men and women at cut-rate prices. Barr-ee Station recently opened a catalog outlet, (804) 974-1604, in Charlottesville on U.S. 29 in the Seminole Square shopping center.

The Garment District at 1509 University Avenue, (804) 296-1003, caters to university women with its fashionable clothing at reasonable prices. Don't miss the great shoe shop downstairs. For traditionalists, **Eljo's**, 3 Elliewood Avenue, (804) 295-5230, has been selling preppie clothes for more than 40 years, offering the best of Southwick, Corbin and Gitman.

Freeman-Victorious Framing, 1413 University Avenue, (804) 296-3456, not only does framing, but also sells antique prints and posters, mirrors and other fine gifts.

Also on University Corner is **Willie's Hair Design**, (804) 295-1242, a full-service salon serving men and women in the university and larger Charlottesville community. Located at 22 Elliewood Avenue, Willie's validates for both nearby parking garages.

On the athletic front, **Blue Wheel Bicycles**, 19 Elliewood Avenue, (804) 977-1870, sells fine bicycles at competitive prices, along with a good selection of accessories. This bike shop has been around for more than 24 years. **Ragged Mountain Running Shop**, 9 Elliewood Avenue, (804) 293-3367, has a great selection of running and aerobic shoes at very competitive prices. **Mincer's**, 1527 University Avenue, (804) 296-5687, is open seven days a week and has been selling university sportswear for more than 41 years.

At Barracks Road and Emmet Street is a unique shopping enclave made up of dozens of delightful specialty shops and a few department stores within walking distance (just watch the traffic).

For a vast selection of women's shoes, check out **Scarpa** at 2114-A Barracks Road, (804) 296-0040, where the styles go from collegiate casual to formal in all the top brands in all price ranges. At nearby **Talbot's** at 1027 Emmet Street, (804) 296-3580, you'll find a premier selection of classic apparel and accessories in a comfortable, homelike atmosphere. (Roanoke has a Talbot's too.) This store is especially popular with the community and UVA population.

Shenanigans at 2146 Barracks Road, (804) 295-4797, is a great place to find children's books, toys, stuffed animals, dolls from around the world and children's music, including sing-along videos. True to its name, **Whimsies** at 2142 Barracks Road, (804) 977-8767, has fanciful and spunky children's wear, including clothes for infants to preteens. It's next door to Shenanigans. For those who answer to the call of the wild, head to **Blue Ridge Mountain Sports**, 1121 Emmet Street, (804) 977-4400, for camping, canoeing, backpacking, hiking and outdoor outfitting needs.

Virginia's best is showcased in **The Virginia Company** at 1047-B Emmet Street, (804) 977-0080, on the Island behind Ruby Tuesdays Restaurant. A great selection of gifts, food, wine, books, music and much more — all with the Old Dominion mark of quality — is for sale here seven days a week.

Nature by Design, 1107-B Emmet Street, (804) 977-0080, is a fascinating shop for folks of all ages, selling such variety as polished rocks for less than a dollar and driftwood water fountains at $1,300. Jewelry, bird feeders, garden accessories, chimes, agate bookends, puzzles, games and more all have a touch of nature.

Keller & George moved to a larger location at 1149 Millmont Street, (804) 293-5011. Here you'll find the popular Jefferson cup along with fine jewelry and distinctive and unusual gifts. **Andrew Minton Jewelers**, 1115-C Emmet Street, (804) 979-7672, sells fine contemporary and antique jewelry.

Plow & Hearth, 1107-C Emmet Street, (804) 977-3707, sells beautiful outdoor ornaments and furniture made of wrought iron, cedar and other sturdy materials as well as a large variety of garden accessories. The shop's bird feeders are also extremely popular.

For women, **Levy's** at 2120 Barracks Road, (804) 295-4270, sells gorgeous, sophisticated sportswear and bathing suits downstairs and formal wear and snappy business suits on the upper level.

In nearby Seminole Square, (804) 296-4141, is an exquisite furniture store that has been furnishing homes in Central Virginia since 1926. **Gilmore, Hamm and Snyder Inc.**, 2109 India Road, (804) 973-8114, sells quality furniture by such manufacturers as Stickley, Brown Jordan, Pennsylvania House and Hickory Chair along with hand-woven Oriental rugs, lamps, pictures, mirrors and window treatments.

Les Fabriques, (804) 975-0710, recently moved to the Shoppers World Shopping Center. You'll find designer and bridal fabrics, buttons and other accessories, at the new location at 1422 Seminole Trail. It also sells top-brand sewing machines.

Historic Downtown Mall

We've already described some of the shops in the **downtown pedestrian mall**, (804) 296-8548, that specialize in exquisite handcrafts and antiques. All told, there are nearly 160 stores and restaurants in the historic district. But we'd also like to mention a few of the delightful specialty shops, most of which are owner-operated.

One of the most interesting places to browse is the **Old Hardware Store**, (804) 977-1518, a block-long building that houses a restaurant and soda fountain, several specialty food bars and shops selling just about everything — gold and silver jewelry, games, wrought iron and much more. The Old Hardware Store at 316 E. Main Street is aptly named; it operated from 1895 to 1976 and was once the premier hardware store in central Virginia. Not only did it sell rope and tools and other hardware, but you could also find fine china and silver there, along with everyday crockery and eggs and other staples. Just like the old days, the Old Hardware Store still has something for everyone. **Harlan & McGuire Jewelers**, (804) 977-8012, has a nice little shop here with a pretty selection of gold and gemstones.

Timberlake Drugstore, (804) 296-1191, may be small in size, but it's big in history. This small shop at 322 E. Main Street has been around since 1890 and is one of the few places around with an old-fashioned soda fountain. The drugstore still sells cosmetics, prescriptions and candies and will develop your film, but it also offers a deli menu featuring old-fashioned thick milk shakes (vanilla, chocolate, strawberry and cherry) available in regular or "extra thick." Or maybe you feel like a sundae, banana split or an ice cream float. For those without a sweet tooth, Timberlake's menu includes sandwiches, croissants and breakfast foods.

Another outstanding specialty shop on the downtown mall is **Palais Royal**, 311 E. Main Street, (804) 979-4111, which has the finest in French designer linens, robes, towels and blankets. **The Gemstone Collection**, 413 E. Main Street, (804) 293-4367, has a beautiful display of gems and minerals as well as designer sterling and gold jewelry. Custom designs are available too. **Art Needlework Inc.**, 124 E. Main Street, (804) 296-4625, is a great source for needlepoint and knitting patterns. You'll also find other supplies, including beautiful yarns, many imported and hand-dyed, in wool, cotton, silk, mohair and angora.

Speaking of animals, **The Cat House**, (804) 984-2287, is a charming shop at 102 Fifth Street S.E., chock full of clever gifts for the cat lover. There's something for the pet and owner alike, including stuffed animals, puzzles, clothing, jewelry, kitty-shaped backpacks, headbands and barrettes, mailboxes, gift wrap and catnip toys. There's even a small corner for the dog lover who dares to venture inside. Also at the store, pick up Rita Mae Brown's T-shirts, caps and bumper stickers and some of her autographed "Mrs. Murphy" mystery books that the famed author co-wrote with her feline friend Sneaky Pie.

The mall has several fine Oriental rug shops. **Purcell Oriental Rug Company Ltd.**, 107 W. Main Street, (804) 971-8822, specializes in Afghan tribal nomadic rugs. Right next door at 105 W. Main, **T.S. Eways**, (804) 979-3038, carries a wide assortment of Oriental rugs.

Market Street Wineshop and Gourmet Grocery, 311 E. Market Street, (804) 296-3854 or (800) 377-VINE, just a few blocks off the mall, is a gathering place where everybody seems to know everyone else, but if you're a first-time visitor you'll receive the same friendly welcome as the regulars. The store has one of the state's largest selections of wine and beer, from the old and rare to the good and cheap. The shop has been so popular, the owners added another Uptown store at 1448 Seminole Trail in the Shoppers World Shopping Center.

If you'd rather do all your shopping inside an air-conditioned mall, plan a trip to **Fashion Square**, (804) 973-9331. There are more than 70 shops and services from Sears to Ann Taylor. If you have a sweet tooth, stop by the Kohr Bros. Frozen Custard stand. The mall is at the intersection of U.S. 29 and Rio Road.

Nelson County

You'll find a nice selection of shops in and around Wintergreen Resort. The Mountain Inn in the resort itself has several nice spots, including **Blue Ridge Mountain Sports**, (804) 325-2156, which sells quality outdoor sportswear and accessories. It also rents movies, day packs, kid carriers and VCRs. **The Hodge Podge II**, (804) 325-1456, at the resort offers a delightful mix of gifts, toys, stationery and imported foods and wines. **Thomas Ashfield Galleries**, (804) 325-7717, also at Mountain Inn, is a contemporary craft gallery with handcrafted jewelry, pottery and a variety of other metal, wood and glass items.

The **Stedman House**, (804) 361-2560, at the bottom of Wintergreen Mountain at 2788 Rockfish Valley Highway in Nellysford, is a home-decorating center, though the shop also sells beautiful furniture, art, antiques and accessories.

Across the street from the Stedman House in the Valley Green Center is the **Valley Green Art & Craft Co-op**, Va. 151 in Nellysford, (804) 361-9316, which sells country crafts, jewelry, porcelain dolls, miniature furniture, stained glass, wearable fiber art, original photography and the works of various artists.

Antiques

Several antiques shops are also nearby Wintergreen. **Bear Creek Antiques**, 3.5 miles south of Nellysford on Va. 151, (804) 361-9322, sells a bit of everything, including mountain and primitive pieces. Just down the road at

193 Roberts Ridge Lane, **Past Time Antiques**, (804) 361-1273, sells a variety of collectibles and country furniture. **Tuckahoe Antique Mall**, (804) 361-2121, also in Nellysford at 4202 Rockfish Valley Highway (also known as Va. 151), has a large selection of antiques with 50 shops under one roof.

Afton, off Va. 151 and U.S. 250, attracts many antique shoppers to three stores, all within walking distance from each other on Va. 6, a winding little road that runs between Va. 151 and U.S. 250. **Antiques at Afton**, (540) 942-2993, specializes in antique furniture, pottery, glassware, tools and linens. **Afton House Antiques**, (540) 456-6759, offers fascinating collections of antique furniture, arts, crafts, dolls and home furnishings, while **Whitehouse Antiques**, (540) 942-1194, has American period pieces from country to formal. The shop also caters to the dealer trade and has new inventory weekly.

Further south in Colleen, located at the crossroads of Va. 56 and U.S. 29, you'll find the **Four Brothers Packing House** at 4137 Pyebrook Highway, (804) 263-8577, specializing in antiques, collectibles and American origin furniture, and **Four Brothers Antiques**, 92 Spade Road, (804) 263-4854, selling collectibles, glass, Oriental furniture and jewelry.

Lynchburg

Antiques

A phenomenal array of antique stores — nearly 20 in all — bring collectors and browsers to this historic and cultural city. For a list of them all, contact the Lynchburg Visitor Center at (804) 847-1811.

For a whirlwind tour of downtown shops, visit **Redcoat Gallery & Antiques**, 1421 Main Street, (804) 528-3182, and **Sweeney's Curious Goods**, 1220 Main Street, (804) 846-7839. There's also a concentration near River Ridge Mall off Candlers Mountain Road, beside Liberty University.

Handcrafts

Virginia Handcrafts Inc., (804) 846-7029, part of the Farm Basket shopping complex at 2008 Langhorne Road, will keep you wandering around all day. It's a casual shop where browsers and their children are welcome. This unique store features a collection of American crafts, many of which are made by Virginians, including kaleidoscopes, game boards, pottery and jewelry. These are displayed among planters, fountains, lamps and much more than can possibly be described here. The atmosphere is just plain fun!

Adjoining it is the **Farm Basket Shop**, 2008 Langhorne Drive, (804) 528-1107, where you can browse through rooms of carefully chosen gift items from around the world. Children can entertain themselves with an imported wooden train in a toy department that also overflows with stuffed animals, dolls and baby gifts. You can create custom invitations and announcements by computer. A mail-order catalog is available. If hunger strikes, stop for a cucumber sandwich at the complex's restaurant, which has some of the best homestyle food in the area. The Farm Basket's fruit is locally grown in their own mountain orchards. This is a Lynchburg landmark not to be missed!

Outlets

Lynchburg has 14 terrific outlets and discount stores. A complete list is available from the visitor center, (804) 847-1811.

The granddaddy of them all, the first shoe company south of the Mason-Dixon line (founded 1888) and the most famous, is **Craddock-Terry Shoe Factory Outlet**. You can find a division of this factory outlet, **Masseys Super Shoes**, (804) 847-3535, at 601 12th Street. You can choose from among 300,000 pairs of shoes in stock from the national Masseys catalogs and — the best part — get up to a whopping 70 percent off. You'll see the billboards with the gigantic plastic pairs of red high heel pumps as you come into town on major roads. The store specializes in hard-to-find sizes and widths. Shoe lovers will recognize national brand names such as Rockport and American Gentleman. It's worth an overnight stay for an average family just to buy seasonal shoes and see the sights of Lynchburg at the same time. Another fine shoe outlet is **Consolidated Shoe Store**, 10200 Timberlake Road, (804) 237-5569.

For clothes and accessories, try **Carolina Hosiery Connection**, 525 Alleghany Avenue,

(804) 846-5099, and **Tultex Mill Outlet**, Forest Plaza West Shopping Center on Old Forest Road, (804) 385-6477. For mall-lovers, **River Ridge Mall** next to Liberty University, is the area's largest mall. For the largest Tultex collection, known worldwide, go to Martinsville, home of Tultex. It borders the Blue Ridge and also has furniture outlets.

Specialty Shops

For both specialty shopping and terrific eating, go to the **Community Market** at the corner of Main and 12th streets, (804) 847-1499, established in 1783. You'll find homemade crafts, Virginia-made goods and baked goods. Something is always going on at the Market, the hub of Lynchburg activity since the days of Thomas Jefferson. Jefferson scared local citizens by biting into a tomato, long thought to be a poisonous fruit. This market and the one in Roanoke are centerpieces of Blue Ridge life and a joy to behold.

For best-sellers, regional histories, travel guides, children's books and every kind of book in between, stop in at **The Bookstore**, (804) 384-1746, in the Boonsboro Shopping Center, 4925 Boonsboro Road.

Smith Mountain Lake

General and Specialty Stores and Services

Smith Mountain Lake has two major shopping areas: **Bridgewater Plaza** on Va. Route 122 at Hales Ford Bridge, home of the official Smith Mountain Lake Partnership Visitor Center, and **Village Square** on Va. 122/655 in Moneta.

Hales Ford is the very center of lake life. Here you'll find enough interesting little shops to poke around in while the kids play miniature golf at **Harbortown Golf**, (540) 721-1203, or play games at the arcade. On summer weekends, live entertainment draws crowds; during the rest of the year, the steady seasonal stream of boats and visitors from around the world are often entertainment enough. Bridgewater Plaza's anchor, in addition to the miniature golf course, is **Bridgewater Marina and Boat Rentals** and **Bridgewater Para-Sail**, (540) 721-1639.

Lovers of fine art will enjoy **The Little Gallery**, (540) 721-1596, where you can find one-of-a-kind treasures and see the works of well-known artists as well as emerging local ones. **Gifts Ahoy**, (540) 721-5303, will delight children and has the lake's most unique collection of gifts, greeting cards and Beanie Babies. The Plaza also has the refreshing **Ice Cream Cottage**, (540) 721-1305, where your family can get such cooling fare as flavored shaved ice or ice cream in a waffle cone.

Diamond Hill General Store, just 4.5 miles west of Va. 122 at the corner of Diamond Hill Road and Horseshoe Bend, (540) 297-9309, is not simply a restored, living museum. It is also a gift shop, a Christmas shop, a New York-style deli and an antique shop. This landmark general store opened in 1857 as Debo's General Merchandise. The Debo family owned and operated the store for 135 consecutive years. Carl and Christine Brodt refurbished and reopened the store in 1992. Guests are invited to sign the register and sip fresh coffee around an old potbellied stove. Next door is the original post office building where James Debo presided as the first postmaster. It now holds an antique shop. In the old Debo residence you can find the year-round Christmas shop, specializing in Santas, and the gift shop, featuring wood carvings, personalized signs, Virginia wines, Virginia pottery and much more.

Smith Mountain Flowers, (540) 297-6524, has flowers for any occasion. They can also special order fruits, candies and other gifts to satisfy your basket or bouquet needs. **Atkins Lakeshore Gallery**, 13105 Booker T. Washington Highway at Westlake Commons, (540) 721-7267, specializes in P. Buckley Moss works, handmade furniture, baskets and textiles. Definitely don't forget to visit **Cindy's Candy Cupboard** across the street at 13314 Booker T. Washington Highway at Food Lion Plaza. It has more than 200 kinds of candy and is a great place to take children. They also have sugar-free offerings.

Close to Village Square is the Lakewood Professional Center. A wonderful gift shop well-worth the visit is **Season's Home Accessories** on Va. Route 16, (540) 721-7400, with accents and decorations for the home, garden and dock. Here, you'll find items unique to the lake including welcome signs, flags and books along with sculpture and ceramics. Across the street, on Va. 16, is the new **Westlake Wildlife Gallery**, (540) 721-4414, featuring limited-edition prints, collectible plates, decoys and sculptures.

Beyond these centers, other shops are either general or specialized and far-flung. **Classic Collections**, (540) 297-2804, on Va. 122, north of Hales Ford bridge, has quilts, pottery, baskets, custom-designed flags, teddy bears, bird carvings and oak rockers. The **Old Hales Ford Country Store**, (540) 721-5504, nearly 4 miles north of Hales Ford bridge, has souvenirs and just about anything else you need while enjoying the lake. Recently, it has also added a garden center with a wide variety of plants, trees, shrubbery and flowers.

Bedford County

Antiques

Bedford County has nearly 20 antique stores within a close radius of each other. In downtown Bedford at 201 N. Bridge Street, is **Bridge Street Antiques**, (540) 586-6611, specializing in furniture, tools, silver and primitives. Books, toys and Virginia antiques can be found downtown at **Hamiltons**, 155 W. Main Street, (540) 586-5592. Farther out of town, you'll find **Old Country Store**, a mile west of Bedford on Va. 460, (540) 586-1665. Thirty dealers do business at **The Peddler Antiques** on Va. 854 between routes 811 and 221, (804) 525-6030. You'll find many shops between Lynchburg and Bedford. For a complete list, call the Bedford Area Chamber of Commerce at (540) 586-9401.

Outlets

If you love pottery and enjoy seeing how it's made, travel to **Emerson Creek Pottery**'s factory in Bedford County (take Va. 43 S. to Va. 725 E. — Peck's Road — about 10 miles from Bedford). The company's product line is sold in all 50 states and is becoming widely collected as fine art. A showroom here houses a permanent display of the pottery's private collection. Established in 1977 as a small studio of two artisans, the Emerson Creek Pottery now employs several people for each step of the pottery process. The distinctive

handpainted patterns are a part of what makes Emerson Creek so well-known. The retail shop, (540) 297-7884, provides tour schedules. The seconds shop occupies an 1825 log cabin next to the factory. Along with great bargains, you'll find occasional unusual pieces, first runs and specialties. Outside you can have lunch at the picnic table, wander through the flower gardens or relax on a bench.

Franklin County

General Stores

Don't leave Franklin County without a visit to **Boone's Country Store**, (540) 721-2478, a few miles from the intersection of Va. 122 at 23 Country Road, the winding mountain road to Roanoke. Run by German Baptists, the store has the most heavenly sticky buns, pies, cakes, rolls and homemade entrees this side of Amish country. The store also sells country items, piece goods, books and cards. If you want to take home an authentic reminder of German Baptist country, don't miss Boone's.

Handcrafts

For handcrafted items for the home, curtains and decorations, as well as hand-painted and hand-made woodcrafts, travel the main road between Roanoke and Rocky Mount, U.S. 220. There you'll discover **Sew Much and More**, 19590 Virgil H. Goode Highway, (540) 483-2496. They specialize in alterations, but you'll also find custom-made children's clothes at this shop. Downtown Rocky Mount is the location of **From the Heart**, 265 Franklin Street, (540) 489-3887, a store with a unique assortment of gift items, local art, toys, pottery, linen and antiques.

Outlets

Southern Lamp & Shade Showroom, 19858 Virgil H. Goode Highway, (540) 483-4738, on U.S. 220 near Wirtz, has a great selection of lamps and shades at less than retail prices. It's well-worth visiting if you're shopping for lighting. In Rocky Mount, **Virginia Apparel Outlet**, 721 N. Main Street, (540) 483-8266, has a fine selection of clothing for the entire family at outlet prices.

New River Valley

Blacksburg

Antiques

Antique stores are spread out all over the New River Valley, especially in the Blacksburg area. Downtown, there are **Grady's Antiques**, 208 N. Main Street, (540) 951-0623; **Other Times LTD**, 891 Kabrich Street, (540) 552-1615; and **Heirloom Originals**, 609 N. Main Street, (540) 552-9241. They each have a good selection of collectibles and decorative antiques.

Specialty Shops

In the downtown, a very special store that started out as a hole in the wall several decades ago has since grown to be one of the most popular art supply and overall neat-stuff stores in western Virginia. Everyone in the know in the New River Valley knows this is **Mish Mish**, (540) 552-1020, which probably should be renamed Hodge Podge. It's at 204 Draper Road. Shoppers of any age could spend the entire day there looking at everything from the finest art supplies and watercolors to a rainbow of Silly Putty.

You'll want to stop at **Printer's Ink**, 801 University City Boulevard, (540) 552-5676, at University Mall, for all your books, magazines, greeting cards and gift items from Hallmark and other popular designers. **For the Birds**, (800) 742-4737, is filled with items both whimsical and practical, all bird-oriented. The shop at 880 University Boulevard has bird feeders, houses and seed, books and tapes, binoculars, bird-themed clothing and gifts and a large selection of garden items (birdbaths, fountains and little critters for your yard).

Sixty specialty shops and Peebles Department Store are among the stores at **New River Valley Mall**, 782 New River Road off U.S. 460 in Blacksburg, (540) 381-0004. The specialty stores, along with Peebles, really are a cut above those you find in other western Virginia shopping malls. The mall also wins your heart with free wheelchairs, high chairs in the food court, strollers and special programs.

Christiansburg

Antiques

Cambria Emporium at 596 Depot Street in Christiansburg, (540) 381-0949, is the best place in Montgomery County to find tiny antique treasures and surprises. The big, red, three-story building in the historic Cambria area of the county is a landmark in itself, constructed in 1902 and renovated several years ago as an antiques mall housing 20 dealers. Here, among 20,000 square feet of space, you can find every antique imaginable in a pleasant, old-time setting. It's open, airy and uncluttered.

You'll find glassware, furniture, dishes, quilts, vintage clothing and fine china. Along with those, you'll run across small reminders of the past that will make you ooh and ahh! For the antique lover, Cambria Emporium is definitely worth an overnight in this charming town. The Oaks bed and breakfast inn nearby is the perfect place to stay. Don't forget to go upstairs to see Casey's Country Store, a room laid out like a general store of the 1900s. A counter sign reads, "If it ain't priced, it ain't for sale, folks!" That's the spirit of Cambria Emporium.

Floyd County

General Stores

Without a doubt, counterculture-flavored Floyd County has the most diverse, interesting shopping of any area in the New River and, some might say, the entire Blue Ridge. **Floyd County General Store**, 206 S. Locust Street, (540) 745-4563, is the essence of that idea. For more than 75 years, Floyd's has been the center of Floyd County entertainment, nightlife and culture. It has become famous not only for its merchandise, but also for its famous Friday and Saturday Night Flatfooting Jamborees (see our Arts chapter). Owner Freeman Cockram's landmark store was rescued from debt several years ago by the community that cherishes it as its cultural center, in a move reminiscent of old-fashioned note burnings and barn raisings. As a general store, it offers a plethora of merchandise including

Springtime is a fine time to visit local outdoor markets.

potted possum and bib overalls, sold from an old-fashioned candy counter.

Down the road a piece is another interesting general store, **Poor Farmers Market**, (540) 952-2670, a combination grocery store, deli and gift shop on U.S. 58 in Meadows of Dan, just off the Blue Ridge Parkway. This hub for locals and tourists alike got its start when owner Felecia Shelor told a local farmer she'd buy his produce and then peddle it whole-sale. The business boomed, and the store has grown 10 times its original size since 1983. Its deli serves great lunches, with such favorites as fried apple pies and the Hungry Hillbilly sandwich. The owner's life story is as interest-ing as the store: she rose from a life of poverty as a 15-year-old bride to a store owner with 15 employees. You'll love this place, and the prices are great!

Handcrafts

When you're traveling the Blue Ridge Park-way looking for a unique Blue Ridge gift, don't miss **New Mountain Mercantile**, (540) 745-4ART, a shop at 114 Locust Street, 6 miles from Milepost 165.2 in Floyd. It's filled with many handmade items with representation of more than 150 artists and crafters. Browse through stunning tie-dyed and batik clothing, dolls, pottery, jewelry, handcrafts made by art-ists inspired by Native American Indians, per-fume made of essential oils, candles (both herbal and decorative), stained glass, quilts, pottery, original framed art, field guides and books on subjects such as herb gardening and gift making. You'll also find music, instru-ments and handtuned wind chimes. The store is run by three sensitive, savvy women — Theresa Cook, Kalinda Wycoff and Christine Byrd — who know great buys when they see them. Their store also serves as a Floyd County information center of sorts. Their "Here and Now" Art Gallery features new exhibits monthly. New Mountain Mercantile rates as one of the outstanding handcraft stores in the entire Blue Ridge. They also have a branch store at Tanglewood Mall in Roanoke. You never know which bluegrass artist will be per-forming out front to lure you in.

Specialty Stores

A direct contrast to a simple country moun-tain way of life, **Chateau Morrisette**, (540) 593-2865, the sixth-largest winery in Virginia,

is a delightful stop, not only to buy wine and baked goods at wholesale prices, but as a terrific gourmet place for lunch (see our Restaurants and Wineries chapters).

Wintergreen Farm Sheepskin Shoppe, (540) 745-4420, specializes in sheepskin products, of course, but also has fine American handcrafts, antiques and unique walking sticks. While there, visit the turn-of-the-century Farmstead Museum and Woodwright Blacksmith Shop. It's on U.S. 221, 2 miles south of Floyd.

Bluegrass and old-time music lovers will want to see the largest distributor of such music in the world, **County Records or County Sales**, (540) 745-2001, at 117A W. Main Street. Requests come in from the four corners for their old-time fiddle music and gospel albums.

Outlets

Better than an outlet store, with more fabric than you could ever find in any retail store, **School House Fabrics** on Locust Street, (540) 745-4561, is a dream come true. An old three-story schoolhouse has been renovated and filled with everything from specialty fabrics to buttons and beads. What is amazing is how organized and well-grouped this massive mania of yard goods is. Each room is arranged according to fabric; for example, a downstairs room is devoted to bridal fabrics, lace, veils,

beading and wedding goods. Out back, an extra building contains large reels of upholstery fabric, tapestry and some remnants.

Giles County

Handcrafts

The New River Valley Arts and Crafts Guild operates a dynamic **Fine Arts Center Shop** run solely by volunteers, (540) 626-3309, in a mobile unit next to what used to be the Old Pembroke School on the main drag, U.S. 460. More than 50 categories of handcrafts are available from 30 working artists, with such original works as snake canes, baskets, quilts, pottery, birdhouses and wood workings. Also available are gallery paintings from local artists. There's also a year-round Christmas Corner.

Radford

One dandy antique shop can be found in Radford. It is **Grandma's Memories**, 237 First Street, (540) 639-0054.

Encore! Artful Gifts, 1115 Norwood Street, (540) 639-2015, is the best place in the city to find unique gifts and original fine art. Merchandise ranges from the very unusual to the very trendy. Discover eclectic folk art, Toys

That Touch the Senses and truly unique cards, gift items and packaging. Also unique to the store is its variety of coffee beans.

Pulaski County

Pulaski County and Main Street Pulaski offer the most tremendous shopping surprises of any place in the rural Blue Ridge. It's a Blue Ridge town, where time seems to have stood still just for the benefit of tourists. While Pulaski County's unusual shops have been established for some time, newcomers to downtown Pulaski within the past four years will think they're dreaming when they see what has happened to a formerly neglected downtown area. Roscoe Cox, a Pulaski native and retired executive, took up the town's languishing Main Street program seven years ago and, within eight months, had 20 new stores and restaurants doing business within two blocks of the town's newly rebuilt courthouse.

Some stores already there even before the revival are worth the trip. Theda and Rudolph Farmer of **Theda's Studio**, 89 W. Main Street, (540) 980-2777, have been in the portraiture business for almost 60 years, and a visit to their shop is like taking a trip through time. Original tin-roofed ceilings and arresting pictures of brides from the '50s and '60s will take you back. With an outside barber pole that still turns, **Sani-Mode Barber Shop**, 81 W. Main Street, (540) 980-6991, is like looking through the window into a Norman Rockwell painting. The prices of haircuts are a throwback to that time, as are the lines of barber chairs from the '40s and '50s. This is a priceless — we repeat, priceless — experience that may not be on the Americana landscape for much longer.

Specialty stores include **C&S Galleries**, 5635 Old U.S. 11, (540) 674-0232, an authorized P. Buckley Moss dealer and at 21 W. Main Street, the **Fine Arts Center** for the New River Valley, (540) 980-7363, which has been serving the arts and culture of the New River Valley for nearly two decades. In this spacious setting you'll find furniture, glassware, rugs, quilts, baskets and jewelry. Nationally known artists Annie Moon and Pam Tyrell are represented here.

Further down the street is **Casimir Company**, 69 W. Main Street, (540) 980-5199. It specializes in posters, open-edition prints and full-service custom framing and accessories. There is also a gallery of original artwork. Also, don't miss **Upstairs, Downstairs**, 27 W. Main Street, (540) 980-4809, handpainted furniture downstairs and a series of small boutiques upstairs. You'd find furniture like this for four times the cost in the metropolitan areas. Don't forget to stop at the charming Victorian-style coffee shop upstairs for a relaxing break. Nearby is The Count Pulaski Bed & Breakfast and Gardens. Main Street Pulaski's main thrust, however, is first-class antique stores. It has succeeded wildly in this area. The list is long and still growing. By the time you read this, who knows how many first-class, unusual stores will have been attracted to Main Street Pulaski!

General Stores

Pulaski County offers some unusual specialty shopping in unique settings. **Draper Mercantile** on Va. 658, (540) 980-0786, two minutes off I-81 at Exit 92, is a revitalized 1880s general store, doctor's office and fire station in what was old downtown Draper. Now it's a discount place to buy, among other things, the largest display of Ridgeway grandfather, wall and mantle clocks in Virginia. You also can buy, at a 40 to 60 percent discount, High Point, North Carolina, showroom furniture, gifts, crafts, floral arrangements, reproduction toys and Christmas ornaments. If you can't take it with you, the gracious owner, Lee LaFleur, will arrange to have it shipped to your home.

Specialty Stores and Outlets

Christmas store buffs, don't you dare miss the opportunity of a lifetime at **Newbern Molding**, makers of PJ's Carousel Collection. You can find this store in Fort Chiswell on Va. 2, just off I-81, (540) 637-NOEL. **PJ's Carousel Village** in historic Newbern is the original home of the famous full-size and miniature carousel horses, right next to the factory where they are manufactured. Factory seconds are available. The Carousel Village is 3,500 square feet of fun! Be sure to have some ice cream in the old-fashioned parlor.

Alleghany Highlands

Alleghany, Bath and Highland Counties

Antiques

The Highlands are sprinkled with charming little shops in quaint downtowns and along out-of-the-way country roads in the counties of Alleghany, Highland and Bath. It's a junket you're bound to enjoy, whether you're hunting for top-quality antiques or just out enjoying the scenery.

Always unique, **Always Roxie's**, 622 Main Street in Clifton Forge in Alleghany County, (540) 862-2999, specializes in antiques, gifts and collectibles including doll houses and miniatures. Its slogan is, "We can help make your mini-house a mini-home." The shop carries railroad items, crocks, jewelry and glassware and cherished teddies.

Lovers of quilts and high-quality, unusual quilted gifts and handcrafts should head for **Quilts Unlimited**, (540) 839-5955, a Homestead Resort shop on Cottage Row in Bath County. It handles both new and antique quilts along with a fine selection of regional handcrafts.

In Highland County, plan a visit to **High Valley Antiques and Collectibles**, U.S. 220, (540) 474-5611, which occupies a pre-Civil War era log home.

General Stores

Over in McDowell, just off U.S. 250, you'll come across **Sugar Tree Country Store and Sugar House**, (540) 396-3469, a 19th-century country store featuring maple products, apple butter, pottery and baskets. The store, in the scenic Bullpasture Valley, is a must-see during the annual Highland Maple Festival, when it has tours inside of the modern-day syrup operations. Highlights of the festival are outdoor demonstrations of old-time methods of making maple syrup in iron kettles. The country store offers maple products available by mail-order.

Handcrafts

In Alleghany County visit the **Alleghany Highlands Arts & Crafts Center**, 439 E. Ridgeway, (540) 862-4447, in downtown Clifton Forge, off I-64, for fine arts and handcrafts. The center is a nonprofit organization run by a professional arts administrator and volunteer staff that encourages creativity and appreciation of the visual arts. Items for sale include pottery, wooden wares, jewelry, stained glass, needlework, drawings, fiber arts, prints, watercolors and oil paintings.

Also visit **The Crafts Shops of Covington Inc.**, 120 W. Main Street, (540) 962-0557. Handcrafted pottery, textiles, glass and other high-quality collectibles for you and your home are on display seven days a week. To ensure high standards of workmanship and creativity, samples of each artist's work are reviewed before they are permitted to sell and work on site.

In Bath County, shops in **The Virginia Building** at The Homestead offer country crafts such as dolls, rugs, candles, baskets, tin and pottery.

Highland County's Gallery of Mountain Secrets on Main Street in Monterey, (540) 468-2020, is a treasure of traditional arts and fine crafts. It's a very special store, down from the historic Highland Inn, that offers jewelry, pottery, wooden and quilted items and decorative accessories. Also on Main Street, **Highland County Crafts**, (540) 468-2127, gives a touch of country to all its gifts. It offers a Christmas corner and maple syrup and homemade preserves.

Outlets

It's worth a trip to the Alleghany Highlands just to shop at the **Bacova Guild Factory Outlet** on Main Street in Hot Springs, Bath County, (540) 839-2105. You've seen the Bacova Guild's many silk-screened gifts, including mailboxes and doormats, in leading outdoor catalogs such as Orvis and L.L. Bean. The Bacova Guild's owners provided every family in Bath County with a free silk-screened mailbox — a county trademark undoubtedly unmatched in the United States and perhaps the world. The wildlife-motif items are made in

Bacova, a charming village erected in the early 1920s as a lumber mill's company town. In 1965 the village was totally restored by philanthropist Malcolm Hirsh, whose brother, Philip, owns Meadow Lane Country Lodge in Warm Springs. A complete line of decorative, yet useful, gifts are at least 20 to 40 percent off regular prices. Summer shopping can yield an incredible Christmas gift bonanza!

Specialty Stores

Across the Alleghany County border in Greenbrier County, West Virginia, shops at the **Greenbrier Resort** will remind you of those in New York City. They include a toy store and fabulous boutiques.

Bath County's Homestead Resort offers a great array of shops including **The Gift Caboose**, (540) 839-5457, with gifts for all occasions and ages. After opening seven specialty shops in two years, The Homestead recently added several new retail venues, including **The First Lady**, (540) 839-7612, which features ladies' dresses, designer sportswear and accessories. Other Homestead stores are **Classic Bath**, (540) 839-7866, with soaps, lotions and perfumes; **The Homestead Collection**, (540) 839-7866, with home accessories and gifts; **Hobby Horse**, (540) 839-7946, featuring toys and clothing for children; **1766**, (540) 839-7743, with logoed apparel and gifts; **Southern Taste**, (540) 839-7991, complete with a range of items for the kitchen; and **William S. Flynn Men's Apparel**, (540) 839-7999.

Highland County has the unique **Ginseng Mountain Store**, (540) 474-5137, off U.S 220, six miles north of Monterey. Hours of operation are "by chance and always by appointment." You can get choice spring lamb cut to your specification, sheepskin products, stoneware, maple syrup and woven and braided rugs. The store has added a bed and breakfast accommodation for visitors to this rugged land. It has two bedrooms, sleeping as many as six, along with a full kitchen and Jacuzzi. A recent addition to the store is the Saddle Shop. Another great place is **The Personal Touch**, Main Street, Monterey, (540) 468-2145, which carries handcrafted dolls, cut and pierced lampshades and stained glass. You can also find antiques, quilts and books.

The Blue Ridge boasts the highest number of caves of any mountain range in North America.

Attractions

In addition to satisfying your soul with beautiful sights and friendly people, the Blue Ridge of Virginia will arouse your curiosity and pique your interest with its wide variety of attractions. You'll never grow tired of the scenic wonder of underground caverns, the historical insight of the region's many museums and historic homes or the pure fun of many off-the-beaten path destinations.

Elvis Presley lives on in Roanoke, where he is honored by a private citizen at Miniature Graceland, and maple sugar is celebrated at its own museum in Highland County. Also in Highland, you can attend Bear Mountain Outdoor School and learn Blue Ridge country survival skills such as building a log cabin. Alleghany County has one of the largest railroad archives in the United States, the province of the C&O Railroad Historical Society.

Historically, the Charlottesville area is one of the country's best-known tourist cities, with such attractions as Montpelier, Monticello and Ash Lawn-Highland, the former homes of three of our greatest presidents. A half-million visitors a year make the trek to the neoclassical mansion designed by the third president of the United States, Thomas Jefferson. Farther south is Jefferson's summer getaway at Poplar Forest in Bedford County. In the hills of Pulaski County, visitors stroll through an 1810 village in Old Newbern and see what life was like nearly two centuries ago.

History buffs will find the region's libraries an important source of information. In Lynchburg, Jones Memorial is one of the nation's foremost genealogical libraries. Virginia Tech's Carol Newman Library has the fifth-largest microfilm collection in the United States and Canada.

There's probably not a small town in the nation with as many military museums as Lexington, with its VMI Museum, George C. Marshall Museum, Stonewall Jackson House and Lee Chapel. In Roanoke, To The Rescue Museum houses an international tribute to the millions of lives touched by the volunteer rescue squad movement and honors the father of the movement, Julian Stanley Wise.

Some museums honor forgotten geniuses, for example the Cyrus McCormick Museum in Rockbridge County, dedicated to the inventor of the first successful reaper. Every county seat seems to have its own museum for recording local history. One, in Botetourt County, records the history of a county seat that once was an English land grant stretching the whole way to the Mississippi River.

Covered wooden bridges are so common in the Blue Ridge that locals nearly take them for granted. Virginia's first covered bridges were built around 1820, and hundreds more were erected in the decades that followed. Many of them fell into disrepair and were demolished or replaced with uncovered bridges. But a few of these favorite courting spots of yesteryear have been preserved. Of the seven covered wooden bridges accessible to the public in Virginia, the Blue Ridge claims the bridge deemed oldest and most unusual, Humpback Bridge in Covington, Alleghany County.

If it's other-world exploration you desire, you've come to the right region. The Blue Ridge boasts the highest number of caves of any mountain range in North America. So many miles of them exist under Virginia's outer skin that several have never been completely explored. In other words, no end has been found!

Visit just one cave and you will realize that America's history doesn't stop at ground level. Another world lies down under, millions of years old. Caving, also called spelunking, is a unique experience: surrounded by an unearthly silence, you can hear the steady drip of calcite solution as it forms stalactite icicles and stalagmite gardens at the modest rate of one inch every 125 years.

Most visitors to the area opt to tour one of the many commercial caverns; six of them are easily accessible from major interchanges of the Skyline Drive or I-81. Though some of these tours can be a bit hokey, padded with silly jokes and gimmicks from the tour guides, cavern guides nevertheless provide fascinating scientific information about the formation of the caves.

If commercial caves are too tame for you, get down and dirty in one of Virginia's many wild caves with Highland Adventures, P.O. Box 151, Monterey 24465, (540) 468-2722 (they also do rock climbing, mountain biking and foraging classes). Owner Rick Lambert takes groups on daytrips in one of 17 caves throughout the Alleghany Mountains. He will personalize trips for groups and even do overnight treks on which spelunkers can enjoy the unique experience of sleeping in a cave. The outfitter supplies gloves, helmets, lamps and guides; you provide the old clothes and knee pads for crawling.

Cave temperatures average 54 degrees year round, so it's a cool, damp and usually dark experience. Of course, all the commercial caverns are lighted, but wearing a sweater or jacket is always a good idea. On a hot day, you can't beat the caverns' natural air conditioning.

Almost all the caverns have interesting histories peppered with stories of Native Americans, soldiers and adventurous children who stumbled across passageways leading to hitherto unseen wonders. But, unfortunately, some caves bear the scars of souvenir hunters, a practice that has been halted by the Virginia Cave Act. Explorers of wild caves now know to "take nothing but pictures, leave nothing but footprints."

Enjoy making your choices from the attractions listed in this chapter. Be sure to look at our Civil War, Kidstuff, Horse Country and Wineries chapters for ideas of other things to do. Hours and prices may change, so be sure to call ahead. Good luck if you're trying to see it all!

www.insiders.com
See this and many other **Insiders' Guide®** destinations online.
Visit us today!

Shenandoah Valley

Frederick County

Libraries

Archives in the Handley Regional Library
Braddock and Piccadilly sts., Winchester
• (540) 662-9041

Hundreds of history buffs travel here to do genealogical research in the library's archives, particularly on ancestors who fought in the Civil War. Aside from amassing a collection of more than 400,000 books, the library itself is also a magnificent structure. Listed on the National Register of Historic Places, the original building (it opened in 1913) was designed in the Beaux Arts style. Created to represent a book, the rotunda served as the spine with two wings representing the open pages. Corinthian columns stand guard in front, while the dome is covered with a copper top on the outside and stained glass on the inside. A new wing was added in 1979 called the "grandson leaning against the grandfather." The library is open from 1 to 9 PM Tuesday and Wednesday and 10 AM to 5 PM Thursday, Friday and Saturday.

Museums

Abram's Delight Museum
1340 S. Pleasant Valley Rd., Winchester
• (540) 662-6519

Abram's Delight, the oldest house in Winchester, was built in 1754 of native limestone with walls 2 feet thick. A restored log cabin on the lawn is from the same period. Abram's Delight is beautifully refurbished and furnished with period pieces. It's open Monday through Saturday from 10 AM to 4 PM and Sunday noon to 4 PM April 1 through October. Admission is $3.50 for adults, $3 for seniors, $1.75 for children ages 6 to 12 or $8.75 for a family ticket. You can save by buying a block ticket for entrance to this museum and two other historic sites in town, Stonewall Jackson's Headquarters and George Washington's Office Museum. Block tickets cost $7.50 for adults, $6.50 for seniors and $4 for children. Family block tickets are $20. Groups of more than 20 pay $7 for adults, $6 for seniors.

George Washington's Office Museum
32 W. Cork St., Winchester
• (540) 662-4412

Part of this old log-and-stone building was used by Washington when he was colonel of the Virginia Regiment protecting the 300-mile-long frontier to the west. It's open 10 AM to 4 PM daily (noon to 4 PM Sunday) April 1 through October. Admission is $2 for adults, $1.50 for seniors and $1 for children ages 6 to 12.

Kurtz Cultural Center
2 N. Cameron St., Winchester
• (540) 722-6367

Just a short walk from the downtown pedestrian mall is the historic building housing the Old Town Welcome Center and Gift Shop, several displays and a gallery with changing art exhibits. The prestigious Julian Wood Glass Junior Collection opened in 1996, featuring 18th- and 19th-century decorative art, furniture and paintings. In other parts of the center, a permanent interpretive exhibit called "Shenandoah — Crossroads of the Civil War" details the Shenandoah Valley's major battles. A Patsy Cline display contains records, photos, belongings and videos of the Winchester-born country singer. The cultural center is open from 10 AM to 5 PM Monday through Saturday and noon to 5 PM Sunday. Admission is free, except to the Julian Wood Glass Collection, which costs $3.

Other Historic Attractions

Belle Grove Plantation
U.S. Hwy. 11, Middletown
• (540) 869-2028

Belle Grove, c. 1794, is an 18th-century plantation, working farm and center for the study of traditional rural crafts. The National Historic Trust site was the home of Maj. Isaac Hite Jr. and his family for more than 70 years. Hite was a grandson of one of the first permanent settlers in the Shenandoah Valley. Thomas Jefferson was actively involved in Belle Grove's design, thanks to some family connections. Hite married the sister of James Madison, who was a close friend of Jefferson. In fact, James and Dolley Madison spent part of their honeymoon visiting the Hites at Belle Grove.

Belle Grove hosts a variety of special activities throughout the year, from the Shenandoah Valley Farm Craft Days in early June to the Battle of Cedar Creek Living History Weekend in mid-October. A very nice gift shop and quilt shop are also at the site.

The plantation is open to the public April through mid-November from 10:15 AM to 3:15 PM daily (1:15 to 4:15 PM Sunday). Admission is $5 for adults, $4.50 for seniors and $2.50 for children ages 6 to 12. Belle Grove is a mile south of Middletown on U.S. 11; take Exit 302 from I-81, then head west on Va. Route 627 to U.S. 11.

Glen Burnie Manor Home and Gardens
100 W. Piccadilly St., Winchester
• (540) 662-1473

Open to the public for the first time in 1997, Glen Burnie is the home of Winchester's founder, Col. James Wood. Wood built the original house in the early 1750s, and his son, Robert, replaced the log and stone structure with a Georgian brick manor house in 1794. The house remained in the Wood family until it was inherited by Julian Wood Glass Jr. in 1952. Glass renovated the houses and designed the formal gardens on the 264-acre working farm. He also furnished the home with 18th-century furniture and art, including works by John Singleton Copley, Gilbert Stuart and Rembrandt Peale. At his death, Glass established the Glass-Glen Burnie Foundation to preserve the home and his art collection. (The first in a series of exhibits of the artwork can be seen at the Kurtz Cultural Center through 1999.) The home is open from 10 AM to 4 PM Tuesday, Wednesday, Friday and Saturday and from noon to 4 PM Sunday. The $8 fee also will allow you to visit the art exhibit in the Kurtz Cultural Center.

Stonewall Jackson's Headquarters
415 N. Braddock St., Winchester
• (540) 667-3242

Jackson used the private home of Lt. Col. Lewis T. Moore as his headquarters during the Civil War from 1861 to 1862. Jackson's office remains much as it was during his stay, and the house contains artifacts of Jackson, Turner Ashby, Jed Hotchkiss and other Confederate leaders. The house is open from 10 AM to 4 PM daily (noon to 4 PM Sunday) April 1 through October. Admission is $3.50 for adults, $3 for seniors and $1.75 for children.

If you plan on stopping by several sites, consider the block tickets. The block ticket will get you in Stonewall Jackson's Headquarters plus George Washington's Office Museum and Abram's Delight Museum. Block tickets cost $7.50 for adults, $6.50 for seniors and $4 for children. Family block tickets are $20.

Other Attractions

Patsy Cline Gravesite
Patsy Cline Memorial Hwy., Va. Rt. 522 S., Winchester • (540) 667-2012

Thousands of people come to Winchester each year to pay their respects to one of country music's most beloved singers, Patsy Cline. She was born on September 8, 1932, in nearby Gore and went on to star on the Grand Ole Opry. A year after "I Fall to Pieces" hit No. 1 on the country record charts, Cline was killed in an airplane crash in Tennessee in 1963. A bell tower was erected in her memory at the Shenandoah Memorial Park where she is interred. Several local highways, including Va. 522, have been renamed in her honor. Those wishing to visit the grave should enter the north gate and take the first right to a bench on the left.

Clarke County

Historic Attractions

The Burwell-Morgan Mill
Va. Rt. 255 and Va. Rt. 723, Millwood
• (540) 837-1799

In 1782 Lt. Col. Nathaniel Burwell and Brig. Gen. Daniel Morgan decided to start a joint venture — a flour and grist mill. During the Civil War, both armies bought feed and supplies from the mill. In 1876 a second floor was added, and the mill continued to operate until 1953. Today the mill is back in operation grinding meal and flour with the wooden gears dating back to the 1750s. Just as it did almost 200 years ago, the great wheel turns under a splash of water. The mill is open for tours April 1 through October 31 from 10 AM to 5 PM Thursday through Sunday. A $3 donation is requested.

Historic Long Branch
Va. Rt. 624, Millwood
• (540) 837-1856

This 400-acre estate in the heart of Virginia's hunt country has been owned by a series of famous men, including Lord Culpeper, Lord Fairfax and Robert King Carter. In fact, George Washington helped survey the property. In 1788 Robert Carter Burwell inherited the land and began to build the mansion along the plans suggested by Benjamin Henry Latrobe, the architect who designed the U.S. Capitol. The property was handed down to Maj. Hugh Mortimer Nelson and Abram Hewitt, but by the 20th century, this large estate was declining. Henry Z. Isaacs, a Baltimore textile executive, bought the property in 1986, and in three short years, restored it to its early grandeur. The estate is decorated with hand-painted wallpaper and 18th- and 19th-century antiques — the dining room chairs are identi-

INSIDERS' TIP

Even if it's a warm summer's day, don't forget to take a sweater along when you visit any of the caverns along the Blue Ridge. The temperature in the caverns remains in the mid-50s year round.

cal to those in the White House. Long Branch is open for guided tours from noon to 4 PM weekends only from April through October. There is also a special weeklong Christmas tour the first week in December. Admission is $8.

Other Attractions

The State Arboretum of Virginia
Va. Rt. 2, Box 210, Boyce
• (540) 837-1758, (540) 837-1458

Also known as the Orlando E. White Arboretum, this research center for the University of Virginia is on 170 acres of Blandy Experimental Farm. You can drive along a circular route or stroll through the grounds and enjoy a picnic lunch. Explore one of the most extensive boxwood collections in North America or rest beneath stands of beeches, magnolia and maples. Printed trail guides and information on current programs are available at the Visitor's Pavilion. The Arboretum is open year-round from dawn to dusk. Admission is free. Guided tours are available by appointment.

Shenandoah County

Caverns

Shenandoah Caverns
Off I-81 at Exit 269, south of Mount Jackson • (540) 477-3115

Shenandoah Caverns, taking its name from the Native American word for "daughter of the stars," was discovered in 1884 during the building of the Southern Railway. The grotto is an estimated 11 million years old and is the closest underground attraction to I-81. It's also the only one in Virginia with an elevator, an advantage to visitors who are disabled, elderly or just plain tired. Bacon Hall, a formation named for its hanging slabs of striped iron oxide and calcite, has been featured in *National Geographic*. Other notable points on the tour are the Grotto of the Gods, Vista of Paradise and Rainbow Lake.

The caverns recently opened a new exhibit, American Celebrations on Parade. This unusual attraction features a variety of parade and window display paraphernalia that the cavern owners have collected over the years. You'll find all kinds of interesting things, including several 22-foot bears used in the Tournament of Roses Parade and moving characters from seasonal window displays from stores across the United States. Nearby attractions include Skyline Drive, New Market Battlefield and its Civil War museums and the Meems Bottom covered bridge.

Shenandoah Caverns is open year round; hours depend on the season. Admission to both the caverns and American Celebrations on Parade is $11.50 for adults and $5.50 for children ages 5 to 14. Group rates are available upon request.

Covered Bridges

Meems Bottom Bridge
Va. Rt. 720 off U.S. Hwy. 11,
Mount Jackson

Just north of Harrisonburg in Rockingham County and less than a half-mile from busy I-81, visitors can step back in time at Meems Bottom Bridge. The 204-foot, single-span Burr arch truss crosses the north fork of the Shenandoah River 2 miles south of Mount Jackson on U.S. 11. The bridge takes its name from the Meems family who owned the Strathmore estate west of the Shenandoah River. The original 1893 structure was rebuilt in 1979, almost three years after arsonists burned it. It had been burned before, in 1862, when Stonewall Jackson went up the valley ahead of Union general John C. Fremont, before the battles of Harrisonburg, Cross Keys and Port Republic. The structure was rebuilt, only to be destroyed again by a flood in 1870. The one-lane bridge is open to automobile traffic and is a good side excursion from New Market, a major destination for Civil War buffs just 6 miles south of the bridge.

Museums

Bedrooms of America Museum
9386 Congress St., New Market
• (540) 740-3512

This sounds like a sleeper of a museum, but actually it's a fascinating place if you like old furniture and want to learn more about American antiques. Eleven rooms of authentic furniture represent every period of America's bedrooms, from William and Mary (c. 1650) through art deco (c. 1930). The rooms are also furnished with period accessories, bed coverings, curtains and wall coverings.

The museum is housed in a restored 18th-century building used for a time by Confederate Gen. Jubal Early as his headquarters during the Civil War. It's open 9 AM to 5 PM daily (except Christmas Day). A large gift shop on the bottom floor carries everything from antiques to moccasins. Admission is $2 for adults, $1.50 for seniors, $1.25 for children ages 8 to 14 and free for those younger than 8. The group rate for 10 or more is $1.25.

Museum of American Cavalry
298 W. Old Cross Rd., New Market
• (540) 740-3959

On the New Market Battlefield in the home of Confederate Maj. Christiona Shirley is an unusual collection chronicling the development of the cavalry from Jamestown through Vietnam. Three galleries in the 3,000-square foot museum display arms, armor, full-scale mounted figures, uniforms, maps and period artwork. The museum shop sells books, artifacts and original and reproduction militaria. The museum, on the corner of Old Cross Road and Collins Drive, is open daily 9 AM to 5 PM April through November. Admission is $5 for adults, $2.50 for children 6 to 12 and free for those younger than 6.

New Market Battlefield Historical Park and Hall of Valor Museum
8895 Collins Dr., New Market
• (540) 740-3101

In the spring of 1864, a wavering Confederate line was reinforced with teenage cadets from Virginia Military Institute. This museum chronicles their brave but tragic stand and has some interesting displays of VMI professor Stonewall Jackson (see our Civil War chapter). The museum is open 9 AM to 5 PM daily. Admission is $5 for adults, $2 for children ages 7 to 15 and free for younger children.

New Market Battlefield Military Museum
9500 Collins Rd., on Va. Rt. 305,
New Market • (540) 740-8065

Fashioned after Robert E. Lee's Mount Vernon home, this museum stands on the sloped hill where the Battle of New Market began in May 1864. More than 2,000 original artifacts are arranged chronologically in 108 displays, including Stonewall Jackson's family Bible and Gen. George Armstrong Custer's spurs. Custer left his books behind when he had to flee quickly to avoid capture by Confederate troops. There also is a 30-minute film on the Civil War, while outside, 15 monuments mark strategic points on the 8-mile battlefield. (See our Civil War chapter.) The museum is open from 10 AM to 4 PM daily from March 15 to December 1. Admission is $6, $3 for children ages 6 to 14 and free for those younger than 6.

Museum of American Presidents
130 N. Massanutten St., Strasburg
• (540) 465-5999

New in 1996, this fascinating museum displays presidential artifacts, including James Madison's desk, on which he likely wrote the *Federalist Papers*; a lock of George Washington's hair; and many documents featuring presidential signatures. Combining education and entertainment, the museum displays biographical sketches of all 42 presidents. The one-room schoolhouse, a hands-on area for children, features reproduction Colonial costumes and toys. Admission is $3.50

INSIDERS' TIP

In the 1950s, Saturday night at the movies meant going to a drive-in. During their hey-day there were more than 6,000 drive-in theaters across the United States. Today that number has dwindled to about 800. You can catch a part of Americana at several spots along the Blue Ridge, including Winchester, Fort Union and Lexington.

for adults, $2 for seniors and children ages 6 to 17 and free for those younger than 6. Year-round hours are 10 AM to 5 PM daily and noon to 5 PM Sunday. It's closed New Years, Easter, Thanksgiving and Christmas.

Warren County

Caverns

Skyline Caverns
U.S. Hwy. 340, Front Royal
• **(540) 635-4545, (800) 296-4545**

Sixty-million-year-old Skyline Caverns, at the foothills of the Blue Ridge near the Skyline Drive, has a unique solarium entrance where green shrubs border the cave to create a most attractive welcome. Three running streams traverse the core of the cave; one is stocked with trout as an experiment in adaptation. Fat and thriving, the fish require chopped pork each week to make up for a lack of vitamin D. Another unusual aspect is anthodites, called "orchids of the mineral kingdom," the only such rock formations in the world. They grow at a rate of one inch every 7,000 years!

Skyline is noted for its simulated scenes of reality, such as the Capitol Dome, Rainbow Trail and the Painted Desert. Two large gift shops, a snack shop and picnic area are on the grounds. Kids enjoy the outdoor Skyline Arrow, a miniature train that carries them on a half-mile journey through the woods.

Skyline Caverns, near the north entrance of Shenandoah National Park, is open year round, with hours depending on the season. From June 15 through Labor Day, the hours are 9 AM to 6:30 PM. Admission is $10 for adults, $5 for children ages 6 to 13 and free for children younger than 6. Discounts are available for AAA, military and seniors. Reservations are accepted but not required.

Museums

Warren Rifles Confederate Museum
95 Chester St., Front Royal
• **(540) 636-6982**

Mosby's Rangers, Stonewall Jackson, Robert E. Lee, Jubal Early, J.E.B. Stuart and Confederate spy Belle Boyd all saw action in Warren County. Uniforms, flags, pictures and other relics of their feats are displayed here. The museum and gift shop, which is owned and operated by the Warren Rifles Chapter of the United Daughters of the Confederacy, is open from April 15 to November 1, weekdays 9 AM to 4 PM and Sunday noon to 4 PM. Admission is $2 for ages 13 and older. Discounts are available for groups or members of AAA or AARP. If you call during closed months, no answering machine or service will pick up your call. Write to the museum if you would like to arrange a specialty tour. The zip code is 22630.

Page County

Caverns

Luray Caverns
U.S. Hwy. 211, Luray • **(540) 743-6551**

Each year nearly a half-million people visit Luray Caverns, the largest known cave on the East Coast, to see the colorful natural cathedral with the world's only Stalacpipe Organ. Stalactites are tuned to concert pitch and accuracy and are struck by electronically controlled, rubber-tipped plungers to produce music of symphonic quality. An hour-long conducted tour transports visitors through a wonderland of vast chambers, some 10 stories high. Memorable formations include the Fried Eggs, the enormous Double Column and Pluto's Ghost. Placid, crystal-clear pools such as Dream Lake reflect the thousands of stalactites above. One of the largest chambers, the Cathedral, has been the setting for more than 300 weddings. A wishing well has produced more than a half-million dollars for charity. Topside, you'll find three gift shops and a restaurant. Don't miss the Luray Singing Tower, a carillon of 47 bells, the largest weighing 7,640 pounds, the smallest 12 pounds. Recitals are given seasonally; call for hours. A self-guided tour of the Historic Car & Carriage Caravan is included in the caverns admission.

The central entrance to Skyline Drive is only 10 minutes from the caverns. Luray Caverns is open year round at 9 AM. Admission is $14 for adults, $5 for children ages 7 to 13 and $12 for adults older than 62. Children 6 and younger are admitted free.

Museums

Luray Caverns Car and Carriage Caravan
U.S. Hwy. 211 Bypass, Luray
• **(540) 743-6551**

This museum next to Luray Caverns grew from the car-collecting hobby of the caverns' president, H.T.N. Graves. Among the vehicles are Rudolph Valentino's 1925 Rolls Royce, a Conestoga wagon, an ornate sleigh and an 1892 Benz, one of the oldest cars in the country. All 140 items, including cars, coaches, carriages and costumes, are fully restored. Admission is included in your ticket to Luray Caverns ($12 adults, $5 children). The caravan is open every day from 9 AM until one hour after the last cavern tour (7 to 8 PM depending on the time of year).

Other Attractions

Luray Singing Tower
U.S. Hwy. 211 Bypass, Luray
• **(540) 743-6551**

Across from the Luray Caverns is a tower containing a carillon of 47 bells, the largest weighing 7,640 pounds and the smallest 12 pounds. Free recitals are given on weekends at 2 PM during March, April, May, September and October. From June through August, the bells peal at 8 PM Tuesday, Thursday, Saturday and Sunday. Listen from outside on the grounds. There is no fee.

Rockingham County

Caverns

Endless Caverns
Off I-81 at Exit 257, New Market
• **(540) 740-3993**

On October 1, 1879, two boys and their dog chased a rabbit up the slope of Reuben Zirkle's farm. The rabbit disappeared under a boulder. The boys moved the boulder, and before their astonished eyes appeared a great shaft of Endless Caverns. No end has ever been found to the labyrinth of winding channels and vast rooms, which now are lighted artfully and dramatically for visitors. Snowdrift and Fairyland are two of the most popular formations. Of all the caverns, Endless is the one that makes you feel as if you're venturing into uncharted, rugged territory, and its outdoor scenery is most beautiful.

Just as interesting are the historic native limestone buildings constructed during the 1920s. On the wide porches of the Main Lodge, visitors are invited to rest, rock and relax while enjoying a sweeping view of the Shenandoah Valley. The stone lodge is cooled in the summer and warmed in winter by air from the caverns. Nearby, Endless Caverns' 100-site campground sits at the foot of Virginia's Massanutten Mountains, adjoining George Washington National Forest.

On I-81, you can't miss the sign for Endless Caverns; it's the largest outdoor billboard in the Eastern United States, standing 35 feet high and 500 feet long.

Endless Caverns is open year round except Christmas Day. The caverns open at 9 AM throughout the year. Closing hours vary: 5 PM from mid-March to mid-June and after Labor Day to mid-November; 4 PM from mid-November to mid-March; and 7 PM from mid-June to Labor Day. Admission is $10 for adults, $5 for children ages 3 to 12 and free for those younger than 3.

Museums

Reuel B. Pritchett Museum
Va. Rt. 257, Bridgewater College
• **(540) 828-5462**

The Rev. Reuel B. Pritchett bequeathed his collection of rare artifacts to Bridgewater College in 1954. The 10,000-piece collection features more than 175 rare books, including a three-volume Bible printed in Venice in 1482 and a medieval book of Gregorian chants made and hand-copied by a monk. There are also a cuneiform brick dating to 600 B.C., a Chinese Mandarin gown, a Kiowa chieftain's headdress, wooden carpentry tools, swords, coins and glassware. The museum, in the lower level of Cole Hall, is open from 1 to 5 PM Monday through Friday. Admission is free.

Shenandoah Valley Folk Art & Heritage Center
115 Bowman Rd., Dayton
• **(540) 879-2681**

This museum has a 12-foot electric relief map of Stonewall Jackson's Valley Campaign of 1862. The map fills an entire wall and lets you see and hear the campaign battle by battle. The museum also displays many artifacts of the Shenandoah Valley's history, a Civil War exhibit and Valley folk art. The center also includes a genealogical library. The Heritage Museum Store sells genealogical and valley-related books and gifts. Hours are Monday and Wednesday through Saturday 10 AM to 4 PM and Sundays 1 to 4 PM. Admission is $4 for adults, $1 for children ages 5 to 18 and free for those younger than 5.

Virginia Quilt Museum
301 S. Main St., Harrisonburg
• **(540) 433-3818**

Quilts represent a rich American heritage, combining practicality, skill and creativity. Enjoy this history at the Quilt Museum, which displays beautiful works by both early and contemporary artisans. You will also learn about the role of quilts in American cultural life. The museum is open Monday and Thursday through Saturday from 10 AM to 4 PM; Sunday hours are 1 to 4 PM. Adults pay $4 admission; seniors and students with IDs, $3; and kids 6 to 12, $2. Children younger than 6 get in free. Group rates are also available.

Warren House Life Science Museum
17 Grace St., Harrisonburg
• **(540) 568-6906**

This James Madison University museum has a large display of stuffed mammals and an impressive collection of live reptiles.

Snakes, spiders, an iguana and a giant 8-inch African millipede are among the moving, breathing exhibits. Kids should enjoy crawling around the dinosaur cave that JMU students created for them. Equally interesting are the collections of Native American relics, seashells, birds and butterflies from around the world. (See our Kidstuff chapter.) The museum is open from 9 AM to 3 PM Monday through Friday and from 9 AM to noon on Saturdays during the academic year. The times may vary because the museum is staffed by student volunteers, so you may want to call ahead before you make a trip. During the summer, guided tours are available by appointment only. Admission is free.

Other Historic Attractions

The Daniel Harrison House (Fort Harrison)
N. Main St., Dayton
• **(540) 879-2280**

This historic 18th-century (c. 1749) stone house, just north of Dayton, was a natural fort to which Daniel Harrison added a stockade and an underground passage to a nearby spring. What appear to be loopholes set in the house's stone walls for firing rifles at Indians gave rise to the name Fort Harrison. Free guided tours are available. The house is open 1 to 4 PM on weekends from late May through October and for special events in November to April. The house also hosts community events such as the Dayton Autumn Festival in October, the Christmas Craft Show at Thanksgiving and the 12th Night Celebration in January.

Lincoln Homestead and Cemetery
Va. Rt. 42, Harrisonburg

Abraham Lincoln's father, Thomas Lincoln, was born in Rockingham County, and his ancestors were buried here in a little cemetery 7.5 miles north of Harrisonburg. The house

The Albemarle County Courthouse dates back to 1763.

now standing at the old Lincoln homestead is privately owned, so please respect that when you visit the cemetery.

Sporting Events

Although most sports-minded visitors are in the Blue Ridge to play, some want to watch others play. The area has a lot to offer in college competition, especially basketball and football. You'll want to get tickets early, because the locals are avid fans.

The Valley Baseball League
Harrisonburg • (540) 568-6154

One of the oldest amateur baseball leagues in the country, the Valley League is sanctioned by the NCAA because it features college players, many of whom go on to play professional ball. Mo Vaughn played here. Harrisonburg, Front Royal, New Market, Staunton, Waynesboro and Winchester have franchised teams in the circuit. Starting the first weekend in June, the league plays 40 regular-season games, with all six teams competing in the playoffs. Games are scheduled for every day of the week, with most beginning at 7:30 PM.

James Madison University
Harrisonburg • (540) JMU-DUKE

JMU has 27 intercollegiate teams but charges admission only to football, basketball, soccer and baseball games. When the men's basketball team plays at home, the whole town turns out or tunes in. The Dukes have advanced to post-season play five of the past eight seasons under coach Charles G. "Lefty" Driesell. Sherman Dillard, who played his college ball at James Madison, returned to take over the head coaching duties in 1997-98. The JMU women also added a new coach, Bud Childers, in 1997. The Dukes have made six NCAA basketball playoff appearances. Men's and women's games are played at the Convocation Center on the east side of I-81.

JMU's football team has been in four NCAA playoffs and made the 1994 NCAA I-AA final eight. The baseball squad is the only Virginia team to have played in the College World Series; it also played in the 1995 South Regional Tournament. Other nationally ranked sports at the college are field hockey (1994 national champions and 1995 national semifinalist), archery (three national championships), men's soccer (1994 and 1995 NCAA final eight, seven NCAA playoffs), women's lacrosse and soccer (1995 and 1996 NCAA tournaments).

Women's lacrosse and men's and women's soccer teams play at the JMU Soccer and Lacrosse Field at Reservoir Street (capacity 1,860) on the east campus. Baseball's home is Long Field (capacity 1,200), and football is played at Bridgeforth Stadium (capacity 12,500).

Call the ticket office at the number above to purchase tickets or find out game schedules.

Augusta County

Caverns

Grand Caverns
Off I-81 at Exit 235, Grottoes
• **(540) 249-5705**

Grand Caverns, within Grand Caverns Regional Park, is one of the oldest and most spectacular caverns in the Shenandoah Valley. The public has been coming here since 1806, including Thomas Jefferson, who rode horseback from Monticello to see the site. During the Civil War, Gen. Stonewall Jackson quartered his troops within this massive stone fortress after the Battle of Port Republic. Union soldiers also visited the cave; their signatures still can be seen penciled on the walls. In better times, the Grand Ballroom, which encompasses 5,000 square feet, was the scene of early 19th-century dances for the socially prominent. Cathedral Hall, 280 feet long and 70 feet high, is one of the largest rooms in Eastern caverns. Massive columns and the rare "shield" formations, whose origins are a mystery to geologists, are highlights.

It's open 9 AM to 5 PM on March weekends, and daily April through Halloween. Admission is $10 for adults, $6 for children ages 3 to 12, free for children younger than 3 and $9 for senior citizens and active military. Rockingham County residents pay half-price.

Museums

Frontier Culture Museum
U.S. Hwy. 250 W., Staunton
• **(540) 332-7850**

Somehow "museum" doesn't seem an appropriate word for the living, breathing outdoor Frontier Culture Museum. Authentic farmsteads have been painstakingly brought from Old World Europe and reconstructed here. Original gardens, hedges, pastures and even road layouts have been duplicated, along with the old ways of survival. You can tour Scotch-Irish, 18th-century German, American and English farmsteads staffed with knowledgeable, articulate interpreters. Also authentic are the farm animals, including lambs, chickens, cows and kittens, making this a fine attraction for children.

The museum recently added an 18th-century forge, or blacksmith shop. This one-room, thatched-roof stone structure was brought over from Ireland. If you are lucky, you will catch the resident blacksmith demonstrating how the generations-old tools and equipment are used.

Throughout the year, the museum hosts more than 100 special events, such as Lantern Tours at Christmas and the Traditional Frontier Festival the weekend after Labor Day, with crafts, food and entertainment.

The museum is open 9 AM to 5 PM daily for most of the year (10 AM to 4 PM December 1 through March 15). The facility is closed Thanksgiving, Christmas and New Year's days. Admission is $8 for adults, $7.50 for seniors and $4 for children. Special rates are available for preregistered groups of 15 or more.

To find the museum, take Exit 222 off I-81, then go west on U.S. 250.

Waynesboro Heritage Museum
Main St., Waynesboro
• **(540) 943-3943**

This historic building on the corner of Main Street and Wayne Avenue has served the banking needs of the people of Waynesboro since 1908. Today it houses the city's historical treasures. You can still see inside the large walk-in vault, but all around are reminders of Waynesboro's past. There is a case of arrowheads and tools from the Indians who stopped by and planted crops. There is a bill of sale for a slave and notices from the tannery that closed when the chestnut blight swept through the area. There are reminders of war — shoes from Union and Confederate soldiers, a World War I canteen and pistol belt, a Japanese officer's sword taken from the beach at Iwo Jima during WWII. There's even a collection of international dolls, ranging from an Indonesian Rod Puppet and Russian Nesting Matryoshkas to our own colonial era Applehead, Nuthead and Corncob dolls. Hours are 1 to 4 PM Tuesday through Thursday and Sunday afternoons. It's open from 10 AM to 4 PM Friday and Saturday with extended hours from 6 to 8 PM on the first Friday of every month.

Woodrow Wilson Museum and Birthplace
18 to 24 N. Coalter St., Staunton
• **(540) 885-0897**

Woodrow Wilson's birthplace has been carefully restored to appear as it would have when he lived there as a child. Throughout the 150-year-old Greek Revival-style house are furniture and other personal items belonging to the Wilsons, including the family Bible in which Woodrow Wilson's birth was recorded. You'll also find an array of period pieces typical of the antebellum era.

The museum is a tribute to our nation's 28th president, who was born here in 1856. Displays chronicle his life as a scholar, Princeton University president, governor and statesman. Seven exhibit areas include rare artifacts, photographs, personal possessions and the furnishings of Wilson's study at Princeton. The displays do not shy away from the controversies Wilson generated in his lifetime, from the way in which he alienated wealthy trustees and alumni as Princeton's president to his lack of support for women's suffrage as America's president. Of course, the displays also highlight the reforms Wilson brought about as the nation's leader. The museum houses Wilson's beloved Pierce-Arrow automobile.

The museum and birthplace are open daily 9 AM to 5 PM (10 AM to 4 PM December through February except Thanksgiving, Christmas and New Year's days). Admission is $6.50 for adults ($5.75 for seniors and AAA members), $4 for students ages 13 and older and $2 for ages 6 to 12. Group rates are available.

Other Attractions

Natural Chimneys
Off Va. Rt. 731, Mount Solon
• **(540) 350-2510**

A mere 500 million years ago, layers of limestone began to form from sediment under an ancient sea that once covered the Shenandoah Valley. Today, seven of those rock formations can be seen at Natural Chimneys Regional Park. The "chimneys" range in height from 65 to 120 feet, but each includes a 12-inch band of lava about 6 feet up from the ground. One of the chimneys leans 13.5 feet, approximately the same as the Leaning Tower of Pisa. The park also includes campsites, a swimming pool, stage and picnic shelters and hosts two jousting tournaments each year (see our Horse Country chapter). Admission is $5. The park is open daily from 9 AM to dusk from March through October.

Statler Brothers Complex
501 Thornrose Ave., Staunton
• **(540) 885-7297**

The Statler Brothers, world-famous country singers, make their home in Staunton and have their own museum and office complex in town. On display are mementos collected by the band in 30 years of performing. Free tours of the complex take place at 2 PM every Monday through Friday. The gift shop, open weekdays from 10:30 AM to 3:30 PM, sells albums, cassettes, compact discs, T-shirts, sweatshirts and other souvenirs. A tip from those in the know: if you really want to see the Statler Brothers in the flesh, hang out until after the museum closes. That unusual tour time does serve a purpose. You may catch them leaving the building on days when they are in town. If you are a Statler Brothers fan, you will know that tours and taping of their weekly TNN cable program take them away from Staunton regularly.

Lexington/ Rockbridge County

Caverns

Natural Bridge Caverns
**U.S. Hwy. 11 off I-81 at
Exit 175 or 180, Lexington**
• **(540) 291-2121, (800) 533-1410**

Here's a cavern with its own ghost! For more than 100 years, people have been hearing the plaintive voice of a woman deep within the limestone passages. The first time it happened in 1889, men working in the caverns abandoned their ladders, fled and refused to go back. Their tools and lanterns were found in 1978. The last time the ghost was heard was 1988, when six people on the final tour of the day heard a distinct moaning sound, which continued throughout the guide's narrative. In all cases, it is documented that those present had an eerie feeling and fled the premises without hesitation. The caverns, at Virginia's Natural Bridge complex, offer a guided, 45-minute tour 347 feet underground. The pathways are winding and steep in areas, so walking shoes are suggested.

Topside, see Natural Bridge and the Wax Museum. The Caverns Gift Shop is the largest in the valley, with 10,000 square feet of space; the "rock" and "mineral" candies are sure to delight youngsters. Colonial-style Natural Bridge Hotel features sumptuous buffets.

The cavern is open March through November, 10 AM to 5 PM daily. Admission is $7 for adults, $3.50 for children ages 6 to 15 and free for those younger than 6. A special combination ticket to see all three attractions is $15 for adults and $7.50 for children ages 6 to 15.

Museums and Historic Attractions

George C. Marshall Museum and Library
VMI Parade Grounds, Lexington
• **(540) 463-7103**

The Marshall Foundation was founded in 1953 at the suggestion of President Harry Truman to honor the memory of Gen. George C. Marshall. Marshall was the only American military hero to win a Nobel Peace Prize, for his plan to reconstruct Europe following World War II. Winston Churchill said of Marshall, "Succeeding generations must not be allowed to forget his achievements and his example." Marshall also was former Army Chief of Staff and Secretary of State and Defense. Presidents Johnson and Eisenhower dedicated the museum in 1964. Visitors can see a stirring movie and striking photographic display, including the hauntingly stark, black-and-white photos of the faces of children of war-torn Europe.

The museum is open from 9 AM to 5 PM daily. Admission is $3 for adults and $1 for children ages 7 to 18; a senior citizen discount is available.

Lee Chapel and Museum
**Washington & Lee University,
Lexington** • **(540) 463-8768**

Civil War buffs won't want to miss the beautiful Lee Chapel and Museum, the focal point of the campus where Confederate great Robert E. Lee served as president for five years after the war. Lee's remains are buried here, and you can see the famous Edward Valentine statue of a recumbent Lee. The museum is open 9 AM to 5 PM Monday through Saturday from April through October and closes one hour earlier October through April. Sunday hours are 2 to 5 PM.

McCormick Farm
**U.S. Hwy. 11 N. to Va. Rt. 606 or
Exit 205 off I-81, Steeles Tavern**
• **(540) 377-2255**

This 635-acre farm, 20 miles north of Lexington, is the home of Cyrus McCormick, who invented the first successful mechanical reaper at age 22. McCormick Farm is part of the Virginia Tech College of Agricultural and Life Sciences and a Virginia Agricultural Experiment Station. Visitors may tour the blacksmith shop, gristmill, museum and McCormick family home, all National Historic Landmarks. McCormick's 1831 invention launched a new era in agriculture, an age of mechanization that not only changed life on the farm but also made it possible for millions of people to leave

Photo: The Roanoke Valley Convention and Visitors Bureau

Dixie Caverns in Salem was discovered when a dog fell through a hole in the mountain.

the land and enter an industrial society. The site is open 8:30 AM to 5 PM daily.

Stonewall Jackson House
8 E. Washington Ave., Lexington
• (540) 463-2552

Stonewall Jackson House, owned and operated by Stonewall Jackson Foundation, is the only home the famous Confederate general ever owned. The house was restored in 1979 and is furnished with period pieces, including many of Jackson's personal possessions. The house, which is listed on the National Register of Historic Sites, is open to the public daily for guided tours of the rooms. In addition to tours and exhibits, the Stonewall Jackson House sponsors a variety of educational programs through the Garland Gray Research Center and Library, on the office level of the museum. Educational activities include in-school programs, internships, lectures, workshops and scholarly symposia. It is open 9 AM to 5 PM Monday through Saturday and 1 to 5 PM Sunday. Hours extend to 6 PM in June, July and August. The museum is closed

on Thanksgiving Day, Christmas Day, New Year's Day and Easter Sunday. Admission is $5 for adults and $2.50 for youth ages 6 to 17. Children younger than 6 are admitted free of charge.

VMI Museum
VMI Parade Grounds, N. Main St.,
Lexington • (540) 464-7232,
(540) 464-7334

The VMI Museum, on the lower level of Jackson Hall on the VMI Campus, brings the nation's history to life. Other exhibits tell American history through the lives and service of VMI faculty. Both Gen. Stonewall Jackson and Gen. George W. Custis Lee taught at VMI. Open 9 AM to 5 PM daily, the museum is closed holidays.

Zoos

Natural Bridge Zoo
U.S. Hwy. 11, off I-81 at Exit 175 or 180
• (540) 291-2420

Next to Natural Bridge Village and Resort,

this 25-acre zoo is also an endangered species breeding center. It has the largest petting area in Virginia and elephant rides for the kids. For two decades the zoo has been raising generations of endangered species, including four generations of the scarlet macaw, Siberian tigers, ring-tailed lemurs and Himalayan bears. Elegant giraffes, graceful antelopes, huge camels, curious ostriches and many monkey families make this collection of animals and birds Virginia's largest and most complete. The zoo's most recent addition is a baby white tiger named Mohan.

On weekends, children can ride Asha, the African elephant, for $2.50. Enjoy the thrill of mingling with tame deer, gentle llamas and cute, fuzzy miniature donkeys. The family will enjoy large covered picnic pavilions and a well-stocked gift shop. Hours of operation are 9 AM to 6 PM seven days a week. Admission is $6 for adults and $4 for children ages 3 to 12.

Other Attractions

Boxerwood Garden
963 Ross Rd., Lexington
• (540) 463-2697

Boxerwood Garden is an absolute horticultural treasure located just minutes from historic downtown Lexington. The late Dr. Robert S. Munger (father of world-renowned photographer Sally Mann) began this collection of more than 2,400 specimen plants spread over 15 acres when he retired from medicine in 1957. For more than 30 years, Dr. Munger collected rare and unusual trees and shrubs, tagged with its name and the date he planted it. Hundreds of varieties of dwarf conifers, magnolias, dogwoods, rhododendrons, azaleas, Japanese maples and more adorn the grounds, along with an occasional (and equally unusual) piece of man-made art. Some species are among the last of their kind on Earth.

For years Boxerwood Garden was not open to the public. Only the privileged few gained access to the pristine natural sanctuary, named for Dr. Munger's 13 boxer dogs. Karen "KB" Bailey was one of those few; the doctor was her mentor for a number of years before his death, bestowing his knowledge on an eager and capable student. In 1997,

after years of dedication to the garden, KB and co-owner Hunter Moehring purchased Boxerwood. They have opened the garden to the public in an attempt to preserve and continue the legacy of Dr. Munger. KB welcomes the opportunity to share her knowledge and horticultural techniques; guests are welcome to work in the garden alongside her. The Orchard House (see our Bed and Breakfasts chapter) is a small guesthouse located in the midst of the arboretum and can be rented for $160 per night. Weekly rates are also available. The property is also available for weddings, receptions and other special occasions.

Boxerwood Garden is open for self-guided tours from 9 AM to 4 PM Thursday and Friday, 9 AM to 1 PM Saturday and 1 to 4 PM on the first Sunday of each month from March through November. Guided tours are available by appointment. A contribution of $4 per person is suggested.

Buffalo Springs Herb Farm
Raphine Rd., Raphine • (540) 348-1083

This unique 18th-century farmstead offers nearly everything an herbal devotee needs. The "big red barn" has herbal products, dried flowers and designs, garden books, accessories and a program room. Several gardens and a plant house are also on-site. Buffalo Springs hosts Don Haynie and Tom Hamlin schedule various programs and workshops throughout the season as well. The herb farm season runs from April through mid-December. Hours are 10 AM to 5 PM Wednesday through Saturday and 1 to 5 PM Sundays in April and May and from September through mid-December. The farm is closed during the winter.

Carriage Tours of Historic Lexington
Lexington Visitor Center,
106 E. Washington St., Lexington
• (540) 463-5647

The Lexington Carriage Company will take you back in time to the 19th-century pace of this historic town. Horsedrawn carriages will transport you past sites like the Stonewall Jackson House, Lee Chapel and Washington & Lee University and through the historic downtown and residential districts. Professional carriage drivers/tour guides narrate the tours. Be advised that carriage tours take 45-50 minutes and do not make stops along the way.

Tours begin across from the Lexington Visitor Center. They are offered daily (including holidays) from April 1 through October 31 from 10 AM to 4:30 PM; summer hours (June through August) are 9 AM to 5 PM. Tours are cancelled in the event of inclement weather. Fare is $1 for ages 3 and younger, $3 ages 4 through 6, $6 ages 7 through 13, $9 ages 65 and older and $10 for ages 14 through 64. Groups of 10 or more must make reservations. Discounts are available for groups of 10 or more and groups of 30 or more.

Ghost Tour of Lexington
Various sites • (540) 348-1080

This 1.3-mile candlelight walk through the back streets and alleyways of historic Lexington is not for the skittish! Guides introduce visitors to some intriguing and chilling ghost stories while trekking after some of the town's long-departed residents. Witness firsthand the unexplained phenomenon that has occurred nightly in the Stonewall Jackson Cemetery since the tour began. Victorian-style seance re-creations can also be arranged.

Tours are late May through October at 8:30 PM nightly. Admission is free for children younger than 3, $6 for ages 4 to 10 and $8 for ages 11 and older. Tickets must be purchased in advance at Shear Timing Hair Salon, 17 S. Randolph Street in downtown Lexington. Reservations are strongly advised for groups of 10 or more.

Historic Garden Week
Various locations • (540) 463-3777

History and garden aficionados flock to Lexington in the spring for its incomparable Historic Garden Week. Each April (the date changes yearly), civic-minded residents open

their historic homes and gardens to an appreciative public. Many of the residences are furnished with family heirlooms and gorgeous antiques and have ornate gardens.

Holiday in Lexington
Downtown Lexington sites
• (540) 463-3777

For two weeks in December, this 19th-century college town welcomes you to its historic downtown district sparkling with minilights and white candles. Events include tours of historic properties and homes, music, galas, theater and overall festivity. If you like Christmas in Williamsburg in eastern Virginia, you should try it western Virginia style.

Hull's Drive-In Theatre
Va. Rt. 5, Lexington
• (540) 463-2621

One of the last auto drive-in theaters left in Virginia, Hull's is worth a visit for a dose of nostalgia. From the well-groomed grounds to the syrupy snowballs, Hull's Drive-In is one of the premier mom-and-pop operations anywhere. Nothing's changed since 1950. It's open weekends at dusk mid-March through November.

Mock Convention
Washington & Lee University, Lexington
• (540) 463-8460

This is an event worth waiting for every four years. Held only during presidential election years (look for the next one in the year 2000), W&L's nationally known Mock Convention has been called "the nation's foremost and most accurate predictor in presidential politics." The Convention has earned this reputation by correctly predicting the presidential nominee of the party out of power 16 of 21 times. In 1996 they again chose correctly, selecting Senator Bob Dole as the GOP nominee. It has been wrong only once since 1948,

INSIDERS' TIP

Even if you've never considered yourself a history buff you should take time out to visit some of the many historic homes of Virginia's Blue Ridge. Activities like living history weekends at Belle Grove Plantation and Independence Day activities at Poplar Forest bring history to life.

predicting Senator Edward Kennedy as the 1972 Democratic nominee.

The Convention itself is filled with political speeches, platform fights and 1,600 student delegates who have spent months researching the attitudes of the states they represent. The result is an event that is covered nationally and broadcast live around the world on C-Span. Harry Truman, Richard Nixon, Jimmy Carter, Bill Clinton, Dan Quayle, Newt Gingrich, Bill Bennett, Michael Dukakis and Mario Cuomo have addressed past Conventions.

Lest you get the idea that the Convention is all work, the event begins with a long, elaborate parade featuring dignitaries and a competition in which students try to outdo each other with outlandish floats. The 1996 extravaganza included a float created as a spin-off of the movie *Deliverance* that was the prize-winning West Virginia entry.

Wade's Mill
Va. Rt. 606, Raphine
• **(540) 348-1400**

This working water-powered grist mill, c. 1750, is listed on the National Register of Historic Places. Not only does Wade's Mill offer a variety of stone-ground flours, but it also has pottery and basketry by local artists. All products are available by mail. Cooking classes and other special events may also be arranged. The mill is open 10 AM to 5 PM Wednesday through Saturday and 1 to 5 PM Sunday from April to the Sunday before Christmas. It is closed on Sundays in June, July and August.

Roanoke Valley

Botetourt County

Museums and Historic Attractions

Botetourt Museum
Court House Complex
Fincastle • **(540) 473-8394**

Botetourt County (pronounced BOT-uh-tot), named in 1770 for Lord Botetourt of England, once stretched to the Mississippi River,

encompassing what is now parts of West Virginia, Kentucky, Ohio, Indiana and Illinois. Fincastle was the historic county seat. The museum, which attracts thousands of visitors annually, is sponsored by the Botetourt County Historical Society. Programs, especially those dealing with genealogy, are open to the public. The museum plays a cooperative role in historic Fincastle's annual fall Old Fincastle Festival, one of the largest festivals in the Roanoke Valley (see our Annual Events and Festivals chapter). Museum hours are 10 AM to 2 PM Tuesday, Thursday and Saturday, 2 to 4 PM Sunday and upon request.

Craig County

Museums and Historic Attractions

Craig County Museum
Main and Court sts., New Castle
• **(540) 864-7023**

Dedicated Craig County residents are lovingly restoring this c. 1910, three-story brick hotel as a repository for Craig County's past. They've already restored several bedrooms to just as they were in the old hotel and have established a genealogy library for those tracing their roots in this rural, scenic town. Operated by the Craig County Historical Society, which also sponsors the Craig County Fall Festival in October, the museum's potential as a first-class attraction is just beginning to be fulfilled as a work in progress. It is open Monday through Wednesday from 1 to 4 PM.

Roanoke and Salem

Caverns

Dixie Caverns
5753 W. Main St., Salem
• **(540) 380-2085**

Dixie Caverns offers breathtaking netherworld formations along with a gift and pottery shop, rock store, Christmas shop and campground. Tour guides first take visitors up the mountain instead of down into it, pointing out the spot where a dog fell through a hole

The region's summer baseball leagues provide hours of sporting entertainment.

and led to the discovery of the caverns. The pet's owners also found evidence that the Native Americans of Southwest Virginia used the cave for shelter and food storage. Some of the most popular formations on the cavern tour are the Turkey Wing, Magic Mirror and Wedding Bell, where dozens of couples have been united.

Outside, there's also lots to do and see. The Dixie Caverns Pottery displays thousands of gifts in a shop open daily year round from 9 AM to 6 PM. Other shopping options include a basket shop, a shop named Christmas in Dixieland and a Rock and Mineral Shop, with its famous polished-stone wheel. The campground is open all year for RVs and campers. For anglers, the Roanoke River is nearby.

Summer hours are 9 AM to 7 PM daily. The caverns are also open the rest of the year from 9:30 AM to 5 PM daily. Admission for adults is $6, $3.50 for children ages 5 to 12 and free for children younger than 5. Dixie Caverns is just south of Roanoke off I-81 at Exit 132.

Museums and Historic Attractions

Catholic Church Museum
624 N. Jefferson St., Roanoke
• **(540) 982-0152**

The history of the Catholic Church in the Roanoke area is depicted in artifacts and memorabilia in this three-room museum in the former Saint Vincent's Orphan Asylum and Convent on the grounds of Saint Andrew's Church, a landmark structure built in 1900. The impressive Gothic-style building looms above the downtown commercial landscape. The museum facilitates research into the history of the Roanoke area through cemetery and orphanage records and files maintained on the Catholic churches and their members in the region and through its library collection.

You can buy religious articles and books here. Operated by the Catholic Historical Society of the Roanoke Valley, the museum is open 10:30 AM to 2 PM Tuesday or by appointment.

Harrison Museum of African-American Culture
523 Harrison Ave. N. W., Roanoke
• **(540) 345-4818**

A regional Roanoke showcase for African-American culture, the Harrison Museum is on the Virginia Historic Landmarks Register as the first public high school for black students in western Virginia. The museum's stated mission is to research, preserve and interpret the achievements of African Americans, specifically in western Virginia, and to provide an opportunity for all citizens to come together in appreciation, enjoyment and greater knowledge of African-American culture.

Since its opening in 1985, the museum has offered art and historical exhibits in its galleries and the Hazel B. Thompson Exhibition Room. The permanent collection of local artifacts and memorabilia has grown from a few objects to several thousand. Thanks to the generosity of donors, Harrison Museum owns an impressive African collection, which includes masks, bronze sculptures, paintings, furniture and textiles. Schools and organizations may borrow several traveling exhibits and displays. One of its most popular undertakings is the annual Henry Street Heritage Festival held on the last Saturday in September (see our Annual Events and Festivals chapter). It's a festive celebration of African-American heritage; it was held on the Henry Street site for its first four years, then relocated to Elmwood Park in downtown Roanoke in 1994.

The Museum store and gift shop offers Afrocentric art, books, cards, jewelry and African art. Museum hours are 10 AM to 5 PM Tuesday through Friday and 1 to 5 PM Saturday and Sunday. For group tours contact the curator.

History Museum of Western Virginia
Center in the Square, Levels 1 and 3, One Market Sq., Roanoke
• **(540) 342-5770**

The rich heritage of Roanoke unfolds before you in the galleries of the History Museum of Western Virginia, run by a dedicated group of society preservationists. Prehistoric artifacts acquaint you with life in the Valley before Colonial settlement, through the frontier era and boom days of the Norfolk & Western Railroad and into the present. You will see re-creations of an 1890 country store, fashions from the 1700s to the 1990s and lifestyles from wigwams to Victorian parlors.

For 1999 the museum has several revolving exhibits, including "The Big Picture" and the "Piedmont Airlines Aviation" display. "The Big Picture" includes a collection of recently restored panoramic photographs of Roanoke taken between 1910 and 1935. The "Piedmont" display includes photographs of the airline's early history, model airplanes and a hands-on area for children to explore aviation. The History Museum Gift Shop on the first floor sells handmade quilts, historic maps, genealogical charts, books and vintage toys. The gift shop offers unique items for every age and interest. Additional information on educational programs, group tours and special events is available by calling the museum.

The museum is open 10 AM to 4 PM Tuesday through Friday, 10 AM to 5 PM Saturday and 1 to 5 PM Sunday. Admission is $2 for adults, $1 for senior citizens and children ages 6 to 12 and free for children younger than 6.

The Salem Museum
801 E. Main St., Salem • **(540) 389-6760**

The Salem Museum is in the Williams-Brown House. That's easy. What was a little difficult for a while was finding the Williams-Brown House, c. 1840, which was slated to be torn down until a group of Salem residents towed it from its original location to a safer destination just a quarter-mile away. Run by volunteers of the Salem Historical Society, the museum focuses on a range of topics, from adventures and hardships of the Civil War to the leisure of a summer sojourn at the Lake Spring Resort Hotel. A gift shop and a gallery for rotating historical exhibits are also on the premises. Hours are 10 AM to 4 PM Tuesday through Friday and noon to 5 PM Saturday. Admission is free.

Science Museum of Western Virginia and Hopkins Planetarium
Center in the Square, Levels 1, 4 and 5, One Market Sq., Roanoke
• **(540) 342-5710**

The Science Museum is a fun place for adults and children to explore the wonders of science through hands-on experiences. Broadcast a weather report and see yourself on TV, or visit the touch tank. You can make lightning in the Physics Arcade and see the stars in Hopkins Planetarium, where you'll explore the reaches of the universe and then come back down to Earth for lectures, movies and special events such as technology expos and wildflower pilgrimages. Children will especially enjoy the museum's newest galleries: BodyTech, which demonstrates how the body works, and The Science Arcade, which explores color, sound and light. Children also like the first floor Science Museum Shop, which sells educational toys that are so much fun kids don't have a clue that they're learning while they play.

Exhibits change frequently, ranging from roaring mechanical dinosaurs and real sharks to giant insects and animated life-size animals of the future. The first-class planetarium has hosted dancing laser shows and imaginative narratives on the creation of Earth and the stars. It's a great place to spend an afternoon in Roanoke.

The museum is open 10 AM to 5 PM Monday through Saturday and 1 to 5 PM Sunday. Admission is $5 for adults, $4 for senior citizens, $3 for ages 3 to 12 and free for those younger than 3. If you want to see the exhibits and the Planetarium, tack an additional $1.30 on the museum price. To see just the Planetarieum, it's $2.60.

To the Rescue National Museum
Tanglewood Mall, 4428 Electric Rd. S.W., Roanoke • (540) 776-0364

To the Rescue, the only permanent national museum dedicated to volunteer lifesaving, brings an international spotlight to Roanoke as the birthplace of the rescue squad movement. Julian Stanley Wise never forgot when, as a 9-year-old Roanoker, he stood helplessly by as two men drowned when their canoe capsized on the Roanoke River. He vowed then that he would organize a group of volunteers who could be trained in lifesaving. He did.

In 1928 he and his crew of N&W Railway workers became the first volunteer rescue squad in America to use lifesaving, rescue and first aid techniques on victims. Later, they were the first to use iron lungs during the polio epidemics that struck the country. They pioneered the Nielson method of lifesaving and modern-day cardiopulmonary resuscitation.

Famous museum expert Conover Hunt, a Virginia native whose major project was The Sixth Floor, the JFK Museum in Dallas, oversaw the creation of the exhibit, which includes dramatic hands-on interactive videos and displays. The quality and brilliance shows. The exhibit includes artifacts from 31 states and three countries. To the Rescue also houses the VA Hall of Fame. Additionally, exhibits include the National EMS Memorial, recogniz-

ing 99 men and women from 30 states who gave their lives while saving others. Hours of operation are 10 AM to 9 PM Monday through Saturday and 1 to 6 PM Sunday. Admission is $2 for adults and $1 for children.

Virginia's Explore Park
3900 Rutrough Rd., Roanoke
• (540) 427-1800

Virginia's Explore Park, a living history museum and nature center at Blue Ridge Parkway Milepost 115, allows visitors to experience the rich cultural heritage and natural beauty of western Virginia just minutes from Roanoke. Eighteenth- and early 19th-century buildings carefully moved to the park's Blue Ridge Settlement include homes, barns, a schoolhouse, a blacksmith/wheelwright shop and other structures. They serve as the physical backdrop for living history interpreters who demonstrate the lifeways of the 19th-century settlers. Attractions also include a live exhibit on regional Native American culture, where an exact replica of a pre-European-contact Tutelo Indian village is under construction. An 18th-century frontier fort/settlers' cabin complex is also under construction. In addition, visitors can enjoy 6 miles of hiking trails winding through beautiful river-gorge scenery and wooded areas.

Special events, such as Days of Revolution, Fort Days, Traditions in Appalachia, the Fall Harvest Festival, classes and workshops take place throughout the year. Call for details about upcoming events and a free events calendar.

Virginia's Explore Park is open 9 AM to 5 PM Friday through Monday from April through October. Admission is $6 for adults and $4 for students (ages 6 to 18). Children younger than 6 are admitted free when accompanied by a parent or guardian. Special event prices may apply. Group rates are available for groups of 15 or more.

Virginia Museum of Transportation
303 Norfolk Ave., Roanoke
• (540) 342-5670

This official transportation museum for the state is in a restored freight station next to the Norfolk Southern main line. Exhibits include the largest collection of museum rolling stock

Ruby the tiger is a favorite attraction at the Mill Mountain Zoo in Roanoke.

on the East Coast (you can even climb aboard a caboose or a railway office car); antique autos, trucks, carriages, buses and trolleys; an O gauge model train on 4 tiers of track; and a model circus train exhibit. The Class J, #611 steam locomotive is on permanent display.

The Main Gallery exhibit, "The Claytor Brothers: Virginians Building America's Railroads", highlights the brothers' contributions to transportation. "Moving the Rocks that Moved the Nation" shows the part coal played in America's industrialization.

In 1999 the Virginia Museum will host the Cool Wheels Festival beginning Aug. 31. Along with classic cars, you also can marvel at the third annual ugly pickup contest. Other events on tap this year include a Spring Rail Fair in early May and the Haunted Railyard in October. The Oct. 29 event gives young goblins an alternative twist on the Halloween haunted house.

Of special interest to history and railroad buffs is the museum's Resource Library and Archives, which includes photograph, film, periodical and book rooms. It is also the repository for the Association of American Railroads' entire photograph collection.

The museum's gift shop sells prints by area artists, toys, books, souvenirs and more. The museum is open 10 AM to 5 PM Monday through Saturday and noon to 5 PM Sunday. It is closed on Mondays in January and February. Admission is $5 for adults, $4 for senior citizens, $3 for children ages 3 to 18 and free for those younger than 3. Group rates are available.

Spectator Sports

The Roanoke Express
Hockey Roanoke Inc., 4502 Starkey Rd. S.W., Roanoke • (540) 989-GOAL

Roanoke's professional hockey franchise continues to sell out the house for miles

Costumed interpreters demonstrate open-hearth cooking
at the American Frontier Museum in Staunton.

around. It's one of the area's most popular winter spectator activities. The season runs from October through March at the Roanoke Civic Center on Tuesday, Friday and Saturday, with a few exceptions. The team performs in the East Coast Hockey League, which includes 19 teams from nine different states. Season tickets are available. Individual tickets are $6 to $10 a person. There is no lack of action, both on the ice and in the stands.

The Roanoke Wrath
1948 Franklin Rd., Roanoke
• (540) 344-8565

The Roanoke Wrath exploded into the United States Premier Development Soccer League in 1997. Also affiliated with the United States Amateur Soccer Association, the team is able to draw talent from both college and professional ranks without compromising college eligibility. Home games are played at Victory Stadium on Reserve Avenue in Roanoke. The season starts in May and runs through the summer to mid-August with games at 7:30 PM. Admission is $3 for adults and $2 for children.

Salem Avalanche
1004 Texas St., Salem • (540) 389-3333

As the top Class A affiliate for the Colorado Rockies baseball team, the Avalanche live happily in the sports-crazed Roanoke Valley City of Salem, where they have a new, state-of-the-art stadium. April through September, 140 games are on the agenda, half at home at Salem Memorial Baseball Stadium. You can hear the Avalanche games on radio station 1240 WROV-AM. General admission is $3. Take Salem Exit 141 off I-81, adjacent to the Salem Civic Center.

Zoos

Mill Mountain Zoo
Off Blue Ridge Pkwy., Roanoke
• (540) 343-3241

On top of Roanoke's Mill Mountain, off the Blue Ridge Parkway and alongside the famous Roanoke Star, is an accredited 3-acre zoo operated by the Blue Ridge Zoological Society of Virginia. One of its main attractions is Ruby the Siberian Tiger, who received local and national attention during a two-year fund drive to build a new habitat at the zoo. Thanks to donations, Ruby also has her own watering hole for use in the summertime. The tiger is just one of the 40 plus species exhibits of mammals, birds and reptiles. Other animals include snow leopards, red pandas, Japanese macaques and much more. There is also a discovery center, Camp Wildcat, for kids of all ages. Special events and educational programs are offered throughout the year, and the zoo is available for birthday parties and other private parties. The zoo is open daily, 10 AM to 5 PM, except Christmas Day. Admission is $5 for adults, $4.50 for senior citizens, $3 for children younger than 12 and free for kids younger than 2. Group rates are available. The Mill Mountain Zoo, in cooperation with the Roanoke Jaycees, operates a miniature train for an additional fee. The zoo's concession and souvenir stands are open during the summer.

Picnic facilities, a wildflower garden and a breathtaking overlook view of Roanoke are nearby. You can get to the zoo off I-581; follow the signs off the Elm Avenue exit to Jefferson Street and take a left on Walnut Avenue.

Other Attractions

Center in the Square
One Market Sq., Roanoke
• (540) 342-5700

This complex is the home of the Art Museum of Western Virginia, The Arts Council of the Blue Ridge, Mill Mountain Theatre, History Museum of Western Virginia and the Science Museum of Western Virginia and Hopkins Planetarium. Resident organizations' hours vary. Roanoke's Center in the Square, visited by nearly 400,000 annually, is unique in America and proved itself unique in the world in 1996 at a United Nations awards forum showcasing the best in urban development. The center received the 1997 Bruner Award for Urban Excellence. It is the best-attended cultural center in western Virginia and attracts even more patrons than Richmond's Valentine Museum.

Five resident organizations coexist in a restored 1914 warehouse anchoring Roanoke's historic city market. A sculptural spiral staircase symbolizes how these five organizations have come together to create a richer cultural life in western Virginia.

A confetti-like sculpture, a gift by the famous Dorothy Gillespie, hangs on one wall. In the heart of shops, galleries and restaurants, Center in the Square is the binding cultural tie in the life of a growing, vibrant downtown and a must-see while in Roanoke. You can make some great buys on items with a science, art or history theme in the center's three member stores.

Fifth Avenue Presbyterian Church Window
301 Patton Ave. N.W., Roanoke
• (540) 342-0264

In 1903 the Rev. Lylburn Downing, pastor of Fifth Avenue Presbyterian, an African-American church, commissioned a stained-glass window to honor Confederate general Stonewall Jackson. The Rev. Mr. Downing had been a member of the Sunday school class Jackson had established for slaves at his own church in Lexington. Although the church burned down in the 1920s, the unusual window was spared and then included in the rebuilt church, where it serves today as a symbol of racial harmony. The window may be viewed Tuesday and Thursday from 10 to 11 AM.

Jefferson Center
540 Campbell Ave., Roanoke
• (540) 343-2624

The Jefferson Center opened its doors in August 1993. Located in the beautifully refurbished Jefferson High School, which was built in 1924, it is now home to 21 nonprofit organizations as diverse as the Roanoke Symphony & Choral Society, a day-care center, the City's police academy, Mental Health Association and Clean Valley Council. There is also a memorabilia room containing yearbooks, newspapers and awards from the center's days as a high school. You'll also want to visit the Museum of Theatre History on the second floor, a collection of artifacts from beautiful old theatres once located in the city.

The building itself was built in the English Classical Revival style. You will marvel at the sculptured ceiling in the old main entrance and the beautiful restoration of the marble and terrazzo floors. Fitzpatrick Hall, the most recently renovated area, won an award from the American Institute of Architects. The Fralin Atrium is stunning as well, with its chandeliers and a sculpture of Horace Fralin.

The final stage of renovation will undertake the building of a 900-seat performance hall. This hall will become home to Opera Roanoke, the Roanoke Symphony & Choral Society and the Roanoke Ballet Theatre (see our Arts chapter).

Miniature Graceland
605 Riverland Dr., Roanoke
• (540) 56-ELVIS

The King lives! You'll find him in miniature in this southeast Roanoke neighborhood beneath the Roanoke Star. He's rockin' — revolving, actually — in perpetual glory on the stage of a miniature auditorium before an audience of adoring Barbies. Kim and Don Epperly's private collection has attracted visitors from all over the world. In the spring of 1995, it seemed as if the entire community turned out to help the Epperlys spruce the place up, since both had been ill. We're pleased to say everything looks great again, and this folk-culture extravaganza continues.

Kim Epperly, former editor of the international "The Wonder of You" newsletter dedicated to the late Elvis Presley, is the heart and soul behind keeping the memory of the entertainer alive. Her husband has crafted replicas of Presley's estate, which fill their side yard. The display is lighted nightly and fans are invited to stroll through the grounds and hear an Elvis song wafting over the loudspeaker.

The Epperlys have shown their private collection at an opening on January 10, Presley's birthday, at the History Museum of Western Virginia — it was a blockbuster. In April 1995, a life-size statue of Elvis was erected and dedicated to the children who lost their lives in the Oklahoma bombing.

Inside the basement of her home, Epperly maintains her own personal museum of Elvis artifacts, including Love Me Tender shampoo and conditioner, full-size mannequins sculpted with auto body compound to look like Elvis' features and newspaper clippings of when the King first visited Roanoke. Each year, the Epperlys add something new to the yard. Don

Epperly has done most of the construction from scrap wood, based on pictures or descriptions from his wife. Some of the features include his airport, a privacy fence, Sun Studios and the Civic Center. Visitors are welcome anytime.

East of the Blue Ridge

Loudoun County

Museums and Historic Attractions

Aldie Mill
Va. Rt. 50, Aldie • (703) 327-6118

For the first time in 26 years, the historic Aldie Mill opened to the public in the spring of 1997. Built in 1807, this five-story brick mill will be open from noon to 5 PM Sundays from May through October. Tours include a look at artifacts from the mill and early machinery used to grind grain. In 1981, the mill was donated to the Virginia Outdoors Foundation by the Douglass family. There is no charge to tour the mill, but donations are appreciated. Aldie Mill is just west of the Va. Route 50 and Va. Route 15 intersection in the village of Aldie.

Dodona Manor
232 Edwards Ferry Rd. N.E., Leesburg
• (703) 777-1880

Gen. George C. Marshall served as U.S. Secretary of State and is well-known abroad for the Marshall Plan, a post-World War II reconstruction plan he drafted for Europe. He lived right here in Virginia, and visitors can now tour his home in Leesburg. Tours run from 10 AM to 4 PM on Friday, Saturday and Monday. Admission is $5, with children younger than 6 admitted free. There are discounts for seniors and groups of 10 or more.

The Loudoun Museum
14-16 Loudoun St. S.W., Leesburg
• (703) 777-7427

Follow the history of Loudoun County, from the days Native Americans toiled the land to the time President John F. Kennedy, Gen. George C. Marshall and entertainer Arthur Godfrey made their homes in Virginia's "Hunt

Country." This museum includes a collection of Native American artifacts and a hands-on display showing how they made stone tools. You can also see Nicholas Minor's plans to develop a town in Leesburg, plus Civil War items from the nearby Battle of Balls Bluff. A video program helps put the experience in perspective. Books, maps and toys are among the items for sale in the museum shop. Hours are 10 AM to 5 PM Monday through Saturday and 1 to 5 PM Sunday. Admission is $1 for adults, 50¢ for children 12 and younger.

Morven Park
17263 Southern Planter Ln., Leesburg
• **(703) 777-2414**

The Greek Revival mansion and estate, which was once the home of Virginia governor Westmoreland Davis, is listed on the National Register of Historic Places and is a Virginia Historic Landmark. The house is furnished with fine antiques and curios that the Davises collected on their travels around the world. On the grounds are gardens, an extensive carriage museum and a Museum of Hounds and Hunting, which contains foxhunting memorabilia from Colonial days (see our Horse Country chapter).

The estate, maintained through a trust established by the late Mrs. Davis, is one of the country's finest equestrian centers, staging fall and spring steeplechase races, horse shows, three-day events, foxhunts and carriage competitions. Morven Park's mansion, gardens, Museum of Hounds and Hunting and Mrs. Robert C. Winmill Carriage Collection are open to visitors noon to 5 PM Tuesday through Friday, 10 AM to 5 PM Saturday and from 1 to 5 PM Sunday from April 1 to October 31 (weekends only in November). Special Christmas tours are held every day except Monday from December 6 to 21. Self-guided tours cost $6 ($5 for seniors, $3 for children ages 6 to 12 and free for those younger than 6).

The Naturalist Center
741 Miller Dr. S.E., Leesburg
• **(703) 779-9712, (800) 729-7725**

You couldn't properly call this a museum because this center is so interactive. Here in this branch of the Smithsonian Institution visitors interested in natural history can delve into their own investigations. Visitors become amateur scientists, with access to the center's large collection of plants, rocks, fossils, insects and animals, aided by scientific equipment, books and references. This study gallery is for kids (10 and older) and adults. A smaller exhibit with some hands-on activities has been set up to entertain younger children while older family members tour the main exhibit. (See our Kidstuff chapter.) Admission is free. Hours are 10:30 AM to 4 PM Tuesday through Saturday.

Oatlands Plantation
20850 Oatland Plantation Ln., Leesburg
• **(703) 777-3174**

This magnificent Federal/Greek Revival-style house was built in 1803 by a descendant of Robert "King" Carter using bricks molded on the property and wood from a nearby forest. The 261-acre estate is renowned for its historic formal gardens in which something always seems to be blooming. Oatlands is a striking venue for spring point-to-point races, the popular Oatlands Sheepdog Trials and Farm Days in May, the June Celtic Festival and other events. Hours are 10 AM to 4:30 PM daily (1 to 4:30 PM Sunday) from April through December. Admission to the mansion is $6 for adults; garden admission costs $3. Seniors and children ages 12 through 18 pay $5 for the mansion, $3 for a garden tour. Those younger than 12 get in free.

Culpeper County

Museums

Museum of Culpeper History
140 E. Davis St., Culpeper
• **(540) 825-1973**

To coincide with the 250th anniversary of Culpeper County, the Museum of Culpeper History is moving to a larger location in mid-1999. The museum's collection is currently displayed in the 800-square-foot structure on East Davis Street, but will soon have room to expand when it moves to the renovated Williamsburg-style 4,000-square foot site, where U.S. 29 and U.S. 15 converge. The exhibits tracing the history of Culpeper County from the age of the dinosaurs to the 20th century will occupy a minimum of 2,500 square feet of the single level building. The collection

The Oatlands Plantation in Leesburg is famous for its formal gardens. The house was built in 1803.

includes dinosaur track fossils cut from the quarry 5 miles east of the city, Native American artifacts and Civil War relics. Also on the new grounds is a recently restored 18th-century log cabin that museum officials believe is the oldest existing structure in the town. Hours are 11 AM to 5 PM Monday through Saturday. Admission is free.

Madison County

Complementing all the natural sites in this area are several zoos and animal attractions and other centers that both children and adults will enjoy.

On the Wild Side Zoological Park
U.S. Hwy. 29, 1 mile south of Madison
• (540) 948-4000

This small but diverse zoo emphasizes natural habitats so that animals can feel secure in their environment. Most of the zoo's animals were raised on a nearby farm of one of the park's owners and managers, Pam Mogensen. You can see Festus the bear and some of the only reindeer in the state. The centerpiece exhibit for the park is the spider monkey cage, where these social little creatures put on a show. The reptile room showcases a variety of snakes, alligators and lizards. You'll also see exhibits of elk, swan, parrots, cranes, mountain lions, porcupines, deer, llamas, African wildcats and more. Although animals and people are protected by various barriers, visitors may touch animals that are willing to be touched, according to park managers. The park is open 10 AM to 6 PM daily. Admission is $6 for adults, $4 for children 3 to 12 years old and free for those younger than 3. Group rates are available.

Orange County

Museums and Historic Attractions

James Madison Museum
129 Caroline St., Orange
• (540) 672-1776

This downtown museum offers several permanent exhibits, one celebrating the life and times of Madison and his important contributions to the American political system. Visitors may even watch a short video about Madison and his home, Montpelier. Artifacts include furnishings from Montpelier, some of his presidential correspondence and a few of Dolley Madison's belongings. Another permanent exhibit details the history of Orange; other exhibits change regularly. The museum is open on weekdays from 9 AM to 4 PM and Saturday from 1 to 4 PM, March through November. Admission is $4 ($3 for seniors and AAA members) and $1 for kids ages 6 to 16.

Montpelier
Off Va. Rt. 20, Montpelier Station
• (540) 672-2728

The gracious home of President James Madison and his beloved wife, Dolley, opened for public tours in 1987. The restoration of Montpelier, which changed hands six times after Dolley Madison was forced to sell it to settle debts, is a work in progress. The archeological work and architectural research are ongoing, which makes Montpelier an exciting place to visit. You may hear from the enthusiastic staff about a new discovery on the 2,700-acre property the same day it happens!

Unlike Jefferson, Madison did not document the fine details of his everyday existence. The uncovering (and literally, in some cases, unearthing) of what Montpelier was like in Madison's time is painstaking. Also, unlike Monticello, where lines form for hours and tours are rather regimented, you can dally at Montpelier and even brainstorm with a tour guide.

Montpelier was first settled by Madison's grandparents in 1723. After the completion of Madison's second presidential term, Dolley and James retired to the estate, where their legendary hospitality kept them in touch with world affairs. Madison was the primary author of the Constitution and one of the authors of the Federalist Papers. He was a proponent of freedom of religion and education in Virginia and served as second rector of the University of Virginia. His public life spanned 53 years and included services as a delegate to the Continental Congress, member of the Virginia

House of Delegates, U.S. Congressman, Thomas Jefferson's Secretary of State and U.S. President for two terms.

Montpelier was owned by the duPont family for decades before it was bequeathed to the National Trust for Historic Preservation in the 1980s. The duPonts built major additions to the home and planted elaborate formal gardens. The biggest challenge for Montpelier's new owners, the National Trust, was what to do about all the new rooms and interior changes. They considered doing away with the duPont imprint and restoring the property to its original Madisonian form. But they struck a compromise, with the exterior and landscape keeping their 20th-century appearances, along with three duPont rooms in the house. The rest of the mansion's museum is being reconfigured as Madison-period rooms based on the results of research.

Guided tours cover the main floor of the 55-room mansion, and visitors are encouraged to stroll through the grounds and see the barns, stables, bowling alley and the garden temple Madison built over his ice house. Dolley and James Madison lie in a cemetery on the grounds along with a number of Madison family members.

One of the legacies of Marion duPont Scott, who made her home at Montpelier from 1928 until her death in 1983, is the annual Montpelier Hunt Races, which take place on the first Saturday in November (see our Horse Country chapter).

Montpelier is about 25 miles north of Charlottesville off U.S. 20 near Orange. It is open daily from 10 AM to 4 PM March through December and weekends only in January. Admission is $6 ($5 for seniors and AAA members) and $1 for children ages 6 to 12.

Albemarle County

Museums and Historic Attractions

Ash Lawn-Highland
James Monroe Pkwy. off Va. Rt. 795,
Charlottesville • (804) 293-9539

This 535-acre estate was the home of James Monroe, our nation's fifth president, who fought in the American Revolution under George Washington and went on to hold more offices than any other U.S. president.

As ambassador to France, Monroe negotiated with Napoleon for the Louisiana Purchase, which doubled the size of the country. During his presidency, Monroe established the nation's first comprehensive foreign policy, later called the Monroe Doctrine, to prevent further European colonization of the Americas.

Ash Lawn-Highland is about 2 miles from Thomas Jefferson's Monticello, off I-64. The mansion holds many of Monroe's possessions, and his boxwood gardens, now occupied by magnificent peacocks, are carefully tended. Livestock, vegetable and herb gardens and Colonial craft demonstrations depict life 200 years ago on the plantation.

Special events include summer musicals and operas performed in English, the Virginia Wine Festival in May, Plantation Days on the Fourth of July weekend, a Midsummer Eve Gala and Christmas candlelight tours.

The Monroe estate is owned and maintained as a working farm by Monroe's alma mater, the College of William and Mary. Ash Lawn-Highland is open daily 9 AM to 6 PM March through October and 10 AM to 5 PM daily from November through February. Admission is $7 for adults, $6.50 for seniors and $4 for children ages 6 to 11. Group rates are available for groups of 15 or more. A special President's Pass available at the Visitors Bureau (804) 293-6789 costs $20 ($18.50 for seniors) and also includes tours of nearby Monticello and Michie Tavern. Ash Lawn is closed Christmas Day, New Year's Day and Thanksgiving Day.

Hatton Ferry
Va. Rt. 625, Scottsville • (804) 296-1492

Long before steel bridges spanned the rivers of Virginia, ferries were needed to carry people and their cargo from one side of the river bank to the other. The Hatton Ferry in southern Albemarle County is one of only two poled ferries still in operation in the United States. The Hatton Ferry started carrying cargo at its present location more than 100 years ago. When the Virginia Department of Trans-

portation decided it was no longer needed as a public service, three groups got together to save the ferry as a historical artifact. The Department of Transportation, the Albemarle County Historical Society and Albemarle County jointly maintain and operate Hatton Ferry on a reduced but fixed schedule. You can take a free historical ride across the James River from 9 AM to 5 PM on Fridays, Saturdays and Sundays from mid-April to mid-October. Rides are contingent on water conditions, so it is a good idea to call the society or the Visitors Center at (804) 977-1783 or (804) 296-6777 before you go.

Michie Tavern
683 Thomas Jefferson Pkwy.,
Charlottesville • (804) 977-1234

Historic Michie Tavern (pronounced "micky") is one of the oldest homesteads remaining in Virginia and was originally set along a well-worn stagecoach route near Earlysville, about 17 miles away. To accommodate the many travelers seeking food and shelter at their home, the Michie family opened it as a tavern in 1784. In 1927 the tavern was dismantled piece by piece, moved by truck and horse and carriage and reassembled on its present site. This historic move garnered the tavern a Virginia Historic Landmark designation.

Today, visitors to Monticello and Ash Lawn-Highland can still stop by the tavern for a hearty Southern-style meal. The tavern museum offers continuous tours of rooms decorated with 18th-century Southern furniture and artifacts. Next door, a 200-year-old converted slave house called The Ordinary offers a Colonial buffet of fried chicken, black-eyed peas, stewed tomatoes, coleslaw, potato salad, green bean salad, beets, homemade biscuits, corn bread and apple cobbler from 11:15 AM to 3:30 PM (11:35 AM to 3 PM November through March) for around $10.

The Sowell House, c. 1822, recipient of a 1995 Preservation Award, was relocated to Michie Tavern in 1993. Now a part of the museum tour, the house offers a unique glimpse into 19th-century rural life in Virginia.

Michie Tavern also houses the small Virginia Wine Museum in its basement. Next door in the Meadow Run Grist Mill is a general store where visitors can buy Virginia wines, specialty foods and crafts.

The Michie Tavern Museum is open year round from 9 AM to 5 PM except Christmas and New Year's Day; the last tour goes out at 4:20 PM. Admission to the museum is $6 for adults, $5.50 for seniors, $2 for children ages 6 to 11 and free for those younger than 6.

Monticello
Va. Rt. 53, (Thomas Jefferson Pkwy.) Charlottesville • (804) 984-9822

Thomas Jefferson's home, one of the country's finest architectural masterpieces, is such a popular tourist attraction that long lines are inevitable during the peak season of summer and early fall. Start early; you can always grab a snack at the lunch stand, which is open from 10:30 AM to 3:30 PM daily April through October.

Jefferson began construction of Monticello in 1769 when he was just 26, and he often longed to retire there during the most active part of his political career. Work on Monticello continued for 40 years, during which Jefferson made many alterations.

Jefferson's wide-ranging interests made him an avid collector of sculpture, maps, paintings, prints, Native American artifacts, scientific instruments and fine furniture, and these objects kept his house quite cluttered. Today, Monticello is filled with original furnishings and many of Jefferson's other possessions. It gives one the feeling that he'll return from Washington at any moment.

Though he was our nation's third president, the author of the Declaration of Independence and an international statesman, Jefferson apparently disliked politics. He wrote to his daughter Martha in 1800, "Politics is such a torment that I would advise every one I love not to mix with it."

Though he did not shirk his duty to his country and its fragile democratic system, he indulged his other interests at Monticello, especially horticulture and garden design. Included are ornamental and vegetable gardens, two orchards, a vineyard and an 18-acre ornamental forest. He experimented with more than 250 varieties of vegetables and herbs, many

of which are grown today in his 1,000-square-foot vegetable garden. Monticello's Thomas Jefferson Center for Historic Plants, the first of its kind in the nation, sells historical plants and seeds in the garden shop from April through October. Monticello is on Va. Route 53, 3 miles southeast of Charlottesville. Take Exit 121 off I-64 and follow the signs. The mansion and grounds are open daily from 8 AM to 5 PM March through October and 9 AM to 4:30 PM the rest of the year (closed Christmas Day). Written tour information is available in several languages.

Admission is $9 for adults, $5 for children ages 6 to 11 and free for children younger than 6. Group rates are available. It's possible to save on the cost of adult admission to Monticello, Ash Lawn and Michie Tavern by buying a $20 President's Pass ($18.50 for seniors) at the Charlottesville/Albemarle Convention and Visitors Bureau at Va. Route 20 S. and I-64 near Monticello.

Charlottesville/Albermarle Visitors Center
600 College Dr. off Va. Rt. 20 S., Charlottesville • (804) 293-6789

A permanent exhibition shows aspects of Jefferson's domestic life at Monticello. Nearly 400 objects and artifacts, from his pocketknife to a porcupine-quill toothpick, are on display, many for the first time. You can view an award-winning film, *Thomas Jefferson: The Pursuit of Liberty*, daily at 11 AM and 2 PM in the exhibition theater, with additional showings in the summer. The center is open from 9 AM to 5:30 PM daily March through October and 9 AM to 5 PM the rest of the year. Admission is free. The museum shop is a great source of brass, porcelain, crystal, pewter and silver pieces and reproductions made exclusively for Monticello.

Rotunda and University of Virginia
McCormick Rd., Charlottesville • (804) 924-7969

Free historical tours of Mr. Jefferson's "academic village" are offered daily from the Rotunda, which Jefferson designed in the style of the Pantheon. Since 1825 the university has been renowned for its unique architectural design. In 1976 the American Institute of Architects voted Jefferson's design for the university the most outstanding achievement in American architecture.

Along with his authorship of the Declaration of Independence and the Statute of Virginia for Religious Freedom, the university was an achievement for which Jefferson wished to be remembered. He called it the "hobby of his old age," quite an understatement. Not only was Jefferson the principal architect, but he also helped select the library collection, hire faculty and design the curriculum. He was one of the major financial contributors and succeeded in securing public funding for the school.

It was his ardent lobbying for public education in Virginia that led to the establishment of the university in the first place. Jefferson had studied at the College of William and Mary in Williamsburg, but he felt the state, which then encompassed West Virginia, needed a major university. He accomplished all this during his retirement at Monticello, from which he often watched the university's construction with his telescope.

The rotunda was completed in 1826, the year Jefferson died.

You can take a free tour of the central grounds from the Rotunda at 10 and 11 AM and 2, 3 and 4 PM daily, except for three weeks at Christmas. Reservations are not necessary. If you ask, tour guides will point out Edgar Allan Poe's former dorm room. Poe, by the way, left the university prematurely after running up a huge gambling debt he couldn't pay.

Scottsville Museum
Va. Rt. 20, Scottsville
• (804) 286-2247

The Albemarle County seat until 1762, Scottsville is an old river town on the James River, about 20 miles south of Charlottesville on Va. 20. In and around the town are 32 authentic Federal buildings, one of the four or five largest concentrations of Early Republic architecture in the state. The town also has a local-history museum, originally a Disciples Church built in 1846, on E. Main Street that opened in April 1998.

Virginia Discovery Museum
524 E. Main St., Charlottesville
• (804) 977-1025

On the east end of the historic downtown mall is a dynamic place for children ages 2 to 10 and their families. You'll find hands-on exhibits and programs about science, history and the humanities. (See our Kidstuff chapter.) Classes and summer camps include everything from computer operation to photography, juggling, dancing and space exploration. The museum even has the real 18th-century Showalter Cabin from Rockingham County and costumes in which the children can play dress-up. Special exhibits change every few months. An art room with an array of materials invites children to create at their own pace, and a gallery space displays their creations for about three weeks. The facility is open Tuesday through Saturday from 10 AM to 5 PM and Sunday 1 to 5 PM. Admission is $4 for adults and $3 for seniors and children younger than 13. ASTC members are admitted free.

Virginia Museum of Natural History
104 Emmet St., Charlottesville
• (804) 982-4605

Admission is free to this unique museum, where you can view changing exhibits of fossils and minerals. You'll also see a changing natural history exhibit on subjects ranging from caves to endangered species. If you are already on the University of Virginia grounds, this makes for an interesting stop. Hours are 8:30 AM to 4:30 PM Tuesday through Friday. Children's activities are held occasionally and can be quite fascinating. Call for more information.

Sporting Events

University of Virginia
Charlottesville • (804) 924-UVA1,
(800) 542-UVA1 (in-state)

Football games at Scott Stadium have become so popular it's hard to get tickets at the last minute. The expansion of the Carl Smith Center at Scott Stadium will add 4,000 new seats for the 1999 season, but tickets will still be at a premium. Through 1998, the Cavaliers have chalked up 12 consecutive winning seasons in the Atlantic Coast Conference and have advanced to six consecutive bowl games. Last year they even set a record attendance at the Peach Bowl in Atlanta. Although UVA didn't win the game, Coach George Welch was named the NCAA's Coach of the Year by the Metropolitan New York Football Writers Association. Welsh, who has been the head coach of the Cavaliers for the past 16 seasons, became the winningest coach in ACC history in 1997. For those reasons, orange-garbed UVA alumni flock to the games in record numbers, hollering "Wahoo-Wah!" after every score. True fans will be hard pressed to pull themselves away from the television on Sunday afternoons, too, with a plethora of graduated Hoos to watch playing in the NFL. Heading the long list of pro players are wide receiver Herman Moore of the Detroit Lions, running back Terry Kirby of the San Francisco 49ers, linebacker Chris Slade of the New England Patriots and rookie running back Tiki Barber of the of the New York Giants. Two former greats, Bill Dudley and Henry Jordan, have been inducted into the NFL Hall of Fame. If you want to be a part of this scene, call the above numbers for ticket information.

The winning women's basketball team continues to gain a widespread following under Coach Debbie Ryan. In 1999, Ryan became only the sixth coach in the nation to record 500 wins at one school. On their way to their 16th straight NCAA tournament appearance, the Cavaliers had been ranked in the AP or *USA Today* poll for a record-setting 278 consecutive weeks. The team advanced to the NCAA Final Four in 1990, '91 and '92. The women also boast an impressive list of alumni. Dawn Staley, who won a gold medal in the 1996 Olympic Games, is one of the premiere players for the Charlotte Sting in the WNBA. Other professional stars include Wendy Palmer of the Utah Starzz, Tora Suber of the Charlotte Sting and Val Ackerman, president of the WNBA. Both men's and women's basketball games are played in the 8,457-seat University Hall.

If you're a soccer fan, you can watch two of the top teams in the nation play home games at UVA. The men's soccer team won four NCAA Division I championships (1991 to 1994) and

tied for a fifth in 1989. The women's team, which has played in the NCAA tournament for nine times in 10 years, advanced to the final four in 1991. Klockner Stadium, home of the Virginia soccer and lacrosse programs, opened in the fall of 1992. It's a great place to watch games, with seating in the stands or on a pleasant grassy bank.

Lacrosse is another winning sport at UVA. The women's team advanced to the NCAA Tournament's Final Four the 1991 through 1994 seasons and won the NCAA Division I championship in 1991 and 1993. The men's team was the runner-up in the 1994 NCAA Division I tournament and advanced to the Final Four again in 1995.

UVA hosts the Cavalier Classic Golf Tournament every spring, drawing some of the top players in the country to Charlottesville's Birdwood Golf Course.

Nelson County

Museums

Walton's Mountain Museum
Schuyler Community Center, Va. Rt. 617, Schuyler • (804) 831-2000

Earl Hamner Jr., whose early years were chronicled in the popular television series, grew up in tiny Schuyler. The museum dedicated to Hamner and *The Waltons* opened to great fanfare several years ago in the same school where the Hamner youngsters learned their ABCs. The museum, made possible by a state grant and support from Hamner and community leaders, is actually a series of former classrooms that recreate sets from the television program. You'll find copies of actual scripts, photo displays that juxtapose Hamner's real family with the television actors and all manner of memorabilia. Visitors can also watch a video documentary of interviews with Hamner, former cast members and episodes from one of the most endearing television series ever. The school is a stone's throw from the old Hamner homestead.

Schuyler is between Charlottesville and Lynchburg, a few miles off U.S. 29. From the first Saturday in March through the last Sunday in November (excluding major holidays), museum hours are 10 AM to 4 PM. Admission is $5 ($4 for seniors and members of groups of 20). Children 12 and younger are admitted free.

Lynchburg

Museums and Historic Attractions

Anne Spencer House and Garden
1313 Pierce St., Lynchburg
• (804) 846-0517

Anne Spencer was an internationally recognized African-American poet of the Harlem Renaissance period of the 1920s. Her poems are included in the *Norton Anthology of Modern Poetry*. Behind her home is the garden and accompanying cottage, Edan Kraal, built for her by her husband as a place where she could write. Hillside Garden Club has beautifully restored the garden. Revered the world over for her intellect, Spencer entertained many great leaders and artists of her day, including Dr. Martin Luther King Jr., Supreme Court Justice Thurgood Marshall, scientist Dr. George Washington Carver, sports legend Jackie Robinson, Congressman Adam Clayton Powell (who honeymooned there) and the legendary singers Paul Robeson and Marion Anderson. House tours are by appointment only. The garden is open 24 hours a day, seven days a week.

Jones Memorial Library
2311 Memorial Ave., Lynchburg
• (804) 846-0501

The Jones Memorial Library, opened in June 1908, is the second-oldest public library in Virginia. One of Virginia's foremost genealogical libraries, the Jones is known for its vast records: 30,000 volumes specializing in genealogical, historical and Lynchburg holdings. The collection includes Revolutionary War records, family histories and genealogies, general works on the Civil War, enlistments, Virginia county and state court records and census reports. Records from England, Ireland and Scotland include heraldry information. A

Certified Genealogist and a Certified Genealogical Records Specialist are both on staff to provide assistance for in-house research. This gem is probably one of the most underutilized treasures of the Blue Ridge.

The library is open 1 to 9 PM Tuesday and Thursday, noon to 5 PM Wednesday and Friday and 9 AM to 5 PM Saturday; it's closed Sunday and Monday.

Lynchburg Museum at Old Court House
Court St., Lynchburg • (804) 847-1459

The historical treasures of one of America's legendary tobacco centers can be discovered in Lynchburg's 1855 Old Court House, now restored to its Greek Revival elegance and home of the Lynchburg Museum. From the native Monacan tribes who inhabited the banks of the historic James River to the bustle of 19th-century industry and the tragedy of the American Civil War, relics of a developing community bear silent testimony to the struggle for a nation. Changing exhibits challenge visitors to reflect on Lynchburg's many contributions to the history of our country. Exhibits are open daily 10 AM to 4 PM, but the museum is closed on holidays. Admission is $1.

Confederate Section, Old City Cemetery
Pest House Medical Museum
Fourth and Taylor sts., Lynchburg
• (804) 847-1811

The Confederate Section of the historic Old City Cemetery serves as the final resting place for more than 2,200 individually marked graves of Confederate soldiers from 14 states. A monument to the memory of the 99 soldiers who died of smallpox in the Pest House during the war is near the entrance to the adjacent Confederate section. Many interpretive tablets and a variety of brochures are available at the Information Gatehouse and throughout the recently restored cemetery. Antique roses and period plantings contribute to the horticultural significance and beauty.

Nearby is the Pest House Medical Museum, depicting conditions in the House of Pestilence quarantine hospital during the Civil War. A second room is furnished as Dr. John

J. Terrell's office when he practiced medicine in the area during the late 1800s.

The cemetery is free and open daily, dawn to dusk. Guided tours are available by appointment at a price of $2 for adults and $1 for students.

Point of Honor
112 Cabell St., Lynchburg
• (804) 847-1459

This fully restored 19th-century plantation mansion is a remarkable example of Federal-style architecture where visitors can experience the lifestyle of one of Virginia's most remarkable families. Point of Honor is the home of Dr. George Cabell Sr., friend and personal physician to Patrick Henry. It was also home to Mary Virginia Ellet Cabell, one of the founders of the Daughters of the American Revolution. Newly re-created kitchen and stable buildings provide unique glimpses into an era now long past. Even the unusual name "Point of Honor" remembers fog-shrouded mornings of long ago when sword and pistol duels were fought on the lawn.

Tours of the house and gardens are available daily 10 AM to 4 PM. Point of Honor is closed on holidays. Admission is $5 for adults, $4.50 for senior citizens, and $1 for youths, with children younger than 6 admitted for free.

The Chapel at the University of Virginia is part of Thomas Jefferson's "academic village."

Red Sox. The team, which is now affiliated with the Pittsburgh Pirates, plays in the 4,000-seat City Stadium. Half of the 140 games per season are played at home. All games are broadcast on radio station WJJS-AM. General admission is $4.

Spectator Sports

Lynchburg Hillcats
City Stadium, Lynchburg
• (804) 528-1144

Lynchburg has had a baseball team in its midst for more than 100 years. Since 1966, the Hillcats have been entertaining fans east of the Blue Ridge as a Class A member of the Carolina League. The Lynchburg team has been affiliated with many clubs along the way, including the New York Mets and the Boston

Bedford County

Museums and Historic Attractions

Bedford City/County Museum
201 E. Main St., Bedford
• (540) 586-4520

Visitors can see a collection of artifacts and memorabilia showing the story of Bedford, a charming city at the foot of the Peaks of Otter, a Blue Ridge Parkway attraction. The exhibits begin with early natives of the region and progress through the mid-20th century. Here, you'll see Native American relics, Revolutionary War and Civil War artifacts, clothing, flags, quilts and more. Research assistance is available for genealogists outside Bedford. Hours are 10 AM to 5 PM Monday through Saturday. Admission is $1 for adults and 50¢ for children.

Poplar Forest
Va. Rt. 661, Forest
• (804) 525-1806

Poplar Forest, Thomas Jefferson's personal, year-round retreat, continues to be restored, and visitors are invited to get an up-close perspective on the painstaking renovations. Archaeologists continue to explore the grounds for clues about Jefferson's plantation community. Various exhibits display artifacts discovered at the slave quarter site, Jefferson's "Wing of Offices" and other excavations. During the former President's time, this was a working tobacco farm spanning 4,812 acres. It was also the site of one of his most outstanding architectural achievements — an unusual octagonal home and its accompanying elaborate landscape. Thomas Jefferson and his wife, Martha, inherited the plantation from her father. Jefferson would travel three days by horseback to reach his retreat away from the bustle at Monticello, his home in Charlottesville. Family members often joined him on visits to his "Bedford estate" where he pursued his passions for reading, writing, studying and gardening. July 4 is the best time to visit, since actors in period attire staff the home and speak the language of the day, transporting you back to 1815. The event is free and takes place from noon to 5 PM. Picnicking is encouraged.

Poplar Forest's huge, ancient boxwoods are incredible to see on the beautiful grounds. The staff's enthusiasm for this cultural treasure is highly contagious. Open 10 AM to 4 PM Wednesday through Sunday from April through November, Poplar Forest is open on major holidays except Thanksgiving. The last tour begins at 3:45 PM. Group rates and tours are available by appointment. Admission is $5 for adults, $4 for senior citizens, $3 for college students and $1 for children ages 12 to 18. Younger children are admitted free.

Other Attractions

Elks National Home
931 Ashland Ave., Bedford
• (540) 586-8232

A spacious retirement home used as a set in the Disney movie *What About Bob?*, the Elks National Home for retired members of this fraternal organization is best-known for its annual Christmas light display. Men from every state work all year to give western Virginia's children a Christmas show worth driving to see. The rest of the year, the beautiful grounds are open for visitors.

Holy Land USA Nature Sanctuary
Va. Rt. 6, Bedford • (540) 586-2823

This 250-acre nature sanctuary represents the Bible Lands of Israel. Visitors can imagine the life, journeys and deeds of Jesus Christ along a 3-mile trail in the beautiful Blue Ridge close to the Peaks of Otter. You have to use your imagination to envision the Biblical scenes outlined for Bible research and study, but many find inspiration from the visit. No admission fee is required to walk on your own. A fee is charged, however, for riding guided journeys, which must be booked in advance.

Campbell County

Red Hill, Patrick Henry National Memorial
Brookneal • (804) 376-2044

Red Hill is the last home and burial place of the famous orator, first governor of Virginia and champion of individual rights, Patrick Henry. The Red Hill museum/visitors center and historic buildings showcase the world's largest collection of Patrick Henry memorabilia, including the famous Peter Rothermel painting, *Patrick Henry Before the Virginia House of Burgesses*. There is also a 15-minute introductory video on Patrick Henry and Red Hill.

You can visit Henry's house, law office and other plantation buildings, and the grounds contain the Henry family cemetery and the national champion osage orange tree. Red Hill, which Henry called "one of the garden spots of Virginia," offers a breathtaking view of the Staunton River Valley. The memorial is open 9 AM until 5 PM daily except November through February, when it closes at 4 PM. It is closed Thanksgiving, Christmas and New Year's Day. Admission is $3 for adults, $1 for students and children.

Franklin County

Museums and Historic Attractions

Blue Ridge Institute
Ferrum College, Ferrum
• (540) 365-4416

Visitors are often astounded that a small Methodist-related college in Franklin County, Virginia, has taken on the role of preserving a cultural heritage to the extent and level of visibility that Ferrum College has done. The result, the Blue Ridge Institute, along with the Blue Ridge Farm Museum and its Folklife Festival, places Ferrum among the nation's most important colleges culturally. Its archives contain thousands of photos, videotapes, phonograph records, vintage books and manuscripts, all treasure troves of Appalachian scenes and people, Shenandoah Valley beliefs, Southwest Virginia folktales and African-American and Caucasian folk music from throughout Virginia. People of English, Scot, Irish, African and German descent will be especially interested in the distinct identities reflected in Blue Ridge music, crafts, foods, beliefs and customs formed after their forebears came to America. The Institute is open Monday through Friday 8 AM to 4:30 PM. Archives are open by appointment

Blue Ridge Institute Museums
Ferrum College • (540) 365-4416

The Blue Ridge Institute of Ferrum College, the State Center for Blue Ridge Folklore, presents the folkways of the region and Virginia as a whole through two unique museum facilities. The Blue Ridge Farm Museum, which presents the history and culture of early Southwest Virginia settlements, features a c. 1800 German-American farmstead with log house, outdoor oven, outbuildings, livestock and gardens revealing the daily life of settlers who came from the German communities of Pennsylvania and the Shenandoah Valley.

All buildings are authentic and were moved from their original Blue Ridge locations. Heirloom vegetables flourish in the gardens, vintage breeds of livestock shelter by the barn, and costumed interpreters work at farm and household chores true to early life in the region.

Both historical and contemporary folkways engage the visitor in the Institute's Museum Galleries. Two rotating exhibits showcase the rich texture of Virginia folklife in music, crafts, art and customs. The Museum Galleries are the only facilities in the Commonwealth dedicated exclusively to the presentation of traditional culture. The Farm Museum is open weekends from mid-May through mid-August, Saturday 10 AM to 5 PM and Sundays 1 to 5 PM. Admission is $3 for adults and $2 for children and senior citizens. Museum Galleries are open year round Monday through Saturday 10 AM to 4 PM. Admission is free.

Booker T. Washington National Monument
Hardy • (540) 721-2094

Booker T. Washington was born into the legacy of slavery, spending the first nine years of his life in bondage on this small tobacco farm. It was from this unlikely beginning that Washington achieved international recognition as an educator, orator, unofficial presidential advisor, founder of Tuskegee Institute and African-American leader. Begin your tour of his birthplace by watching the slide show and seeing the exhibits at the visitors center.

This is the most famous attraction in Franklin County and with good reason. From the beautiful, restored farm and its animals to the hike up Plantation Trail, this monument offers a scenic, historic sojourn into a time when slavery was a way of life in America. The site is open daily 9 AM to 5 PM, except for Thanksgiving, Christmas and New Year's Day. Admission is free.

New River Valley

Montgomery County

Museums and Historic Attractions

Smithfield Plantation
Virginia Tech campus, off U.S. Hwy. 460 Bypass on Va. Rt. 314, Blacksburg • (540) 231-3947

Built by Col. William Preston in 1772, Smithfield Plantation has been extensively restored and is a Virginia Historic Landmark. It was the birthplace of two Virginia governors, James Patton Preston and John Buchanan Floyd, and was briefly the home of a third, John Floyd Jr. Hours are 1 to 5 PM Thursday through Sunday April 1 through November 1. (Note that the last tour begins at 4:30 PM.) Admission is $4 for adults and $1.50 for children 12 and younger. To arrange a group tour for 10 or more visitors, call Alice Payne at (540) 552-2108.

Spectator Sports

New River Valley Speedway
Radford • (540) 639-1700

The New River Valley Speedway is a NASCAR sanctioned .416-mile paved oval track running under the Winston Racing Series banner. The Late Model Stocks are the featured division of the speedway, with supporting divisions including Limited Sportsman, Late Model Trucks, Pure Stocks and Mini Stocks. Also competing on occasion throughout the year are Enduros and Mini Cups. A family atmosphere prevails, and no matter what your preconceptions about racing, this is a sport for all ages to enjoy. Monster truck shows, car shows, concerts, kids events and other special activities are also held during the year.

Races are held every Saturday night from April through September. Admission is $10 for adults and $1 for children younger than 12.

Virginia Tech
U.S. Hwy. 460 Bypass, off I-81, Blacksburg • (540) 231-6726

Hokie football is big — make that BIG — in western Virginia. Virginia Tech has reached a new pinnacle of success the past six years with high national rankings and six straight bowl trips. The Hokies have a huge following.

In 1998, the Hokies advanced to their sixth straight bowl game, meeting Alabama in the freezing rain in the inaugural Music City Bowl in Nashville. When the two teams last squared off in 1973, the Crimson Tide won 77-6. In fact, Alabama had defeated the Hokies in all 10 of their previous meetings, but this time Virginia Tech took charge, 38-7, to upend the university that had earned 12 national championships.

Tech's 1995 squad defeated Texas in the Nokia Sugar Bowl in New Orleans. The next year Tech set a new school record, winning 10 regular season games, before losing to power-packed Nebraska in the FedEx Orange Bowl in Miami. In 1997, Tech faced North Carolina in the Gator Bowl, but lost 42-3.

Virginia Tech football is so big that if you want to catch a game, go as early as you can to avoid the traffic jams on the roads leading off I-81 onto U.S. 460 to Lane Stadium/ Worsham Field (capacity 51,000) in the heart of the Virginia Tech campus. Thousands of tailgating fans will join you in the parking lot. It's simply the main event for this part of the Blue Ridge, with wild, roaring crowds and lots of pageantry and fun!

For those interested in the game itself, be aware that Tech is in the Big East Football Conference, one of the most prestigious leagues in the country. They rival other Big East teams including Miami, Syracuse, West Virginia and Boston College. Tech's mascot is a turkey sporting maroon and orange.

Famous Tech football player graduates include Bruce "The Sack Man" Smith, who won the Outland Trophy in 1984; George Preas, who played with the Baltimore Colts; and Don Strock, a longtime quarterback with the Miami Dolphins. Quarterback Jim Drukenmiller was picked in the first round of the NFL draft by the San Francisco 49ers and continued to make headlines during the 1997 NFL season. Former

Tech wide receiver Antonio Freeman helped lead the Green Bay Packers to back-to-back appearances in the Super Bowl.

Virginia Tech basketball is also BIG — both the men's and women's variety. Bobby Hussey, who took over the reins when long-time coach Bill Foster retired, coaches the men's team. The women's basketball team had a banner year under second-year coach Bonnie Henrickson. In 1998-99 she was named Atlantic 10 Coach of the Year as the Hokies won the regular season title with a 25–1 record and earned their first ever national Top 10 ranking. Point guard Lisa Witherspoon was named the league's Player of the Year. Two of Tech's most famous basketball players are Dell Curry and Bimbo Coles, both now playing in the NBA.

Basketball games are held in Cassell Coliseum, adjacent to the football arena. You can reach the coliseum by exiting I-81 onto U.S. 460 and heading straight to the Virginia Tech campus.

Other Attractions

Selu Conservancy and Retreat Center
Radford University • (540) 831-5108

Selu (pronounced "say-loo") is Radford University's 376-acre "outdoor classroom" of woods, wetlands and meadows bordering the Little River, 5 miles from campus. A hiking trail, a boathouse and dock and the recently completed retreat center complement Selu's natural invitation to learning. Future plans include a science laboratory building and observatory and a living history museum.

University Libraries
Virginia Tech Campus, Blacksburg • (540) 231-6170

The University Libraries include the Carol M. Newman Library (main building) and four branch libraries: Art and Architecture, Geology, Veterinary Medicine and Northern Virginia Graduate Center. Collections include 1.9 million printed volumes, 17,000 magazines or journals, 5.9 million microforms, 120,000 maps, government documents and 130,000 audiovisual and machine-readable pieces. The

Special Collections Department is a particularly rich depository in the history of southern Appalachia, the Civil War, science and technology and railroad history.

Giles County

Covered Bridges

Sinking Creek Bridge
Va. Rt. 601, Giles County

Near the beautiful Appalachian Trail in the New River Valley's Giles County stands a modified Howe truss built across Sinking Creek, just a half-mile north of Newport. Built in 1916, the 70-foot Sinking Creek Covered Bridge was left in place when a modern bridge was built in 1963. The bridge is no longer used for automobiles. Visitors are welcome to explore the bridge — on foot, of course. This area also boasts two other covered bridges, however, they're located on private farms. The Newport countryside is worth exploring for its quaint, country setting. To get to the bridge, take Va. 601, which is a half-mile west of U.S. Highway 42.

Museums and Historic Attractions

Andrew Johnston Museum & Research Center
Main St., Pearisburg • (540) 921-5000

This restored brick house next to the Post Office is home to a genealogy library and historic Giles County displays. It is open by appointment.

Pulaski County

Museums and Historic Attractions

Historic Old Newbern & Wilderness Road Regional Museum
New River Historical Society, Va. Rt. 611, off I-81, Newbern • (540) 674-4835

Eighteen historical buildings comprise part of the 57 properties of the Old Newbern Na-

tional Historic District, a neighborhood originally planned by early settlers. Newbern served
as Pulaski County's seat from 1839 to 1893,
when the courthouse was destroyed by fire.
This interesting tour takes you through the historic buildings, some already renovated and
some in the process, including a slave cabin,
pre-Civil War church, buggy shed and small
weather-boarded barn. The museum is filled
with historical artifacts relating to life in the
New River Valley and some Civil War artifacts.
It also sponsors a Civil War Re-enactors' Boot
Camp and Civil War Weekend (Pulaski County
is the site of the famous Battle of Cloyd's Mountain). Three special fund-raising dinners are
held each year, and the Annual Newbern Fall
Festival is held on the second weekend of
October. Nearby are some great shops and
restaurants. Museum hours are 10:30 AM to
4:30 PM Tuesday through Saturday and 1:30
to 4:30 PM Sunday.

Pulaski County Courthouse
52 W. Main St., Pulaski • (540) 980-7750

The Pulaski County Courthouse, originally
constructed in 1896, has been restored after
being destroyed by a fire in December 1989.
The New River Heritage Exhibits offer a display detailing the local history of African Americans, including a profile of Mr. Chauncy
Harmon. Mr. Harmon, his wife Lucy, and several other teachers, with the support of the
Virginia NAACP and Thurgood Marshall, Special Counsel for the NAACP, brought petitions
for equalization in Pulaski schools in the 1950s.
Their efforts led to one of only a handful of
public school court cases in which the NAACP
prevailed before winning Brown v. the Board
of Education. The courthouse is open Monday through Friday 9 AM to 5 PM. The building is wheelchair-accessible.

Pulaski Railway Station
20 N. Washington Ave., Pulaski
• (540) 980-1991

In the late 1800s, Pulaski was a major stop
along the Norfolk & Western Railroad route.
N&W donated this railway station, constructed
in 1886, to the town in 1989. The Raymond F.
Ratcliffe Memorial Museum, located in the station, houses model railroads and exhibits arti-

facts from the town's history. The railway station is open from 8:30 AM to 5 PM Monday
through Friday and 1 to 4 PM Saturday and
Sunday.

Spectator Sports

Pulaski Rangers
Calfee Park, Pulaski • (540) 994-8624

The Pulaski Rangers baseball team, rookie
team for the Texas Rangers, plays at historic
Calfee Park. Built in 1935, this unique ballpark
has been pictured in *Sports Illustrated*, *National Geographic* and *Life* magazines. The
Rangers play about half of their season at
home against other Appalachian League
teams like the Martinsville Phillies and the
Bristol White Sox. The season runs June
through August. Single games begin at 7 PM,
doubleheaders at 6 PM. General admission is
$3. Call for a schedule of games.

Floyd County

Mabry Mill
Mile 176, Blue Ridge Pkwy.
• (540) 745-4329

Undoubtedly the most scenic and most-
photographed place on the Blue Ridge Parkway, Mabry Mill has been called one of the
most picturesque water mills in the United
States. It still grinds flour for buckwheat cakes
and produces some of the most delicious cornmeal you can buy for Southern-style corn
bread. Mabry Mill also is a workshop of live
crafts (many for sale), music and exhibits that
show a way of life a century ago. The site has
a restaurant.

Wythe County

Thomas J. Boyd Museum
295 Tazewell St., Wytheville
• (540) 223-3331

Here's where you can learn more about
the people and historic places in Wythe
County. Wytheville's first fire truck — dating
from 1855 — is prominently displayed along
with farm equipment, relics from the Civil War

and artifacts from the local mining industry. The museum is open from 10 AM to 4 PM Tuesday through Saturday from April through October. Admission is $2, $1 for ages 6 to 12.

Alleghany Highlands

Alleghany County

Covered Bridges

Humpback Bridge
Off I-64, Alleghany County

Known as the "granddaddy of them all," Humpback is Virginia's oldest standing covered bridge and the nation's only surviving curved-span covered bridge. Built in 1835 as part of the Kanawha Turnpike, the graceful, 100-foot arched span rises 8 feet over Dunlap Creek. It is within viewing distance of I-64, off the Callaghan Exit between Covington, Virginia, and White Sulphur Springs, West Virginia. Its hump design is unique in the Western Hemisphere. Only one other bridge, in France, is similarly constructed.

During autumn, the Humpback Wayside, between Virginia's breathtaking Allegheny and Blue Ridge mountains, is a popular picnic area. Visitors can stroll through the bridge and wade in the shallow creek below to admire the structure's hand-hewn oak timbers. Milton Hall, a historic bed and breakfast inn with gorgeous gardens, is close by (see our Bed and Breakfasts and Country Inns chapter).

Bath County

Museums and Historic Attractions

Bath County Historical Society Museum
Courthouse Sq. • (540) 839-2543

Artifacts of Bath County and the Indian and Civil wars — books, apparel and photographs — are prominent here. The museum also has a genealogy library, which is rapidly expanding due to a newly donated computer with CD-ROM dedicated to genealogical information. Also, generous donations (in memory of a former member of the board of directors) are being used to acquire more materials. The historical society has published a history of the county and other books of historic Bath County information. The museum is open 8:30 AM to 4:30 PM Monday through Friday.

Bear Mountain Outdoor School & Lodge
U.S. Hwy. 250, Hightown
• (540) 468-2700

Bear Mountain Outdoor School could not be more picturesque: it's located on a 600-acre mountain farm at 4,200 feet in Highland County, at the headwaters of the Potomac River. Programs and retreats here merge practical experience with a refreshing vacation break from the fast track. Workshops, seminars and retreats are hands-on, stressing real projects, resources and skills. There are primarily weeklong and weekend offerings from April through October, including a variety of outdoor and rural pursuits. For example, the hand-hewn log building or timber-framing seminars are hands-on sessions for do-it-yourselfers led by qualified instructors who are experts in their fields. Retreats emphasize environmental appreciation.

The Lodge, rustic cabins and outdoor teaching areas in this remote setting are conducive to adventure. Other outdoor activities include hiking, biking, caving, trail rides and fishing. Meals focus on natural foods, and evening activities heighten the enjoyment of this mountaintop vacation. All programs include lodging, meals and instructional materials. Bear Mountain can design custom programs for small businesses, public and private schools, families and organized groups to include team-building, environmental awareness, hiking and more. Call Thomas Brody, owner/director, for a schedule, workshop outlines or references.

Rates are $40 per day, with no charge for children younger than 12. Special rates are available for schools and groups. Guests may accompany a workshop participant for lodging and meals only.

Chesapeake & Ohio Historical Society

312 E. Ridgeway St., Clifton Forge
• **(800) 453-2647**

This international railroad historical society deals with the history of the Chesapeake & Ohio Railway. Its predecessors and successors operated in Virginia, West Virginia, Kentucky, Ohio, Michigan, Indiana and Ontario. The organization's archives division has one of the largest institutional collections devoted to a single railway, including more than 100,000 ink-on-linen original engineering drawings, 50,000 mechanical drawings and 50,000 photographic images, dating from the 1870s to 1980s. A library contains thousands of books, magazines and pamphlets devoted to railroad history in general and C&O history in particular. The Society also owns 19 pieces of historic original C&O railroad equipment, some of which is open for display by appointment, and some in storage awaiting restoration. Several passenger cars have been restored and are used to interpret the railway experience at special events in Clifton Forge and over several states. The premier restored passenger car is the dining car Gadsby's Tavern. The Society, which has more than 2,700 members in 50 states, produces the annual Chessie Calendar, carrying on an unbroken tradition begun by the railway in 1934. The archives and gift shop are open 8 AM to 5 PM Monday through Saturday year round.

Maple Museum

U.S. Hwy. 220, Monterey
• **(540) 468-2550**

In the land of maples is a museum celebrating old-time sugaring. See a replica of a sugar house, where you can watch sugar- and syrup-making demonstrations. Tools and equipment used by sugar makers throughout the years are displayed. Old-timers who can't otherwise get to the real sugar camps will find this especially interesting. It is open daily.

Even the most jaded city children have been spotted making an amazing transformation from being bored to having some hidden chord struck by history and the beauty of the great outdoors.

Kidstuff

If your kids are looking for big metropolitan areas full of amusement parks, video games and Disney-type make-believe, don't aim for the Blue Ridge. However, if you and your family are looking for a break from the artificial and searching for something real, you're heading in the right direction. Even the most jaded city children have been spotted making an amazing transformation from being bored to having some hidden chord struck by history and the beauty of the great outdoors.

The Blue Ridge offers adults and children many opportunities to experience and explore the kinds of places that don't exist anywhere else. We have natural wonders such as Shenandoah National Park, caverns and Natural Bridge in the Shenandoah Valley, and museums such as the New Market Hall of Valor, To the Rescue Exhibit and the Science Museum in Roanoke. In the Horse Country stretching from Loudoun County to Albemarle County, children are thrilled to see horse shows, steeplechases and fox hunts. Lexington's Virginia Horse Center has a plethora of events that children will enjoy. And the jousting tournaments at Natural Chimneys in Augusta County are a real treat — for all ages actually. But parents be warned: exposing your children to such events may lead them to begging you to buy a pony or horse.

Much of the Blue Ridge is rural, which means that there's a county or local fair near almost any destination. What kid wouldn't be fascinated by the farm animals (often shown by children) and the carnivals and games that usually accompany these highlights of the harvest season (see our Annual Events and Festivals chapter). Many resorts and inns in the Blue Ridge appeal to families, so you may be able to plan a trip to our neck of the woods without looking any farther than our chapters on Resorts, Hotels and Motels, and Bed and Breakfast and Country Inns — but think of all the temptations you'd miss!

Shenandoah Valley

Frederick County

Apple Blossom Festival
135 N. Cameron St., Winchester
• (540) 662-3863

Winchester becomes a boomtown every spring during the Apple Blossom Festival (see our Annual Events and Festivals chapter). The sweet scent of apple blossoms fills the air, and each year a different celebrity serves as the marshal of the festival's showcase — the grand feature parade. With events running from 8 AM to midnight for five straight days, it's easy to find something to do. There's an arts and crafts festival, concerts, races, athletic events, a midway with carnival rides and, of course, a circus. While some of the activities are free, you will need tickets for concerts and the circus. Ten dollars will get you in the circus; $6 if you are younger than 12 or older than 62.

Shenandoah Valley Discovery Museum
54 S. Loudoun St., Winchester
• (540) 722-2020

Dress up like a doctor in the mini-hospital emergency room or enjoy playing with the simple machine in the Apple Packing Center. This hands-on, interactive museum for children features permanent displays, a take-apart climbing wall, even snakes. The museum is on the Loudoun Street Pedestrian Mall, and is open from 9 AM to 5 PM Tuesday through Saturday and 1 to 5 PM Sunday. The cost is $3, $2 each for groups of 10 or more.

Winchester Book Gallery
185 N. Loudoun St., Winchester
• **(540) 667-3444**

A short walk down the pedestrian mall is this two-story book shop. The entire upstairs level of the Winchester Book Gallery is devoted to children's books, and you might also find a few maps, dolls, stuffed animals and videos. Check it out from 10 AM to 5 PM Monday through Saturday.

Jammin' Gym
1107 Berryville Ave., Winchester
• **(540) 667-5266**

This smoke-free, gum-free and sock-wearing playground is a great place to take the kids when the hotel pool is closed. Jammin' Gym features an indoor roller coaster. In fact, everything is indoors, including games, laser tag, ladders, tubes, slides and a ball bin for running, jumping and climbing. There also is a special area for children younger than 4 and a full-service restaurant. Admission is $4 for ages 4 and older; those younger pay their ages. Adults accompanying children get in free. Game tokens are a quarter, ride tickets are $1.25 and Laser Runner tickets cost $3.50. Package deals are available.

Virginia Farm Market
1881 N. Frederick Pike, Winchester
• **(540) 665-8000**

Good grief Charlie Brown, this place has the largest display of pumpkins in the area. During the fall pumpkin harvest season, the Virginia Farm Market even opens a "Pumpkin Patch," a maze that the young ones can explore. It's free. Open seven days a week, the market features fresh fruit, preserves, apple cider, baskets and plants. There also will be more than a dozen varieties of locally grown apples on sale during apple season. The indoor-outdoor market is open from April through December. Call before you go; the hours will vary.

Dalke's Family Drive-In
U.S. Hwy. 11, Stephens City
• **(540) 869-2175**

Less than 10 drive-in theaters remain in

www.insiders.com

See this and many other **Insiders' Guide®** destinations online.

Visit us today!

Virginia, including this one just 1 mile south of Stephens City. Dalke's Family Drive-In shows different double-features on two screens nightly during the summer. There are also a refreshment stand and a playground for the young ones. The box office opens at 8 PM, with the first film starting at dusk. In 1998, adults paid $5.50, while children 12 and younger were admitted for free.

Saturday Night Showcase
Sherando Park, Stephens City
• **(540) 665-5678**

Bring a blanket or lawn chair to Sherando Park to enjoy this cultural arts series. The Saturday Night Showcase, offered free throughout the summer, features a variety of musicians, mimes and dance troupes. Plan to get there a little early so you can picnic, ride a paddleboat, swim in the public pool or stroll along the park's nature trails. From I-81 take the Stephens City exit to Va. 277.

Appleland Sports Center
4490 Valley Pike, Stephens City
• **(540) 869-8600**

South of Winchester is this miniature golf park and driving range. Kids can play miniature golf or take a swing in one of nine new batting cages, while parents try their luck on the driving range. There are 33 grass tees with sand traps. A bucket of balls ranges from $3 to $8, while mini-golf costs $4, $2.50 if you're between the ages of 6 and 12. For $1, you can take 15 hits in the batting cage. Weather permitting, Appleland is open from 9 AM to 10 PM daily from March through November.

Rinker Orchards Inc.
1156 Marlboro Rd., Stephens City
• **(540) 869-1499**

If you are visiting this area during apple harvest, it's great fun to go out in the orchards and pick your own apples. Rinker Orchards (just south of Winchester) will give you and your family that experience. The orchard even caters to the smallest family members, who can pick their own apples on easy-to-reach dwarf and trellised trees. The cost varies with the seasons. The season is short though, usually running from mid-September to early-October. You never know what else you might find. On any given weekend, the orchard hosts bake sales, pony rides and a craft shop.

Belle Grove Plantation
Cedar Creek Battlefield, Middletown
• (540) 869-2028

For Civil War history, the re-enactment of the Battle of Cedar Creek takes place every October at historic Belle Grove Plantation on the very battlefield where the fighting took place. (See our Civil War chapter for more information on the house and grounds.)

Wayside Theatre
7853 Main St., Middletown
• (800) 951-1776

Wayside Theatre (see our Arts chapter) often has family comedies and musicals, such as *Oliver!,* that are suitable for children.

Clarke County

Dinosaur Land
U.S. Hwy. 522, White Post • (540) 869-2222

Get your picture taken while you sit in King Kong's hand. The 20-foot replica of the movie icon is a crowd favorite at this outdoor prehistoric forest. More than 35 exhibits bring kids face to face with life-size reproductions of dinosaurs that roamed the earth during the Mesozoic era. Tours of the park are self-guided. Admission is $2.50 for children 2 to 10 and $3 for those older than 10.

During the summer, the hours are 9:30 AM to 6:30 PM. It closes at 5:30 PM from March to Memorial Day and at 5 PM in November and December. The park is closed in January and February.

It's easy to find: Dinosaur Land is at the intersection of U.S. 522 and U.S. 340 between Winchester and Front Royal.

Warren County

Skyline Drive
3655 U.S. Hwy. 211 E., Luray
• (540) 999-3500

The Blue Ridge's greatest resource is its natural beauty, so this is a great place to introduce your children to nature. Starting at Front Royal, you can enter the magic world of the Skyline Drive, a road that squiggles along the crest of the mountains all the way to Waynesboro, where it joins the Blue Ridge Parkway (see our Blue Ridge Parkway and Skyline Drive chapter). The Drive and Parkway run through national parks, where deer and other wild creatures will be easy to spot from your car. The cost is $10 per car, $5 for pedestrians and bicyclists. To make the experience even more special for your children (and you), plan to stay at one of the campgrounds or lodges in this unspoiled area.

Skyline Caverns
U.S. Hwy. 340, Front Royal
• (540) 635-4545, (800) 296-4545

One of three swift underground streams is stocked with fat trout that dart about in easy view in this underground wonder. Youngsters will also marvel at the cave formations inside Skyline Caverns, including the unusual anthodites or "cave orchids" for which Skyline is noted. Above ground is the Outdoor Skyline Arrow, a miniature train that carries children on a half-mile journey through a real tunnel. (See our Attractions chapter.) The caverns are off Interstate 66 at Exit 6.

Front Royal Canoe Company
U.S. Hwy. 340 S., Front Royal
• (540) 635-5440, (800) 270-8808

Front Royal is where the north and south branches of the Shenandoah River join in their rush to the sea. The waterfront below the U.S. 522 bridge draws boaters, swimmers and an-

---

INSIDERS' TIP

Remember your camera when planning outings with kids. Their wide-eyed expressions are priceless, especially if you're going to a farm or horse show.

glers during warm weather. The Front Royal Canoe Company (see our Recreation chapter), can put you and your family adrift on any summer day. On the average, a day trip will run $26 to $42 for canoers; $14 for $22 for a kayak. If rowing is more effort than you want to expend, try tubing, where the river will do all the work for you. It only costs $12. Rent an extra tube to carry your lunch and spend the day lazily drifting; kids will enjoy swimming spots along the way.

Shenandoah County

Stonewall Jackson Museum at Hupp's Hill
U.S. Hwy. 11 S., Strasburg
• (540) 465-5884

For a more educational experience, the whole family should learn from a visit to this park conveniently located near the intersection of interstates 81 and 66. This interpretive center for the Battle of Cedar Creek and the role of the Shenandoah Valley during the Civil War offers hands-on exhibits and activities. It even has a children's room with costumes to try on, wooden horses to ride and a Civil War camp with a tent and camp furniture. Visitors are encouraged to learn about the era through touching, seeing and experiencing what life was like during the Civil War period. (See our Civil War chapter for more information on Hupp's Hill.)

Bryce Resort
1982 Fairway Dr., Bayse • (540) 856-2121

This Shenandoah County resort offers a wide range of family accommodations and activities (see our Resorts chapter), including skiing, grass skiing, horseback and pony riding, mountain biking, in-line skating and tennis. A large private lake with beach provides for all sorts of water activities.

Shenandoah Valley Music Festival
221 Shrine Mont Cir., Orkney Springs
• (800) 459-3396

There is musical entertainment five weekends each summer at the Shenandoah Valley Music Festival (see our Arts chapter.) Held outdoors at the Pavilion on the grounds of the former Orkney Springs Hotel, the festival also hosts special events for kids, such as the production of *Hansel and Gretel* in 1996. On symphony weekends, there are free concerts for kids. You can bring along an adult for $5.

Page County

Luray Caverns
U.S. Hwy. 211 Bypass, Luray
• (540) 743-6551

Beneath the surface of the ground is the world's only stalacpipe organ. Luray Caverns (see our Attractions chapter) also features a Car and Carriage Caravan above ground, which contains antique cars, carriages, coaches and costumes dating back to 1625.

Shenandoah River Outfitters
6502 S. Page Valley Rd., Luray
• (540) 743-4159

Hook up with Shenandoah Outfitters for a leisurely day on the south fork of the Shenandoah River. Rent canoes, inner tubes and kayaks year round. The first trip starts at 8 AM, and the last departs at 1 PM. You can rent a tube for $14. Canoes average $25 to $46 for trips ranging from one to five hours. Kayaks cost $30 a day.

Down River Canoe Company
884 Indian Hollow, Bentonville
• (540) 635-5526

You also can explore the south fork of the Shenandoah with canoe, kayak, inner tube or raft from Down River Canoe Company from April 1 to October 31. Daily rentals are $37 to $49 for a canoe, $21 to $28 for a kayak and $10.50 to $14 for a tube. Rafts will run you anywhere from $44 to $107 depending on the number of people in your group. Down River is open from 9 AM to 6 PM during the week and from 7 AM to 7 PM on weekends.

Luray Reptile Center and Dinosaur Park
1087 U.S. Hwy. 211 W., Luray
• (540) 743-4113

Luray also has one of the state's largest reptile collections for kids who appreciate the creepy crawlies. The Luray Reptile Center and Dinosaur Park also has a petting zoo with tame deer, llamas and other creatures. Counting

Outdoor adventures are what kidstuff is all about.

Photo: Wintergreen Resort

A hook and line guarantee a good time.

the zoo, there are more than 300 animals in 70 exhibits. The center is open daily from 10 AM to 6 PM. Admission is $5, $4 for children ages 3 to 12.

Rockingham County

Purcell Park
Monument Ave., Harrisonburg
• **(540) 434-2319**

Parents will be interested in several small parks in Harrisonburg, including Purcell Park with its picnic shelters, a 1.5-mile-jogging trail and a kids' castle. There also is a lake for fishing in the summer and ice-skating in the winter. Two lighted softball diamonds, a Little League field, Midget League football field and tennis courts will attract the sports-minded youngster.

Hillandale Park
Hillandale Ave., Harrisonburg
• **(540) 434-2319**

Explore a reproduction log cabin at Hillandale Park, or play basketball, practice archery or jog. The Harrisonburg park has a 1.3-mile jogging and exercise trail, 12 picnic shelters and a small playground.

PJ's Arcade and Pizzeria
1940 Deyerle Ave., Harrisonburg
• **(540) 564-1766**

On rainy days try PJ's. This indoor playground for kids 12 and younger offers great indoor adventure. There are arcade games, pool tables, air hockey, even a big jungle gym. Sorry, you have to be 10 or younger to play on the jungle gym. There's no cost to get in, but bring plenty of quarters for the games. During the summer season, the park is open from 11 AM to 9 PM Monday through Thursday, 11 AM to 10 PM Friday, 10 AM to 10 PM Saturday and from noon to 9 PM Sunday.

George Washington and Jefferson National Forests
112 N. River Rd., Bridgewater
• **(540) 828-2591**

For bigger adventure, the newly merged George Washington and Jefferson National Forests is a stone's throw away with lakes for swimming, miles of hiking and 25 campgrounds ranging from primitive to ones with electrical hookups, showers and toilets. There's outdoor fun from one end of the Blue Ridge to the other. In fact, there's even an Eastern National Children's Forest Trail just 18 miles from Covington on Va. 613. (See our

Recreation chapter for more on the national forest.)

Valley Golf Center
141 Carpenter Ln., Harrisonburg
- **(540) 432-9040**

Play a round on the 18-hole miniature golf course, while the adults practice on the driving range. The Valley Golf Center is open from 10 AM to 10 PM Tuesday through Saturday and from noon to 10 PM Sunday and Monday. You'll pay between $3 and $6 for a bucket of balls, while miniature golf runs $3.50 or $2.50 for ages 6 to 12. There's a pro shop, too, if you need new equipment.

Skatetown USA
100 Miller Cir., Harrisonburg
- **(540) 433-1834**

You can have your pick of old-fashioned fun or new-age excitement at Skatetown. After you've taken a spin on the roller-skating rink, test your commando skills in the new laser tag arena. The black-lit maze is filled with fog as you try to hunt down your opponent before you get zapped. Prices range between $3 and $5. The hours vary, so call before you go.

Bull Pen
1945 Deyerle Ave., Harrisonburg
- **(540) 433-2243**

There is something to do here for just about every young athlete. Aside from batting cages, Bull Pen also has off-the-board basketball and go-carts. You can shoot hoops for $3.50 or take a swing at 14 balls for $1. Go-carts cost $3.50, but you must be 10 years old and at least 58 inches tall to take a drive. If not, you can ride with an adult. Bull Pen is open noon to 10 PM Monday through Friday with extended hours on Saturday and Sunday.

Eastern Mennonite University Planetarium
1200 Park Rd., Harrisonburg
- **(540) 432-4400**

Eastern Mennonite University offers a more enlightening experience at its planetarium and museum. There's a half-hour program in the planetarium, then you tour the museum at your own pace. The 2 PM programs are only held on certain Sundays throughout the year, so call for an appointment. The cost is $1.50.

Warren House Life Science Museum
17 Grace St., Harrisonburg
- **(540) 568-6906**

James Madison University operates this museum, where kids can see a variety of live creatures, from snakes and iguanas to spiders and giant millipedes. Kids also can crawl around in the Dinosaur Cave or view a small replica of a rain forest. It's a small museum, but well-done. (For more information, see our Attractions chapter.)

Massanutten Resort
Va. Rt. 644, Harrisonburg
- **(540) 289-9441**

East of Harrisonburg is Massanutten Resort, with golf and great skiing for families. Special programs help develop junior skiers into racers (see our Skiing chapter). The family-oriented resort offers a host of programs geared to children, including crafts, miniature golf and pond fishing. You can even rent mountain bikes for $6 an hour.

Augusta County

Grand Caverns
Off I-81 at Exit 235, Grottoes
- **(540) 249-5705**

It's a wonder this area doesn't fall into some subterranean passage. One of the oldest caverns in the Shenandoah Valley, Grand Caverns includes a 5,000-square-foot underground "ballroom." Look for the "shield" formations too. (See our Attractions chapter.)

Frontier Culture Museum
U.S. Hwy. 250 W., Staunton
- **(540) 332-7850**

Staunton's greatest attraction for children is its fascinating Frontier Culture Museum (see our Attractions chapter), where fields and livestock are tended exactly the way European and early American farmers used to do it. From cows to chickens to kittens, the animals will help make this a fun-filled day for children, and many festivals here throughout the year (see our Annual Events and Festivals chapter) are geared to families. Authentic farm areas have been re-created with costumed interpreters demonstrating life of the frontier culture.

Gypsy Hill Park
Churchville Ave., Staunton
• (800) 332-5219

This is a favorite place for young and old. Athletes can choose between the lighted softball fields, Little League diamonds, tennis courts, a swimming pool and horseshoe pits. There are the usual swings, picnic areas and even a bandstand (free concerts are held here weekly in the summer), but the big draw to Gypsy Hill is the duck pond. Take a few pieces of bread to feed the ducks and swans, but don't let your fingers get too close.

Virginia Metalcrafters
1010 E. Main St., Waynesboro
• (540) 949-9432

Older children (and parents) will enjoy a visit to the showroom of Virginia Metalcrafters, where you can watch brass being molded. Artisans create a variety of items, including candlesticks, lamps and trivets. Oh, and your parents might like to know that they can purchase these artworks at 25 percent below the suggested retail price. Virginia Metalcrafters is open from 9 AM to 5 PM Monday through Friday, 9 AM to 4 PM Saturday and from 1 to 5 PM Sunday.

A Touch of Love
416 W. Main St., Waynesboro
• (540) 942-3844

Doll lovers will delight in this shop, where more than 2,000 specialty dolls are on display. While you may find a few play dolls, most of the items in this store are collectibles, including dolls from 80 doll artists. A Touch of Love is open from 10 AM to 5 PM Monday through Saturday.

Collector's Choice
18 W. Beverley St., Staunton
• (540) 885-8572

Staunton has its own doll shop, Collec-

tors' Choice, which also specializes in figurines, boxes and other small collectibles. You might find a few stuffed animals too. The shop is open from 10 AM to 6 PM Monday through Friday and 10 AM to 5 PM Saturday.

Candy Shop
Va. Rt. 608, Stuarts Draft
• (540) 337-0298

This a favorite stop for those with a sweet tooth. The Candy Shop sells Hershey products, some of which are made in the Hershey plant in Stuarts Draft. This unique country store carries much more than just candy — rocking horses, wind chimes and quilts make it a fun stop. (See our Shopping chapter.)

Sherando Lake Recreation Area
Off Va. Rt. 664, Lyndhurst
• (540) 942-5965

Just 14 miles south of Waynesboro is Sherando Lake, a recreational haven between two lakes. Family camping units are available on a first-come, first-served basis (see our Recreation chapter). Plus there's hiking, swimming, boating and fishing. If you don't want to camp, the cost is $8 a carload for day use.

Shenandoah Acres Resort
Va. Rt. 660, Stuarts Draft
• (540) 337-1911, (800) 654-1714

Raft races for all ages are held the last weekend in July at Shenandoah Acres Resort. An excellent place for family fun, there's camping, horseback riding, tennis and minigolf (see our Recreation chapter). For a daytrip, you can enjoy the sand-bottom lake and picnic at one of many tables and grills surrounding the lake. The cost is $6, $4.50 for children ages 6 to 11. The young ones get in free. Minigolf is $3.50, and horseback riding costs $8 for a 25-minute ride, $15 for the hour trail.

INSIDERS' TIP

There's always something for children to do at the Frontier Culture Museum in Staunton. The 1999 calendar includes 50 programs for the entire family to enjoy, culminating with a Year 2000 Gala Celebration on December 31. Call (540) 332-7850 for schedules and information.

Humpback Rocks
Near Mile 5.8, Blue Ridge Parkway
• **(540) 564-8300**

At nearby Humpback Rocks, the National Park Service has re-created a typical pioneer mountain farm as it might have appeared just before the turn of the century. You can explore the farm and hike up to the rocks — for free (see our Recreation chapter for more information). A picnic area and comfort station are nearby.

Blue Ridge Soap Box Derby
200 S. Forest Ave., Waynesboro
• **(540) 943-5907**

Start your engines. Well, these racecars may not have engines but they are powered by a lot of hard work and determination. After a brief hiatus, soap box racing returned to Waynesboro in 1994 and today it ranks as one of the largest races in the country. For one Saturday in mid-May, Main Street is blocked off so that kids ages 9 to 16 can show off how they cared for their own vehicles — not to mention their driving skills. The competition is friendly, but tough. In fact, Mark Stephens, a representative from Waynesboro's 1997 competition, won the National Soap Box Derby championship in Akron, Ohio. It doesn't cost a thing to watch, but if you want to race, the entry fee can go as high as $474 if you need a car. It's only $50 if you build one yourself.

Lexington and Rockbridge County

History is a major reason families come to Lexington and Rockbridge County — Civil War history (Robert E. Lee and Stonewall Jackson), World War II history (George C. Marshall) and natural history (Natural Bridge).

George C. Marshall Museum and Library
VMI Parade Grounds, Lexington
• **(540) 463-7103**

This is a nice vacation for families or a perfect destination for school field trips. Large pre-scheduled children's groups can partici-

pate in "Try On A Piece of History." The museum staff coordinates this program in which pieces of uniforms are used to bring history alive. Children can also take part in scavenger hunts at the museum. Older children and teens may gain perspective on the impact of war through a photographic display that includes black-and-white photos of the children of war-torn Europe. Admission is $3 for adults, $1 for ages 7-18. School groups are free (see our Attractions chapter).

Stonewall Jackson House
8 E. Washington St., Lexington
• **(540) 463-2552**

Young visitors to Stonewall Jackson House are provided with small slates at the beginning of guided tours. They can then enjoy playing "detective" by locating each of the items listed on the slate as they walk through the house. Kids also enjoy exploring the antique toy reproductions in the gift shop.

Admission is $5 for adults and $2.50 for ages 6-17 (see our Attractions chapter).

VMI Museum
VMI Parade Grounds, N. Main St., Lexington • (540) 464-7334, (540) 464-7232

This museum has a special display of a typical cadet's room in the barracks that always fascinates children. The Virginia Military Institute cadets in uniform and the Friday afternoon full dress parades are always of special interest to children. Throughout most of the year, except during breaks and exams, cadet guides give tours of the VMI Post (see our Attractions chapter).

Carriage Tours of Historic Lexington
Lexington Visitor Center, 106 E. Washington St., Lexington
• **(540) 463-5647**

The Lexington Carriage Company operates this nearly hour-long tour of many of Lexington's historic sites. Older children, especially those who've not had the opportunity to get up close and personal with horses, will enjoy a ride on this forgotten mode of transportation. Carriage Tours do not make stops along the way, however, so parents of young or antsy children might want to consider the length of the 45-minute (or longer) tour.

Carriage rides cost $1 for ages 3 and younger; $3, ages 4 to 6; $6, ages 7 to 13; $10, ages 14 to 64; and $9, ages 65 and older. (See our Attractions chapter.)

Virginia Horse Center
Off I-64 W. at Exit 55, Lexington
• (540) 463-2194

The horse center hosts all kinds of horse shows, but the ones that are of particular interest to children are the miniature horse shows and the pony club shows. In addition, the center hosts rodeos, auctions and living history Civil War encampments, which are a delight for children of all ages! (See our Horse Country chapter.)

Natural Bridge of Virginia
Natural Bridge • (540) 291-2121

From Natural Bridge, one of the seven wonders of the natural world, to gigantic, breathtaking caverns and a wax museum featuring behind-the-scenes tours of how the figures are made, Natural Bridge of Virginia has something to please every child. Not only are the natural surroundings sublime, but the resort also puts on an enthralling light and sound show nightly, *Dramas of Creation*. (See our Resorts chapter.)

Lime Kiln Theatre
Lime Kiln Rd. • Box Office,
14 S. Randolph St., Lexington
• (540) 463-3074

Lexington's summer professional outdoor theater presents musicals, plays and concerts in "the most unusual theatre setting in the United States" — a real kiln used 100 years ago. The productions are often family-oriented, and each year there are some special shows scheduled for children. (See our Arts chapter.)

Sweet Things
106 W. Washington St. • (540) 463-6055

Lexington's homemade ice-cream parlor is a special delight for children of all ages. You can even watch the homemade cones being made.

Roanoke Valley

Roanoke

Many families come to Roanoke via the Blue Ridge Parkway, since the Capital of the Blue Ridge is the largest metropolitan area off one of the most popular and beautiful roads in the United States. Cultural attractions and shopping await below in downtown Roanoke. The Mill Mountain Exit off the Parkway takes you down the mountain to Roanoke, which offers cultural attractions for both adults and children.

Shopping is a major reason tourists visit Roanoke. Roanoke's historic City Market interests children with colorful seasonal produce peddled by farmers wearing straw-brimmed hats and arts and crafts sold by Floyd County flower children dressed in tie-dyed T-shirts. You never know what you'll find in the farmer's booths in the city market, but you can be sure it will be fresh, beautifully presented and an attraction unto itself. Whatever the season, kids will delight in everything from handmade Easter eggs and Christmas greenery to fresh peaches and strawberries.

There's enough to do in Roanoke to keep you and your family occupied for a solid week or so. Call the Roanoke Valley Convention & Visitors Bureau, (800) 635-5535, for its latest calendar of events and shopping, attraction and restaurant guides.

Mill Mountain Zoo & Star
3 miles off Blue Ridge Pkwy., Roanoke
• (540) 343-3241

Mill Mountain itself offers a nice campground and the scenic overlook of the Mill Mountain Star, a 100-foot-high man-made metal star that glows at night. The Mill Mountain Zoo is a small but interesting zoo that children love. There, they can ride the Zoo Choo, see Ruby the Tiger or get acquainted with wildlife both exotic and indigenous to the area. (See our Attractions chapter.)

Wertz's Country Store and Wine Cellar Inc.
City Market, 215 Market St. S.E., Roanoke
• (540) 342-5133

Children who have never been into an old-style general store with good food, candy and antiques will love visiting Wertz's. Owner Ezra Wertz is recognized in tourism circles as the most-photographed man in Roanoke!

Good Things On the Market
City Market, 212 Market St., Roanoke
• (540) 343-2121

You can find this candy store right across from Wertz's. It is a must-see for children — and for the inner child of most grownups. There, you'll find the childhood staples of gumdrops and licorice along with fancier, trendy candy and the latest gimmicks in the confectionery world, all packaged to delight any sweet tooth.

Nuts & Sweet Things
City Market Building, 32 Market Sq.,
Roanoke • (540) 344-3717

This store, in the City Market Building, which has been bustling with activity since 1922, is another place for candy-lovers. The large festival marketplace showcases shops, gifts, food, crafts and special events under a neon-light sculpture. At the center is a culinary arcade where more than a dozen restaurants offer a taste of American and international cuisine, so something is bound to appeal to the younger set.

B&D Comics
802 Elm Avenue S.W., Roanoke
• (540) 342-6642

This store is subsidized by a millionaire whose collector's passion is comics. You are sure to find what you — er, your children — are looking for.

Center in the Square
One Market Sq., Roanoke
• (540) 342-5700

This cultural complex of Roanoke was named one of the best attractions in the world by the United Nations in 1996. It was an old warehouse before being transformed into a home for the Science Museum of Western Virginia, Roanoke Valley Historical Society and Museum, Mill Mountain Theatre, the Art Museum of Western Virginia (with ArtVenture, just for kids) and the Arts Council.

Kids will easily stay occupied for the day visiting each of these attractions. (See our Attractions chapter.)

Science Museum of Western Virginia and Hopkins Planetarium
Center in the Sq., Levels 1, 4, and 5,
One Market Sq., Roanoke
• (540) 342-5710

This museum celebrated its 28th anniversary in 1998. Interactive exhibits ranging from colorful lasers to holograms keep the kids busy, and afterwards you can catch the latest Hopkins Planetarium show. Both the museum and planetarium rate high on every child's list of what's fun to do in Roanoke. Its gift shop on the ground level is full of items large and small to intrigue every child's imagination. (See our Attractions chapter.)

History Museum of Western Virginia
Center in the Square, Levels 1 and 3,
One Market Sq., Roanoke • (540) 342-5770

This permanent exhibit offers the history of the area, emphasizing the railroad, which launched the city as a crossroads of transportation. Children enjoy seeing the miniature general store of yesteryear and an exhibit of vintage clothing. Special exhibits might range from D-Day to Elvis Presley's birthday. A gift shop on the ground level offers a treasure of books that are wonderful keepsakes. (See our Attractions chapter.)

Art Museum of Western Virginia
Center in the Square, Levels 1 and 2,
One Market Sq., Roanoke
• (540) 342-5760

The art museum offers special exhibits for children, such as cartoon originals. Its permanent collection of pictures and sculpture is worth a visit as well. (See our Arts chapter.)

ArtVenture
Center in the Square, One Market Sq.,
Roanoke • (540) 342-5768

This interactive art center for children is open Saturdays only from noon to 4 PM. It is a special place where children can occupy themselves with hands-on art activities under the supervision of dedicated art museum volunteers.

Mill Mountain Theatre
One Market Sq., Roanoke
• (540) 342-5740

This energetic theater group always has children in mind and offers special programming, such as *Beauty and the Beast* in 1996, along with its general crowd-pleasers, ranging from *The King and I* to *Scrooge*. Its cast and directors are some of the best in the nation. (See our Arts chapter.)

Virginia Museum of Transportation
303 Norfolk Ave., Roanoke
• (540) 342-5670

In this restored freight station is where Roanoke proudly displays its railroad heritage. Here, the kids will find history larger than life as they stand beside steam engines and vintage locomotives. They can climb aboard a caboose or stroll through a railway post office car and the largest rolling stock collection in the East. A true delight is the gift shop which is stocked with every child's dreams. (See our Attractions chapter.)

Harrison Museum of African-American Culture
523 Harrison Ave. N.W., Roanoke
• (540) 345-4818

This museum, located in a renovated school, traces the history of the African-American experience. Its colorful displays of beautiful African artifacts are well worth a visit. (See our Attractions chapter.)

To the Rescue National Museum
Tanglewood Mall, 4428 Electric Rd., Roanoke • (540) 776-0364

This is the official national museum of the lifesaving movement. Here, children can fulfill all their emergency and rescue fantasies with interactive exhibits, a simulated car wreck and documentary footage. Don't miss this gem in the city that gave birth to the volunteer rescue squad movement. (See our Attractions chapter).

Grandin Movie Theatre
1310 Grandin Rd., Roanoke
• (540) 345-6177

This is one of the few ornate theaters the wrecking ball hasn't destroyed. You can see classics and modern movies for the best prices in town. This cavernous, popcorn-scented architectural masterpiece will thrill children who may have never seen anything like its tiled floors, mahogany candy cases and ornate decor. (See our Arts chapter.)

Virginia's Explore Park
3900 Rutrough Rd., Roanoke
• (540) 427-1800

This park, entering its sixth year, consists of reconstructed buildings and barns showing the lifestyle of yesteryear. Interpreters authentically demonstrate the lifeways of 18th-century pioneers. It's one of the area's most popular attractions for school children because of its beauty, pristine environment and showcase of what life was like for our great-great-grandparents. (See our Attractions chapter.)

The Virginia Chili Cook-off
Market Sq., Roanoke • (540) 342-2028

Thousands throng the City Market during the first weekend of May to sample the chili and showmanship that go along with "Three-Alarm Chili." (See our Annual Events and Festivals chapter.)

Community School Strawberry Festival
Downtown City Market, Roanoke
• (540) 563-5036

This event takes place a block down from the Chili Cook-off during the first weekend of May. Here children can sample homemade shortcakes and real whipped cream and assorted strawberry delicacies. (See our Annual Events and Festivals chapter.)

Festival in the Park
Downtown Roanoke
• (540) 342-2640

This is a two-week-long celebration of music, entertainment, food and fun that attracts several hundred thousand people to sample an incredible array of festivity. It happens the last weekend in May and the first weekend in June. Special children's programming is ongoing, with theater, drama, special acts and the fabulous Children's Parade where thousands of children decorate their bikes and march alongside gigantic helium balloons. It's "Macy's in Miniature," some say. (See our Annual Events and Festivals chapter.)

Macado's
120 Church Ave., Roanoke
• **(540) 342-7231**

Kids won't be bored while dining at Macado's, known for its outrageous decor ranging from the Three Stooges circling overhead in an airplane to car bodies suspended in air. The food is pretty good too, with a wide choice of sandwiches kids will love. (See our Restaurants chapter.)

Star City Diner
108 S. Jefferson St., Roanoke
• **(540) 343-9301**

You can't miss this restaurant because of the hula-hoop waitress and Big Boy statues on the roof. The menu is extra long and lots of fun reading. Choosing is the problem!

Chuck E. Cheese's
4059 Electric Rd., Roanoke
• **(540) 989-8193**

Bring out the earplugs for your basic loud and boisterous outing to a child's idea of Heaven. There are lots of rides and video games, and, yes, they do serve food. The pizza is quite tasty, a minimal comfort to long-suffering adults trying to hold a conversation above the happy, hollering kids.

Discovery Zone
4037 Electric Rd., Roanoke
• **(540) 772-2715**

The perfect place for rainy days, Discovery Zone offers what seems like miles of tunnels, ball pits, climbing ladders and fun! All kids need is lots of energy. Parents can actually relax while kids play and wear themselves out. A snack bar offers pizza and soft drinks. Kids younger than 10 will be happily entertained here.

East of the Blue Ridge

Loudoun County

Oatlands Plantation
20850 Oatlands Plantation Ln., Leesburg
• **(703) 777-3174**

Oatlands Plantation (see our Attractions chapter) has some marvelous activities for children, including sheep dog trials, steeplechases, Civil War re-enactments and Draft Horse and Mule Day, when the gentle giants of the horse world compete in obstacle races and log pulls. Every June there is a Celtic Festival featuring musicians, storytellers and face painting.

Morven Park
17263 Southern Planter Ln., Leesburg
• **(703) 777-2414**

Leesburg's magnificent Morven Park (see our Attractions chapter) is the scene of many exciting horse activities, including steeplechases, horse shows and carriage driving competitions. The carriage museum on the grounds has items of special interest to children, including small sleighs and carts and a marvelous toy carriage collection.

Naturalist Center
741 Miller Dr. S.E., Leesburg
• **(703) 779-9712, (800) 729-7725**

Older children will enjoy a visit to the Naturalist Center, a part of the Smithsonian Institution's National Museum of Natural History. Children 10 and older can study natural history using the center's collections, scientific equipment and books. Children become true scientists under the guidance and direction of the center's staff. A smaller exhibit with some hands-on activities has been set up for younger children, who must wait while older kids use the main study gallery. This unique learning center will eventually move to the Mall in Washington, D.C., when construction of its permanent home is completed. Take advantage of it now, while it's in the quiet setting of Virginia's countryside!

My Friends & Me
118 South St. S.E., Leesburg
• **(703) 777-8222**

Doll collectors take note: if you are shopping in Leesburg's historic downtown, a shop that may be of interest is My Friends & Me. Known for its artist bears series, the shop also sells teddy bears and dolls for collectors of all ages. The shop is open from 11 AM to 6 PM Tuesday through Saturday and from 1 to 5 PM Sunday.

Washington and Old Dominion Rail Trail
21293 Smiths Switch Rd., Ashburn
• **(703) 729-0596**

The Washington and Old Dominion Rail Trail runs right through Leesburg and is a delightful place for biking and hiking. This multiuse trail begins at Purcellville and continues east toward Washington, D.C. For information on the trail, call the Northern Virginia Park Authority at (703) 352-5900 or write 5400 Ox Road, Fairfax Station, VA 22039. For those who didn't bring along a bicycle, call Bicycle Outfitters, (703) 777-6126. You can rent a bike for $5 an hour or $20 a day.

Balloons Unlimited
2946 Chainbridge Rd., Oakton
• **(540) 554-2002, (703) 281-2300**

The more adventurous children may enjoy a hot-air balloon ride, a great way to see the area around Loudoun County. Balloons are launched twice a day — around sunrise and late evening — from April through November. The hour-long ride costs $150, young children pay half-price.

Fauquier County

C.M. Crockett Park
62 Culpeper St., Warrenton
• **(540) 788-4867**

The C.M. Crockett Park — a 100-acre park with a 109-acre lake — offers a wide range of activities, from boat rentals, hiking and fishing to special events on weekends at the park's Waterside Amphitheater. Open from 7 AM until dusk, the park has four picnic shelters, plus areas to play volleyball or pitch horseshoes. An entrance fee is charged on the weekends at $3 for resident and $5 for nonresident vehicles.

Warrenton Pony Show
U.S. Hwy. 29 Bus., Warrenton
• **(540) 347-9442**

Fauquier County is the hotbed of horse country with countless steeplechases and horse shows including the marvelous Warrenton Pony Show in late June (see our Horse Country chapter for specifics).

Marriott Ranch
5305 Marriott Ln., Hume
• **(540) 364-3741**

Saddle up for a western trail ride at the Marriott Ranch. Every day but Monday, you can take a guided trail ride of the farm's 4,200-acre Texas longhorn cattle operation. (See our Recreation chapter.) Reservations are required, and the minimum riding age is 10. The whole family might want to take a spin on a hayride or a stage coach, too.

The Flying Circus
Va. Rt. 644, Bealeton
• **(540) 439-8661**

The Flying Circus, south of Warrenton, puts on a different air show every Sunday from May through October (see our Annual Events and Festivals chapter). These are precision aerobatics airshows complete with wing walking and skydiving. Rides are available at the shows, which feature antique open cockpit biplanes. The park has a concession stand and picnic grounds. The gates open at 11 AM, with the shows beginning at 2:30 PM. Admission is $10, $3 if you are between the ages of 6 and 12. The circus is right off U.S. 17. Just follow the signs.

Lake Brittle
4354 Lake Brittle Rd., Gainsville
• **(540) 349-1253**

North of Warrenton visitors will find the 77-acre Lake Brittle. Although you can't swim or camp here, rowboats and canoes are available to rent, and fishing is allowed. A concessions stand and picnic facilities are also on site. The lake opens one hour before sunrise and closes one hour before sunset, year round. You can rent a rowboat for $7, or if you would like one with a motor, it costs $16 per day.

Sky Meadows State Park
11012 Edmonds Ln., Delaplane
• **(540) 592-3556**

Just west of Middleburg, Sky Meadows State Park offers camping, horse trails, picnic areas, fishing and eight hiking trails, including a 3.6-mile stretch of the Appalachian Trail (see our Recreation chapter). The 1,863-acre park is open daily 8 AM to dusk, and entrance fees are required ($2 on weekends, $1 on weekdays). Children ages 3 to 13 pay $1 everyday. If you would like to stay overnight, the camping fee is $8.

Dominion Skating Center
1550 N. Main St., Culpeper
• **(540) 825-3141**

Ever wonder what your parents did for fun when they were young? Well, slip on a pair of roller skates and slide back in time. You can glide across the pecan hardwood floors at this 24-year-old skating rink. It's open from 7 to 9:30 PM Wednesdays, and 7:30 to midnight Fridays and Saturdays. A good time for family fun is during the 2 to 4:30 PM sessions on Saturdays and Sundays. Afternoon admission is $2 and, if you don't bring your own skates, you can rent a pair for 75¢. At night the entry fee is $4. If you work up an appetite, don't worry: the snack bar offers pizza, hot dogs, chips, drinks and ice cream.

Madison County

On the Wild Side Zoological Park
U.S. Hwy. 29, Madison • **(540) 948-4000**

Feed a camel or pet a reindeer at Central Virginia's newest zoo. On the Wild Side Zoological Park features a range of exotic animals, from the park's centerpiece spider monkeys to porcupines, gelded deer and ostriches (see our Attractions chapter). Zoo owner Pam Mogenson raised most of the animals on her 5-acre Madison County farm. Children have a chance to get up close to some animals in a petting area, where sheep and goats will snuggle up for attention. Admission to the zoo is $6, $4 for children 3 to 12 years old.

Rose River Vineyard and Trout Farm
U.S. Hwy. 33, Syria • **(540) 923-4050**

A nice stop for the whole family (see our Wineries chapter), this 177-acre farm operates a winery and trout farm, where kids will enjoy watching the fish in their raceways or lanes. Rose River Vineyard and Trout Farm also has two stocked trout ponds. Just buy some corn bait, borrow one of the farm's fishing poles (they are happy to lend them out) and pay only for what you catch. The farm borders the

Shenandoah National Park and has picnic sites and hiking trails.

Graves Mountain Lodge
Off Va. Rt. 670, Syria • **(540) 923-4231**

If the family gets hungry, stop in at Graves Mountain Lodge, just a mile away, for a magnificent country spread. The lodge is so popular, it's probably best to call ahead for reservations (see our Restaurants chapter). Graves Mountain Lodge also offers horseback riding, swimming, hiking and tennis.

Albemarle County

Virginia Discovery Museum
524 E. Main St., Charlottesville
• **(804) 977-1025**

The Downtown Mall in Charlottesville is a great place for family fun, and the Virginia Discovery Museum is the perfect place to start. Activities include hands-on exhibits, costumes, science programs and an art room especially for children (see our Attractions chapter.) Special events are held throughout the year. Ask about the log cabin.

Charlottesville Ice Park
230 W. Main St., Charlottesville
• **(804) 979-1-ICE**

On the other end of Charlottesville's Downtown Mall is the Charlottesville Ice Park (see our Recreation chapter). This indoor ice-skating rink — yes, you can skate year round — rents skates and offers lessons. It's a beautiful new building, and your family should enjoy the unique experience ice skating on even the hottest days. Public skating times vary, so be sure to call ahead. You might even make it to one of the pick-up hockey hours. Prices average about $5 to $6.

Old Michie Theatre
221 E. Water, Charlottesville
• **(804) 977-3690**

Just off the mall, the Old Michie Theatre entertains families with puppet shows and main stage productions. Husband-and-wife team Frances Furlong and Steven Riesenman work hard to give children quality entertainment in a relaxed atmosphere. They even keep puppets in the lobby for young ones who can't sit still during performances. (See our Arts chapter.)

Community Children's Theatre
Charlottesville • (804) 961-7862

Charlottesville has another organization that brings stage entertainment to kids. The Community Children's Theatre arranges for professional shows to come to the Charlottesville Performing Arts Center for one-night performances throughout the year (see our Arts chapter). The shows, which included *Swiss Family Robinson* and *Roller-skate Express,* are well-done and worth the effort.

Planet Fun
3005 Berkmar Ave., Charlottesville
• (804) 975-4FUN

For more physical recreation, the Planet Fun just off U.S. 29 provides plenty of action. The park has a bumper boat pond with a waterfall, go-carts, batting cages, miniature golf, an arcade, concessions and a soft play center for younger kids. The park is open daily from 10 AM to 10 PM with extended hours on Friday and Saturday. Prices vary for individual activities. Bumper boat rides are $3.50 and $1 for passengers. You have to be at least 48-inches tall to get behind the wheel. Go-carts — you must be 12 or older and stand 60-inches tall to ride alone — are $3.50. To get a little batting practice, you can spend $25 an hour in the batting cage or take 15 swings for $1. Miniature golf rates are $4.25, $3.50 for seniors and children younger than 12. Soft play, $4 for unlimited time, is only for children younger than 12. And quarters will get you tokens for the arcade games. Whew, that should keep you busy.

The Game Place
112 W. Main St. Ste. 2, Charlottesville
• (804) 984-1040

Come in, sit down and play. That's the kind of store you'll find in The Game Place on Charlottesville's historic Downtown Mall. Kids of all ages are invited to pull up a chair and test out their skills with all types of board games. In fact, the shop even holds tournaments almost every Saturday. Midweek sessions of Magic cards also are quite popular.

Not counting the chess sets, you can buy games ranging in price from $2 to $70.

Kegler's
2000 Seminole Tr., Charlottesville
• (804) 978-3999

Just down U.S. 29 is Kegler's, where bowling, miniature golf and an arcade should entertain all. Bowling is $2.85 an hour, or you can play golf for $3.75. They also have pool tables and dart boards. A restaurant, lounge and nursery on site make this a fun family outing. Kegler's is open from 10 AM to 11 PM Monday through Wednesday, 10 AM to midnight Thursday, 10 AM to 1 AM Friday and from noon to 11 AM Sunday. Don't forget your bowling shoes.

Shenanigans
2146 Barracks Rd., Charlottesville
• (804) 295-4797

One local toy store is worth mentioning: Shenanigans, in the Barracks Road North Shopping Center. It's a small shop with lots of interesting dolls, games, costumes and books. Drop by 10 AM to 8 PM Monday through Friday, 10 AM to 6 PM Saturday or noon to 5 PM on Sunday.

Whimsies
2142 Barracks Rd., Charlottesville
• (804) 977-8767

Next door to the toy store is Whimsies, a children's clothing store where you'll find expensive, but beautiful, finely made children's clothes. Shop hours are 10 AM to 7 PM weekdays, 10 AM to 6 PM Saturday and noon to 5 PM Sunday.

Soda Fountain at Timberlake's Drugstore
322 E. Main St., Charlottesville
• (804) 296-1191

Step up to the soda fountain and order an old-fashioned thick milkshake. They come in vanilla, chocolate, strawberry and cherry — regular or extra thick. This spot has been a Charlottesville tradition since the 1890s. You can treat yourself to a sundae, banana split, float or cone or, if you're in the mood, try something from the deli menu. Since it's a drug store, your parents can even get a prescription filled or drop off vacation film to be developed. The Fountain is open from 8:45 AM to 6 PM Monday through Friday and from 9 AM to 5 PM Saturdays.

University of Virginia
Alderman and Massie sts., Charlottesville
• **(804) 924-UVA1**

If your kids are into sports, you've got a smorgasbord of events here (see our Attractions chapter). Athletic events at the University of Virginia run the full gamut from seven home football games to polo and are exciting outings for children. There are also sports camps for young athletes every summer led by members of UVA's coaching staff.

Monticello
Va. Rt. 53, Charlottesville • (804) 984-9800

Charlottesville is steeped in history, and many children will enjoy the "old-fashioned" houses and odd furnishings of landmarks such as Monticello. The home of President Thomas Jefferson is open daily for tours (see our Attractions chapter). And, be sure to ask why Jefferson cut a hole in the floor for his clock.

Ash Lawn-Highland
Va. Rt. 95, Charlottesville • (804) 293-9539

Tour the home of President James Monroe or try to drop by when there's a special event (see our Annual Events and Festivals chapter). Children of all ages can come fly their kites and participate in contests during Kite Day at Ash Lawn, an early May occasion. If you are visiting in the summer, check out the music, puppetry and drama for children at 11 AM Saturdays from July to mid-August. Admission to the outdoor Summer Saturday series is only $4. Don't forget to take along a picnic, and watch for the colorful peacocks. They roam all around the grounds.

James River Reeling and Rafting
Main and Ferry sts., Scottsville
• **(804) 286-4FUN**

Just south of Charlottesville in Scottsville,

Learning new things is part of the fun at many Blue Ridge museums and attractions.

the whole family can drift down the James River on a tube or try a faster pace in a canoe. James River Reeling and Rafting can outfit the whole family. Tubing costs $12, and you can rent a cooler tube for your picnic basket and beverages for another $5. Canoe trips range from the $30 4-mile float to the $75 overnight trip. (Find out more in our Recreation chapter.)

James River Runners Inc.
10082 Hatton Ferry Rd., Scottsville
• **(804) 286-2338**

The scenery is exquisite and the experience of floating down the James River is truly relaxing. Just let the current carry your inner tube. The cost is $12, $5 for a cooler tube. Canoe rides range from $30 for a 3-mile trip to $88 for an overnight adventure. James River Runners also has kayaks, ranging from $16 to $22, and four- and five-man rafts for $16 per person. (See our Recreation chapter for information.)

Balloon Adventures
Boars Head Inn & Sports Club, U.S. Hwy. 250 W., Charlottesville
• **(800) 476-1988, (804) 971-1757**

Take flight in one of the largest passenger balloons in America — 11 stories tall! Chief Pilot Rick Behr, a licensed commercial balloon pilot with more than 3,000 hours of experience, will fly you over scenic Charlottesville and surrounding green fields and woodlands of Albemarle County. Flights are every day at sunrise April 1 through Dec. 1 and in March by appointment. Evening flights are also available. Trips average an hour. Reservations are recommended, especially for weekends. Rates are $135 per person for morning flights and $185 per person for evening rides.

Nelson County

Waltons Mountain Museum
Va. Rt. 617, Schuyler • (804) 831-2000

Even if your children haven't seen *The Waltons'* reruns, they'll enjoy the Waltons Mountain Museum just west of Charlottesville (see our Attractions chapter). This museum is dedicated to Nelson County native Earl Hamner Jr., the creator of the hit TV show, and his wonderful family. The museum, in the school where the Hamners studied, is a grouping of sets from the series, with actual scripts, photos and memorabilia. Kids can see videos of special shows and interviews with Hamner and the cast.

Wintergreen
Va. Rt. 664, Wintergreen • (800) 325-2200

Wintergreen Resort, about 50 minutes from Charlottesville, has loads to do for children — skiing, swimming, horseback riding, hiking, camp programs, craft workshops, canoeing — and plenty for parents as well (see our Resorts chapter). During the summer, Wintergreen offers children's daily and weekly programs geared for ages 2 to 5 and 6 to 12. In the cooler winter months, kids 17 and younger ski for free when accompanied by an adult on Family Days.

Lynchburg

Lynchburg is the major metropolitan city in this part of the Blue Ridge, and history and shopping beckon in many forms for the children to have an enjoyable day.

Masseys
601 12th St., Lynchburg • (804) 847-3535

You wouldn't think that a shoe store would interest kids, but you'll want to trot them into Masseys, a downtown outlet and a division of

Craddock-Terry Shoe Factory, where children can eyeball a pair of size 21 shoes! The more than 300,000 pairs of shoes includes a great children's selection (and a big selection of socks to go with them). The prices are often real bargains, and it's worth a night over in Lynchburg for the variety and savings before heading back to school. (See our Shopping chapter.)

The Farmer's Market
Memorial Ave. at the River Front Blvd.

Here's another busy, bustling, wonderful place for young people. This open-air arena offers everything from homemade candy and baked goods to beautiful fruits and vegetables for the viewing and eating.

Pest House Medical Museum and Confederate Cemetery Old City Cemetery
Fourth and Taylor sts., Lynchburg • (804) 847-1465

Here children can take a tour of Dr. John Jay Terrell's medical office with its 1860s hypodermic needles and primitive medical instruments. The amputating blades used on Civil War soldiers always attract grave attention and bring the war down to a more human level that kids don't always get from a textbook. (See our Civil War and Attractions chapters.)

Point of Honor
112 Cabell St., Lynchburg • (804) 847-1459

This restored home of Dr. George Cabell gives a slice of 19th-century life. Children are fascinated to hear that the name comes from the gun duels fought on its lawn! And most school children have heard Patrick Henry's "Give me liberty or give me death!" speech, so take them to Red Hill, which was home to the famous lawyer and his 17 — yes, 17! — children. They can see Henry's home, original law office, kitchen and garden as they were before his death. (See our Attractions chapter.)

Poplar Forest
Va. Rt. 661, Forest • (804) 525-1806

This is Thomas Jefferson's summer home.

It is being renovated and offers indoor and outdoor views of painstaking historical restoration through ongoing archeological digs. Kids are always fascinated with Jefferson's solidly designed outdoor solid-rock privies. (See our Attractions chapter.)

Smith Mountain Lake

Bridgewater Plaza
Va. Rt. 122 at Hales Ford Bridge

Hales Ford Bridge is the center of life at Smith Mountain Lake. At Parrot Cove or Bridgewater Marina, you can rent pontoons, Jet Skis or go Parasailing. Your family can even rent a 51-foot-long houseboat at Parrot Cove. Call ahead to reserve so you won't be disappointed. They're not cheap; Jet Ski rentals go for $60 an hour! If you want to go fishing, look up some good guides, such as Bob King, in the "Fishing" section of our Recreation chapter.

You can call the Smith Mountain Lake Chamber/Partnership at (540) 721-1203 to learn the names of other guides. Although you can do some impromptu lake expeditions in your rented boat, you may want an expert to show you where the action is. If it's rainy, Bridgewater Plaza has a terrific arcade with nearly 50 different video and skill games offering tickets for prizes. The ice-cream parlor is right next door and you can eat your treat either sitting on the decking on a pretty day or inside if the mercury is rising. There are several nice gift shops for browsing.

Gifts Ahoy
Bridgewater Plaza, Hales Ford Bridge
• **(540) 721-5303**

The selection is quite impressive for a small shop with toys both children and adults will enjoy. Here, you may find Beenie Babies or huge stuffed animals along with greeting cards and seasonal displays.

The Little Gallery
Bridgewater Plaza, Hales Ford Bridge
• **(540) 721-1596**

This small treasure has unique crafts and paintings, many lake-oriented. At Christmas, this is the only place we know where Santa

Parasails into a shopping center to hand out candy to good girls and boys on the deck outside.

Smith Mountain Lake State Park
Off Va. Rt. 626 S. • (540) 297-4062

You won't be disappointed at this park. Relatively new, the beach is beautifully situated looking at the mountains, and a nearby campground and Turtle Island make an enchanting voyage from the beach for the little ones.

Sal's Pizza
Fairway Village, Westlake Corner on Booker T. Washington Hwy.
• **(540) 721-8904**

This restaurant is authentically Italian, very inexpensive and serves large pizzas. The wonderful salad bar appeals to adults and youngsters alike. (See our Restaurants chapter.)

Bedford

Bedford City/County Museum
201 E. Main St., Bedford
• **(540) 586-4520**

Children can soak up history effortlessly at the Bedford City/County Museum with its Civil War artifacts and other well-displayed items. Bedford is about 20 miles from the park at the lake. (See our Civil War and Attractions chapters.)

Elks National Home
931 Ashland Ave., Bedford
• **(540) 586-8232**

At Christmas, one of the biggest displays of lights in the United States is showcased here at the Elks National Home. The retired Elks work on the exhibit all year, and it shows come December. (See our Attractions chapter.)

Franklin County

Booker T. Washington National Monument
Va. Rt. 122, Hardy • (540) 721-2094

This place is centered around the famous

educator's birthplace. The video on how a 9-year-old rose above slavery to become one of the most inspirational leaders of his time will fascinate everyone. The film addresses Washington's hard life and meager existence and is a historic sojourn into a time in America when slavery was a way of life. The site also has a beautiful restored farm — with lots of farmyard animals contained with split-rail fences — that will uplift you after viewing Washington's triumph over hardship.

Blue Ridge Institute Museum
Ferrum College, Ferrum • (540) 365-4416

Here you can find an 1800 German-American working farmstead with log house, oven, outbuildings, pasture and garden that demonstrates the lifestyles of early colonists. Also visit the Blue Ridge Institute with its many exhibits and archives, which are internationally recognized for excellence. Exhibits have included toys, walking sticks, canes and quilts. (See our Attractions chapter.)

Blue Ridge Folklife Festival
Ferrum College, Ferrum • (540) 365-4416

At this festival, children can play games from the 1800s, see workhorses bigger than trucks and eat fare such as flannel cakes with original recipes. It's wonderful, wholesome fun for the entire family, and even city kids are in awe when they leave.

Wythe County

Historic Millwald Theatre
Main Street, Wytheville • (540) 228-5031

You can watch the latest movies in Virginia's oldest motion picture theater in continuous operation. This grand old building showed its first film in August 1928 and it's still going strong. During the summer Millwald hosts two shows nightly with a 2 PM matinee on Sundays. From September to May, you can catch a 7:30 PM movie Sunday through Thursday. There are still two shows each on Friday and Saturday. The price is pretty reasonable. In 1999 it's just around $3 for the young ones, about $5.50 for mom or dad.

New River Valley

Blacksburg and Radford

Virginia Tech
Blacksburg • (540) 231-5396

The New River Valley is synonymous with Virginia Tech, the state's largest land-grant university. It's a 45-minute drive down I-81 from Roanoke. Tech in itself is the major attraction in Blacksburg and one the children will enjoy touring. City children will enjoy the perfect farm animals and agricultural experimental stations that raise extraordinary farm livestock and hybrid crops, the likes of which you won't see anywhere else.

The most popular spot at Tech is the Duck Pond. Small children are enchanted by the pampered fowl who lord over the spot and hold court for visitors. Brazen at times, they've no qualms about coming to the kids to get a snack. These ducks are definitely more intelligent than most and definitely more aggressive!

For kids who like to bike, Blacksburg has some of the nicest bike trails in the nation, so bring your bikes.

Cascades State Park
Off Va. 623, Pembroke • (540) 265-5100

One of the biggest attractions in western Virginia can be found right outside of Blacksburg, 20 minutes from U.S. 460, at this beautiful park. College students and people from all over the nation come to hike the trail to the fabulous Cascades waterfall. It's recommended for children who can hike 3 miles and is no — we repeat, no — fun for small ones. Plan on keeping your eye on adventurous children of all ages to prevent falls off the waterfall. (See our Recreation chapter.)

Radford Bisset Park Pool
off Norwood St. • (540) 731-3633
Blacksburg Public Pool
Graves Ave. • (540) 961-1103

If you're thinking about going swimming, the town pool at Blacksburg and the city pool at Radford, home to Radford University, are two of the nicest in the Blue Ridge. The park at Radford, beside the New River, is a joy for children. They can walk or bike beside the New River and then picnic in the gazebo. It's one of the most impressive, inexpensive things a family can do and has to be one of the most wonderful parks in the Blue Ridge due to its New River setting.

Pulaski County

Claytor Lake State Park
Off I-81 at Exit 33 • (540) 674-5492
This lake south of Radford is a man-made body of water lined with clean, white sandy beaches, boat rentals and a beautiful campground. It's a good base for sightseeing throughout the Valley.

Floyd County

Floyd County General Store
Floyd County • (540) 745-4563
This store will be a treat for any child. Tins of canned possum, roadkill and other country eye-openers make this a must-see, and the tiny stores offering arts and crafts usually have lots of homemade wooden toys and folk crafts.

Alleghany Highlands

The Homestead Resort
Va. Rt. 34, Hot Springs • (800) 838-1766
At The Homestead, children can join the resort's KidsClub. This is a daily program with different topics each day. These include Senses Day, Magnet Day and Tree Day. The activities last from 9 AM to 3 PM and include free play, movies, experiments, art, pool activities and bowling. The kids will learn to make their own kaleidoscope, underwater world, door-knob signs and much, much more. The cost for a full day is $45, including lunch. Variations of this price depend upon whether the kids want a whole day or half day. There are many other attractions at The Homestead, including shops and restaurants. The kids will have no problem being entertained no matter what they do. (See our Resorts chapter.)

Greenbrier Resort
U.S. Hwy. 60, White Sulphur Springs, W.Va. • (800) 624-6070
Here children can enjoy a wide variety of attractions. These include the surrounding shops around the resort as well as the snack bars. Prices for an ice-cream sundae are a little high at the Greenbrier, but the ambiance is worth the extra cost just to hear the kids "ooh" and "ahh" at the fancy desserts and elegant surroundings. The shops include both toy stores and boutiques with some rare finds you'd expect to see on Fifth Avenue. Some items are reasonably priced while others are outrageous. They're guaranteed entertainment for a Sunday afternoon. (See our Resorts chapter.)

Blue Bend
Alvon, W.Va. • (304) 536-1440
This is a favorite swimming hole in the Monongahela National Forest in nearby Alvon, West Virginia. Some say the swimming spot got its name because that's the color swimmers turn when they hit the icy water. Kids love the idea. (See the listing for Monongahela National Forest in our Recreation chapter.)

The largest colony of artists in residence in the country, the Virginia Center for the Creative Arts, is in the remote foothills of the Blue Ridge in Amherst County.

The Arts

Whew! For a relatively sparsely populated region, the Blue Ridge of Virginia offers abundant and diverse opportunities for arts and cultural experiences. Listing the best and brightest is a difficult task, since they're all backed by energetic people who believe strongly in the cause they promote.

Fine arts, folk art, history and pop culture blend well in these Blue Ridge counties. Maple sugar is celebrated at its own museum in Highland County. Alleghany County has one of the largest railroad archives in the United States, the province of the C&O Railroad Historical Society.

If music is your leisure choice, try Friday night flat-footing at Floyd County General Store where fiddles, autoharps and a 1940 jukebox hold forth. Or, you can attend chamber music fests at Garth Newel Music Center in Bath County, where you'll probably rub elbows with jet-setters who patronize The Homestead Resort.

Historically, the Charlottesville area is one of the country's best-known tourist cities, with such attractions as Montpelier, Monticello and Ash Lawn-Highland, the former homes of three of our greatest presidents. A half-million visitors a year make the trek to the neoclassical mansion designed by the third president of the United States, Thomas Jefferson. Farther south is Jefferson's summer getaway at Poplar Forest in Bedford County. In the hills of Pulaski County, visitors stroll through an 1810 village in Old Newbern and see what life was like nearly two centuries ago.

Theater opportunities range from movies to live performances. Worldly chic Charlottesville, home to numerous movie stars and directors, hosts the biggest names in the movie business during its annual Virginia Film Festival. More than 20,000 people show up to view film classics and hobnob with celebrities, who usually attend the opening gala.

If historical drama is more to your liking, you can attend Virginia's outdoor drama, *The Long Way Home*. This stirring true saga of Mary Draper Ingles's capture by Indians and escape home through nearly 1,000 miles of wilderness to Radford has riveted audiences for 25 years.

No matter how small, nearly every community in the Blue Ridge has its own performing theater group, some comprised of as few as a dozen people, as in sparsely populated Giles County. In small-town Lexington, Lime Kiln Theater enjoys a national reputation for its open-air plays and musical performances in a magical setting. Staunton residents Robin and Linda Williams of public radio's *A Prairie Home Companion* with Garrison Keillor are regulars. Middletown's Wayside Theater, just south of Winchester, attracts patrons from Washington, D.C., to its summer performances, which often include big-name actors who love the area.

Museum buffs will find a surprising range and quality of offerings in the Blue Ridge. The works of world-famous artist P. Buckley Moss, "the people's artist," whose annual revenues have been estimated well into the millions, can be seen in her private retreat and museum at Waynesboro.

Not to be underestimated for the role they play in the region's arts and culture are the diverse programs underwritten by colleges and universities. The contributions of academic giants such as Virginia Tech in Blacksburg and the University of Virginia in Charlottesville are immeasurable.

The largest colony of artists in residence in the country, the Virginia Center for the Creative Arts (affiliated with Sweet Briar College), is in the remote foothills of the Blue Ridge in Amherst County. And tiny Ferrum College in Franklin County is the nation's most important repository of Blue Ridge culture through its Blue Ridge Farm Museum, Institute and Folk Life Festival.

Education in the arts doesn't begin on the college level. In culturally rich Lynchburg is the Virginia School of the Arts, one of the few secondary schools in the nation tailored for these pursuits.

The cultures of many ethnic groups are celebrated in the Blue Ridge. In Roanoke, the Harrison Heritage Museum for African-American Culture exists to celebrate and remind western Virginia of the rich contributions of its black citizenry. In her day, African-American poet Anne Spencer was a celebrity in Lynchburg, entertaining a steady flow of world dignitaries at her home and grounds, which are now open to the public by appointment. In her meticulous garden, she chatted with Martin Luther King Jr., Paul Robeson, Marion Anderson, Thurgood Marshall, Dr. George Washington Carver and Jackie Robinson. Congressman Adam Clayton Powell even honeymooned there.

Enjoy making your choices from the attractions listed. Hours and prices may change, so be sure to call ahead.

www.insiders.com
See this and many other **Insiders' Guide®** destinations online.
Visit us today!

Shenandoah Valley

Frederick County

Theater

Shenandoah Summer Music Theatre
Shenandoah University, 1460 University Dr., Winchester • (540) 665-4569
Student actors, singers and dancers perform four lively musicals June through August, Wednesday through Sunday, at the university. A subscription to all four shows is $58 for Friday and Saturday nights, $54.40 for other nights and matinees, with discounts for seniors and children for matinees only.

Wayside Theatre
7853 Main St., Middletown
• (540) 869-1776, (800) 951-1776
The second-oldest professional theater in the state brings the best of Broadway to the valley from June to December. The company's professional actors from New York and around the country perform comedies, dramas, musicals and mysteries in an intimate downtown theater. The 1997 playbill included *Marvin's Room* and the British farce *A Bed Full of Foreigners*. Wayside stages *A Christmas Carol* every winter. The theater is in the middle of this little town, which you'll find by taking Exit 302 from I-81.

Tickets range from $17 to $20. Children 17 and younger pay $7.50. There are group discounts for groups of 20 or more. The theater is wheelchair-accessible.

Shenandoah and Page Counties

Visual Arts

John Sevier Gallery
Congress St. and Old Cross Rd., New Market • (540) 740-3911
Set in a little log cabin in the heart of the downtown, this gallery specializes in art by Shenandoah Valley artists. It also sells locally made crafts such as woodwork, ornaments, stained-glass windows and fine photographs. One wall is set aside for an Artist of the Month display. The gallery is open from 10 AM to 5 PM Thursday through Monday.

Dance

Plains Promenaders Square Dance Club
Luray • (540) 896-7913
This group of about 60 dancers meets for classes and workshops every Tuesday night September through May at the Plains Elementary School in Timberville. Members get together for dances on the second and fourth Saturdays each month. Some of the more advanced dancers also perform at special events and festivals around the area, including Heritage Days at Skyland. The group has been around for about 28 years.

Music

Shenandoah Valley Music Festival
221 Shrine Mont Cir., Orkney Springs
- **(800) 459-3396**

This 36-year-old outdoor summer music festival features symphony pops, classical masterworks, folk, jazz and Big Band music, all performed on the grounds of the former Orkney Springs Hotel, a popular spa and mineral springs resort at the turn of the century. Evening concerts are held on weekends between Memorial Day and Labor Day in a rustic open-air pavilion. Arts and crafts shows featuring regional artisans take place on the hotel's front lawn on the symphony concert weekends.

Another festival tradition is the old-fashioned ice cream social held next to the pavilion before each concert. Don't worry about your attire. It's casual and relaxed. Admission prices and concert times vary. Tickets for the 1997 season ranged from $11 to $16 for adults. Student and children's tickets were $7 and $4, respectively. You might want to call in advance, especially if you want seating under the pavilion. The show will go on, rain or shine. For information and a free season brochure, contact the festival's Woodstock headquarters.

Many guests picnic on the grounds before concerts.

Rockingham County

Visual Arts

Sawhill Gallery
JMU campus, Duke Hall, Harrisonburg
- **(540) 568-6407**

This free gallery exhibits five or six shows of diverse art during the year. The summer exhibition is traditionally geared for children. Sawhill is open seven days a week during the academic year, weekdays only during the summer. Call ahead to confirm hours.

Theater

Court Square Theater
Liberty St., Harrisonburg
- **(540) 564-1998**

This renovated, historic building in the heart of downtown Harrisonburg is home to live performances, films and concerts. When the facility opened in 1998, the Blue Ridge Theater Festival moved in as the resident professional drama troupe. From May to October the company performs a series of six plays, including *Shenandoah*, a dramatic musical set in the Shenandoah Valley. During the past four years, the Blue Ridge Theatre Festival also has staged shows in historical settings in Hungary, Romania, the Czech Republic, Moldavia and at the Edinburgh Festival in Scotland. The local plays cost just under $15, or dinner-and-theater packages can be arranged with the new Calhouns Restaurant and Mirco Brewery. Once a month, Court Square Theater hosts a popular music series that has already booked 10,000 Maniacs, Leon Russell and Seldom Scene, to name a few. Concert prices vary, but are usually in the $15 to $20 range. The movies — which are more in the line of art-house films instead of the likes of an *Armageddon* — cost about $5.50.

James Madison University Masterpiece Season Series
JMU campus, Wilson Hall, Harrisonburg
- **(540) 568-7000**

This 20-plus event series features a wide array of shows. JMU faculty and staff put on theater, dance and music performances. Professionals also come in to do family and encore shows, ranging from the Vienna Boys Choir and the Richmond Ballet to *A Chorus Line* and *Some Like It Hot*. Shows run Sep-

---

INSIDERS' TIP

Summer is a great time to see outdoor theater and music productions at unique venues such as Lexington's Lime Kiln Theatre and the Ruins at Barboursville, once the estate of Virginia governor James Barbour.

tember through April. Admission varies from $5 for the JMU productions to $20 for the road companies.

Latimer-Shaeffer Theatre
JMU campus, Harrisonburg
• **(540) 568-7000**

In addition to James Madison theater, music and dance department shows, this on-campus theater also holds summer performances. Two children's shows in June and one family show in the summer round out the venue's offerings. Admission ranges from $5 to $8.

Shenandoah Shakespeare Express
U.S. Hwy. 33, Thomas Harrison Middle School, Harrisonburg • (540) 434-3366

This globe-trotting company of 12 actors stages the Bard's plays the way they used to be seen — on a bare stage, surrounded by an audience on three sides. Clad in black slacks, turtlenecks and tennis shoes, this company strips away 400 years of accumulated theatrical trappings to focus on the language of the plays. The formula has worked for young and old alike. Since the company started in 1988, SSE has performed in 40 states and five countries. The troupe has done hundreds of shows at high schools and universities across the country, and the actors came back home to open the 1997 season fresh off a sold-out run at the Folger Shakespeare Library in Washington, D.C.

If you hit Harrisonburg during the summer, you're in luck. The troupe stages seven weeks of repertory action at the Thomas Harrison Middle School. Show times are 7:30 PM Tuesday through Friday and 2 and 7:30 PM Saturday. Tickets are $9, $7 for students and seniors and $5 for children 12 and younger. The 1997 playbill included *Love's Labor's Lost*, *A Midsummer Night's Dream* and *Henry IV, Part 1*.

Call for a schedule. The Express may show up in a town near you.

Augusta County

Visual Arts

Shenandoah Valley Art Center
600 W. Main St., Waynesboro
• **(540) 949-7662**

This nonprofit cultural center has been an all-volunteer organization for more than 12 years. An affiliate of the Virginia Museum of Fine Arts in Richmond, the center provides a forum for artists of all diversities to exhibit their works. Housed in a beautiful old former residence downtown, the center holds art exhibits, music and drama performances, workshops and classes for children and adults. The center also sponsors readings of prose and poetry and even music-appreciation lectures. The galleries are open 10 AM to 4 PM Tuesday through Saturday and 2 to 4 PM Sunday. Admission is free.

Staunton-Augusta Art Center
1 Gypsy Hill Park, Staunton
• **(540) 885-2028**

An old pump house at the entrance to the beautiful Gypsy Hill Park in Staunton is headquarters for this art center, an affiliate of the Virginia Museum. It puts on 10 exhibitions a year, displays art by area elementary and high school students every March and exhibits works of local artists throughout the year. In addition, the art center offers classes and workshops for children and adults throughout the year. The third Saturday every May, the center hosts a huge outdoor art show of works by more than 100 artists. In the fall, the center is converted into an "arts for gifts" shop, where local crafters can display their wares. The cen-

---

INSIDERS' TIP

The first Friday of the month is a special day for art lovers. That's the day when cities such as Charlottesville and Leesburg play host to a flurry of open houses at art galleries, studios and shops. Drop by and enjoy free refreshments and you might just get a chance to meet the featured artists.

P Buckley Moss. **MUSEUM**
Waynesboro, Virginia

*Exhibiting works by one
of America's most popular
artists...*
Free Admission * Guided Tours
* Museum Shop

Open daily, 10-6; Sunday 12:30-5:30
I-64, Exit 94 (540) 949-6473

ter is open from 9 AM to 5 PM weekdays. Admission is free.

Valley Framing Studio & Gallery
328 W. Main St., Waynesboro
• (540) 943-7529, (800) 821-7529

Valley Framing Studio is the area's most comprehensive art gallery, carrying the largest inventory of artwork in Central Virginia. The gallery specializes in limited edition prints and represents nearly 100 percent of the major print publishers in the art world. The work of artists such as Bev Doolittle, Robert Bateman, Steve Lyman, Charles Wysocki and Charles Frac is available here. Civil War and aviation art lovers will recognize works by Troiana, Kuntsler, Gallon, Harvey, Phillips and Kodera. Valley Framing also has an extensive inventory of local and regional artists' prints, bronzes and ceramics. The gallery is open year round from 10 AM to 5 PM Monday through Friday and 10 AM to 3 PM Saturday and by appointment.

Museums

P. Buckley Moss Museum
2150 Rosser Ave., Waynesboro
• (540) 949-6473

The museum dedicated to this former resident of Augusta County resembles many of the large houses built by early 19th-century settlers. Since the early 1960s, Moss has found her inspiration and much of her subject matter in Shenandoah Valley scenery and in the area's Amish and Mennonite people. Although the artist was born in New York, she moved here in the mid '60s.

Born with what later was diagnosed as dyslexia into a family of high achievers, Moss was ridiculed and taunted as a child for her lack of academic prowess. She hid her childhood sorrow in her painting, and eventually her family recognized her artistic genius. As a result, she now uses her foundation profits, guided by the worldwide Moss Society, to help needy children. Whenever she travels, she makes it a point to visit pediatric hospital centers to encourage children.

The museum's displays examine the symbolism in her work and her sources. Guided tours are available. The museum and shop are just south of I-64 at the Waynesboro West Exit 94. The hours are 10 AM to 6 PM Monday through Saturday and 12:30 to 5:30 PM Sunday. Admission is free.

Theater

Fletcher Collins Theater
Deming Hall, Mary Baldwin College, Staunton • (540) 887-7189

Every academic year the theater department at this women's college produces four

Musical instruments of the Blue Ridge region are frequently exhibited at the Blue Ridge Institute at Ferrum College.

Photo: Richard T. Nowitz/The Roanoke Valley Convention and Visitors Bureau

or five major plays, ranging from musicals by Gilbert and Sullivan to Shakespearean productions and several modern and experimental plays. Call for schedules. Admission prices range from $3 to $6.

Oak Grove Players
232 W. Frederick St., Staunton
• **(540) 885-6077**

This amateur theater company produces five plays every summer in the middle of a grove of oak trees 2 miles west of Verona. Founded in 1954 by Fletcher Collins, the retired head of Mary Baldwin College's theater department, Oak Grove Players is one of the oldest amateur outdoor theaters in the country. A lot of patrons picnic on the grounds before the plays, which range from *The Lion in Winter* to *The Foreigner*. Admission is by season subscription only, although patrons are allowed to buy tickets for their out-of-town guests. The Oak Grove Players were the first to perform *The Nerd*, a play by the late Larry Shue, who still has family in Staunton. The shows run nightly at 8:45 PM starting in June.

ShenanArts Inc.
Staunton • (540) 248-1868

ShenanArts is a nonprofit performing arts company that produces a variety of plays and musicals and hosts a retreat for playwrights every summer at the Pennyroyal Farm, c. 1808, just north of Staunton. Performances take place at the Pennyroyal Farm in warm weather and at a variety of other locations in the winter. The arts corporation also offers theater programs for youth, one of which led to a full-blown production of a rock opera, *The Wall*, in 1992. A touring company performs throughout Virginia and West Virginia. One of the traveling shows is a play about AIDS geared for teens and performed entirely by teenage actors. The annual Shenandoah Valley Playwrights Retreat has been going on for more than 20 years and hosts writers from all over. The 1997 season included a Theater for Youth series and a Cabaret Series designed for grownups. Patrons could see all three youth plays for $18, while the Cabaret's $15 to $19 ticket also served up coffee and dessert. *Love Letters* and *All I Really Need to Know I Learned in Kindergarten* were just two of the entrees last season.

Waynesboro Players
Various locations, Waynesboro
• (540) 885-4668

This nonprofit amateur theater made up of actors from Waynesboro, Staunton, Augusta County and surrounding areas has been around since the 1940s. They perform three plays a year, in addition to some dessert-theater offerings at local schools and community centers. Most of the plays are performed at the Waynesboro High School auditorium. Tickets range from $7 to $9. Contact Bill Robson at the above phone number.

Music

Shakin'
Downtown Staunton sites • (800) 332-5219

It seems almost everyone in Staunton turns out for this outdoor summer concert series.

All kinds of bands, from rock 'n' roll to country, perform at a downtown location every Thursday from 6 to 8 PM. One year Mary Baldwin College hosted the festivities; but for the past couple of years, Shakin' shook the Johnson Street parking lot near the recently refurbished train station. Call for locations and dates. The music party runs mid-May through August. This is another freebie.

Stonewall Brigade Band
Gypsy Hill Park, Staunton
• (800) 332-5219

This is reportedly the oldest continuously performing band in the nation. Formed in 1855, the band gave its first public concert before the Civil War. Today local musicians keep the tradition alive with free performances every Monday night at 8 PM during the summer months. If you went every week, chances are you still wouldn't hear the band's entire repertoire. Playing between 10 to 20 songs each show, the Stonewall Brigade Band performs nearly 150 different songs each season. There is one exception: each show ends with the National Anthem.

Queen City Acoustic
909 Clemmer Ln., Staunton
• (540) 886-5362

Joe Dockery, a chiropractor by day and musician by night, had a plan to bring some of the top performers in the folk music industry to Staunton. He knew that many of the stars traveled the I-81 corridor from shows in Philadelphia and Washington, D.C., to other gigs in Charlotte, N.C., and Atlanta. Why not, he reasoned, offer them another chance to perform along the route? So in 1998, he created Queen City Acoustic, a nonprofit corporation that stages a series of six Thursday night concerts in the Cabaret space at McCormick's Restaurant. He got the idea after watching a concert at the Birchmere in D.C. "I like seeing the performers really close up," he said. "It's just much more of an intimate experience. It adds to the soulfulness of the art." Among the stars booked for the 1999 series were Christine Lavin, Patty Larkin, Garnet Rogers, Freyda Epstein with Missy Raines and Jim Hurst, Steve Forbert and Greg Brown, whose music has been featured in several motion pictures.

Prices for the concerts range from $15 to $20. You can save about $3 if you call in advance.

free, ships purchases and accepts most major credit cards.

Rockbridge County

Visual Arts

Art Farm Galleries
Va. Rt. 39, near the Virginia Horse Center, Lexington • (540) 463-7961

Chinese artist and teacher I-Hsiung Ju started the Art Farm in 1975 as a "farm to raise young artists." A retired professor of art at nearby Washington & Lee University, Dr. Ju conducts summer workshops in the traditional Chinese method of painting. Students come from all over the country to live for a week at the farm and learn from Dr. Ju. The first and second floors of a remodeled house display the artist's paintings and serve as both galleries and classrooms. Many of his works are reasonably priced; all are beautiful.

Artists in Cahoots
1 Washington St., Lexington • (540) 464-1147

This well-filled gallery is run by a cooperative of local artists and crafters who somehow manage to put out beautiful works of art at reasonable prices. The collection encompasses paintings, prints, etchings, photographs, ceramics, jewelry, decoys, sculpted art glass, wood and metal crafts. The Treasure Trove contains Sandage jewelry designs, the extraordinary metal and clay sculptures of Milenko Katic, Virginia clay jewelry and Lexington commemorative pottery by Maureen Worth, Margaret Carroll's expanded designs in stained glass, innovative works by photographer Nathan Beck and paintings by Roy and Pauline Petteson. Feather textured decoys by John Owen complete the array. The artists staff the shop themselves and chat with patrons as they create. The shop gift wraps for

Theater

Lime Kiln Theatre
Lime Kiln Rd. • Box Office, 14 S. Randolph St., Lexington • (540) 463-3074

The Roanoke Times called it "one of the most agreeable spots in the Western World." Performances at the outdoor Theater at Lime Kiln celebrate the history and culture of the Southern mountains. What makes the place unique — even enchanting — is its setting in what was once a limestone quarry. Lime Kiln is best known for its annual musical, *Stonewall Country*, a rollicking tribute to local Civil War hero Thomas "Stonewall" Jackson. Robin and Linda Williams, favorites of Garrison Keillor's *A Prairie Home Companion* and long-time friends of Lime Kiln, wrote the music for *Stonewall Country*. Audiences return year after year to experience this Shenandoah Valley summer tradition. Also performed is *Glory Bound*, by local playwright Tom Ziegler, who also wrote *Apple Dreams*, which debuted to rave reviews at Lime Kiln in 1993. The 1997 bill also included the 1996 Regional Playwriting Contest winner, *Uncivil War*, by John J. Wooten. You can also catch the renowned Folk Tale Festival, wholesome entertainment for the whole family, which is an annual event at Lime Kiln.

Lime Kiln's popular Coors Concert Series always offers an eclectic slate of musicians. This Sunday-night concert series features nationally known musicians performing bluegrass to zydeco music.

Lime Kiln has picnic areas with tables and grills, and vendors sell some food and drinks. The site is wheelchair-accessible and has a big-top tent in case of bad weather, so performances take place rain or shine. Group rates are available.

INSIDERS' TIP

Lights! Action! Camera! The Blue Ridge has been the setting for many television programs and movies, including *Lassie*, *What About Bob?*, *Dirty Dancing*, *Sommersby* and *The Waltons*, based on the Nelson County upbringing of its creator, Earl Hamner Jr.

Virginia Film Festival

For four days in October, the stars shine a little brighter in Charlottesville. But you won't need to cart along a refracting telescope. A simple movie ticket will give you one of the best views in town.

For the past 12 years, the Virginia Film Festival has brought some of the biggest stars in show business to venues across the city. Screenwriters, critics, directors, producers and, yes, even those who have made their living in front of the camera come to town to share their old classics, preview their works in progress or just give their views of life in Hollywood.

Over the past decade, Film Festival-goers have been treated to insights from some of the best in the business, including Gregory Peck, Sidney Poitier, Robert Duvall, Eva

Marie Saint, Charlton Heston, Ann Margaret, Fay Wray, Nick Nolte, local resident Sissy Spacek and the late Jimmy Stewart and Robert Mitchum. But Bob Chapel, chair of the hosting Drama Department at the University of Virginia, said that "no other honored guest has had a career that has been so expansive in regards to working in film and theater and the television industry" than 1997's featured guest, Jason Robards.

"I did some of the early television," Robards said with a gruff laugh. "But not many people saw it. I was going to be on television one night and, my wife, she got on the roof and looked around to see where there was a television antenna. Nobody had a set back then.

"She saw an antenna, so she went down four blocks and rang the bell at this walk-up apartment and said, 'My husband is on television, can I ...?' They said 'Oh, yes, please come in.' And she watched it with them."

Fifty years later, Robards's audience has grown substantially. The two-time Oscar winner (for *All the Presidents Men* and *Julia*) recently starred with former Albemarle County resident Jessica Lange in *A Thousand Acres*. But, as Film Festival fans found out, acting wasn't Robards first love.

Although his father, Jason Robards Sr., was an actor, the younger Robards tried like the dickens to avoid show business. He had seen his father's career shine on the stages of New York but dim under the glare of Hollywood's searchlights. So young Jason joined the Navy. In fact, he was at Pearl Harbor when the Japanese attacked.

"I thought I was going to stay in the military 20 years, retire when I was 37 and then live on my pension," the silver-haired actor said with a good-natured grin before the start of festival opening reception. "After the war came along, I thought I better get out."

It was during his Navy days that Robards was introduced to the work of Eugene

— continued on next page

Photo: Ron Batzdorff

Jason Robards was a guest at the 1997 Virginia Film Festival in Charlottesville.

Long Day's Journey Into Night, starring from left, Jason Robards, Dean Stockwell and Katharine Hepburn, was shown at the 1997 Virginia Film Festival.

O'Neill, America's only Nobel-winning playwright.

"I was on a flagship, and they had a library and I saw a book," he said. "The book was *Strange Interlude*. I said 'Oh, this has got to be a risqué, book, I think I will take it and see what it looks like.'"

But the book turned out to be a play, a play that would eventually tug Robards into the acting life.

"I was not an actor," he said shaking his head. "My father was an actor. But he discouraged me from being an actor, and I discouraged myself. But that book was the first thing that really got me going. Then I saw O'Neill in an original production of *The Iceman Cometh*. It mesmerized me. So 10 years later, when they were doing a revival of the play, I begged them to put me in."

He landed the part and for years polished his craft on stage, mainly in plays by O'Neill. When he agreed to attend 1997's Virginia Film Festival, it was only fitting that Robards should bring along a Eugene O'Neill film, *Long Day's Journey Into Night*.

"I never made a film until I was almost 40," the Academy Award-winning actor said. "It was always done to make an alimony payment. I didn't take it very seriously. Oh, I love going to the movies, but I didn't want to be in them. I was born in the theater."

But again, Mr. O'Neill helped Robards alter his opinion. When Hollywood decided to film *Long Day's Journey*, Robards had been living the role on stage for two years.

"I wanted to do it because of O'Neill," Robards said. "I think he is our greatest playwright. *Long Day's Journey* is really a picture of a play. It's not a screenplay. It's exactly like the play."

Robards drew a standing ovation when he introduced the 1962 classic at 1997's Film Festival. Hundreds of fans — who paid $6 for the treat — stuck around after the movie to hear Robards talk about O'Neill, the film and co-stars Katherine Hepburn, Ralph Richardson and a young Dean Stockwell.

— continued on next page

"I got to do it on stage and do it on the screen," he said. "That doesn't happen too often. Usually they recast for the screen . . . but they kept me. And this time I wasn't doing it for the money. I was doing it because I had respect for the material. I was doing it because I loved it."

The festival's fans seemed to love the opportunity hear the inside story. And that's what the Virginia Film Festival brings to the community — a chance to be entertained and educated.

Of course, Robards's story is just one of many that has fascinated movie lovers over the last dozen years. Roger Ebert, Rip Torn and director Arthur Penn were among the featured guests who visited in 1998. Ebert, the only film critic ever to win a Pulitzer Prize, drops by the festival every other year to conduct his popular shot-by-shot workshop (he maintains a busy schedule that won't allow him to attend every year). Aside from writing for the *Chicago Sun-Times*, his reviews are syndicated in 305 newspapers in the United States, Canada, England, Japan and Korea, and he compiles a nearly 1,000-page movie guide every year. His 1995 *Video Companion* featured an essay on Robert Mitchum's visit to the Virginia Film Festival, while his 1996 edition included a story on his local "Pulp Fiction" workshop. Ebert's three-day, six hour sessions have, by far, been among the most popular events in the local festivals, selling out well in advance of opening night. Last year Ebert and a few hundred viewers analyzed Michelangelo Antonioni's 1966 hit *Blowup*. Ebert also appeared on a panel discussion with Torn and Penn after the opening-night screening of *Mickey One*.

Penn, director of such classics as *Bonnie and Clyde* and *Little Big Man*, is president of the Actors Studio. Torn, an alumnus of the legendary Actors Studio school, joined Penn to discuss the role the studio had in nurturing talented stars, the likes of Marlon Brando, James Dean and Paul Newman. Penn also was on hand for a screening and discussion of his film *Alice's Restaurant*, while Torn introduced his 1973 film, *Payday*. Most people probably remember Torn for his roles as Zed in *Men in Black* and as Artie in the hit HBO series *The Larry Sanders Show*. He also is the first cousin of Albemarle County resident Sissy Spacek.

All told at the 1998 festival, more than 35 films were screened over a four-day period, ranging from the classic *West Side Story* to the premier of Paul Rodriguez's new film *Melting Pot*.

Each year the festival also includes a couple of free panels, where would-be screenwriters or hopeful producers can pick up a few pointers on how to get started in the business. But for those who just love to rub elbows with the bigwigs, the Festival offers several special events, including an opening night gala ($40) and a Saturday night reception ($15). To find out who will be the featured guests this October, call (800) UVA-FEST. The curtain will rise on October 21.

The organization sponsors the Regional Playwriting Contest, which it started in order to encourage the creation of plays relevant to this region and as an outreach to the community. During the fall, winter and spring, Lime Kiln's resident artists go to area schools, clubs and civic and senior groups and, when schedules permit, accept bookings throughout the summer as well.

Plays run Tuesday through Saturday, and concerts are performed on Sunday from Memorial Day through Labor Day. Performances begin at 8 PM nightly.

Music

Lenfest Center for the Performing Arts
Washington & Lee University, Lexington
• (540) 463-8000

W&L's Lenfest Center is the cultural heart of Lexington, offering lively arts, including national performers in concert, W&L's own University-Rockbridge Symphony Orchestra and other music department performances. The center offers a Concert Guild Series, Theater Series and Lenfest Series featuring performances to appeal to all artistic tastes.

Roanoke Valley

Roanoke

Visual Arts

Arts Council of the Blue Ridge
Center in the Square, Level 1, 20 E. Church Ave., Roanoke • (540) 342-5790

The heart and soul of the cultural community in the Roanoke region, this council provides services and information to its more than 70 member organizations and artists throughout the Blue Ridge region. The Arts Council has taken the lead in urban homesteading, focusing on downtown living areas. In 1998, it showcased downtown apartments. Programs include a quarterly newsletter; the City Art Show, a regional juried art exhibition held annually; Art in the Window, which offers free display space for artists and children; the Perry F. Kendig Award for Outstanding Support of the Arts; and the regional High School Art Show. The Council also published *Blueprint 2000*, the first community-wide cultural plan in the region and is currently implementing many of its recommendations. Through a grant from the NEA, the Council established an after-school arts program, published a regional cultural directory, built a kiosk advertising cultural events in downtown Roanoke and established a funding resource center. Office hours are Tuesday through Friday 9 AM to 5 PM.

Art Museum of Western Virginia
Center in the Square, Levels 1 and 2, One Market Sq., Roanoke • (540) 342-5760

The Art Museum of Western Virginia emphasizes American art of the 19th and 20th centuries. Collections include works by Hudson River school of artists and contemporary American painters, printmakers and photographers. The museum has also acquired a fine Japanese print collection. Many works by Auguste Rodin are available for viewing. The sculpture court holds impressive pieces, and the folk art gallery presents works by artists of the southern mountains. Museum education programs feature lectures, family days, tours, films, performances, classes and workshops. Its rotating exhibitions are of regional, national and international significance. ArtVenture is an interactive art center for children. You can purchase regional American crafts and folk art in the museum store. The museum is open 10 AM to 5 PM Tuesday through Saturday and 1 to 5 PM on Sunday.

Theater

Grandin Movie Theatre
1310 Grandin Rd., Roanoke • (540) 345-6177

Yes, you can still see a movie in a gorgeous cinematic theater like the ones that prevailed years ago throughout America. Julie Hunsaker and the Lindsey family have rescued this fine structure, one of Roanoke's greatest cultural treasures. Comedian Bill Murray of *Saturday Night Live* and *Ghostbusters* fame did a benefit for the Grandin, remarking that places like the Grandin should never be forgotten or destroyed. You can see classics and newer movies for the best prices in town, often $1.95 specials. This cavernous, popcorn-scented architectural masterpiece will thrill its guests, especially children who have never seen anything quite like the tiled floors, mahogany candy cases and ornate decor of the Grandin.

Mill Mountain Theatre
One Market Sq., Roanoke • (540) 342-5740

"New York quality in the Blue Ridge" is how this year-round professional theater has been characterized. Enjoying an association with Actor's Equity Association, Mill Mountain Theatre has become known as one of the best regional theaters in the country based upon its new and original works, lavish musicals, innovative classics, creative children's plays and musicals and dramas. Each October, the annual New Play Competition culminates in the finalists' plays being presented in the Theatre B facility as part of the Norfolk Southern Festival of New Works. A family-oriented musical is scheduled for the winter holiday season, followed by a classic later in the winter. Spring ushers in a comedy or drama followed by two musicals in the summer. Tickets are reasonably priced and vary according to performance date and time.

In addition, once a month from October through June, the Theatre presents Centerpieces, free script-in-hand readings of new plays at a bring-your-lunch series. Educational and drama enrichment programs round out the offerings. Mill Mountain Theatre recently celebrated its 34th year of continuous operation. It attracts performers such as Donna McKechnie, the Tony Award-winning star of *A Chorus Line*, who chose this venue for a pre-New York tryout. Others, such as Robert Fulghum (who worked with the Theatre to develop a dramatization of his books), Sheldon Harnick and Stephen Schwartz, have all been in residence at MMT.

Music

Opera Roanoke
The Jefferson Center, 541 Luck St., Roanoke • (540) 982-2742

Standing ovations are the norm for Opera Roanoke, Southwest Virginia's professional opera company. Led by Artistic Director Craig Fields, the company engages up-and-coming singers in innovative productions. Opera Roanoke presents its productions at Roanoke's Mill Mountain Theatre and at Roanoke College's Olin Theater in Salem. Favorites such as Mozart's *The Magic Flute* and Leoncavallos's *I'Pagliacci* are showcased with top talent who portray the passion, humor, beauty and tragedy of life. Breaking away from the tried and true at times, the company recently presented Monteverdi's *L'Orfeo*, one of the first operas ever written.

Opera Roanoke goes an extra step by projecting English translation supertitles over the stage to be sure that opera goers can follow every turn of the plot. Before each performance, an informal lecture, "Director's Notes," enlightens, educates and entertains both the novice and opera buff.

The Roanoke Symphony Orchestra and Roanoke Valley Choral Society
541 Luck Ave., Ste. 200, Roanoke • (540) 343-6221

Quality performances, superb musicians, innovative programs and exceptional guest artists are the hallmarks of the Roanoke Symphony and Roanoke Valley Choral Society. New Music Director and Conductor David Wiley's first season lead the organization to sold-out concerts and rave reviews. Wiley is also an accomplished pianist and composer.

The orchestra was founded in 1953 and is the only professional orchestra in Virginia west of the Blue Ridge Mountains. The Roanoke Valley Choral Society, a 100-voice community chorus that performs with the orchestra, joined with the RSO in 1994. In addition to the Monday Night Classics series, which consists of classical symphonic and choral works, RSO&RVCS also offers a pops series, a family series, and special-event concerts, which include contemporary and popular music.

The RSO&RVCS has three affiliate organizations that support it both financially and in human resources: The Roanoke Symphony Volunteer Association, The Friends of the Roanoke Symphony and The New River Valley Friends. It is also supported by national and regional grants and individual and corporate contributions. Education is a major focus through a Youth Symphony and annual educational concerts.

The RSO&RVCS has an impressive record of guest artists. Tony Bennett, Willie Nelson, Roberta Flack, Chet Atkins, Norman Krieger, Leon Bates, Bruce Hornsby, Richard Stoltzman and many other respected musicians have performed with the group. The orchestra and choral society have a live recording of Beethoven's

Historic re-creations offer a chance to travel back in time.

"Symphony No. 9" and has plans for another recording in April 1998.

Literary Arts

Literary Festival
Hollins Theatre, Hollins University, Roanoke • (540) 362-6224

This small university in the foothills of the Roanoke Valley has fostered an amazing number of talented authors. Three alumni — Annie Dillard, Henry Taylor and Mary Wells Ashworth — won Pulitzer Prizes. Margaret Gibson and Madison Smartt Bell were nominated for National Book Awards and Margaret Wise Brown is known far and wide for her children's classics, including *The Runaway Bunny*. Others, such as Tama Janowitz (*Slaves of New York*) and Elizabeth Forsythe Hailey (*A Woman of Independent Means*) have seen their work turned into movies. Hollins also started one the country's first writers-in-residence programs and, word has it, Nobel Prize winner William Golding was living at the college when his *Lord of the Flies* became a best-seller. Nancy Parrish even penned a book about the university's literary reputation, *Lee Smith, Annie Dillard and the Hollins Group*. Since 1960, Hollins has celebrated its success with an annual literary festival in early April. During its 39th festival in 1999, Hollins combined its annual event with the dedication of the new Wyndham Robertson Library. Robertson, a 1958 graduate, was a former editor of *Fortune* magazine. Among those who attended the 1999 festival were Taylor, Dillard, Smith, Janowitz, Parrish, Gibson, Bell, Jill McCorkle, Elizabeth Morgan and writer-in-residence Brendan Galvin, author of *Sky and Island Light*.

East of the Blue Ridge

Rappahannock County

Visual Arts

Middle Street Gallery
Corner of Gay and Middle sts., Washington • (540) 675-3440

This nonprofit artists' cooperative features

museum-quality paintings, photography and sculpture. Exhibitions change monthly, and classes are offered for adults and children. The gallery is open Friday through Sunday from 11 AM to 6 PM and by appointment.

Theater and Music

The Theatre at Washington
Gay and Jett sts., Washington
• **(540) 675-1253**
This theater is known for its professional dramatic and musical performances, including the noted Smithsonian at Little Washington chamber music series. Call for a free brochure. Tickets range from $10 to $15. Children get in for half price.

Ki Theatre
Gay and Jett sts., Washington
• **(540) 675-1616**
This is actually a performing arts center that serves as home to two groups: Ki Theatre and the Ki Community Arts program. The first is made up of Obie-award winning playwright and performer Julie Portman and musician Paul Reisler. The two create original plays, which they perform at Ki Theatre and at locations across the country. Reisler scores the productions and Portman writes and performs them.

Ki Community Arts program unites local professional and amateur talent in the fields of theater, dance, music, storytelling and the visual arts.

Call the box office to find out schedules and ticket information.

Orange County

Visual Arts

Ed Jaffe Gallery
108 Main St., Orange • (540) 672-2400
A traditional carver, Ed Jaffe exhibits his

work in a museum-like setting. Sculpture, mostly done in marble, and oil pastels by Jaffe are on display and for sale in this 5,000-square-foot studio and gallery situated in the heart of Orange. If the flag is out front, the gallery is open. In case the artist is working, just ring the bell and wait. Jaffe will show you around. If you are traveling any distance, please call ahead.

Beth Gallery and Frederick Nichols Studio
U.S. Hwy. 33, Barboursville
• **(540) 832-3565**
Artist Frederick Nichols Jr. has his studio and gallery in a renovated general store across from the railroad tracks. He calls his work "photo-impressionism." He does enormous colorful landscapes of Blue Ridge scenes using either oil paint or a silk-screen process. A friendly fellow, Nichols will give tours through the gallery and studio. The gallery is open daily by chance or by appointment. Nichols' career took off a few years ago when he won top honors at an international print exhibition in Japan.

Theaters

Four County Players
Barboursville • (540) 832-5355
This 25-year-old theater company out of Barboursville produces Shakespearean plays, full-scale musicals and children's productions. Most productions are performed at the Barboursville Community Center. But in August Shakespeare productions are staged in a most magical setting: the ruins of what was once the estate of James Barbour, governor of Virginia (1812 to 1814), Secretary of War and ambassador to the Court of St. James. Thomas Jefferson, a friend of Barbour's, designed the house, but it was destroyed by fire on Christmas Day 1884. Overgrown boxwoods tower over the ruins, adding to the air of enchantment about the place. The award-win-

ning Barboursville Vineyards are within walking distance. Among the works staged recently were *The Sisters Rosensweig* and *Greater Tuna*.

Call for a season brochure and ticket information. Admission prices range from $4 to $14, depending on the performance.

Albemarle County

Visual Arts

Biscuit Run Studios
981 Old Lynchburg Rd., Charlottesville
• (804) 977-5411

A father and son team produce stone-and-glass sculptures at this production and display gallery. Their works can be seen in front of many public buildings in the Charlottesville area and a few in Roanoke. David and Christian Breedan call their style "old-fashioned abstract." Sculptures range from 6 inches to 20 feet. Stop in and see the artists in action. Someone is usually on hand from 7 AM to 7 PM every day. The gallery is two miles off U.S. 64 at the Fifth Street Exit.

Fayerweather Gallery
Fayerweather Hall, Rugby Rd.,
Charlottesville • (804) 924-6122

This university gallery next to the Bayly Art Museum has regular exhibits by faculty, student and contemporary artists, so it's naturally where the staff of the UVA Art Department likes to hang out. Fayerweather is open Monday through Friday from 9 AM to 5 PM.

Frances Christian Brand Galleries
111 Washington Ave., Charlottesville
• (804) 295-5867

Call before you drop by this eclectic gallery, which is actually a private home containing the art collection of Frances Christian Brand, now deceased. Cynthia Brand, her granddaughter, gives tours by appointment and likes to have people over for coffee while they admire the rooms full of pre-Colombian pottery, Mexican art, African masks and sculptures, and paintings done by Frances Brand. Tours are free, but donations are accepted.

McGuffey Art Center
201 Second St. N.W., Charlottesville
• (804) 295-7973

A renovated elementary school within walking distance of historic Court Square and the downtown pedestrian mall houses this arts cooperative begun in 1975 with city support. Its light, airy rooms have been transformed into more than 32 studios where you can sometimes watch artists and crafters work. Studios also house dancers. The center has two galleries, an excellent gift shop and the independently run Second Street Gallery. Exhibits, tours and gallery talks are available to the public from September through July. McGuffey offers classes in children's art, printing, painting, papermaking and drawing. Hours are 10 AM to 5 PM Tuesday through Saturday and 1 to 5 PM Sunday.

Second Street Gallery
201 Second St. N.W., Charlottesville
• (804) 977-7284

Looking for a space to showcase contemporary works, 11 area artists got together in 1973 and started the first artist-run alternative gallery in Central Virginia. In 1991, the National Endowment for the Arts named Second Street one of two model art organizations in the country. A free opening reception and gallery talk usually kicks off a new exhibit each month. Works by artists from Virginia, Connecticut, Ohio and Massachusetts were featured in 1997. Second Street also holds special programs, tours and workshops throughout the year. The gallery, in the renovated McGuffey Art Center, is open from 10 AM to 5 PM Tuesday through Saturday and 1 to 5 PM Sunday.

Gallery Neo
108 Second St. N.W., Charlottesville
• (804) 979-0563

This two-story independently owned gallery has been showcasing contemporary work since 1994. While Neo schedules several group shows throughout the year, its monthly exhibitions usually showcase the work of a single artist. In 1997, the displays ranged from works by area artists to a special presentation by Christopher Makos. Makos, an internationally known photographer, was a member of pop icon Andy Warhol's inner circle of friends. Neo is open from 10 AM to 5 PM Monday through Friday and on the weekends by chance or by appointment. You might want to call if you are planning a weekend visit.

bozART Gallery
211 W. Main St., Charlottesville
• (804) 296-3919

Twenty-four artists make up this cooperative effort. They take turns staffing the space, and every month a different artist's work is featured in the front of the gallery. The rest of the exhibit area is devoted to the other members. A new show opens the first Friday of each month with a reception from 6 to 9 PM. If you can't make it for the free food and drink, drop by to see the artwork from noon to 7 PM Tuesday through Sunday.

Newcomb Hall Artspace Gallery
Newcomb Hall, UVA campus,
Charlottesville • (804) 924-3286

The University of Virginia's budding artists have a home again. This student-run gallery operated as a "gallery without walls" while Newcomb Hall was undergoing renovations. Resourceful students found that construction fences made wonderful oversize canvases in the interim, but now the young artists can hang their works indoors once more on the third floor of Newcomb. Not only do students have a place to host their shows, they also bring in an ever-changing variety of art, including panels from the heartbreaking AIDS quilt.

V. Earl Dickinson Building for the Humanities and Social Sciences
Va. Rt. 20 and I-64, Charlottesville
• (804) 961-5203

Piedmont Virginia Community College opened this brand new $7.1 million facility in August 1998. A major boost to the arts in the Charlottesville area, this 36,000-square-foot multi-level building is home to a 500-seat theater, a black box theater for rehearsals and smaller productions, an electronic music lab, classrooms, artist studios with floor-to-ceiling windows and a double art gallery with 140 feet of exhibition space. A smaller gallery in PVCC's main building also offers monthly exhibitions of students' works. The new gallery hosts works by local, state and national artists. The college also stages plays throughout the school year, and hosts concerts and dance performances by students as well as visiting artists. There is no charge to stop by and view art exhibits, but fees will vary with staged shows. The galleries are open 9 AM to 10 PM Monday through Thursday, 9 AM to 5 PM Fridays and 1 to 5 PM Saturdays.

Under the Roof
1017 W. Main St., Charlottesville
• (804) 971-1327

Part contemporary furniture store and part espresso bar, Under the Roof exhibits a wide variety of works mainly by local artists. A new exhibit is displayed about once every two months. Hours are 10 AM to 7 PM Monday through Saturday and noon to 5 PM Sunday.

Museums

Bayly Art Museum
Rugby Rd., Charlottesville
• (804) 924-3592

The University of Virginia's own modern museum has a permanent collection of ancient pottery, sculpture and some paintings, along with special, short-term exhibitions such as photographs by David Plowden or 19th-century Japanese prints. Italo Scanga, a sculptor from the University of California, San Diego, served recently as artist-in-residence. String quartets and other classical music groups also perform here at certain times during the year. The Bayly hosts lectures, workshops and arranges members' trips to other regional galleries. The museum is open Tuesday through Sunday from 1 to 5 PM. Tour groups should call (804) 924-7458 to arrange an appointment.

INSIDERS' TIP

For other Arts-and-Culture offerings, be sure to check out our Annual Events and Festivals chapter.

Theater

Community Children's Theatre
Charlottesville • (804) 961-7862

Since 1953 this company has brought affordable family theater to the Charlottesville community. Professional actors perform in four productions a season, which have recently included *Pippi Longstocking* and *Swiss Family Robinson*. Tickets, $6 in advance or $8 at the door, are sold at the door an hour before curtain and at other locations around town prior to performances. The theater offers children's workshops in the winter with an artist in residence. Performances are held at the Charlottesville Performing Arts Center. Call for a brochure and a schedule.

Heritage Repertory Theatre
Culbreth Rd., UVA, Charlottesville
• (804) 924-3376

This highly praised professional theater produces a series of five plays from late June through early August at the University of Virginia. The productions vary from musicals and comedies to light dramas and thrillers. Superb acting, directing and set design make this series well worth the effort. In conjunction with UVA's Department of Drama, Heritage served as the originating stage for two Broadway-bound productions: *A Few Good Men* with Tom Hulce and *The Roads to Home*, written and directed by Pulitzer Prize-winning Horton Foote and starring Jean Stapleton.

Ticket prices vary widely from $9 to $23, depending on showtime. Call after June 1 to receive a free brochure.

Live Arts
609 E. Market St., Charlottesville
• (804) 293-7595

Live Arts, one block off the Downtown Mall, is home to a resident theater company, the Live Arts Theater Ensemble. A local favorite, LATE produces everything from original plays to well-known Broadway musicals in an intimate setting. The theater began in 1990 in Charlottesville and is working at becoming a professional company. The center hosts theater, dance, poetry readings, performance art and music events and provides a space in which other groups may perform. Call to hear a recording of the latest calendar of events. Tickets are usually priced between $10 and $12. You can knock $3 off the price if you become a Live Arts member.

The Old Michie Theatre
221 E. Water St., Charlottesville
• (804) 977-3690

Professional puppet shows and main-stage plays at this theater entertain young audiences throughout the year. A husband and wife team, Frances Furlong and Steve Riesenman, run the theater, now in its 12th season. Their drama school offers classes during the academic year and a full-day summer camp. The repertoire features classic and new plays for children, from *The Wizard of Oz* to *Old English Folktales*. Every fall, the main-stage selections include *The Legend of Sleepy Hollow*. Tickets range from $5 to $6 for all ages. Those younger than 24 months get in free. Puppet season passes are also available for $28. Call for schedule and tickets. Ask about reduced group rates. They welcome birthday party groups.

University of Virginia Department of Drama
UVA, Charlottesville
• (804) 924-3376

This is UVA's main student theater group, producing at least six high-quality major stage shows every academic year on two stages. The Culbreth Theater seats 595, while the smaller Helms Theater suits a more intimate setting of 160 to 200. Productions have ranged from *Macbeth* and *Fiddler on the Roof* to *Hair* and *A Raisin the Sun*. Prices vary, so call the box office between 10 AM and 6 PM Monday through Friday for a schedule.

Dance

Chihamba
Allied Ln., Box 3286, Charlottesville
• (804) 296-4986

The Chihamba of Dancescape celebrates and educates people about African cultures through music and dance. Ongoing programs include concerts, lecture demonstrations, workshops and African craft sessions in beading, weaving, tie-dying, leather work, mask making and sand painting. Dance performances often feature live African drumming and are really something to watch. The company recently added Chihamba Junior for children ages 4 through 13. Chihamba also sponsors the annual African-American Cultural Arts Festival the fourth Saturday in July at Washington Park, featuring entertainment, venders, food and activities throughout the day. Call to find out about upcoming performance dates.

The Miki Liszt Dance Company
201 Second St. N.W., Charlottesville • (804) 295-7973

Based at the McGuffey Art Center, this nonprofit company performs locally, conducts workshops with guest artists and offers lectures and demonstrations in nursing homes, schools, hospitals, libraries and museums. Its mission is to expose audiences to new currents in dance performance while giving regional dancers the opportunity to create and perform new work. The company also sponsors the annual Community Children's Dance Festival in the spring.

Music

Ash Lawn-Highland Summer Festival
James Monroe Pkwy., Charlottesville • (804) 293-9539

Every summer the festival's professional opera company stages a repertory of two operas and a classic musical at the restored home and gardens of President James Monroe. It's perfect for the opera novice; all the shows are sung in English. Those more in tune with the genre will enjoy the cast's skill. Members of the 1997 company have sung with companies across the United States, including the Metropolitan Opera. All performances are held in the estate's scenic Boxwood Gardens or, in the event of rain, under the new pavilion. Other festival events include a music at twilight series — ranging from Mozart duets to toe-tapping Appalachian fare — every Wednesday night and children's programs on Saturday mornings. Opera tickets range from $15 to $22. Music at Twilight is $10, $9 for seniors

and $6 for students. Picnicking is encouraged before the shows. In fact, you can even reserve a catered gourmet dinner if you don't want to pack your own basket. Ash Lawn-Highland also hosts a variety of events throughout the year. Call to receive a free brochure.

Old Cabell Hall
UVA, Charlottesville • (804) 924-3984

Situated at the south end of the famous college lawn, this newly renovated auditorium has been restored to its turn-of-the-century grandeur. Home to more than 80 concerts throughout the academic year, Cabell hosted violinist Cho-Liang Lin and cellist Janos Starker in 1997. The beautiful, bowl-shaped concert hall has wonderful acoustics, making this a favorite venue for musicians. Offerings include a symphony series, artist faculty series, jazz ensemble and the Tuesday Evening Concert Series, a Charlottesville tradition for more than four decades. Tickets are usually $4 to $6 but can go up to $18 for some performances. The box office will be happy to mail you a free brochure or take your ticket reservations. Call between 10:30 AM and 5 PM Monday through Friday.

Prism Coffeehouse
214 Rugby Rd., Charlottesville • (804) 97-PRISM

This nonprofit volunteer organization presents folk, acoustic and traditional music from around the world in a casual smoke-free, alcohol-free setting. Formed in 1966, the Prism is one of America's oldest surviving coffeehouses. The Coffeehouse hosts concerts each weekend from September through May, and local songwriters meet here for jam sessions. The last Thursday of each month is a free acoustic blues night, while the fourth Tuesday is set aside for a beginner's old-time jam session. It's a happening place; call to hear an extensive recording of the events calendar or to reserve tickets. Weekend performances usually cost between $12 and $14.

Tuesday Evening Concert Series
Old Cabell Hall, UVA campus, Charlottesville • (804) 924-3600

Since November 30, 1948, the Tuesday

Evening Concert Series has given Charlottesville audiences the opportunity to hear some of the world's finest classical musicians. Over the last 50 years, the playbill has read like a list of Who's Who, including Grammy winning cellist Yo-Yo Ma, soprano Dame Joan Sutherland, flutist Jean-Pierre Rampal, violinist Pinchas Zukerman and Russian violist Yuri Bashmet. Today people travel from as far as Winchester and Richmond to attend the six-concert series. Because the series is so popular, tickets are hard to come by. Your best bet is to get a subscription to the entire series, but individual tickets — if there are any remaining — go on sale at the box office two weeks before each concert. There is also a waiting list for any returned tickets. Individual tickets for the 50th anniversary season, which ran from October 6, 1998, to April 6, 1999, were $22 for orchestra seating, $18 for loge and balcony. Season tickets were $110 and $90.

The Westminster Organ Concert Series
190 Rugby Rd., Charlottesville
• (804) 293-3133

Held every year at Westminster Presbyterian Church, this series of concerts offers organ music combined with other instruments and singers. Professional local and visiting musicians make these superb performances. The church's Taylor and Boody tracker-action pipe organ, styled after 17th-century German organs, was handcrafted in the Shenandoah Valley and plays beautifully. The five-concert series is held Friday evenings at 8 PM September through April. The 1997 season featured organists from the Lincoln Center and Oppenau, Germany. Concerts are free.

Literary Arts

Virginia Festival of the Book
Charlottesville • (804) 924-3296

Charlottesville confirms its status as Virginia's writers' capital with this festival. The event attracted more than 100 writers to four days of programs in 1997. Designed to celebrate the book in all its forms, the festival brought in a record attendance of 13,725. The 187 programs, which include book fairs, lectures, signings, panel discussions and readings, are mostly free. John Grisham, bestselling author and Albemarle County resident, was the keynote speaker at the sold-out luncheon one winter. Also on the impressive list of writers who attended in '97 were former U.S. Poet Laureate Rita Dove, Gay Talese, Barbara Parker, Madison Smartt Bell, Donald Justice, Sharyn McCrumb, George Garrett, Nikki Giovanni and Mary Lee Settle. The festival, now in its sixth year, is held in late March at various sites across the city.

Virginia Film Festival
UVA campus, Charlottesville
• (804) 924-FEST, (800) UVA-FEST

This festival is dedicated to celebrating and exploring the unique character of American film. It lasts for four days in late October and brings leading actors, filmmakers, scholars, critics and the public together to discuss American film in a serious way. Dozens of films are shown at venues throughout Charlottesville, most followed by fascinating discussions with representatives from the films.

The event has attracted national attention by featuring special events that honor the history of American film. These have included a 50th anniversary "encore premiere" of *Mr. Smith Goes to Washington*, with its star, the late James Stewart, in attendance.

Other renowned actors and filmmakers who have participated in the festival include Gregory Peck, the late Robert Mitchum, Sissy Spacek (a Charlottesville-area resident), Charlton Heston, Sidney Poitier, Robert Duvall, John Sayles, Ann Margaret, Eva Marie Saint and Roger Ebert.

This stimulating and exciting event is well worth factoring into your fall vacation. More than 8,700 attended last fall. Special discount hotel-and-event package rates are available. Admission prices are reasonable — slightly lower than commercial theater tickets — though premieres and galas cost more. The Academy Award-nominated *Shine* was among the list of premieres in 1996. Call to receive a free catalog and ticket information.

Amherst County

Theater

Virginia Center for the Creative Arts
Mt. San Angelo, Sweet Briar
• (804) 946-7236

Located on the beautiful Mt. San Angelo Estate, this surprising artistic treasure is just outside of Lynchburg in Amherst County. It is the nation's largest continually operating working retreat for professional writers, artists and composers. Artists who visit from abroad are often the leading creative forces in their own countries. Some of the most important exchanges between artists worldwide take place here. The Virginia Center for the Creative Arts is supported in part by the Virginia Commission for the Arts and is affiliated with Sweet Briar College, a private woman's college.

Because the VCCA is a working retreat for artists, the buildings are not normally open to the public. The VCCA holds special exhibits and meet-the-artist receptions in the Camp Gallery during the summer which are open to the public. Other public events, such as poetry readings with international writers-in-residence, are cosponsored with Sweet Briar College.

Lynchburg

Visual Arts

Lynchburg Fine Arts Center
1815 Thomson Dr., Lynchburg
• (804) 846-8451

The 1998-99 season marks the 36th anniversary of the Lynchburg Fine Arts Center. An affiliate of the Virginia Museum of Fine Arts in Richmond, the center serves the region with live theater performances in its 500-seat theater; classes and workshops in drama, art, dance and music; and exhibits by area artists in the center's two galleries. The Lynchburg Regional Ballet Theatre is the center's resident dance company, performing two ballets each season and offering classes in ballet, tap and jazz for all ages and levels. The cos-

tume shop has more than 5,000 costumes, which the public may rent.

Maier Museum of Art
Randolph-Macon Woman's College, 1 Quinlan St., Lynchburg
• (804) 947-8136

Known for its collection of 19th- and 20th-century American paintings, the Maier Museum of Art at prestigious Randolph-Macon Woman's College displays works by artists including Winslow Homer, James McNeill Whistler, Mary Cassatt and Georgia O'Keeffe. Also featuring special exhibitions and programs, this tremendous community asset is well worth the visit for art lovers. The museum is open September through May from 1 to 5 PM Tuesday through Sunday, with summer hours from 1 to 4 PM Wednesday through Sunday.

Theater

Cherry Tree Players
4925 Boonsboro Rd., Lynchburg
• (804) 384-4577

The Players is a group of artists, musicians, business people, directors, technicians and others who have come together to advance the arts and theater in the Lynchburg area. Recent productions have included *The Importance of Being Earnest* and *Pippin*. There is an active children's and youth theater as well. Admission is $10 for adults. No children younger than 6 may attend.

Other Cultural Attractions

Virginia School of the Arts
2240 Rivermont Ave., Lynchburg
• (804) 847-8688

The Virginia School of the Arts, a nonprofit residential and day school for talented high school students, is dedicated to preparing young people for careers in the performing arts and furthering their academic studies. Graduates often attend colleges or universities on full scholarship, and many have joined prominent professional companies. It is one of only six such schools for the arts in America, and students come from throughout the United States. Its arts faculty includes professional performers who contribute greatly to Lynchburg's culture.

Bedford County

Sedalia Center
1108 Sedalia School Rd., Big Island
• (804) 299-5080

The Sedalia Center, "for the art of living and the living arts," is a regional, nonprofit organization offering programming in the arts, culture, environmental awareness, health and inner development. It offers classes, workshops, seminars, coffeehouse performances and special events that, the Center mission states, ignites and nourishes the creative process in each person. The center's modern building is set on 14 acres in the foothills of the Blue Ridge near Big Island. Special events include dancing, storytelling, art and music festivals and the Country Fair, held on the third Saturday of October. Sedalia Center Stages are held the second Saturday of every month and are always a sure bet for great music — the summer season is held on the outdoor stage.

Among the more than 100 classes and workshops offered are those in oil, watercolor, sculpture, pottery, dance, Tai Chi, yoga, meditation, use of active solar heating, conservation and landscape design. Black Powder Blasts offer competitions in early-American skills with muzzle-loaded rifles, tomahawks and knives. A small but dedicated group of creative people makes the Sedalia Center the heart of a special culture for people of the Blue Ridge foothills.

Franklin County

Theater

Blue Ridge Dinner Theatre
Ferrum College, Sale Theatre in
Schoolfield Hall, Ferrum
• (540) 365-4335

Now in its 20th season, the Blue Ridge Dinner Theatre continues to operate on the three guiding principles of theater: discovery,

wholesome family entertainment and celebration. It also serves up a great luncheon or dinner in combination with everything from murder mysteries to great historical masterpieces. Adjacent to the Blue Ridge Institute, the Dinner Theatre also offers theatergoers tours of the facility. Ferrum's theater group, the Jack Tale Players, continues the legacy through acting out legends of the South. Members of the audience are invited to discuss issues related to the day's performance with guests and senior members of the BRDT staff at a free discussion series, the Greenroom Dialogues.

Performances are varied, with hours at 12:15 PM and 6:45 PM. Admission for the matinee luncheon and performance is $13.50 for adults and $8.50 for children younger than 14. Evening dinner and performance admission is $16.50 for adults and $11.50 for children. Special group rates are available for groups of 10 or more. Reservations are recommended for all performances.

New River Valley

Montgomery County

Visual Arts

Armory Art Gallery
201 Draper Rd., Blacksburg
• (540) 231-4859

One of several art galleries at Virginia Tech, Armory Art Gallery is operated by the school's Department of Art and Art History as an educational and outreach program. The 1,000-square-foot gallery, in the Old Blacksburg Armory, has a year-round rotation of exhibits by national or regional artists, work by student artists and other shows of community interest. The gallery is open Tuesday through Friday from noon to 5 PM and Saturday from noon to 4 PM.

Burde Outdoor Sculpture Court
Radford University, Radford
• (540) 831-5754

This display of sculpture in a unique open-air museum setting features pieces from the entire region. Most work is highly contemporary, produced in a variety of media including metal, wood and cement. The collection is designed to represent all styles of contemporary sculpture.

Flossie Martin Gallery
Radford University, Radford
• **(540) 831-5754**

This modern facility occupies 2,000 square feet on the beautiful Radford University campus. The combination gallery and museum features rotating exhibits of both regional and nationally known artists.

The gallery's roster has included Andy Warhol, Winslow Homer, sculptor Dorothy Gillespie and a collection of narrative yarn paintings by Huichol Indians of the Mexican Sierra Madre. Hours are 10 AM to 4 PM Monday through Friday, noon to 4 PM on Sunday and extended hours of 6 to 9 PM on Thursday during fall and winter.

Bondurant Center for the Arts
1115 Norwood St., Radford
• **(540) 831-5324**

In 1998 Radford unveiled a new cultural center in what had once been one of the premiere shopping stores in the downtown area. As in many towns across the country, when shoppers switched to malls, many downtown shops began to suffer. But a million-dollar transformation has given this Norwood Street center a boost, making way for a restaurant, several businesses, a multi-use room capable of accommodating 300 people for special events and a second floor dedicated to the visual arts.

Radford University stages ongoing exhibits here throughout the year. The gallery hours are 1 to 5 PM Monday through Friday and 1 to 4 PM Sundays.

New River Valley Arts Council
Christiansburg
• **(540) 381-1430**

This active organization publishes an arts directory; a lively quarterly magazine, *Expressions*; and a roster of local artists. It's a rich source of information on the arts in the region.

Perspective Art Gallery
Squires Student Center, Blacksburg
• **(540) 231-5200**

Also at Virginia Tech, Perspective Gallery offers a range of artistic styles and media by artists ranging from internationally known professionals to students. The gallery, a facility of the University Unions and Student Activities, also offers talks and receptions where the public can meet featured artists.

XYZ Cooperative Gallery
223 N. Main St., above College Inn, Blacksburg • **(540) 231-5547**

XYZ was created through a cooperative venture by Virginia Tech art students, and the gallery continues to be student coordinated and staffed. A lively exhibit gallery, it sponsors continuing shows that are characterized by their vitality and unique range.

Theater

The Long Way Home Outdoor Drama
Ingles Homestead Amphitheater, Radford
• **(540) 639-0679**

Virginia's only historical drama, now in its 29th season, relates the true story of Mary Draper Ingles' capture and daring escape from Shawnee Indians. In July 1755 during the French and Indian Wars, Mary, along with her two sons, Thomas and George, and her sister-in-law Bettie Draper were captured at Drapers Meadows (now the Virginia Tech Campus in Blacksburg). They were taken North to about present-day Portsmouth, Ohio, where Mary was separated from her family. Forced to travel west 800 miles to make salt for the tribe, she made a heroic escape and traveled about 800 miles in 45 days back to Radford to warn of an upcoming attack. The saga is re-enacted on the very spot where Mary Ingles lived out her days upon her return to the New River Valley, in the Ingles Homestead Ampitheater.

The drama is performed in summer, usually late June through the end of August, Thursday through Sunday evenings at 8:30 PM. A walking tour down the historic Wilderness Road takes place each evening of performance at 7 PM. Admission is $10 for adults and $5 for children 12 years and younger. Babies in arms are free. Group discounts are available for parties of 15 or more. Call for information on Special Performance nights and for group reservations. From I-81 take Exit 105, follow Va. 232 for .7 mile toward Radford and take Norwood Street/First Street west to the amphitheater.

Theatre Arts Department, Virginia Tech
Blacksburg • (540) 231-5335

The New River Valley's cultural richness comes in great part from Virginia Tech's presence, and theater is no exception. The only theatre arts department in Virginia to have both its graduate and undergraduate programs accredited by the National Association of Schools of Theatre, Virginia Tech's has received more awards from the American College Theatre Festival than any other college or university in the Southeast. The Theatre Arts Department at Tech stages about 20 productions each year, including comedies, dramas, musicals and new plays.

Virginia Tech hosts four subscription shows during the academic year. The school has three theaters: Haymarket Theatre at Squires Student Center, Black Box Theatre in the Performing Arts Building and Squires Studio Theatre. All productions are open to the public. Don't miss Tech's Summer Arts Festival.

Other Cultural Attractions

The Montgomery Museum and Lewis Miller Regional Art Center
300 S. Pepper St., Christiansburg
• **(540) 382-5644**

A Valley-wide project to promote Montgomery County's rich history and arts, this center is in a mid-19th-century home of American and Flemish bond brick made from local materials, with hand-hewn oak beams and rafters. A curious aspect of the manse portion of the house is a step-up feature in the back rooms, thought to be a carry-over from Colonial days when some people believed that evil spirits bearing illness traveled the night air along floors.

The house contains both historic and contemporary works, including exhibits and shows of Southwest Virginia artists and crafters. It also houses a genealogical research area, historic small-press library and archives. The Center is open 10:30 AM to 4:30 PM Tuesday through Saturday and 1:30 to 4:30 PM on Sundays, or by appointment.

Radford University College of Visual and Performing Arts
Radford University, Radford
• **(540) 831-5141**

The university offers the public solo and ensemble music performances, theater, ongoing gallery exhibits, classical ballet, Big Band music, jazz and modern dance and opera performances. Call the university for a schedule.

Giles County

Visual Arts

The Mountain Lake Gallery
Va. Rt. 700, Mountain Lake Resort
• **(540) 626-7121**

While at Mountain Lake, check out its gallery, home of the popular, whimsical Bob Evans Knobbits. The gallery features all local arts and crafts including hanging art, jewelry, pottery and sculpture. Hours are 10 AM to 5 PM daily from Memorial Day through Labor Day.

New River Valley Arts and Crafts Guild
U.S. Hwy. 460, Pembroke
• **(540) 626-3309**

Handcrafted treasures are both made and sold in the New River Valley Arts and Crafts Guild in the heart of Pembroke. Here you will find everything from items crafted in the mountain tradition to present-day crafts. Approximately 25 members display and sell their crafts at the gallery.

Summer hours are 10 AM to 5 PM Tuesday through Saturday and 1 to 4 PM Sunday. Winter hours are 11 AM to 4 PM Tuesday through Saturday and 1 to 4 PM Sunday. Due to inclement weather conditions, it is best to call ahead in winter.

Theater presentations and other cultural activities abound in this area.

Pulaski County

Visual Arts

**The Fine Arts Center
for the New River Valley**
21 W. Main St., Pulaski
• (540) 980-7363
This facility is the cultural hub of the New River Valley, featuring contemporary works, music shows, private collections and amateur and professional artists. It is housed in a storefront building considered a prime example of Victorian commercial architecture. Built in 1898, the Center has been designated a Virginia Historic Landmark.

Floyd County

Visual Arts

Old Church Gallery
110 Wilson St., Floyd
• (540) 745-4849
In this 1850 Greek Revival building, art ex-hibits are adjacent to the history room. A century-old copper still used to make moonshine whiskey is on display. The gallery has an active quilter's guild, a monthly literary group, an arts and crafts workshop and children's programs in the summer. The gallery is open 10 AM to 4 PM Saturdays from April through December.

Other Cultural Attractions

Floyd County General Store
S. Locust St., Floyd
• (540) 745-4563
The culture of mountainous Floyd County doesn't get any better than this! At 7 PM Friday night, folks start showing up with fiddles, harmonicas, banjos and guitars, and what follows is a Floyd County tradition. The flat-footing begins, old-timers reminisce, and the music that is the lifeblood of Floyd County mountain spirit soothes the wounds of the work week. This free gathering is an endangered cultural species that is personally financed by Freeman Cockram, who believes Floyd Countians need such a place to gather. Don't miss this landmark!

Alleghany Highlands

Alleghany and Highland Counties

Alleghany Highlands Arts & Crafts Center
439 E. Ridgeway St., Clifton Forge
• (540) 862-4447

The galleries' changing exhibits feature works by Alleghany Highlands artists and those from other areas. Among the fine regional art and handcrafted products of juried quality on sale here are pottery, wooden ware, jewelry, stained glass, note cards, baskets and fiber arts. The center is open 10 AM to 4:30 PM Monday through Saturday May through December and during the same hours Tuesday through Saturday January through April.

Historic Stonewall Theatre
510 Main St., Clifton Forge
• (540) 863-9606, (540) 862-1234

Country music Hall of Famers Tex Ritter, Roy Rogers and Gene Autry once performed in this grand old theater. Located on the eastern tip of what has been called the Golden Triangle of Country Music, other stars stopped by on their way to Kentucky and Tennessee, including Burl Ives, Tom Mix, Lash LaRue and the original Drifters. In 1991 Appalfolks of America, a nonprofit corporation based in Clifton Forge, was given the theater as a charitable donation and what had become a twin cinema was converted back into a performing arts center. Today the three-story building that dates back to 1904 hosts performances almost every Saturday and some Fridays. Stop by and you can hear a wide variety of concerts by country, bluegrass, gospel and Junior Opry performers.

Stonewall also stages dramas by the Clifton Forge Players, the Stonewall Children's Theatre and actors from nearby Lime Kiln, plus it has even hosted occasional variety shows and tributes to Martin Luther King Jr. and Elvis Presley. Most shows are in the $5 to $6 range, but prices are higher for the bigger-named

acts. Robin and Linda Williams from Garrison Keillor's *A Prairie Home Companion* radio show and Grammy-nominated folk singer John McCutcheon were among last year's entertainers.

The Highland County Arts Council
P.O. Box 175, Monterey 24465 • no phone

The Highland County Arts Council has provided children's programs and artists in residence who go into the schools. Other projects are a Maple Festival crafts booth, Highland-style dance classes and storytelling.

Alleghany Highlands Arts Council
185 Maple Ave., Covington
• (540) 962-6220

The Alleghany Highlands Arts Council has been bringing professional performing arts events into the community for 45 years and has been called one of the most successful entertainment and cultural series in the state. The performing arts series has included performances by the Barter Theatre Troupe, Judy Collins, Marie Osmond and Leon Bates. The Young People's Theatre Series takes educational theatre, musical and dance productions into area schools. The AHAC also provides ways for residents to become involved in the performing arts. The Alleghany Highlands Chorale consists of 45 singers who give two major concerts per year and perform at such places as The Homestead. The Alleghany Highlands Orchestra, conducted by Marie Carpenter, is a full orchestra of 38 members. For more information on schedules and tickets, call the Arts Council office.

The Craft Shops of Covington
120 W. Main St., Covington
• (540) 962-0557

This regional craft market features more than 110 crafters displaying their handmade country, traditional and Victorian crafts. Included are wood carvings, jewelry, quilting, ceramics, paintings, photographs, stained glass, dried and silk wreaths and floral arrangements, jumpers, furniture, bird houses, gift baskets, cookbooks and a year-round Christmas shop with ornaments and a large variety of decorations. The Shops are open 10 AM to

6 PM Monday through Saturday and 12 to 5 PM Sunday.

Bath County

Music

Garth Newel Music Center
Hot Springs • (540) 839-5018

For 25 years now, from among the giant hemlocks, the hills of Bath County come alive with the sound of music. The importance of the Garth Newel Center to the culture of the Alleghany Highlands and western Virginia cannot be underestimated. Musicians, students and awe-inspired audiences come together in this unspoiled mountain area to hear music by the likes of Beethoven, Bach, Mozart, Haydn, Schubert, Schumann, Brahms and Dvorak, in an enchanting mountain setting. The Center features the Garth Newel Chamber Players. It provides an intensive residential Chamber Music Study Program for serious young musicians, who receive full scholarships. The architecture and acoustics of Herter Hall provide the perfect ambiance for chamber music and create a unique sense of being outdoors while actually indoors! Before the performance, many visitors have made it a tradition to join friends for a picnic on the grounds.

The Garth Newel Summer Chamber Music Festival begins in July with concerts every Saturday at 5 PM and every Sunday at 3 PM through August 31. Garth Newel now offers visitors a Saturday evening Music and Champagne Supper for a minimum of 12 and a maximum of 50 guests. Reservations are required. Tickets can be purchased in advance or at the door. Single admission tickets are $12.

The Celebrated Composers Series, held on various Sunday afternoons throughout the fall, winter and spring, also includes a post-performance reception with an offering from chef Arlene Di Cecco. Single admission tickets are $15.

Throughout the fall, winter and spring, Garth Newel hosts Music Holidays with guests in residence and Music Holidays Overseas. These events encompass beautiful chamber music performances, gourmet meals, fine wines and convivial company.

Some of our annual gatherings pay homage to such diverse edibles as garlic, apples, wine, tomatoes, molasses, poultry and more.

Annual Events and Festivals

Not a season passes in Virginia's Blue Ridge and its foothills that some group isn't finding a way to celebrate it. You will have plenty to do each month all around the 14-county region: craft shows, antiques sales, historic commemorations, agricultural fairs, horse shows and races, athletic competitions and some of the best fun you'll find anywhere in traditional holiday observances. Imagine the Shenandoah Valley sky ablaze with fireworks on Independence Day, or conjure up a sense of patriotic pride as this history-rich region celebrates the birthdays of such famous Americans as Thomas Jefferson, George Washington, James Madison and the South's famous generals, Robert E. Lee and Stonewall Jackson.

Let your taste buds lead the way as folks gather around to sample their favorite foods served with a big helping of fellowship. The Virginia Chili Cook-off in Roanoke is one such event, and the Highland Maple Festival in Monterey (with syrup-making demonstrations and plenty of maple-flavored goodies) is another. Other gatherings pay homage to such diverse edibles as garlic (and its humble brother, the ramp), apples in every form (especially apple butter!), wine, tomatoes, molasses, poultry and more. Fall festivals usually feature the entire harvest — so save up your calories.

Music, running the gamut from hoedowns to symphonies, is almost always on the program. Don't miss the Old Fiddler's Convention — the original and largest such event — and other cultural extravaganzas. Many activities are held at the region's beautiful historic mansions, such as Montpelier, Monticello and Ash Lawn-Highland.

In the Hunt Country from Leesburg to Charlottesville, steeplechases are a sporting and social staple. Informal point-to-point races in early February lead into the spring chasing season, which features race meetings in such wonderful venues as Leesburg's Oatlands Plantation and Morven Park, Middleburg's Glenwood Park, Charlottesville's Foxfields and Montpelier, and Great Meadow, in The Plains. After a summer hiatus for horse shows, including the historic Warrenton Horse Show and the Upperville Colt and Horse Show (the country's oldest show), steeplechasing resumes in the fall (see our Horse Country chapter).

The list that follows is a sampling of some of the bigger events — and a lot of smaller ones too — that can entertain you for a weekend or longer. Where possible, we have given dates or approximate times of the month when these events occur. You should always call ahead to confirm times and specifics. Happy festing!

January

Virginia Special Olympics
Va. Rt. 664, Wintergreen
- **(800) 932-4653**

Wintergreen Resort hosts this annual snow-skiing competition for mentally challenged athletes. Alpine races are on the agenda at this event, usually held in mid-January. There is no cost to watch.

Livestock Auction
7074 John Marshall Hwy., Marshall
• (540) 364-1566

On the second Saturday of every month, a horse auction is held at the Fauquier Livestock Exchange. You can bid on almost any type of horse, from draft horses to ponies and mules. Such sales were once commonplace in rural America but are now a rarity. There's no cost to watch.

Hunt Country Winter Antiques Fair
28050 Oatlands Plantation Ln., Leesburg
• (703) 777-3174

More than 35 selected exhibitors from New England to the Carolinas sell 17th- to 20th-century furniture, porcelain, jewelry and other collectibles at the National Guard Armory during this three-day fair. It's usually held either the second or third weekend of the month. Admission is $5.

Annual Charlottesville Antiques Show
235 McIntire Rd., Charlottesville
• (804) 296-8018

More than 40 dealers display their wares at the Omni Hotel on the Downtown Mall for this show. Usually held the first weekend in January, the 1999 show marks the 15th year of the annual gathering. Appraisals are available.

Birthday Convocation for Robert E. Lee
Washington & Lee University, Lexington
• (540) 463-3777

The venerable general is saluted on his birthday, January 19, at Lexington's Lee Chapel. The event is free.

Birthday Celebration for Stonewall Jackson
Washington & Lee University, Lexington
• (540) 463-3777

The South's second-greatest hero gets his due at this city-wide festival on January 21, beginning on the grounds of Washington & Lee University. The event is free.

Friday Night Jamboree at Floyd County General Store
S. Locust St., Floyd • (540) 745-4563

Every Friday night at 7 PM folks gather for great bluegrass music, flat-footing and fellowship. People bring their fiddles, harmonicas and guitars for an evening of entertainment and relaxation. Admission is free. (See our Arts chapter.)

Fiddle, Banjo and Dance Club
New River Community College, Dublin • (540) 674-3611

The club meets every second Saturday of the month throughout the year at the New River Community College Campus in Edwards Hall. As many as 1,000 participants come to sing, dance and listen to bluegrass and old-time mountain music. It's free.

February

African-American Heritage Month
U.S. Hwy. 250 W., Staunton
• (540) 332-7850

The Frontier Culture Museum hosts several events during February that examine African-American contributions to early American growth. In years past events have included a drama on 19th-century African-American relationships. Most events are free, but you will have to pay admission to the museum. In past years it was $8 for adults and $4 for children.

Valentine's Day Weekend
Va. Rt. 664, Wintergreen
• (804) 325-2200

Parties, special ski challenges and events for the kids top off this annual festival at Wintergreen Resort. Cupid can even be seen tossing Hershey Kisses to skiers as he patrols the slopes.

Loudoun County Civil War Roundtable
Va. Rt. 7, Leesburg • (540) 338-7550

Winter's a good time to drop by Douglas Community School to attend this ongoing meeting, which features a forum by various

Civil War authorities. This group meets the second Tuesday of every month, except July and August. For $20 the whole family can join the membership.

African-American History Month at Monticello
VA. Rt. 53, Charlottesville
• (804) 984-9822

In keeping with the practice begun by Dr. Carter G. Woodson, the founder of black history commemorations who was also born nearby, Monticello celebrates the contributions of African Americans to the history of Virginia and our nation. Take a plantation community tour every weekend in February. Monticello Plantation life interpreters lead visitors along Mulberry Row, the plantation "street," where African-American slaves lived and labored, and the south dependencies, including the kitchen and cook's rooms. Or, enjoy the African-American History Month Lecture series on Saturdays at the nearby Monticello Visitors Center Theater in the Charlottesville/Albemarle Visitors Center at Rt. 20 S and I-64, (804) 984-9856. In 1999 speakers included Liz Cherry Jones, a local African-American weaver and fabric artist, who discussed black weavers in the 19th-century Virginia Piedmont region. These events are free.

Shrine Circus
Roanoke Civic Center,
710 Williamson Rd., Roanoke
• (540) 981-1201

The first Thursday through Sunday of February brings the Shrine Circus to the Roanoke Civic Center much to the delight of children and adults. Enjoy animals, trapeze artists and lots of clowns. General admission runs at about $8 for adults and $4 for children. Reserved seats are $10 for adults and $6 for children.

Groundhog Day at Mill Mountain Zoo
Mill Mountain Zoo, Roanoke
• (540) 343-3241

Join Roanoke's mayor and other local officials at Mill Mountain Zoo's Weather Station to find out if that rascally groundhog sees its shadow. According to legend, if the groundhog sees its shadow, there are six more weeks of winter; if not, spring is just around the corner. There are children's activities, hot refreshments and the debut of the zoo's resident groundhog in celebration of this day. The ceremony starts at 10 AM and activities continue until 5 PM. Zoo admission is $5 for adults, $3 for children younger than 12 and free for those younger than 2.

Southwest Virginia Boat Show
Roanoke Civic Center, 710 Williamson Rd., Roanoke • (540) 981-1201

This late-February event draws fishing enthusiasts and other water lovers to the Roanoke Civic Center to see the variety of boats and marine supplies on show and for sale. Admission price is $4.50.

Archduke Music Holiday
Va. Rt. 220, Hot Springs • (540) 839-5018

A renowned cultural hub, the Garth Newel Music Center hosts special holiday weekends for lovers of chamber music, gourmet meals and fine wine. Enjoy the black-tie affair on Friday and other special activities throughout the rest of the weekend. Past admission price was $75.

March

President James Madison's Birthday
Va. Rt. 20 S. Montpelier Station
• (540) 672-2728

Every year on March 16 Montpelier hosts a celebration to honor the birthday of the fourth president of the United States. There is a celebration at the cemetery, usually featuring the Marine Corps Band. Other events follow at the house. There is no charge.

Festival of the Book
145 Ednam Dr., Charlottesville
• (804) 924-3296

Celebrate the book in all its forms with dozens of events and more than 100 writers. Programs for all ages include book fairs, storytelling, seminars, readings and book signings at locations throughout the city (see our Arts chapter). Except for the luncheon and closing reception, events are free at this festival that takes place the last weekend in March. National Book Award winner Alice McDermott was the featured speaker at the 1999 luncheon. Past participants have included John Grisham, Tami Hoag and David Baldacci.

MDA Car Show
Roanoke Civic Center, 710 Williamson Rd., Roanoke • (540) 981-1201

Antique, late-model cars and trucks can be found on display at the Roanoke Civic Center in mid-March. Admission is $5 for adults and $2.50 for children.

St. Patrick's Day Parade
Jefferson St., Roanoke • (540) 853-2889

Downtown Roanoke "sports the green" during this weekend parade that's fun for the whole family. It's free to watch.

Confederate Winter Camp
5240 Wilderness Rd., Newbern
• (540) 674-4835

Experience camping during the Civil War period through demonstrations by Confederate re-enactors. See them outside the Wilderness Road Regional Museum. Admission is free.

Highland County Maple Festival
Various locations, Monterey
• (540) 468-2550

This festival, celebrated for two weekends in mid-March, takes place across Highland County, that rugged, gorgeous region bordering West Virginia, just west of Staunton. Begun in 1948, the Maple Festival has been named in the Southeast Tourism Society's Top 20 Events for the past 10 years. Look for 75,000 visitors to flock to this rural area that has a population of just 2,500. During the festival, you can visit local sugar camps and watch the actual process of syrup-making. There's also an arts and crafts show, a maple queen contest and ball, dances, including the maple sugar hoedown, and plenty of opportunities to scarf down pancakes with maple syrup,

maple donuts and fresh fried trout. The events are free, but you'll pay for food.

April

Easter Egg Hunt
U.S. Hwy. 11, Middletown
• (540) 869-2028

Celebrate the Easter holiday with the annual Easter Egg Hunt at Belle Grove Plantation on the Saturday before Easter. There are also other games for kids. Activities are geared for children up to age 10. Cost is $2 per child.

Historic Garden Week
Locations throughout Virginia
• (540) 644-7776

Called "America's largest open house," the doors of more than 250 private homes and gardens throughout the Commonwealth open for the annual Garden Week tours in late April. This event celebrated its 66th year in 1999. Charlottesville, Staunton, Harrisonburg, Roanoke and the Front Royal areas are just a few of the popular touring regions. Prices may vary with locations, but tour block tickets usually range from $10 to $20 per event. If you would like to drop in on a single house or garden, the price is generally $3 to $5. For a $5 donation, you can get a 200-page guidebook detailing the tours. Just write to: Garden Club of Virginia, 12 E. Franklin Street, Richmond 23219.

Champagne and Candlelight Tour
James Monroe Pkwy., Charlottesville
• (804) 293-9539

This enchanting evening tour of the Ash Lawn-Highland home of President James Monroe is always held during Historic Garden Week. Period music is performed during tours of the Federal-style home, and you'll revel in the beautiful gardens, which are illuminated with 1,000 candles. The cost is $8 for this special event.

INSIDERS' TIP

If you're really into attending annual events, the Virginia Division of Tourism puts out a monthly calendar free for the asking. Call (804) 786-2051 or write them at 901 E. Byrd Street, Richmond 23219.

Easter Traditions
U.S. Hwy. 250 W., Staunton
• **(540) 332-7850**

Rolling, tossing, dyeing and trundling eggs are just a few of the activities that take place on the historic farmsites at the Frontier Culture Museum in April. You can learn about past Easter observances, traditions and foods. The event is free, but you will need to pay the regular admission to the museum: $8 for adults, $7.50 for seniors, $7 for students and $4 for children ages 6 to 14.

Local Colors
Market Sq., Roanoke • (540) 342-5700

This local celebration of cultural diversity is held annually at the historic Farmer's Market and on surrounding streets. More than 40 ethnic and cultural groups are represented in a parade of flags and through food, song, dance, music, artifact exhibits, ethnic dress and international children's games. The event is free.

Zoobilation for Conservation
Roanoke • (540) 343-3241

Mill Mountain Zoo celebrates with music and special programs in conjunction with Roanoke Valley Earth Day. Children can learn about the planet, conservation and enjoy food and drinks throughout the zoo and park. Admission is $5 for adults, $4.50 for seniors and $3 for children 2 through 12.

Vinton Dogwood Festival
Various locations, Vinton
• **(540) 983-0613**

This community next to Roanoke celebrates spring in late April every year with a parade, band competition, an antique car show, music, food, crafts, bike races, a long-distance run, an evening of country music and more. The events are free.

Leesburg Flower and Garden Festival
King and Market sts., Leesburg
• **(703) 777-1368**

Downtown Leesburg is transformed into a botanical garden with plants, gardening equipment and supplies for sale as well as entertainment and food. Both King and Market streets are blocked off for this festival on the third weekend in April. Cost is $2, $1 for children 6 to 12.

Warrenton Farmers Market
Fifth and Lee sts., Warrenton
• **(540) 347-1101**

Local farmers sell vegetables, pork, flowers, plants and freshly baked goods and crafts every Saturday from mid-April through December. The market is also open for business on Wednesdays from mid-May through December. It's free to get in.

Graves' Mountain Spring Fling
Va. Rt. 670, Syria • (540) 923-4231

Rain or shine, Graves' Mountain Lodge celebrates spring the last weekend of April with fly-fishing demonstrations, bluegrass music, cloggers, arts and crafts, hayrides and horseback rides. Admission and parking are free. You also can sample some rainbow trout or have a hot dog at the picnic area.

Thomas Jefferson Birthday Commemoration
Va. Rt. 53, Charlottesville
• **(804) 984-9822**

Admission to Monticello's grounds and gardens is always free on April 13, the birthday of Virginia's best-known renaissance man — U.S. President, Secretary of State, scholar, architect, collector and horticulturist Thomas Jefferson. The morning celebration features a wreath-laying ceremony at Jefferson's grave site.

Crestar 10-Miler
Alderman St., Charlottesville
• **(804) 293-6115**

The city's largest foot race (fourth-largest in Virginia) is usually held the first Saturday in April, commencing at the University of Virginia's University Hall. If you would like to participate in the event, which celebrates its 15th year in 1999, call to get a brochure. It's free if you want to watch.

Dogwood Festival
McIntire Rd., Charlottesville
• **(804) 961-9824**

This popular community event now in its

50th year features a queen's coronation, fireworks, a carnival and barbecue. It culminates in a grand parade that shows off Charlottesville at its springtime best. It's usually held for two weeks in mid-April. There is no charge for most events, but you will need some cash if you want to ride the carnival rides and eat the barbecue.

Doo Dah Day
Pleasant Valley Rd., Winchester
• (540) 662-7732

It's a family day of fun at this annual event on the last Saturday in April at Jim Barnett Park. There are games, food, live entertainment and a parade. Spiderman even makes an annual appearance. It costs $4 to get in.

Court Days
Market and First sts., Charlottesville
• (804) 296-8548

Held in historic Lee Park in downtown Charlottesville on a non-Easter weekend in April, this arts and crafts festival features considerable local talent. Pottery, stained glass, jewelry and woodwork are among the wares sold here. Admission is free.

Fridays After Five
Downtown Mall, Charlottesville
• (804) 296-8548

This free outdoor concert series is held at the city's new Downtown Mall amphitheater. Bands are usually local. This event is held 5:30 to 8 PM Fridays through September.

Garden Day at Point of Honor
112 Cabell St., Lynchburg
• (804) 847-1459

A re-created garden party on the lawn where gun duels were once fought gives the home its name. Floral and food displays typical of the early 19th century are shown, and tea is served in the afternoon. The event is held in late April. Admission in 1999 was $12.

Spring Garden Show
Main St., Lynchburg • (804) 847-1499

This is a gardener's field day in late April at the Community Market, where landscapers, florists and nursery operators display their products and where gardening techniques are demonstrated. Entertainment and food add to the festivities. The events are free.

Brush Mountain Arts and Crafts Fair
Radford University Commons, Radford
• (540) 552-4909

Quilters, potters, weavers, decoy carvers and other artists show their wares at the juried festival held in this art-loving college town. This event is held Palm Sunday weekend at the Radford University Dedmonds Center. Admission is $2.

May

Shenandoah Apple Blossom Festival
135 N. Cameron St., Winchester
• (540) 662-3863

This five-day celebration, usually held the first full weekend of May, is a salute to the area's apple-growing industry. You'll find high-quality arts and crafts shows, numerous parades, live music, a 10K race and a circus. (See our Kidstuff chapter.) Actor Dan Ackroyd, singer Pat Boone, former coach Red Auerbach and Olympic gold medal swimmer Amy Van Dyken will be among the special guests for the 72nd annual event in 1999. Some events are free. The circus costs $14 for adults, $9 for children 12 and younger.

Spring Fly-In
491 Airport Rd., Winchester
• (540) 662-5786

Homebuilt, experimental and World War II aircraft owners compete for prizes and share their aviation interests with the public at the Winchester Regional Airport. This is not an air show — all the exhibits are static displays — but in 1997, a B-17 flew in to give rides. Donations are accepted at the gate. The Fly-In is in mid-May, one week after the Apple Blossom Festival.

Ash Lawn-Highland Virginia Wine Festival
James Monroe Pkwy., Charlottesville
• (804) 293-9539

On May 22 and 23, take in the first major wine festival of the year at the historic home of

James Monroe. The festival features craft demonstrations, gourmet food, entertainment, house tours and wine tastings from Central Virginia wineries. The festival costs $10, but you will need a little extra to sample the food.

Virginia Mushroom and Wine Festival
414 E. Main St., Front Royal
• (540) 635-3185, (800) 338-2576
This Main Street celebration started as a salute to the shiitake mushroom and grew to include arts and crafts, food, wine tastings, live music, clogging, open-air theatrical performances and rides for the kids. (Adults may also like the 60-foot slide.) It's usually held the second weekend in May. Last year it cost $5 for the wine tasting.

Newtown Heritage Festival
U.S. 11, Stephens City • (540) 869-3087
Catch the eighth annual festival of crafts, art, artisans, parades, children's rides, food and entertainment as Stephens City celebrates the heritage of Newtown. The free events take place throughout the small town of Stephens City. Look for the festival in the third weekend in May.

Folk Arts and Crafts Festival
U.S. Hwy. 11, Weyers Cave
• (540) 885-5960, (888) 750-2722
The focus here is on local artisans, many of whom exhibit solely at this festival, but others from North Carolina, Pennsylvania and Washington, D.C., also have attended. The show is usually held the first weekend in May at Blue Ridge Community College and includes foods ranging from country ham sandwiches to pork rinds. There's also live entertainment around the clock, including bluegrass, country and Irish music. It's free.

Mayfest
46 E. Main St., Luray • (540) 743-3915
Luray's normally serene Main Street and

the town park are transformed into a frenzy of activity the third Saturday in May in a celebration reminiscent of the old-fashioned street festivals. The street is lined with crafters, antique dealers and vendors with flowers, plants and herbs. Food, live music by Shenandoah Valley bands, pony rides, llamas, arts activities, go-cart rides, dancers and the performance of a traditional Maypole dance add to the fun. Historic buildings are open for tours too. Admission to the events is free.

Re-enactment of the Battle of New Market
George Collins Pkwy., New Market
• (540) 740-3212, (540) 740-3101
This event is centered around a skirmish and living history exhibit on Saturday and a full battle re-enactment on Sunday closest to May 15, the date of the 1864 Civil War battle. The event is held at Battlefield State Historic Park. Cost is $5; free for those younger than 12.

Shenandoah Valley Music Festival
221 Shrine Mont Cir., Orkney Springs
• (540) 459-3396
Classical music is performed live in a concert series from May to August. Shows are performed in an outdoor pavilion next to the former Orkney Springs Hotel, a massive pre-Civil War building (see our Arts chapter). Get there early for the ice-cream socials held before every concert. Arts and crafts shows are also held those weekends. Tickets run $11 to $16 for adults, $4 to $7 for children.

Gun Show
U.S. Hwy. 11, Harrisonburg
• (540) 434-0005
The Rockingham County Fairground hosts this annual weapons display featuring all kinds of guns, including antiques and collectibles on the Saturday and Sunday of Memorial Day Weekend. The Fairground is a half-mile south of Harrisonburg. Cost is $4.

INSIDERS' TIP

Although many festivals are held outdoors, dogs are not always welcome participants. You might want to give the event organizers a call before you take Fido along for the ride.

Memorial Day Horse Fair and Auction
U.S. Hwy. 11, Harrisonburg
• (540) 434-4482

This annual tradition is the largest horse auction in the Shenandoah Valley. Held at the Rockingham County Fairgrounds, it also features Western wear and horse equipment. It's free, unless you have the high bid on a horse.

Annual Shenandoah Antiques Expo
Off I-64, Fishersville • (804) 846-7452

This 19-year-old event is one of the largest gatherings of dealers and collectors in the region. Approximately 500 dealers from up and down the East Coast attended past events at Augusta County Expoland. The show is usually held the second weekend of May with another planned for October. General admission tickets are around $3 per day.

Wool Days
U.S. Hwy. 250 W., Staunton
• (540) 332-7850

Sharpen the shears, the sheep are ready! The Frontier Culture Museum does it the old-fashioned way, from shearing to washing, carding and spinning during the first week in May. It doesn't cost anything to watch interpreters shear the museum's flock of sheep, but you will have to pay the general admission to get in the museum. Last year it was $8 for adults $7.50 for seniors, $7 for students and $4 for children.

Art in the Park
1 Gypsy Hill Park, Staunton
• (540) 885-2028

This downtown Staunton outdoor art show features more than 100 local and national artists, including a large number of wildlife painters. The event, which also offers entertainment and food, is held at the city's beautiful Gypsy Hill Park usually the third weekend of May. It's free.

Blue Ridge Classic Soap Box Derby
Main St., Waynesboro
• (540) 943-5907, (540) 948-6868

Waynesboro plays host to one of the largest soap box derbies in the United States, usually the second weekend in May. Drivers ages 9 to 16 show their driving skills down Main Street in their own home-made cars. In 1997, Mark Stephens of nearby New Hope advanced from the local competition to win the World Championship in Akron, Ohio. There's no fee to watch.

Spring Wildflower Symposium
Va. Rt. 664, Wintergreen
• (804) 325-8169

Every May, Wintergreen Resort invites prominent specialists to lead workshops, lectures and other educational programs about wildflowers. More than 65 field trips, lectures and workshops are presented by well known botanists, photographers and artists. There are also guided hikes, wildflower sales, photography displays and entertainment. The symposium is usually held the second weekend of May. Cost is $85, and does not include accommodations.

Memorial Day at Wintergreen Resort
Va. Rt. 664, Wintergreen
• (804) 325-2200

Ring in the holiday with lots of activities for the whole family, including hayrides, rock climbing, magic shows, mountain tales, craft workshops and a seafood buffet. There is a nominal fee for most events, around $6, except for the buffet, which is more.

Culpeper Day
Davis St., Culpeper • (540) 825-7768

This community-wide street festival is a tradition held the first Saturday of May featuring regional crafts, bluegrass and country music and all types of food from shish kabobs to funnel cakes. Admission is free. The Museum of Culpeper also will be open for tours.

The Flying Circus
Va. Rt. 644, Bealeton • (540) 439-8661

The first weekend in May is usually the opening airshow for The Flying Circus at Bealeton, southwest of Warrenton on U.S. 17 and Va. 644. Airshows, balloon rallies and car shows are held on the grounds every Sunday through October. (See our Kidstuff chapter.) Admission is around $10, $3 for those ages 6 to 12.

Oatlands Sheep Dog Trials
28050 Oatlands Plantation Ln., Leesburg
• (703) 777-3174

This highly entertaining weekend fete (typically the second week of May) champions the herding instincts of border collies. Watch handlers use whistles to command their dogs to guide the sheep. It takes place at glorious Oatlands Plantation, just outside of Leesburg in the heart of the Virginia Hunt Country. Crafts, music, sack races and food add to the festivities. Last year's event cost $8. It's more if you want to tour the mansion.

Delaplane Strawberry Festival
11012 Edmonds Ln., Delaplane
• (540) 592-3556

Crafts, hayrides, clowns, games, pony rides and a petting zoo are part of this strawberry harvest celebration held at Sky Meadows State Park usually on Memorial Day weekend. Sample strawberry shortcake and sundaes or take home fresh strawberries and jam. The cost is $10 per car.

Wilderness Civil War Re-enactment
Off Va. Rt. 628, Orange
• (703) 787-9483

The Wilderness event is one of the two largest re-enactments on the East Coast. Nearly 5,000 re-enactors, including 150 on horseback, stage a major battle each day on a private farm five miles north of Orange. It features living history, encampments, music, period antiques and crafts, plus kids' activities. The event is usually held the third weekend of May. Admission is around $10.

Graves' Mountain Festival of Music
Va. Rt. 670, Syria • (540) 923-4231

This three-day bluegrass concert series, held the Thursday, Friday and Saturday after Memorial Day, brings in folks from around the region to Graves' Mountain Lodge. Bring a lawn chair. The cost of a three-day pass last year was $39 in advance.

Dolley Madison's Birthday
Va. Rt. 20 S., Montpelier Station
• (540) 672-2728

This is an annual celebration on May 20 at Montpelier, 4 miles from Orange, including a ceremony honoring the former first lady at the cemetery on the grounds. There is no charge.

Annual Kite Day
James Monroe Pkwy., Charlottesville
• (804) 293-9539

At Ash Lawn-Highland, home of President James Monroe, the fields are open to children and the young at heart for kite-flying. Both designs and flights are judged for prizes. It costs $1 to come watch, and it's free for kite flyers. If you don't have one with you, they have kites on sale in the gift shop.

Crozet Arts and Crafts Festival
Park Rd., Crozet • (804) 977-0406

Claudius Crozet Park, 12 miles west of Charlottesville, is the venue for this nationally ranked show, always held on Mother's Day weekend. It's a wonderful opportunity to see and purchase a variety of arts and crafts. Admission fee is $3.50.

North-South Skirmish Association Spring Nationals
U.S. Hwy. 522, Gainesboro
• (540) 662-3424

The North-South Skirmish Association honors Civil War soldiers by staging shooting competitions with authentic uniforms and original or reproductions of firearms. You can watch mortar, cannons, revolvers, carbine and musket fire at the 96th national event in mid-May. There also will be a ladies' dress competition at Fort Shenandoah. Antiques, books and clothing will be on sale. Admission is free.

Neighborhood Art Show
Main St., The Plains • (540) 253-5177

Collages, sculptures, ceramics and paintings by artists young and old are displayed at Grace Episcopal Church Parish House, usually the second weekend in May. Admission to the Friday night gala for this 51-year-old event is $10. General admission prices were $7 for families or $5 per person last year.

Of Ale and History Beer Festival
U.S. Hwy. 11, Middletown
• (540) 869-2028

Try unlimited samples of microbrewed beers from more than 20 brewers at the third annual event in mid-May at Belle Grove Plantation. There is also live entertainment and plenty of food. The cost is $15 at the gate, $13 if you pay in advance.

Exhibition of Sporting Art
17263 Southern Planters Ln., Leesburg
• (703) 777-2414

The works of nearly 30 equine artists is the focal point of this monthlong event, which marked its 14th year in 1999. It is held at Morven Park's Museum of Hounds and Hunting. There is an opening-day reception for members only. Admission fee for the park is around $6.

Old Town Spring Festival
Main St., Warrenton • (540) 347-4414

Country and bluegrass music, dancing, clogging demonstrations, crafts and a petting zoo take over Main Street in historic Old Town Warrenton usually the third Saturday in May. It's free.

Celebrate Virginia
Lexington/Rockbridge County
• (540) 463-3777

The focus is on the heritage of the community, Robert E. Lee, Stonewall Jackson, the colleges (Washington & Lee University and Virginia Military Institute), antiques, horse shows, downtown Lexington and the Maury River. These free events near the end of May are part of a statewide celebration of Virginia. Lexington hosts a different event every year and, in 1999, Natural Bridge will receive a National Historic Landmark designation as part of the festivities.

Theater at Lime Kiln
Lime Kiln Rd., Lexington
• (540) 463-3074

Memorial Day begins the summer season at Lime Kiln, an outdoor theater that's nationally recognized for presenting original plays and musicals relating to Virginia's culture and history. Plays and concerts take place under the stars in an enchanting setting, the ruins of an actual lime kiln built in the 1800s. Plays are performed Tuesday through Saturday until Labor Day. On Sunday nights, some of the best and brightest in the music business perform jazz, blues, folk and bluegrass music at Lime Kiln. Admission prices range from $8 to $16 depending on the event.

Ghost Tours of Lexington
Streets of Lexington • (540) 348-1080

Come experience the "ghosts" of Lexington after the sun sets during this late-May event. Narrated ghost tours of the town begin nightly in the summer through Labor Day, and then continue only on the weekends through October. Reservations are required. Admission is $8 for ages 11 and older, $6 for ages 4 to 10 and free for children younger than 3.

Bonnie Blue National Horse Show
Va. Rt. 39 W., Lexington
• (540) 463-3777

You'll see all breeds of horses at this major event in mid-May at the Virginia Horse Center (see our Horse Country chapter). The events are free for spectators.

Art Museum of Western Virginia Sidewalk Art Show
Market Sq., Roanoke • (540) 342-5760

Sculpture, photography, watercolors, prints and more are on display in the market district during Roanoke Festival in the Park weekend around the end of May. Admission is free.

The Virginia Chili Cook-off
Market Sq., Roanoke • (540) 342-2028

Thousands of connoisseurs pour into Roanoke's historic farmer's market the first Saturday in May to indulge themselves. Don't forget to head down the block for some home-

---

INSIDERS' TIP

In vintage Virginia fashion, one of the state's largest sporting events, the Virginia Gold Cup in Fauquier County, is also its biggest social event. Insiders arrive early, stay late and, in between, eat, drink, gossip and place private bets on the race.

made strawberry shortcake at Community School's Strawberry Festival. The events are free. Free tastes of chili are given out, but you'll pay for strawberry shortcake.

Community School Strawberry Festival
Downtown City Market, Roanoke
• **(540) 563-5036**

This event takes place one block down from the Chili Cook-off during the first weekend of May. Be sure to save room!

Roanoke Festival in the Park
Roanoke • (540) 342-2640

This two-week-long celebration beginning Memorial Day weekend includes one of the East Coast's largest sidewalk art shows, a river race, concerts, fireworks, children's games, ethnic foods, bike and road races and a children's parade. During the second week, a carnival is held at the Civic Center. General admission is free, and events cost extra.

An Evening of Elegance
2111 Memorial Ave., Lynchburg
• **(804) 847-8688**

This annual fund-raiser for the Virginia School of the Arts is always held in early May. Internationally acclaimed dancers perform with local students at the E.C. Glass Auditorium. This gala benefits the Dame Margot Fonteyn Scholarship Fund. Tickets range from $25 to $100.

Fair by the James
Downtown Lynchburg
• **(804) 528-3950**

This Midways Fair is held downtown near the James River. It has live entertainment, livestock, artists, crafts, food and much more. This event is part of the Virginia State Fair. General admission is free, but events and rides may cost extra.

May Fest
off U.S. Hwy. 460 E., Concord
• **(804) 993-2185**

This wine and food festival is held on a farm, Stonewall Vineyards, in the rolling hill country outside of Lynchburg in mid-May. It includes wine tasting, tours and plenty of mu-

sic. Admission is $7, which includes a wine tasting and a souvenir glass.

June

Heritage Fair
336 Belle Grove Rd., Middletown
• **(540) 869-2028**

See craft demonstrations the way they were done in days of old at this 32-year-old tradition at Belle Grove Plantation. The event, the last weekend in June, features demonstrations along with wagon rides, exotic animals, live music and country fare. Admission is in the $5 range, with a reduced price for those younger than 12.

Polo, Wine & Twilight Dine
Va. Rt. 17, The Plains • (540) 635-7627

Enjoy a day of horse sport, food and fine wine from Oasis Vineyard on Fridays from June through September at Great Meadow. It costs $10 per vehicle to watch the games. You will need to call in advance if you want a tailgate dinner.

Vintage Virginia Wine Festival
Va. Rt. 17, The Plains
• **(800) 277-CORK**

Forty wineries take part in this early June weekend event on the grounds of Great Meadow. More than 100 vendors display their arts and crafts at Virginia's largest wine festival, and other features include gourmet food from 30 restaurants, jazz, reggae and pop music, rides and children's entertainment. More than 40,000 people attended last year's event. Admission is around $19, $16 in advance.

Shenandoah Valley Bach Festival
1200 Park Rd., Harrisonburg
• **(540) 432-4367**

The second week in June is filled with professional concerts and events celebrating the works of Bach and Mendelssohn at Eastern Mennonite University. Aside from the three main concerts, the annual event includes films, free noon chamber music recitals and a Bach Boutique featuring hand-crafted art by local artisans. Last year, $15 would get you in the main concerts.

Ash Lawn-Highland's Summer Festival

While a student at the University of Virginia 22 years ago, Priscilla Little had a bright idea of how to spend her summer vacation. Today, hundreds of people organize their vacations around her grand plan.

Little, a singer who was working on her master's degree at UVA, enjoyed opera, but there were few places in the Charlottesville area, including Mr. Jefferson's University, where one could relish the stratospheric, high-speed coloratura of one of Mozart's arias. In other words, she was looking for a place to sing. So she founded the Ash Lawn-Highland Summer Festival.

"She came up here and asked if she could do a couple of one-act opera performances," said Judith Walker, general manager of Ash Lawn-Highland's festival for the past 12 years. "They said, 'Yes,' and she put on an all-local production."

Little did Little realize that on the eve of Ash Lawn's 20th anniversary, her after-school project, which had blossomed into one of the most respected summer opera programs, would be recognized internationally. The June 1997 issue of *Money* magazine named Ash Lawn-Highland Summer Festival one of the "20 top warm-weather opera companies in the world." That placed the Albemarle County company in the same league with Italy's La Scala Opera, Germany's Munich Opera Festival and Austria's Salzburg Festival. As grand as that may sound, Ash Lawn prides itself in taking the highbrow out of opera.

"It's a real easy way for people to experience opera for the first time," Walker said.

— continued on next page

Photo: Ash Lawn-Highland

Madame Butterfly was one of three performances staged at Ash Lawn-Highland's Summer Festival in 1997.

"You can bring your bottle of wine and have a picnic before the show. It's outdoors, so you don't have to get dressed up, and all the songs are sung in English."

Set amid the relaxing centuries-old boxwood gardens at President James Monroe's historic home, the festival erases the intimidation factor for the opera novice. For the connoisseur, the fully staged productions at Ash Lawn are a rare treat. Past cast members have performed at the New York City Opera, the Washington Opera and the Metropolitan Opera.

"We spend two days auditioning in New York," Walker said, "and from 10 AM to 5 PM both days, we hear singers every four minutes. But we have been blessed with some exceptional singers. They come because they have the opportunity to sing the principal roles — at a very young age — that they wouldn't have the opportunity to sing at a major opera house."

The Marriage of Figaro, The Wizard of Oz and *Susannah* will be performed in 1999. But the 10-week Festival includes more than opera. Its Music at Twilight series features a different musical performance every Wednesday night, ranging from Broadway show tunes to Appalachian hoedowns. There's something for the younger generation too. Visiting puppeteers, storytellers, theater companies and singers perform in the Summer Saturdays series for children. And there is even a free lecture series for those who want to know the behind-the-scenes stories about the operas. Of, course, that was Little's plan. Her first mini-festival in 1978 included two one-act operas, lectures and a concert of African-American music. Her free performances drew 800 fans. Today, that number is closer to 10,000 each summer.

"Over the years, it evolved into two full-length operas and a musical," Walker said. "In the beginning we borrowed lights from UVA. A lot of the costumes came from there. It was a real community effort, and it still is. We bring in 40 singers and musicians, and each one of them is housed by members of the community all summer long. That is very unusual."

Oh, and one of the other great things about going to Ash Lawn's Summer Festival is that you don't have to fork out hundreds of dollars for a front-row seat at Salzburg. In recent years, tickets for Ash Lawn's operas and musicals ranged from $14 to $22. The 8 PM shows run from June through mid-August. For information on Ash Lawn-Highland's Summer Festival, call (804) 293-4500.

Bluemont Concert Series
Central and Northern Virginia
• (703) 777-6306

Enjoy music under the stars during this summer outdoor concert series held in Warrenton, Leesburg, Middleburg, Winchester, Culpeper and Luray. Each town has a concert each week, beginning mid-June. Musicians such as Grammy-nominated John McCutcheon and Robin and Linda Williams rotate venues. Call for a calendar of the family-oriented concerts. Admission is $3.

Mowing Day
U.S. Hwy. 250 W., Staunton
• (540) 332-7850

On the third Saturday in June, watch the staff at the Frontier Culture Museum compete in an old-fashioned mowing contest and learn the tools and techniques of mowing. There is no charge to watch, but you will need to pay to get in the museum: $8 for adults, $7.50 for seniors, $7 for students and $4 for children.

Hall of Fame Joust
Va. Rt. 936 Mt. Solon • (540) 350-2510

Four levels of competitors vie for jousting titles at Natural Chimneys Regional Park. Look for this event about the third Saturday in June (see our Horse Country chapter). It costs $5 to get into the park.

Confederate Memorial Service
West of Pleasant Valley Rd., Winchester
• (540) 662-1937

The more than 3,000 Confederate soldiers

Graves Mountain Apple Festival in Syria celebrates one of our most treasured commodities — crisp mountain-grown apples.

buried in the Stonewall Jackson Cemetery are honored in this June 6 service sponsored by the Turner Ashby United Daughters of the Confederacy, Chapter 54. The event will celebrate its 133rd annual service in 1999. There is no charge.

Annual Sun and Sand Beach Weekend
Va. Rt. 660, Stuarts Draft
• (540) 337-1911

You'll need plenty of energy for this one! Held at Shenandoah Acres Resort, this weekend is a nonstop summer festival of volleyball, mini-golf, sand-castle building contests, various water contests and a DJ dance on Saturday night. This is always held the third weekend in June. It costs $6 for those 12 and older, $4.50 for ages 6 to 12 and free for the young ones.

Greater Shenandoah Valley Fair
U.S. Hwy. 340, Waynesboro
• (540) 943-9336

Hop on the amusement rides, buy cotton candy, listen to country music or watch the automobile action at this weeklong event at the fairgrounds in late June. There is a lot of smashing and bashing in store during the championship demolition derby, but the main event is the stock car race on the Eastside Speedway oval.

Nelson County Summer Festival
Va. Rt. 653, Lovingston • (804) 263-5239, (800) 282-8223

Held in late June, this is a family-oriented, upscale festival on the lovely grounds of Oak Ridge Estate south of Lovingston. It features two days of traditional and contemporary music, crafts and wine from four local wineries. Children will enjoy the animals, puppets and Tom Sawyer's Fence Painting game. It costs $10, $5 more if you want to tour the house.

Miss Virginia Pageant
710 Williamson Rd., Roanoke
• (540) 981-1201

This annual event, which takes place around the end of June at the Roanoke Civic Center, produces the state's Miss America contestant. Young women from all over the state compete to win scholarships. Admission is around $10.

Roanoke Valley Horse Show
1001 Roanoke Rd., Salem
• (540) 375-4013

Held in mid-June at the Salem Civic Center, this is one of the top all-breed horse shows on the East Coast. It usually attracts about 800 entries from across the United States. Admission is around $5.

Ash Lawn-Highland Summer Festival
James Monroe Pkwy., Charlottesville
• (804) 293-4500

This potpourri of music is highlighted by opera and musical theater productions, a Music at Twilight concert series with traditional and contemporary musical performances and a Summer Saturdays family entertainment series. (See our Arts chapter.) Prices vary.

Festival Around Town
Pearisburg Community Ctr., Winona Ave., Pearisburg • (540) 921-2644

This beautiful town near the Appalachian Trail hosts this all-day arts and music fete on the third Saturday of June. You can come celebrate early on Friday night when the Lion's Club hosts its kick-off barbecue dinner. Admission is free.

Count Pulaski Festival
Downtown Pulaski • (540) 994-8636

Held in downtown Pulaski, this festival commemorates the renovation of the town's railway station. The event is focused on railroad and transportation and includes activities such as boat shows, car shows, music, arts and crafts and a railroad exhibit. Admission is free.

International Bass Bonanza
Covington • (540) 962-2178

This fishing event is held every year at Lake Moomaw in the Allegheny Mountains. The elusive largemouth bass is the featured attraction. There is no admission price to watch, but competitors must pay a $60 entry fee.

Chautauqua Festival in the Park
Downtown Wytheville • (540) 228-6855

In the late 19th century, the Chautauqua (pronounced sha-TAUK-wa) movement became a popular form of adult education and entertainment in the United States. In the 1920s, Wytheville was a stop on the Chautauqua circuit of traveling caravans with their tents and performances. The lectures, music, drama and children's activities were popular until the Great Depression aided in its demise. But in 1985, the Chautauqua Festival was revived in Wytheville and for 14 years has been a growing source of both entertainment and education. For nine days in late June at locations around this scenic southwest Virginia community, you can sample food, participate in a hot air balloon rally, watch a parade, hear concerts, go to the circus, test your taste buds in the pepper eating contest, take in the art exhibits or listen to the winners read from their works in the annual writing contest. Most events are free.

July

Fourth of July Celebration
Davis St., Culpeper • (540) 825-4416

Enjoy an old-fashioned parade, arts and crafts, games and fireworks in downtown Culpeper and at the town's Yowell Meadow Park. It's free, but bring along some money for the covered-wagon rides.

Fourth of July Celebration
Cadet St., New Market • (540) 740-3432

This Shenandoah Valley town hosts a big family celebration with a lot of music, food, games, a parade and fireworks at Community Park at the south end of Cadet Street. Admission is free.

INSIDERS' TIP

You don't have to be an expert to enjoy wine. Wine festivals give you the opportunity to sample a lot a different varieties so you can find the ones you like. The bigger events, such as Vintage Virginia, often offer free seminars on wine tasting.

A little music will liven up any festival or event.

Piedmont Family Fair
Va. Rt. 605, Arlie • (540) 347-2334

This July 4 celebration, in its eighth year in 1999, is at the Arlie Conference Center from noon to 5 PM. There's plenty to see and do for the whole family, including puppet shows, miniature horses, hay rides, jugglers, concerts, antiques, a Civil War encampment, sheep dogs, vintage cars and llamas. Last year it cost $10 for a carload.

Monticello Independence Day Celebration
Va. Rt. 53, Charlottesville • (804) 984-9822

New citizens from the Charlottesville area are naturalized each Fourth of July on the grounds of Thomas Jefferson's Monticello. A fife and drum corps provides music at this moving event, attended usually by nearly 1,000 people. Past speakers have included Gen. Colin L. Powell, former chairman of the Joint Chiefs of Staff of the Department of Defense, and the Honorable Andrew Young, former U.S. ambassador to the United Nations. Admission to the outdoor ceremony is free. You will have to pay the general admission if you want to tour the house. (See our Attractions chapter.)

Frederick County Fair
U.S. Hwy. 11, Clearbrook • (540) 662-9002, (540) 667-8739

An old-fashioned country fete starts the last Monday in July and runs through Saturday at the county fairgrounds north of town. It features food, arts and crafts, a demolition derby and Miss Frederick County Fair Pageant and a tiny miss pageant for 4- and 5-year-olds. Admission is $4.

Annual Raft Race
Lake Rd., Stuarts Draft • (540) 337-1911

At Shenandoah Acres Resort, folks of all ages race around a measured course in inflatable rafts. Winners receive cash prizes at the late-July event. There is no cost to enter, but you will have to pay the general admission fee to get into the resort. Last year it cost $6 for adults, $4.50 for children ages 6 to 11.

Plantation Days at Highland
James Monroe Pkwy., Charlottesville • (804) 293-9539

At Ash Lawn-Highland, James Monroe's 535-acre estate, merchants, crafters, servants and soldiers are depicted in a celebration of early American life. More than 20 crafters and artisans in period costumes demonstrate and sell their work the first weekend in July. Visitors can also enjoy 18th-century music and games. Tickets are $2 in addition to the regular $7 admission fee.

Graves' Mountain Fourth of July
Va. Rt. 670, Syria • (540) 923-4231

Graves' Mountain Lodge celebrates the Fourth of July with a fireworks display at 9 PM. Admission is free.

Fourth of July Firemen's Carnival
Park Rd., Crozet • (804) 823-6178

Claudius Crozet Park, 12 miles west of Charlottesville, is the venue for this four-day festival with rides, games, food, fireworks and a parade on Saturday. There is no charge, but it costs a dollar to park.

Orange County Fair
Va. Rt. 20, Montpelier • (540) 672-1361

This late-July celebration of rural life features animal exhibits, country music, games and food. You won't want to miss the fiddle contest, draft horse pull or the skunk drag races. Admission to the 1997 event was $5, $3 for children ages 5 to 15.

Pig Roast at Horton Cellars
U.S. Hwy. 33, Gordonsville
• (540) 832-7440

Every year in mid-July, this Orange County winery hosts an annual pig roast, complete with music and wine. It's a popular event, so reservations are needed. Last year's prices were in the $15 range.

Festival of Virginia Wines
Va. Rt. 664, Nelson County
• (804) 325-8171

Wintergreen Resort hosts this annual event featuring wine tastings from 11 Virginia wineries, crafts, workshops, classical and jazz music, and a vintner's dinner. The event is usually held the last Saturday of July. Festival admission is $10. The dinner is $68 per person, and reservations are required.

Fourth of July Jubilee
Va. Rt. 664, Nelson County
• (804) 325-8180

At Wintergreen Resort you'll find games,

entertainment and a grand fireworks display. More than 30 artisans will display their crafts at the July 2 through 4 event. You also can ride the chairlifts. There is no charge for the craft show and fireworks display.

Summer Music Festival
Va. Rt. 664, Wintergreen
• (804) 325-8180

The Wintergreen Performing Arts Council stages a series of concerts ranging from chamber music to full orchestra in the John Evans Performing Arts Center at Wintergreen Resort in July. Fireworks follow the Fourth of July concert. Ticket prices vary from $7.50 to $20.

Rockbridge Regional Fair
Va. Rt. 39 W., Lexington
• (540) 463-3777

Come spend the day at this county fair held at the Virginia Horse Center. It includes a variety of livestock, entertainment, carnival rides, food and competitions. There's a minimal price to park but no admission charge.

Fourth of July Hot Air Balloon Rally
VMI, Lexington • (540) 463-8719

This Fourth of July event features the launching of 14 different balloons at the VMI grounds throughout the weekend. There's also food, games, music and fireworks. It's free.

Music for Americans
Roanoke • (540) 853-2889

At Roanoke's Victory Stadium, this Fourth of July celebration features a performance by the Roanoke Symphony Orchestra, the community chorus and fireworks. Admission is free.

Virginia Commonwealth Games
Various locations, Roanoke
• (540) 343-0987, (800) 333-8274

Produced by Virginia Amateur Sports in Roanoke during the third weekend of July, this sports festival is for men and women of all ages and abilities. This Olympic-style competition includes such sports as basketball, karate, tennis and chess as well as many others. Admission to opening ceremonies, held at the Roanoke Civic Center, is $4 for adults and free to children 10 and younger. Some of the sporting events are free, while others charge a minimal admission.

Vinton July Fourth Celebration
814 E. Washington St., Vinton
• (540) 983-0613

The fireworks celebration is held every year at the Vinton War Memorial. Admission is free.

Salem Fair and Exposition
1001 Roanoke Blvd., Salem
• (540) 375-4013

For two weeks beginning July 1, this old-time country fair holds forth at the Salem Civic Center, both indoors and outside. Carnival rides, games, food, concerts and livestock judging go on for the duration of the event. A bake-off attracts some of the best cooks in the Roanoke Valley. General admission is free, but some events cost extra.

Independence Celebration
Va. Rt. 661, Lynchburg • (804) 525-1806

This is not your typical Fourth of July party. At Poplar Forest, interpreters will portray the lives of local citizenry during Thomas Jefferson's time. The fun includes early 19th-century craft demonstrations, music, wagon rides and a lot of food. Admission is free.

July Fourth Celebration
Bedford • (540) 586-7161

The Blue Ridge lights up under a blazing night sky during this event held at Liberty Lake Park. Also part of the celebration is music, food and face painting. Admission is free.

Blue Ridge Draft Horse and Mule Show
Ferrum College, Ferrum
• (540) 365-4416

Young and old alike enjoy seeing these magnificent beasts show their beauty and strength at an old-time farm country setting at Ferrum College. This event takes place to-wards the end of July and includes string music, contests and costumed interpreters. The price is $5 for adults and $4 for children.

Fourth of July Celebration
Norwood St., Radford • (540) 731-3634

At Radford's Bisset Park you'll find gospel music, craft shows, food vendors and fireworks. All events take place along the New River and are free.

New River Valley Horse Show
Dublin • (540) 980-1991

This is the largest such event in the New River Valley. It is held around the second weekend in July and includes various horse breeds.

July Fourth Celebration
Clifton Forge • (540) 862-4246

This is the largest Independence Day spectacle in the Alleghany Highlands. It's free.

August

Rockingham County Fair
Off U.S. Hwy. 11, Harrisonburg
• (540) 434-0005

The Los Angeles Times named the Rockingham County Fair one of the 10 best rural county fairs in the United States. Virginia's largest agricultural county salutes its agrarian roots with exhibits, livestock and a tractor pull during the third week of August. The 1999 fair features country music star Billy Ray Cyrus. It's seven days of nonstop action with a petting zoo, a circus, bull riding and a demolition derby. Admission is $5, with an extra charge for the main stage concerts.

Natural Chimneys Joust
Va. Rt. 936, Mt. Solon • (540) 350-2510

Here's an anachronism. "Knights" from several states congregate to joust for a shining ring. Bluegrass music fills the air, and the

---

INSIDERS' TIP

October events attract many visitors already in the region for fall foliage. It's a great time to attend an apple-butter festival or grape harvest event — but plan early, as the Blue Ridge is busy in autumn.

seven castle-like towers of Natural Chimneys form a spectacular backdrop. The event, which has been held since 1821, takes place the third Saturday in August. (See our Horse Country chapter.) Admission is $5.

Airshow Festival
Va. Rt. 644, Bealeton • (540) 439-8661

In mid-August, the Flying Circus near Warrenton hosts a weekend of aerial fun. You can even take a ride in the open cockpit of a biplane before or after the show. The 12-minute rides cost $30 per passenger.

Lucketts Fair
Lucketts Community Center, 42361 Lucketts Rd., Leesburg • (703) 771-5281

Be sure to come to the Lucketts Fair, a summer tradition for 27 years during the last weekend in August. Enjoy bluegrass music, quality crafts including furniture, paper cutting, pewter, woven rugs, quilts, forged iron, stained and beveled glass and many others, as well as antiques and old-time demonstrations in spinning and butter churning. For the little ones, there is juggling, music and magic and old-fashioned games, including a watermelon seed spitting contest. After building up an appetite, choose from a vast variety of down-home food, including barbecue platters, hand churned ice cream, country ham sandwiches, pork rinds, roasted corn on the cob and more. The price is only $3, and free for children younger than 6. Stick around for the fruit pie baking contest in the afternoon.

Virginia Wine Festival
Va. Rt. 17, The Plains • (540) 253-5001, (800) 520-9670

The oldest wine festival in the Commonwealth is held in late August on the grounds of Great Meadow. It's an event featuring more than 40 of the state's finest wineries, food, arts and crafts, music and wine lectures. Tickets to the 24-year-old festival are priced just below $20.

Shakespeare at the Ruins
Va. Rt. 777, Barboursville • (540) 832-5355

The Four County Players and Barboursville Vineyards in Orange team up to produce this annual theater, wine and dinner evening. Enjoy a Shakespearean play staged outdoors at the historic ruins of Gov. Barbour's mansion in early August. Call for prices.

Oak Grove Folk Music Festival
Va. Rt. 612, Verona • (540) 885-3000

This annual festival, in its 21st year in 1999, is an intimate, family-oriented weekend where you can hear local and national folk acts under the trees at Virginia's oldest outdoor theater. Claire Lynch and the Front Porch String Band headlined a recent show. Tickets were $12 for each of the three sessions or $25 for a weekend pass. Food and beverages are available.

Blessing of the Vineyard
14141 Hume Rd., Hume
• (540) 635-7627, (800) 304-7656

Oasis Winery hosts this annual event the third weekend of August. It features a blessing ceremony, harvest feast, entertainment and tastings. If you want to go, it's a good idea to make reservations at least two months in advance. Tickets, including the meal, are about $69.

Albemarle County Fair
Off U.S. Hwy. 29, North Garden
• (804) 296-5803

This annual event is usually held at the end of August and features old-fashioned country fun with rides, games, contests, live bands, food and a variety of crop and animal exhibits. Tickets are $4 for adults and $1 for children ages 6 to 12.

Greene County Fair
Va. Rt. 230, Stanardsville
• (804) 985-8282, (804) 985-7622

Enjoy food, music, exhibits and rides at this annual fair. Along with the usual dairy, sheep, beef and market hog shows, events include such acts as a ventriloquist, cloggers, country and bluegrass bands plus frog-jumping, turkey-calling and horseshoe-pitching contests. Tickets to get in are $3.

August Court Days
Various locations • (703) 777-0519

More than 200 costumed characters interpret Leesburg's Colonial history in street vignettes in downtown Leesburg. A children's fair, music and crafts are also featured. This Colonial-era street fair is held usually the third weekend of August. Look for the Scottish Army troops representing the king to take on the buckskinners from the valley. The fest costs $5, and children younger than 12 get in free.

Page Valley Agricultural Fair
Collins Ave., Luray
• **(540) 743-3915, (540) 843-FAIR**

Animal, crop and homemakers' exhibits are part of this fair, which also includes a tractor pull, parade, demolition derby and live music. It is usually held in mid-August. Admission to the fair is $4.

Madison County Fair
Va. Rt. 687, Madison
• **(540) 948-4455**

Come on down to this old-fashioned county fair with a carnival, tractor pull, pet show and fireworks. This event is usually the last Saturday in August at the Young Farmers Grounds on Va. 687. Admission is free.

Rockbridge Community Festival
Main St., Lexington • (540) 463-3777

This festival is held along downtown Main Street. It includes the usual festival activities such as music, arts and crafts, food and live entertainment. It's free.

Vinton Old-Time Bluegrass Festival and Competition
Vinton • (540) 983-0613, (540) 345-8545

This event is held around mid-August every year at the Vinton Farmers Market. Not only can you enjoy music by well-known musicians, but also you can listen to individual and band competitions. Don't forget to stop by and check out the crafts and carnival. It's free.

Thomas Jefferson's Tomato Faire
Main and 12th sts., Lynchburg
• **(804) 847-1499**

This early August agrarian festival starts at 6 AM with tomato and canned good competitions, live entertainment and handmade crafts.

It's held at the downtown Community Market and is free.

Stepping Out
Main St., Blacksburg
• **(540) 951-0454**

This major downtown festival is always held the first weekend in August and is free. Music and food are plentiful as merchants seek ways to attract people downtown.

Newport Agricultural Fair
Giles County • (540) 544-7469

One of the oldest agricultural fairs in Virginia, this free Giles County community event has judged food and agriculture exhibits and livestock competitions, bluegrass music and horseshoe and jousting tournaments happening the second weekend of August.

September

Celebrating Patsy Cline Weekend
Various sites, Winchester
• **(540) 662-4135, (800) 662-1360**

A series of activities held on September 4-6 pays tribute to the legendary country singer who was born in Winchester. Past events have included a buffet meal, a reunion dance with music provided by members of Patsy Cline's band and a concert by George Hamilton III. The cost will vary depending on the events, but the proceeds go toward establishing a Patsy Cline Museum in Frederick County.

Taste of the Mountains Main Street Festival
Main St., Madison • (540) 948-4455

This is a chance to watch craftspeople at work as they demonstrate basket weaving, woodcarving, glass blowing, chair caning, furniture making, quilting, spinning, bark-basket making and beekeeping. You'll want to tear yourself away to listen to Appalachian tunes played on dulcimers and harps and watch the footwork of the clog dancers. A petting zoo for the kids and plenty of mountain-inspired food add to the fun. It's free. Since nearly a mile of Main Street has been blocked off for the fair, park at Madison High School on U.S. 29 and ride the free shuttle.

Photo: Lexington Downtown Development Association

Art on the Green, a juried art show, draws visitors to Hopkins Green in downtown Lexington every October.

Grand Caverns Bluegrass Festival
Off I-81 at Exit 235, Grottoes
• **(540) 249-5705**

Grand Caverns Regional Park hosts the annual music festival in early September. Nationally recognized bands perform in the two-day event and other activities include arts and crafts booths, food, volleyball and horseshoe games and half-price tours of the caverns. Past musical lineups have included the Nashville Bluegrass Band, the Orangeblossoms and Alvin Breeden and the Virginia Cutups. Campers are welcome. Tickets are $23, $21 in advance.

Apple Harvest Arts & Crafts Festival
Pleasant Valley Rd., Winchester
• **(540) 662-3996**

This fall festival at Jim Barnett Park features apple butter-making and pie contests, live music and arts and crafts galore. It is usually held the third weekend in September. Admission is about $3.

Bottle and Pottery Show and Sale
Millwood Pike, Winchester
• **(540) 877-1093**

This mid-September show and sale of antique bottles, pottery, postcards and small collectibles, sponsored by the Apple Valley Bottle Collectors Club, has been an annual happening for 23 years. It's held at Winchester National Guard Armory off I-81 at U.S. 50 W. There's a $1 donation at the door.

Annual Harvest Festival
3659 Ox Rd., Edinburg
• **(540) 984-8699**

Shenandoah Vineyards hosts an all-day festival the first Saturday of September, giving visitors a chance to stomp grapes, munch barbecue, browse through arts and crafts vendors and demonstrations, dance and, of course, sample wine. There's also pony rides, a barrel-rolling contest, live bluegrass and dance bands and a BMW Car Club show and competition. Tickets are $7, $3 for designated drivers.

African-American Culture Day
Davis St., Culpeper • (540) 825-4416

African-American artifacts, history telling and culture sharing are among the events at this free outdoor street festival on the second Saturday in September. There is also music, food, arts and crafts and a Civil War re-enactment.

Constitution Day Celebrations
Va. Rt. 20 S., Montpelier Station
• (540) 672-2728

Enjoy free admission to tour Montpelier, the home of President James Madison, the father of the Constitution. This is an opportunity to better understand the man who contributed so much to the founding of our government. The daylong event commemorating the anniversary of our nation's charter includes Colonial games for children and music by a drum-and-fife corps.

Annual Orange Street Festival
Davis St., Orange • (540) 672-5216

For more than 20 years, Orange has blocked off three blocks along east and west Davis Street for its free street festival. On the first Saturday of the month, the streets are filled with crafts, food, children's rides and live entertainment.

Virginia's Natural History Weekend Retreat
Va. Rt. 664, Wintergreen
• (804) 325-8172, (804) 325-8169

At Wintergreen Resort, natural science experts lead walks, field trips, lectures and slide presentations during this weekend event usually held in mid-September. Scientists, museum curators and college professors lead programs on Virginia natural history, including slide lectures on bats, fossils, wetlands, Indians, birds and reptiles. Registration is $85 and does not include accommodations.

Edinburg Ole Time Festival
Various sites, Edinburg
• (540) 984-8521

The town celebrates its anniversary with cookin' and eatin', cloggin' and joggin', and walkin' and talkin'. This annual event sponsored by the local Chamber of Commerce is held over three days in mid-September and features crafts, demonstrations, antiques, concerts, dances, a walking tour, Civil War re-enactments and a rubber-duck race. Prices vary according to the events. A shuttle bus runs from the parking lot at Valley Baptist Church.

Fall Hunt Country Antiques Fair
28050 Oatlands Plantation Ln., Leesburg
• (703) 777-3174

More than 100 dealers exhibit antiques during this event held at Oatlands Plantation the third or fourth weekend of September. The $7 tickets do not include admission to the house.

Apple Harvest and Butter Making Festival
Various sites in Nelson County
• (804) 263-5036

Enjoy apple butter and apple cider, cooked in giant kettles over an open fire at this fest, held throughout the county in late September and October. For more than 25 years, local orchards have staged these special events throughout the harvest season. Call for locations and times. Among the orchards participating are A.T. Davidson & Sons, Dickie Brothers Orchard, Drumheller's Orchard, Fitzgerald Orchard, Silver Creek-Flippin Seaman Orchards and Saunders Brothers Inc. Admission is free.

Great Grape Celebration at Tarara
Tarara Vineyard and Winery,
13648 Tarara Lane, Leesburg
• (703) 771-7100

This fourth annual celebration of the fall harvest is not to be missed. View the crushing of the grapes and tour the cave winery. Taste wines from 12 Virginia wineries along with a variety of delicious foods. Wine seminars, live entertainment, arts, crafts and even hayrides and a farmers market are there for your enjoyment. Tickets are $10 in advance, $15 at the gate.

Fauquier County Fall Farm Tour
Various sites, Fauquier County
• (540) 347-4414, (800) 820-1021

Seven farms in Fauquier County, including a longhorn ranch, dairy farm, emu ranch, flower and produce farm, beef cattle farm, thoroughbred horse farm and Mariott Ranch were included in last year's annual tour. There is plenty to see and do, including hayrides, a petting farm, beekeeping and miniature horses. Food includes emu burgers, hot dogs and ice cream. Events are free, but food costs extra.

Belle Grove Antique Show
U.S. Hwy. 11, Middletown
• (540) 869-2028

More than 60 antique dealers are on hand for this annual show held on Labor Day weekend at the historic Belle Grove Plantation. Last year admission was $7, and that included a tour of the house. It's easy to find; take Exit 298 off I-81 and turn north on U.S. 11.

Annual Rockbridge Food and Wine Festival
Theatre at Lime Kiln, Lime Kiln Rd.,
Lexington • (540) 463-5375

This early September fest offers something for everyone: exotic autos, live music, seminars, food and wine tastings, and presentations by the Lime Kiln players. Admission is $12 in advance and $15 at the door.

Rockbridge Mountain Music and Dance Festival
Glen Maury Park, 10th Ave.,
Rockbridge County
• (540) 261-7321, (540) 261-2880

This free annual event is held at Glen Maury Park under the pavilion. Activities include fiddle and dance workshops, flat-footing, old-time bands and called dances.

Fincastle Festival
Roanoke St., Botetourt County
• (540) 473-3077

Historic Fincastle celebrates its Scotch-Irish roots at this free two-day festival held downtown the second weekend of September. Arts, music, games and merchant open houses await visitors.

Henry Street Heritage Festival
Henry St., Roanoke • (540) 345-4818

This is an annual celebration of African-American culture in a neighborhood close to downtown Roanoke the last weekend of September. The day includes ethnic food, music, entertainment and children's activities. The events are free.

Olde Salem Days
Main St., Salem • (540) 772-8871

This is a downtown celebration held the second Saturday in September. Its focus is on antiques and crafts and it's free. You'll also enjoy music and children's activities.

Kaleidoscope
Various locations, Lynchburg
• (804) 847-1811, (800) 732-5821

This is Lynchburg's big annual fall festival that lasts nearly a month. It includes a children's festival on the third Saturday, a major antiques show with 100 dealers, a riverfront music jamboree with barbecue, a craft show, bike race and teddy bear parade. Thousands of runners participate in the 10-mile race. Admission to most events is free.

Boones Mill Apple Festival
U.S. Hwy. 220, Boones Mill
• (540) 483-9542

This tiny community rallies enormous resources to stage a major parade and social event along U.S. 220. Look for major politicos among the common folk at this free event held the third Saturday of September.

Claytor Lake Arts and Crafts Fair
Pulaski County • (540) 980-7363

This is a popular Labor Day weekend event for the whole family. About 50 local craftspeople bring their best work to sell. Good Appalachian-style vittles such as hotcakes and apple turnovers are available. Admission is free.

October

Fall Fly-In
491 Airport Rd., Winchester
• (540) 662-5786

Homebuilt, experimental and World War II aircraft owners compete for prizes and share their aviation interests with the public at the Winchester Regional Airport. One year, visitors got to take a ride in a real B-17. Donations are accepted at the gate.

Arborfest at the State Arboretum
U.S. Hwy. 50, 9 miles east of Winchester
• **(540) 837-1758**

Celebrate multicultural gardening traditions the second Sunday in October at the State Arboretum with music, lectures, children's activities, entertainment and the curator's fall tour of the arboretum. There is also an apple tasting and bulb sale. It's free, but donations are accepted.

Crozet Arts and Crafts Festival
Park Rd., Crozet • (804) 977-0406

Claudius Crozet Park, 12 miles west of Charlottesville, is the venue for this nationally ranked show, always held the second weekend of October. This 18-year-old event includes more than 120 crafters, music and food, and a clown has been known to show up too. The cost is usually less than $5.

North-South Skirmish Association Fall Skirmish
off U.S. Hwy. 522 N., Gainesboro
• **(540) 662-3424**

Members of the North-South Skirmish Association fire old weapons at breakable targets in the 97th national event, held the first full weekend of October at Fort Shenandoah. A ladies' dress competition is also held, and there is a large sutler area. Sutlers were people who followed the Civil War soldiers and sold goods. The modern-day sutlers will have books, period clothes and antiques. Admission is free.

Shenandoah Valley Balloon Fest
U.S. Hwy. 50, Millwood
• **(540) 837-1856, (800) 662-1360**

Take a ride in one of 25 hot air balloons and see the fall foliage at its peak during this weekend event in mid-October at historic Long Branch, Robert Burwell's 1811 Greek Revival mansion. Other activities include an antique fire engine display, bluegrass music, hay rides, carnival rides and mansion tours. Last year admission was $20 per carload or $5 per individual. Balloon rides are extra.

Battle of Cedar Creek Living History and Re-enactment
U.S. Hwy. 11, Middletown
• **(540) 869-2064**

This re-enactment is held on the site where the original Civil War battle was fought on October 19, 1864. The annual memorial takes place at Belle Grove Plantation on the weekend closest to October 19. Various symposiums and workshops are held throughout the days, and you also can watch artillery, infantry and signal corps demonstrations. Last year, admission was $8.

New Market Heritage Days
Main St., New Market
• **(540) 740-3212**

The Shenandoah Valley town salutes its German, Scottish and Irish heritage at this weekend festival capped by a large parade. There are pony rides for the children and two craft shows. It's free.

Page County Heritage Festival
Collins Ave., Luray • (540) 743-3915

This Columbus Day weekend festival brings to mind the old-time county fairs with music, clogging shows, wagon rides, apple cider, home-cooked food, a steam and gas engine show and a Saturday Chili Cook-Off. More than 170 crafters display their wares. The festival is held at the Page County Fairgrounds. An admission will be charged.

Elkton Autumn Days Festival
B St., Elkton • (540) 298-9370

This outdoor festival is held the third weekend in October. Features include home-cooked food, a car show, square dancing, clogging and live entertainment. More than 100 crafters also display their wares in front of Elkton Elementary School. There is no admission fee.

Aldie Harvest Festival
U.S. Hwy. 50, Aldie • (703) 327-6742

This quaint village bursts with life in mid-October with a festival centering around the restoration of the town's double-wheel 1810 mill. More than 300 crafters and artists take part in the day's activities, which include a

Civil War encampment, food and music throughout the town. It's free.

Traditional Frontier Festival
U.S. Hwy. 250 W., Staunton
• **(540) 332-7850**

This is a good time to visit the Frontier Culture Museum, which hosts this annual festival on October 16-18. Come and enjoy traditional crafts and entertainment from Germany, England, Ireland and America at the museum's living-history farms, and sample English scones, Scottish meat pies and German bratwurst. The cost is $8 for adults and $4 for children.

Virginia Fall Foliage Festival
Broad St., Waynesboro
• **(540) 943-2093, (540) 949-8513, (540) 949-8203**

This festival happens usually the first two consecutive weekends in October. Features include a 10K run, an arts and crafts show with more than 200 exhibitors, a chili cookoff and a lot of good food made with apples, including apple dumplings, apple butter and cider. There's also face painting and balloons for the kids. No admission is charged.

Graves' Mountain Apple Harvest Festival
Va. Rt. 670, Syria • **(540) 923-4231**

Celebrate apple-harvest season with the folks at Graves' Mountain Lodge the second and third weekends of October. Festivities include arts and crafts, apple-butter making, hay rides and horseback rides. You can also pick apples in the lodge's orchards. Don't miss the homemade Brunswick stew cooked in black kettles over an open fire each day. Admission and parking are free.

Fall Fiber Festival & Sheep Dog Trials
Va. Rt. 20 S., Montpelier Station
• **(540) 672-2935**

The stars are the sheep, llamas, angora and cashmere goats, and angora rabbits who provide the raw materials for the spinning, weaving and shearing demonstrations. Sheep dog trials take place both days of the event,

which is usually held the first weekend in October at Montpelier, home of James Monroe. Forty vendors also are on hand to exhibit and demonstrate their fiber crafts. A corner has been set up where children can learn to spin and weave. Last year admission cost $6 for those 16 and older.

Monticello Bacchanalian Feast
U.S. Hwy. 250 W., Charlottesville
• **(804) 296-4188**

This evening feast at the Boar's Head Inn includes a seven-course meal with Virginia wines and entertainment. It's usually held on one of the first Fridays in October to kick off the Monticello Wine and Food Festival. In 1998, tickets were $65. Call for a reservation.

Monticello Wine and Food Festival
U.S. Hwy. 250 W., Charlottesville
• **(804) 296-4188**

Held at the Boar's Head Inn, this early to mid-October festival is a chance to taste many of the wines made in Virginia and view exhibits of the state's many wineries and vineyards. There also is an exhibit of crafts on hand plus samples of gourmet foods. Last year tickets were $12 at the door or $8 in advance.

Virginia Film Festival
Culbreth Rd., Charlottesville
• **(804) 924-FEST, (800) UVA-FEST**

Filmmakers, scholars, movie stars and the public will explore TechnoVisions at the 12th annual Virginia Film Festival on October 21-24, 1999. This year's theme will examine the emergence of new technology from the dawn of filmmaking to today's Internet. Bring along your 3D glasses for screenings of Alfred Hitchcock's *Dial M for Murder* and Andy Warhol's *Frankenstein*. More than 60 films, videos and CD-ROMs will be presented, along with guest speakers and free panels on how to break into the business. Past participants in the film festival include such stars as Gregory Peck, Jimmy Stewart, Nick Nolte, Robert Duvall, Charlottesville's own Sissy Spacek and Jason Robards (see the Close-up in our Arts chapter). While some receptions may cost in the $40 range, tickets to the movie screenings were $6 last year.

Dayton Autumn Celebration
Main and College sts., Dayton
• **(540) 879-9538**

This Rockingham County town greets fall the first Saturday in October with live comedy and country music, food, 200 arts and crafts exhibits and children's games. There is no cost. The festival also runs a free shuttle bus from satellite parking areas.

Crafters Fair
Va. Rt. 617, Schuyler • (804) 831-2000

This fair is held in late October at the Waltons Mountain Museum in Schuyler, near Charlottesville, where Earl Hamner Jr. grew up and gained the inspiration for the wonderful family television series *The Waltons*. It's a good chance to see the work of local crafters and meet up with other fans of the popular TV show. It's free.

Christmas at the Kurtz
2 N. Cameron St., Winchester
• **(540) 722-6367**

From mid-October to Christmas Eve, artisans from the Shenandoah Valley display handmade and unique arts and crafts at the Kurtz Cultural Center. There are also craft demonstrations on the weekends. Admission is free.

Craig County Fall Festival
Downtown New Castle • (540) 864-5010

Breakfast and lunch are served in the old brick hotel as a part of this street festival in mid-October. Live entertainment, an antique car show, crafts and a Civil War re-enactment are all part of the fun. The events are free.

Harvest Festival on the Market
Downtown Roanoke • (540) 342-2028

Every fall folks pour into the streets of Roanoke's Historic City Market for horse-drawn carriage rides, lessons in scarecrow building, hot cider and live bluegrass. The event is usually held during mid-October. It's free.

Roanoke Railway Festival
303 Norfolk Ave., Roanoke
• **(540) 342-5670**

The Virginia Museum of Transportation celebrates the Roanoke Valley's rail heritage with a weekend of model train exhibits and an antique car show. There's also nostalgic entertainment, a huge rail-related crafts show, children's activities, bus tours and other transportation-related activities. Admission is $5 for adults, $4 for seniors and $3 for students.

Annual Zoo Boo
Roanoke • (540) 343-3241

It's a Halloween party at the Mill Mountain Zoo that gets bigger every year. Children dress up and party among the animals. Admission is $5 for adults and $3 for children.

Affair in the Square
Campbell Ave., Roanoke
• **(540) 342-5708**

This event combines entertainment, food, beverages and dancing on every level of Center in the Square and has become an annual custom for many residents of Southwest Virginia. It takes place the second Saturday of October. Admission is $40 per person.

Wine Festival
Smith Mountain Lake
• **(540) 721-1203, (800) 676-8203**

On the last Sunday in October, more than a dozen of Virginia's best wineries converge at Bernard's Landing and Resort for a festival on the beautiful lake. Chamber music, wine tastings and good food make this one of the area's more sophisticated festivals. Prices are $15 to taste or $5 for general admission.

Roanoke Symphony Polo Cup
off Main St., Salem • (540) 343-6221

Come enjoy an afternoon of action with professional polo teams at Roanoke County's Green Hill Park. This early October event, sponsored by the Roanoke Symphony, includes a day of food, fashion and fun. Admission is around $10.

Virginia Garlic Festival
U.S. Hwy. 29, Amherst
• **(804) 946-5168, (800) 732-5821**

The 5-acre Rebec Vineyards hosts this mid-October celebration, and several Virginia wineries participate. The wonderful food will please epicures. A Garlic Queen dressed in a giant bulb with sprouts shooting from her head has been known to make an appearance. You can also find music and arts and crafts. Admission with wine-tasting for adults is $12; general admission is $6 and $ 2 for children ages 2 to 11. Tickets are a little more if purchased at the gate.

Amherst County Apple Harvest and Arts and Crafts Festival
U.S. Hwy. 29, Amherst
• (804) 847-7435

More than 100 crafters display their works, along with apple products and special entertainment at Amherst County High School in late October. Admission is free.

Main Street Music Festival
Main St., Lynchburg • (804) 847-1499

An afternoon in early October finds the Community Market replete with blues, jazz and gospel music. This free multicultural event also has a variety of ethnic foods and cultural exhibits.

Harvest Festival
Community Market, Main St., Lynchburg
• (804) 847-1499, (800) 732-5821

This end-of-October festival features Virginia-made products and crafts, square dancing and country music. Children go crazy with the costume contests and community pumpkin-carving. It's free.

Blue Ridge Folklife Festival
Ferrum College • (540) 365-4416

On the fourth Saturday of October, Ferrum College showcases regional folklife with this blockbuster festival, now in its 26th year. Visitors experience the tastes, sights and sounds of western Virginia folk culture as demonstrated by local residents. More than 40 Blue Ridge crafters demonstrate basket making, instrument making, cane carving, tobacco twisting and a variety of other folk arts. Many of these items are available for sale as well. The South's thriving auto culture is featured along with vintage steam and gas-powered farm machinery. There are horse pulling, mule jumping and log skidding contests. The Virginia

State Championship Open Water and Treeing Coon Dog contests are held throughout the day. A delicious variety of foods are always on hand and there are three performance stages featuring music and storytelling. Many of these demonstrations are getting to be extinct as the old-timers die, so if you want to see the Blue Ridge as it was, make it a point to go to the festival. It's crowded, but a lot of fun. The festival is held from 10 AM to 5 PM. Admission, which includes a tour of the Farm Museum, is $5 for adults and $4 for children and senior citizens.

Sedalia Country Fair
1108 Sedalia Rd., Big Island
• (804) 299-5080

At this fair held the second Saturday in October you can find animal events, antique and new farm machinery, exhibits and food, glorious food. Admission is free.

Historic Appomattox Railroad Festival
Downtown Appomattox • (804) 352-8268

During this mid-October free event, festivities include a parade, antiques displays, live music, memorabilia, food and children's activities. The festival commemorates the donation of the depot to the town.

Halloween Jazz at Stonewall Vineyards
off U.S. Hwy. 460 E., Concord
• (804) 993-2185

Just east of Lynchburg is another winery, Stonewall Vineyards, which hosts this relaxing weekend event in late October. Come dressed in costume to enjoy live jazz, gourmet food and local wines. A blanket or chair is recommended. Admission is $5 with costume, $6 without.

Smith Mountain Lake Fall Festival
Various locations, Moneta
• (540) 721-1203

On Columbus Day weekend, Smith Mountain Lake's six or so communities all host festivals, forming a virtual ring of events around the lake. You'll find arts and crafts shows, an antique car show, a flea market, traditional folkway demonstrations and more. The events are free.

MS Home Tour Gala
Various homes, Smith Mountain Lake
• (540) 297-8687, (800) 676-8203

This national award-winning fund-raiser for Multiple Sclerosis showcases the grandest homes on the lake. Homes are accessible by either land or water. Don't miss this event for show-and-tell for a good cause. It's held around the first weekend of October at 10 different homes each year. Tickets are $12 in advance.

Radford Highlanders Festival
Main St., Radford • (540) 831-5182

A joint partnership between the city of Radford and Radford University, this event celebrates the area's Scotch-Irish heritage. Appalachian traditions and activities include Highlander games, music, dancing, crafts, storytelling and food. The events are free.

Newbern Fall Festival of Arts and Crafts
5240 Wilderness Rd., Newbern
• (540) 674-4835

Held at the Wilderness Road Museum in mid-October, this free event is filled with the spirit of the Appalachian Mountains through and through. Square dancing, antiques, crafts and stagecoach rides are just a few of the activities you can find here.

Fall Foliage Festival
Downtown Clifton Forge
• (540) 862-4969

The autumn glory of Alleghany County serves as an incredible backdrop for this arts and crafts festival held the third weekend in October. You can find music, craftspeople, an art show and various other activities featuring the Appalachian heritage. The festival is free.

November

Threshing Party
U.S. Hwy. 250 W., Staunton
• (540) 332-7850

Workers at the Frontier Culture Museum show how farmers in different parts of the world harvest grain at this two-day event in late-November. It's free with your admission to the museum. Last year's rates were $8 for adults and $4 for children.

Christmas at Oatlands Plantation
28050 Oatlands Plantation Ln., Leesburg
• (703) 777-3174

Special Christmas events begin here the day after Thanksgiving and continue through Christmas. The mansion is dressed for the holidays, and living history presentations are staged on weekends. Call for events and times. Most programs in the day cost $8.

Culpeper Christmas Open House
Davis St., Culpeper • (540) 825-4416

Downtown Culpeper comes alive with Christmas activity in late November: carriage rides, caroling, stories and refreshments. Christmases past have featured old-fashioned demonstrations, including sausage making, weaving and blacksmithing. To make sure you're in a festive mood, the open house launches the start of the downtown merchants' Christmas sales. There is no charge.

Festival of Trees
Jefferson Ctr., Roanoke • (540) 344-0931

Local charities and businesses benefit the Mental Health Association by erecting and decorating large themed Christmas trees. This annual event held on Thanksgiving weekend delights everyone who loves Christmas decorations on beautiful trees. The event is free.

Greening of the Market
Market Sq., Roanoke • (540) 342-2028

To decorate for the holidays, downtowners hang live wreaths in the historic market area, and strollers enjoy free steaming apple cider.

Lighting of the Community Christmas Tree
Lee Plaza, Roanoke • (540) 981-2889

Everyone is invited to Lee Plaza at City Hall for this annual event held Thanksgiving weekend. It's free.

Stocked Market Holiday Bazaar
1001 Roanoke Blvd., Salem
• (540) 375-3004

More than 100 booths in the Salem Civic Center feature crafts and gifts during this mid-

November event. A $5 admission fee will get you in for three days.

Christmas at the Market
Main St., Lynchburg • (804) 847-1499, (800) 732-5821

This colorful event is always held at the end of November at the downtown Community Market. Come enjoy a variety of hand-crafted Christmas items from more than 100 vendors. The kids will love the music and Mr. and Mrs. Santa Claus. Admission is free.

Santa at the Lake
Smith Mountain Lake • (800) 676-8203

Where else would Santa arrive by parasail? It's a real thrill when the boat pulls in and the rosy-cheeked man with the white beard descends from the skies over Smith Mountain Lake and onto the dock at Hales Ford Center — truly a unique experience for the youngsters. This event takes place Thanksgiving weekend and is free.

Franklin County Fall Arts and Crafts Festival
Rocky Mount • (540) 483-9542

This free festival is usually held the weekend before Thanksgiving. Downtown merchants gather together their best local wares for the event.

December

Holiday House Tour
2 N. Cameron St., Winchester • (540) 667-3577

Tour five of Winchester's homes decorated for the holidays the first Sunday of the month. The tour includes a mix of old and new homes in and around Old Town. Check by the Welcome Center in the Kurtz Building for locations and costs. In years past, the tour was $10.

Celebrate spring at the Apple Blossom Festival in Winchester.

Photo: Virginia Division of Tourism

Abram's Delight Candlelight Tour
1340 S. Pleasant Valley Rd., Winchester • (540) 662-6550

This 1754 house is dressed up in period greenery for the holidays. Free tours are given the first weekend in December.

First Night Winchester
2 N. Cameron St., Winchester • (540) 722-6367

The town's annual New Year's Eve celebration of the arts features more than 40 different artists entertaining the public at sites throughout Winchester. It's a family-oriented, alcohol-free celebration. Buy a button for $7, and you will have access to all the venues.

Christmas Candlelight Tour
336 Belle Grove Rd., Middletown • (540) 869-2028

Belle Grove Plantation decked out in its holiday splendor is a grand way to celebrate the season. The tour is usually offered mid-through late December. Admission is $7.

Candlelight Christmas Tour
46 E. Main St., Page County • (540) 743-3915

Take a candlelight tour of Page County's

historic bed and breakfasts the second weekend of December. About seven inns are included on this tour. In 1998 the price was $12, $6 for ages 5 to 12. If you stay at one of the participating inns, it's free.

First Night Harrisonburg
Various locations, Harrisonburg
• **(540) 433-0279**

This is a nonalcoholic New Year's Eve community arts celebration for all ages. More than 20 musical, drama and dance performances are staged at seven locations around the city. Simply buy a button for about $8, $6 in advance, and go to as many events as you like. Children younger than 5 get in free.

Woodrow Wilson Open House
18 N. Coalter St., Staunton
• **(540) 885-0897**

Entertainment, birthday cake, punch and holiday decorations are part of Woodrow Wilson's birthday party celebration on December 28 at his birthplace. There also are some special Victorian amusements geared for the children. It's free.

First Night Augusta
Downtown Staunton
• **(540) 949-8203, (540) 886-2206**

A variety of music from classical to country can be heard at this New Year's Eve celebration for the entire family. Adults will enjoy line dancing, a visual arts display along Main Street, gospel and folk music, dramatic readings, cloggers and magic tricks. A series of children's activities begin early in the afternoon with a parade, quilt painting, face painting and pony rides. The event was free in 1998, but participants were required to get a festival button for admittance in several of the venues.

Traditions of Christmas Past
U.S. Hwy. 250 W., Staunton
• **(540) 332-7850**

Throughout the month opportunities abound for you to tour the Frontier Culture Museum's living farms by lantern at night and to learn about how America's early settlers and their kin prepared for Christmas. Children may attend gift-making workshops. This is a popular event, so getting tickets in advance is advisable. The tickets cost $10 for adults and $5 for children.

Christmas Open House at Morven Park
17263 Southern Planter Ln., Leesburg
• **(703) 777-2414**

The mansion is decorated with turn-of-the-century ornaments, the fireplaces are ablaze and a 12-foot-tall Christmas tree fills the Great Room with its pine fragrance. It looks as if the late Virginia governor Westmoreland Davis and his wife might walk through the door at any moment. The open house is held most days throughout the month. Last year the standard tour price was $6, $5 for seniors and $3 for children ages 6 to 12.

First Night Leesburg
King and Market sts., Leesburg
• **(703) 771-2707**

This family event rings in the New Year with a candlelight procession to the courthouse. This celebration of the arts includes singing, puppet shows, storytelling, mimes and plenty of food. Tickets are $7. Those younger than 6 get in free.

Christmas in Historic Old Town Warrenton
Main St., Warrenton • (800) 820-1021

Warrenton is full of holiday cheer with Santa visits, horse-drawn carriage rides, caroling and more starting the first Friday in December and running every weekend until Christmas. There is a $1 to $2 charge for rides.

First Night Warrenton
Various locations, Warrenton
• **(800) 820-1021**

This family celebration features more than 50 musical and theatrical performances throughout Old Town Warrenton. Festivities culminate in a candlelight gathering on the Old Courthouse steps. Admission was is around $7.

Holiday Homes Tour
122 Main St., Orange County
• **(540) 672-1653**

Tour bed and breakfast inns, Montpelier, James Madison Museum and other historic sites the first Saturday of the month. Advance

Street festivals are common throughout the year in the Blue Ridge.

sales to the 1998 event — which toured home places more than 125 years old — were $15 in advance and $20 at the door.

Annual Yuletide Traditions at Ash Lawn-Highland
Va. Rt. 795 (James Monroe Pkwy.), Charlottesville • (804) 293-9539 (804) 293-9539, (804) 977-1234

Included in the holiday activities throughout December at the historic home of James Monroe are Christmas By Candlelight evening tours and historic re-enactments as well as Gingerbread and Lace, a celebration with caroling, ornament-making, tree-trimming and refreshments. Cost runs around $8. After Christmas, you can attend afternoon holiday concerts at Ash Lawn-Highland.

Annual Yuletide Traditions at Michie Tavern
683 Thomas Jefferson Pkwy. (Va. Rt. 53), Charlottesville • (804) 977-1234

An array of Christmas delicacies is served for a Yuletide feast in the Ordinary at historic Michie Tavern in mid-December. There also are ballroom dancing, candelight tours and activities for the children during the weekend. The feast costs $25, $12.50 for children ages 5 to 10.

Annual Yuletide Traditions Monticello
Va. Rt. 53 (Thomas Jefferson Pkwy.), Charlottesville • (804) 984-9822

The home of Thomas Jefferson holds guided holiday tours several evenings before Christmas, with period dancing in the parlor, food demonstrations in the kitchen and refreshments in the museum shop. Last year the cost was $10, $5 for children ages 6 to 11. There's also a holiday wreath workshop at the Monticello Visitors Center.

First Night Virginia
Downtown Charlottesville • (804) 296-8269

The first and the biggest of the First Night events in the state, this alcohol-free family-oriented New Year's Eve celebration of the arts is held in various locations in the downtown area from 3 PM to 1 AM. Nearly 100 acts

are booked for the night's entertainment, ranging from blues to bagpipes and comedy to concerts, and ends with a gigantic fireworks display. Purchase a button — the cost is around $10 for adults and $5 for children younger than 12 — and it will be your key to getting into all the events.

Appalachian Mountain Christmas
Va. Rt. 664, Wintergreen • (804) 325-8180

During Christmas week, the resort celebrates with horse-drawn carriage rides, ornament and Appalachian craft workshops, wandering minstrels, jugglers and clowns and an old-fashioned carol sing. The fees for the workshops average $10, and reservations are required.

Holiday Traditions in Lexington
Various locations, Lexington • (540) 463-3777

Visiting Lexington is always nice, especially when it is the Christmas season. Activities range from a 10K road race to a candlelight procession. Other free activities include a tree-lighting ceremony, caroling and a Christmas House tour.

Community Tree Lighting
Hopkins Green Park, downtown Lexington • (540) 463-3777

Lexington's mayor is joined in the annual tree lighting by glee club singers from Virginia Military Institute and Washington & Lee University. It's free.

Dickens of a Christmas
Market Sq., Roanoke • (540) 342-2028

Roanoke's City Market is the place for carriage rides, chestnut roasting, ice carvings, hot cider and holiday music on the first three Fridays in December. It's free.

First Night Roanoke
Market Sq., Roanoke • (540) 342-2640

This nonalcoholic New Year's celebration in the downtown City Market area was cited in 1998 by the Southeast Tourism Society as one of the Top 20 events in the southeast. The fun includes a Chinese dragon processional, costumed characters, ice-skating for kids, holiday music, hot cocoa and a "Resolution Wall," where you can write your New Year's resolution for the world to see. The night ends with a huge display of fireworks. In advance, admission is $7 for adults and $3 for children. On the night of the event, admission is $9 and $5 for children.

Ye Olde Salem Christmas
Main St., Salem • (540) 375-3057

Early in December Salem celebrates the season with carriage rides, children's activities, food and open houses. Also enjoy a parade and ice sculptures. The events are free.

Amos Alonzo Stagg Bowl
1001 Roanoke Blvd., Salem
• (540) 375-3004, (800) 288-2122

Salem Stadium hosts the NCAA Division III football championship in mid December each year. Admission is $8 in advance or $10 the day of the game for adults. Children and students get in for $5.

The Living Christmas Tree
Thomas Rd., Lynchburg • (804) 239-9281

Hear a spectacular 100-voice choir and see 50,000 lights adorn this 40-foot tree at Thomas Road Baptist Church. The is no admission charge.

Christmas at Point of Honor
112 Cabell St., Lynchburg
• (804) 847-1459, (800) 732-5821

This is a celebration of the joyous season as it would have been in the 1820s. Held in early December at Point of Honor, a mansion built by Patrick Henry's doctor, George Cabell, the event is an opportunity to revel in the color and aroma of festive greens and sing along with a local group performing 19th-century carols. Admission is free.

Scrooge Day
Main St., Lynchburg • (804) 847-1499

Always the last Saturday before Christmas, this is the day to take care of last-minute shopping at the downtown Community Market. You'll find handmade gifts, stocking stuffers, home-baked treats, wreaths, greenery and trees. Admission is free.

Diamond Hill Christmas Candlelight Tour
Lynchburg • (804) 528-0747

Come tour four homes in Lynchburg during the Christmas season. Each will have music and a candlelight dinner. Don't forget to make your advance reservations for this event happening the first weekend in December. Admission is $8.

Patrick Henry Women's Auxiliary Christmas Tea
Brookneal • (804) 376-5216

Enjoy Christmas tea, Colonial style, at Red Hill. Patrick Henry's home is decorated with period trimmings, and refreshments and holiday music add to the holiday mood. Admission is free.

Christmas Lights at Elks National Home
931 Ashland Ave., Bedford
• (540) 586-8232

Retired Elks work all year to get ready for one of the grandest displays of Christmas lighting in Virginia every December. Drive through and see years of innovative decorations by these retired fraternal associates. It's free to drive through.

Deck the Halls Open House
5240 Wilderness Rd., Newbern
• (540) 674-4835

Visit the Wilderness Road Regional Museum for a rustic Christmas to remember. It's free to enter.

Along both Skyline Drive and the Blue Ridge Parkway you'll find lodges, cabins and campsites where you can spot deer, raccoons and black bear from your doorstep.

Blue Ridge Parkway and Skyline Drive

It's like stepping back in time. Imagine driving almost the entire length of an East Coast state without seeing fast food restaurants, tractor trailers or glaring billboards. In Virginia this miracle is made possible by a scenic stretch of highway that begins in Front Royal as Skyline Drive, runs the length of Shenandoah National Park and becomes the Blue Ridge Parkway near Waynesboro. From Waynesboro, the Parkway meanders 469 miles, all the way to the Great Smoky Mountains in North Carolina, offering magnificent views of valleys, forests and mountain ranges along the way.

Construction of Skyline Drive began in 1931, spurred on by President Herbert Hoover, who spent many a weekend at his fishing camp in the area. As the story goes, Hoover was riding his horse along the crest of the Blue Ridge Mountains one day in 1930 when he turned to a companion and said: "These mountains are made for a road, and everybody ought to have a chance to get the views from here. I think they're the greatest in the world."

The road was built by local farmers, who were paid from drought relief funds. The Civilian Conservation Corps pitched in to build rock walls, picnic areas and scenic overlooks. The 105-mile-long Skyline Drive was finished on August 29, 1939, during the administration of Franklin D. Roosevelt.

Today it costs $10 per vehicle to enter Skyline Drive at any point. That fee and the 35 mph speed limit help keep the road free of commuters and speeders. Pedestrians and bicyclists pay $5.

Unfortunately, the crystal-clear visibility of a half-century ago has given way to occasional hazy conditions brought on by worsening pollution, much caused by coal-burning power plants in the Ohio Valley and from as far away as northern Indiana. The haze is worst during summer months. Shenandoah National Park officials do a visibility check every day at 1 PM and post the results around the park by 2 PM. If you want to know what the visibility is like before you go, contact one of the entrance stations that post the information daily: Front Royal, (540) 635-5258; or Rockfish Gap, (804) 943-8764. A weather recording is available at (540) 999-3500.

Just like Shenandoah National Park, the Blue Ridge Parkway is governed by the National Park Service but is a separate and distinct facility. The legislated purpose of the Parkway was to link Shenandoah National Park with Great Smoky Mountains National Park in North Carolina and Tennessee by means of a scenic highway. This goal was accomplished in 1936 and was recognized worldwide as a significant engineering achievement. The designers often took the long route, which would have been avoided by conventional highway builders, to provide access to scenic, historic and natural features of the region. The route follows the mountaintops at an average elevation of 3,000 feet. Unlike Skyline Drive, there is no charge for access to the Blue Ridge Parkway.

Both Skyline Drive and the Parkway are very popular destinations. Shenandoah National Park officials estimate they have two million visitors a year during the peak seasons of summer and fall. In October you can even see the cars lined up on the Rockfish Gap Exit off I-81 waiting to enter the Parkway and the Drive.

Along both Skyline Drive and the Blue Ridge Parkway you'll find lodges, cabins and campsites where you can spot deer, raccoons and black bear from your doorstep. Waysides (grills and coffee shops) offer souvenirs, fudge, ice cream and Southern specialties such as Virginia ham, blackberry cobbler and buckwheat pancakes. Drive slowly when you pull into the parking lot: curious deer have been known to walk right up to the cars.

Of course, hundreds of restaurants, motels, hotels and bed and breakfast inns pepper the area near Skyline Drive and the Parkway, but this chapter includes only places on these scenic highways. The facilities in Shenandoah National Park are operated by ARAMARK, a concessionaire for the National Park Service. Some of the restaurants and accommodations along the Blue Ridge Parkway are privately owned and operated, which we have noted in individual listings. This is because the Parkway's boundaries are quite narrow in places, bordering private property where people live or make a living.

Accommodations, restaurants and snack bars described in this section are organized from north to south. Locations are identified by mileposts, beginning with 0.6 at the Front Royal Entrance Station. The numbering system starts over when Skyline Drive meets the Blue Ridge Parkway at Rockfish Gap.

For more information about the scenic highways, contact one of the following:

• ARAMARK Shenandoah National Park Lodges, P.O. Box 727, Luray 22835; (800) 999-4714, for accommodations and restaurants

• Shenandoah National Park Headquarters, 3655 U.S. Highway 211 E., Luray 22835; (540) 999-3500

• National Park Headquarters, 400 BB&T Building, Asheville, North Carolina 28801; (828) 298-0398 or (828) 271-4779

These offices will send you directories and strip maps of the drives.

Skyline Drive

Visitor Centers

If it's your first trip to Skyline Drive, you might want to start off at one of the visitor cen-

ters. There's so much to see and do, and the friendly staff can get you started in the right direction. The centers can provide you with maps of the park, trails and facilities, and they also sell books and more comprehensive guides to the area and its people. The park staff also will have the most up-to-date information about wildlife, changes in trail conditions and upcoming ranger programs. Skyline Drive has two visitors centers that are open from 9 AM to 5 PM daily from March 28 to November 2. The hours are reduced in the winter. Both centers have restrooms, water fountains and phones.

Dickey Ridge Visitor Center
Mile 4.6 • (540) 635-3566

Near the Front Royal entrance to Skyline Drive, this former dining hall was built in 1938 and converted into a visitor center in the 1950s. From here you have a view of Chester Gap to the east and Massanutten to the west. This center usually closes in the winter.

Harry F. Byrd Sr. Visitor Center
Mile 51 • (540) 999-3283

Fifteen miles north of the Swift Run Gap entrance off U.S. Highway 33, this visitor center offers a scenic view of a large centuries-old meadow. Opened in 1966, the center is near the park's largest and most popular campground, Big Meadows.

Overlooks

It's a three-hour nonstop trip from Front Royal to Rockfish Gap. However, if you wish to stop and enjoy the view, which we recommend you do, there are more than 70 scenic overlooks along the 105-mile Skyline Drive. Aside from affording breathtaking views of the Shenandoah Valley to the west and the Virginia Piedmont to the east, several overlooks have picnic tables and access to hiking trails. Most will have signs explaining the views. Here is just a sample:

Stony Man Overlook
Mile 38.6, Elevation 3,100 ft.

Look to your left and you can see what appears to be a man's face in the second-highest peak in the park, Stony Man Mountain. You also can see New Market Gap and the town of Luray. One of the larger overlooks along the drive, Stony Man has running water, flush toilets and a picnic table. You also can hook up with the Appalachian Trail from here.

Franklin Cliffs Overlook
Mile 49, Elevation 3,140 ft.

History buffs will find this spot interesting. From here you can look out over the Shenandoah Valley and see where Gen. Thomas J. "Stonewall" Jackson led his Confederate troops through what is now the little town of Stanley. His 25,000 men struggled up over the Blue Ridge through Fishers Gap in November 1862 on their way to victory in Fredericksburg. There are two placards here on Jackson and his campaign.

Hikes

One of the most popular activities on Skyline Drive is hiking. There are nearly 500 miles of trails, including some 95 miles of the Appalachian Trail. Some of the most popular lead to waterfalls. Here are some of the favorites. See our Recreation chapter for more hiking information.

Limberlost Trail
Mile 43

Dedicated in September 1997, Limberlost is the park's first wheelchair-accessible trail. This gently winding loop is 1.3 miles long with a crushed greenstone walkway. The trail passes by old homesites and crosses Whiteoak Canyon Run. It includes a wooden boardwalk through the wetlands, a footbridge over the run and many benches along the way.

Hawksbill Trail
Mile 45.6 and 46.7

There are two parking lots that lead to this 2-mile round-trip hike. Be prepared. It's a steep climb to the summit of Hawksbill Mountain, the highest point in the park at 4,051 feet. At the top, there is an observation platform, picnic table and shelter.

Dark Hollow Falls Trail
Mile 50.7

This is one of the most heavily trafficked trails in the park. It will take you to the bottom of Dark Hollow Falls, a 71-foot waterfall that cascades over greenstone. It's a 1.4-mile round-trip hike from the parking lot.

Lodges

Skyland Lodge
Mile 41.7 • (540) 999-2211, (800) 999-4714

This is the first lodging facility you reach when driving south on Skyline Drive from the Front Royal entrance. George Freeman Pollock, one of the people instrumental in establishing the Shenandoah National Park, built a private resort, Stony Man Camp, with cabins and a dining hall on this site in 1894.

The Skyland facilities sit at 3,680 feet — the highest point on Skyline Drive — and several of the 177 guest rooms overlook the Shenandoah Valley. Skyland offers a variety of lodgings, including rustic cabins, motel-style lodge rooms and suites. Some are equipped for individuals with disabilities. Amenities include a glass-walled dining room and the Tap Room, which offers live entertainment nightly during the summer. Guest rooms do not have phones, but some have televisions. Service shelters have pay phones and ice and soda machines.

Skyland is a lively place for a family vacation. Adults can take guided horseback trips, and children may ride ponies. The playground has swings, bars, seesaws and plenty of grass and dirt. An amphitheater serves as an outdoor classroom where the National Park Service conducts educational programs. Naturalists lead hikes along numerous trails near the lodge in spring and summer and offer evening programs on such topics as bird-watching, wildflowers and acid rain. You can also gaze through a telescope at the brilliant stars. Skyland's gift shop is stocked with mountain crafts, photo supplies, daily papers and magazines. The lodge has meeting rooms and audiovisual equipment to accommodate conferences.

Rates range from $79 to $88 per night for a single lodge unit on weekdays to $155 per night for a one-bedroom suite on weekends. Rustic cabin rooms are $46 to $77 per night on weekdays and $48 to $79 per night on weekends. The lodge is usually open from late March to the end of November.

The most popular month is October, that magical time of brilliant color in the Blue Ridge. Room rates are slightly higher this month. Reservations are often made a year in advance for these autumn nights. It's not a bad idea to make reservations well in advance for summer nights too.

Big Meadows Lodge
**Mile 51.3 • (540) 999-2221,
(800) 999-4714**

Nine miles south of Skyland Lodge you'll come to a clearing, the only large treeless area in the Shenandoah National Park. The Byrd Visitor Center and the Big Meadows Wayside overlook the meadow, which was probably the result of fire set either by lightning or by Native Americans to encourage the growth of wild berries. The Park Service keeps the area clear to this day, and it's an excellent place for visitors to see a diversity of wildlife, including berries and wildflowers.

The resort is a short drive from the meadow. The main lodge was built in 1939 by mountain labor using stone from the Massanutten Mountains across the Shenandoah Valley. Paneling throughout the building came from native chestnut trees that grew in the Big Meadows area. This variety of tree is nearly extinct today because of the chestnut blight in the early 1930s.

The resort includes 11 rustic cabins and 70 motel-style rooms. The main lodge's 21 rooms offer the warm, rustic atmosphere of the historic lodge, while the cabins with fireplaces sit among the trees. The most modern units feature king-size beds, fireplaces and sitting areas with televisions. The main lodge has an outdoor deck where guests can lounge by day and stargaze by night. For a quarter you can look more closely at the stars through a telescope.

The lofty central room of the main lodge is a casual place where you can relax and enjoy the valley view. Several board games are available, and a lot of comfortable sofas and chairs and a fireplace create a relaxed ambiance. The dining room offers a tremendous view of the Shenandoah Valley. On a clear day you can enjoy the panoramic vista 40 miles across the entire Appalachian Range into West Virginia. The Tap Room, made cozy by a fireplace, is open from 4 to 11 PM.

Big Meadows Lodge offers naturalist activities and a children's playground, and Byrd Visitor Center, where exhibits illustrate the park's history and the folkways of its former inhabitants, is nearby.

The retreat is open from early May through October. Rates range from $60 per night in the main lodge on weekdays to $125 per night for a one-bedroom suite on weekends. Rates are slightly higher in October.

www.insiders.com

See this and many other **Insiders' Guide®** destinations online.

Visit us today!

Cabins

Lewis Mountain Cabins
**Mile 57.5 • (540) 999-2255,
(800) 999-4714**

For a tranquil experience, you can spend the night in one of the cabins on Lewis Mountain, where rooms have no phones or televisions to disturb the peace. The heated cabins have furnished bedrooms and private baths, with towels and linens provided. Cooking is done in connecting outdoor areas equipped with fireplaces, grills and picnic tables.

The cabins are open from mid-May through October. Rates range from $55 per night on weekdays for a single-room cabin to $83 per night on weekends for a two-room cabin. Rates are slightly higher in October.

Potomac Appalachian Trail Club Cabins
**118 Park St. S.E., Vienna
• (703) 242-0315, (703) 242-0693**

If you're game for a bit of backpacking, the Potomac Appalachian Trail Club maintains six cabins and seven three-sided shelters in the backcountry of the park. The shelters, which provide protection from the elements, are along the Appalachian Trail at intervals of

Watch for deer roaming the parking lot at the Loft Mountain Wayside.

12 to 20 miles. You must have a valid backcountry camping permit for three or more nights. These free permits are available at any of the ranger stations, entrance stations or the park headquarters on Va. Route 211 east of Luray and 5 miles west of Skyline Drive.

The cabins provide a bit more comfort than primitive camping, and staying in one can be a gritty or sublime experience, depending upon your perspective. You must hike in, gather your own firewood and draw your own water from a nearby spring. Each cabin has a table, woodstove and/or fireplace, bunks and a pit toilet. There are mattresses and blankets, but you should bring your own sleeping bag or bedding. There's no electricity, so you must also have your own source of light. The cabins are equipped with pots, pans and dishes. The cabins are Range View (Mile 22.1), Cronin (Mile 37.9), Rock Spring (Mile 41.1), Pocosin (Mile 59.5), Doyles River (Mile 81.1) and Jones Mountain (accessible from Criglersville, but not from Skyline Drive). Range View can accommodate up to eight people, while Jones Mountain sleeps 10. The others can house 12. Prices range from $12 to $20, with a $10 surcharge if there are seven or more people in your party.

All cabins are locked, so you must get a key from the PATC by mail before your visit. For reservations, call or write the PATC at the address above. The cabins are popular, so reserve early.

Campgrounds

Shenandoah National Park operates five campgrounds along Skyline Drive. All campgrounds have a 14-day limit, allow pets, do not accept credit cards and are closed in the winter. Many sites accommodate tents, tent trailers and recreational vehicles. However, water and electric hookups are not available for RVs. Shower and laundry facilities are near all but two of the campgrounds. For more information, refer to our Recreation chapter.

Mathews Arm Campground
Mile 22.2 • (540) 999-3397

Mathews Arm reopened 117 of its 181 sites in September 1997 for self-contained vehicles only. The campground was closed in 1993 due to budget shortfalls, but increased entrance fees at Shenandoah National Park helped raise enough funds to reopen the facility. Mathews Arm is available on a first come, first served basis. Cost is $10. There are no showers or laundry facilities.

Big Meadows Campground
Mile 51 • (800) 365-2267

The largest campground on the drive with 227 sites, Big Meadows is also the most popular. If you are planning on camping in the summer or fall, you must make reservations. Cost is $17 per night. A campstore, laundry facilities and a gas station are nearby.

Lewis Mountain Campground
Mile 57.5 • (540) 999-3397

This 31-site campground is often full in pleasant weather, especially on weekends and holidays. It's first come, first served, so plan to arrive early. It costs $14 per site, per night. Amenities include a laundry and coin-operated concessions.

Loft Mountain Campground
Mile 80 • (540) 999-3397

There are more than 200 sites at Loft Mountain, and you can usually find a spot except on the weekends. This, too, is first come, first served. The cost is $14 per night. There is a campstore nearby with coin-operated concessions and laundry facilities.

Dundo Campground
Mile 83.7 • (540) 298-9625

This campground is open for any bonafide nonprofit organized group. It's primitive tent camping with pit toilets, running water, picnic tables and grills. There are only seven campsites here with a maximum of 20 people per site. (You must have eight people to be considered a group.) The cost is $30 per night. Reservations are required.

Backcountry Camping

For those who prefer a little more seclusion, backcountry camping is allowed in most areas of the park, but permits are required. Tents may be set up as long as they are one half mile from the developed areas, such as picnic grounds or other campgrounds. Campers also should be one quarter of a mile from the Skyline Drive and other roadways in the park and be out of sight of any trail or other backcountry campsites. If you prefer to rough it, be aware that campfires and glass containers are not allowed in the backcountry. Also,

park officials recommend that you take along about 20 feet of rope. It's a good idea to hang your food from a tree in airtight containers to prevent unwanted visits from bears. Permits are available at the entrances, visitor centers or the main business office. If you have your trip planned out a month in advance, you can request a permit by mail. Call (540) 999-3500.

Places to Eat

Elkwallow Wayside
Mile 24.1 • (540) 999-2253

Open from April to early November, this campstore has a small selection of groceries and camper supplies, a gift shop and grill service.

Panorama Restaurant
Mile 31.5 at U.S. Hwy. 211
• (540) 999-2265

This is the place for that hearty breakfast before hitting the trail. Panorama serves three meals a day on weekends and lunch and dinner on weekdays from April to mid-November. Lunch and dinner menus often include local specialties such as fried catfish and country ham along with staples such as hamburgers, homemade pizza, sandwiches, soups and salads and soft-serve yogurt. There also is a gift shop for souvenir hunters.

Skyland Lodge
Mile 41.7 • (540) 999-2211

One of the best views on the drive is from the window tables in this glass-walled dining room, which offers full meals every day from late March through November. The Stony Man (corned-beef hash topped with poached eggs) and the four-cheese omelet are breakfast standouts. Menus change, but dinner selections often include prime rib, trout with pecan butter, eggplant or chicken Parmesan and vegetable-stuffed ravioli. The Tap Room has a limited bar menu to go with the beer, wine and spirits dispensed daily from midday to late evening.

Big Meadows Wayside
Mile 51 • (540) 999-2221

The coffee shop has carry-out service and

a menu similar to the Panorama Restaurant listed previously. Lunch and dinner are served daily from late March through November. It's also a service station and campstore.

Big Meadows Lodge
Mile 51.2 • (540) 999-2221

A four-cheese omelet, Belgian waffles and blueberry pancakes are breakfast features. Lunch offerings include veggie burgers and a hearty Reuben. The dinner menu has savory fried chicken, baked Virginia trout, catfish and chicken scallopini. The restaurant is full-ser-

vice May through October. The Tap Room offers a limited bar menu well into the evening.

Loft Mountain Wayside
Mile 59 • (804) 823-4515

This campstore/gift shop sells crafts, souvenirs, foodstuffs and gas. The grill serves hamburgers, hot dogs and the like. It's open weekends only April through mid-May then daily from morning until early evening through November 3.

There are several picnic tables outside on

Waterfalls

It's the second-most asked question in the Shenandoah National Park: "Where can I see a waterfall?" The question came up so often that the staff at the park was eager to find a quick reply.

"We asked Joanne Amberson if she would write a book for us," said Greta Miller, executive director of the Shenandoah Natural History Association. "She is a retired English professor who volunteers here at the park . . . and she likes to hike."

Amberson had trekked the paths to all of the waterfalls along Skyline Drive many times.

"Since I was an ex-English professor, they knew I could write," she said. "It was a lot of hard work, but it was fun to do."

Amberson is used to putting up with hard work to do what she loves. For years the Rappahannock resident spent countless hours commuting from her home in Virginia to teach at Prince George's Community College in Maryland. When she retired five years ago, she signed on as a volunteer at the park. Today her long treks are mostly on foot.

"I didn't know anything about hiking until 1970," Amberson said. "But, now, I have been hiking for 27 years."

Of course, asking Amberson which hike is her favorite is a lot like asking Florence Henderson which is her favorite Brady.

"They are all beautiful," she said. "The South River Falls has a sheer drop, and you can get fairly close to it. You can just sit there and see the whole mountain behind you. But for every person, a different falls would fit their personality. Jones River Falls is short, but it is exquisitely beautiful. Each one is unique, and each one has its own personality."

By far and away, Dark Hollow Falls is the most visited waterfall on Skyline Drive because it is the closest to the Drive and requires the shortest hike — 1.4 miles round-trip. Although Amberson describes it as a moderate climb, it descends pretty quickly alongside Hogcamp Branch, a small stream that gradually widens.

"The one thing they all have in common is that you have to walk down to see them," Amberson said.

And as they say in waterfall circles, those who walk down, must hike back up to the car. In the summer the Dark Hollow Falls trail can be quite crowded with families, older folks and people wearing shoes that give the impression that a hike was a spur-of-the-

— continued on next page

moment idea. For the climb back up, there are several places to sit and enjoy the ferns and wildflowers.

"There are 15 major waterfalls in the park, but the book gives you nine hikes," Amberson said. "There is an arduous hike on one trail that would lead you to five more falls."

While only a true hiker will want to follow the steep and rocky path to those five smaller falls, the main hike to Whiteoak Canyon Falls is another of the more popular attractions. The round-trip hike of 4.6 miles leads to the second-highest falls, but even this hike seems to attract more experienced hikers. Most come prepared with hiking boots and water bottles. Although it is longer than Dark Hollow, this trail has a gradual decline through an old hemlock forest, where 400-year-old trees are bigger around than two people. You get a splendid view from the top of the cliffs directly across the falls as it cascades 86 feet down the canyon. You can sit here, even with the treetops, and listen to the splash of the falls.

"There must be an attraction between people and water," Amberson said. "It is all very refreshing. It makes you feel like sitting and meditating and contemplating."

While the falls are picturesque and peaceful, be advised that we're not talking Niagara here. In fact, in warm weather some of the falls will dry up to a trickle.

"In a dry summer the falls can have no water at all," Amberson said. "So the best time to go see them is in the spring and early summer . . . unless we have had a lot of rain. The Rose River Falls is perhaps the second easiest to get to (2.6-mile hike), but it is one that is good to go to in the spring. When there is a lot of water, it falls in four parallel streams. You are in the woods surrounded by hemlocks. It is just beautiful."

Also, if it's a dry season, you might want to postpone your trip to Overall Run Falls. Before you trek the 6.4 miles to tallest falls in the park, be aware that your only view may be of Massanutten Mountain. Overall Run Falls will have little to no water in a dry summer, Amberson said.

The park's new booklet is filled with such helpful hints for those who really want to see the falls.

"The book gives you a complete map of each hike, directions and my statement on what is easy and hard," Amberson said. "Of course, it is all relative. What may be hard for one is easy for another, but I give my assessment."

Hike to Waterfalls in the Shenandoah National Park is available at each of the entrance stations on the Skyline Drive. It costs $2. For more information, call the Shenandoah Natural History Association at (540) 999-3582.

Oh, yes. The most asked question in the park is "Where can I get something to eat?"

— continued on next page

Photo: Anne P. Causey

The popular Whiteoak Canyon Falls is the second-highest waterfall in the park.

Shenandoah National Park's Most Visited Waterfalls

Fall	Height	Mile Post
Overall Run No. 1	29 feet	22.2
Overall Run No. 2	93 feet	22.2
Whiteoak No. 1	86 feet	42.6
Whiteoak No. 2	62 feet	42.6
Whiteoak No. 3	35 feet	42.6
Whiteoak No. 4	41 feet	42.6
Whiteoak No. 5	49 feet	42.6
Whiteoak No. 6	60 feet	42.6
Cedar Run	34 feet	45.6
Rose River	67 feet	49.4
Dark Hollow Falls	71 feet	50.7
Lewis	81 feet	51.2
South River	83 feet	62.8
Doyles River No. 1	29 feet	81.8
Doyles River No. 2	63 feet	81.8
Jones Run	42 feet	84.1

a wooden deck, where you can enjoy a snack while you watch the deer.

Picnic Areas

If you decide to bring your own food, there are seven picnic facilities along Skyline Drive with tables, restrooms, water fountains and even fireplaces. From north to south are: Dickey Ridge at mile 4.7, Elkwallow at 24.1, Pinnacles at 36.7, Big Meadows at 51.2, Lewis Mountain at 57.5, South River at 62.8 and Loft Mountain at 79.5 You may also find other picnic tables at overlooks, visitor centers and lodges.

Fishing

Although the streams are relatively small, fishing is allowed in 30 spots in the Shenandoah National Park. You may fish year round, but only artificial lures and lures with single hooks are allowed. Many of the trout streams are "catch and release," so it's a good idea to check with the visitor centers or entrance stations to find out the latest rules and regulations. You will need a Virginia fishing license.

Blue Ridge Parkway

Visitor Centers

Even if its not your first trip on the parkway, it might be a good idea to stop by one of the four visitor centers in Virginia. Mother Nature can alter the course of a trail or close a campground, so it's best to get the latest information. Each center has free maps, books for sale, exhibits, picnic tables, bathrooms and updates on ranger programs. The centers are open 9 AM to 5 PM daily in the summer, weekends only in early spring and late fall and are closed in the winter. Besides the visitor centers, you could try the ranger's office in Vinton at (540) 857-2490. Another way to obtain general information about the Parkway is to call Plateau District office at (540) 745-9660. While most of the Parkway visitor centers and facilities are closed from the first of November to the end of April, this office remains open.

Humpback Rock Visitor Center
Mile 5.8 · (540) 943-4716

This center is near the Rockfish Gap entrance to the Blue Ridge Parkway. Outside is an easy quarter-mile self-guided trail through a reconstructed farmstead. There's a group of log buildings, most dating back to the 1880s, that represents a typical pioneer homestead — a cabin, spring house, chicken coop and barn.

James River Visitor Center
Mile 63.6 • (804) 299-5496

From this center, there is a self-guided trail that will take you to the restored canal locks on the James River. Before railroads became the favored way to "ship" freight, engineers looked for easier ways to get their goods up river. In the mid-1800s, 49 miles of canals were built through the Blue Ridge. A footbridge will give you a good view of the river.

Peaks of Otter Visitor Center
Mile 86 • (540) 586-4357

You can see a living history demonstration on weekends at the Johnson Farm, a homestead dating back to the 1800s. It has been restored to the way it looked in the 1920s. A trail around the farm is 2.1 miles. There also is an amphitheater, museum, naturalist program, nature walks and a 23-acre lake near this popular center.

Rocky Knob Visitor Center
Mile 169 • (540) 745-9662

This quaint center is in a converted gasoline station. It offers a series of activities, including a naturalist program, campfire talks and guided hikes. The visitors center overlooks the Rock Castle Gorge, where three trail systems intersect. There is a strenuous 10.8-mile loop trail into the gorge.

Overlooks

If you don't like to hike, you can still see a lot of the great outdoors without ever leaving your car. According to the folks at the Roanoke headquarters, the road was designed to have an overlook at almost every mile. That means there are literally hundreds of overlooks scattered between Rockfish Gap in Virginia and Great Smoky Mountains National Park in North Carolina. Here are a couple of examples:

The Priest Overlook
Mile 17.6

The Priest is the tallest in what has been called the "religious mountains," including Little Priest, the Cardinal, the Friar and the Bald Friar. There is a picnic table here and a short trail to a scenic pedestrian overlook.

Yankee Horse Ridge Overlook
Mile 34.4

Word has it that this is where a Union soldier's horse fell and had to be shot. You can see a reconstructed spur of an old logging railroad by following the trail to Wigwam Falls. There's an interpretive sign and picnic table at this overlook.

Hikes

With more than 100 trails along the Blue Ridge Parkway, there is bound to be something to suit every hikers' fancy. Among the most popular trails are Humpback Rocks and Rock Castle Gorge (see our Recreation chapter). We also have listed a sample of easy, moderate and difficult paths.

Falling Water Cascades National Scenic Trail
Mile 83.4

You can divide this trail into two parts or hike it as one continuous loop. It's a 1.6-mile moderate walk to see the cascades. Watch your step; the wet rocks can be slippery. Look for the thicket of rhododendron.

Flat Top Trail
Mile 83.5

This one's for avid hikers. The 4.4-mile

INSIDERS' TIP

Rustic cabins along the Appalachian Trail are a comfortable way to camp without having to sleep on the ground. Be sure to book these shelters early because low prices and unique settings make the cabins popular.

stretch leads to the highest of three main peaks in the area, Sharp Top, Flat Top and Harkening Hill. This trail across Flat Top Mountain levels off at 4,001 feet at a picnic area. Be sure to wear good shoes for hiking. It is a strenuous climb. This popular trail also has the distinction of being listed in the National Register of Historic Trails.

Sharp Top Trail
Mile 86

Another popular hike, this trail leaves the camp store and climbs to the summit of Sharp Top Mountain, an elevation of 3,874 feet with a 360-degree panoramic view. The 1.5-mile hike is strenuous but one of the best sites to watch the sun rise. Park officials report seeing numbers of hikers heading up the trail in the early morning hours. At one time, Sharp Rock was thought to be the tallest peak in Virginia. A stone from the mountaintop even sits at the Washington Monument in D.C. with that distinctive but incorrect heading. If you would like to go to the top, but don't think you are up to the hike, a bus will take you up most of the route, except for the last 1,500 feet.

Mabry Mill Trail
Mile 176.2

This is for the beginner who likes to see something more than nature. This easy half-mile trail takes you to E.B. Mabry's grist mill, saw mill, blacksmith shop and other outdoor exhibits. You may even see actors re-creating old-time skills in the summer and fall.

Accommodations

Peaks of Otter Lodge
**Mile 86 • (540) 586-1081,
(800) 542-5927 in Va.**

Unlike the lodges in Shenandoah National Park, Peaks of Otter is open year round. The lodge setting is idyllic, a valley surrounded by gentle mountains and facing a beautiful lake. Each room has two double beds, a private bath and a private balcony or terrace overlooking the lake. The rooms have no televisions or phones.

The lodge's restaurant serves hearty Southern fare and has a sumptuous salad bar.

The gift shop sells fine Virginia crafts, stationery, books, jellies and more.

You can also camp at Peaks of Otter (see the listing below). Park rangers give talks on nature topics during the peak season, and hikers can trek along miles of well-marked trails near the lodge.

Rates are about $76.68 for two people per room weekdays or weekends; slightly higher in October and on holiday weekends.

Rocky Knob Cabins
Mile 174 • (540) 593-3503

Seven cabins were built in the 1930s for the Civilian Conservation Corps workers who constructed much of the Blue Ridge Parkway. They have no fireplaces and no other source of heat, so it's understandable that they are only open from late May through Labor Day. The cabins have completely furnished electric kitchens but no bathrooms. However, private showers and laundry facilities are in a bathhouse within 200 feet of each cabin. Rates are about $48.50 for two and $5 for each extra person. You may make reservations by calling after 10:30 AM weekdays or in the evenings. Or you can write to: Rocky Knob Cabins, Route 1, Box 5, Meadows of Dan, VA 24120.

Doe Run Lodge Resort and Conference Center
**Off Parkway near Mile 189, Fancy Gap
• (540) 398-2212, (800) 325-6189**

This family-oriented year-round private resort in Fancy Gap sits on beautiful Groundhog Mountain and offers tennis, swimming, saunas and golf. Choose from poolside chalets, town-house villas, tennis center chalets and single-family residences. See our Resorts chapter for complete details.

Campgrounds

The Parkway has nine developed campgrounds with tent and recreational vehicle sites (no water or electric hookups), including four in Virginia.

All campgrounds have restrooms (no showers), sewage dumping stations and telephones. Grills and tables are provided at each site.

Campgrounds are open late April through October. You are limited to stays of 14 consecutive days from June 1 through Labor Day and 30 days total for the calendar year. Reservations are not accepted, but you probably won't need them. Do, however, plan to make camp early during the peak summer months or the fall foliage season.

All campgrounds charge $10 per site for up to six people and $2 for each additional person. Leashed pets are allowed. While the campground and other facilities typically don't open until the end of April, if there has been a mild winter with little storm damage, there is a chance that the park superintendent may decide to open some facilities earlier in the season.

In 1999, Roanoke Mountain Campground, Peaks of Otter Campground and picnic area, and Humpback Rock picnic area opened the first weekend in April. Call ahead if you are planning an early spring outing.

Otter Creek Campground
Mile 60 • (828) 298-0398

It's a cool and peaceful setting here beneath the hemlock, oak and pine trees. Otter Creek is the smallest campground, but there is room for 45 tents and 24 RVs.

Peaks of Otter Campground
Mile 86 • (828) 298-0398

Peaks of Otter, a half-mile east of Mile 86 on Va. 43, is one of the area's most popular campgrounds because of its beautiful lakeside setting. There are 82 tent sites and 59 hookups for RVs or trailers. There are plenty of spots to picnic with 62 tables on hand. Fishing is allowed, and there is a campstore and gas station nearby.

Roanoke Mountain Campground
Mile 120.5 • (828) 298-0398

If you are worried about finding a camping spot or want to avoid crowds, Roanoke Mountain is one of the lesser-used campgrounds. It's also handy if you would like to take a daytrip to nearby Roanoke or Mill Mountain. It has 74 tent sites and spaces for 30 RVs.

Rocky Knob Campground
Mile 167.1 • (828) 298-0398

At 3,100 feet, this is the highest campground in Virginia's section of the Parkway. Rocky Knob has 81 places to stake a tent and 28 lots for RVs. There are 72 picnic tables, 15 miles of trails and plenty of spots to fish nearby. You might want to check out the Chinese chestnut trees.

Backcountry Camping

The Blue Ridge Parkway has one backcountry camping area near Rock Castle Gorge. Campers must apply for a free permit from the Rocky Knob Visitor Center. Call (540) 745-9662 or drop by the center at Milepost 169. Campers may park their cars at the visitor center and pick up the trail from there.

Places to Eat

Whetstone Ridge
Mile 29 • (540) 377-6397

This casual dining spot near Montebello serves hearty fare from early May through October, with breakfast specialties such as buckwheat pancakes. The simple dinner menu lists fried chicken, hamburger steak, flounder and country ham. Don't miss the warm apple dumpling for dessert.

Otter Creek Restaurant and Craft Shop
Mile 60.8 • (804) 299-5862

You can have breakfast all day long at Otter Creek, including bacon and eggs plus buckwheat, cornmeal, buttermilk or just plain pancakes. If you would like a little something traditional for your dinner, there are the usual family favorites: fried chicken, hamburger steak, fish and country ham. The restaurant is next to a year-round Otter Creek campground and small craft shop and is open mid-April through mid-November.

Mary's Rock Tunnel in South Portal of Skyline Drive makes an interesting diversion.

Peaks of Otter Lodge
Mile 86 • (800) 542-5927

Friendly service and hefty portions make this a popular dining spot among locals and travelers alike. Like the lodge, the restaurant is open year round. Breakfasts are the stick-to-your-ribs sort, and lunch specials include big salads, burgers and ham steak with buttered apples. The dinner menu offers Southern dishes such as barbecued ribs and country ham, as well as prime rib and tenderloin steak. The coffee shop prepares picnic lunches for guests wanting to eat outdoors.

Mabry Mill Coffee Shop
Mile 176 • (540) 952-2947

A single menu is available throughout the day at this coffee shop at Mabry Mill, a famous pioneer attraction along the Parkway. Country ham, barbecue, and corn and buckwheat cakes are specialties plus you can get breakfast any time of day. Mabry Mill is open from late April through October.

High Country Restaurant at Doe Run Lodge
Off Parkway near Mile 189, Fancy Gap • (540) 398-2212

Open year round, this privately owned restaurant serves breakfast, lunch and dinner six days a week. (It's closed Mondays.) The menu is seasonal and offers such gourmet selections as she-crab soup, venison, fresh rainbow trout from Doe Run's stocked pond, lamb, duck, steaks and country ham. The restaurant also prepares picnic lunches. The hours are limited in the winter, but lodging is available year round.

Picnic Areas

Of the 14 designated areas for picnicking along the Blue Ridge Parkway, six are in Virginia. They each include picnic tables, fireplaces, drinking water and comfort stations. From north to south are: Humpback Rocks at mile 5.9, James River at 63.6, Peaks of Otter at 86, Smart View at 154.5, Rocky Knob at 169 and Ground Hog Mountain at 189.

Fishing

Fishing is allowed in certain spots along the Parkway, but it is a good idea to check with the local ranger for rules about creel limits and what type of bait is allowed. Regulations are usually posted at each fishing area, but they will vary from site to site. Designated "special waters" in Virginia include Abbott Lake, Little Stoney Creek and Otter Lake. In special waters, fishing lures are limited to a single-hook artificial lure. A Virginia fishing license is valid in all Parkway waters. No special trout license is required.

Sixty percent of the Civil War's battles were fought in Virginia.

The Civil War

Civil War attractions draw thousands of history buffs to the Blue Ridge each year. Battlefield restoration is increasing in light of this demand, including restorations of Hanging Rock Battlefield in Salem and Brandy Station Battlefield in Culpeper County, rescued in 1996 by the Brandy Station Foundation. The heavy tourism traffic has led to a flurry of antique store banners proclaiming their stash of Civil War memorabilia.

Men dressed in Civil War uniforms and women in hoop skirts gather regularly at balls such as the Bonnie Blue Ball in Richmond, which celebrated the 100th anniversary of the Museum of the Confederacy, established in 1996. Although these events attract criticism, including blasts from former Virginia governor Douglas Wilder who condemns them as "a celebration of slavery," scholars agree it's important to understand the Civil War era in its many and varied aspects. To this end, Virginia's Blue Ridge offers a wealth of information and firsthand experiences.

Academic groups frequently schedule Civil War seminars, such as a recent one titled "Hunter's Raid" at Virginia Western Community College. Any of the chambers of commerce in the Blue Ridge can provide information on times and locations of these sessions.

The War Between the States was, as the poet Walt Whitman described, "A strange, sad war." More Americans lost their lives in the Civil War (1861 to 1865) than in both world wars combined. And of all the states involved in the conflict, none suffered as much trauma as Virginia did, say some historians. Although the Old Dominion was one of the last states to leave the Union, its strategic geographic position among seceding states made it a natural battleground for clashes between the two armies. Beginning with the war's first major battle at Bull Run (First Manassas) and ending with the South's surrender in the tiny, peaceful village of Appomattox Court House near Lynchburg, 60 percent of the Civil War's battles were fought in Virginia. One borderline Shenandoah Valley city, Winchester, changed hands from Confederate to Federal control no fewer than 72 times. Thousands of men from both sides heeded the call to arms and never returned; 700,000 people died in the war, 400,000 of them victims of germs rather than bullets. Untold acres of family farms were laid to waste. Is it any wonder that more than 130 years later the War Between the States is not forgotten?

The Blue Ridge not only is the site of some of the bloodiest battles of the Civil War but also is home to one of the country's most noted Civil War scholars and authors, history professor James I. Robertson Jr. of Virginia Tech. He is past executive director of the U.S. Civil War Centennial Commission, and his book, *Civil War! America Becomes One Nation*, an illustrated history for young readers, probably best answers questions about the war in a way young and old can clearly understand. Robertson, whose book has been nominated for a Pulitzer Prize, teaches a Civil War class that is one of the hottest tickets on campus. His enthusiasm for Civil War history comes as no surprise, since his great-grandfather was Gen. Robert E. Lee's cook. Robertson's book takes into account the political and socioeconomic mood of the 1860s and the events that set off a movement the South anticipated would be over within weeks, but which, in fact, lasted four years and marked a turning point in American history. Robertson's biography of Stonewall Jackson, released in 1997, already has become a best-seller.

The fact the Confederacy even survived for the duration of the war was in large measure due to the military leadership of Virginia's Blue Ridge generals, Lee and Thomas J. "Stonewall" Jackson. As the story goes,

Jackson's nickname came out of the battle of First Manassas. Gen. Barnard Bee of South Carolina pointed to Jackson's troops and shouted, "There stands Jackson like a stone wall." In addition to his legendary nickname, Jackson's Rebel yell became his battle signature. To this day, the U.S. Army regularly conducts staff rides into the Shenandoah Valley for its officers, following the course of Jackson's famed Foot Cavalry.

When discussing the role the Blue Ridge played in the Civil War, Robertson emphasizes the Shenandoah Valley's two important geographic characteristics: first as a spear pointing into the North and second as the "Breadbasket of the Confederacy." The number of major battles in the region attests to the constant wrenching for control of the Valley, which prompted Jackson, often called the "pious blue-eyed killer," to push his men so hard in the spring of 1862 that their shoes fell apart in the fields.

The war in the Blue Ridge is fraught with tragic moments in military history. One of the most heartbreaking was the Battle of New Market on May 15, 1864, which is often re-traced and its startling events re-enacted. On that rainy Sunday afternoon, 247 Virginia Military Institute cadets advanced side by side with veteran Civil War infantrymen into hellish cannon and rifle fire. The soldiers forged onward with parade-ground precision, using each step to free the other from the furrows of mud caused by the heavy rainstorm. The Confederate commander of Western Virginia, Maj. Gen. John C. Breckinridge, had enlisted the cadets to join his ragtag force of 4,500. The cadets marched forward, their muzzle-loading muskets slung over shoulders destined to bear a far heavier load, their VMI flag leading the way. Looming ahead was a battle that would go down in American history as one of the most valorous and one of the last Confederate victories in the Shenandoah Valley. As the smoke of the battle cleared, 10 cadets lay dead, including Cadet Thomas G. Jefferson, 17, descendant of our nation's third president. Another 47 cadets were wounded.

Visitors can retrace the soldiers' steps by touring the New Market Battlefield Historical State Park and its museum, the Hall of Valor, which has displays of Civil War muskets, uniforms, tintype photos, day-to-day accessories, and a replica of the type of cannon captured by the cadets. Many visitors find it to be one of the most stirring of all the Blue Ridge Civil War sites, fascinating young and old alike with its sense of history and urgency.

Beyond the Shenandoah Valley, Southwest Virginia was also a region of vital importance to the Confederacy, Robertson points out. Through it ran the Virginia and Tennessee Railroad, the only lifeline between Richmond and the West. The lead mines at Austinville, the saltworks at Saltville and the coal mines throughout the region provided the embattled South with essential natural resources. The May 1864 Battle of Cloyd's Mountain near Dublin in Pulaski County remains the largest engagement ever fought in Southwest Virginia. A future president, Col. Rutherford B. Hayes, was a hero of that battle. Today only a marker commemorates the site.

Roanoker Gary C. Walker, author of *The War in Southwest Virginia* and *Hunter's Fiery Raid Through Virginia's Valleys*, outlines in great detail the way the war was fought in this region of Virginia. He captures the mood of the area, geographically a third of Virginia, which broke away to rejoin the Union and form its own state, West Virginia. Walker's book on Maj. Gen. David Hunter, who was known for his unquenchable hatred of slavery, shows how Hunter wreaked his vengeance upon Southwest Virginia before its secession. States Walker, "Civilian property became an official military target. Both men and women were arrested without charge. Routinely, Southern ladies and their crying babies were forced from their homes with nothing but the clothes on their bodies. Their manor houses were plundered and burned before their horrified eyes." In Hunter's books, one can almost smell the smoke, feel the perspiration drip from the brow and hear the heart pound as the lines clashed and the men fell with hideous and gaping wounds.

Walker also is a consultant to the growing

www.insiders.com

See this and many other **Insiders' Guide®** destinations online.

Visit us today!

Photo: K.B. Gatz-Broadway

A Civil War re-enactment details the lives of Confederate soldiers.

number of hobbyists who participate in Civil War battle re-enactments all along the East Coast. The most recent Blue Ridge addition was Roanoke County's re-enactment of Hunter's Raid at Green Hill Park. A mid-October re-enactment at Cedar Creek in Middletown, which includes open camps, drills, dress parades, demonstrations of military and civilian life and a special education symposium, is part of an effort by the Cedar Creek Battlefield Foundation to save the battlefield's 158 acres from development by raising $450,000. The visitor center, book shop and other annual battle re-enactments also have helped stave off the bulldozers.

The Battle of Cedar Creek in 1864 marked the end of Confederate dominion over the Shenandoah Valley and its essential food supplies. It also marked the end of famed Gen. Jubal Early's career and of the war-weariness that had plagued the North. (A private trust fund was established in 1996 to preserve Early's home in Red Valley, Franklin County.) This battle also put to rest any hopes the Confederacy may have had for a negotiated peace. The victory freed Gen. Philip Sheridan and his men, including Gen. George Custer (who had the misfortune of tangling later with Chief Sitting Bull at the Battle of Little Big Horn) to play

crucial roles in the final battles of the Civil War the following spring.

If you've never seen a battle re-enactment, you're in for a real experience. Authenticity is a must. Sack cloth, shell jackets and frock coats are required of all participants on the field. Eyeglasses must be of period construction. Only period footwear is allowed, preferably mule hide with square toes and wooden pegs. Uniforms must be woolen. Many of the soldiers carry their own original binoculars, pistols and bayonet rifles. No, they don't use real bullets, but they do use real gunpowder. For schedules of battle re-enactments throughout the country, write the *Camp Chase Gazette*, P.O. Box 707, Marietta, Ohio 45750.

Hundreds of monuments, museums and battle re-enactments await you in the Blue Ridge of Virginia. The region also has more than 250 historic markers that serve as on-the-spot history lessons. In the following pages, we list only actual sites where you can see or do something. For a complete list of Virginia Civil War battlefields and markers, write the State of Virginia, 1021 E. Cary Street, Richmond 23219 or call (804) 786-2051. Another great guide is Robertson's book, *Civil War Sites in Virginia, a Tour Guide*, published by the University Press of Virginia. And our sister publi-

Re-enactments

It doesn't matter what the season, there is some type of Civil War-related activity planned every month of the year. There are mock battles, symposiums, lectures, demonstrations, drills — you name it. The largest such event in Virginia, the Grant vs. Lee 1864 Re-enactment, will bring more than 10,000 re-enactors to the Brandy Station Battlefield in Culpeper County on June 18–20. In what is called the "largest engagement of Blue and Gray since Appomattox," weekend warriors will replay the battles of the Wilderness, Cold Harbor, Laurel Hill, Spotsylvania Courthouse and Yellow Tavern. To help celebrate the 135th anniversary of these battles, there also will be cavalry demonstrations, music, authors, artists and sutlers (also known as vendors) selling food, period merchandise and antiques. Advance tickets are $10 a day, $24 for a three-day pass. Below are just a few of the re-enactments you'll find along the Blue Ridge:

March 6:	Battle of Waynesboro, (540) 949-8203
April 10–11:	Battle of Appomattox Courthouse, (804) 352-0493
April 17–18:	Battle of Stanardsville at Oak Ridge Estate, (804) 263-8676
May 15–16:	Battle of New Market, (540) 740 3212
June 18–20:	Grant vs. Lee at Brandy Station, (888) 696-3340
August 1–2:	Ball's Bluff Re-enactment at Ida Lee Park, (703) 777-1368
August 27–29:	Third Winchester Battle and 10 Mile March, (301) 665-1400
October 15–17:	Cedar Creek Battlefield, (540) 869-2064

cation, *The Insiders' Guide® to Civil War Sites in the Eastern Theater*, describes 15 tours anyone interested in the Civil War — including kids — will enjoy.

Unless otherwise noted, admission is free of charge.

Shenandoah Valley

Gen. Stonewall Jackson's Headquarters
515 N. Braddock St., Winchester
• **(540) 667-3242**

From this brick house, Jackson commanded his forces in defense of the strategic Shenandoah Valley. The French-style house contains artifacts of Jackson, his cavalry chief Gen. Turner Ashby and others. From April through October, hours of operation are Monday through Saturday from 10 AM to 4 PM and Sundays from 12 to 4 PM. It is open weekends only in November and December. Admission is $3.50 for adults and $1.75 for children.

Stonewall Jackson Memorial Cemetery and National Cemetery
Several blocks east of business district, Winchester

These two cemeteries are located across the street from each other. Buried in the Stonewall Jackson Cemetery are 3,000 Confederate soldiers, including 800 who are unknown. Also buried here is Confederate Gen. Turner Ashby. National Cemetery is one of the largest national cemeteries in Virginia and includes more than 4,500 Union soldiers, half of them unidentified. Some of the action of the Third Battle of Winchester in 1864 was fought in this vicinity.

Belle Grove Plantation
Cedar Creek Battlefield, Middletown
• **(540) 869-2028**

Spared during the Civil War even though it served as Gen. Philip Sheridan's headquarters during the decisive 1864 Battle of Cedar Creek, Belle Grove was built between 1794 and 1797 with the design assistance of Thomas Jefferson. James and Dolley Madison

Tours de Force

With more than 200 Civil War sites sprinkled across the commonwealth, it could take weeks just figuring out what to see and how to get there. Well, Mitchell Bowman has been out with his shovel and hammer, making things a lot easier for tourists.

"We have 226 sites across the state about the Civil War, where there have never been markers before," said Bowman, executive director of new Virginia Civil War Trails Inc. "What we are doing is turning Virginia into one great big outdoor museum. All of our markers will explain what actually happened on that site."

Each of the markers is also linked by a series of trailblazing red-white-and-blue signs.

Close-up

"The second thing we wanted to do was link entire campaigns and regions together so it will make it a lot easier to understand," he said.

The partnership of federal, state and local governments and private citizens spent four years and $2.2 million dollars to create Virginia's Civil War Trails. In fact, they divided the state into five driving trails.

Along the Blue Ridge, you can follow Stonewall Jackson's exploits on the **Shenandoah Valley Avenue of Invasion** trail or you can see where Col. John S. Mosby slipped past Union forces along the **1861-1865 Northern Virginia Crossroads of Conflict** trail.

Photo: Mary Alice Blackwell

The trails give visitors an opportunity to walk in the soldiers' footsteps. The buildings still stand and the railroad still runs in the beautiful countryside of Fauquier County, where Jackson, not yet nicknamed "Stonewall," hurried his troops onto train cars for the trip to Manassas in July 1861. March with Jackson west of Staunton into the rugged Allegheny Mountains, using the same backcountry dirt roads he did in 1862. Experience the horror with the citizens of the Shenandoah Valley as Union Gen. David Hunter orders the burning of fields, barns and homes in 1864. Or wander among the soldier graves at Old City Cemetery in Lynchburg or others in Loudoun, Staunton and Winchester. You can even travel to Appomattox Courthouse and stand in the reconstructed house where Lee surrendered.

Lee's Retreat, the **1862 Peninsula Campaign** and **Lee vs. Grant: The 1864 Campaign** are the other three trails that link the state's history.

"We started out with 'Lee's Retreat' and

— continued on next page

An example of the signs linking Civil War Trails sites.

Stonewall Jackson Memorial Cemetery in Lexington
contains the remains of the legendary general.

we just finished putting in 36 markers in the Valley," Bowman said. "We have put in 170 markers so far, but we keep finding more."

The nonprofit corporation also plans to put in several waysides, including one in the Shenandoah Valley and another in McDowell.

"We want to give people easy access to the sites," Bowman said. "We want them to be able to park their cars and go on a little hike, if they like."

You can obtain an informational packet on Virginia's Civil War Trails by calling (888) CIVIL WAR. The package contains a statewide Civil War Trails map, a full-color battle map and a newspaper featuring descriptions of all the sites and a calendar of events.

honeymooned here. Today the house and grounds exemplify the home and working farm of a wealthy Federalist planter. From April through October, the plantation is open Monday through Saturday from 10 AM to 4 PM and Sunday from 1 to 5 PM. Admission is $5 for adults, $2.50 for ages 13 to 17 and $2 for ages 6 to 12.

Cedar Creek Battlefield Foundation Re-enactment
Cedar Creek Battlefield, Middletown
• (540) 869-2064, (888) OCT-1864

The Cedar Creek Battlefield Foundation is dedicated to the historic interpretation and preservation of this 1864 battlefield — a Civil War battle in which both Confederates and Federals claimed victory. Plan to stop at the Visitor Center overlooking the battlefield for a personalized presentation of the events of the battle and a visit to the bookshop featuring the 1864 Valley Campaign. The Annual Re-enactment and Living History is held in October by approximately 3,500 re-enactors with artillery, cavalry and infantry demonstrations daily as well as an afternoon battle. Admission to the re-enactment for adults is $8, children 12 and younger are free. All proceeds go to the preservation of the battlefield. The hours of operation for the museum are Monday through Saturday from 10 AM to 4 PM and Sunday 1 to 4 PM from April 1 through November 1 only. There is a small admission fee for the museum. For more information write: P.O. Box 229, Middletown 22645.

Cedar Creek Relic Shop
7841 Main St. • (540) 869-5207

Cedar Creek Relic Shop has the largest collection of authentic Civil War relics for sale in the Shenandoah Valley, with sales benefiting the restored battlefield. The inventory includes swords, bayonets, carbines, muskets, buttons, plates, artillery shells, tintypes, documents and other relics of the Civil War era. The store also sells tapes and books and buys and sells antique weapons from other eras in addition to those from the Civil War. The staff here take pains to be certain that memorabilia is truly Civil War vintage, which is not always true at roadside antique stands. The shop is open year round, but you need to call for the various weekend hours.

Stonewall Jackson Museum at Hupp's Hill
U.S. Hwy. 11 S., Strasburg
• (540) 465-5884

Adjacent to trenches built by the 1st and 3rd brigades of the second division, 6th U.S. Corps, on October 20, 1864, the Stonewall Jackson Museum at Hupp's Hill serves as an interpretive center for the Civil War in the Shenandoah Valley. It exhibits Jackson's 1862 Valley Campaign with an impressive collection of Civil War artifacts. Reproduction weapons and uniforms can be touched. The children's room features discovery boxes, costumes to try on, wooden horses to climb on and a Civil War camp with tent and camp furniture. Hours of operation are Monday through Saturday 10 AM to 5 PM and Sundays noon to 5 PM. The museum is closed on New Year's Day, Easter Sunday, Thanksgiving and Christmas. Admission is $3 for adults, $2 for children ages 6 through 17 and free for children younger than 6.

Strasburg Museum
E. King St., Strasburg • (540) 465-3175

The exhibits at the Strasburg Museum include many high-quality Civil War and railroad relics. The blacksmith, cooper and potter's shop collections are especially noteworthy. Hours of operation are 10 AM to 4 PM daily from May through October. Admission is $2 for adults and $1 for children.

Belle Boyd Cottage
101 Chester St., Front Royal
• (540) 636-1446

This cottage museum, dedicated to the famed Confederate spy, teenager Belle Boyd, depicts life in Warren County and Front Royal during the Civil War. Belle was famous for the information she gathered that helped Jackson win the Battle of Front Royal on May 23, 1862. Hours of operation are 10 AM to 4 PM Monday through Friday from November through April. The museum is open the same hours May through October with additional hours on weekends from noon to 4 PM. Admission is $2 for adults and $1 for students.

Warren Rifles Confederate Museum
95 Chester St., Front Royal
• (540) 636-6982

Included in this museum is memorabilia from spy Belle Boyd and generals Lee, Jackson, Early and Ashby. The collection also has an abundance of other Civil War artifacts. From April 15 through November 1, the museum is open Monday through Friday from 9 AM to 5 PM and Saturday and Sunday from noon to 5 PM.

Prospect Hill Cemetery
540 Prospect St., Front Royal
• (540) 635-5468

Within the cemetery you will find two significant memorials. The first one, Soldier's Circle Monument, stands over the graves of 276 Confederate dead. The second, Mosby Monument, is flanked by two Parrott rifled cannons and is a memorial to seven members of a Confederate group named Mosby's Rangers, who were illegally executed as spies in 1864.

Edinburg Mill
U.S. Hwy. 11, Edinburg • (540) 984-8521

Built in 1848 on the banks of Stoney Creek, the Historic Edinburg Mill operated as a grist mill until 1978 when it was converted to its present day use as a restaurant. In 1864, the mill was spared from being burned by Gen. Sheridan's soldiers when local women pleaded for the livelihood of the Shenandoah Valley. Aside from its Civil War history, the Edinburg Mill is also noted for its child ghost — Frankie. Killed on October 22, 1898, when his clothing became entangled in machinery at the mill, 11-year old Frank Hottle is thought to still roam the large confines of the building. Many strange and unexplainable events have occurred over the years.

Herbert Barbee Confederate Monument
E. Main St., Luray

Herbert Barbee, an Italian-trained sculptor of international note, got the idea for this statue when, as a youth, he saw a Confederate sentry standing in Thornton Gap during a snowstorm. The muzzle of the soldier's gun was pointed down to keep out the snow. With donations coming in from Virginia, Maryland and even the northern states of New York and Pennsylvania, Barbee chose to place his creation in his hometown of Luray. It was different from other monuments, because the soldier was ragged. He has no socks, his shoes have holes and his clothes are tattered. When the statue was dedicated in 1898, many thought Barbee was crazy to place his monument on the outskirts of the town, but as the area has expanded, the Herbert Barbee Confederate Monument is now in the center of Luray.

New Market Battlefield Historical Park
8895 Collins Dr., New Market
• (540) 740-3101

New Market Battlefield State Historical Park, owned and operated by Virginia Military Institute, offers a perspective on one of America's most dramatic eras and is one of Virginia's finest Civil War museums. Visitors can view cannons in a field where in 1864 6,000 Federal soldiers clashed with 4,500 Confederates, including the famous VMI cadet corps desperately recruited from the college to help the South's cause. It was the first and only time in American history that an entire student body fought in a pitched battle.

The Hall of Valor, focal point of the 300-acre battlefield park, presents a concise, graphic survey of the entire Civil War. Exhibits highlight significant events of the war chronologically. Visitors can view two films, including a stirring account of the cadets' baptism by fire and one about Stonewall Jackson, a former VMI professor. You will see a life-size artillery unit, a model railroad, exquisitely sculpted soldiers and four battle scenes among the three-dimensional exhibits in the Virginia Room.

The c.1825 Bushong farmhouse, around which part of the battle raged, still stands with its reconstructed blacksmith shop, meat and loom house, wheelwright shop, oven, henhouse and other artifacts of daily life in the 1860s. The home served as a hospital after the battle. Scenic pathways lead to the "Field of Lost Shoes," where the mud was so thick soldiers' mulehide shoes were often irretrievable. The celebrated Shenandoah River flows nearby.

The park is open daily, except holidays, from 9 AM to 5 PM. Admission is $5 for adults and $2 for children ages 6 to 15.

New Market Battlefield Military Museum
9500 Collins Dr. on VA. Rt. 305,
New Market • (540) 740-8065

Perched atop a small hill on the battlefield, the Military Museum is a faithful replica of Gen. Robert E. Lee's beautiful Arlington House. The focus of the collection is primarily Civil War and is one of the largest collections of its kind. Because the exhibit also spans other eras of American history, the total collection is said to be the largest of military memorabilia from the American Revolution to the present. Among the items you can see here are relics, uniforms, headgear, edged weapons, flags, personal items, weapons, letters, maps, artwork, currency, stamps, medals and other revealing icons of life in America's past.

The museum's gift shop features more than 900 book titles, primarily about the Civil War. The museum is open March 15 through December 1, daily from 9 AM to 5 PM. Admission is $6 for adults and $3 for ages 6 to 14.

Shenandoah Valley Folk Art & Heritage Center

Harrisonburg-Rockingham Historical Society, Bowman Rd. and High St., Dayton
• **(540) 879-2681**

Known formerly as the Warren-Sipe Museum, the expanded and upgraded museum is highlighted by a huge electrified relief map with accompanying audiocassette outlining Stonewall Jackson's Valley Campaign of 1862, which targeted control of the Shenandoah Valley. The artifacts, photos and paintings in the collection help illustrate significant events of the Civil War in Rockingham County. Don't miss it for a blow-by-blow depiction of Jackson's campaign.

In addition to its focus on the Civil War, the museum now showcases traditional arts of the Shenandoah Valley. Genealogy research is available, and many Civil War scholars take advantage of this free service. The Heritage Museum Store sells books on numerous topics, including the Civil War, local tales and legends and genealogy. The museum is open February through December on Wednesday through Saturday from 10 AM to 4 PM and Sundays from 1 to 4 PM.

Fort Harrison

off Va. Rt. 42 S., Dayton
• **(540) 879-2280**

Guided tours are available of the home of Daniel Harrison, brother of Harrisonburg founder Thomas Harrison. The stone house was a natural fort used by settlers during Indian attacks in the 18th century, and it also served as a refuge from fighting during the Civil War. Donations are encouraged to help finance restoration of the site. The site is open May 31 through October 31, on weekends from 1 to 4 PM.

Stonewall Jackson Memorial Cemetery

300 block of S. Main St., Lexington

Marked by Edward Valentine's bronze statue of the general, Stonewall Jackson Memorial Cemetery contains the remains of the 39-year-old leader of battle, who died May 10, 1863, from wounds received at the Battle of Chancellorsville. Historians note the irony of the statue, which faces south, as probably the only time Jackson ever turned his back on his enemy. Approximately 400 other Confederate soldiers also are buried here. You will also see the graves of John Mercer Brooke, who developed the concept of the ironclad ship, the *Merrimac*, and William Washington (1834-1870), well-known artist of the Civil War period who is especially known for his painting of the *Battle of Lantane*.

Stonewall Jackson House

8 E. Washington St., Lexington
• **(540) 463-2552**

Built in 1801, the only home Jackson ever owned is furnished with his personal possessions. A brief slide show and guided tours interpret Jackson's life as a citizen, soldier, VMI professor of natural philosophy, church leader and family man. Guided tours of the home and restored garden are given every half-hour. The museum shop specializes in books, prints, quilts, samplers and reproductions of antique toys. Hours of operation are Monday through Saturday from 9 AM to 5 PM and Sundays from 1 to 5 PM. In June, July and August the museum stays open until 6 PM. It is closed Thanksgiving, Christmas, New Year's Day and Easter. Admission is $5 for adults, $2.50 for ages 6 to 17 and free to children younger than 6.

INSIDERS' TIP

While in the area, Civil War buffs may want to take a side trip to Manassas National Battlefield Park Visitor Center. You can take a walking tour of the battlefield, where Confederate troops fended off Union forces in two major battles in the early stages of the war. It's only a 25-mile drive from Leesburg along U.S. Highway 15 and Va. Route 234.

Virginia Military Institute and Museum
VMI Parade Grounds, N. Main St., Lexington • (540) 464-7334

Founded in 1839 as the nation's first state military college, VMI is known internationally as the school of the citizen-soldier and often is called the "West Point of the South." In Civil War lore, it is known for the officers and men it contributed to the Confederacy. At the center of campus, in front of the Cadet Barracks, is a statue of Gen. Stonewall Jackson. Nearby are cannons from the Rockbridge Artillery. The famous statue, *Virginia Mourning Her Dead*, a monument to the VMI cadets who fell at New Market, stands on the parade grounds. In the VMI Museum in Jackson Memorial Hall is a mural of the historic cadet battle charge. The museum is open year round, except holidays, daily from 9 AM to 5 PM.

Washington & Lee University
Main St., Lexington • (540) 463-8768

Robert E. Lee served as W&L's president in the five years after the Civil War. The focal point of the school's beautiful front campus is Lee Chapel, where the remains of Lee and most of his family are entombed. Edward Valentine, who created the statue of Stonewall Jackson in the Jackson Memorial Cemetery on Main Street, also sculpted the chapel's famous pose of the recumbent Lee. A museum in the chapel's basement focuses on Lee's life, and his office is preserved as he left it. The museum is open Monday through Saturday from 9 AM to 5 PM and Sunday from 2 to 5 PM.

Roanoke Valley

Hanging Rock Battlefield Restoration
I-81, Exit 141, at Orange Market via Va. 311, Roanoke • (540) 389-5118

Hanging Rock Battlefield is the latest battlefield restoration taking place and is the terminus of the old Catawba Branch Railway greenway being built in Roanoke County and the city of Salem. Spearheading this task is the Hanging Rock Battlefield & Railway Pres-ervation Foundation, comprised of nine preservation and governmental groups. The foundation's objective is preserving the site of this important battle and allowing Civil War buffs access.

In case you visit before restoration is complete, you'll find most of the work taking place around Buzzard's Roost, behind the Orange Market. The 6-acre site overlooks Hanging Rock and Mason's Creek. Kiosks and descriptive memorials to the battle will be included in the exhibits.

East of the Blue Ridge

Balls's Bluff Battlefield
Ball's Bluff Regional Park, Ball's Bluff Road, Leesburg • (703) 777-1368

On Oct. 21, 1861, a force of 1,700 Union soldiers crossed the Potomac River to meet an equal force of Confederates from the defenses of Leesburg. The battle resulted in 900 Union casualties, including their commander, Col. Edward Baker, a U.S. Senator and friend of Abraham Lincoln. The Confederacy lost 155 soldiers, including many local men serving with the 8th Virginia Infantry. The Ball's Bluff battle resulted in the creation of the Joint Congressional Committee on the Conduct of the War which investigated Union defeats and corruption in the federal war effort. Battlefield Park's National Cemetery contains Union dead. To learn more about this site, follow the interpretive trails maintained by the Northern Virginia Regional Park Authority.

Aldie Mill
Va. Rt. 50, Aldie • (703) 327-6118

Built from 1807 to 1809, Aldie Mill was owned by Henry Moore during the Civil War. Moore sold provisions to both Union and Confederate forces in Loudoun County. It served as a common resting place for Union patrols because of the available feed for their horses. It was here in March of 1863 that Confederate Col. John Singleton Mosby and 17 of his men surprised and defeated 59 of the 1st Vermont Cavalry. Mosby, known as the Gray Ghost, left his job as a Bristol lawyer to enlist when Virginia seceded. He organized a group of "partisan rangers" who went on a guerrilla rampage from Leesburg to Fairfax Courthouse. Aldie Mill also was the site of two other battles involving Mosby's troops in 1861.

Mount Zion Old School Baptist Church
Va. Rt. 50, east of Gilbert's Corner
• (540) 687-6681

At this 1851 church, Col. John S. Mosby held his first rendezvous with his men to initiate partisan activities behind Union lines. The church also was used during the Gettysburg campaign as a field hospital for hundreds of Union and Confederate cavalrymen. Church pews were broken up to make coffins for the Union dead, who were buried in the adjacent cemetery. During the war, the church was also used as a barracks and a temporary prison for local Confederate sympathizers arrested during Union sweeps through the area. The church was the site of a major skirmish between Mosby and the Union Cavalry in July 1864, which left more than 100 Union casualties. Mosby lost eight men.

Exchange Hotel and Civil War Museum
400 S. Main St., Gordonsville
• (540) 832-2944

This historic building started in the mid-19th century as Virginia's Exchange Hotel, a resting place for passengers on the Virginia Central Railway. During the Civil War, the hotel became the Gordonsville Receiving Hospital, and the Confederacy brought wounded soldiers here from nearby battlefields. The museum houses many good exhibits and artifacts, especially its medical displays. Special medical re-enactments take place in the spring and fall. The museum is open mid-March through mid-December from 10 AM to 4 PM Tuesdays through Saturdays, and Sunday afternoons during the summer. The cost is $4 for adults.

Jackson Statue
Fourth St., Charlottesville

This statue, created by Charles Keck, is of a bareheaded Jackson galloping forward on his favorite mount, Little Sorrel.

Lee Statue
Park between First and Second sts., Charlottesville

The work of sculptors H.M. Shrady and Leo Lentelli, this is an equestrian statue of Lee.

University Cemetery
Alderman and McCormick rds., north of UVA Football Stadium, Charlottesville

Even during the Civil War, Charlottesville was known for its healthcare facilities, many of which treated military patients. The remains of 1,200 Confederate soldiers lie in University Cemetery, most of them victims of disease. A bronze statue of a bareheaded Confederate soldier is at the center.

Daniel Monument
Intersection of Park Ave.,
Ninth and Floyd sts., Lynchburg

John Warwick Daniel was a member of Gen. Jubal Early's staff who went on to become a distinguished orator and U.S. Senator. This monument to the "Lame Lion of Lynchburg," so named for Daniel's wound at the Battle of the Wilderness, was created by Sir Moses Ezekiel, a famous postwar sculptor.

Lynchburg Museum at Old Court House
901 Court St., Lynchburg • (804) 847-1459

The tragedy of the Civil War is apparent from the exhibits on display in this historical representation of Lynchburg's history. The city was at the center of Confederate supply lines, making it a frequent Union target. The museum is housed in Lynchburg's 1855 Old Court House, one of Virginia's outstanding Greek Revival civil buildings. The museum is open daily, except holidays, from 10 AM to 4 PM. Admission is $1.

Pest House Medical Museum and Confederate Cemetery
Old City Cemetery, Fourth and Taylor sts.,
Lynchburg • (804) 847-1811

The Confederate Section of the historic Old City Cemetery serves as the final resting place for more than 2,200 individually marked graves of Confederate Soldiers from 14 states. Nearby

is the Pest House Medical Museum. One room depicts conditions in the House of Pestilence quarantine hospital during the Civil War. The second room is furnished as Dr. John J. Terrell's office when he practiced medicine in the area in the late 1800s. A monument to the memory of the 99 soldiers who died of smallpox in the Pest House during the war is near the entrance to the adjacent Confederate section. Many self-interpretive tablets and a variety of brochures are available at the Information Gatehouse and throughout the recently restored cemetery. Antique roses and period plantings contribute to the horticultural significance and beauty. The museum and cemetery are open daily from sunrise to sunset for self-guided tours or by appointment.

Spring Hill Cemetery
Fort Ave., Lynchburg

Buried here is Gen. Jubal Early, who saved the city of Lynchburg from destruction during 1864 when he ran empty railroad cars up and down the tracks to convince the Yankees that Confederate reinforcements were arriving for a major battle. The Union forces retreated, and Lynchburg was saved from the destruction of Gen. David Hunter.

Southern Soldier Statue
Monument Terrace, center of downtown, Lynchburg

Honoring heroes of all wars, a statue of a Southern infantryman stands at the top of Monument Terrace. It was designed by James O. Scott and erected in 1898.

Riverside Park
2240 Rivermont Ave., Lynchburg

Here you will find a fragment of the hull of the canalboat *Marshall*, which transported the body of Jackson from Lynchburg to Lexington for burial in 1863.

Appomattox Court House National Historical Park
Off U.S. Hwy. 460, 20 miles east of Lynchburg, Appomattox • (804) 352-8987

If you're going to Lynchburg to see Civil War history, just 20 minutes farther will put you at Appomattox, where our nation reunited on April 9, 1865. A restored village appears the same as the day generals Grant and Lee ended the war with a handshake. Living-history exhibits are held during the summer. Appomattox hosts the famous Railroad Festival every autumn (see our Annual Events and Festivals chapter). The park is open daily from 9 AM to 5 PM.

Bedford City/County Museum
201 E. Main St., Bedford • (540) 586-4520

This interesting local collection includes a number of artifacts from the Civil War, including weapons, flags, photos and personal effects. The museum is open Monday through Saturday from 10 AM to 5 PM. Admission is $1 for adults and 50¢ for children.

Longwood Cemetery
Bridge St., Bedford

A Civil War monument marks the final resting place of soldiers who died at one of five Confederate hospitals in and around Bedford. A tall obelisk stands over the single grave of 192 soldiers and a nurse.

New River Valley

Pulaski County

The Wilderness Road Regional Museum
Newbern • (540) 674-4835

Operated by the New River Historical Society, the museum consists of six historic structures on a 6-acre tract. The collection includes a number of Civil War displays, including a drum, since the area is close to Cloyd's Mountain, site of Southwest Virginia's major Civil War battle (May 9, 1864). Each year, the museum has a Civil War Weekend in mid-June. Hours of operation are Tuesday through Saturday from 10:30 AM to 4:30 PM and Sunday from 1 to 4:30 PM.

Alleghany Highlands

Highland County

McDowell Presbyterian Church
U.S. Hwy. 250 W., McDowell

McDowell is the site of the second major battle of Jackson's valley campaign; a roadside marker commemorates the event. Inside the village is McDowell Presbyterian Church, used as a hospital during and after the fighting.

Virginia's Wine Country

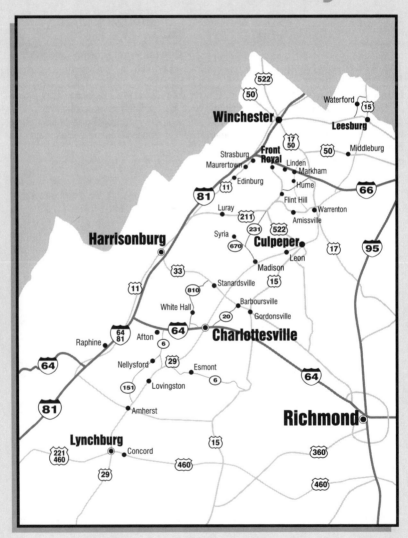

Wineries

Twenty years ago, you might have been right in fashion sipping a mint julep or iced tea on a summer afternoon in the Blue Ridge. Today, corks are popping from Leesburg to Pulaski.

In less than two decades, Virginia winemaking has grown from a struggling cottage industry to a burgeoning international force. The industry transformation has been, and continues to be, remarkable. The state's winery count has increased from 6 in 1979 to 52 in 1998. Last year Virginia was the nation's 12th-largest commercial grape-growing state and was ranked sixth among vinifera wine growing states.

These changes make it an exciting time to visit Virginia wineries. Visitors get a close-up view and firsthand taste of the fruits of our winemakers' labors. You can find out for yourself why *The Wine Spectator* calls Virginia "the most accomplished of America's emerging wine regions" and why Virginia wines continue to win national and international awards at an impressive rate.

Since Thomas Jefferson's time, growers have suspected that Virginia soils and high elevations, which minimize summer heat and lengthen the growing season, would make ideal grape-growing conditions. The Shenandoah Valley, both climate- and soil-wise, has been favorably compared to Germany's Moselle Valley, a famous Riesling region, and the Piedmont is said to share many of the same characteristics with the Bordeaux region of France.

But it wasn't until the 1980s that the industry really took off, in part because of support from state officials. In 1985 the Virginia General Assembly created the Virginia Winegrowers Advisory Board to promote winemaking in the state. The Assembly also set up a research team to provide grape growers with the technical support necessary to produce a healthy crop.

The results of these efforts and the efforts of individual wineries are here for us all to enjoy. Winery tours in Virginia are wonderful in many ways. Not only do visitors get to taste a wide variety of wines, but they can do so in spectacular settings. Our wineries offer everything from majestic pastoral scenes to impressive mountain views at high elevations. Most have areas for picnickers, so take along lunch or brunch and make a day of it.

As you plan your winery tours, look at the maps in this chapter and consider visiting three or four wineries in a day. Around Charlottesville, Front Royal and Middleburg, numerous daytrip options are available. In Charlottesville, for example, Oakencroft, White Hall and Autumn Hill vineyards are nestled together, as are Jefferson and Totier Creek. Each of these clusters make excellent daytrips. Around Middleburg, you can visit Swedenburg, Piedmont and Meredyth, and outside Front Royal you'll find Oasis, Linden and Naked Mountain vineyards.

We suggest you not try to do too much in one day; it is much better to savor each stop and each view. So chart your course carefully, and don't forget to call ahead to confirm winery hours, which can change.

If you're lucky, you'll be in the area when one of the wineries hosts a festival or open house. Spring and fall are big festival times. In May, Front Royal hosts the annual Virginia Mushroom and Wine Festival, Tarara Vineyards holds a Virginia Wines and Cheeses of the World Festival, and Mountain Cove Vineyards sponsors a Fiesta de Primavera with music, crafts and tastings of new wines. In October festivals range from the small annual Harvest Fest at Rockbridge Vineyard to the large Smith Mountain Lake Festival with more than a dozen wineries represented. (See our Annual Events and Festivals chapter.) For a complete listing of festivals and events, we recommend an excellent annual guide to Virginia's wineries that is available free from the Virginia Wine Marketing Program, VDACS, Division of Marketing, P.O. Box 1163, Richmond 23218; (800) 828-4637.

The following is a complete list of wineries of the Blue Ridge region, beginning with those in the Shenandoah Valley. Wineries are organized alphabetically within their geographic region. The cost of tours and tasting in most wineries is free unless otherwise noted. Some wineries will charge a small fee for group tastings.

www.insiders.com

See this and many other
Insiders' Guide®
destinations online.
Visit us today!

Shenandoah Valley

Deer Meadow Vineyard
199 Vintage Ln., Winchester
• **(540) 877-1919, (800) 653-6632**

Owner Charles Sarle made his first commercial wines in 1987, after retiring from a career as a mechanical engineer. He had been a home winemaker for 10 years. He and his wife, Jennifer, operate the winery on their 120-acre farm southwest of Winchester. They produce Cabernet Sauvignon, Chardonnay, Seyval Blanc, Chambourcin and Golden Blush — a wine from an American hybrid. This small, rustic vineyard is open March through December. Tours are offered from 11 AM to 5 PM Wednesday through Sunday and most Mondays and holidays.

To reach the vineyard from U.S. 50, go south on Va. 608 for 6.5 miles; turn left on Va. 629 and drive 1 mile to the winery on the right. From U.S. 55, travel north on Va. 600 then go straight on Va. 608 and 8 miles to Va. 629.

Guilford Ridge Vineyard
328 Running Pine Rd., Luray
• **(540) 778-3853**

Owners John Gerba and Harland Baker planted these vines in the early 1970s and began winemaking in the mid-1980s. The Page County winery cultivates 4 acres of hybrid grapes and uses Bordelaise winemaking methods to produce their Red Page Valley, Et Delilah (light red) and Pinnacles (crisp white).

Visitors to the 80-plus acre farm have an opportunity to see a variety of animals — llamas, peacocks, goats, sheep and a potbellied pig — that make their home here. Call ahead to arrange a visit and purchases; tastings are offered to groups of eight or more year round. There is a small fee for group tastings. Tours of the winery are not available.

Guilford Ridge is easy to find. From the traffic light at the intersection of U.S. 340 and U.S. 211 Business in Luray, go south 4 miles on U.S. 340 Business and west 1 mile on Va. 632.

Landwirt Vineyards
8223 Simmers Valley Rd., Harrisonburg
• **(540) 833-6000**

This winery has been growing grapes since 1984, when owner Gary Simmers planted 16 acres of vines. Simmers is a dairy farmer whose family has lived and farmed in this part of Rockingham County for generations. In fact, the vineyards are in an area named Simmers Valley. In 1994 Simmers decided to stop selling his grapes to a nearby winery and start producing his own wines; two years later he sold his first vintages and picked up 14 medals along the way. Landwirt produces Chardonnay, Pinot Noir, Cabernet Franc, Cabernet Sauvignon and Riesling, the winery's most prolific variety with 6 acres of Riesling grapes planted. The winery is open for tours and tastings from 1 to 5 PM Saturday and Sunday and other times by appointment.

To get to Landwirt, take Exit 251 off Interstate 81. Travel north on U.S. 11 for 5 miles, turn left on Va. 806 and proceed 2.5 miles, going straight at the intersection of Va. 806 and Va. 619 for a half-mile. The winery is on the right.

North Mountain Vineyard & Winery
4374 Swartz Rd., Maurertown
• **(540) 436-9463**

North Mountain Vineyard's 10 acres are situated on property in northern Shenandoah County that has been farmed since the late 1700s. The vineyard was established in 1982

Photo: Lexington Visitors Bureau

Rockbridge Vineyard in Raphine has more than 5 acres of grape vines.

when proprietor Dick McCormack planted some 8,000 vines of Chardonnay, Vidal and Chambourcin. At the winery building, which was built in 1990 and modeled after a European-style farmhouse, you can taste North Mountain's award-winning Chardonnay, Vidal Riesling, red, blush and spiced apple. The winery's large picnic area overlooks the vineyard. North Mountain is open for tours and tastings from 11 AM to 5 PM on weekends and holidays. Large groups should call ahead for an appointment.

From I-81 take Exit 291 at Toms Brook, go west on Va. 651 for 1 mile to Mt. Olive. Turn left on Va. 623 and go 2 miles, turn left on Va. 655 and follow signs for a half-mile to the winery.

Rockbridge Vineyard
30 Hillview Ln., Raphine
• (540) 377-6204, (888) 511-9463

Shepherd and Jane Rouse own this expanding 13-acre winery, which is housed in a renovated 19th-century dairy barn. Shepherd was the winemaker at Montdomaine Cellars but is now trying his hand on his own patch of land while also working as the winemaker at Oakencroft Vineyard in Charlottesville. In just

a few short years, Rockbridge Vineyard, between Staunton and Lexington, has brought home a series of gold medals and the Governor's Cup for its 1995 V'Dor dessert wine. The 47-acre farm sits at 2,000 feet elevation, so it is a wonderful spot on hot summer days. The breezy hillside is great for picnics, and the Rouses will even lend you a blanket if you want to enjoy a picnic spot. Rockbridge produces Chardonnay, Riesling, Cabernet, Pinot Noir, Vidal Ice Wine and several other blended varieties. Tours and tastings are offered from noon to 5 PM Saturday and Sunday in April, November and December and Wednesday through Sunday from May to October. The vineyard is closed January to March.

From I-81, take Exit 205 to Va. 606. The vineyard is 1 mile west on the right.

Shenandoah Vineyards Inc.
3659 S. Ox Rd., Edinburg • (540) 984-8699

The Shenandoah Valley's first winery grows 14 varieties of grapes on 40 acres. The winery itself is on the lower level of a renovated Civil War-era barn, which also houses a small gift shop and tasting room. Owner Emma Randel lives in the restored log house where her mother was born. In this peaceful setting with sweeping mountain views, the winery produces Chardonnay, Riesling, Cabernet Sauvignon, Merlot and several blends, including Shenandoah Blanc, Shenandoah Ruby and Cabernet Blanc. In 1995, Shenandoah's Chardonnay was named one of the best white wines in the state. The winery is open for tastings from 10 AM to 6 PM daily March through December and from 10 AM to 5 PM in January and February; it is closed Thanksgiving, Christmas and New Year's Day. Tours are given hourly from 11 AM to 5 PM. A large picnic area has wonderful views of surrounding mountains.

To find the vineyards, turn off I-81 at Exit 279 in Edinburg. Go west on Stoney Creek Road then right on S. Ox Road. The winery is 1.5 miles on the left.

East of the Blue Ridge

Afton Mountain Vineyards
234 Vineyard Ln., Afton • (540) 456-8667

This winery lies on a southeastern slope of the Blue Ridge at 960 feet, just minutes from the end of Skyline Drive and the beginning of the Blue Ridge Parkway near Afton, a village known for its antiques and mountain crafts. The winery and its 17 acres of vineyards offer magnificent views of the Rockfish River Valley and the mountains immortalized in Edgar Allan Poe's "Tale of the Ragged Mountains." The winery sells breads, cheeses and meats, which can be enjoyed from a scenic picnic area. Wines include Chardonnay, Cabernet Sauvignon, Gewurztraminer, Riesling, Merlot and Pinot Noir. The winery is open for tours and tastings from 11 AM to 5 PM Friday to Monday during January and February. From March through December, the winery is open from 10 AM to 6 PM daily except Tuesdays. Afton is closed Easter, Thanksgiving, Christmas and New Year's Day.

If you are traveling from Charlottesville, go west on I-64 to Exit 107. Continue west on Va. 250 for 6 miles to Va. 151 S. Stay on this road for 3 miles to Va. 6 W., which you travel on for 1.8 miles to Va. 631. Go south 1.2 miles to the winery entrance. From Staunton, go east on I-64 to Exit 99. Travel east on Va. 250 for 1.3 miles to Va. 6 E. Drive 1.7 miles to Va. 631 south; the winery entrance is 1.2 miles farther.

Autumn Hill Vineyards/ Blue Ridge Winery
301 River Dr., Stanardsville
• (804) 985-6100

The setting for this small, award-winning winery is a high plateau northwest of Charlottesville. Owners Avra and Ed Schwab left Long Island for Virginia in the mid-1970s. Ed, who ran an interior design firm, had grown weary of the rat race. Deciding to try winemaking, the couple planted the first stage of their vineyards in 1979; they now have 13 acres of vines. Their European-style wines include Chardonnay, Riesling, Blush, Cabernet Sauvignon, Cabernet Franc and Merlot. The winery is open to visitors only two weekends: the last weekend in March and the first weekend of November. Phone sales are available year round.

To get to Autumn Hill from Charlottesville, drive north on U.S. 29 until you get to the stoplight at U.S. 33 in Ruckersville. Go west on U.S. 33 for 2 miles to Quinque, turn left at Va. 633 and proceed 6.5 miles, ending at Va. 603. Turn left and travel 1 mile to the winery on the left.

Barboursville Vineyards
Va. Rt. 777, Barboursville • (540) 832-3824

Barboursville wines have won more awards than any other vineyard in Virginia including this year's Governor's Cup for its Cabernet Franc. Try the Chardonnay Reserve. It was selected as one of the top 25 Chardonnays produced in the United States, and it was recently served at the embassy in Paris.

Zonin, the giant Italian wine firm, owns the 830-acre winery, which includes a cattle farm and the imposing ruins of a mansion designed by Thomas Jefferson for Virginia governor James Barbour. The site is a registered Virginia Historic Landmark and has many prime picnic spots. Barboursville produces more than 25,000 cases of wine a year from 125 acres of grapes. The wines at Barboursville are more in the European style, fresh and clean with subtle complexity, and include the popular Chardonnay, Riesling, Sauvignon Blanc,

Cabernet Franc, Pinot Noir, Traminer Aromatico, Malvaxia, Barbera and Sparkling Brut. Tours are available from 11 AM to 4 PM Saturdays. Tastings and sales are offered from 10 AM to 5 PM Monday to Saturday and from 11 AM to 5 PM on Sundays except major holidays.

At the intersection of Va. 20 and U.S. 33, follow Va. 20 S. for 200 yards. Turn left on Va. 678 and go a half-mile, make a right on Va. 777 (Vineyard Road) and another right at the first driveway. Then follow the signs.

Breaux Vineyards
13860 Harpers Ferry Rd., Hillsboro
• **(540) 668-6299**

Friends of Paul and Alexis Breaux must have good taste. "I made some homemade wine and our friends and neighbors kept after us to make more," Paul Breaux said. So on April 18, 1998, Breaux Vineyards became the 50th winery in the state. Ten months later, Breaux had won 15 medals in a series of wine competitions. When Paul and Alexis purchased their 400-acre farm in western Loudoun County, the property came with 18 acres of 14-year-old grapevines. They planted 10 more acres and, with the help of winemaker David Collins, quickly sold more than 2,200 cases of their first vintage. They plan to have more than 7,000 cases ready for their second season. Madeleine Chardonnay, named for his 8-year-old daughter, is one of Paul's favorites. The winery also produces Seyval Blanc, Vidal Blanc, Riesling, Viognier, Cabernet Franc, Cabernet Sauvignon, and what is thought to be one of the state's first Late Harvest Sauvignon Blancs. Paul Breaux keeps a twin-engine plane nearby to take him back and forth from his real estate company in Nags Head, N.C., but someone will be on hand for tours and tastings from 11 AM to 6 PM Thursdays through Mondays from May through October. Hours are 11 AM to 5 PM from November through April. The winery is closed on major holidays. Their Napa-meets-Mediterranean–style tasting room offers a view of their hillside vines on Short Hill Mountain. You may bring along a picnic or sample some of Breaux's light gourmet fare. Large groups are asked to please call ahead.

From the Northern Virginia area, go west on the Dulles toll road to Greenway. At Leesburg, take Va. 7 west for three miles to the Va. 9 Hillsboro exit. Go eight miles to Hillsboro then another 1.5 miles to Va. 671, also known as Harpers Ferry Road. Bear right on Va. 671 and the winery sign will be one mile ahead on the right.

Burnley Vineyards
4500 Winery Ln., Barboursville
• **(540) 832-2828**

One of the oldest wineries in Albemarle County, Burnley Vineyards produces 11 wines that include Chardonnay, Cabernet Sauvignon, Riesling, Spicy Rivanna and Daniel Cellars Somerset dessert wines. Lee Reeder and his father planted their first vines in 1976, the year after nearby Barboursville Vineyards opened. In 1984 father and son started the winery. Today they produce about 6,000 cases a year from grapes grown on their own 25 acres and from a small, private vineyard in Luray. Their wines have won more than 100 awards in state, national and international competitions.

Tastings are offered in a room with a cathedral ceiling and huge windows overlooking the countryside. The winery is open Friday through Monday from 11 AM to 5 PM in January, February and March; from April through December, hours are 11 AM to 5 PM daily. Group tours or evening visits can be arranged in advance.

INSIDERS' TIP

Several wineries in Virginia offer their own accommodations. Prince Michel Winery has luxury suites with living rooms and fireplaces. Burnley Vineyards offers a fully furnished house with a balcony overlooking the vineyards. Tarara Vineyard and Winery opened a four-room bed and breakfast, while Sharp Rock's accommodations include two cottages.

If you are heading from Charlottesville, go north 15 miles on Va. 20 and then turn left on Va. 641. Go one-third of a mile to the winery. From the intersection of U.S. 33 and Va. 20, take Va. 20 S. for 2 miles then turn right on Va. 641, proceeding less than a half-mile to the winery.

Dominion Wine Cellars
1 Winery Ave., Culpeper • (540) 825-8772

In 1985 a group of 20 growers formed the Virginia Wineries Co-op and contributed their grapes to launch the Dominion label. Today the cooperative idea continues under the direction of the Williamsburg Winery, which now owns the Dominion facilities. Most of the original growers still produce grapes for Dominion, which has only a few acres of its own vines. Dominion grapes come from across the state to produce Blanc de Blanc, Chardonnay, Late Harvest Vidal, Cabernet Sauvignon and Riesling. Williamsburg Winery labels are also available at the vineyard. A courtyard with umbrella-covered picnic tables and a scenic deck makes a nice picnic spot. Dominion Wine Cellars is wheelchair-accessible. Tours and tastings are offered Monday through Saturday from 10 AM to 5 PM and Sunday from 11 to 5 PM; the winery is closed on major holidays.

From U.S. 29 Bypass, take the Culpeper Exit at Va. Route 3 then travel west to McDevitt Drive, where you turn right to Winery Avenue.

Farfelu Vineyard
13058 Crest Hill Rd., Flint Hill
• (540) 364-2930

This small winery in Rappahannock County has been revitalized in recent years. It was one of the first Virginia wineries to receive a commercial license as a farm winery and produced its first wines in 1975. Owner Charles Raney, a former United Airlines pilot, produces Cabernet Sauvignon, Chardonnay and red and white picnic wines from 7.5 acres of vines. The 86-acre property has a picnic area and hiking trail along the Rappahannock River. Tours and tastings are available from 11 AM to 4:30 PM daily, but Raney asks that visitors telephone in advance. Tours and tastings are free for small groups and $1 a person for

groups of 10 or more. The winery is closed in January and February.

You can reach the winery from U.S. 66. Take Exit 27 at Va. 647; go 12.5 miles to the winery gate on the left.

Gray Ghost Vineyards
14706 Lee Hwy., Amissville
• (540) 937-4869

This small vineyard opened in the spring of 1994 on a 22-acre farm in Rappahannock County. Using grapes from their 9 acres of vines as well as from five other small Rappahannock vineyards, owners and winemakers Cheryl and Al Kellert produce Chardonnay, Cabernet Sauvignon, Vidal Blanc, Seyval Blanc, Cabernet Franc and Victorian White. The winery has a canopied picnic area and a large display of wine glasses. Tours and tastings are available from 11 AM to 5 PM on Friday, Saturday and Sunday and are free for small groups. Large groups of 10 or more should call ahead for an appointment. The vineyard is 11 miles west of Warrenton on U.S. 211.

Hill Top Berry Farm and Winery
2800 Berry Hill Rd., Nellysford
• (840) 361-1266

Like many couples, Marlyn and Sue Allen needed something to do after the kids went off to school. "We lived here for 22 years," Marlyn Allen said. "When the kids graduated from college we decided we were going to do something we wanted to do." Seven years ago, they planted some berry bushes — a lot of berry bushes. In fact, they have six acres of blackberries alone, not counting their raspberries, boysenberries, plums, peaches, apples, grapes . . . and shiitake mushrooms. During the first weekend in July, they usually open their gates for a pick-your-own blackberry day, but along the way Marlyn began to save a few berries to make some homemade wine. When friends tasted a sample of his blackberry wine, they encouraged him to make more. So, the Nelson County couple decided to give it a go. In March 1999, they opened their own small winery and planned to release about 1,500 gallons of their "true to the fruit" wines. Hill Top is open from noon to 5 PM

Thursday through Saturday, 1 to 6 PM Sundays and other times by appointment.

From Charlottesville, go west on I-64 to Crozet, Exit 107. Turn left on U.S. 250 west and another left on Va. 151 south. After about 10 miles, turn left at Tuckahoe Antique Mall on Va. 612. Bear to the right across the bridge and the winery will be at the top of the hill on the left.

Horton Cellars Winery/
Montdomaine Cellars
6399 Spotswood Tr., Gordonsville
• (540) 832-7440

In the early 1980s Dennis Horton searched the vineyards of southern France for grapes that would thrive in Virginia's warm climate. He settled on the Viognier, a variety used in some of the world's finest wines. He and his business partner, Joan Bieda, harvested the first crop from their 65 acres in Orange County in 1991 and made it into wine at Montdomaine Cellars, a noted Cabernet producer that Bieda and Horton later purchased. In 1993 Horton Vineyards made the first crush at its new underground stone cellars and offered tastings in a delightful vaulted-ceiling tasting room. Horton's Viognier and other Rhone varieties have done well in national competitions, but try the Norton as well. This native Virginia grape produced Monticello's prize-winning clarets in the 1800s. The vineyard is open for tours and tastings from 10 AM to 5 PM daily.

From Gordonsville, drive west on U.S. 33 for 4 miles to the winery entrance on the right. From U.S. 29, head east on U.S. 33 for 8 miles to the winery on the left.

Jefferson Vineyards
Va. Rt. 53, Charlottesville
• (804) 977-3042, (800) 272-3042

This vineyard, between Monticello and Ash Lawn-Highland, is situated on the same stretch of rolling land once owned by Philip Mazzei, the 18th-century wine enthusiast who helped convince Thomas Jefferson to plant vines. Though Jefferson was never able to grow grapes successfully here, Jefferson Vineyards has been able to, cultivating 16 acres of European vinifera — the same variety that Mazzei tried to grow.

Today winemaker Michael Shaps, who studied and trained in France's Burgundy region, produces Cabernet Franc, Pinot Noir, Cabernet Sauvignon, Chardonnay and Riesling at Jefferson Vineyards. Tours and tastings are available from 11 AM to 5 PM daily. The winery has a small gift shop, a pleasant picnic table area under a grape arbor and a deck with views of the surrounding mountains. The quaint, renovated barn that houses the tasting room can be booked for private parties.

To get to the vineyard take I-64 to Exit 121A, heading toward Scottsville. Immediately past the traffic light, turn left onto Va. 53. The winery entrance is 3 miles on the right.

Linden Vineyards
3708 Harrels Corner Rd., Linden
• (540) 364-1997

Linden has 13 acres of vines and leases an additional 6 acres at Flint Hill to produce about 5,000 cases a year of Chardonnay, Seyval, Cabernet, Sauvignon Blanc and Riesling-Vidal. The latter is a blend that does not require aging and produces a young, fresh wine with 48 percent Vidal and 52 percent Riesling. Well-designed and meticulously maintained, the winery was started in the spring of 1987. The comfortable tasting room offers a view of the vineyards against a mountain backdrop, and the grounds have picnic areas. Tours and tastings are available from 11 AM to 5 PM on weekends January through March and Wednesday through Sunday from April through December. The winery is also open some holiday Mondays but is closed Thanksgiving, Christmas and New Year's Day.

From Interstate 66 take Exit 13 at Linden and go east 1 mile on Va. 55. Then turn right on Va. 638 and travel 2 miles. The winery is on the right.

Loudoun Valley Vineyard
38638 Old Wheatland Rd., Waterford
• (540) 882-3375

This 25-acre vineyard has one of the best views in the area, and owners Hubert and Dolores Tucker have capitalized on it. Their glass-walled tasting room overlooks the Short Hill Mountains and the vineyard land, upon which Mosby's Rangers camped during the Civil War. The Tuckers produce Chardonnay, Pinot Noir, Riesling, Cabernet Sauvignon, Merlot and Zinfandel wines, and they recently added Poire, their first dessert pear wine. Tours are available from 11 AM to 5 PM on weekends January through March and Wednesday to Sunday April through December. Tours and tastings are free, except for large groups, who should call ahead for an appointment.

You can reach the vineyard from Leesburg by going west on Va. 7 for 2 miles to Va. 9. Go west on Va. 9 and drive another 5 miles to winery on the right.

Meredyth Vineyards
Va. Rt. 628, Middleburg • (540) 687-6277

This pretty Fauquier County vineyard is among the most prized in Virginia, with excellent offerings of 15 wines, including Seyval Blanc, Cabernet Sauvignon, Riesling and Chardonnay. Meredyth is situated on a beautiful 216-acre farm outside of Middleburg along the edge of the Bull Run Mountains, foothills to the Blue Ridge that are also among the oldest mountains in the world. Josephine and Archie Smith III open the vineyard for public tours from 11 AM to 5 PM every day except Christmas, Thanksgiving and New Year's Day. The vineyard store is open from 11 AM to 5 PM daily. There is a $1 charge for tastings.

From I-66 turn west on Va. 50 to Middleburg. Turn south at the traffic light and go 2.5 miles to Va. 628 (Logan's Mill Road). Turn right and go 2.5 miles to the winery. The entrance is on the right.

Mountain Cove Vineyards
1362 Fortune's Cove Ln., Lovingston
• (804) 263-5392

In 1974 Mountain Cove owner Al Weed became the first person in Central Virginia to plant grape vines. A native of Brooklyn, N.Y., Weed left a career in investment banking and moved with his family to the Nelson County farm in 1973. He planted French hybrid grapes, believing they were more hardy and prolific than other vines. Today he produces several blends of reds and whites as well as a tasty peach wine called LaAbra Peach. Weed built most of the winery and the rough-sawn oak

tasting room himself. The vineyard is open from noon to 6 PM Saturday and Sunday in April and Wednesday through Sunday from May through December. For other times call ahead. The vineyard is closed Christmas, Thanksgiving, Easter and New Year's Day.

To get to Mountain Cove from Lovingston go north on U.S. 29 and turn left on Va. 718. Make a right on Va. 651 (Fortune's Cove Lane), and the winery is on the right.

Naked Mountain Vineyard
Leeds Manor Rd., Markham
• (540) 364-1609

This chalet-like winery sits on the east slope of the Blue Ridge, east of Front Royal in Fauquier County. A picnic area on the 8-acre vineyard offers sensational views. Owners Bob and Phoebe Harper produce a wonderful Chardonnay, Riesling, Sauvignon Blanc and Cabernet Sauvignon. They use traditional methods of winemaking, including fermentation and aging in French oak barrels. The winery has a spacious tasting room on the second floor surrounded by a deck. Tours are offered from 11 AM to 5 PM on weekends and holidays during January and February and Wednesday through Sunday (and holidays) March to December. Groups of 10 or more should call ahead for an appointment.

From Washington, D.C., drive west on I-66 to Exit 18 at Markham. Go north on Va. 688 for 1.5 miles to the winery.

Oakencroft Vineyard and Winery
1486 Oakencroft Ln., Charlottesville
• (804) 296-4188

Owner Felicia Warburg Rogan heads the Jeffersonian Wine Grape Growers Society, a group that won Charlottesville the title of Wine Capital of Virginia and initiated the annual Monticello Wine and Food Festival in the early 1980s. The winery is situated on a bucolic farm west of the city, a beautiful site surrounded by rolling hills and overlooking a large pond. A big red barn houses the winery, tasting room and gift shop. Oakencroft produces a variety of wines including Chardonnay, Blush, Cabernet Sauvignon and Merlot. Tours and tastings are given from 11 AM to 5 PM on weekends in March, 11 AM to 5 PM daily April

Thomas Jefferson: Food and Wine Connoisseur

He wanted to be remembered for three things.

Never mind that Thomas Jefferson was twice elected president of the United States; he was a reluctant politician. At his request, his proudest accomplishments were carved on his headstone: Author of the Declaration of American Independence and of the Statute of Virginia for religious freedom and father of the University of Virginia.

But between his accomplishments in politics, law, science and education, Jefferson managed to develop a keen appreciation for culinary delicacies. In fact, he has been called this country's first gourmet. He loved fine food and wine. He followed this interest from beginning to end — that is, from garden to table.

Few people realize that Jefferson was an avid collector of recipes and wine. With his knowledge of Europe's finest vineyards, Jefferson was the wine advisor to several presidents and, at George Washington's request, selected the first wines to be stocked in the White House. Though he didn't actually cook, he passed recipes along to friends and gathered them for his own chefs.

In Jefferson's writings, researchers have found grocery lists, wine inventories and recipes. They discovered receipts for hundreds and hundreds of bottles of wine. As president he spent about 10 percent of his $25,000 salary on wine; Jefferson estimated that he needed about one bottle of wine for every 3.5 people served.

Jefferson certainly was not a drunkard; he simply valued wine. "No nation is drunken where wine is cheap and none sober, when the dearness of wine substitutes ardent spirits as a common beverage," he wrote. In fact, he was vehemently opposed to luxury taxes on wine, insisting wine was an "innocent gratification" and a "healthy substitute" to whiskey.

Most wines Jefferson served were ordered from Europe. European tastes, particularly French, had a large influence on him. He served almost five years as Minister to France, and it was in this time that his study of and devotion to food and wine blossomed. In France he began gathering his favorite recipes. He brought two important ones back to the United States. The first is what some believe may be this country's first ice cream recipe. He served this dish at the White House, to the delight of many diners.

The second was a recipe for pasta, which he brought back along with the United States' first pasta mold. Jefferson's daughter used the mold to create a dish with Parmesan cheese. Later, American cooks turned this entree into an American classic: macaroni and cheese.

Though Jefferson was heavily influenced by French food and wine, he also enjoyed the robust flavors of Virginia cooking. At least once during his presidency, Jefferson wrote to Monticello cooks for a muffin recipe that he said his French cook could not do properly. And one White House guest remarked that the president served "half French and half Virginia" to his diners. Jefferson's meals, by the way, were famous for their elegance, innovation and abundance.

His love of food and wine extended to the garden, where Jefferson spent many hours recording and observing his plants. Remember that 150 years ago, Americans were still experimenting with soils to find out what could grow here. At his Albemarle County home, Monticello, Jefferson experimented with an enormous variety of fruits

— continued on next page

and vegetables, many grown with seeds and saplings he brought back from Europe. Today the Monticello gardens have been carefully restored following Jefferson's own plans, and garden tours at Monticello are well worth the effort (see our Arts chapter).

Some of Jefferson's agricultural projects were successful and others were not. His peach and apple orchards did wonderfully. But, despite prolonged efforts, he never successfully grew olives, grapes or rice.

It wasn't from lack of trying. Jefferson believed successful winemaking depended on native grapes. In 1773 he gave 2,000 acres near Monticello to Italian farmer Philip Mazzei in hopes of launching a new indus-

Photo: R. Lautman/Monticello

Jefferson was an avid entertainer. Here, in Monticello's dining room, he served many lavish and bountiful meals.

try for the colony. But Mazzei's efforts ended with the start of the Revolutionary War.

Jefferson's many attempts to start a vineyard at Monticello were among the first in Virginia. Today many of Virginia's dozens of winemakers consider Jefferson their premier champion. "He was a promoter," said Peter Hatch, director of gardens and grounds at Monticello. "He left a legacy of gentle stewardship of the land."

As a promoter, Jefferson never lost hope that grapes would grow in Virginia soils. He wrote: "We could, in the United States, make as great a variety of wines as are made in Europe, not exactly the same kinds, but doubtless as good." He was right. More than 50 vineyards across the state produce wine, with many of these wineries just minutes from Monticello.

Jefferson attributed his long life — he died on July 4, 1826 at the age of 83 — to regular exercise and a healthy diet. Who could disagree? He could have written the lifestyle recommendations that today's doctors prescribe. Jefferson's genius is evident in so many areas of his life, but who would have guessed that part of his legacy would include the promotion of progressive ideas about food and wine? He was a man ahead of his time, and we can only be thankful that he was.

through November and daily from noon to 6 PM in December. Call for appointments in January and February.

From U.S. 29 in Charlottesville, drive west on Barracks Road (Va. 654) for 3.5 miles. The winery entrance is on the left.

Oasis Vineyard
14141 Hume Rd., Hume
• **(540) 635-7627, (800) 304-7656**

This vineyard and winery sit on a spectacular stretch of land facing the Blue Ridge Mountains. From 100 acres of vines, Oasis produces Chardonnay, Riesling, Merlot, Gewurztraminer, Cabernet Sauvignon and three types of champagne using traditional French methods. Owners Dirgham Salahi and his Belgian-born wife, Corinne, purchased the property in the mid-1970s and planted French hybrid grapes as a hobby. They soon learned that the soil was well-suited for grape growing and turned their hobby into a business. Although much of Oasis's wine is sold at the winery, it is also carried by some independent vintners and served by many restaurants in Virginia and Washington, D.C. Tastings are offered daily from 10 AM to 5 PM, and tours are at 11 AM, 1 PM and 3 PM daily. Tastings and tours are $3 and include a sampling of up to eight wines and an Oasis wine glass. Large groups are welcome by appointment.

From I-66 take Exit 27 at Marshall. Turn left upon exiting and then right onto Va. 647 and travel 4 miles. Turn right on Va. 635 and go 10 miles. The winery is on the left. You also can get there from Front Royal and Skyline Drive. Drive south on U.S. 522 for 7 miles, then turn left on Va. 635 and go 1 mile.

Peaks of Otter Winery
2122 Sheep Creek Rd., Bedford
• **(540) 586-3707**

Nancy and Danny Johnson opened Virginia's "smallest" winery in 1996. The new winery actually is part of the 250-acre Johnson's Orchard, which has been in the Johnson family for five generations. Since more than 100 acres is devoted to fruit, the Johnsons specialize in "Fruit of the Farm Wine" featuring apple, peach, nectarine, pear, berry and other fruit wines. At selected times of the year, the Johnsons open a petting area where children get a chance to see some of the orchard's farm animals. The winery is open daily from 7 AM to 7 PM from mid-August to mid-November. Call for an appointment at other times.

From the Blue Ridge Parkway, exit at Milepost 86 onto Va. 43. Go south for approximately 4 miles and turn right onto Va. 682. Go another 4 miles and turn right at Va. 680. Go 1 mile, and the sign will be on the right. Or if you are traveling on Va. 460, exit north on Va. 680. Go 5 miles, and you will see the sign on the left.

Piedmont Vineyards and Winery
2546D Halfway Rd., Middleburg
• **(540) 687-5528**

Virginia's first commercial vinifera vineyard is on Waverly, a 100-acre pre-Revolutionary War farm. Family-owned and operated, these 37 acres of vines were planted in 1973. Today the winery produces about 5,000 cases a year of Chardonnay, Hunt Country White, Pinot Gris and Cabernet Sauvignon. Tours and tastings are available from 10 AM to 4 PM daily except major holidays; large groups should call ahead for an appointment and expect to pay $2 per person. A picnic area is on the grounds for the use of visitors.

You can get to Piedmont from Middleburg by traveling approximately 3 miles south on Va. 626. From I-66 take Exit 31 to Va. 245 at the Plains then take an immediate left onto Va. 626.

Prince Michel de Virginia Vineyards
U.S. Hwy. 29, Leon • **(540) 547-3707, (800) 869-8242**

Prince Michel Vineyards, the largest wine producer in the state, sits just south of Culpeper. The vineyard is the only Virginia winery with an extensive museum about wine and an exclusive restaurant with a French chef. The winery's owner, Jean Leducq, made his fortune in the industrial laundry industry and now lives in Paris. His dream to have his own winery came true in 1983 in the Blue Ridge foothills. His wines have become wildly popular, selling throughout the mid-Atlantic region. Prince Michel also recently opened a wine shop and gift shop in Williamsburg.

The museum's diverse collection includes

Photo: Buddy Mays/Virginia Division of Tourism

This beautiful wine basket is from Oakencroft Vineyard near Charlottesville.

photos showing the process of grape-crushing. Some shots taken in Burgundy show two naked men in a barrel with the grapes, stirring and ventilating them. (Rest assured, this is not a technique applied at Prince Michel!) Visitors will also find a collection of every Mouton Rothschild label from 1945 to 1984, many of which were designed by famous artists such as Picasso, Salvador Dali and Georges Roualt. The winery has a special room for viewing a video documentary about the history of wine, the process of making it and Prince Michel Vineyards.

A self-guided tour takes visitors throughout the winery and features displays that describe the winemaking process. The tour ends at the gift shop, which sells everything from elegant wine canisters to scarves, wine-related jewelry and, of course, the wine itself. Visitors can sample wine or drink it by the glass at an attractive bar inside the gift shop.

Some of the vineyard's award-winning wines include Chardonnay, Riesling, Gewurztraminer, Cabernet Sauvignon, Merlot and Virginia Brut, a sparkling wine. Rapidan River Vineyards, also in Leon, is one of the Prince Michel family of vineyards. It produces fine Rieslings and Gewurztraminer (sold at Prince Michel) but is not open for visitors. Prince Michel is open for tours and tastings from 10 AM to 5 PM daily except major holidays. For $2 you can sample four wines or pay $3 to sample all of Prince Michel's wines. Read more about the Prince Michel Restaurant in our Restaurants chapter or call (800) 800-WINE for reservations.

The vineyard is 10 miles south of Culpeper on U.S. 29. From Madison go north 8 miles on U.S. 29. The winery is on the west side of U.S. 29.

Rebec Vineyards
2229 N. Amherst Hwy., Amherst
• (804) 946-5168

Richard Hanson has been making wine as a hobby for 37 years. In 1987 he decided to turn commercial. In their earliest winemaking years, he and his wife, Ella, could boast that their winery was the smallest in Virginia. That's no longer true, though Rebec Vineyards is still a small operation producing about 1,000 cases annually from 10 acres of vines. Their farm has been home to Ella Hanson's family since the mid-1800s. Her mother was born in the house where the Hansons live, and Ella grew up just 2 miles away. Built in 1742, the house was recently added to the list of National Historic Landmark designations. It has been home to the family of Gov. William Cabel and U.S. Vice President William Crawford. Rebec wines include Chardonnay, Cabernet Sauvignon, Riesling and Gewurztraminer.

Since 1991 Rebec Vineyards has hosted the Virginia Garlic Festival, an October event that features the crowning of a garlic queen, a garlic-eating contest, live music, good food and a lot of Virginia wine. The winery, made of wood from a 250-year-old tobacco barn, is open for tours and tastings from 10 AM to 5 PM daily March 15 through December 15 and by appointment the rest of the year.

The vineyard is on the west side of U.S. 29, just 5 miles north of Amherst and 11 miles south of Lovingston.

Rose River Vineyards and Trout Farm
U.S. Hwy. 33, Syria • (540) 923-4050

Rose River, with both the winery and the trout farm to entertain young and old, is a great stop for families. This 177-acre farm has 14 acres of grapes and two trout ponds stocked with fish raised on site. Visitors can use one of the farm's fishing poles and buy corn bait on the premises; you pay only for what you catch ($2.88 a pound). The kids will enjoy watching the trout in their raceways (lanes filled with fish). The vineyard's wines include Cabernet Sauvignon, Chardonnay, Peach and Blush. Each bottle comes with an elegant silk-screened label, and personalized labels are available.

The farm borders the Shenandoah National Park and has picnic sites and hiking trails. If you pass through Syria near lunch or dinner time, stop in at Graves Mountain Lodge, just a mile down the road from Rose River. You'll be delighted by their wholesome country fare, but don't forget to call ahead for reservations (see our Bed and Breakfasts and Country Inns chapter). Winery tours and tastings are offered from 11 AM to 5 PM on weekends from April to mid-December, from 11 AM to 5 PM Thursday through Monday during October and at other times by appointment. The Trout Farm is open 9 AM to 5 PM Saturday and Sunday.

To get to the vineyard from Syria go west on Va. 670, passing Graves Mountain Lodge, and turn left on Va. 648.

Shadwell-Windham Winery
14727 Mountain Rd., Hillsboro
• (540) 668-6464

They may have skipped a generation or two, but the Bazaco family is back in the wine business. Dr. George Bazaco's great-grandfather was a sheriff, but he also grew grapes in northern Greece. When young George went to study medicine in Italy, he also picked up a desire to grow grapes. In the mid-1980s, the Bazacos planted eight acres of grapes on their 300-acre farm in Loudoun County. Four years ago, they began making small amounts of Cabernet Sauvignon, Merlot, Cabernet Franc, Sauvignon Blanc, Riesling and Virginia Chardonnay and Viognier blends. In 1999 they released about 650 cases using the traditional European methods of winemaking. Tastings at Shadwell-Windham are a real treat. Bazaco's mother usually fixes a pan of baklava, so that visitors can have a little taste of Greece. The working farm is a beautiful spot for a picnic, and the winery hosted a wedding in 1998 with the lake and stately weeping willow trees as a backdrop. The winery is open the second and fourth full weekends of every month from March through November. It will also open from December through February as weather permits. The hours are 11 AM to 6 PM Saturdays and 1 to 5 PM Sundays.

If you are in the Washington D.C. area, take U.S. 66 west to Va. 267 (Dulles Access road) to the Greenway. Take the exit for Va. 7 west and proceed to Hillsboro exit at Va. 9

INSIDERS' TIP

Virginia wines are popular items in many gourmet shops throughout the Blue Ridge. If you can't visit the winery, look for its label as you shop.

Photo: Virginia Division of Tourism

Chateau Morrisette in Meadows of Dan commands a spectacular view from a 3,500-foot mountaintop.

west. Go 7.3 miles then turn right on Mountain Road (Va. 690 north). Windham Farm is one mile away on the left.

Sharp Rock Vineyards
5 Sharp Rock Rd., Sperryville
• **(540) 987-9700**

This five-acre vineyard sits in one of the most beautiful spots in Virginia, directly across an open field from popular Old Rag Mountain. Sharp Rock bottled its first vintage in 1997 and currently produces four wines, a barrel fermented Chardonnay, a Chardonnay Reserve fermented in new French oak barrels, a Cabernet made in the Bordeaux style, and a Sauvignon Blanc. Californians David and Marilyn Armor bought the Rappahannock County property in 1990, two weeks after their first visit to the area. With David serving as winemaker, Sharp Rock is a small, hand-se-

lected grape operation. The couple produced 500 cases of wine in 1999. The Armors also run the Sharp Rock Farm Bed and Breakfast for those who like a quiet stay in the pristine Virginia countryside (see our Bed and Breakfasts and Country Inns chapter). They restored the main house and other buildings on the 23-acre farm, some dating back to 1792 and 1864. The winery and tasting room is in the barn rebuilt from old wood. The tasting room floor was taken from a 250-year-old building in Charlottesville. Sharp Rock Vineyards is open for tours and tastings on Saturdays and the first full weekend of every month — noon to 5 PM Saturdays and 1 to 5 PM Sundays. From March through November the winery is open from noon to 5 PM Saturdays and by appointment.

To get to the winery from Charlottesville, take U.S. 29 north to Madison. Turn left on Va.

INSIDERS' TIP

With so many wineries within easy driving distances, it's easy to visit several in one day. But don't overdo it. Even though the samples may appear small, they can add up. Make sure you have a designated driver.

231 north and go 12 miles to Va. 601. Turn left and go about one mile. Sharp Rock Farm is on the right at the intersection with Va. 707.

Stonewall Vineyards
Va. Rt. 721, Concord • (804) 993-2185

This family-operated winery is halfway between Appomattox and Lynchburg. From their 14 acres of vinifera and French and American hybrids, owners Larry and Sterry Davis and their son, winemaker Bart Davis, produce Claret, Cabernet Sauvignon, Chardonnay and Cayuga. They also make a mead wine called Pyment that is a medieval blend of wine, honey and spices. Using their own vines, purchased grapes and grapes from leased vineyards, the Davises produce about 5,000 cases of wine a year. They recently added a new tasting room. Tours and tastings are offered from 11 AM to 4 PM daily.

From Lynchburg drive east 12 miles on U.S. 460. At the Concord traffic light, turn north on Va. 608, drive 5 miles then turn left on Va. 721. The winery is 100 yards on the left.

Swedenburg Estate Vineyard
23595 Winery Ln., Middleburg
• (540) 687-5219

Named after its proprietors, Wayne and Juanita Swedenburg, this family-owned vineyard consists of more than 15,000 grapevines on the 130-acre Valley View Farm, which has been under continuous cultivation for more than 200 years. The winery produces European-style premium wines, including Cabernet Sauvignon, Pinot Noir, Chardonnay, Riesling and Chantilly. The vineyard is open from 10 AM to 4 PM daily.

The winery is 1 mile east of Middleburg on U.S. 50. Or, if you are traveling from I-66, drive west on U.S. 50 for 21 miles to the Valley View entrance on the left.

Tarara Vineyard & Winery
13648 Tarara Ln., Leesburg
• (703) 771-7100

R.J. "Whitie" and Margaret Hubert own this 50-acre vineyard in Loudoun County and age their premium wines in a 6,000-square-foot cave at the edge of the Potomac River. Winemaker Richard Donley produces Chardonnay, Charval, Cabernets, Cameo, Cabernet Reserve, Merlot, Pinot Noir and Terra Rouge. Visitors can tour the cave and enjoy tastings from 11 AM to 5 PM Thursday through Monday; Tuesday and Wednesday by appointment; and weekends only in January and February. Groups larger than 10 should reserve in advance. The vineyard grounds have picnic and meeting facilities. If you don't want to pack your own basket, gourmet picnics are catered by the Red Fox Inn.

From Leesburg go north on U.S. 15 for approximately 8 miles to Lucketts. Go right on Va. 662 for three miles to the winery on the left.

Totier Creek Vineyard
1652 Harris Creek Rd., Charlottesville
• (804) 979-7105

This family-owned vineyard was planted in 1982 and '83 just south of Charlottesville in the Green Mountain range, a series of foothills east of the Blue Ridge. Owner/vintner Jamie Lewis ages his wines in a variety of oak barrels. His wines are known for their distinctively clean, light taste — produced in the tradition of many Italian wines — though he does produce fuller, oakier wines as well. The winery sells three types of Chardonnay, Merlot, Cabernet Sauvignon, Cabernet Franc, Pinot Noir, Riesling and Blush. Totier Creek wines are primarily available at the vineyard or at wine festivals.

Tours and tastings are offered from 11 AM to 5 PM Wednesday through Sunday and weekends only from Christmas to March 1. Bring a picnic lunch to enjoy on the winery deck. A banquet facility on the grounds will seat up to 160 people.

To get to Totier Creek take Exit 121A off of I-64 and follow Va. 20 S. past the Thomas Jefferson Visitors Center for 10.5 miles. Turn right on Va. 720 and travel 1 mile.

White Hall Vineyards
Break Heart Rd., White Hall
• (804) 823-8615

It didn't take long for White Hall Vineyards to establish itself as a state-of-the-art winemaking facility. After planting vines in 1991, the facility opened for tours and tastings in 1996, just in time to showcase their award-winning 1994 wines. That first harvest earned eight medals at state wine competitions, and things only got better. The 1995 wines collected 12 more medals and the coveted Governor's Cup for their Cabernet Sauvignon.

Brad McCarthy served as assistant winemaker at Horton Vineyards, Montdomaine Cellars and Rockbridge Vineyard before becoming winemaker at White Hall. Owners Edith and Tony Champ had searched the East Coast for a spot to build a winery and grow grapes. Tony Champ was retired from the fiber industry in New York City, and both had always dreamed about operating a winery. They settled on White Hall, just outside Charlottesville, where they bought a scenic 300-acre tract of land with breathtaking views of the Blue Ridge Mountains. The winery produces Chardonnay, Merlot and Cabernet Sauvignon from 14 acres of grapes. Tours and tastings are available daily from noon to 5 PM. If you plan on visiting on a weekday, call first. The vineyard is closed on major holidays.

From U.S. 29 in Charlottesville, go west on Barracks Road (Va. 654) to White Hall. From I-64 take the Crozet Exit and go east on Va. 250. Make a left turn on Va. 240 (which turns into Va. 810) to White Hall. Continue north on Va. 810 then turn left on Va. 674 (Break Heart Road). The winery is 1.5 miles from the turn.

Willowcroft Farm Vineyards
38906 Mt. Gilead Rd., Leesburg
• (703) 777-8161

Small but selective describes this 10-acre vineyard on top of Mount Gilead. The winery is housed in a rustic barn with a splendid view of the nearby Blue Ridge. Owner Lewis Parker creates some of the Piedmont's finest Cabernet Sauvignon, Chardonnay, Riesling, Seyval and Cabernet Franc. Each September he invites the public to help harvest grapes, a special hands-on experience few people have the opportunity to enjoy. The vineyard is open for

tours and tastings from 11 AM to 5 PM Wednesday through Sunday or by appointment.

To get there from Leesburg, head south on U.S. 15, making a right turn onto Va. 704. Then make an immediate left onto Mt. Gilead Road. The winery is 3.1 miles on the right.

Wintergreen Winery, Ltd.
Va. Rt. 664, Nellysford • (804) 361-2519

In the beautiful Rockfish Valley adjacent to Wintergreen Four Seasons Resort, this Nelson County vineyard offers spectacular views all seasons of the year. Part of the original High View plantation built by the Rodes family, the land has been in agricultural use since the early 1800s, producing tobacco, wheat, barley, hay, apples and now grapes. Award-winning wines include Chardonnay, Cabernet Sauvignon, Riesling, Blush, Three Ridges White, Governor Nelson White and Mill Hill Apple wine. The facilities are open for tours and tastings daily from 10 AM to 6 PM except in February and March when the winery is open from noon to 5 PM. It is closed on major holidays. Wintergreen has a picnic area and gift shop.

From I-64 exit west onto Va. 250 and proceed to Va. 151, turning south and traveling 14 miles. Turn west onto Va. 664 and go a half-mile to the winery entrance on the right. From the Blue Ridge Parkway, take the Reed's Gap exit. Turn east onto Va. 664, and the winery is 5 miles on the left.

Southwest Virginia

Chateau Morrisette
Meadows of Dan • (540) 593-2865

This remote winery commands a view from a 3,500-foot-high mountaintop farm bordering the Blue Ridge Parkway in Floyd and Patrick counties. Since 1983 wines have been made here in a traditional European style, using a combination of stainless-steel tanks and oak barrels for aging and fermentation. Built of native stone and wood, Chateau Morrisette has an underground wine cellar, reminiscent of the Bourdeaux countryside. Facilities include a tasting room, restaurant and large scenic deck with a view of Buffalo Mountain, the second-highest peak in Virginia.

Chateau Morrisette hosts a monthly "Black Dog" jazz concert series the second Saturday of each month from June to October. Live jazz, tastings, tours and gourmet lunches make this an exciting event. Call ahead to confirm time and admission charge.

Wines include Chardonnay, Merlot, Black Dog, Black Dog Blanc, Sweet Mountain Laurel, Our Blue Dog and Cabernet Sauvignon. Tours and tastings are available for $1 from 10 AM to 5 PM Monday through Saturday and 11 AM to 5 PM Sunday except major holidays. The restaurant is open for lunch Wednesday through Sunday and for dinner Friday and Saturday.

You can get to the winery from the Blue Ridge Parkway. At Milepost 171.5, turn west on Black Ridge Road and make an immediate left on Winery Road. The winery is a quarter-mile on the right.

Villa Appalaccia Winery
Va. Rt. 1, Box 661, Floyd
• (540) 593-3100

Susanne Becker and Stephen Haskill are willing to go the extra mile for their winery. The husband and wife, both microbiologists, work in Chapel Hill, N.C., during the week. He's a researcher at the college. She works for the EPA. But on the weekends, you will find them at their hillside winery in Floyd County. After a sabbatical in Northern California, the couple had planned on planting a few vines for their own enjoyment. Instead they filled four acres with 2,200 vines. This year they added more Pinot Grigio, bringing their Sycamore Creek Vineyard to a total of 12 acres. This family-run vineyard puts an emphasis on Italian-style wines. The reds include Toscanello and Sangiovese, with a dry rose, Cappriolo. Pinot Grigio, Liciro and Simpatico are three of their white wines made from Italian varietals. Villa Appalaccia also features a Tuscan-style tasting deck with an inspiring view of the picturesque Rock Castle Gorge. Visitors are treated to Italian bread with pesto, cheese and other Italian specialties. During the cooler months, you might want to stop by the tasting room to sample some minestrone along with the wines. The hours are 11 AM to 5 PM Thursday, Friday and Saturday from April through November and other times by appointment. Because of local restrictions, the winery is closed on Sundays.

Villa Appalaccia is right off the Blue Ridge Parkway between mileposts 170 and 171. To get there, take I-64 west to I-81. Go south to the second Christiansburg exit at Va. 8. Go east through Floyd and six more miles to the Parkway. Go south on the Parkway for 5.2 miles to Va. 720. Turn left and follow the gravel road 300 yards to the winery.

Attending a horse event
not only gives you the
chance to see beautiful
country and fine horses
but also to
people-watch.

NO POSTAGE
NECESSARY
IF MAILED
IN THE
UNITED STATES

BUSINESS REPLY MAIL

FIRST-CLASS MAIL   PERMIT NO. 80   HELENA   MT

POSTAGE WILL BE PAID BY THE ADDRESSEE

FALCON PUBLISHING INC
PO BOX 1718
HELENA   MT   59624-9917

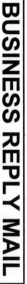

FALCON® has books for every adventure…where-to-go guidebooks on hiking, climbing, birding, mountain biking and many other outdoor recreational activities; how-to books on essential outdoor skills; field guides; travel guides; driving guides; giftbooks that capture your favorite state; and quality books on the legendary American West.

Photo by Michael Sample

FALCON®

To locate the bookseller nearest you and for a complete list of titles call **1-800-582-2665.**

☐ YES! Please send me a free catalog.

Name: _____

Address: _____

City: _____

State: _____ Zip: _____

visit us on the web at: www.falconguide.com

Horse Country

Whether clearing fields or carrying soldiers from Bull Run to Appomattox, horses have played a vital role in the history of the Shenandoah Valley. Today, their workload may not be as physically demanding, but horses still have a major impact on Virginia's economy.

The Virginia Horse Center has brought millions of dollars to the Lexington and Rockbridge areas. Celebrating its 10th anniversary, the center is a showcase for equine versatility. Year-round events include everything from barrel racing to dressage.

East of the Blue Ridge, stretching from Loudoun to Albemarle counties, is Virginia Hunt Country, an area devoted to the centuries-old sport of riding to the hounds and the accompanying lifestyle. Because of this singularity of purpose, the area has managed to keep development at bay, preserving large estates and horse farms.

Natural adjuncts to fox hunting are horse shows and steeplechases, activities that are easily accessible in this region and thrilling to watch. Attending a horse event not only gives you a chance to see beautiful country and fine horses but also to people-watch. The Hunt Country is crawling with celebrities from politics or the entertainment industry who have homes in the Middleburg/Upperville or Charlottesville areas. Here are some of the most popular places to catch the action. Also see our Annual Events and Festivals chapter for information on specific events.

Fox Hunting

The area hosts more than a dozen historic hunts, which go out several times a week from fall through spring, including holidays. If you want to watch the blessing of the hounds or follow the chase by car, plan ahead. The best way to track down races is through *The Chronicle of the Horse*, a weekly publication

that produces an annual hunt roster issue in September. *The Chronicle*, (540) 687-6341, will send you a copy for $1.50. The roster lists race days and secretary numbers for all the hunts in the United States; the secretaries can tell you exact times and locations.

At least once a year, usually on the first Saturday in December, the Middleburg Hunt meets at the historic Red Fox Tavern in Middleburg and rides down Main Street, hounds and all. Contact the Red Fox, (540) 687-6301, ext. 2, for details.

Horse Shows

Paper Chase Farm Inc.
U.S. Hwy. 50, Middleburg • (540) 687-5255

Head east on U.S. 50 from Middleburg, and you'll spot the impressive rings, jumps and barns of Paper Chase, a facility owned by Jan Neuharth, daughter of *USA Today* founder Al Neuharth. About two dozen weekend or Sunday shows are held here each year. Admission to the shows is free. This equestrian center also offers riding lessons and instructional clinics with Olympic riders several times a year.

Upperville Colt and Horse Show
U.S. Hwy. 50, Upperville • (540) 592-3858

This weeklong hunter/jumper show begins the first Monday of June. Show events start at 8 AM and continue until dark. Several thousand spectators visit the show each weekday, and about 10,000 make it to the big show, the Budweiser Grand Prix, on Sunday. Admission is $5 for adults and free for children younger than 12.

The Roanoke Valley Horse Show
Salem Civic Center, 1001 Roanoke Blvd.
• (540) 389-7847

Rated "A" by the American Horse Show

Association, this June event has been a national standout in horse-lovers' country and is celebrating its 28th year. The show is sponsored by the Roanoke Valley Horsemen's Association. It attracts more than 1,000 entries nationwide for prizes totaling more than $300,000, including a grand prix purse of $50,000. It's the only indoor, air-conditioned show in Virginia and continues to be one of the top multibreed shows in the United States.

This is a truly special community effort that over the years has plowed more than $1 million back into community projects. Tickets are $5 weekdays, $10 Friday and $12 Saturday and are available by calling the Salem Civic Center at (540) 375-3004.

www.insiders.com

See this and many other **Insiders' Guide®** destinations online.

Visit us today!

Warrenton Horse Show
U.S. Hwy. 29 Bus., Warrenton
• (540) 347-9442

Founded in 1899, the Labor Day Warrenton Horse Show is one of the few major horse shows in which only one ring is utilized. Find a seat, stay put and let the action unfold before you. The grounds are also home to the annual Pony Show in late June and the Summer's End show in August. Tickets to the Labor Day Show on September 4 to 6 are $5 plus $1 for the shaded grandstand; the other two shows are free.

Commonwealth Park
13256 Commonwealth Pkwy., Culpeper
• (540) 825-7469, (914) 876-3666

Though it's off the beaten path on U.S. Highway 522, this horse center has 900 stalls and eight competition rings that are busy most of the time with hunter/jumper and cutting horse shows and a couple of horse trials. More than 30 events are scheduled each year, attracting the Olympic-class riders who live in the area. Admission to the events is free; call for a schedule.

Tea Time Farm
Off Va. Rt. 151, Afton • (540) 456-6156

Best-selling author Rita Mae Brown, who was active in forming Charlottesville's Pied-

mont Women's Polo Club, is also the driving force behind Tea Time. The equestrian center, which faces the Blue Ridge Mountains and is skirted by the Rockfish River, is an idyllic setting for horse shows, clinics, polo and fox hunting. In 1993, Tea Time revived the Oak Ridge Fox Hunt Club, founded in 1887. As a spectator, you can watch the start and finish of the hunt club's fox hunts at Tea Time or at the nearby Oak Ridge Estate. Call to see what's going on during your visit to the area. You can also go on a trail ride or take a riding lesson from the folks at Tea Time. The 500-acre farm offers fabulous views of Nelson County and the Blue Ridge.

Virginia Horse Center
Off I-64 W. at Exit 55, Lexington
• (540) 463-2194

A showcase for the Virginia horse industry and one of the top equine facilities in the United States, the $12 million Virginia Horse Center is home to several premier national horse shows and three-day events and the annual Virginia Horse Festival in April.

The indoor arena complex has 4,000 spectator seats and a 150-foot-by-300-foot show arena. The facility can house 575 horses in permanent stalls and more than 196 in portable interior stalls. The center has two winterized barns, an enclosed schooling area, an on-grounds restaurant and 48 camper hookups. Outdoor facilities include the lighted Wiley Arena, four all-weather dressage arenas, a speed events ring, an announcer's pavilion, pre-novice through preliminary cross-country courses and a 5-mile hunter trial course.

With all these amenities, something is going on here almost all the time, from polo matches to draft-horse pulls. In addition to horse competitions, the center hosts rodeos, auctions, concerts, living-history Civil War encampments, Jack Russell terrier races, therapeutic riding demonstrations and foxhound demonstrations.

To find the center from Interstate 81, take Lexington Exit 191 to I-64 W. Proceed on I-64 W. to Exit 55, then follow the signs for 2 miles

Photo: The Roanoke Valley Convention and Visitors Bureau

Whether ridden for work or pleasure, horses play vital roles in life in the Blue Ridge.

to the center. If you'd like a tour, be sure to call beforehand.

Combined Training

Combined training, also called three-day eventing or horse trials, is a discipline dating back to the training of war horses in Europe. It's also one of the most exciting horse sports to watch. Dressage, performed on the first day, is the ballet of horse sports, requiring great discipline. On the second day is an endurance phase involving long gallops and jumping through a challenging cross-country course. The third day, horses and riders are put through a structured course of fences to test the horses' agility, soundness and willingness after the stress of the cross-country. The Blue Ridge area hosts several world-class events.

Morven Park Horse Trials
41793 Tutt Ln., Morven Park, Leesburg
• (703) 777-2890

During the first week of October, you can catch the action over cross-country jumps designed by Olympian Bruce Davidson. Davidson often is in the competition along with other world-class competitors. The backdrop for the event is a splendid white-columned mansion, once the home of Virginia governor Westmoreland Davis and his spunky, side-saddle-riding wife. Treasures the couple collected during a lifetime of world travel are on display in the mansion. The mansion, gardens, the Museum of Foxhounds and Hunting and the Carriage Museum are open during the event; admission to the mansion and both museums is $6. Admission to the trials is free.

Morven Park also hosts a variety of shows every weekend from April to October, including hunter/jumpers and steeplechases. Admission to most events is free. Call for schedules and information.

Middleburg Horse Trials
Va. Hwy. 626, Glenwood Park, Middleburg
• (540) 687-5449

Top riders participate in this event, which is held the final weekend in September. The

Middleburg area is home to many Olympic riders, so the level of competition is high (though a new course has recently been added for novice riders). At Glenwood Park, which is also a steeplechase and horse show venue, spectators can see almost all of the course from the stands. Admission to the trials is free. Glenwood Park is 1.25 miles north of Middleburg on Va. 626, also called Foxcroft Road.

Combined Driving

One of the most colorful and elegant equestrian sports is competitive carriage driving. Competitions often are paired with three-day events because of their similarity. On the first day, drivers execute a series of dressage movements, much like a skater's compulsory figures. The second day is devoted to the marathon, a grueling cross-country dash through streams and around natural and man-made obstacles. In the third phase drivers dressed in formal attire wheel their teams through an intricate pattern of cones.

Local driving clubs also get together for pleasure rides or driving shows, such as the fall show at Middleburg's Foxcroft School (see our Annual Events and Festivals chapter). The Piedmont Driving Club in Boyce, (540) 955-2659, is your best source for information.

Endurance Riding

This is now an Olympic sport, but it's not the easiest competition for spectators to watch.

Old Dominion 100-mile Ride
4-H Center, Front Royal
• (540) 933-6991

Held in June, the Old Dominion is one of the most respected competitions in the country and often is a tune-up for the Olympics or World Championships. Riders camp overnight with their horses at the 4-H Center in Front Royal in preparation for a 5 AM start. Each rider has 24 hours to cover 100 miles of rugged terrain and is pulled from the competition if the horse fails to pass the frequent veterinary checks along the way. If you want to put out a little effort, you can hike to one of the veterinary checks or the river crossing to watch the horses come through. Call before you go, because they change the locations of the check stations each year. You probably won't want to hang around for the finish. Winners come in as darkness is falling, and the rest straggle in throughout the night.

Jousting

Maryland's state sport also has a loyal following in Virginia. Though it's patterned after the rivalry of knights of old, today's sport is done not in armor but in T-shirts and jeans. Despite the informal dress, you have to admire the skill of the riders who, at a full gallop, thread their lances through a series of three steel rings. The horse and rider usually cover the 90-yard course in less than eight seconds. We've listed the two major jousting events in Virginia.

Natural Chimneys Jousting Tournament
Mount Solon • (540) 350-2510

Listed as America's oldest continuously held sporting event, the Mount Solon tournament has been at the Natural Chimneys Regional Park every year since 1821. It started out as a contest to see which of two men would marry a local damsel, but today thousands visit the scenic park to watch riders from Virginia, West Virginia, Maryland and Pennsylvania test their marksmanship. Admission to the park is $5. Bring along a blanket and picnic basket. If you want to stay longer, campsites are available, but call first since they fill up fast. The seven towering rock formations at Natural Chimneys also serve as the backdrop for the annual Hall of Fame Joust in mid-June.

Ruritan Joust
Va. Hwy. 688 off I-66, Hume
• (540) 364-2889

The Ruritan Joust has been going on at the old school grounds on the edge of Hume for more than 30 years. Bring a blanket and a cooler for an afternoon of watching, but save room for the pièce de résistance, the barbecue, which has been cooking underground all night. Local folks serve it up with all the fixings. Held the third Saturday in August, the joust recently added an antique car show and

The Virginia Horse Center in Lexington has one of the
top equine facilities in the United States.

Jack Russell terrier races to the day-long list of activities.

Dressage

Break out your top hat, white gloves and tails! The elegant and ancient art of dressage can be found sprinkled throughout the Blue Ridge. Although the basic tenets of dressage date back to 400 B.C., most folks are probably more familiar with those famous white Lipizzan stallions from the Spanish Riding School in Vienna, Austria.

Dressage is the classic art of riding, where the rider uses subtle shifting of his weight, a squeeze of a leg or a pull on the reigns to lead his horse through a series of serpentine figures, sideways movements and smooth transitions from a trot to a halt. But don't let the formal attire fool you, dressage is also a very competitive sport.

Although Virginia may be better known for its thoroughbreds and steeplechase races, dressage shows, competitions and workshops can be seen at Morven Park in Leesburg, (703) 777-2890, and the Virginia Horse Center in Lexington, (540) 463-2194.

To find out if an event corresponds with your visit, check with the Virginia Dressage Association at (540) 347-0363.

Fancy Hill Farm
100 Equus Loop, Natural Bridge
• (540) 291-1000

This equestrian center between Lexington and Natural Bridge off I-81 boards, trains and offers riding lessons as well as offering a variety of shows, clinics and competition. Three large outdoor rings and an indoor arena allows for hunter-jumper competition and dressage schools year round. For the past several years, Fancy Hill has hosted International Dressage Clinics, sponsored by Spring Creek Dressage Ltd. Nicole Uphoff-Becker and Albrecht Heidemann were among participants for the April 1999 clinic. Uphoff-Becker, who has made four visits to Fancy Hill, was a record-setting rider for Germany in the Olympics. She and her horse, Rembrandt, won four gold medals in individual and team competition at the

Games in Barcelona, Spain, and Seoul, Korea.

Hunt Country Stable Tour

Trinity Episcopal Church
Annual Stable Tour
U.S. Hwy. 50, Upperville • (540) 592-3711

A dozen farms open their stables every year for this Memorial Day weekend event, which draws carloads of tourists. It's a rare opportunity to see places where horses live better than people, including philanthropist Paul Mellon's Rokeby Farm and the late Redskins owner Jack Kent Cooke's Kent Farm. Proceeds of the tour go into the church's outreach budget and a program to feed the hungry in Washington, D.C. Hours are 10 AM to 5 PM Saturday and Sunday. Tickets, good for both days, are $12 in advance and $15 after mid-May. For an extra $8, you can drop by Trinity Parish Hall for a catered country lunch.

Historic Garden Week
Various sites • (804) 644-7776

This tour is huge, covering more than 250 homes and estates in 31 areas across Virginia. Visitors may buy block tickets, ranging in price from $10 to $20, for a tour of five or six properties, which often include the homes of wealthy horse folks with interesting stables and horses. One year, the Middleburg tour visited an estate with extensive training grounds for the family's Olympic hopefuls. The Warrenton Hounds were shown at another stop. Historic Garden Week is scheduled for a week around the end of April. Call to get a copy of the guidebook and to find stops near you.

Polo

Middleburg Polo
Kent Field, U.S. 50 W. to Va. Rt. 624, Middleburg • (703) 777-0775

Kent Field is one of the oldest polo pitches in the area. It bore the name of Phipps Field, for the famous New York racing family, through the ownerships of Paul Mellon and Virginia Sen. John Warner. The late Jack Kent Cooke, owner of the Redskins football team, later purchased the land from Sen. Warner. Against the pretty backdrop of Goose Creek, teams play on Sunday afternoons from mid-June to September. The atmosphere is relaxed, and the action fast-paced. The games begin at 1 PM. Admission is $5 per person. From U.S. 50 turn at Goose Creek Bridge and watch for the "Polo Today" signs.

Virginia Polo Center
1082 Forest Lodge Ln., Charlottesville • (804) 979-0293, (804) 977-POLO

The University of Virginia turns out some of the finest intercollegiate polo players in the country. Interest runs high among the student body when the UVA polo team plays arena polo at the Virginia Polo Center on Friday nights during the school year.

Polo is also a popular sport among the horsey set in Charlottesville. The Charlottesville Polo Club and the Piedmont Women's Polo Club defend themselves against area teams at the center from mid-May through September. Admission is usually $3; call for times.

Roanoke Symphony Polo Cup
Green Hill Park, Diuguids Ln. off Main St., Salem • (540) 343-6221

Roanokers' opportunity to "Ponder the Ponies and Promote the Notes" has gone professional to include U.S. Polo Association-ranked teams in its match. Events feature a high-level 14-16-goal match. Crowds travel from throughout the mid-Atlantic and Northeast regions to attend this festive fund-raiser for the Roanoke Youth Symphony. Past events featured the Virginia Highlands Pipe and Drums Corps Dressage exhibition and the Virginia Tech Veterinary School display. Since 1996, the Polo Cup has featured works by a Virginia artist, including Beth Shively in 1997. The traditional divot-stomping is held at halftime. Not only does the polo tournament provide a unique cultural experience, but it also allows patrons of the arts to enjoy good food and fun together. Proceeds benefit the Youth Symphony and educational programs.

General admission is reasonable (about $10 including parking) so that the revelry is accessible to all. For a hefty fee, however, you can rent tables for tailgate parties and tents for private groups. These range in cost from approximately $170 to $1,450, depending on the size of tent or table you choose. Concessions are available during the activities. Tent and tailgate patrons have their names listed in the program as a gesture of appreciation, and corporate sponsors enjoy premium field position and recognition. The 1999 event is September 25.

Point-to-Point and Steeplechase Races

While both styles of competition feature races over fences, steeplechases generally offer big-money prizes and are sanctioned by the National Steeplechase Association. Point-to-points are sponsored by local hunts. While they often have top-notch steeplechase horses and riders in the field, point-to-points usually are attended by folks in mud boots and jeans. The fancy clothes and hats are saved for steeplechases. Either is good fun and a perfect excuse to prepare a sumptuous tailgate lunch.

Virginia has more steeplechases (about two dozen) than any other state and has as many point-to-points. Contact the Virginia Steeplechase Association in Middleburg, (703) 777-2414, for a schedule. If you're visiting the Blue Ridge between March and November, you can catch a race almost any Saturday. Here are some of the biggest races (see our Annual Events and Festivals chapter for more).

The Virginia Gold Cup Races
Great Meadow, The Plains
• (540) 347-2612, (800) 69-RACES

For the past decade, this 74-year-old classic has been run at Great Meadow, an excel-

lent facility owned by newspaper magnate Arthur Arundel. It seems that all of Capitol Hill attends this see-and-be-seen event. Lavish tailgate parties are in full swing long before the first race at 1:30 PM. All tickets are sold in advance, and you should arrive when the gates open at 10 AM to get a parking place, see the pre-race demonstrations and cruise the booths. General admission parking, which admits a maximum of six per vehicle, costs about $60. The Gold Cup takes place the first Saturday in May, Kentucky Derby Day.

Great Meadow is also the venue for the International Gold Cup the third Saturday in October. This race attracts almost 30,000 folks each year. General admission parking, which admits six people per vehicle, costs about $40 in advance, $50 the day of the race. The Great Meadow Exit off I-66 is well-marked.

Foxfield Races
Garth Rd., Charlottesville
• (804) 293-9501

Foxfield hosts two major steeplechase meetings each year, events that draw top 'chasers and 20,000 spectators, some from as far away as New Jersey. Races are traditionally held the last Saturday in April and the last Sunday in September. The six-race card starts at 1 PM and features flat and jumping races. You'll want to get there early, though, to get a good parking spot and begin tailgating.

Although hot dogs and soft drinks are sold at the course, sophisticated tailgate parties have become the norm. The scene is straight out of *Town and Country* magazine, with women in hats and smart outfits and men in natty tweeds. It's not unusual to see folks sipping champagne and nibbling caviar from silver plates on the back of a Rolls or BMW.

General admission costs $15 in advance ($5 for parking) and $20 at the gate ($10 for parking). Depending upon location, you can also reserve a parking spot for anywhere from $70 to $200, which includes four admission

---

INSIDERS' TIP

Virginia's state dog is the American foxhound. Ask folks around Middleburg and Upperville about the Great Foxhound Match there at the turn of the century. The American hounds handily out-hunted the British hounds.

tickets. Call to purchase advance tickets or to find out ticket office locations in Charlottesville.

The Foxfield Race Course is 5 miles west of the Barracks Road Shopping Center.

Middleburg Spring Races
Glenwood Park, Va. Rt. 626, Middleburg
• (540) 687-6545

This is the oldest steeplechase in the state, looking forward to its 80th anniversary in 2000. Usually held the third Saturday in April, the event attracts up to 10,000 spectators to the 112-acre park. The purses are big, reaching a total of $140,000 in 1997, and the races feature top steeplechase jockeys and horses.

You can buy food on the race grounds, but most folks usually bring their own picnics for tailgating. The gates open at 10:30 AM to allow for ample socializing before the races begin around 2 PM. Admission is $12 on race day ($10 in advance) and includes parking. Glenwood Park is 1.25 miles north of Middleburg on Va. 626, also called Foxcroft Road.

Montpelier Hunt Races
Off Va. Rt. 20, Montpelier Station
• (540) 672-2728

This is the only public sporting event held at the home of a U.S. President. Set against the rolling hills of Orange County and the historic backdrop of James Madison's home, the Montpelier Hunt Races have become one of the key stops on the National Steeplechase Association circuit. Top horses and riders come from across the country compete in this annual event held on the first Saturday in November.

The race has a long and rich history. The duPont family bought Montpelier in 1900, and in 1927 Marion duPont Scott (she married the actor Randolph Scott) and her brother, William, welcomed local folks and the well-to-do to their home for the first race. Sixty-three years later, the Montpelier Hunt is still a favorite whether you come dressed in cutoffs or khakis.

A general admission ticket will get you in for $10, or you can pay up to $2,000 for a reserved spot in the special hospitality area. Parking is $5 in advance, $10 on race day.

Jack Russell terrier races usually begin around 10:30 AM for those who want to arrive early and set up their tailgate parties. Bring your fancy basket and participate in the Dolley Madison tailgate competition. The first race begins at 12:30 PM. The main house is open for tours too (see our Attractions chapter).

Over the Fences

Here's a schedule of steeplechases and point-to-point races. Call to confirm starting times and locations.

Casanova Hunt Point-to-Point: February 20 at Mt. Sterling Farm in Warrenton, (540) 788-4806

Rappahannock Hunt Point-to-Point: February 27 at Thornton Hill Farm in Sperryville, (540) 547-2810 or (540) 371-5349

Blue Ridge Hunt Point-to-Point: March 6 at Woodley Farm in Berryville, (540) 837-2262

Warrenton Hunt Point-to-Point: March 13 at Arlie Race Course, (540) 347-1888 or (540) 347-5095

Piedmont Fox Hounds Point-to-Point: March 20 at Salem Course in Upperville, (540) 592-3032 or (540) 592-3035

Farmington and Keswick Point-to-Point: March 21 at Montpelier Race Course at Montpelier Station, (804) 980-9926

Orange County Hunt Point-to-Point: March 27 at Locust Hill Farm in Middleburg, (540) 687-6060

Old Dominion Hounds Point-to-Point: April 3 at Ben Venue Farm in Ben Venue, (540) 364-4573 or (540) 363-1507

Loudoun Hunt Point-to-Point: April 11 at Oatlands in Leesburg, (703) 777-8480 or (540) 338-4031

Middleburg Spring Races: April 17 at Glenwood Park in Middleburg, (540) 687-6545 or (540) 687-6595

Fairfax Hunt Point-to-Point: April 18 at Belmont Plantation in Leesburg, (703) 787-6673

Foxfield Spring Race: April 24 at Foxfield in Charlottesville, (804) 293-9501

Middleburg Hunt Point-to-Point: April 25 at Glenwood Park in Middleburg, (540) 338-5231

Virginia Gold Cup: May 1 at Great Meadows in The Plains, (540) 347-2612

Bull Run Hunt Point-to-Point: May 2 at Brandywine Park in Culpeper, (703) 866-0507

Glenwood Races: September 11 at Glenwood Park in Middleburg, (540) 687-3455

Fairfax Races: September 18 at Belmont Plantation in Leesburg, (703) 532-2257 or (703) 787-6673

Foxfield Races: September 26 at Foxfield in Charlottesville. (804) 293-9501

Virginia Fall Races: October 2 and 3 at Glenwood Park in Middleburg, (540) 687-5662

Morven Park Steeplechase Races: October 9 at Morven Park in Leesburg, (703) 777-2414

Bedford County Point-to-Point: October 10 at Wolf Branch Farm in Forest, (540) 586-1051

International Gold Cup Races: October 16 at Great Meadows in The Plains, (540) 347-3455

Middleburg Fall Races: October 30 at Glenwood Park in Middleburg, (540) 687-3455

Montpelier Hunt Races: November 6 at Montpelier Race Course at Montpelier Station, (804) 980-9926

In this spectacular setting are recreational opportunities for every budget, from the camper on a shoestring to the golfer luxuriating at a nationally acclaimed resort.

Recreation

Recreation: It's a concept we learn in kindergarten that stays with us all our lives. The whole world loves to play. Historically, visitors came to the Blue Ridge Mountains to partake of pristine waters and gaze upon lofty peaks, a tonic for body and soul. That's still true today — but mostly they come to play.

With so many leisure activities in the Blue Ridge, the wise visitor will plan an itinerary well in advance. However, getting sidetracked is also a regional pastime, hazardous only to a tight vacation schedule, certainly not to the spirit or health.

It is to the Blue Ridge that Virginia owes much of its international recognition in the realm of outdoor recreation. The big draw, of course, is the scenery. Mother Nature blessed Virginia's Blue Ridge with lush vegetation, sparkling streams and mountain peaks that dress in dazzling colors for fall and pristine white in winter. Between the mountains are valleys patchworked with fields of grain and grassy meadows in which languid dairy cattle graze among wildflowers. Many small towns are postcard images, with covered bridges and steepled churches that withstood the Civil War.

In this spectacular setting are recreational opportunities for every budget, from the camper on a shoestring to the golfer luxuriating at The Homestead or The Greenbrier, two of our nation's most acclaimed resorts.

Among the region's greatest recreational treasures are its parks and forests. Two national forests with acres of precious wilderness have become one — the George Washington and Jefferson National Forests. The Shenandoah National Park, Virginia's mountain playground, is also here. State parks, including Claytor, Douthat, Sky Meadows and Smith Mountain Lake, offer recreational opportunities galore, from horseback riding to cross-country skiing.

Two outdoor mega-attractions are here also — the Bikecentennial Trail that spans the country from Williamsburg, Virginia, to the West Coast, and the Appalachian Trail, stretching from Maine to Georgia. Natives in small towns take for granted a continuing stream of blaze orange-clad backpackers and bikers enjoying country byways.

Blue Ridge forest preserves offer some of the finest fishing and hunting in the Southeast. Some hunters and anglers prefer to go it alone, while others enlist local guides who know the way of the woods and streams. Licenses can be obtained at a variety of stores.

Most visitors come to see rather than stalk, and they're never disappointed. The hills are home to black bear, deer, turkey, small game and a variety of songbirds.

There's bountiful water in the region — fresh mountain streams, rivers and lakes, including Smith Mountain Lake, the state's largest inland body of water. These lakes and waterways offer the popular sports of boating, swimming, rafting, canoeing and tubing — a pastime especially enjoyed by college students who tow a "refreshment" tube stocked with cold drinks and snacks. It's a great way to spend a hot summer afternoon.

If your idea of a hazard is a sand-filled bunker on the edge of a tiered green, you'll find a plethora of excellent public, semiprivate and resort courses in the Blue Ridge.

As you're probably beginning to suspect, choosing an activity in the Blue Ridge Mountains is like trying to select a meal from a mile-long Virginia buffet. There are far too many recreational opportunities to list completely in these pages. We highly recommend that you send for brochures and guides offered by the Commonwealth of Virginia and tourism and recreation associations. This is especially important for many camping areas that require reservations. Look for information contacts listed within the various recreation categories in the following pages. Then go out there and have fun! You'll be in good company.

Boating

Canoe Outfitters

The Blue Ridge region has many reputable canoe outfitters. Several are along the South Fork of the Shenandoah River, which meanders between the Massanutten and Blue Ridge mountain ranges before joining the Potomac River at Harpers Ferry, West Virginia. These outfitters also rent rubber rafts, kayaks and tubes, the local's craft of choice for a lazy afternoon of drifting with the current.

Other outfitters are near the James River, the longest and largest river in Virginia. Only Lexington's James River Basin Canoe Livery leads canoe trips down both the Maury and the James rivers.

Farther southwest, in Giles County, the New River Canoe Livery in Pembroke runs trips down the magnificent New River, reputed to be second only to the Nile as the oldest river on Earth. (Atypical of most rivers, the New flows north.)

Most canoe outfitters will only allow you to travel down familiar waters, unless you're an expert and willing to assume the risks (financial and otherwise) of canoeing a less-traveled tributary. Generally speaking, a single fee includes the canoe rental, paddles, life jackets, maps, shuttle service and an orientation. The shortest trips cost anywhere from $25 to $30 per canoe, while longer all-day trips range from $45 to $55. Tubing costs much less.

Here are some good places to rent boats and equipment in the Blue Ridge region, from north to south.

Front Royal Canoe Co.
U.S. Hwy. 340 S., Front Royal
• **(540) 635-5440, (800) 270-8808**
This outfit, 3 miles south of the entrance to Skyline Drive, rents canoes, kayaks, rafts, tubes and flat-bottom boats on the South Fork of the Shenandoah River from mid-March through mid-November. Trips range from leisurely fishing to mild whitewater adventures. Multiple-day excursions also can be arranged. Canoe daytrips cost between $26 and $42. Reservations are recommended but not required. Shuttle service for privately owned canoes and watercraft is available. (See our Kidstuff chapter for more information.)

www.insiders.com

See this and many other **Insiders' Guide®** destinations online.

Visit us today!

Downriver Canoe Company
884 Indian Hollow, Bentonville
• **(540) 635-5526**
This company rents canoes and kayaks for exploring the South Fork of the Shenandoah River, a good waterway for novices and moderately experienced canoeists. Detailed maps describing the river course and the best way to negotiate it are provided. The maps also point out the best camping areas, picnic sites, swimming holes and fishing spots. Daily rentals run from $37 to $49. (See our Kidstuff chapter.)

Multiple-day trips can also be arranged. Reservations are recommended, but last-minute canoe trips are often possible. Open April 1 through October 31, this company also has a shuttle service for people with their own canoes. Rafting and tubing trips also are available.

River Rental Outfitters
2047 Rocky Hollow Ln., Bentonville
• **(540) 635-5050**
"Bring us your weekend . . . and we'll do the rest!" is this business's motto. It offers canoe and tube rentals on the Shenandoah River and organizes fishing, camping, hiking and biking trips. The outfitter will custom-design a weekend vacation for the entire family, including packages with the nearby Skyline Bend

INSIDERS' TIP

Don't forget to yield. When hiking, give uphill hikers and horse riders the right of way. On the water, non-powered sailboats have the right of way in most circumstances.

Farm, Warren County's oldest licensed bed and breakfast inn.

Open March 15 through November 1, River Rental also opens on weekends in November by reservation. Reservations are strongly recommended for any weekend or holiday. The business also rents kayaks, fishing equipment and camping gear and sells fishing tackle and all kinds of supplies. Fishing packages are available.

Shenandoah River Outfitters
6502 S. Page Valley Rd., Luray
• **(540) 743-4159**

This outfit offers canoe, kayak and tube rentals and canoe sales. It also organizes overnight trips complete with tents and sleeping bags (see our Kidstuff chapter). Situated on the Shenandoah River between the Massanutten Mountain Trails and the Appalachian Trail in the George Washington section of the national forest, this company is open year round. Canoe rental averages $25 to $46 a day. Reservations are recommended.

James River Runners Inc.
10082 Hatton Ferry Rd., Scottsville
• **(804) 286-2338**

This outfitter, 35 minutes south of Charlottesville, specializes in family canoe and rafting trips on the James River. Owners Christie and Jeff Schmick can arrange a variety of outings suitable for children older than 6. They also arrange day and overnight trips for larger groups — even conventions. A special two-day package features canoeing for 9 miles the first day, camping overnight by the river and tubing the next day.

Canoe rentals cost $30 for a 3-mile trip, $44 for 9 miles and $88 for an overnight excursion. Sit-on-top kayaks are less expensive: $16 for 3 miles; $22 for 9 miles. Four- and five-person rafts are available for $16 per person.

Group tubing trips can be arranged, and groups of 25 or more get a discount. Tubes rent for $12 each, $5 for a cooler tube. Reservations are necessary for groups and recommended for small parties. James River Runners is open March through October.

James River Reeling and Rafting
Main and Ferry sts., Scottsville
• **(804) 286-4FUN**

This business offers canoe and tubing trips for people at all levels of experience. It specializes in customizing overnight trips to suit the customer's fancy. "Describe what you want and let us design a trip for you," reads its brochure. Trips can be organized for convention groups, which get a 10 percent discount when 11 or more boats are rented. The company maintains a permanent campground on the river and offers two-day canoeing/rafting packages.

It will cost around $30 per boat for a 4-mile trip. The 12.5-mile float, which usually runs four to six hours, costs $45. For fishermen specializing in smallmouth bass, there is a $35 package for about two to three hours. Overnight excursions cost about $75. Tubing costs $12. Add $5 more if you would like a cooler tube.

The headquarters is on the corner of Main and Ferry streets in downtown Scottsville at the James River Trading Post. Here you'll find fishing and camping supplies and anything else you might have left behind. It's open March 1 through October 31.

James River Basin
Canoe Livery Ltd.
1870 E. Midland Tr., Lexington
• **(540) 261-7334**

This outfit arranges day and overnight trips down both the Maury and James rivers. You can take an adventurous run down Balcony Falls, the mighty rapids where the James breaks through the Blue Ridge Mountains. Or you can spend a couple of hours paddling down a slow stretch of the beautiful Maury. The staff gives a solid orientation, with instructions on safety and basic canoeing strokes. A video program also familiarizes canoeists with the stretch of river about to be boated.

James River Basin is open from 9 AM to 5 PM daily from May 1 to September 30 and by appointment anytime during the rest of the year. In 1997 James River canoe trips ranged between $42 and $50. Canoe trips down the Maury were $23 to $48. Kayaks were less expensive. Two-day overnight trips range from $76 to $80. Tack on two more days for $34 a day.

New River Canoe Livery
Pembroke • (540) 626-7189

Owner Dave Vicenzi rents canoes for trips along the New River in Giles County. The easiest trip is on the 7 miles of river between Eggleston to Pembroke, but the most popular outing is an 11-mile run from Pembroke to Pearisburg, which has several Class II (intermediate) whitewater rapids. When the water is high in the spring, Vicenzi allows customers to canoe down Walker and Wolf creeks, tributaries of the New River. Multiple-day trips can also be arranged, but customers must supply their own camping gear. The Livery is open 10 AM to 6 PM Tuesday through Saturday from April through October.

Wilderness Canoe Company
Va. Rt. 130 and U.S. Hwy. 11, Natural Bridge • (800) 4CANOE4, (540) 291-2295

This company specializes in river trips lasting from two hours to two days. The James River headwaters provides quiet recreation for paddlers of all ages, and the staff here can make this outdoor adventure safe and fun. The retail store has its own Wilderness Canoes, kayaks, fishing boats, bait and tackle, T-shirts, snacks and drinks. Class I and II rapids are available on request. The store is at the intersection of Va. 130 and U.S. 11. You can rent a two-man canoe for $45, a kayak for $25, an inner tube for $5 or a four-person raft

for $75. During the four-hour trip, the guides make several stops to explore the land along the Wilderness Area. The Canoe Company recently purchased 50 acres of land near the river, so tent camping is now available for $10 a night. Sites include a picnic table, fire ring and lantern stand.

Tangent Outfitters
1055 Norwood St., Radford
• **(540) 674-5202**

You can canoe the New River or bike the New River Trail State Park with equipment from Tangent Outfitters. Not only does Tangent rent mountain bikes, but it also offers a wide assortment of river fun. You can rent your own Dagger Legend Royalex canoes for $30 a day or $110 a week. But if you are more of a beginner, you might want to sign up for one of four guided trips. For $15 you can take a 4-mile float down the New River. A 6-mile trip costs $18, a 10-mile intermediate trip over Class I and II rapids is $21. There also is 6 PM to dusk Sunset Canoe Trip for $15. Lunches are available for an additional $5. Ask about the guided fishing trips. You can hook up with some smallmouth bass for $125 per person.

Other Boating Possibilities

Let's not forget boating on Virginia's beautiful lakes. Boats can be rented at several state parks in the heart of the mountains. Generally, boats here are available on weekends beginning in mid-May and daily from Memorial Day through Labor Day weekend.

At **Douthat State Park**, (540) 862-8100, near Clifton Forge, you can rent rowboats and paddleboats on a 50-acre lake stocked with trout. This park is listed on the National Register of Historic Places for the role its design played in the development of parks nationwide. Rowboats and canoes rent for $4 an hour; paddleboats cost $5.

INSIDERS' TIP

To operate a boat in state waters, you must have a Certificate of Number (also known as a registration card), a temporary Certificate of Number or a temporary Registration Certificate. For details, dial the Department of Game and Inland Fisheries (804) 367-6892.

Photo: The Roanoke Valley Convention and Visitors Bureau

A day spent fishing in Virginia's mountain streams may fulfill your wildest dreams.

Rowboats and paddleboats are also available on a 108-acre lake at **Hungry Mother State Park**, (540) 783-3422, in the far reaches of Southwest Virginia, near Marion. Rowboats rent for $3.50 an hour or $15 a day. Paddleboat rental is $3.50 for a half-hour and $5 an hour. No gas-powered engines are allowed on the lake.

In Pulaski County, about an hour southwest of Roanoke, you can rent rowboats to take out on 4,500-acre **Claytor Lake**, (540) 674-6000. Boats and supplies also can be found at several private concessionaires along the 21-mile lake. Claytor Lake has one of the only full-service marinas in the state park system.

Fairy Stone State Park, (540) 930-2424, offers boating on its 168-acre lake adjoining Philpott Reservoir. Just minutes from the Blue Ridge Parkway, Fairy Stone is in Patrick County. Rowboats rent for $4 an hour, $16 a day or $80 a week. Paddleboats and hydrobikes cost $5 an hour.

Smith Mountain Lake has 500 miles of winding shoreline, and 20,600 acres of sparkling waters also offer countless possibilities for boating. About a dozen places rent various types of boats, from pontoons to motorboats and houseboats. For information and brochures, contact the Smith Mountain Lake Visitors Center at (800) 676-8203.

You also will find ample boating opportunities in the George Washington and Jefferson National Forests, including the 43.5-mile **Gathright Dam** and **Lake Moomaw**, (540) 962-2214, 19 miles north of Covington. The largest lake in the National Forest, Lake Moomaw is popular for boaters. You have to bring your own boat, but there is a full-service marina and two boat ramps.

Camping

From primitive campsites to modern RV campgrounds with all the amenities, camping in the Blue Ridge Mountains is a four-season activity.

Forests cover two-thirds of Virginia, with most of it in the Blue Ridge Mountains. Camping here is a huge industry, offering an inexpensive, family-oriented recreational pastime whether you prefer KOA Kamping Kabins with all the comforts of home or a remote spot in the woods flat enough for your tent. At Blue Ridge campgrounds, you'll usually find swimming holes in cool mountain streams or lakes and copious hiking trails. Some places even have boat rentals and horseback riding.

National Forest Campgrounds

In the George Washington and Jefferson National Forests, most family camping is on a first come, first served basis. Group camping is one of the exceptions for which reservations can be made up to 120 days in advance — and must be made at least 10 days in advance. No rental cabins or other lodging is available in national forest campgrounds. If you want to bring along your pets for company, you can, but dogs must be leashed. Call (540) 265-5100 for reservations or information.

State Park Campgrounds

Seven state parks in the Blue Ridge have campgrounds, and four also have cabins. Reservations for campsites and cabins must be made by calling the **Virginia State Parks Reservation Center** at (800) 933-PARK. Depending upon availability, reservations may be made up to the day before arrival or by Thursday for a weekend arrival. Payment must be made within 14 days after the reservation is made and prior to arrival by credit card over the phone. Or you may mail a check, providing there is sufficient time to assure arrival of payment. Reservations may be made up to 11 months in advance. The maximum camping period is 14 days in any 30-day period. Leashed pets are permitted. Overnight facilities open March 1 and close the first Monday in December.

Raymond "Andy" Guest Shenandoah River State Park
Va. Rt. 340, Warren County
• **(540) 622-6840**

This new park, scheduled to open in May 1999, lies along the Shenandoah River in Warren County. For now, vehicular access is prohibited, but you can get to certain areas by boat if you have a special-use permit. Camping permits are available through Sky Meadows State Park.

Sky Meadows State Park
11012 Edmonds Ln., Delaplane
• (540) 592-3556

Twelve primitive campsites are available by way of a .75-mile trail at this park in Fauquier and Clark counties. The site, two miles from the Appalachian Trail, includes tent pads, fire rings, a lean-to shelter, pit toilets and nonpotable water.

Smith Mountain Lake State Park
Va. Rt. 1, Huddleston • (540) 297-6066

This park located 40 miles between Lynchburg and Roanoke has 50 primitive campsites with individual picnic tables and fire grills. Cold-water showers are available.

Holliday Lake State Park
Va. Rt. 2, Appomattox • (804) 248-6308

Located just a few miles from Appomattox National Historical Park, Holliday offers campers 30 sites with electric and water hookups.

Douthat State Park
Va. Rt. 1, Milboro • (540) 862-8100

One of six original campgrounds built by President Roosevelt's Civilian Conservation Corps, Douthat rents 25 log cabins and five concrete lodges. The cabins, lodges and lakefront restaurant were all built by the CCC. Douthat also has 92 campsites on three campgrounds and 15 group campsites at this park that covers portions of Bath and Alleghany counties.

Claytor Lake State Park
4400 State Park Rd., Dublin
• (540) 674-5492

There are 12 lakefront cabins available for rent on a weekly basis at this Pulaksi County park. Those who prefer to rough it can choose from 321 campsites in four campgrounds. Electrical and water hookups are available at 44 sites.

Fairy Stone State Park
Va. Rt. 2, Stuart • (540) 930-2424

This, too, was one of six original state parks opened by the CCC in 1936. Covering parts of Patrick and Henry counties, Fairy Stone offers eight log cabins and 16 concrete block cabins. The log cabins were part of the original facilities. The park also includes 51 campsites with electric and water hookups.

Developed Campsites

Developed campsites can accommodate one piece of camping equipment and/or one motor vehicle and a maximum of six people. Expect a grill, picnic table and access to bathhouses on site.

Cabins

Housekeeping cabins ranging from one room to two bedrooms are available in Claytor, Douthat, Fairy Stone and Hungry Mother state parks. During Memorial Day to Labor Day, a week's stay is required, unless there is availability within the month before the arrival date. A two-night minimum stay is required at all times. Reservations are required. Douthat and Hungry Mother state parks have lodge facilities that accommodate up to 15 guests.

Group Camping

Group camping is available with water/electric sites at Douthat and developed sites at Fairy Stone, with a minimum group of three sites required. Natural Tunnel has a large group camping area that accommodates up to 50 people for $48 per night.

Expect to pay the following camping fees (nightly rates): primitive sites, $8; developed

---

INSIDERS' TIP

No answer? If you're the type who likes to finalize your vacation plans in advance, remember that some of the sites, including many parks, boating facilities and swimming areas, operate seasonally. If you can't get anyone on the phone, try again later.

sites, $11 to $12; electric/water hookup sites, $14 to $17; pet fee, $3 per night per pet; cancellation fee, $5.

Cabin rates are based on three seasons that vary by park and size of cabin. Weekly rates range from $240 to $496. Extra beds cost $3 per night, and pet fee is $5 per night per pet. The cancellation fee is $20 if more than 30 days in advance; within 30 days of arrival it's $20 per night cancelled.

Organizations and Information Sources

For camping and visitor information and maps, we suggest the following sources:

Virginia Hospitality and Travel Association (private campgrounds), 2101 Libby Avenue, Richmond 23230; (804) 288-3065

George Washington and Jefferson National Forests, 5162 Valleypointe Parkway, Roanoke, 24019-3050; (540) 265-5100

National Forest group camping reservations, (800) 280-2267

Shenandoah National Park, Route 4, Box 348, Luray 22835; (540) 999-2243, (800) 778-2851

Virginia State Parks, Department of Conservation & Recreation, Division of State Parks, 203 Governor Street, Suite 306, Richmond 23219; general information, (804) 786-1712; brochures and reservations, (804) 225-3867, (800) 933-PARK; TDD number, (804) 786-2121

Blue Ridge Parkway Camping, 2551 Mountain View Road, Vinton 24179; (540) 857-2213

U.S. Army Corps of Engineers (Philpott Lake, Bassett only), Wilmington District, Philpott Lake, Route 6, Box 140, Bassett 24055; (540) 629-2703

Virginia Division of Tourism, Bell Tower on Capitol Square, Richmond 23219; (804) 786-4484

Shenandoah Valley Travel Association, P.O. Box 1040, New Market 22844; (540) 740-3132

Fishing

Naturalist Henry David Thoreau once commented, "In the night, I dream of trout-fishing." In Virginia's Blue Ridge, anglers see their dreams become reality in clear, cold mountain streams, rivers and lakes. Visitors can rest easy at night knowing that, at any given moment, millions of fish are surging upstream or lying tantalizingly in wait in stone river recesses.

An aggressive conservation effort by the state is partly responsible for the plentiful fishing in the Blue Ridge. For example, the mountain streams found in Shenandoah National Park are one of the last completely protected strongholds of the native Eastern brook trout. Savvy Virginia tourism experts report that since Robert Redford's naturalistic film on fly fishing, based on the book *A River Runs Through It*, the numbers of fly-fishing anglers in Virginia have been thicker than the black flies their artificial bait imitates. But don't worry — the out-of-the-way waters far outnumber those that aren't.

Here are a few tips about the best places to catch fish: brown trout — Lake Moomaw, Mossy Creek and Smith River; largemouth bass — James River; smallmouth bass — James River, Smith Mountain Lake, Claytor Lake and Lake Philpott; striped bass — Claytor Lake and Smith Mountain Lake; and walleye — Smith Mountain Lake, Philpott Lake, Claytor Lake, Carvins Cove and the Roanoke River.

And now for bragging rights! To name a few state records: smallmouth bass, 7 lbs., 7 oz., New River; Roanoke bass, 2 lbs., 6 oz., Smith Mountain Lake; striped bass, 45 lbs., 10 oz., Smith Mountain Lake; walleye, 14 lbs., 2 oz., New River; and northern pike, 31 lbs., 4 oz., Motts Run. By the time you read this, some of these records might already be broken.

Figures for citation fish are equally impressive. In 1996, the James River set the record with 551 citations, followed by Smith Mountain Lake with 314 citations, the New River with 149, Claytor Lake and Philpott Reservoir with 108 and Lake Moomaw with 94.

Photo: Tod Kenworthy

The Blue Ridge Mountains are a hiker's paradise.

The primary objective of this section is to direct you to some of the Blue Ridge's classic streams, rivers and lakes — the ones where anglers aren't so close that they're crossing lines. After you get to your spot, you might want to rough it on your own. Or you can hire a guide.

The Virginia Department of Game and Inland Fisheries recommends literally hundreds of fishing places. You can find out about real gem daytrips. An especially fun one for lovers of both fishing and horseback riding is the package offered by **Virginia Mountain Outfitters** in Buena Vista, near Lexington. Trips range from one to five days and include a clinic. Call Deborah Sensabaugh at Outfitters, (540) 261-1910, to find out more.

Farther north, in the charming tin-roofed town of Edinburg, **Murray's Fly Shop** is a good place to find out where you can fish in the Shenandoah Valley for the really big ones. Proprietor Harry Murray is the author of several books, including *Trout Fishing in the Shenandoah National Park*, and promises to help you catch fish. Murray offers numerous

clinics and can be reached at (540) 984-4212 for a complete list.

Wintergreen Resort in Nelson County offers Fly Fisher's Symposiums. Call Chuck Furimsky at (800) 325-2200 for more information on fishing and lodging at this first-class resort, which also offers great golfing and skiing. Also for fly fishing, go westward in Bath County to **Meadow Lane Lodge**, site of a former Orvis Fishing School on the Jackson River. Call (540) 839-5959.

For details and the widest array of locations, the Department of Game and Inland Fisheries' *Virginia Fishing Guide* is a must. Traditionally, topographic maps published by the U.S. Geological Survey have been the most useful sources of information for anglers. These maps can tell you whether streams flow through open or forested land, how steep the land is and where tributaries enter. Instructions on how to get both guides are listed at the end of this fishing section.

We hope you're now excited about all the fishing possibilities. But, don't forget your license, which can be obtained from some county circuit court clerks, city corporation court clerks and a variety of other authorized agents. The first Saturday and Sunday in June have been designated as Free Fishing Days in Virginia. No fishing license of any kind is required for rod and reel fishing except in designated trout-stocked waters. A detailed booklet describing licensing requirements, game fish size and catch limits, special regulations (specific to certain areas) and other regulations can be obtained from the Virginia Department of Game and Inland Fisheries (see address at the end of this section).

Fishing Licenses

Unless otherwise specified, resident license requirements apply annually to all persons who claim the Commonwealth of Virginia as their legal domicile. Nonresident fees apply annually as well, unless otherwise indicated. A 50¢ issuance fee, added to each of the following licenses, is not included in our listed fee.

Resident

County or city resident to fish in county or city of residence, $5 per year

State resident to fish only, $12

To fish statewide for five consecutive days in private waters or public waters not stocked with trout, $5

State and county resident to trout fish in designated trout-stocked waters, $12 (in addition to regular fishing license)

Age 65 and older, $1

Virginia lifetime license, $250

Nonresident

Nonresident to fish only, $30 per year

To fish for five consecutive days statewide in private waters or public waters not stocked with trout, $6

To fish in designated trout-stocked waters, $30 (in addition to regular fishing license)

Virginia lifetime license, $500

Safety Suggestions

Regardless of whether you're testing the waters of the Blue Ridge as an experienced angler or a novice, it doesn't hurt to remember safety at all times, especially cold-weather hazards. Although getting away from it all is most of the fun, don't forget to let somebody know where you are. Despite the best of precautions, you could fall in at some point. In hot weather, it's an inconvenience. In cold weather, which is most of the year, it can be fatal. Many anglers do not realize that hypothermia can strike when the temperature is in the 40s. Prevention is always best — wear waders with rough soles when fishing in streams and wear a life preserver when fishing in rivers and lakes. And don't forget to look out for snakes (timber rattlers and copperheads are the two poisonous species) and ticks, the latter of which are "fishing" for you!

Lakes

The following are some favorite fishing areas of the Blue Ridge. Source material for complete listings is included at the end of this Fishing section.

Rivianna Reservoir
Charlottesville area

Anglers consider this the best bet for fishing in the area surrounding this historic city. It supports good populations of bass, crappie, bream and channel cats, with occasional walleye and muskie. There is a public boat ramp near the filtration plant of the Charlottesville water-supply reservoir, which may be reached from U.S. Highway 29 north of Charlottesville by taking Va. Route 631 (Rio Road) or Va. Route 743 west to Va. Route 659 or Va. Route 676. The ramp is at the end of Va. 659.

Lake Moomaw
Bath, Alleghany counties

This flood-control reservoir was completed in 1981 with the closing of the Gathright Dam on the Jackson River. Ever since, its 43-mile shoreline has been a popular playground for residents of Alleghany, Bath and Highland counties. Much of the shoreline is adjacent to the Gathright Wildlife Management Area. Crappie fishing is outstanding, with 1.5-pounders common. There is an equal complement of largemouth and smallmouth bass. Thirty-seven citation rainbow trout have also been pulled from the lake. For more information, call the

James River Ranger District in Covington, (540) 962-2214.

To reach the lake, get off I-64 at Exit 16 and follow U.S. Highway 220 to Va. Route 687 then to Va. Route 641 and Va. Route 666. The access point is 16 miles from the interstate.

Smith Mountain Lake
Bedford, Pittsylvania, Franklin counties

Striped bass are prevalent at Smith Mountain Lake, which has been the source of numerous citation fish. More anglers appear to be converting to fishing live bait over artificial. A real pro, who has been fishing the lake since its beginnings with Appalachian Power Company in the '60s, says the secret to landing big stripers is live shad, which can be caught at dockside in casting nets.

The state's largest striper, 45 pounds 10 ounces, was caught here in 1995. At the rate these whoppers are growing, that record might soon be surpassed. If you're serious about getting one of the big ones, a professional guide is a great idea. Some good ones are R.M. King, (540) 721-4444; Dave Sines, (540) 721-5007; or Spike Franceschini, (540) 297-5611. They'll try to ensure you don't go home with only tales about the one that got away.

The lake provides a lot of camping and recreational opportunities, including a swimming beach, through Smith Mountain Lake State Park, (540) 297-4062. To reach the lake from U.S. 460, take Va. 43 to Va. 626 S.

Claytor Lake
Off Va. Rt. 660, Pulaski County

This lake, also impounded by Appalachian Power, on the New River near Dublin, is known for its fantastic white bass fishery, producing many citations annually. Claytor has traditionally been a good flathead catfish lake, too, with fish up to 25 pounds or more. Crappie also have shown good growth rates. Claytor Lake State Park, (540) 674-5492, provides fine marinas, camping, cottages and a swimming beach. The lake is accessible by taking Exit 101 from I-81 to Va. 660. Follow this road for 3 miles to Claytor Lake.

Hungry Mother Lake
Off Va. Rt. 16, Smyth County

In the rustic highlands of its namesake,

Hungry Mother State Park, (540) 783-3422, near Marion, this lake provides good fishing for largemouth bass, bluegill and crappie (up to 13 inches). Camping is available, as are boat rentals. To reach the lake, take Exit 47 off I-81 to U.S. 11, which you follow into Marion. At the second stoplight, turn right onto Va. 16.

Resources

State Publications

For the total scoop on fishing, the following titles are available from the Virginia Department of Games and Inland Fisheries, 4010 Broad Street, P.O. Box 11104, Richmond 23230-1104, (804) 367-1000: *Virginia Wildlife Calendar*, *Virginia Fishing Regulations* and *Virginia Fishing Guide*.

U.S. Geological Survey Maps

Contact the Distribution Branch, U.S. Geological Survey, Box 25286, Federal Center, Denver, Colorado 80225 for individual maps.

Virginia Topographic Maps

An outstanding collection of Virginia topographic maps is the *Virginia Atlas & Gazetteer*, published by the DeLorme Mapping Company, P.O. Box 298, Freeport, Maine 04032.

Lake and River Maps

Contact the Alexandria Drafting Company, 6440 General Green Way, Alexandria 22312.

Books on Trout Streams

We recommend two great trout stream books: *Virginia Trout Streams*, by Harry Slone, published by Backcountry Publications; and *A Fly Fisherman's Blue Ridge*, by Christopher Camuto, published by Henry Holt & Company.

Golf

Virginia is building a reputation for producing some of the finest players and courses in the country. Sam Snead, Lanny Watkins, Curtis Strange and Vinny Giles are all home-grown talents. Arnold Palmer, Jack Nicklaus and Gary Player also have come to the Commonwealth to design some of the most exciting new places to play.

Virginia has more than 150 golf courses, many of which are in the mountains and valleys of the Blue Ridge, including three of the country's top golf resorts. The diverse topography of the region means that the courses vary widely, providing a never-ending challenge that draws visitors back year after year. The fact that Blue Ridge links are generally greener and 10 to 15 degrees cooler in the summer is another draw. The quality of golf here, like the quality of life, is always nothing short of outstanding.

In this section we have listed a few of the best-known public, semiprivate and military courses. Our list is by no means complete; we've simply tried to give you a sampling of what the state's top courses in the Blue Ridge have to offer. For more information on Virginia links, we recommend the following sources: Virginia Golf Association, (804) 378-2300; Golf Promotions in Virginia, (800) GOLF-NVA; and Golf Virginia Resorts Association, (800) 93-BACK9.

Carper's Valley Golf Club
1401 Millwood Pike, Winchester
• **(540) 662-4319**

Tree-lined fairways and gently rolling hills dominate this 150-acre course at the top of the Shenandoah Valley. Four lakes add to the scenic and competitive layout along the 6125-yard par 70 course. There's a short tight par 3 and a long open hilly par 5, but you will want to make sure your drive is accurate on the fourth hole. A severe dogleg left to right, this signature hole is heavily forested. The greens fee is $22 on the weekend and holidays and $16 during the week. Carts rent for $12 per rider for all 18 holes or $8 apiece for nine holes. Carts are required until noon on weekends and holidays.

Meadows Farms Golf Course
4300 Flat Run Rd., Locust Grove
• **(540) 854-9890**

In 1993 nursery magnate Bill Meadows opened this Orange County course, a beautifully landscaped layout that boasts the country's longest hole. At nearly a half-mile long, this 841-yard, par 6 has brought the course plenty of national attention. Two ponds come into play as you go up hills on this challenging dogleg right. Your best bet is to hit your tee shot short of the first pond, hit over the pond, then if you can carry the other pond on your third shot, you should be about 75 yards from the green. But don't forget to watch out for the clover-shaped bunker. Meadows recently added nine more holes, bringing the total to 27. The par 72 Island to Long is 6312 yards, the par 72 Long to Waterfall is 6320 yards, while par 70 Island to Waterfall is 5560 yards. On the waterfall you actually drive your cart behind a 60-foot waterfall then walk across a swinging bridge to get to the tee. On weekdays combined greens and cart fees run $29, $24 for seniors. On Fridays the cost is $34 and $29. Greens and cart fees on Saturday and Sunday are $39. You may walk the course on Monday through Thursday. Just knock five bucks off the price. Meadows Farms is just west of Fredericksburg.

Caverns Country Club
910 T.C. Northcott Blvd., Luray
• **(540) 743-7111**

Near the famous Luray Caverns, this course offers the unique experience of golfing near cave openings, though it can be quite tricky getting your ball out of these hazards. The first hole sets the tempo on this hilly 6499-yard, par 72 course. No. 1 is a long par 5 that measures about 500 yards. The greens fees are $19 Monday through Thursday and $28 on the weekend. Add an additional $11 per person if you want a cart.

Bryce Resort and Golf Course
1982 Fairway Dr., Bayse
• **(540) 856-2124, (800) 821-1444**

Although this Shenandoah County resort is built right beside a mountain, golfers will enjoy a relatively flat course. It does takes a few challenging turns, starting right off the bat with a long par 5 dogleg on the first hole. On the back nine, No. 15 is one of the most picturesque holes on the course, a 140-yard par 3 with a pond off to the right. Quite a few creeks also come into play over the 6024-yard, par 71 course.

There is also a miniature golf course nearby. Bryce, a golf and skiing resort, is near the West Virginia border (see our Resorts chapter). Cart and greens fees are $30 for weekdays and $45 on the weekends.

Shenandoah Valley Golf Club
134 Golf Club Cir., Front Royal
• (540) 636-2641, (540) 636-4653

Some of the best golfers have tested their skills here at Shenandoah Valley. Once used as a qualifier for the Kemper Open, this Warren County club hosts the Mid-Atlantic PGA twice a year. This 27-hole par 72 course offers golfers three distinctively different looks over 6399 yards, ranging from rolling hills to flat land in the valley. There's not much room for error on the Red nine. Also called the "old course," it is known for its narrow fairways and small greens. The White is filled with par 3s, all tight and tricky, while the Blue is the most difficult with a mixture of blind holes. The par 3 No. 2 on the Blue course is definitely a postcard hole. If you're looking for scenery, Shenandoah keeps a full-time flower gardener, and it shows with stunning flower beds throughout. Combined cart and greens fees range from $21 to $44.

Bowling Green Golf Club
838 Bowling Green Rd., Front Royal
• (540) 635-2024

Front Royal's premier golfing spot has two challenging 18-hole courses. The North is a 6085-yard par 71, while the south course plays a par 70 over 5587 yards. The older North course should offer more of a challenge. Greens fees during the week are $17 in the mornings, $12 in the afternoons. Weekend rates are $36 in the morning and $21 after noon. Carts range from $10 to $15. Walkers aren't allowed until 2 PM on weekends during the summer months.

Shenvalee
9660 Fairway Dr., New Market
• (540) 740-9930, (540) 740-3181

This course opened its first nine holes in 1927. The second nine, added later, is more difficult, with a creek wandering in and out of the course. In 1993-94 a third nine was built, giving a somewhat open feel to the gently rolling course. Several holes are longer than 400 yards, adding considerable difficulty. Both the Old-to-Creek and Miller-to-Old are 5600-yard par 72 courses. The Creek-to-Miller is a 5636-yard par 71. Greens fees range from $34 to $38, while carts are an additional $13 to $26. Walking is not permitted on the Miller course.

The Homestead Resort
U.S. Hwy. 220, Hot Springs
• (540) 839-7740, (800) 838-1766

The nation's oldest first tee is still in use at The Homestead Resort in Hot Springs, near golf legend Sam Snead's estate. After generations of ownership by the Ingalls family, the resort is now run by Club Resorts Inc., the same folks who resurrected North Carolina's Pinehurst.

Of the resort's three courses, The Cascades is acknowledged as one of the best mountain layouts in the country and has hosted six USGA championships. The par 70 6282-yard course has three of the prettiest finishing holes to be found anywhere, with a stream, two ponds and a small waterfall adding challenge as well as beauty. There is room for daring shots on the par 4 10th and par 5 17th holes, but the short par 3 18th over water is definitely one of the most memorable.

The Homestead Course, dating back to the 1890s, is one of the state's oldest. It's easier to score on the shorter par 72 5796-yard course, so this has become a favorite with the resort's overnight guests. Add in the 6200-yard par 72 Lower Cascades, and there are 54 excellent holes at The Homestead. In fact, The Cascades is the only course in the state to be rated in the nation's top 100 by both *Golf Digest* (39th) and *Golf Magazine* (43rd).

Cart and greens fees range from $95 to $125 for resort guests. Those who just come for a round on the links will pay between $125 and $160. It's one price whether you walk or ride. Caddies are available. The Homestead's Golf Advantage School specializes in instruction to adults and children.

The Greenbrier
300 W. Main St., White Sulphur Springs, W.Va. • (800) 624-6070

A top-rated resort, The Greenbrier is just 30 miles south of The Homestead in West Vir-

Tennis, anyone?

ginia. It may be just outside of our Blue Ridge region, but its so close that a true golf fanatic won't want to pass this by. Readers of *Condé Nast Traveler* have voted The Greenbrier one of the best courses in the Lower 48.

This exclusive resort (see our Resorts chapter) has three historic courses, including a classic designed by the legendary Jack Nicklaus. The 6311-yard par 72 Greenbrier course is heavily wooded with water coming into play on several holes along the front nine. Lakeside, completed in 1962, has been recognized for its use of the land. The shorter par 70 6068-yard course also is peppered with several water hazards. The 6353-yard Old White, dating back to 1913, also is a par 70. Picking a signature hole here is like pointing to one diamond in a tennis bracelet, but an unforgettable twosome are No. 2 and No. 16 that surround the lake on the Greenbrier course. Greens fees are $95 for resort guests and $200 for nonregistered guests. Carts are an additional $18 per person.

Stoneleigh
35271 Prestwick Ct., Round Hill
• (540) 338-4653

Some say a round at Stoneleigh is like a trip across the Atlantic, thanks in part to its

designer Lisa Maki. Maki, who studied in Scotland, structured out the par 72, 6709-yard course with a series of stone walls and sloping angles. In fact, a stone wall fronts the green on the much-talked-about No. 2 hole. The hole plays uphill to a very small green, but once you're there it's worth it. You can look out on a 20-mile view of the Northern Virginia suburbs. Stoneleigh is on the verge of going private, so if you feel you're a pretty fair shotmaker, don't wait too long to try this course. Play is limited on the weekend, but open to the public anytime during the week. Combined greens and cart fees range from $48 to $58. Carts alone are $12 per person.

Algonkian
47001 Fairway Dr., Sterling
• (703) 450-4655

This long 7015-yard course bordering the edge of the Potomac River is operated by the Northern Virginia Regional Park Authority. Designed by Ed Ault, the Loudoun County course plays like two entirely different nines. The front is flat and open. Because of its long spacious fairways, Algonkian remains one of the metro area's most popular courses. (It's only 30 miles from Washington, D.C., and 15 miles from Tyson Corner.) Adding to the challenge is the tight tree-lined back nine, which requires careful shot placement. Greens fees will run from $18 to $22, while carts rent for $26 for two people. Along with the golf course, Algonkian's 800-acre park includes something for the whole family, including an outdoor swimming pool; 18-holes of miniature golf; a children's playground with swings, slides, seesaws and a nature trail; 12 river-side vacation cottages; boat launch access to the Potomac River; and picnic areas.

Landsdowne Golf Club
44050 Woodbridge Pkwy., Leesburg
• (703) 729-4071

Designed by Robert Trent Jones Jr., Landsdowne has been called one of the finest courses in the Washington, D.C. area. The back nine cuts through woods and runs adjacent to the Potomac River. The par 3 15th hole over water is a standout. The forgiving front nine, with its lush zoysia fairways, is more open. Cart and greens fees range from $55 to $90. All golfers are required to take a cart.

Raspberry Falls Golf and Hunt Club
Va. Rt. 15, Leesburg • (703) 779-2555

You can get an idea of what it's like to play the deep bunkers found on British Open courses at Gary Player's signature designed course in Leesburg. The 6296-yard par 72 course was built on an old hunt club property in 1996. Water comes into play on only two holes at Raspberry Falls, but stacked sod bunkers can make things challenging on all but one hole. Watch out for No. 18 — this par 5 is a long 550-yard dogleg. Greens and cart fees are $55 Monday through Thursday and $65 on the weekends. Walking is allowed.

Birdwood Golf Course
200 Ednam Dr., Charlottesville
• (804) 296-2181, (800) 476-1988

The Boar's Head Inn's golf course has challenged young golfers for years. In fact, Birdwood has been ranked one of the top 10 collegiate courses in America by *Golf Digest*. A favorite of orange and blue clad University of Virginia students, the 18-hole par 72 course has also hosted the NCAA East Regional Golf Tournament, the National Ladies Public Links

Championship and the Virginia State Amateur Golf Championship. Designed by Lindsay Evans, this tough course has a demanding finish, including the par 3 No. 14 hole. It may be short, but the plush green sits right on an island. Once private, this 6821-yard championship course is now open to the public. Birdwood offers individual instruction, group clinics, video swing analysis, a pro shop and the "19th Hole" for food and beverages. Carts rent for $18 to $12, while the combined cart rental and greens fees will range from $20 to $55 depending on the time of year.

Wintergreen Resort
Va. Rt. 151, Nellysford • (804) 325-8250

This Nelson County resort is consistently ranked among the nation's top golf destinations. Stoney Creek was rated the 34th best course in the country by *Golf Digest*, while Devils Knob has been picked as one of Virginia's top 10. In 1990 designer Rees Jones cut the ribbon on the Stoney Creek course, a 6341-yard par 72 valley layout. This roomy 18-hole course features bold mounding, similar to what is found on many British courses. You will want to watch out for the 410-yard 4th hole. The par 4 plays pretty straight, but there is a water hazard just right of the green.

Last year, Jones returned to unveil the brand new Tuckahoe Nine at Stoney Creek. It has already been hailed as the most challenging and beautiful of the Wintergreen courses. The look is a little different than Stoney Creek's original 18, with more elevated tees, greens and water. The ninth hole is the longest at 586 yards, but the 457-yard par 4 first hole is the most elevated tee on the course and is bordered on the right side by a lake.

Devils Knob, the highest course in the state at 3,850 feet, was designed in the 1970s along a challenging, yet surprisingly level mountain ridge. Because of its elevation, Devils Knob offers a comfortable 70 to 85 degree temperature in the spring and summer. Tree-lined fairways can be found throughout the 6003-yard course. If you are hoping to make the par 70 on this 18-hole course, good luck with the 600-yard double dogleg on No. 7.

Greens fees for both courses are $60 midweek and $72 Friday through Sunday. Discount rates are available for those staying at Wintergreen. Cart fees are $16.50. Walking is permitted, but you will have to pay a trail fee (close to the same as the cart fee). See our Resorts chapter for more about Wintergreen.

Laurel Ridge Golf Club
Va. Rt. 15, Palmyra • (804) 589-3730

Laurel Ridge, 20 miles east of Charlottesville in Fluvanna County, is a welcome new daily-fee course in a golf-hungry Central Virgina. Designed by Brian Smith, the par 72 6375-yard course is sculpted from the rolling hills and framed by the forested Blue Ridge. The practice area includes a large driving range, pitching area and putting green. The 4,000-foot clubhouse is computerized so you can line up with the VSGA handicap system. Inside there are locker rooms, a pro shop and Mulligans Restaurant, serving from a grill menu from 11 AM to 3 PM. The locals like to lunch here. Although the staff at Laurel Ridge say they are too new — the club opened in 1997 — to have a signature hole, No. 5 is a challenging par 4 dogleg over water. Greens fees are $18 to $24, while cart rental is $12 per person, $8 if you only play nine holes. This is a soft-spike only course, but if you come by an hour before tee time, the staff will replace your metal spikes with soft ones for a $5 fee.

Ivy Hill Golf Club
1327 Ivy Hill Dr., Forest • (804) 525-2680

This championship course is a 6147-yard, par 72 challenge. With the mountains as a backdrop, it's a very scenic course, but it's also quite hilly. Because of the terrain, the staff tries to discourage golfers from walking — however, the adventurous may hike the course with bag in tow after 2 PM on the weekends. Although the front nine is open, there still isn't room to spray the ball too much. The back nine is a lot tighter and truly a challenge if you play from the tips. The par 4, 500-yard 7th hole is a standout. A 285-yard tee shot should

put you in a landing area with little more than 200 yards to get to the green. Just bend the ball a little right to left to get there. Cart and greens fees are $20 to $25 weekdays and $25 to $30 on the weekends.

London Downs
1400 London Dr., Forest • (804) 525-4653

Another championship course, London Downs is a par 72 public course measuring 6347 yards. The course was designed over gently rolling hills, but take extra care when approaching No. 7. You will have to carry a water hazard on the 150-yard hole to make par in three shots. Greens fees are $16 during the week and $21 on weekends. Carts are an additional $10, but you may walk if you're up to a little exercise.

Ole Monterey
1112 Tinkercreek Ln., Roanoke • (540) 563-0400

A public course built in 1926, Ole Monterey was designed by golfing legend Fred Findlay. The 6287-yard par 71 layout is solid, and the holes are challenging. A long par 4 on No. 11 gives a view of what's in store. This uphill hole plays 418 yards from the white tees with a straightaway 465 from the blues. Greens and cart fees are $14 and $12 during the week, $29 on the weekend. During the summer months, walking is not allowed on weekends until after 3 PM.

Countryside Club
1 Countryside Rd., Roanoke • (540) 563-0391

A generally forgiving, open layout, this course features several difficult par 3s. One particularly difficult par 3 is the downhill No. 16 over water. Most of the generous land area over the gently rolling hills makes it an enjoyable 6018-yard par 71 course. Weekend greens and cart fees are $37. It's $29 if you can go during the week. Before noon on weekends and holidays, a cart is mandatory.

Blue Hills
2001 Blue Hills, Roanoke
• (540) 344-7848

The price is right and the scenery is beautiful at this public Roanoke course. Built at the foot of a mountain, the par 71 course is 5937-yards of gently rolling hills. The long par 5 on No. 13 may present a challenge, but water comes into play on several holes. Greens fees are $18 during the week, $20 on the weekend. Carts rent for $10 per person.

Hanging Rock
1500 Red Lane Ext., Salem
• (540) 389-7275, (800) 277-7497

With so many rolling hills, some have dubbed Hanging Rock a "roller coaster of elevation changes." No hole probably illustrates the moniker better than its signature par 4 No. 5. You start out with a tee shot from high above, follow up with a mid-range second stroke, but then you have a decision to make. There are two greens. One is a straightaway shot, but it's straight uphill. All you can see is the flag on this blind shot. Your other option is the green that is flanked by water on three sides. In fact the entire 18-hole par 72 course designed by Russell Breeden is surrounded by streams, boulders and trees, not to mention a superb view of the mountains. Seventy-five different tees allow you to play Hanging Rock anywhere from 4691 yards to 6828. The course was named one of the top three courses in Virginia by *The Golfers Guide* readers survey. Carts rent for $12, but the combined cart and greens fee ranges from $34 to $42. Walkers are allowed on weekdays and late Saturday afternoons.

Olde Mill Golf Resort
Va. Rt. 1, Laurel Fork • (540) 398-2638

This resort at Groundhog Mountain is a scenic, challenging and relatively unknown gem designed by Ellis Maples in the 1970s. Just off the Blue Ridge Parkway, the 6185-yard course is naturally hilly with lots of lakes and streams. In fact, water comes into play on 13 holes. If you hope to match the par 72, the 10th hole could pose a few problems. You must drive from an elevated tee to a fairway surrounded on three sides by water. *Golf Digest* awarded Olde Mill four out of five stars. Greens fees are $26 Monday through Thursday and $36 on Friday through Sunday. Carts rent for $13. Olde Mill is closed December 1 through March 1.

Draper Valley
2800 Big Valley Rd., Pulaski
• (540) 980-4653

Draper Valley is one of the golfing jewels in the southwestern portion of the state. Long hitters have been coming here in droves, with more than 35,000 rounds of golf played here each year. Tom McKnight, a 44-year-old golfer from nearby Galax, honed his talents here. In 1998, a national television audience watched the three-time Virginia State Amateur champion advance to the finals of the U.S. Amateur in upstate New York. He had plenty of opportunity to practice his big ball at Draper Valley. Stretching out to 7046 yards, this par 72 course designed by Harold Louthern features wide fairways and large greens with picturesque mountain backdrops. Since it was built over farmland, there are not many trees, but there are a number of blind spots with holes playing down hill or back up on the mountainside. No. 9 is a gem with a scenic overlook of the lake and mountains, but the true test comes on all the par 3s with more than 190 yards from tee to green. Greens fees range from $25 to $30, with cart rental at $10.

Westlake
360 Chestnut Creek, Smith Mountain
Lake • (540) 721-4214

Golfers can test their skills at Westlake. Designed by Russell Breeden, Westlake is a par 72 course. Hilly and narrow, the 5878-yard course is quite challenging, especially the last hole. No. 18 is a long par 4 dogleg right to left that ends with a water hazard right next to the green. Greens fees and carts are $29.50, $34.50 on the weekends. Walking is allowed in the late afternoon.

Hiking

It almost goes without saying that Virginia is a hiker's paradise. Last year *Walking* magazine named the Skyline Drive and Blue Ridge Parkway two of the country's most scenic routes leading to national park trails. And that is only the beginning.

It would be difficult to give a comprehensive list of hikes, but we can give you a small sampling. You might like the most popular and easily accessible or perhaps you're drawn to the more remote in the rural parts of the state. We have thousands of trails crossing over diverse terrain, enough to fill several books. In fact, many good reference books have already been written on the subject. Among the them, we recommend: *Trails of Virginia* by Allen de Hart (probably the most complete guide), *Walking the Blue Ridge* by Leonard M. Adkins, *Hiking Virginia* by Randy Johnson and *Hiking Virginia's National Forests* by Karin Wuertz-Schaefer.

If you're uneasy about planning your own outing in unfamiliar country, **Mountain Memory Walks**, (540) 253-9622, in The Plains organizes two- to seven-day hiking trips in the Blue Ridge, with lodging in comfortable inns. The folks at area camping and outdoor stores can also be enormously helpful in trip planning. **Blue Ridge Mountain Sports** in Charlottesville, (804) 977-4400, not only carries a plethora of hiking and camping guides, but their hiking and camping experts will also guide you in organizing a Virginia outing. They can even pull up local weather conditions and forecasts on their computer to aid you in your plans. Other camping outfitters include **Rockfish Gap Outfitters** in Waynesboro, (540) 943-1461.

Here's a selection of hiking opportunities in or near the Blue Ridge.

Appalachian Trail

Conservationist Benton MacKaye had a dream in 1921: to construct a hiking trail that would continuously connect the states along the Appalachian Mountain chain. His proposed "experiment in regional planning" was begun in 1922 and completed in 1937. This famous trail traverses 2,100 miles and 14 states from Georgia to Maine. In 1948, the first hiker walked the entire trail; today about 100 hikers every year complete the walk. The entire hike takes four to six months to finish.

Impressively, more than 500 miles of the Appalachian Trail (AT) — about a quarter of its total distance — wind through Virginia. The portion of the trail that runs through the Shenandoah National Park, starting in Front Royal and ending at Rockfish Gap at I-64, is considered by veteran hikers to be one of its most beautiful sections. The trail also passes through the Mount Rogers National Recreation Area, a spectacular stretch of land in Southwest Virginia that includes the state's two highest peaks.

Hikers can find countless access points to the state's 500 miles of Appalachian Trail, and a variety of trips, day-long or much longer, can be planned around the trail. Perhaps the best guides to the AT are published by the Appalachian Trail Conference, the governing body of the trail. The organization puts out guidebooks to every section of the trail, complete with maps and access points. Four of these books are devoted to the Virginia-area trails: *Appalachian Trail Guide for the Shenandoah National Park*, *Appalachian Trail Guide for Southern Virginia*, *Appalachian Trail Guide for Northern Virginia and Maryland* and *Appalachian Trail Guide for Central Virginia*. Except for the Shenandoah National Park guide, the books do not cover side trails. These guides are available at most camping stores and outdoor outfitters.

A large section of the AT in Virginia (from the Shenandoah National Park north) is maintained by the Potomac Appalachian Trail Club. The club operates seven three-sided shelters and six fully enclosed cabins along the trail.

INSIDERS' TIP

If you are planning a hearty day hike, remember it could take a good 3 to 4 hours to go 3.5 miles. Be sure to start early enough so that you can get back before nightfall. It might also be a good idea to take along a flashlight, just in case.

For reservations or more information about this section of the AT, contact the club at 118 Park Street S.E., Vienna 22180, (703) 242-0693. The southern portions of the AT in Virginia are maintained and promoted by eight different trail clubs; for more information on these clubs and their coverage areas, contact the Appalachian Trail Conference headquarters in Harper's Ferry, West Virginia, at (304) 535-6331.

Shenandoah National Park and Skyline Drive

The Shenandoah National Park is a narrow park that follows along the Blue Ridge Mountains for almost 75 miles. Its 194,327 acres contain about 100 miles of the Appalachian Trail and 421 miles of other hiking paths. These range from rugged climbs up steep, rocky terrain to easy nature trails with interpretive guideposts. A new Limberlost Trail was recently completed to give easy access to baby strollers and wheelchairs. (See the Blue Ridge Parkway and Skyline Drive chapter for more information.)

Excellent hiking maps and trail guides to the Shenandoah National Park are available at both visitor centers and entrance stations on the Skyline Drive and by mail from the Shenandoah Natural History Association, Route 4, Box 348, Luray 22835, (540) 999-3581.

The Shenandoah National Park and Skyline Drive begin at Front Royal and end at Rockfish Gap just east of Waynesboro. A few of the unique day hikes in the park are described below.

Fox Hollow Nature Trail
Mile 4.6, Skyline Dr.

Park in the Dickey Ridge Visitor Center to take this 1.2-mile circuit hike. This trail passes by the remnants of the Fox Family homesite — a walled cemetery, the family's house, a concrete-enclosed spring and an old mill stone — a reminder of the displaced residents who once lived on this mountain before the government decided to build the drive. (The ruins

of nearly 5,000 farm buildings can be found throughout the park.)

White Oak Canyon Falls
Mile 42.6, Skyline Dr.

This is a popular and pleasant trail to the second-highest falls (86 feet) in the park. The 4.6-mile round-trip hike starts easily crossing the Limberlost Trail. The trail grows steeper as it enters the canyon. From a rock outcropping you will find a perfect view of the falls spilling over the canyon ledge. You may continue on to see five more falls, ranging from 35 to 62 feet, but the trail becomes steep and narrow and adds an additional 2.7 miles to your trip.

Big Meadows
Mile 51.3, Skyline Dr.

Big Meadows, one of the few large treeless fields in the park, is great for hiking. Depending upon the season, you'll find wildflowers here that don't grow in the woods and strawberries and blueberries along the path. This is also an excellent place to see a diversity of wildlife, since many animals depend on this grassy area for sustenance. This is a 132-acre meadow, the largest of its kind in the park, so you may wander until your heart's content.

Old Rag
Va. Rt. 600, near Nethers

To reach one of the park's most celebrated peaks, you have to leave the Skyline Drive and hike back in. There are two ways to get to the summit, but both start outside the park. A 7.2-mile circuit hike starts at the parking lot at Weakley Hollow Fire Road. Follow the blue blazes along the Ridge Trail. This is a steep and strenuous climb over, around and between granite boulders, but it is also the most interesting because of these unique obstacles. These narrow rock-walled corridors are the remains of the dikes through which lava flowed 700 million years ago. If you don't mind a longer walk, you can avoid the boulders on your trip back to the car by taking the Saddle Trail to the Weakley Hollow Fire Road.

A second and easier climb to the summit is the 5.4-mile hike starting at Berry Hollow parking lot. Just follow the fire road to the Saddle Trail. This too is a steep climb, but you will bypass the boulders in the other hike. There are two shelters and a spring along this route.

Blue Ridge Parkway

Rockfish Gap is the gateway to the Blue Ridge Parkway, the 469-mile-long scenic route that passes through the Cherokee Indian Reservation in North Carolina. The National Park Service maintains dozens of trails near the Parkway that are highly accessible, even for the laziest of walkers. But if you have the energy, you can hike through tunnels of rhododendron leading to rushing waterfalls or out to soaring peaks covered with mountain laurel and spruce.

Hiking in these mountains also provides a glimpse of what life was like for early settlers. It's not uncommon to stumble upon the crumbling rock foundation of an old cabin or a stone wall that used to keep in livestock. The ridges and valleys were inhabited by a few hardy souls when the Park Service began to obtain land for the Parkway decades ago.

Many trails lead to farms and communities that have been reconstructed by the Park Service. For instance, at the Mountain Farm Trail near Humpback Rocks (close to Charlottesville) you might see a ranger posing as a grandma and churning butter on the front porch of an old cabin, while brother John plucks a handmade dulcimer nearby.

Many interpretive programs are offered by the Park Service along Blue Ridge Parkway trails. Rangers conduct guided walks during the heaviest tourist months, talking about everything from endangered plants to old-time farming methods.

Most Blue Ridge Parkway trails are well-marked and easy to find. However, Parkway maps are available at the visitors centers such as the one at Humpback Rocks. Write to the National Park Headquarters at 400 BB&T Building, Asheville, North Carolina 28801, or call (704) 298-0398.

Here is a sample of some of the day hikes along or near the Blue Ridge Parkway. (See the Blue Ridge Parkway and Skyline Drive chapter for more hikes.)

Mountain Farm Trail
Mile 5.8

This quarter-mile-long trail along the Parkway is an easy, self-guiding route that begins at the Humpback Rocks Visitor Center, not too far from Charlottesville. It passes log cabins, chicken houses and a mountaineer's garden, reminders of the everyday life of the Blue Ridge's former inhabitants.

Humpback Rocks Trail
Mile 6.1

This is a steep and rocky section of the Appalachian Trail that can be reached from the Mountain Farm Trail described previously. Then it's a strenuous 4-mile hike to the summit of Humpback Mountain, from which you can see Rockfish Gap and the Shenandoah National Park to the north, the Shenandoah Valley to the west and the Rockfish River Valley to the east. In late spring, mountain laurel and azaleas make this a colorful, fragrant hike.

Rock Castle Gorge Trail
Mile 168.8

This 10.6-mile strenuous loop in northern Patrick County is noted for its high meadows, sweeping views, waterfalls and historical sites en route to the 3,572-foot summit of Rocky Knob. Along the way, you'll see a log shelter built by the CCC in the 1930s and old Rock Castle Pike, a pioneer road for wagons and carriages. Also keep an eye out for the 12-acre jumble of boulders called Bear Rocks, a haven for wildlife. Until the 1920s a mountain community thrived in this rugged area, where the rushing waters of Rock Castle Creek fueled sawmills and grist mills. This hike is one of several in the 4,200-acre Rocky Knob Recreation Area, which has a Park Service visitor center, campground, picnic areas and rustic rental cabins.

George Washington and Jefferson National Forests

If you would like to hike any of the trails in the George Washington and Jefferson National Forests, you should have a map. These trails are used less than the Parkway trails and are not as well maintained.

Photo: The Roanoke Valley Convention and Visitors Bureau

Slip a canoe into a mountain stream for an adventurous getaway.

All told there is a total of 1.7 million acres in Virginia's national forests. While many popular hikes are within easy reach, others are very difficult to get to. Your only access may be down dirt roads. Some trails may even require a little bushwhacking.

For a map of the George Washington or the Jefferson section write to Forest Headquarters, 5162 Valleypointe Parkway, Roanoke 24109-3050, or call (540) 265-5100.

Sherando Lake Recreation Area
Off Va. Rt. 664, Lyndhurst
• (540) 942-5965

Most of the action at Sherando Lake takes place between the two lakes at this popular family campground in Augusta County. But for the landlubber, there are plenty of trails to choose from. The Blue Loop Trail to Torry Ridge and the White Rock Gap trails are recommended for experienced hikers. Blue Loop and Torry Ridge combine for a steep 3-mile circuit hike. White Rock Gap is a little more moderate 2.5 mile climb that will lead you to the Blue Ridge Parkway.

Crabtree Falls Trail
Off Va. Rt. 56 near Montebello

Just off the Parkway, this 3-mile hike in Nelson County leads to the highest cascading falls in Virginia. Its trailhead is a parking lot on Va. 56, a few miles east of Montebello. Five major and several smaller waterfalls tumble down the mountain for a total of 1,200 feet. There are many overlooks along the way. You can see the Tye River Valley from the highest overlook at the upper falls. Hikers are advised to stay on the trails and off the slippery rocks.

Cascades National Recreation Trail
Va. Rt. 623, near Pembroke
• (540) 552-4641

West of Blacksburg you'll find wonderful hikes on the Appalachian Trail and in other recreation areas. One excellent 2-mile day hike follows Little Stoney Creek, which takes you to the 66-foot Cascades waterfall. The Civilian Conservation Corps constructed this beautiful trail in the 1930s. It's well-maintained, with benches along the creek and pretty wooden bridges. During the summer the pathway is lush and heavily shaded, a perfect place to cool off. You can also take a dip in the clear mountain pool at the base of the falls. To get there, go to Pembroke then take the road marked Cascades Recreation Area just east of the Dairy Queen on U.S. Highway 460. There is a $2 parking and picnicking fee.

Mount Rogers
National Recreation Area
5714 Va. Rt. 16, Marion
• (540) 783-5196

Farther west of the Blue Ridge Parkway in Smyth County lies a sliver of land measuring 55 miles long and nearly 10 miles wide. This spectacular area, part of the George Washington and Jefferson National Forests, is often said to resemble the Swiss Alps because of its high plateau and Alpine-like meadows. The area has 400 miles of trails, many of which climb to the crest zone — where Mount Rogers, Whitetop and Iron Mountain reach to nearly 6,000 feet. Mount Rogers Recreation Area is dazzling with its purple rhododendron, dense red spruce and Fraser firs, wild horses and panoramic views.

The Virginia Creeper Trail
Parallels U.S. Hwy. 58, Washington and Grayson counties • (540) 783-5196

A former railroad grade between Abingdon and Whitetop, this trail is 34 miles long and has many starting and stopping points. The easy grade provides a great way to enjoy fall foliage without working up too much of a sweat.

State Parks

The Blue Ridge's state parks offer great hiking opportunities. Some of our favorites are described here.

Sky Meadows State Park
11012 Edmonds Ln., Delaplane
• (540) 592-3556

The easily accessible Sky Meadows in Fauquier County, just outside Paris, was once a working Piedmont plantation. Its 1,863 acres along the eastern slope of the Blue Ridge entice weekend warriors with its maze of hiking

trails, including a 3.6-mile stretch of the Appalachian Trail. (See our Kidstuff chapter for more information.)

Douthat State Park
Va. Rt. 1, Millboro • (540) 862-8100

Douthat State Park, which spans Bath and Alleghany counties, has 40 miles of wooded hiking trails from the long 4.5-mile Stony Run to the short one-quarter mile Buck Lick Trail. Buck Lick was constructed by the Civilian Conservation Corps in the '30s and has 17 interpretive signs about geological features, trees, wild animals, lichens and forest succession.

With 4,493 acres of scenic high ridges, Douthat has more miles of hiking trails than almost any other state park. The park's trails are color-coded and generally in good condition. A hiking map from the visitor center is recommended for long hikes. There is a $1 fee for parking.

Smith Mountain Lake State Park
and Visitor Center
Va. Rt. 626, Huddleston • (540) 297-6066

This 1,506-acre park is not just for water enthusiasts, although it's a great place for swimming at the beach area, paddleboating (rentals available) and boating. The park also offers camping, picnicking, a visitor center, interpretive programs and four short trails, each less than 2 miles long. Cabins are being built and should be completed by fall 1999. The Chestnut Ridge Trail and Turtle Island Trail are open year round. Lake View Trail and Tobacco Run Trail are open when the visitors center is open.

Grayson Highlands State Park
Off U.S. Hwy. 58, Mouth of Wilson
• (540) 579-7092

The Appalachian Trail and more than 9 miles of other trails pass through this scenic 4,754-acre park on the eastern edge of Mount Rogers National Recreation Area. The park has ample camping and picnic facilities. Although the visitor center and camping close the first of December, the park is open year round for hiking and nature observation. There is a dollar a day entrance fee, $2 on weekends during the peak season.

New River Trail State Park
U.S. Hwy. 58, Foster Falls
• **(540) 699-6778**

Following the course of the historic New River, this linear park is a 57-mile trail running from Galax to Pulaski, the longest linear park in the state. The trail, which is frequented by hikers, bikers and horseback riders, has several convenient parking areas and access points along its route. The southern terminus is on E. Stuart Drive (Va. 58) in Galax.

Others

Highland Wildlife Management Area
Off Va. Rt. 615, Highland County
• **(540) 468-2550**

In Highland County, best known for its annual Maple Festival (see our Annual Events and Festivals chapter for details), you'll find endless possibilities for hiking in a 14,283-acre wilderness area that includes three tracks of land, Jack Mountain, Bull Pasture Mountain and Little Doe Hill. One option is a strenuous 5-mile hike up an old fire road to 4,400-foot Sounding Knob, the best-known landmark in the county. The mountaintop has a grazed open area and splendid views. Sounding Knob Trail begins at the junction of Va. 615 and the Buck Hill Road, established by the Civilian Conservation Corps.

Goshen/Little North Mountain Wildlife Management Area
Augusta and Rockbridge counties,
• **(540) 862-8100**

Between Lexington and Staunton on Va. Route 39, the state operates a 34,000-acre wildlife management area. Here, alluring hikes offer solitude and scenic views of the Maury River, the gorge at Goshen Pass and a variety of flora and fauna. Some trails are not named,

including a network that leads across a swinging bridge at Goshen Pass. Some that may be easier to find are the 4.2-mile Guy's Run Trail and 12.8-mile Little North Mountain Trail. Laurel Run Trail, a moderately difficult path, starts near the wayside picnic area at Goshen Pass and travels 2 miles uphill beside a creek coursing down to the Maury River. Rosebay rhododendron, oaks, maples and hemlock decorate the trail.

Old Chessie Trail
Off N. Main St., Lexington
• **(540) 463-3777**

Linking historic Lexington with Buena Vista, this 7 miles of old Chesapeake and Ohio railroad grade is now owned and maintained by the Virginia Military Institute Foundation. The flat, easy path offers glimpses of the Maury River and is bordered by wildflowers in the spring. From U.S. 11 in Lexington, turn on Old Buena Vista Road and go 1 mile. Informal parking is available along the side of the road, or stop by the visitor center in Lexington for directions daily from 9 AM to 5 PM.

Rivanna River Greenbelt Trail
Off Riverside Ave., Charlottesville
• **(804) 971-9798**

This half-mile trail is notable not only for the beautiful views it offers of Charlottesville's Rivanna River but also for its accessibility to people with disabilities. The brownstone trail is also ideal for bikers and joggers. Hikers will find several nice fishing spots along the trail and a fishing pier that is also accessible to the disabled. You'll find this pretty trail in Riverview Park just off Riverside Avenue in Charlottesville.

Ivy Creek Natural Area
Hydraulic Rd., Charlottesville
• **(804) 973-7772**

The 215-acre Ivy Creek Natural Area is an

INSIDERS' TIP

Not only is the Blue Ridge surrounded by national and state parks, there are also very good private campgrounds for the outdoor enthusiasts. The prices may be a bit higher, but many cater to RV owners with electrical and water hookups. Check with local visitor centers for listings.

unspoiled stretch of forest, streams and fields traversed only by footpaths. A network of 6 miles of trails includes self-guided ones. Ivy Creek is 2 miles north of the city. The area is open daily from 7 AM to dark. A new one-story building was constructed in 1997 for indoor educational programs.

Ash Lawn-Highland Historical Trail
James Monroe Pkwy., Charlottesville
• **(804) 293-9539**

Several miles from Charlottesville at Ash Lawn-Highland, a 535-acre estate that was once home to President James Monroe, a historical trail leads through pastures and woods to the top of Carter's Mountain. Ecology markers are posted along the 3-mile-long path, which begins at the museum shop. Ash Lawn is just off I-64, 2.5 miles beyond Thomas Jefferson's Monticello (see our Attractions chapter for more information about Ash Lawn).

Horseback Riding

If you're unable — or unwilling — to explore these mountains on foot, by all means get on a horse, even if it's your very first time. You'll find that your mount is an amiable companion as well as a comfortable means to get to places you'd otherwise miss. If you squint your eyes just right, you can imagine you're an early frontiersman scouting the uncharted Blue Ridge wilderness. Experienced equestrians do it all the time — trailering their horses to state parks or national forests for a day or weekend of riding.

Several equestrian outfitters (particularly in the Shenandoah Valley) offer one- or two-hour rides for beginners, half- or full-day treks for the more experienced and a variety of overnight trips, though steep insurance premiums are causing more outfitters to just focus on beginners.

You can rough it and camp beside a trout stream, grilling fresh trout over a campfire and listening to the whippoorwills at sunset. Or you can say goodnight to your horse at day's end and retire to a cozy country inn. Several inns specialize in guided trail riding, and most horse outfitters offer packages with nearby inns so that you can soak in a hot tub after a long

day's ride (see our Bed and Breakfasts and Country Inns chapter). In this section, we list places that offer guided horseback trips to the public. The Blue Ridge also has many private liveries and horse clubs and a plethora of trails, both public and private.

Maintree Farm
4024 Maintree Rd., Leesburg
• **(703) 777-3279**

This boarding and training operation offers guests a rare opportunity to enjoy prime hunt country. The stable, across from the Loudoun Hunt kennels, takes out a mock hunt every Sunday morning — a delightful two-hour ride. During fox-hunting season, the owners can arrange riding to the hounds with the Loudoun Hunt. If partner Beth Newman rides out with you, ask her how she became one of the country's leading female steeplechase riders.

Group lessons and trail rides are $18 per hour; the mock hunt is $25. Though the stable caters to all levels, only experienced equestrians should expect to ride over fences. Reservations are required.

Massanutten Trail Rides Inc.
751 Mountain Rd., Front Royal
• **(540) 636-6061**

For a taste of the Old West, take a trail ride with Skyline Ranch Resort along the mountain ridges of the George Washington section of the national forest. Western-style rides lasting 90 minutes are $20 per person, $17.50 for children. Children must be 9 or older. Skyline Ranch is a members-only campground, but nonmembers can reserve campsites within a week of their visit on a space-available basis.

Marriott Ranch
5305 Marriott Ln., Hume • (540) 364-3741

This 4,200-acre beef cattle ranch, owned and operated by Marriott International, is home to one of the largest Western trail-ride operations on the East Coast. Rides are usually 1.5 hours long and are available every day of the week except Monday. Rides go out at 10 AM , noon and 2 PM Tuesday through Sunday. Rates are $25 per person on weekdays and $27.50 on weekends; group rates are available. The minimum riding age is 10. The trails run through winding streams, open valleys and wooded hills on the ranch. Horse-drawn buggy, stage coach and haywagon rides also are offered. Reservations are required for all types of rides.

Marriott Ranch also specializes in Western-style corporate special events, such as barbecues and country-and-western dances, as well as business meetings and formal affairs, including wedding receptions and garden parties. Saturday nights in September and October are lively ones at the ranch. "Steak Bake and Boot Scoot" parties include haywagon rides, Western-style steak cookouts, country-and-western dance instruction and Western comedy entertainment. Reservations are required; call for current prices. Lodging is available.

Fort Valley Riding Stable
299 S. Fort Valley Rd., Kingscrossing
• (540) 933-6633

In the middle of the Massanutten Mountains, 1.5 miles from the nearest general store, is scenic Fort Valley and the Twin Lakes Campgrounds, where fat trout seem to just jump into your creel. Horseback riding is $20 per hour, $70 for a half-day guided trip and $100 for an all-day trip that lasts about seven hours. The half- and full-day rides include lunch on the trail. A two-day wilderness ride to some of the mountains' most scenic spots is $200 per person, which includes two trail lunches, a country breakfast, a campfire dinner, sleeping bags and tents.

Shenandoah National Park
Luray • (540) 999-2243

Guided trail rides leave from the National Park's Skyland Lodge several times daily. The route follows the scenic White Oak Canyon trail, which passes several waterfalls. The hour-long ride costs $20.90 per person and must be booked a day ahead. Tours go out daily from April through October and on weekends in November.

Graves Mountain Lodge
Off Va. Rt. 670, Syria • (540) 923-4231

This family-owned and -operated retreat has a heritage of hospitality dating back 130 years. Practice does make perfect, for the rustic mountain lodge has the right mix of life's simple pleasures (see our Bed and Breakfasts and Country Inns chapter). Porch-sitting ranks right up there with hiking, fishing and swimming, especially after you've spent the day wildlife-watching from horseback.

Working closely with the lodge is Tom Seay of Overnight Wilderness Outfitters, (540) 923-5071, who offers full-day rides in the Blue Ridge Mountains for $90, including lunch. Or, take an overnight excursion into the mountains for $125. Half-day rides are $50 per person, and there are shorter rides on the lodge's 50 miles of trails. For $20 you can get an hour-long guided trail ride, but you must be at least 4 feet tall. Stabling and services are available for horse owners, and groups are welcome.

Special times at the lodge are the April Spring Fling Festival, the June Festival of Music and the October Apple Harvest Festival (see our Annual Events and Festivals chapter).

Jordan Hollow Farm Inn
326 Jordan Hollow Farm Rd., Stanley
• (540) 778-2285

This is a wonderful vacation spot for horse lovers. The 145-acre farm is nestled in a secluded hollow between the Massanutten and Blue Ridge mountain ranges, 6 miles south of Luray. You can spend the night in one of the country inn's 21 rooms, dine on "American regional" cuisine and ride horses through lovely meadows or woods. The inn offers at least three beginner trail rides a day, Western-style, for $20 per person per hour. Pony rides are also available for children younger than 12.

Horse owners are invited to stable their horses at Jordon Hollow and enjoy the many miles of scenic trails on the farm. The innkeepers will guide these rides or layout a trail course for experienced riders.

Mountaintop Ranch
1030 Mountaintop Ranch Rd., Elkton
• (540) 298-9542

The folks at this mountaintop ranch between Shenandoah and Elkton are surrounded on three sides by the Shenandoah National Park. Trails lace more than 3,000 acres of unspoiled meadows and forest land. Rides last anywhere from one hour to all day and cost $23 per person for the shortest trip. Other options include a half-day trip for $65 that travels to a waterfall. The full-day $115 rides include lunch and usually run about six hours. Groups of 10 or more receive a discount.

Woodstone Meadows Stable
Va. Rt. 644, McGaheysville
• (540) 289-6152

In the Shenandoah Valley across from Massanutten Resort (see our Resorts chapter), this outfit offers leisurely trail rides in the Massanutten Mountains. Horse and rider are matched according to the rider's ability, and everyone receives basic instructions before taking off. Five-hour trail rides leave daily year round if weather permits. The cost is $25 per person, but you need to make reservations with a credit card or cash payment at least two hours in advance. Riders must be at least 10 years old and 4 feet 8 inches tall. The maximum weight is 230 pounds. Weekday pony rides are available by reservation from April through October for $1 per minute with a 10-minute limit.

Montfair Stables
4579 Slam Gate Rd., Crozet
• (804) 823-5202

This outfit offers half-hour, one-hour, half-day and all-day rides for the beginner or expert, on Western or English saddles. Montfair is 15 miles west of Charlottesville at the foot of Pasture Fence Mountain and stays open year round, weather permitting. Fees are $15 for a half-hour, $25 for one hour and $35 for an hour and a half. Groups of six or more receive a discount. The one-hour rides are very popular, so make your reservations early.

Wintergreen Resort– Rodes Farm Stables
Va. Rt. 613, Nellysford • (804) 325-8260

Guided trail rides in the mountains and Rockfish Valley are offered daily except Wednesdays from mid-March through November. The activities include pony rides for kids, sunset trail rides through Rockfish Valley, riding lessons, horsemanship classes and private rides for advanced riders. Wintergreen is the only resort in America to offer the sport of vaulting, or gymnastics on horseback.

Trail rides (English tack only) last an hour and 15 minutes. The cost is $32 for resort guests and $38 for the public during the week, $5 more on weekends. Pony rides are $15 for resort guests and $18 for other children. Riding lessons are $28 and $32. Reservations are required. (For more information on Wintergreen, see our Resorts chapter.)

River Ridge Ranch
Va. Rt. 1, Box 119-1, Millboro
• (540) 996-4148

This 377-acre ranch about 10 miles from The Homestead in Bath County offers English or Western guided trail rides through unspoiled forests and fields. There's a spectacular view of the Cowpasture River Valley from one of the trails, and riders can count on seeing wildlife during any of the rides. Fees are $35 for an hour's ride or $90 for a half-day ride plus $5 for lunch. Guests at the ranch receive a 10 percent discount.

Highly popular are the Saturday night haywagon rides and cookouts atop River Ridge Mountain. We're not talking hot dogs on a clothes hanger, but New York strip steaks, barbecued chicken or fresh mountain trout grilled over a campfire. Prices are $27.50 for adults, $12 for children.

River Ridge Ranch has two honeymoon cabins, a lodge and another family unit for overnight accommodations. The ranch can accommodate 12 guests, who have access to fishing and swimming in the Cowpasture River as well as hiking. Cabins rent for $120 per night, double occupancy. The family unit can accommodate four to six people for $160 per night, and lodge rooms are $100 per night, double occupancy. All rates include a full country breakfast. River Ridge is open from April 1 to Thanksgiving.

The Homestead Resort
U.S. Hwy. 220, Hot Springs
• (540) 839-5500, (800) 838-1766

Guided trail rides are among the many activities offered at this highly acclaimed resort in Bath County. There are more than 100 miles of trails through beautiful mountain terrain and alongside the resort's golf courses. The riding master can accommodate either English- or Western-style riders. Rides lasting from 45 minutes to an hour are $60 per person, including a mandatory helmet. Rides depart the historic stables across from the hotel on the hour from 9:30 AM to 2:30 PM. Reservations are necessary. Children who are at least 4-feet tall are welcome. (See our Resorts chapter for more on The Homestead.)

Virginia Mountain Outfitters
55 Lost Creek Ln., Buena Vista
• (540) 261-1910

Outfitter Deborah Sensabaugh and her horses stay busy year round on a variety of trips in the Blue Ridge and Alleghany mountains. Half-day trail rides covering about 10 miles of mountain trails are $50 per person, including a hearty picnic lunch.

Full-day rides follow any one of the 100 miles of trails Sensabaugh knows. Tell her what you'd like to see — scenic overlooks, deep woods, mountain streams — and she'll oblige. The price is $85 per person for the seven-hour trip. Sensabaugh also organizes overnight rides and furnishes everything except sleeping bags and personal items. Camping ranges from primitive national forest sites to privately owned campgrounds with full services. In either case, there's always access to water for swimming and fishing, so bring your suits and fishing gear.

Overnighters are $170 per person, which includes all meals from lunch on the arrival day to lunch and an afternoon snack the following day.

For a three- to five-night getaway, sign up for a pack trip covering 75 to 100 miles. Rides take place in all kinds of weather and cover all kinds of terrain, and Sensabaugh offers a generous dose of history and trail lore along the way. These outings cost $90 per person per day — a price that includes all meals, tents and camping gear other than sleeping bags.

Sensabaugh can tailor a ride to your abilities and desires. She also offers discounts for riders staying at Lavender Hills Farm, a nearby bed and breakfast inn (see our Bed and Breakfasts and Country Inns chapter).

Rock 'N' Horse Stable
Va. Rt. 782, Natural Bridge
• (540) 291-2381

Take in the natural beauty on a guided horseback ride along the trails of the lower Shenandoah Valley. Rock 'N' Horse Stable offers year-round trail rides into the Jefferson National Forest. Rides are $20 for an hour, $50 for a half-day ride and $100 for a full day on the trails. The shorter rides pass through wooded areas, while the longer rides pass along more scenic trails. The day-long rate includes lunch on the trail. Riders must be a minimum of 56 inches tall.

Mt. Rogers High Country Outdoor Center
Va. Rt. 603, Troutdale • (540) 677-3900

This family-owned business has many years' experience in providing wilderness adventures in the Mt. Rogers National Recreation area southwest of Floyd and Pulaksi counties. Day rides, covered-wagon trips and pack trips all originate at the Livery Base Camp in Troutdale. All-day rides in the high country, including lunch, are $75 per person for a group of one to three people, $60 per person for four or more. For those who prefer shorter rides, the cost is $15 for an hour, $25 for two.

A most unusual trip is the covered-wagon excursion into the mountains where wild horses still run free. You can ride a horse alongside the wagons, if you like, for $20 more than the usual fare ($45 for one to three people, $40 for four or more). A one-hour wagon ride costs $10 per person. Overnight covered-wagon treks cost $200 per person, including all meals and equipment except sleeping bags. Overnight horse trips with pack mules are $125 per day per person, including meals and equipment other than sleeping bags. Groups of 10 or more receive special rates.

Hungry Mother State Park
2854 Park Blvd., Marion • (540) 783-3422

A few miles north of Marion is a state park known for its beautiful woodlands and placid 108-acre lake in the heart of the mountains.

The diverse topography of the region makes for never-ending challenges on the golf course.

It's also home to Hemlock Haven, an attractive conference center.

At Hungry Mother, half-hour guided trail rides cost $8 per person. If you have small children, let them sit right behind you on the park's gentle horses. The stables are open from Memorial Day to Labor Day. Accommodations at the park include campsites and housekeeping cabins (see this chapter's Camping section for rates).

Hunting

A fellow once commented that he hunted to feed his body and his soul. In the Blue Ridge of Virginia, no hunter goes hungry.

As expected, wildlife is concentrated around farmland or other areas where there is food. With much of the Blue Ridge comprised of the 1.5 million acres of the George Washington and Jefferson National Forests and state lands, food for wildlife is abundant.

An annual $3 stamp is required to hunt in the national forest and can be purchased at most outlets that sell hunting licenses. Maps of the forests are sold through their regional offices listed at the end of this section. Ask about hunting regulations, license outlets and seasons and bag limits for the particular county you plan to visit.

Hunting is allowed in designated areas of five Virginia state parks, including Fairy Stone in nearby Patrick County, Cumberland State Forest and Grayson Highlands State Park in Grayson County. A $5 hunting fee applies for some counties. Also in Patrick County, **Primland Hunting Reserve** in Claudville, a half-hour south of the Blue Ridge Parkway, is a well-known hunting preserve of 10,000 acres specializing in birds, deer and even sporting clays. Call Rick Hill at (540) 251-8012 for details. Guides and dogs are available.

Westvaco Corporation, a huge paper and bleached board milling concern, also offers hunting and fishing permits on vast holdings of company land in Virginia and West Virginia. Westvaco's office address is listed at the end of this section.

The most popular game are squirrel, grouse, bear, deer, bobcat, fox, duck, rabbit, pheasant and quail. For truly adventurous pioneers, muzzle-loading rifles, bow and arrow and other primitive weapons are allowed at various times.

The Blue Ridge is home to most of the record-setting areas for hunting in Virginia. Latest statistics single out Bedford County for having the highest turkey harvest of 498 birds. Bedford also came in second highest for deer, with 5,753. In 1993 Virginia's five north-central mountain counties (Alleghany, Augusta, Bath, Highland and Rockbridge) accounted for a whopping 15,640 whitetail deer harvested.

Whether you're going on your own or signing up with a hunting lodge, you're going to need a valid license, which can be obtained by clerks of circuit courts and other authorized agents (see listings in this section). Licenses and permits are good from July 1 through June 30. Hunting seasons and bag limits are set by the Virginia Department of Game and Inland Fisheries and vary according to county. Some counties are off-limits to hunters of certain species, while others have liberal hunting rules.

Take note that one outstanding hunting lodge is **Fort Lewis Lodge** in Millboro, Bath County. It's a mountain paradise. Call John Cowden at (540) 925-2314.

The best suggestion to assure you are hunting within the bounds of the rules and regulations is to send for the latest pamphlet from the Department of Game and Inland Fisheries, "Hunting and Trapping in Virginia Regulations." The brochure lists everything you need to know about how and where to hunt in the Blue Ridge, or where to find specific game information. It also lists specific license requirements and fees. To obtain the brochure, write or call the **Department of Games and Inland Fisheries**, 4010 W. Broad Street, Richmond 23230; (804) 367-1000.

For other information about where to hunt in the Blue Ridge, write or call the following:

Virginia State Parks, 203 Governor Street, Suite 306, Richmond 23219; (804) 786-1712.

George Washington and Jefferson National Forests, 5162 Valleypointe Parkway, Roanoke 24019; (540) 265-5100.

Westvaco Corporation, Appalachian Woodlands, P.O. Box 577, Rupert, West Virginia 25984.

Ice-skating

Charlottesville Ice Park
230 W. Main St. • **(804) 979-1ICE,**
(804) 984-2151

Opened in 1996, the Charlottesville Ice Park is getting plenty of local and regional attention. Lessons and the Pro Shop cater to both figure skaters and ice hockey players. The rink even has its own hockey team. Public skating times vary, so you will want to call ahead. During the summer months, it's open at 10 AM during the week and 1 PM on weekends. Prices average $5 on weekdays and $6 on weekends. Skate rentals run from 50¢ to $2, depending on the day you go. Weekends, naturally, are more expensive. The ice park is on the west end of the downtown pedestrian mall, close to several theaters, movie houses and a plethora of restaurants and shops.

The Homestead Resort
U.S. Hwy. 220, Hot Springs
• (800) 838-1766, (540) 839-7740

The Homestead Resort in Hot Springs offers ice-skating action outdoors. The Olympic-size rink is at the base of the ski slopes and opens around Thanksgiving weekend. Although it closes for Christmas, skating usually runs from 9 AM to 5 PM daily through the second week in March, weather permitting. The hours are extended on the same evenings that the resort holds night skiing. A half-day pass costs $6 or $5 for children 12 and younger. Skate rental is $4 for a half-day and $2.50 for children. Ski-and-skate packages are available. (See our Resorts chapter for more information on this posh resort.)

Mountain Biking

Virginia's Blue Ridge and neighboring Alleghany Mountains are a mountain biker's mecca. From technically and physically demanding single-track to gravel roads and rider-friendly rail-trail conversions, bikers have a wide range of terrain to suit their abilities.

New in 1996 was Randy Porter's book, *A Mountain Biker's Guide to Western Virginia*, which provides specific descriptions for moun-

tain-biking destinations including woods roads, trails and rough roads west of the Blue Ridge, primarily in the George Washington and Jefferson National Forests.

The majority of public land open to mountain biking is in the George Washington and Jefferson National Forests, which encompass more than 1.5 million acres of mountain lands. The forests are divided into a number of ranger districts, with individual maps available showing most of the trails, forest roads and other significant features for two-wheel travel. The Washington and Jefferson National Forests contain several thousand miles of trails and gravel roads, all of which are open to mountain bikers, with the exception of the Appalachian Trail and those trails within designated wilderness areas.

If you are a beginning mountain-bike rider, you should probably stick to forest development roads until you get the hang of using all the gears on sometimes long climbs and steep descents. While single-track riding — also called narrow trail riding — is often touted as the epitome of the mountain-bike experience, ascents and descents on rough, rocky and sometimes minimally maintained surfaces can be pretty tricky.

For those of you planning to get into the sport of cycling, here are some tips from the *Roanoke Times* on how to avoid injuries: Make certain the bike fits your body and that you have a proper-fitting helmet; Be aware of road and/or trail hazards such as pot holes, branches or rocks; Never cycle too closely behind another mountain biker; Learn proper braking techniques, such as applying the front brake when trying to stop; Purchase a bicycle with good shock absorbers; Do not ride too fast; Ride with a partner at the same skill level.

Regardless of experience, anyone riding in the national forest should heed the following advice:

Since none of the backcountry trails are maintained for continuous riding, you can expect to carry your bicycle across obstacles. Outside of designated wildernesses, you may ride behind the gated and mounded earth tank traps of closed roads. These roads are closed to motorized vehicles but are open to pedal-powered bicycles, horses and hikers.

While riding the trails, anticipate meeting horse riders and hikers. Hold your riding speed down on narrow trails and when approaching blind curves. You should be able to stop in half the distance you can see in front of you. Just as hikers should yield to horse riders, mountain bikers should yield to both horse riders and hikers by stopping and allowing them to pass when meeting head on, or by dismounting and asking to pass when meeting from behind. As the newest user group in the backcountry, mountain bicyclists have to earn the respect of hikers and horse riders, while those more established user groups learn to share the trails with you. Mutual cooperation and courtesy will go a long way toward keeping backcountry trails open to all users.

The following companies offer cycling tours in Virginia:

VCC Four Seasons Cycling, 119 Madison Road, Orange 22960; (800) 245-3868

Vermont Bicycle Touring, Travent International, P.O. Box 711, Bristol, Vermont 05445; (800) 245-3868

Backroads, 1516 Fifth Street, Suite L101, Berkeley, California 94710-1740; (800) 462-2848

For more information on Virginia bicycle clubs, maps and rides, contact the Virginia Department of Transportation, State Bicycle Coordinator, 1401 E. Broad Street, Richmond 23219; (800) 835-1203.

The Big Levels
Along Coal Rd., near Sherando Lake

The Big Levels area near Sherando Lake in the Pedlar Ranger District of the Washington and Jefferson National Forests is a favorite for many mountain bikers. The Big Levels is a great place for pedaling along the relatively flat Reservoir Trail and Orebank Creek Road or any of the myriad unmarked former logging roads that meander through these 32,000 wooded acres.

Washington & Old Dominion Railroad Regional Trail
21st St., Purcellville • (703) 729-0596

Millions of riders in Northern Virginia escape to this 45-mile asphalt route from the Purcellville Train Station trailhead in Loudoun County to Shirlington in Arlington County. It's a fairly flat route and the asphalt paving makes it easier for the whole family to ride. Along the way, you'll pass several restored bridges and traverse a heavily wooded corridor. Closer to Arlington, the trail meets up with the 17-mile Mount Vernon Trail, giving bikers even more options.

Lignite Trail
Off Va. Rt. 685, just past the Fenwick Mines picnic shelter • (540) 828-5195

Hardier and more skillful riders will enjoy this trail as it ascends Bald Mountain via a number of tortuous switchbacks before arriving at the Bald Mountain Primitive Road just off the Blue Ridge Parkway.

Walnut Creek Park
Old Lynchburg Rd, Charlottesville • (804) 296-5844

More than 10 miles of twisting single-track trail in this Albemarle County park is designed with the intermediate rider in mind. There are plenty of challenging climbs and quick descents in the upper portion of the park. For the less experienced, an easier route follows along the lake's dam.

Wintergreen Resort
Va. Rt. 151, Wintergreen • (804) 325-8166

This Nelson County resort recently opened its trails to mountain bikers. With more than

---

INSIDERS' TIP

Outdoor enthusiasts should be aware that hunters may use the same state and national forests during hunting season. It might be a good idea to check with the Department of Game and Inland Fisheries at (804) 367-1000 to find out the dates and locations of Virginia's various hunting seasons.

112 miles covering Wintergreen and the Big Levels area of the George Washington National Forest, there are plenty of routes to occupy hardy riders. The Outdoor Wilderness School at Wintergreen Resort can get you on your way.

North River Gorge Trail
Dry River District, off Va. Rt. 718 to Forest Rd. 95 • (540) 828-2591

This is one of the George Washington section's flatter trails. Beginning mountain bikers may find more comfort along this one. Use the parking lot for Wild Oak Trail.

Hidden Valley Trail
Warm Springs District, off Va. Rt. 621 on Forest Rd. 241 • (540) 839-2521, (800) 628-8092

Beginners may also enjoy this trail because of its flatness. An added bonus to riding on this route is the accessibility of a cool trout stream that runs adjacent to it, great for fishing or just cooling off.

New River Trail State Park
Va. Rt. 48, Galax, • (540) 699-6778

Heading into Southwest Virginia, you'll find this splendid rail-trail conversion that offers fantastic mountain-biking opportunities. The 57-mile New River Trail is actually a state park that runs from Pulaski to Fries and Galax, 29 miles of it adjacent to the New River, thought to be the second-oldest river in the world. Numerous access points are along the way, but your ride will be made easier by purchasing a $4 "Map and User's Guide" and arranging a shuttle through Lanny Sparks at New River Bicycles, (540) 980-1741. His shop is in Draper, the 6-mile point along the trail.

Mountain Lake Resort
Mountain Lake • (800) 346-3334, (540) 552-4641

In 1997, Mountain Lake opened nearly 20 miles of its hiking trails for mountain bikers. The trails are wide, well marked and feature a hard surface with low to no mud. Rated moderate to difficult, they offer a challenge for beginners and the more advanced riders. Two major cycling events were held at Mountain

Lake in 1998. The Misty Mountain Hop, an eight-mile race sponsored by the National Off-Road Bicycling Association, was the highest mountain bike race on the East Coast and the largest sanctioned race in the state. At 4,000 feet above sea level, Mountain Lake's trails offer spectacular views. The other exciting cycling event was the two-day Mountains of Misery Challenge. More than 200 riders were faced with a 5-mile Category I climb to finish at Mountain Lake. Adult and children's mountain bikes — Trek 820s, 830s and 220s — are available for rent along with helmets and child seats at the resort.

The Virginia Creeper Trail
Off Va. Rt. 91, Damascus

Although you'll no longer hear the whistle from the old Virginia Creeper, you'll most certainly enjoy making tracks downhill from Whitetop Station through Damascus and on to the end of the line at Abingdon along the Virginia Creeper Trail. Maintained jointly by the Town of Abingdon and the Mount Rogers National Recreation Area in the Jefferson section of the National Forest, you're sure to enjoy the ease of riding and spectacular scenery along this 33-mile former rail bed. Like the New River Trail, there are numerous access points from which to enter the trail, but many cyclists enjoy arranging a ride through Blue Blaze Shuttle Service, (540) 475-5095, in Damascus and careening downhill from Whitetop Station.

Lori Finley's *Mountain Biking the Appalachians: Northwest North Carolina/Southwest Virginia*, published by John F. Blair, provides a lot of good information about traveling along the Virginia Creeper and New River Trails as well as the Mount Rogers National Recreation Area, (540) 783-5196. According to forest service literature, "Whoever invented mountain bicycles surely had the Mount Rogers National Recreation Area in mind!" Finley has gone the distance to share Mount Rogers' best mountain-biking spots.

In addition, the Clinch Ranger District, (540) 328-2931, of the Jefferson section of the national forest has a brochure available detailing four loop rides. The headquarters for the National Forests is in Roanoke, (540) 265-6054, and a service center for the George Washington section is in Harrisonburg, (540) 564-8300.

Advice on additional places to ride in either section of the national forest is as close as any bike shop or district ranger office. In addition, both Douthat State Park, (540) 862-7200, just north of Clifton Forge, and Grayson Highlands State Park, (540) 579-7092, adjoining the southern edge of the Mount Rogers Recreation Area, allow mountain biking on their trails. Assistant park manager Sandie Purick and the staff at Grayson Highlands have developed what may be the first two mountain-bike trail guides in the Virginia State Park System to help two-wheel travelers find their way around the park.

Swimming

Swimmers who enjoy the outdoors can count on the cool mountain streams, lakes and even waterfalls of Virginia's Blue Ridge for the most refreshing dip they'll ever take.

Municipal pools, such as the Town of Blacksburg's, perched atop a mountain vista, or the City of Radford's, beside the ancient New River, are a panacea to the eye and spirit by virtue of their environmentally beautiful settings.

Some of the best swimming can be found in the area's state parks and national forests. Picture yourself swimming at the bottom of a sparkling waterfall after a 2-mile hike at the Cascades in Pembroke in Giles County. Or how about lying on Claytor Lake's white sand beach in Pulaski County while horseback riders amble by! For the strong in spirit, there's icy cold Cave Mountain Lake near Glasgow. All have sparse but clean and accommodating changing and shower facilities.

Primitive swimming fans will find the 10-mile venture across the West Virginia border to Blue Bend near Covington worthwhile to delight in the coldest water in the Blue Ridge.

Families with small children will be interested in an abundance of private campgrounds with lovely swimming areas overseen by lifeguards. One of the best known is Shenandoah Acres Resort at Stuarts Draft, near the Waynesboro intersection of Skyline Drive and the Blue Ridge Parkway.

Following is an Insiders' list of swimming sites definitely worth the drive from anywhere.

Municipal Pools

War Memorial Pool
Ridgeview Park, at end of Magnolia Ave., Waynesboro • (540) 942-6767

War Memorial Pool, in the center of lovely Ridgeview Park, is surrounded by a playground, tennis courts, a baseball diamond and an open field. The managers of this Olympic-size pool pride themselves on its cleanliness and pleasing view.

Open from Memorial Day to Labor Day, the pool's general admission hours are from noon to 7:30 PM Monday through Saturday and 1 to 7:30 PM on Sunday. Fees are $1 for ages 15 and younger and $2 for folks 16 and older.

Gypsy Hill Park Pool
Constitution Dr., Staunton
• (540) 886-6846

This fairly new L-shaped pool is Olympic-size and has a wading pool. The facility opens for the season around Memorial Day and closes Labor Day. It's open from 11 AM to 6 PM Monday through Saturday and from 1 to 6 PM on Sunday. The fee is $1 for ages 16 and older, 50¢ for ages 1 to 15 and free to children younger than 1.

Roanoke City Pools
Fallon Park Pool, 2024 Dale Ave.
• (540) 853-2206
Washington Park Pool, 1616 Burrell Ave.
• (540) 853-2369

The City of Roanoke Parks and Recreation Department offers two outdoor municipal swimming pools. The pools are both L-shaped and 50 meters in length with a diving well and an additional wading pool for youth younger than 6. The pools are open from Memorial Day to Labor Day. The hours for operation are noon to 6 PM Sunday through Thursday and noon to 8 PM Friday and Saturday. Admission is $2 for ages 16 and older, $1 for ages 6 to 15 and free for children 5 and younger. Both facilities offer swimming lessons and special events and may be rented for special occasions during non-programmed hours.

Charlottesville Municipal Pools

Washington Park Pool, 14th St. and Preston Ave. • (804) 977-2607
Onesty Pool, Meade Ave.
• (804) 295-7532
Crow Pool, Rosehill Dr. • (804) 977-1362
Smith Pool, Cherry Ave. • (804) 977-1960
McIntire Pool, U.S. 250 Bypass
• (804) 295-9072
Forest Hills Pool, Forest Hills Ave.
• (804) 296-1444

The city of Charlottesville boasts six municipal pools: two outdoor (Washington Park and Onesty); two indoor (Crow and Smith); and two wading pools (McIntire and Forest Hills). The outdoor and indoor pools are all 25 yards long, and the facilities feature showers, hair dryers and lockers. The indoor pools are heated. The wading pools are small and shallow, designed for children 12 and younger.

The outdoor and wading pools are open from Memorial Day to Labor Day. The hours for the outdoor pools are noon to 6 PM Monday through Friday and noon to 5 PM Saturday and Sunday. The wading pools are open 10:30 AM to 4:30 PM Monday through Friday and noon to 5 PM Saturday and Sunday. The indoor pools are open year round, but hours are widely varied, so call ahead of time. Admission for nonresidents for the outdoor and indoor facilities is $3.75 for children and $4.50 for adults. There is no charge for the wading pools.

Miller Park Pool

301 Grove St., Lynchburg
• (804) 528-9794

Two play areas and a place for picnics surround this pool in Miller Park. The Olympic-size pool features a high dive and a kiddie area. Lessons are offered each morning. Miller Park Pool is open from Memorial Day through Labor Day. Hours are noon to 7 PM Monday through Friday, 11 AM to 6 PM on Saturday and 1 to 7 PM on Sunday. Admission is $1.75 for all ages. Pass books of 10 tickets can be purchased for $12.50. These can be used for afternoon or evening swim sessions.

Blacksburg Public Pools

Graves Ave. (outdoor), Patrick Henry Dr. (indoor) • (540) 961-1103

Scenery lovers will be thrilled at the panoramic view from the Graves Avenue mountaintop outdoor facility, which is open from 1 to 5 PM Tuesday through Saturday June through mid-August. The fee is 75¢ for ages 3 to 14 and $1 for ages 15 and up. The pool is off S. Main Street, past Blacksburg Middle School. For indoor swimming, Blacksburg's 25-yard indoor pool has six lanes, a sauna, a spa and a diving area. The Blacksburg Aquatic Center is open Monday through Friday from 6 AM to 9 PM, Saturday from 9 AM to 9 PM and Sunday from 1 to 6 PM. The fee until 7 PM is $2.50 for adults and $2 for children and senior citizens. To swim after 7 PM it is $2 for adults and $1.50 for children and seniors. The pool is across from Blacksburg High.

Bisset Park Pool

Off Norwood St., Radford
• (540) 731-3633

Radford's city pool is an Olympic-size swimming pool in Bisset Park, just off Norwood Street, bordering nearly a mile of the scenic New River. Its setting in a 58-acre municipal park makes this pool unique. It is surrounded by six lighted tennis courts, lighted picnic shelters, playgrounds, a gazebo and fitness station. The facility is open May 23 through Labor Day. Hours are Monday through Friday 1 to 5 PM and weekends 1 to 8 PM. Admission is $1 for ages 7 to 15 and $1.25 for ages 16 and older. Children younger than 6 are admitted free with a paying adult.

State Park Swim Areas

Claytor Lake

Off I-81 at Exit 33, near Dublin
• (540) 674-5492

At this beautiful park in Pulaski County, you'll think you're on an ocean beach, with the ample white sand surrounded by a full-service boat marina beside the sparkling water. Camping, horseback riding (rentals available) and sport fishing are also popular at this

4,500-acre lake and surrounding natural areas.

Smith Mountain Lake State Park
Off Va. Rt. 626 S. • (540) 297-4062

This lakefront beach nestled in the tall blue mountains of Bedford County offers a never-ending show of gliding sailboats in the distance. It's paradise for water enthusiasts and has a visitors center with especially good nature programs for the whole family during the summer. Special events include the Ruritans Bass Fishing Tournament in March, an Arts in the Park in June and Ruritan Supper and Festival in September. From U.S. 460, take Va. 43 to Va. 626 S. to access the park and lake.

National Forest Swim Areas

Sherando Lake
I-64 Exit 96, south of Waynesboro
• (540) 828-2591

Sherando Lake, in the George Washington section of the national forest, offers a pristine beach within a natural paradise of camping, boating and fishing. The daily swimming fee is $10 per carload.

Cave Mountain Lake
Off Va. Rt. 781, near Natural Bridge
• (540) 265-5100

This seemingly long trip to isolation is worth it. Cave Mountain Lake Campground, in the Jefferson section of the national forest, is nearby with its unusual picnic tables and sites often surrounded by stone, set amidst large pines and hardwoods. There is a large open field with plenty of sunshine, and the lake is cool and refreshing. It's a real getaway.

From I-81, take Natural Bridge Exit 175 or 180 and turn onto Va. Route 130 at Natural Bridge. Follow this road 3.2 miles, then turn onto Va. Route 759, which you'll follow for 3.2 miles and then turn right onto Va. Route 781. Drive 1.6 miles to the recreation area's paved entrance road.

Cascades Recreation Area
Off Va. Rt. 623 near Pembroke
• (540) 265-5100

Cascades features a 3-mile hike to a 60-foot waterfall. Picture yourself hiking and then jumping into a cool, placid pool of water right under a thundering waterfall. This is one of the most photogenic sites in the New River Valley. Warning: don't try jumping into the water from the cliffs of the waterfall. There have been at least three deaths in recent memory from careless youths who did. This swimming area is not recommended for small children. For more information write George Washington and Jefferson National Forests, 5162 Valleypointe Parkway, Roanoke 24019. To get there from Pembroke in Giles County, return to U.S. 460, head north and west about a mile, then turn right onto Va. 623 to Cascades Recreation Area.

Monongahela National Forest
Blue Bend Recreation Area, west of W.Va. Hwy. 92, near Alvon, W.Va.
• (304) 536-1440

A true "swimming hole," Blue Bend is known for its chilling mountain stream waters surrounded by huge, flat rocks — perfect for sunbathers. Built by Civilian Conservation Corps camp workers during the Great Depression, the rock craftsmanship makes this place unusual. There is no more invigorating feeling in the world than baptism by Blue Bend's waters. Swimming is within view of an authentic swinging footbridge. Primitive camping and picnic tables are nearby in this deeply wooded, out-of-the-way area populated mostly by locals. Don't miss this place, but be prepared for a chilly experience. Blue Bend is said to earn its name from the color of the swimmers' lips when they emerge! From I-64, take the White Sulphur Springs (West Virginia) exit to W.Va. 92; go north 10 miles to Alvon. Turn left at the Blue Bend sign and proceed several miles to the Blue Bend Recreation Area.

It's usually warmer
skiing in the Blue Ridge
than in New England
or out West.

Skiing

Skiing requires two things: mountains and snow. Virginia's Blue Ridge has both in abundance.

Throughout this book we've shown you that the Blue Ridge has more mountains than a redhead has freckles. Wintergreen and Massanutten, two of the region's four ski resorts, have vertical drops of 1,000 feet or better; they don't come any higher south of New York. Those mountains attract the white stuff and can keep it, with temperatures ranging 10 to 20 degrees lower than in the flatlands. Natural snowfall will vary from year to year, but the snow on the slopes stays surprisingly consistent because of aggressive snowmaking and the use of Snomax, a process that makes better snow at higher temperatures. Just because you're not driving in a blizzard doesn't mean they're not skiing up a storm at Wintergreen, Massanutten, Bryce and The Homestead.

There is a catch, but you're going to like it. It's usually warmer skiing in the Blue Ridge than in New England or out West. At Wintergreen you can even ski and play golf the same day. Warm temperatures also account for the popularity of night skiing in the region. All four resorts described in this chapter have lighted slopes, which means more schuss for your buck on a ski trip. And night skiing rates are almost always cheaper than day rates.

You have to sleep sometime, but while you do, fleets of snowcats, highly sophisticated mechanical behemoths, are stalking the slopes, bulldozing moguls, pulverizing icy spots and smoothing trails so that you're greeted with a brand-new surface come morning.

All that high-tech equipment is fueled with money, but area ski resorts are finding they can afford it. In recent years, the Southeast has shown more growth in skier visits and ski lessons than any other part of the country, according to the Ski Virginia Association. Getting all those skiers to the top of the mountain has led to more and faster lifts, including Virginia's first quad chair, at Massanutten.

Blue Ridge resorts also have kept pace with the shredders, those derring-do snowboard enthusiasts, by providing snowboard parks, rental boards and lessons. Wintergreen's snowboarders receive an hour-long lesson free with board rentals. Massanutten and The Homestead even offer the latest craze, snow tubing.

Since skiers have to rest, eat and party too, off-the-slope facilities at our four ski areas offer spas, après ski activities and good restaurants. These are year-round resorts (see our Resorts chapter), so they excel at everything, even keeping nonskiers happy.

"More and more people are discovering that Virginia offers a terrific ski resort experience, with great skiing and activities for the whole family," says Mark Glickman, president of the Virginia Ski Association.

We haven't attempted to give you rates because there are so many variables: whether you ski during the day or at night, rent or bring your own equipment, stay at the ski area or elsewhere or take a private or group lesson. Generally, you can expect to pay $15 to $20 for a full-day midweek lift ticket and $25 to $33 for a weekend day pass. All the resorts have cost-saving packages. Look for some of the best prices on weekdays; you'll also find fewer lines and more room on the slopes Monday through Friday.

Of the four resorts listed here, only The Homestead rents cross-country skis and provides trails. But if you own your own equipment, you can make tracks alongside the Blue Ridge Parkway, Skyline Drive, in Mount Rogers National Recreation Area in Southwest Virginia and almost any place with hiking trails or fire roads.

Just go with friends and always be prepared for emergencies. See our chapter called

The Blue Ridge Parkway and Skyline Drive for further information.

For more ski information, order free brochures from Ski Virginia Association, P.O. Box 454, Nellysford 22958, (800) THE-SNOW.

Shenandoah Valley

Bryce Resort
Va. Rt. 263, Basye
• (540) 856-2121

This intimate, family-oriented ski resort is a little more than an hour from the Washington Beltway and less than three hours from Richmond. A few miles off Interstate 81, Bryce is tucked into the folds of the Shenandoah Mountains. It's owned by the approximately 450 families who own homes there. Many skiers drive to Bryce from the Washington, D.C., area, but the resort is also popular with the locals, particularly on weekday evenings, when they can ski under the lights and then warm up with a hot-buttered rum in the glass-walled Copper Kettle Lounge.

Manfred Locher manages the resort, and his brother, Horst, directs the ski school, the ski area and an extensive racing program. Both have been at Bryce since the resort opened in 1965.

One of Bryce's notable features is its racing program. For more than 20 years, Bryce has sponsored NASTAR races, starting a trend among Southern ski resorts. Every Saturday, Sunday and holiday at 3:30 PM, the NASTAR races begin, offering skiers the chance to test their abilities against the pros. The races are handicapped according to age and gender. Bryce also has a weekend ski program to train skiers for sanctioned U.S. Ski Association races.

Bryce's seven slopes cover 20 acres and are serviced by two double-chair lifts and three rope tows. The resort averages 40 inches of natural snow annually but produces enough to blanket all trails. The broad beginners area is visible from the deck and two lodges at the base. One lodge houses the Copper Kettle Lounge and a restaurant serving hearty breakfasts, lunches and dinner. The second lodge houses a cafeteria, ski rental and repair facility and a ski shop.

The Horst Locher Ski School offers private and group lessons, including a SKIwee program for children ages 4½ to 8.

In the summer, grass skiing is a popular sport at Bryce. Invented in Europe as a summer training method for skiers, grass skiing mimics snow skiing but substitutes short, treadlike skates for skis. Rentals and lessons in grass skiing are offered in the summer and fall.

Condos, chalets and townhouses near the slopes are available for weekend rentals or long-term stays. For lodging information and reservations, call (800) 821-1444. Ski hours are 9 AM to 9:30 PM.

Bryce is 11 miles from I-81. Take Exit 273 at Mt. Jackson and then follow Va. Route 263 W. to Bayse and Bryce Resort.

Massanutten Resort
Va. Rt. 644, Harrisonburg
• (540) 289-9441, (800) 207-MASS

An easy two-hour drive from Richmond, Washington, D.C., or Roanoke, Massanutten Resort sits in the heart of the Shenandoah Valley atop Massanutten Mountain, once a haven for moonshiners. The resort's 14 trails and 68 acres of skiing tower above an attractive, spacious lodge at the base. Inside are a cafeteria, convenience store and glass-walled nightclub with a big dance floor. This place gets really lively on Saturday nights. Another nice feature of the lodge is a large windowed room with tables and chairs where guests can bring their own food, "camp out" during the day and watch the skiing without spending a dime.

The resort gets only about 34 inches of natural snowfall a year but has greatly expanded its snowmaking capability. In Virginia's Blue Ridge, Massanutten has been the first to open and the last to close the past five seasons.

Diamond Jim, a 3,400-foot run with a vertical drop of 1,110 feet, is Massanutten's most challenging slope, starting at the resort's highest point (2,880 feet) alongside ParaDice, the

Photo: Wintergreen Resort

Spend your winter vacation swooshing down snowy mountainsides.

other expert trail. Both are lighted for night skiing and are served by Virginia's first quad chairlift. Ski hours are 9 AM to 10 PM.

Snowboarders have not been left out of the winter fun. A snowboarders-only park with bumps and a quarterpipe is served by its own J-bar lift. Rentals and lessons are also available along with the excitement of participating in fun competitions.

A new activity that has attracted all ages was added in 1997. Massanutten became the first resort in the state to open a snow tubing park. See our Close-up later in this chapter.

Children 5 and younger receive free lift tickets. For children 4 to 12, the Ski Wee program includes lessons, rentals, lift tickets and lunch. On Saturdays and Sundays, one trail is devoted to NASTAR racing. Massanutten Adaptive Ski School, an extensive program for the disabled, is another special feature at Massanutten.

You can take advantage of overnight lodging and ski packages at Massanutten's chalets, villas and hotel rooms and at hotels in nearby Harrisonburg. The resort's supply of overnight accommodations is limited, so reserve early. For those lucky enough to stay "on mountain," a sports complex called Le Club offers indoor swimming, a sauna, outdoor hot tubs, an exercise room, children's movies, table tennis and more.

To get there from I-81, exit onto Va. 33 E. in Harrisonburg. Go 10 miles to Va. 644, where you will see signs to the resort.

East of the Blue Ridge

Wintergreen
Va. Rt. 664, Wintergreen
• **(804) 325-2200, (800) 325-2200,**
Skiing magazine has called Wintergreen

"the South's single-best ski resort," and it continues to live up to its reputation in accommodations, restaurants, shops and other amenities. The mountain has 17 slopes, ranging from a vast beginners area to the Highlands, a three-slope complex with a drop of more than 1,000 feet, and runs up to 4,450 feet long for advanced skiers. The recently added snowboard park features jumps and other obstacles for those who want to take to the slopes on a single board.

Wintergreen's ski patrol is consistently ranked among the best in the nation by the National Ski Patrol Association. In addition, all skiers and snowboarders who rent equipment from Wintergreen are entitled to a free learn-to-ski lesson, another of the resort's efforts to promote safe skiing. Ski hours are 9 AM to 4:30 PM daily. Night skiing is from 5 to 10 PM Sunday through Friday and from 6 to 11 PM on Saturday.

You can ski in the morning and golf at the Stoney Creek course in the afternoon for the price of a ski ticket. The 3,000-foot difference in elevation between the mountaintop and the valley golf course translates into a 10- to 15-degree temperature change that makes it possible for you to golf and ski on the same day.

A summit ski area, the resort's accommodations and facilities are at the top of the slopes. The restaurant and condominium complexes offer extraordinary views up the spine of the Blue Ridge and off to each side. To the west is the Shenandoah Valley and to the east, the Piedmont.

The resort's headquarters is the Mountain Inn, which underwent a spectacular $5 million renovation in 1993. Guests can have a sandwich or hot cappuccino by the fire in the Gristmill lobby or browse an array of shops selling everything from exquisite hand-knit sweaters to Blue Ridge Mountain quilts.

The Wintergarden Spa complex has an indoor pool, a Jacuzzi, hot tubs, saunas, an exercise room and the Garden Terrace Restaurant. Dining at Wintergreen is exceptional in quality and variety. The Copper Mine features gourmet dining in an elegant atmosphere, the Garden Terrace is the place for casual family dining (kids younger than 12 eat free from 5:30 to 6:30 PM), and Cooper's Vantage serves

salads, burgers and cocktails for lunch and dinner. Wintergreen has seven eateries in all plus a grocery store where you can get goods to stock the condo kitchen. The 4,000-square-foot Blue Ridge Terrace offers outdoor barbecue and music on the slopes on weekends. The Treehouse, at the top of the beginner slope, houses the resort's innovative Camp Wintergreen kids' programs for ages 2½ to 12.

From areas north or east of Wintergreen, follow I-64 W. to Exit 107 (Crozet, U.S. 250). Take U.S. 250 W. to Va. 151 S. and turn left. Follow Va. 151 S. for 14.2 miles to Va. 664 and turn right. Wintergreen is 4.5 miles ahead on Va. 664. You can also get to Wintergreen from the Blue Ridge Parkway via the Reeds Gap exit, between Mileposts 13 and 14. Look for the signs.

Alleghany Highlands

The Homestead Resort
U.S. Hwy. 220, Hot Springs
• **(540) 839-1766**

This elegant hotel became the South's first true ski resort when it opened its slopes in 1959. In the 1950s, ski resorts in the North were experimenting with snowmaking. Under the direction of Austrian native Sepp Kober, known as the "Father of Southern Skiing," investors spent nearly $1 million to develop a 3,000-foot slope on Warm Springs Mountain, along with side trails, a ski mobile and a glass-walled lodge with a circular fire pit, ski equipment shops and a rental service. Since then the slopes have grown 200 feet steeper and the runs more challenging and diverse. The four-wheeled ski mobile has been replaced with modern ski lifts. A snowboard park and 260-foot-long halfpipe were added in 1994. At the base of the slopes is an Olympic-size ice-skating rink with instructors close at hand.

On Saturdays and Sundays tubing is added to the list of outdoor events. A two-hour session cost $10 in 1998-99, the Homestead's first winter of snow tubing.

Today The Homestead is renowned for its ski school and family atmosphere. On the resort's ski staff are several young Austrian ski instructors who can accommodate group, private and children's lessons.

Nine runs are open for day and night skiing, and half-day rates are available. The resort offers packages with special rates for families that include accommodations, breakfast and dinner daily, lift tickets and lessons. You'll also want to take advantage of The Homestead's other sporting facilities, exquisite dining and historic spa (see our Resorts chapter). Ski hours are 9 AM to 5 PM on weekdays, 8 AM to 5 PM on weekends and holidays and 6 to 10 PM on Friday and Saturday.

The Homestead is about 200 miles from Washington, D.C. Take Exit 61 (Va. 257) off I-81, go south on Va. 42, then west on Va. 39. Follow U.S. 220 into Hot Springs. For a lengthier but very scenic route, take I-64 W. off I-81 near Lexington, then Va. 39 W. to U.S. 220 into Hot Springs.

Snow Tubing at Massanutten

Now you can experience the thrill of the slopes without the agony of having two boards strapped to your feet. Snow tubing has come to Virginia.

Massanutten Resort opened Virginia's first snow tubing park during the 1997-98 season, and more than 30,000 people sat down in rubber inner tubes and whisked along the 900-foot long runs. Some Massanutten officials even claim that it's the largest such park on the East Coast.

Largest or not, Patrick Causey was willing to drive his family 230 miles from Virginia Beach for just a day of tubing. In fact, he purchased tickets for two sessions.

"It was a fun thing to do," Causey said. "This was a chance to play in the snow. We don't get snow at home (in Virginia Beach). I'd like to do it every year."

Because the snow tubing park is so popular, Massanutten now offers two-hour sessions daily from 9 AM to 9 PM. With six banked lanes and 300 inner tubes, you'd think there would be plenty to go around, but tickets are a hot commodity on these slopes. If you plan on coming on a weekend, arrive early in the morning. Tickets are limited and they sell out fast.

And here's the good part. No special equipment, clothes or lessons are needed. Just let the helpful Massanutten staff members hook your tube to one of the two lifts, and you're on the way to the summit.

Tube riders come in all shapes and sizes, including 2-year-old Jinah Harrell.

Now, all you have to do is sit down and you're ready for the thrill of being a kid again. That's right. You're sledding with abandon down a steep slope . . . with no sticks attached.

Virginia, the first, largest, and wealthiest of the British colonies in Colonial America, has more historic homes than all other states combined.

Real Estate and Retirement

Thinking of buying a house in the Blue Ridge? You can't beat the quality of life. On many occasions, visitors passing through the area have spied the home of their dreams and clinched a deal even before finding new jobs.

Homes in the Blue Ridge can be found to fit every taste. You'll find modern homes perched atop mountain ridges in resorts such as Bryce, Wintergreen and Massanutten or on the fairway at private communities such as Glenmore and Keswick near Charlottesville. If the classics are more your style, the region is rich in tin-roofed Victorians, such as those in Salem or Edinburg, and New York City-style brownstones in downtown Lexington and Lynchburg. If what you want is a primitive log cabin to fix up, check out the Alleghany Highlands or Southwest Virginia. And if you're looking for a farm, consider the horse country of Loudoun and Albemarle counties, the wine region of Warren County, gorgeous Catawba Valley near Roanoke or isolated country estates in Loudoun, Fauquier, Alleghany, Highland or Bath counties.

You don't have to go to the ocean to live near the water. A visit to Smith Mountain Lake's Bernard Landing's condominiums or the townhomes at Mallard Point along Claytor Lake's white-sand beaches will convince you you're already there.

Virginia, the first, largest and wealthiest of the British colonies in Colonial America, has more historic homes than all other states combined. And the Old Dominion zealously guards these treasures, preventing historic structures from giving way to industry and subdivisions. Nearly 100 old homes are open for visitation, mainly those renovated as museums and bed and breakfasts or open during historic garden weeks, and they do change hands. Two real estate companies specializing in historic homes are Mead Associates in Historic Lexington, an affiliate of Sotheby's International, and McLean Falconer in Charlottesville, the chosen city of movie stars and millionaires, who often favor such houses.

Also, *The Charlottesville Area Real Estate Weekly*, issued by the Charlottesville Area Association of Realtors, is a helpful, comprehensive free guide to real estate in the seven-county area. Pick one up at any one of more than 400 locations in the Central Virginia area or receive a copy in the mail by calling (804) 978-4700.

Lucky visitors may stumble upon their dream homes, but your best bet is to let local real estate professionals know that you're looking. Homes in Middleburg, Warrenton, Charlottesville, South Roanoke and Lexington are often sold by word of mouth before they ever see the marketplace. Realtors can also offer guidance on the best schools and shopping areas and the level of satisfaction in the neighborhood you're considering.

Local real estate boards can answer questions about major developments and fair market prices. In this chapter, we've included information about these boards for each region as well as local homebuilders associations, in case you decide to remodel or build and want reputable contractors. Finally, we offer the average price of a home in each region, as provided by the Multiple Listing Service of the Virginia Association of Realtors.

The following organizations can assist you in making regional or statewide comparisons and can answer questions about purchasing or building a home:

Home Builders Association of Virginia, 1108 E. Main Street, Suite 700, Richmond 23219-3534, (804) 643-2797.

Virginia Association of Realtors, P.O. Box 15719, Richmond 23227, (804) 264-5033

Our Real Estate section is followed by information on retirement services offered in the communities of the Blue Ridge.

Real Estate

Shenandoah Valley

Frederick County

The east end of the city of Winchester, a historic city in the northern Shenandoah Valley, and the southern part of Frederick County are growing rapidly. This is in part a result of the westward migration of Washington-based workers, people willing to commute an hour or so to their jobs in order to live in an area that's less crowded and less costly. But the Winchester area also has a good number of industries that keep the real estate market healthy.

Much of Winchester's beauty comes from the graceful old homes along tree-lined streets and row houses built before and during the Civil War. Many of these row houses, which are a short walk from the pedestrian-only downtown mall, are being restored and remodeled. These average from $250,000 to $375,000. You'll also see a lot of old homes that were built partially of stone. In the newer subdivisions, four- to five-bedroom modern homes range from $300,000 to $400,000.

In Frederick County, the average price of three- and four-bedroom homes in 1997 ranged from $130,000 to $220,000. The county has some developments of modestly priced

homes on small lots that can be bought for less.

For more information on real estate in Winchester and Frederick County, contact:

Blue Ridge Board of Realtors, 181 Garber Lane, Winchester 22602, (540) 667-2606

Top of Virginia Building Association, P.O. Box 744, Winchester 22604, (540) 665-0365

Clarke County

Just to the east of Frederick County, in Clarke County, real estate prices are considerably higher. In 1998 the average price of a three- to five-bedroom home in that beautiful, rural county ranged from $200,000 to $220,000. Also in Clarke, an occasional estate in the country was selling for more than $1.1 million. These estates are usually handed down from one generation to the next so they aren't often on the market.

Clarke County boasts quite a few 19th-century manor homes surrounded by rolling pastures, and these have attracted some of the county's wealthiest newcomers, Washingtonians willing to make the long commute to work or wanting a second home for the weekends.

For more information on real estate in Clarke County, contact:

Blue Ridge Board of Realtors, 181 Garber Lane, Winchester 22602, (540) 667-2606.

Top of Virginia Building Association, P.O. Box 744, Winchester 22604, (540) 665-0365

Warren County

Many federal employees and retirees have moved into Warren County, which includes the town of Front Royal, attracted by the beauty of the land, the relaxed pace and lower real estate prices. The most prized properties here are those with a sense of privacy and clear views of the Shenandoah River or the mountains. While some vacation homes could be bought for as little as $70,000 in 1998, prices ranged as high as $350,000, with an average of about $120,000. An historic estate in this county can cost in the millions, but it's rare when one comes on the market. Spacious new homes on the county's two golf courses, Shenandoah Valley Golf Club and Bowling Green, are as high as $400,000, though they average $250,000 to $300,000. These high-end prices are not reflective of the rest of Warren County, where in early 1999 three-bedroom homes ranged from about $85,000 to $120,000. If you're looking for a more secluded spot, there are a few two-bedroom A-frames in Shenandoah Farms and other remote areas that range from $50,000 to $60,000.

For more information on real estate in Warren County, contact:

Blue Ridge Board of Realtors, 181 Garber Lane, Winchester 22602, (540) 667-2606

Top of Virginia Building Association, P.O. Box 744, Winchester 22604, (540) 665-0365

Shenandoah County

Shenandoah County encompasses several quaint, historic towns, including Woodstock, Edinburg and New Market, along with the Bryce Resort community in Basye. Retirees and young couples are always seeking weekend retreats where the average price of a three-bedroom home was $97,000 in 1998.

On U.S. Highway 11, there are a lot of old homes dating back to the Civil War, some still in need of renovation with prices ranging from $90,000 to $100,000. There are new subdivisions, priced in the high $90s, while east of Woodstock homes start at $175,000.

Bryce Resort (see our Resorts chapter) in western Shenandoah County is an entirely different real estate market. The year-round resort community has chalets, condominiums and townhouses near the resort's ski slopes, lake and other facilities. Prices range from $39,000 to more than $500,000, depending upon the size of the property and its proximity to the slopes. (These range from efficiencies to houses that sleep 15 people.) Bryce Resort includes four timeshare developments but only one, Chalet High, is still selling units. Managed by Alexander Properties, Chalet High is a development of chalets and townhouses on the northern end of Bryce Resort's golf course.

For more information about real estate in Shenandoah County contact:

Massanutten Association of Realtors, 129-C S. Main Street, Woodstock 22664, (540) 459-2937

Shenandoah County Homebuilders Association, c/o Barbara Thompson, 225 Taylortown Road, Edinburg 22824, (540) 984-9218

Page County

Page County is more rural, with much of its land tucked between Massanutten Mountain and the Blue Ridge range farther east. Prices are lower in Page County. Riverfront property is usually more expensive and hard to come by (the south fork of the Shenandoah River runs through Page County, and the north fork winds through Shenandoah County).

For the most part, architectural styles are simple — this is a rural, no-frills kind of region. The county has a few interesting old homes, but brick ramblers, Cape Cods and modest, plainly built homes are more the norm. The average sales price in Page County in 1998 was $80,300 for three- and four-bedroom homes.

For more information about real estate in Page County contact:

Massanutten Association of Realtors, 129-C S. Main Street, Woodstock 22664, (540) 459-2937

Rockingham County

In the heart of the Shenandoah Valley, Harrisonburg is one of the fastest growing cities in the state and the seat of Virginia's leading agricultural county, Rockingham. Housing prices in this area accelerated during the 1980s but began leveling off in the '90s. In 1997 the average price of a three-bedroom home ranged from $100,000 to $120,000. You could buy a starter home for as low as $85,000 or a more luxurious house for up to $400,000. In 1998 the average price of homes sold in Harrisonburg and Rockingham County ranged from $109,000 to $131,000.

It's increasingly difficult to find quality historic properties in many areas of the Blue Ridge but not in Harrisonburg and Rockingham County, where a good number of old homes, some needing renovation and others already restored, are often available. It is also fairly easy to find farm properties; dairy and poultry farming are the leading agricultural industries.

Massanutten Village, a year-round mountain resort community, is a 15-minute drive east of Harrisonburg. You'll find chalets, condominiums and townhouses near the resort's ski slopes, golf course, tennis courts and swimming pools. A property owners' association maintains the roads, runs the police department and manages the entire 725-home development. Lots start at $10,000 and go up to $25,000. In 1998, the average price of homes ranged from $86,000 to $114,000.

Six hundred villas and condominiums at Massanutten are timeshares. The units cost from $4,000 to $18,000 for one week per year at the resort. Owners can also swap that week for one at a condominium in Germany, Key West, the Bahamas or any timeshare development that participates in the exchange program.

For more information contact:

Harrisonburg-Rockingham Association of Realtors, P.O. Box 1204, Harrisonburg 22801, (540) 433-8855

Shenandoah Valley Builders Association, P.O. Box 1286, Harrisonburg 22801, (540) 434-8005

Massanutten Homeowners Association, Route 2, Box 819, McGaheysville 22840, (540) 289-9466, (800) 296-6762

Augusta County

Augusta County is growing by leaps and bounds, especially in the Stuarts Draft area close to Waynesboro. A number of industries have built plants there, including Hershey and Little Debbie Bakery, and this has led to a boom in housing. Farther west, more and more people from Washington, D.C., New York and other Northern states are retiring in the Staunton area, drawn to its rich history, pastoral beauty and vibrant downtown.

Average home prices in Staunton, Waynesboro and Augusta County ranged from $90,000 to $108,000 in 1998, with certain areas such as Stuarts Draft on the high end of that figure and Staunton homes generally on

the lower end. A great demand continues from newcomers to the area for big old homes and farmhouses, but both are in short supply. It isn't that they don't exist. These homes just rarely come on the market, and when they do, they go quickly.

Two major residential developments in Staunton are worth mentioning. Ironwood, a private community next to the Staunton Country Club, is characterized by spacious, red cedar homes with private gardens. Baldwin Place is a planned community in Staunton's north end, where the homes, streets and even flora are reminiscent of early American villages. Numerous small, well-maintained developments throughout the county offer 5- to 20-acre parcels.

Staunton's downtown area is being developed into a major tourist area worthy of repeat visits. Developers and families have grabbed up many of the charming, architecturally sound commercial buildings and homes, but a few may still be left.

For more information contact:

Staunton-Augusta Association of Realtors, 1023 N. Augusta Street, Staunton 24401, (540) 885-5538

Augusta Homebuilders Association, P.O. Box 36, Waynesboro 22980, (540) 942-4644

Rockbridge County

Forty percent of Rockbridge County is rolling farmland, but its primary city, Lexington, has a historic downtown that attracts an average home price of $126,700, according to local real estate professionals. A growing sentiment is that the influx of horse-loving "Yankees" attracted by the Virginia Horse Center (see our Horse Country chapter) has pushed the price of homes and real estate to nearly double over the past several years. Wide disparities exist in the cost of farmland estates, which can run anywhere from $200,000 to more than a cool million, and the historic homes downtown that can go for $400,000 on Marshall Street.

Lexington's historic downtown has long been popular for filming period movies. In 1938 Lexington's Virginia Military Institute was the setting for scenes in *Brother Rat*; more than

Photo: Wintergreen Resort

Views like this compel many Blue Ridge visitors to buy real estate in the region.

50 years later, in the summer of 1992, dirt was poured on the streets for the Civil War film *Sommersby*. Lexington has numerous buildings and homes that represent most of the architectural styles prevalent in American communities during the 19th century. You will find Victorian cornices and stoops on Main Street, turreted Gothic buildings at Virginia Military Institute, Roman Revival, slender Tuscan columns and bracketed pediments downtown. The town even has an Italianate villa at 101 Tucker Street that dates to the late 1850s; a central bell tower surmounts its bracketed, overhanging roof. Many of these gems are open for a Christmas holiday tour and again in the spring during Historic Garden Week.

As we stated earlier, Lexington's proximity to the state's Virginia Horse Center has attracted many would-be gentleman farmers. A restored 1820 brick residence and cottage on 82 acres sold recently for about a half-million dollars, but small family farms are available starting at $100,000 (no house). With a house, you'll probably pay at least an additional $75,000. Many such homes are sold by Mead Associates, Realtors, with offices in the historic Jacob Ruff House at 21 N. Main Street, and RE/MAX Town & Country at 31 S. Main Street.

Lexington has average family developments with above-average prices. Homes in the suburban, family-oriented neighborhoods of Birdfield, Mt. Vista and Country Club Hills start at $100,000, with many priced at $150,000 and up. If you're looking for something in the range of $80,000 to $100,000, neighboring Buena Vista offers some nice neighborhoods. The average price of a home in the Lexington and Buena Vista area was listed between $111,000 and $185,000 in 1998.

For more information contact:

Lexington-Buena Vista-Rockbridge Association of Realtors, P.O. Box 797, Lexington 24450, (540) 464-4700.

Roanoke Valley

The average price of a home in the Roanoke Valley runs $125,000. In the Smith Mountain Lake area, populated by retirees and second-home owners, the average price is determined by whether or not a home is waterfront. Lake homes easily average $250,000 to $300,000.

Botetourt and Craig Counties

The growing bedroom community of Botetourt County averages somewhat less — around $112,000 — than the nearby lake area, and finders' fees are often offered for farmland. Others choose to live farther out in rural Craig County and the Catawba Valley, where a wide variety of homes averaging $80,000 and large spreads are easier to find.

Roanoke, Salem and Roanoke County

The city of Roanoke's neighborhoods are well-defined and often bound together by civic leagues and The Neighborhood Partnership, an energetic organization uniting neighborhoods for more than a decade by encouraging pride and fellowship. Popular areas range from pricey Hunting Hills in Southwest Roanoke County, where the average sales price is $316,000, to up-and-coming Wasena, where an average family home in a nice neighborhood can be purchased for $75,000.

Each year, more and more Roanoke County land, including land next to the Blue Ridge Parkway, is being developed with high-end homes. For example, Strawberry Mountain homes average around $316,000. Genteel South Roanoke remains a favorite residential area, with a minuscule turnover in homes, which range in price from $125,000 to $1 million. More affordable but equally nice are such family favorites as Raleigh Court and Penn Forest, where neighborhood block parties and nightly strolls are the norm.

Nearby Salem offers everything from downtown-area, tin-roofed Victorian-style homes with stained glass that can cost as much as $500,000 to the more modest dwellings in Beverly Heights, where young families reside in ranch homes valued from $80,000 to $125,000.

The adjoining town of Vinton offers pricey subdivisions such as Falling Creek, with homes costing more than $150,000, and charming downtown wonders you can still buy for less than $75,000. Figures from 1998 show that the average price of a home sold in the Roanoke Valley area ranged from $104,000 to $139,000.

For more information contact:

Roanoke Valley Association of Realtors, 3130 Chaparrel Drive S.W., Roanoke 24018, (540) 772-0526

Roanoke Regional Home Builders Association, 1626 Apperson Drive, Salem 24153, (540) 389-7135

East of the Blue Ridge

Loudoun County

If you are looking for property in Loudoun, start in Leesburg, the imaginary dividing line of real estate in the county. As a rule of thumb, most of the area west of Leesburg is more rural, while the eastern portion is better suited to the D.C. business crowd. Generally, prices are lower in the west and increase as you get closer to the new developments near Washington Dulles International Airport.

In fact, you can find a mixed bag of homes in Loudoun, ranging from Quaker and pre-Civil War homes to townhouses and condominiums. In the east, Sterling and Sterling Park are two popular neighborhoods, while newer developments in Ashburn Village, Cascades and Lansdowne start at $100,000 for townhouses and the low $200,000s for single-family homes.

You can find the older homes with more acreage in the western communities near Purcellville, Hillsboro and Round Hill. Some of the largest — and most expensive — estates can be found near Middleburg.

County-wide, sales in August 1997 averaged $198,000 with the three-bedroom homes ranging from $89,000 to $299,000. Most, however, fell in the $128,000 to $159,000 price list. Compared with the entire Northern Virginia area, prices were higher overall in 1998, ranging from $214,000 to $243,000.

For more information contact:

Northern Virginia Association of Realtors, 8411 Arlington Boulevard, Fairfax 22116, (703) 207-3200

Fauquier County

Location is everything in Fauquier County. The northern section is more upscale than some of the other surrounding counties because it lies in the heart of Virginia's hunt and wine country. Upperville and The Plains still play host to some of the oldest horse shows in the country. Many homes in the area also date back to the Civil War and have been meticulously restored to their early grandeur. In fact, North Wales, one of Fauquier's most distinguished homes, was listed on the market in 1997 for about $9 million. This estate, with eight cottages on 1,000 acres, is rich with history. Dating back to 1716, it survived both the Revolutionary and Civil wars and was used as a safe haven for slaves as a stop on the Underground Railroad.

If your tastes are a little more modest, southern Fauquier offers many single-family detached homes that run in the $100,000 to $190,000 price range. The areas around Bealeton on U.S. Highway 17 and Remington off U.S. Highway 29 have been strong growth areas. On average, the cost of three-and four-bedroom homes in Fauquier ranges between $156,000 and $300,000.

For more information contact:

Greater Piedmont Association of Realtors, 47 Garrett Street, Warrenton 20186, (540) 347-4866

Rappahannock County

In Rappahannock County land-development rules are strict, ensuring that the quaintness and beauty of this county remain intact. With approximately 6,000 full-time residents (about the same number as lived here 100 years ago), Rappahannock has been able to keep out large-scale development. Only one town, Washington, is incorporated. No stoplights and no chain stores are to be found here, just markets and well-stocked country stores. Thousands of visitors each year seek out the county's wonderful restaurants, bed and breakfasts and antique stores. As you might imagine, real estate is quite valuable in this area, with average three- to four-bedroom home prices in 1998 hovering between $114,000 and $271,000.

For more information contact:

Greater Piedmont Association of Realtors, 47 Garrett Street, Warrenton 20186, (540) 347-4866

Culpeper County

Since this scenic area is still within commuting distance to Washington, D.C., the strongest area of home sales is still in the northern section of Culpeper County. Those who don't mind the drive can often find larger homes with more land for the dollar than is available in the northern counties.

While a few modestly priced townhomes are sometimes listed for less than $100,000, larger farms and semi-custom homes are on the market in the $200,000 to $500,000 price range. In general, the three-bedroom, two-bathroom home is a big seller. In 1998, the average sales of three- and four-bedroom homes in Culpeper County ranged from $113,000 to $165,000.

For more information on Culpeper County contact:

Greater Piedmont Association of Realtors, 47 Garrett Street, Warrenton 20186, (540) 347-4866

Madison County

A rural refuge, Madison County is home to part of the Shenandoah National Park and the scenic Graves Mountain Lodge (see our chapter on Bed and Breakfasts and Country Inns). The development rules are more relaxed here. In 1998 the average price of a home in this area was about $81,000 to $122,000. The homes are mostly three bedrooms, although there are some two- and four-bedroom homes included. It is difficult to find historic Victorian or Colonial homes on the market; instead, the predominant styles are the brick rambler and simpler homes with vinyl siding.

For more information contact:

Greater Piedmont Association of Realtors, 47 Garrett Street, Warrenton 20186, (540) 347-4866

Greene County

One of Virginia's smallest counties in size, nearly one-fifth of Greene's 98,920 acres belong to the Shenandoah National Park. While much of the land is covered by forest and farms, large parcels of property have been earmarked for subdivisions.

Cheaper land and affordable homes have turned Greene County into a popular bedroom community for young families willing to commute the short distance to nearby Charlottesville. In fact, Greene ranked ninth in the state for the highest net migration rate with a population of 13,600 in 1997.

While some older historic buildings line U.S. Highway 33 in Stanardsville, many of the homes for sale are newer constructions. The average home price in 1998 was $97,000.

For more information on homes in Greene County call:

Charlottesville Area Association of Realtors, 2321 Commonwealth Drive, Charlottesville 22901, (804) 973-2254

Blue Ridge Homebuilders Association, 2330 Commonwealth Drive, Charlottesville 22901, (804) 973-8652

Orange County

The real estate market in Orange County, home of James Madison's Montpelier (see our Attractions chapter) and the Barboursville Winery (see our Wineries chapter), is more up-

scale. You will find a diversity of residential properties and prices that are generally lower than in Albemarle County, which includes Charlottesville. Average homes in Orange County cost $101,000 to $175,000 in 1998 for mostly three-bedroom homes. Generally, the homes are scattered across the county because the local government has not allowed the growth of residential neighborhoods. In fact, only 3 percent of its 227,000 acres is developed.

More than 95 percent of Orange County is zoned agricultural and used generally for farming and timber. Land cannot be subdivided into more than four parcels in any four-year period of time, making it is extremely difficult to rezone agricultural land to residential. This is precisely what makes Orange such a desirable place to live for people who can afford the prices of some of the stately estates, antebellum homes and spacious horse and cattle ranches.

For more information on homes in Orange County call:

Greater Piedmont Association of Realtors, 47 Garrett Street, Warrenton 20186, (540) 347-4866

Albemarle County

Albemarle County, which surrounds Charlottesville, works hard to restrict growth and preserve its rural beauty. The local government has targeted Crozet and the Ivy area, a few miles west of Charlottesville, as growth areas and allows some higher-density development, such as the Highlands, a new Crozet subdivision. But the Free Union area and many other parts of the county are slated to remain as rural as possible, with minimum requirements of one residence per 21 acres.

Charlottesville has the dubious distinction of being one of the most expensive areas in Virginia in which to live, second only to Northern Virginia. People of great wealth are drawn to the area, captivated by the beauty of the land, its historic estates and the city's cosmopolitan atmosphere. The many hospitals in the area attract doctors, and jokes abound about the number of lawyers — graduates of UVA who refuse to leave the area. In short, a lot of money floats around this area, and the real estate market has risen to the occasion.

This affluence is especially notable in the stretch of land west of the city along Barracks Road, toward Free Union and east of the city at the Keswick development. In the western area near Ivy, new homes on 3- to 8-acre lots in a subdivision named Rosemont cost $600,000 and up, with lots ranging from $80,000 to $225,000. Near the Farmington Country Club, also west of the city, stately homes run anywhere from $500,000 to more than $2 million. Inglecress is another exclusive development along Barracks and Garth roads, where homes on 3 to 5 acres cost anywhere from $500,000 to more than $1 million. In all three subdivisions, the majority of homes have four or more bedrooms.

Architectural styles of most of these new homes are similar — white columns and symmetrical porticos abound — though the Virginia farmhouse remains a staple in the county and in many subdivisions. Jefferson's Monticello and the University of Virginia are architectural models, at least on the exterior. But inside many new homes you'll find contemporary features such as vaulted ceilings, skylights and open spaces.

The Keswick community gives new meaning to the term "exclusive," even by Charlottesville standards. Sir Bernard Ashley, cofounder of Laura Ashley Company and founder of Ashley House Inc., is also owner and developer of the 600-acre Keswick Estate. This is a private, gated community with a maximum allowable density of about 100 homesites in 2- to 4-acre parcels. Amenities include the Keswick Club, a private-membership golf and leisure club with an 18-hole Arnold Palmer signature golf course and Keswick Hall, a 48-room country house hotel (see our Resorts chapter). Community services include underground utility services (central water and sewage, electricity, natural gas, tele-

phone and cable television), fire and police protection and a rescue squad. The Keswick Estate Homeowners' Association and Keswick Estate Design Review Board are vital organizations here. Architectural controls ensure that all homes will be developed to the same high standards of design and construction. Two- to 6-acre lots are priced at $120,000 to $425,000, with an average price of about $230,000.

Also east of Charlottesville is Glenmore, a private, gated community off U.S. Highway 250. The 1,188-acre community is wrapped around a championship golf course, swimming facility, tennis complex and equestrian center with bridle trails. The community will have only 750 homes at build-out, with homesites on the golf course, in deep woods, on grassy knolls, overlooking the 2.5-mile frontage on the Rivanna River or with views of Thomas Jefferson's Monticello (see our Attractions chapter). Property owners are presently automatically prequalified for membership in the Glenmore Country Club, a privately owned sports and social club with a new $4 million clubhouse and the best in sporting facilities. Elegance prevails, with plans, landscaping and builders subject to approval by the community's Architectural Review Board. Homesites are priced at $100,000 to more than $300,000 for three- to six-bedroom houses. Homes range in value from $350,000 to more than $1 million. Golf cottages with maintenance-free grounds keeping start at $225,000 and go up to $400,000.

More than 100 homes in the Charlottesville area were built between the early 1700s and the Civil War era. Wealthy families, often using royal land grants, began migrating west from Richmond in the early 1700s. Such estates as Plain Dealing, Estouteville and Edgemont are registered historic landmarks. Because so many historic homes are in the area, one or two may be on the market at any given time.

The city, which has no more room for development, has a few beautiful neighborhoods. Gracious old homes are concentrated in the Rugby Road area, but you'll find more modest, rambler-type homes and Cape Cods close to the university. Within a two-block range of Rugby Road are homes that sell for $300,000 to $1 million.

Statistics from 1998 indicate that homes in the Charlottesville and Albemarle County area sold for prices ranging from $139,000 to $256,00.

Some important phone numbers:

Charlottesville Area Association of Realtors, 2321 Commonwealth Drive, Charlottesville 22901, (804) 973-2254

Blue Ridge Homebuilders Association, 2330 Commonwealth Drive, Charlottesville 22901, (804) 973-8652

Nelson County

The character of Nelson County can be defined by its two major tourist attractions. Wintergreen, the state's largest resort, offers a taste of luxury associated with a weekend on the ski slopes (see our Resorts chapter), while the Waltons Museum houses a collection of memorabilia dedicated to a hard-working family that struggled to weather the Great Depression (see our Attractions chapter). While hundreds of tourists are drawn to these Nelson destinations each year, more than 13,000 folks decided to call this diverse county their home.

Nelson, indeed, is an eclectic community. It's home to polo players, best-selling authors, farmers, retirees and — with Charlottesville just a half-hour's drive away — plenty of business commuters. Property can be found to accommodate just about any pocketbook. Look for higher prices as you get closer to Charlottesville and the mountains, but it is possible to find a few modest-priced homes in the southern reaches of the county.

A modest three- or four-bedroom home in Lovingston, Shipman and parts of the county outside the Wintergreen resort area can be found usually starting at $100,000. Add 5 to 10 acres for a small farmette for an average of $110,000 or more. Since much of it is rural, Nelson has many large farms priced at $250,000 to $400,000 or more. It also has its share of large historic or picturesque estates, some costing as much as $1.2 million.

The four-star Wintergreen Resort has luxury condominiums and single-family homes on the ridges overlooking the ski area, Devil's Knob Golf Course and the surrounding mountains. In the valley is a growing community that has at its center the award-winning Stoney Creek golf course and the Rodes Farm Equestrian Center. About one hour from Charlottesville, Wintergreen is secluded from encroaching development by the Blue Ridge Parkway and Shenandoah National Park on the north and west and the George Washington and Jefferson National Forests to the south. More than half of Wintergreen's 11,000 acres have been set aside as permanent, undisturbed wilderness.

The community has its own preschool and primary school, police force and fire department. More than half of the resort's property owners are retired and generally quite active, sometimes only spending part of the year at Wintergreen. Most of the resort's full-time residents are based in the valley at Stoney Creek.

Property owners who are members of the resort's Wintergreen Equity Club receive benefits and privileges that include unlimited skiing, golf, tennis and use of the resort's spa. Membership in this club initially costs $12,500, and annual passes cost $400.

The 1999 price of condominiums ranges anywhere from $45,000 to $350,000, covering efficiencies to three-bedroom constructions. Homes were listed from $150,000 to more than $750,000 and land from $25,000 to $250,000 per lot. These prices often include membership in the owners' equity club.

For more information contact:

Charlottesville Area Association of Realtors, 2321 Commonwealth Drive, Charlottesville 22901, (804) 973-2254

Wintergreen and Stoney Creek at Wintergreen Real Estate, P.O. Box 747, Nellysford 22958, (804) 325-2500, (800) 325-2200

Lynchburg and Bedford and Franklin Counties

Lynchburg and surrounding Bedford County comprise one of the most rapidly growing regions in the state. According to Realtor Alice Smith of Smith & Thurmond Inc., spokesperson for the Lynchburg Realtors, the average selling time for a home is only 115 days.

Among the areas of growth are Ivy Hill, a planned community around Ivy Lake and Ivy

Photo: K.B. Gatz-Broadway

Autumn is one of the most beautiful times of the year in the Blue Ridge.

Hill Golf Course; Poplar Forest, a neighborhood of fine homes on wooded lots carved out of Jefferson's land surrounding his home; Meadowwood, just outside the city on lots averaging 2 to 3 acres; and Meadowridge, homes on 2- to 3-acre lots close to the mountains. Prices in these areas range from $200,000 to $400,000.

In Lynchburg, you'll love the tree-bordered streets lined with two-story brick Colonials graced by manicured lawns. Among the most prestigious and desirable are Peakland Place, Linkhorne Forest, Link Road, Rivermont Avenue and Boonsboro Forest. New growth west of the city is due to land that is ripe for development. In addition, homeowners in several historic districts are turning formerly neglected turn-of-the-century residences into glorious showcases. The most advanced renovation of these historic districts are Diamond Hill and Garland Hill. Close behind are Federal Hill, College Hill and Daniels Hill. In 1998, the price of a home in Lynchburg averaged between $100,000 and $135,000.

South of Lynchburg, Smith Mountain Lake, which straddles the border between Bedford and Franklin counties, attracts upscale buyers seeking waterfront golf communities, second homes and retiree getaways. Most waterfront homes list for more than $200,000. Some more popular communities are Chestnut Creek, Waters Edge, Waterfront and Waverly, with houses ranging in price from $175,000 to $600,000. New in 1996 was the Boardwalk development, where prices start at $260,000. Condo prices at Bernard's Landing (see our Resorts chapter) start in the low $80,000s and in the $70,000s at Striper's Landing.

It's worth a boat trip around Smith Mountain Lake's 500 miles of shoreline just to see the architectural, custom-built splendor of some of the homes. One of the most noted builders of cedar lake homes is Smith Mountain Cedar Homes, perennially a high-volume performer, along with its parent company, Lindal Cedar Homes.

Rural farmsteads and homes in Bedford and Franklin counties are more affordable and more available than in any of the other Roanoke bedroom communities. The average price of a home is less than in Roanoke, at around $70,000. Naturally, the cost of lake property brings up the median, but some real rural bargains still can be found.

For more information, contact:

Lynchburg Association of Realtors, 3639 Old Forest Road, Lynchburg 24501, (804) 385-8760

Builders & Associates of Central Virginia, P.O. Box 216, Forest 24551, (804) 385-6018

Roanoke Regional Home Builders Association, 1626 Apperson Drive, Salem 24153, (540) 389-7135

New River Valley

Montgomery, Giles and Pulaski Counties

The average price of homes sold in the New River Valley ranged from $96,000 to $114,000 in 1998. In Montgomery County, which includes the university towns of Blacksburg and Radford, the high salaries paid to professionals from Virginia Tech and Radford University have driven up the price of homes and land. The price of premium farmland in neighboring Floyd and Giles counties is also affected by the high standard of living.

The New River area is considered one of the five major growth areas of Virginia, according to Realtor E.R. Templeton of Raines Real Estate of Blacksburg. Requests for finders are often found posted on bulletin boards in little towns such as Newport.

Potential homeowners will most likely find Christiansburg and Pulaski the least expensive places to buy a home, ranging from $80,000 to $120,000, according to the local Board of Realtors. The average price of a home was $35,000 higher in nearby Blacksburg.

The downtowns of Blacksburg and Radford offer true small-town atmospheres conducive to leisurely evening strolls, breathtaking parks (especially Radford's Bisset Park along the New River) and the likelihood of meeting others who enjoy an academically stimulating lifestyle. The towns are packed with apartment complexes and townhouses for the thousands of students who live there. The majority of apartments are well-kept, and the students are pleasant and add immensely to the area's quality of life and diverse culture.

Popular family developments near Blacksburg are Foxridge, Heathwood, Toms Creek Estates and Westover Hills, where the average price of a home is $140,000.

In Christiansburg, the same type of development home will average $105,000. Some of Christiansburg's better-known developments are Craig Mountain, Diamond Point, Victory Heights and Windmill Hills.

In Radford, a family can buy a home in Sunset Village for a price on the low end, $50,000 to $80,000, and in the newer developments of College Park and High Meadows for $100,000 to $160,000.

Many New River Valley residents opt to live in the environs of Giles, Floyd and Pulaski counties, where rural living is prevalent. Farms can be expensive since a lot of professionals also like to live out in the country. The quality of farmland varies in each county and it tends to be scarce, due to the area's beauty and proximity to the Blue Ridge Parkway. It probably is least expensive in Pulaski County, where good farmland sells for about $3,000 an acre. Much of the land there is devoted to dairy farms and to raising cattle and hogs.

Numerous second homes have been built in Pulaski County's Claytor Lake area. One development, Mallard Point, near Dublin, is a luxurious waterfront community of gracious townhomes unique to the popular water playground. The spacious two- and three-bedroom units offer amenities such as a whirlpool, individual lighted boat slips and a private tennis court.

Downtown Pulaski is definitely on the rise, due to its dynamic Main Street Program. Professionals from Washington, D.C., and other metropolitan areas are renovating some of the Prospect Street mansions, notable for their witches' caps and winding front porches. An area short on bed and breakfast inns, Downtown Pulaski probably has more old mansions that would lend themselves to this cause than any other place in the New River Valley. It's the next hot spot of New River Valley tourism.

If you're looking for a pleasant family development in Pulaski, consider Mountain View Acres or Newbern Heights, with houses priced from $90,000 to $150,000. Oak View is more expensive at $100,000 to $170,000 but considerably more affordable than a similar development in neighboring Montgomery County.

For more information, contact:

New River Valley Association of Realtors, 811 Triangle Street, Blacksburg 24060, (540) 953-0040

New River Valley Home Builders Association, P.O. Box 2010, Christiansburg 24068, (540) 381-0180

Alleghany Highlands

Highland, Bath and Alleghany Counties

This area, which includes the counties of Highland, Bath and Alleghany, has no organized real estate board, and no Multiple Listing Service records are kept on the average price of a home. But local real estate agents (see listings below) say most homes typically sell for a fourth of the price of their urban counterparts. Another rule of thumb, from Highland County's Building Permits Office, is that the cost of building a new home here is $50 per square foot compared to $89 in Northern Virginia.

The area also is unusual in that much of the rural, mountainous Highland County property is owned by people who don't live there. For example, half of the least-populated county in Virginia is owned by vacationers in the highest county east of the Mississippi. Real estate here is prized for its proximity to The Homestead (see our Resorts chapter), the Potomac and James rivers and hunting and fishing preserves. Here, you can buy farms with miles of split rail fences on emerald-green pastures, maple sugar orchards, wooded tracts, trout farms and cattle farms. It's obvious to visitors

that the sheep outnumber the human population five to one. Many look to this area for retirement.

Real estate professionals in this area who can provide information include the following:

Clarkson & Wallace, Warm Springs, (540) 839-2609

Richardson Real Estate Company, Monterey, (540) 468-2105

Retirement

Determining the perfect place to retire takes planning, with careful consideration of individual tastes and personal needs. The Blue Ridge has numerous agencies and contacts to help you determine where you would be happiest. Here is a list, arranged by region, of helpful agencies or programs. Through these services you'll find tips about personal care programs and local perks such as Cox Cable, Roanoke's free cable TV installation for seniors, "Enjoy the Prime Time of Your Life." Also check with local hospitals, county health departments and social service departments, since many offer ongoing senior services, programs and seminars.

Shenandoah Valley

Agencies

Frederick County Parks and Recreation Department
107 N. Kent St., Winchester
• (540) 665-5678

This recreation department offers an assortment of year-round activities for people 55 and older. Senior Clubs are active throughout the county, and members take regular trips,

---

INSIDERS' TIP

If you're in the market for a retirement community, start early. Allow yourself up to a year to compare and visit locations, especially if you need a large space. Many communities have waiting lists for two-bedroom units, which are tougher to come by.

enjoy varied courses and participate in specially designed fitness classes.

Godfrey Miller Senior Center
28 Loudoun St., Winchester
• (540) 667-5869

Built in 1785, this large stone and brick center is on Winchester's historic pedestrian mall. Activities include programs on arts and crafts, bingo, bridge, music, Bible study and healthcare. There are lunches, picnics, trips, lectures and weekly blood-pressure clinics. Affiliated with the Grace Lutheran Church, the center is open from 10 AM to 3 PM Monday through Thursday.

Shenandoah Area Agency on Aging
207 Mosby Ln., Front Royal
• (540) 635-7141, (800) 883-4122

This agency provides elderly services to seniors in Clarke, Frederick, Page, Shenandoah and Warren counties as well as the city of Winchester. Programs include home healthcare, case management, special activities and home-delivered meals and meals in local senior centers.

Rockingham County Parks and Recreation Department
40 E. Gay St., Harrisonburg
• (540) 564-3160

This program offers lunches, crafts and daytrips for area seniors.

Augusta County Parks and Recreation Department
P.O. Box 590, Verona 24482-0590
• (540) 245-5727

The seniors program at this recreation department focuses on classes and daytrips. Fifty-five Alive driving classes for senior citizens are also held here.

Waynesboro Department of Parks and Recreation
413 Port Republic Rd., Waynesboro
• (540) 949-6505

Seniors in the Waynesboro area meet for lunches, daytrips, craft classes and exercise groups through programs with parks and recreation.

The Valley Program for Aging Services Inc.
325 Pine Ave., Waynesboro
• (800) 868-VPAS

An enormous resource for area seniors, the Valley Program serves Rockingham, Augusta, Rockbridge, Bath and Highland counties. Services aimed at supporting independent living for seniors include case management, transportation, employment help, adult day care, personal care and home-delivered meals.

AHC Hospice of the Shenandoah
P.O. Box 1000, Fishersville 22939
• (540) 932-4193

Hospice provides a wide range of services from clinical care to emotional support for terminally ill patients and their families. This licensed chapter serves Staunton, Waynesboro and Augusta County.

Retirement Communities

Shenandoah Valley Westminster-Canterbury
300 Westminster-Canterbury Dr., Winchester • (540) 665-0156

This nonprofit life-care retirement community is affiliated with the Episcopal and Presbyterian churches but is open to retirement-aged people of all denominations. Services

---

INSIDERS' TIP

In the 1800s about 25 families made up the population of Salem. But when South Salem was annexed in 1953 followed by the eastern corridor in 1960, Salem became the largest town in Virginia with a population of more than 16,050. A walking tour along Main, Clay and Calhoun streets will take you past 22 historical sites that figured in the town's development.

range from independent living to complete on-site healthcare. Located 65 miles from Washington, D.C., this 65-acre campus includes 2.5-miles of walking trails, a 14-acre restricted natural park and vegetable and flower gardens.

Virginia Mennonite Retirement Community
1501 Virginia Ave., Harrisonburg
• (540) 564-3400

The Mennonite Churches of Virginia offer a variety of cottages, apartments, town homes or condominiums at this 43-acre retirement community. If the need arises, there are also assisted living private rooms and long-term nursing care available at Oak Lea with an Alzheimer's wing and garden. Open to all denominations, the campus adjoins Eastern Mennonite University.

Baldwin Park
21 Woodlee Rd., Staunton
• (540) 885-1122

This retirement community close to downtown Staunton has studio and one- and two-bedroom apartments with window boxes and patios or balconies. All services, including meals, housekeeping, laundry and activity programs, are provided. There is no entrance fee.

Roanoke Valley

Agencies

Family Service of Roanoke Valley
3208 Hershberger Rd. N.W., Roanoke
• (540) 563-5316

Family Services offers information about home healthcare, insurance, Medicaid and Medicare. Counseling and other mental-health-issue resources also are available.

League of Older Americans
706 Campbell Ave. S.W., Roanoke
• (540) 345-0451

The LOA publishes a monthly newsletter full of part-time jobs, offers a full-time office and staff for concerns of seniors and sponsors an annual picnic to raise funds for Meals on Wheels. This fund-raiser also allows seniors to mingle, eat fried chicken and discuss important legislation with local politicians.

Retirement Communities

Brandon Oaks
3804 Brandon Ave. S.W., Roanoke
• (540) 776-2600

Brandon Oaks offers several spacious floor plans plus dining, transportation, housekeeping, 24-hour security, an activities director and on-site professional healthcare. The community has 172 units offered as one- and two-bedroom apartments and two-bedroom cottages.

Elm Park Estates
4230 Elm View Rd., Roanoke
• (540) 989-2010

Elm Park Estates is near hospitals, medical facilities and shopping (Tanglewood Mall is across the street). Amenities include a craft room, library, beauty salon and planned daily activities. Studios and one-bedroom and two-bedroom apartments are available. Pets are permitted.

Roanoke United Methodist Home
1009 Old Country Club Rd. N.W., Roanoke • (540) 344-6248

Several types of living arrangements and levels of care are available to people of all faiths at this licensed nursing center with a social worker. The facility has social rooms, an activities staff, a chapel and a large-print library. Guest rooms are available.

The Park-Oak Grove
4920 Woodmar Dr. S.W., Roanoke
• (540) 989-9501

This community offers seven spacious living-quarter designs, varying in size from studios to one- and two-bedrooms units. A wellness staff stays on site. A first floor art gallery has been the scene of numerous exhibits, part of The Park-Oak Grove's ongoing Visual and Performing Arts Series. A visit by Miss Virginia is an annual event. Inquiries are welcomed. Guided tours and complimentary lunches are easily arranged by calling during regular business hours.

East of the Blue Ridge

Agencies

Area Agency on Aging
751 Miller Dr. S.E., Leesburg
• **(703) 777-0257**

This agency publishes a free newsletter, *The Golden Grapevine*, to bring seniors up to date about what is going on in Loudoun County. The agency is a major contact for information and assistance for seniors and their family members. It oversees programs that provide meals, job placement, home care and transportation.

The Retired Senior Volunteer Program lets seniors know where their skills may be needed in the community.

Loudoun County Department of Parks and Recreation
741 Miller Dr. S.E., Leesburg
• **(703) 777-0343**

Leesburg offers a number of programs throughout the city, including the Ida Lee Recreation Center on Ida Lee Drive. Along with a special programs and events, this center houses an indoor pool, spa, gymnasium and exercise and meeting rooms.

Rappahannock-Rapidan Area Agency on Aging
401 S. Main St., Culpeper
• **(540) 825-3100**

You can find out information and referral on community services at one of R-RAAA's five centers. Other services include legal aid, health-insurance counseling, homebound meals, transportation, adult care and a volunteer program that matches senior volunteers with activities in their communities. Centers are in Culpeper, Fauquier, Madison, Orange and Rappahannock counties.

Hospice of the Rapidan
1200 Sunset Ln., Culpeper
• **(804) 825-4840, (800) 676-2012**

Residents in Fauquier, Rappahannock, Culpeper, Madison and Orange counties may benefit from the services of Hospice of the Rapidan. Hospice offers clinical care and emotional support for terminally ill patients and their loved ones.

Albemarle County Parks and Recreation
401 McIntire Rd., Charlottesville
• **(804) 296-5844**

This large department oversees three recreation centers and seven parks over 2,000 acres. Included in its list of activities is a year-round exercise class for senior citizens at the Meadows Community Center in Crozet. This center, off Va. 240 in the western part of the county, has a kitchen and large meeting room. There is no charge for the exercise program.

The Jefferson Area Board for Aging
674 Hillsdale Dr., Charlottesville
• **(804) 978-3644**

Senior services through JABA are many: case management, adult day care, home-delivered meals, personal care, transportation and employment aid. The agency's goal is to support independent living for seniors. Through 11 senior centers and six outreach offices, JABA serves clients in Charlottesville and the counties of Albemarle, Nelson, Greene, Louisa and Fluvanna. Its Center of Adult Eldercare and Rehab offers adult day care, overnight care, a library, a doctor's clinic and a space for occupational, physical and speech therapy. JABA also publishes *Silver Linings*, a free senior-oriented newspaper.

The Senior Center Inc.
1180 Pepsi Pl., Charlottesville
• **(804) 974-7756**

This is an active center in a facility conve-

INSIDERS' TIP

The price of land in the Blue Ridge is considerably lower than in other parts of the country, especially the Northeast and West Coast.

nient to several Charlottesville retirement communities. Members can take part in daily lunches, classes, lectures, exercise groups and entertainment programs. Trips, both daylong and weeklong, are scheduled regularly.

Charlottesville-Piedmont Alzheimer's Chapter
500 E. West Field Rd., Charlottesville
• (804) 973-6122

This association is a great source of education and information about Alzheimer's Disease for patients and their families. Services include support groups, a newsletter, a lending library of books and videos and a caregiver resource file.

Charlottesville Recreation and Leisure Services
800 E. Market St., Charlottesville
• (804) 970-3261

The recreation department in Charlottes-ville offers activities for young and old at seven recreation centers and 25 parks. A part-time staffer was hired just to oversee the senior citizens' programs. Since local residents have access to wonderful programs at the Senior Center and the Jefferson Area Board for Aging, the recreation department gears its services primarily to seniors who are more frail and elderly.

Activities range from ceramics and bingo to road trips to theatrical productions. The staff even takes programs and slide shows to local nursing homes.

Hospice of the Piedmont
1290 Seminole Tr., Charlottesville
• (804) 975-5500, (800) 975-5501

Hospice of the Piedmont includes teams of nurses, social workers, therapists, clergy, counselors, nutritionists and trained volunteers who assist patients and their families in dealing with a limited life expectancy. The Piedmont area Hospice covers the city of Charlottesville plus Albemarle, Greene and Nelson counties.

Central Virginia Area Agency on Aging
3225 Old Forest Rd., Lynchburg
• (804) 385-9070

This agency serves Bedford County as a clearinghouse for home healthcare referrals with all issues pertaining to seniors.

City of Lynchburg Department of Parks & Recreation
301 Grove St., Lynchburg
• (804) 847-1640

This department offers social stimulation to seniors through classes such as aerobics and CPR and trips offered on an ongoing basis.

Southern Area Agency on Aging
433 Commonwealth Blvd., Martinsville
• (540) 632-6442

This agency acts as a clearinghouse in Franklin County for resource referral for health issues, home-healthcare, legislation and senior issues.

Retirement Communities

Branchlands Village
1300 Branchlands Dr., Charlottesville
• (804) 973-9044

Conveniently located near the local senior center and shopping mall, this retirement community offers townhouse and apartment living. Residents have access to a variety of planned activities, transportation services, housekeeping and on-site dining. Exterior maintenance is included.

The Colonnades
2600 Barracks Rd., Charlottesville
• (804) 971-1892, (800) 443-8457

The Colonnades is on 59 acres, nearly half of which is a nature preserve with maintained walking trails. The community offers concierge and supplemental personal services, including transportation, housekeeping and licensed nursing care.

Martha Jefferson House
1600 Gordon Ave., Charlottesville
• (804) 293-6136

Seniors live graciously in this beautiful residence that's located in a wonderful downtown neighborhood. Common living areas are tastefully decorated with antiques and fine furniture. Three meals are served daily. A nursing facility is attached.

Our Lady of Peace
751 Hillsdale Dr., Charlottesville
• (804) 973-1155

This nondenominational, nonprofit facility offers three levels of care: independent living, assisted living and nursing care. Operated by the Catholic Diocese, Our Lady of Peace is close to the Senior Center and shopping mall. Housekeeping, laundry and transportation services are available.

University Village
2401 Old Ivy Rd., Charlottesville
• (804) 977-1800

A beautiful facility with great views of the surrounding countryside, University Village offers apartment living for independent seniors. A registered nurse remains on duty weekdays. A wellness center, concierge, dining room and indoor pool are available to residents.

Valley View
1213 Long Meadows Dr., Lynchburg
• (804) 237-3009

Services at Valley View include meals, housekeeping, transportation, wellness programs and a community center with a hot tub and a visiting nurse, which are included in the monthly rental fee.

The facility has a country store, barber/beauty shop, a games and crafts area and an exercise room.

Westminster Canterbury
501 VES Rd., Lynchburg
• (804) 386-3500

Residents at this community have a choice of eight apartment styles. Services and amenities include a beauty/barber shop, individual climate control, no-scald water control, housekeeping and your choice of dining arrangements (either in your apartment or in the central area).

New River Valley

Agencies

New River Valley Agency on Aging
143 Third St. N.W., Pulaski
• **(540) 980-7720**

This agency provides resources for seniors, including referrals for home healthcare, legislative issues, part-time jobs and retirement communities.

Retirement Communities

Warm Hearth Village Retirement Community
2607 Warm Hearth Dr., Blacksburg
• **(540) 961-1712**

On a 220-acre wooded site, Warm Hearth has 46 one-level townhomes, apartments in three low-rise buildings and apartments for assisted living in a licensed home for adults.

Alleghany Highlands

Agencies

Valley Program for Aging Services Inc.
325 Pine Ave., Waynesboro
• **(800) 868-VPAS**

This agency serves as a clearinghouse for health, legislative and labor issues. It serves Bath and Highland counties.

Every major city in the
Shenandoah Valley has
at least one college
or university, and the
area has several
college preparatory,
parochial and military
boarding schools.

Education

If natural beauty inspires learning, it is no wonder that the Blue Ridge is lined with some of the finest colleges and universities in Virginia. Shoot, why stop there? The University of Virginia and Virginia Tech have both been cited by national publications for their academic excellence. Tech, in the heart of the New River Valley, took a leading role in establishing one of the world's first electronic villages, while "Mr. Jefferson's University" in Charlottesville continues to turn out leaders in medicine, law and business.

Every major city in the Shenandoah Valley has at least one college or university, and the area has several college preparatory, parochial and military boarding schools. The Roanoke Valley is home to Roanoke College and Hollins. Excellent prep schools include North Cross and Roanoke Catholic.

Harrisonburg, the seat of Virginia's leading agricultural county of Rockingham, bustles with academic activity. James Madison University, Eastern Mennonite University and Bridgewater College are within a few miles of each other. To the south, in historic Staunton, are Mary Baldwin College, a Presbyterian-affiliated school for women, and Stuart Hall, Virginia's oldest Episcopal preparatory school for girls.

Washington & Lee University and Virginia Military Institute sit in quaint, historic Lexington. VMI used to be the only public all-male college in the nation, but that ended with the class of 1997-98. In compliance with the Supreme Court's ruling to go coed or go private, the school now admits women cadets.

In addition to Mary Baldwin College, several esteemed private women's colleges are in the mountains and foothills of the Blue Ridge, including Hollins College in Roanoke, Randolph-Macon Woman's College in Lynchburg and Sweet Briar College in Amherst.

South of Roanoke, the New River Valley is home to both Virginia Tech and Radford University, two of the most popular choices in Virginia higher education.

If you're looking for a New England-style preparatory school without the cold weather and high tuition, consider the Blue Ridge. The region has an abundance of high-quality day and boarding prep schools, many with gorgeous mountain campuses and exciting outdoor programs. Virginia is known for fine college preparatory schools such as Notre Dame Academy and Foxcroft School in Middleburg. Randolph-Macon Academy in Front Royal has been turning out stellar students since 1892. South of Front Royal is Wakefield Country Day School, where seniors' SAT scores average 1323 points.

Charlottesville-area prep schools include St. Anne's-Belfield, Woodberry Forest in nearby Orange County and the Miller School of Albemarle. Lynchburg has several prep schools, including the Virginia Episcopal School and the Seven Hills School. Lynchburg is also home to five colleges and two business schools drawing more than 15,000 students each year.

A strict regime is also a way of life at two military boarding schools in the Valley: Fishburne Military School in Waynesboro and Massanutten Military Academy in Woodstock.

Listed in this chapter in geographic order, north to south and east to west, are four-year colleges and some of the better-known preparatory schools in the Blue Ridge region. There are also 23 community colleges in Virginia, including the 114-acre Piedmont Virginia Community College near Monticello in Albemarle County.

Information on any of the two-year colleges is available from the State Council of Higher Education, (804) 225-2137.

Colleges and Universities

Shenandoah Valley

Averett College
Danville • (800) 448-5233

Averett College, chartered in 1859, is a coeducational four-year comprehensive college offering undergraduate and graduate programs to more than 2,200 students. This college is based in Danville, with satellites in Martinsville, Roanoke, Lynchburg, Bluefield, Bristol and Charlottesville. Averett offers more than 30 undergraduate degree options and three master's degree programs. Master of arts degrees in business, education and teaching are offered on Averett's Danville campus. In addition, master of business administration and bachelor of business administration degree classes are offered to working adults at more than 25 locations throughout Virginia, North Carolina and Washington, D.C. Students in Averett's adult M.B.A. and B.B.A. programs earn degrees through night or weekend study. Undergraduate majors range from business to music to education and include hard-to-find majors such as aviation and equestrian studies. Equestrian majors study at the college's 65-acre equestrian center, and aviation classes are held at Danville Regional Airport.

The college offers undergraduates opportunity for additional study through its leadership studies program, honors program and through travel abroad. Averett is currently developing an athletic/convocation complex on its North Campus, located 2 miles from the Danville college's main campus. When completed the complex will include a baseball field, softball field, two soccer fields and 12 tennis courts. The complex's anchor, the E. Stuart James Grant Center, will house a basketball arena, classrooms, faculty/coaches offices and fitness facilities. The complex will serve as an athletic and cultural center both for the college and the surrounding community. Averett

www.insiders.com
See this and many other
Insiders' Guide®
destinations online.
Visit us today!

is associated with the Baptist General Association of Virginia and takes seriously its Christian heritage and its commitment to intellectual inquiry and excellence in all aspects of college life.

Shenandoah University
Winchester • (540) 665-4581

Shenandoah University, a United Methodist-affiliated institution, was founded in 1875 in Dayton, Virginia, and moved to Winchester in 1960. Since then the university has developed into a comprehensive Level V accredited institution of higher education. It offers more than 60 programs of study at the undergraduate, graduate and professional levels in five schools: the School of Arts and Sciences, the Harry F. Byrd Jr. School of Business, the Shenandoah Conservatory, the School of Pharmacy, and the School of Health Professions (nursing, respiratory care, occupational therapy and physical therapy).

In addition to the university's beautifully landscaped 76-acre campus, it also maintains several state-of-the-art facilities in downtown Winchester and the former Winchester Hospital on the campus of the new Winchester Medical Center. It also operates a satellite campus in Leesburg.

Shenandoah University's student body of approximately 2,300 men and women represent 40 states and 28 countries.

Christendom College
**Front Royal • (540) 636-2900,
(800) 877-5456**

This small college was founded in 1977 to inspire and educate Catholic students for church lay leadership. The student body will probably never exceed 450 because of efforts to retain a close community life. The college is situated on a 100-acre campus of gently rolling land surrounded by the Blue Ridge Mountains. Bachelor of Arts degrees are awarded in English, French, history, philosophy, political science and economics, classical studies and theology. The college also offers a two-year Associate of Arts degree.

Eastern Mennonite University
Harrisonburg • (540) 432-4000

Christian values and global concerns are integrated with the learning process at this private college that was founded in 1917 to serve the educational needs of the Mennonite Church. The school has about 1,000 undergraduates, 100 seminary students, 100 graduate students and 100 students enrolled in the new adult degree completion program. This new program is designed for working people who can complete their education without leaving their jobs.

In keeping with the church's heritage of peace and nonviolence, EMU has added a graduate-level conflict transformation program, in which people from all over the world can learn how to mediate conflict.

All students at Eastern Mennonite participate in a cross-cultural experience, from attending seminars in Africa and Europe to working with the Spanish-speaking community in Harrisonburg. The most popular majors are business, education, biology, nursing and social work. The 90-acre hillside campus is in the northern tip of the town of Harrisonburg.

James Madison University
Harrisonburg • (540) 568-6147

Flanked by the Blue Ridge Mountains to the east and the Alleghenies to the west, this beautiful 472-acre campus sits in the heart of the Shenandoah Valley. First called the State Normal and Industrial School for Women, the school opened in 1909 with 209 students and 15 faculty members. Today, with an average enrollment of 13,700, JMU is recognized as one of the top comprehensive coeducational public universities in the country. In April 1997, it was included in *The Student Guide to America's 100 Best College Buys*.

The university offers a wide range of courses on the bachelor and master levels. The school has even recently added a doctorate program in educational counseling. The strongest academic areas include the arts, education, communications, health and human services, business and science and technology.

More than 500 student athletes compete in 13 men's and 14 women's sports. The Con-

vocation Center, a 7,600-seat arena, was added for sports and entertainment events. The campus is within walking distance of downtown Harrisonburg.

Bridgewater College
Bridgewater • (540) 828-8000

This private, Church of the Brethren-affiliated college is 7 miles south of Harrisonburg. Bridgewater has been coeducational since it was founded in 1880. Its average enrollment is 1,000 students, and the most popular majors are business and biology. An excellent music program also attracts many students.

Mary Baldwin College
Staunton • (540) 887-7000

This private women's college enrolls about 1,150 undergraduates and 50 graduates. Close to half of the students are Virginians, and the rest represent 32 states and nine foreign countries. Thirty-three major and even more minor courses of study are offered, and the most popular are art, psychology, sociology, communications and biology. The school is home to several innovative educational programs, including the Virginia Women's Institute for Leadership, the Program for Exceptionally Gifted, the Adult Degree Program and a Master of Arts and Teaching program. The college also has recently added a bachelor of science degree program, and pre-med majors in this program maintain an exceptionally high acceptance rate at medical schools. The pretty campus is within walking distance of downtown Staunton.

Washington & Lee University
Lexington • (540) 463-8400

Washington & Lee University in historic Lexington was founded in 1749 and enrolls about 1,600 undergraduates and 400 law students. *U.S. News and World Report* has rated W&L one of the top bargains for a quality private school education in America. The university offers both bachelor and juris doctor (law) degrees. The 1998-99 school year was a big one for Washington & Lee. It marked the 250th anniversary of the university and the 150th anniversary of its law school.

Its history is rich with historic names. In

1796 George Washington contributed 100 shares of canal stock in the James River Co. to Liberty Hall Academy, a Presbyterian seminary. The grateful trustees changed the school's name to Washington Academy in 1798 and to Washington College in 1813.

Gen. Robert E. Lee rode into town on his horse, Traveller, in 1865 and became the college's president until his death in 1870, at which time the name of the school was changed to Washington & Lee University. While there, Lee established the nation's first journalism program and its School of Law. W&L's gracious campus is designated a National Historic Landmark, with neoclassical brick buildings dating back to the generosity of Washington. Lee Chapel, on the tree-lined colonnade, is a focal point for students, who gather there for lectures, concerts and special events. Lee designed the beautiful chapel and is buried there.

W&L is a charter member of the 14-college Old Dominion Athletic Conference and is a member of NCAA's Division III.

Virginia Military Institute
Lexington • (540) 464-7000

Virginia Military Institute joins W&L in Lexington as a national treasure of tradition. Thomas J. Jackson, the immortal "Stonewall," taught here 10 years before heeding the call of the South in the Civil War. Again this year, VMI leads the nation's publicly supported colleges in endowment per student. VMI has produced some of the most famous leaders in the world as graduates, including Gen. George C. Marshall, class of 1901, author of the Marshall Plan to reconstruct Europe after World War II. A museum in his honor is next to the 12-acre parade ground, as is the VMI Museum that chronicles the history of the Institute. The VMI Post (campus) is a National Historic District, and the Cadet Barracks a National Historic Landmark.

This is the school that was portrayed in Ronald Reagan's film, *Brother Rat*, about VMI"s infamous Rat Line. Women joined the ranks for the first time in August 1997. VMI underwent 13 months of planning for the assimilation of women. Approximately 35 women were among the entering "Rat" class. The 1,200 cadets pursue bachelor degrees in 12 disciplines in the general fields of engineering, science and liberal arts. Undergirding all aspects of cadet life is the VMI Honor Code, to which all cadets subscribe. VMI alumni have distinguished themselves in every American conflict since the Mexican War, including 500 alumni who served in Operation Desert Storm and Desert Shield. The school has 13 intercollegiate athletic teams in NCAA Division I.

Roanoke Valley

Hollins University
Roanoke • (540) 362-6000

Founded in 1842, Hollins College was the first chartered women's college in Virginia. Enrollment is 1,070, with 870 undergraduate women and 200 coed graduate students. Hollins awards a bachelor of arts degree with 31 majors and offers graduate programs in five disciplines: English/creative writing, children's literature, psychology, liberal studies, teaching and a certificate of advanced studies.

Hollins is known internationally for its clinic for stutterers, the Hollins Communications Research Institute. Hollins emphasizes community outreach through its graduate programs, the Women's Center and summer programs for women and rising juniors and seniors in high school.

Hollins enjoys a strong liberal arts focus, with nationally recognized programs in creative writing. Three Pulitzer Prize winners — Annie Dillard, Henry Taylor and Mary Wells Ashworth — graduated from Hollins. Other notable alumna include *Time* publisher Lisa Valk

---

INSIDERS' TIP

Not ready to send your youngster off to boarding school? Try a boarding summer school program at one of the Blue Ridge's many college preparatory schools.

Photo: Jack Hollingsworth/Virginia Department of Tourism

The University of Virginia campus is in Charlottesville.

Long, ABC News correspondent Ann Compton and Elizabeth Forsythe Hailey, author of the best-seller, *A Woman of Independent Means*. Hollins has the first graduate program for the writing and study of children's literature and is also noted for its international concentration. The college hosts more than 200 public events annually, including the New Century Women's Leadership Award.

Nearly half of its students study abroad. One program is offered through Christie's of London for museum and auction house studies. Hollins's sports programs are also well-known in the NCAA Division III and Old Dominion Athletic Conference. Its Riding Center is popular for women who like to take their horses to college with them. No wonder, since its riding team often wins first place at the Nationals.

Roanoke College
Roanoke • (540) 375-2500

Founded in 1842, Roanoke College moved to Salem in 1847 and was chartered as a four-year liberal arts college in 1853. Roanoke is the second oldest Lutheran college in the nation and Virginia's only Lutheran college.

Roanoke offers programs leading to the Bachelor of Arts, Bachelor of Science and Bachelor of Business Administration degrees. Within these programs, 29 majors, 28 minors and 12 concentrations are offered. Roanoke is consistently named as one of the region's best in *U.S. News & World Report*'s "Annual Guide to America's Best Colleges." *Money* magazine also recognizes Roanoke as one of the top 10 colleges in the nation for giving "Dollars for Scholars," financial aid based on merit. About 53 percent of Roanoke's 1,700 students are from Virginia, with the remainder representing 39 states and 14 foreign countries.

Roanoke enjoys a long and distinguished history. Roanoke was one of the few Southern colleges to remain open during the Civil War. Roanoke also placed an emphasis on internationalization long before that idea came into vogue. In the 1870s through the 1890s, President Dreher recruited heavily among the Choctaw in Oklahoma Territory. Many of these students returned to leadership roles in the Choctaw Nation. The first Mexican student came in 1876, and the first Japanese student arrived in 1888. The first two Koreans ever to graduate from an American college or university received their degrees at Roanoke — Surh Kiu Beung in 1898 and Kimm Kiusic in 1903. Roanoke's athletic history is a source of pride for alumni as well as for the Roanoke Valley. In 1938, Coach "Pap" White's Five Smart Boys won the state championship and went on to the national finals of the Metropolitan Basketball Writers Invitational tournament at Madison Square Garden, to which the NCAA and NIT tournaments were then secondary. In 1972, Coach Charles Moir led the Roanoke basketball team to the NCAA Division II championship. In 1978, the men's lacrosse teams followed in their footsteps, winning the Division II title in lacrosse. Self-guided campus walking tour brochures are available at the Admissions Office in Roselawn on High Street.

East of the Blue Ridge

University of Virginia
Charlottesville • (804) 982-3200

"Mr. Jefferson's University" is the hub of the Charlottesville community. With its neoclassical buildings, white porticos and graceful landscapes, the university's grounds are considered among the most beautiful in America.

In 1998 *U.S. News & World Report* ranked the University of Virginia among the top 25 best universities in the country for the fifth consecutive year. Also in the recent survey UVA tied the University of California Berkeley as No. 1 in the nation among the best public universities. The university has succeeded in shaking its reputation of being a party school, notorious among *Playboy* readers and others for its annual Easter parties and infamous mud slide near Fraternity Row. This is due in part to tougher entrance criteria — the number of applications far exceeds the space available for undergraduates. About 60 percent of all in-state applicants get in, and roughly 65 percent of undergraduates are Virginians. But they are smarter, more studious and harder-working than ever.

The University of Virginia is especially noted for its schools of Law and Medicine and for the Colgate Darden Graduate School of Business Administration. The English depart-

ment also ranks among the top in the country. UVA is known across the state for its Center for Public Service, which helps localities by collecting demographic and economic data for use in developing public policy. Total enrollment is about 18,000 graduate and undergraduate students.

Sweet Briar College
Sweet Briar • (804) 381-6100

Sweet Briar College is a nationally ranked, highly selective, independent women's college of the liberal arts and sciences, offering the bachelor of arts or the bachelor of science degree. It is 12 miles north of Lynchburg in Amherst County, on 3,300 rolling acres in the foothills of the Virginia Blue Ridge. The college is known for its laboratory-based and equipment-intensive program in the sciences. Its program in international education, which includes study-abroad in France, Spain, Germany, England and Scotland, attracts students from colleges across the country. Celebrated writer John Gregory Brown forms the core of the college's distinguished creative writing program.

Sweet Briar's all-level riding program, which regularly snags national championships, boasts one of the best on-campus facilities in the country. About 600 women from more than 40 states and 15 foreign countries choose from Sweet Briar's 39 majors, including interdepartmental and self-designed majors. For women older than 25, the college offers the Turning Point Program.

Lynchburg College
Lynchburg • (804) 544-8300, (800) 426-8101

Nestled in the foothills of the Blue Ridge mountains, Lynchburg College is known as one of the most beautiful campuses in the South. An independent, coeducational institution related to the Christian Church (Disciples of Christ), Lynchburg College is one of only two colleges in Virginia featured in *Colleges that Change Lives*, a book by Loren Pope, former education editor of *The New York Times*, that features 40 selected colleges nationwide. The school serves approximately 1,450 undergraduates and 400 graduate students in professional, liberal arts and sciences, and graduate programs.

Two teaching innovations at Lynchburg College that have received wide recognition are the Lynchburg College Symposium Readings (LCSR) program and the Senior Symposium. LCSR incorporates classical reading selections across the curriculum, while in the Senior Symposium, students read selections from the classics, prepare written analyses, and attend weekly lectures to discuss major themes addressed in the readings. Small classes and one-on-one interaction with professors are among the many benefits of an education at Lynchburg College.

Master degrees are offered in business administration, education and counseling. The Corporate M.B.A. program is designed for experienced employees and managers who wish to pursue an M.B.A. with their peers at a level appropriate to their experience. The adult education program, Access, is for students older than 25 who want to earn an undergraduate degree. The Daura Gallery, named for the Catalan-American artist Pierre Daura, hosts several exhibitions featuring the work of local, regional and national artists throughout the year.

Liberty University
Lynchburg • (804) 582-2000, (800) 522-6225

Liberty University is a Christian, comprehensive, coeducational university committed to academic excellence. Liberty serves more than 10,000 students from 50 states and 31 nations at the undergraduate and graduate levels. The school was founded by Dr. Jerry Falwell, the TV evangelist who is also the founder of the Moral Majority. Liberty celebrated its 25th anniversary in the autumn of 1995.

The school adheres to strict fundamental Christian principles. For example, no modern or classical music is permitted in dormitories, and a demerit system with fines is enforced for students caught listening to anything other than Christian music on campus. Liberty is accredited by the Southern Association of Colleges and Schools and offers 75 areas of study. Liberty Baptist Theological Seminary offers master's degrees in Christian education, divinity, counseling and theology.

Liberty's facilities include a 12,000-seat football stadium and the 9,000-seat Vines Convocation Center, which are used by the Flames athletic teams, who compete on the NCAA Division I level. Prospective students or anyone interested in the school is encouraged to visit.

Randolph-Macon Woman's College
Lynchburg • (804) 947-8000

Randolph-Macon Woman's College, a four-year liberal arts college affiliated with the United Methodist Church, serves 700 women from 43 states and 27 countries. It sits on 100 acres near the Blue Ridge, with a 100-acre riding center nearby. For more than a century, women have come to the campus to prepare for a multifaceted life through rigorous academics, opportunities for cross-cultural experiences and an emphasis on community service and involvement. Individual research and the unique sense of community that draw women to the campus are enhanced further by the student-faculty ratio of 9-to-1.

Many students got to work behind the scenes on a major theatrical production in 1998. Valerie Harper, who played Rhoda on the *Mary Tyler Moore Show* and on her own sitcom *Rhoda*, came to the college to work on her one-woman play *All Under Heaven*. The production, based on one of Randolph-Macon's most celebrated graduates Pearl S. Buck, played 15 sold-out performances before Harper took the production Off-Broadway. Buck, the author of *The Good Earth*, was the first woman to win both a Pulitzer Prize and Nobel Prize.

All classes are taught by professors rather than teaching assistants, and the average class has 13 students. The college offers 24 majors as well as many relevant emphases and concentrations. The college's nationally recognized Maier Museum of Art features works by noted American artists including George Bellows, Thomas Hart Benton, Georgia O'Keeffe and James McNeill Whistler. The Across-the-Curriculum Writing Program ensures every student has strong writing skills. Also, many students choose to enhance their studies by going abroad. The Prime Time program is offered for women of nontraditional college age.

The value of asking questions and pursuing knowledge clearly is conveyed to Randolph-Macon students, many of whom further their studies. The college ranks in the top 20 percent of private, four-year institutions nationwide in numbers of graduates going on to earn doctorates. The staff of the Career Development Center provides a one-on-one, four-year career preparation program, assisting students with graduate school and career decisions.

Ferrum College
Ferrum · (540) 365-2121, (800) 868-9797

Ferrum College's 700-acre campus is in the foothills of western Virginia's splendid Blue Ridge Mountains. The region's natural resources enhance the college's curriculum, which combines rigorous academics, a strong experiential learning component and a practical, "real life" emphasis. It's not unusual to find Ferrum students meeting class requirements by rappelling off rocky cliffs in Fairystone State Park, taking and analyzing water samples from nearby Smith Mountain Lake, leading schoolchildren on nature field trips or spending a weekend backpacking through George Washington and Jefferson National Forests.

A private, coeducational, liberal arts United Methodist Church institution founded in 1913, Ferrum offers bachelor degrees in 34 majors as well as a distinctive teacher education program to its 1,100 students. Majors range from business administration to environmental science, from dramatic and theatre arts to international studies, from criminal justice to recreation and leisure.

Ferrum College also makes valuable contributions to the economic, cultural and community life in and around Franklin County. The College houses the Blue Ridge Institute and Museum, which is Virginia's official Center for Blue Ridge Folklore (see our Arts chapter); presents the popular Blue Ridge Dinner Theatre each summer (see our Arts chapter); offers leadership training and team building opportunities to community groups through its high and low ropes courses; and presents a range of art exhibits, concerts, theatrical performances, lectures and sporting events, nearly all of which are free and open to the public.

The college's impact in the community is perhaps communicated most strongly through the service activities undertaken by Ferrum students. Through the Bonner Scholars program, dozens of Ferrum students provide nearly 600 hours of volunteer service to the community each week, while other students and student groups also volunteer their time and talents to a range of service projects and agencies. Students in Ferrum's teacher education program also connect with the community as teacher aides and student teachers, spending thousands of hours annually in local classrooms.

New River Valley

Virginia Tech
Blacksburg · (540) 231-6000

Virginia's largest and most diverse university, Virginia Tech has a pervasive presence in western Virginia as the largest employer in southwest Virginia. The school employs 5,800 full-time employees and has an annual payroll of $250 million. Virginia Tech enrolls nearly 25,000 undergraduate and graduate students and has 73 undergraduate and 120 graduate degree programs. Virginia Tech consists of eight colleges: Agriculture and Life Sciences, Architecture and Urban Studies, Arts and Sciences, Business, Engineering, Human Resources and Education, Veterinary Medicine and Forestry. All 50 states and nearly 100 foreign countries are represented in the student body.

Tech's 3,000-acre main campus is in a town of 32,000 residents, in the scenic Blue Ridge Mountains. As you would expect, many students can't bear to leave Blacksburg after graduation, and legions of them stay to make it a top-notch, stimulating university town. Additional facilities include a 120-room conference center, an 800-acre research farm, the Equine Center, graduate centers in Roanoke, Hampton Roads and the Washington, D.C., metro area and 12 statewide agricultural experiment stations. The Hotel Roanoke Conference Center, 36 miles away, is also partially owned by Virginia Tech.

U.S. News & World Report has ranked Virginia Tech in its top 20 with National Merit Scholars and top 50 nationally in annually sponsored research. Its Corporate Research Center is home to more than 30 companies employing about 600 people. As a land-grant university with a statewide mission, Tech is responsible for Virginia's Cooperative Extension Service, which is carried to 107 Virginia communities. Tech is also a leader among universities in the United States in the use of communications technology. The entire campus is connected with the town of Blacksburg and the world through the unique Blacksburg Electronic Village. The school has gained quite a bit of fame through this bold use of the electronic superhighway. It also is famous for its traditional Cadet Corps.

Tech is a member of the Big East Football Conference and a member of the Atlantic 10 Conference for other sports. It has a 51,000-seat stadium, offering some of the most popular spectator sports in the Blue Ridge. Be prepared for hour-long traffic jams when the Hokies play football at home.

Radford University
Radford • (540) 831-5000

The New River Valley's other major state-supported educational institution, Radford University enrolls more than 8,000 students in this residential community of 14,000. Radford is 36 miles southwest of Roanoke in the Blue Ridge Mountains. In addition to the Graduate College, Radford has five colleges offering bachelor degrees: Arts and Sciences, Business and Economics, Education and Human Development, Waldron Health and Human Services, and Visual and Performing Arts. Special pre-professional programs are offered in law, pharmacy, physical therapy, medicine, veterinary medicine, sports medicine and ROTC. Unique to Radford is its Business Assistance Center. It provides a wide range of services for small- and medium-size businesses in the area and offers opportunities for students to get real life experience doing research and counseling.

As with Virginia Tech, many graduates elect to live and work in this beautiful college town beside the scenic New River. Radford belongs to the Big South Conference and NCAA Division I and offers 20 varsity sports.

Southwest Virginia

Emory & Henry College
Emory • (540) 944-4121

This historic (founded in 1836), private, liberal arts college enrolling 900 students has been cited by *Money* magazine as one of the 100 Best Educational Buys in the nation. *U.S. News & World Report* calls Emory & Henry one of the top 5 regional liberal arts colleges in the South.

Emory & Henry offers 37 majors and special programs, including Appalachian Studies, international studies, pre-med and pre-law. It also ranks with the top 1 percent of U.S. colleges and universities in alumni giving. Students receive the full benefit of a high-quality faculty and a low student-faculty ratio of 14 to 1. It is ideal if you are interested in spectacular mountain views and easy access to the recreational opportunities they afford, including mountain climbing, hiking and bicycling. The college is close to the historic town of Abingdon. As a member of the Old Dominion Athletic Conference, the college boasts six varsity sports for men and women in the NCAA Division III.

Preparatory Schools

Shenandoah Valley

Foxcroft School
Foxcroft Rd., Middleburg • (540) 687-5555

This prestigious boarding and day school for girls in grades 9 through 12 was founded in 1914 by Charlotte Noland, who served as the school's headmistress until she retired in 1955. Miss Charlotte valued such old-fashioned virtues as determination, courage and character, but she wasn't above having a bit of fun. She said she wanted to establish a school that girls "would hate to leave because they loved it." Alumnae will attest to her success.

The school is set among 500 idyllic acres of orchards, fields and streams near Middleburg. Local foxhunts meet frequently at the school, and many of the students participate in the hunt. The school has a definite equestrian tone — 40 percent of the girls are involved in its excellent riding program, using one of the school's 35 horses or their own.

Twenty-five day students and 130 boarders represent 15 countries and 23 states; 30 percent of the students are international. The school is small, but the program is extensive. More than 70 courses, including advanced placement and opportunities for independent study, are available. Classes average 10 students to one teacher.

Notre Dame Academy
35321 Notre Dame Ln., Middleburg
• (540) 687-5581

A 200-acre campus surrounds this coed college preparatory school for day students in grades 9 through 12. The school, founded in 1965, has a strong affiliation with the Roman Catholic Church. Of the 160 students, 60 percent are Catholic, and the faculty of 20 includes eight Sisters of Notre Dame. A dress code calls for skirts, khaki pants and polo or button-down shirts.

Notre Dame offers advanced-placement courses in nine test areas, accelerated programs, independent study and college credit through courses at local colleges. With 18 interscholastic sports available, intramural athletics are also an important part of a student's life here. Notre Dame had one of the first high school varsity Junior Olympic mountain biking teams in the United States, and both its boys' and girls' basketball teams were state ranked.

The school boasts a 100 percent college acceptance rate. The 24 graduates in the class of 1997 were accepted at 71 different colleges, including the Georgetown University, James Madison University, University of Virginia, Old Dominion University, Villanova University and Providence College. The campus is off U.S. 50, west of Middleburg.

Randolph-Macon Academy
201 W. Third St., Front Royal
• (540) 636-5200, (800) 272-1172

This coed boarding school, affiliated with the United Methodist Church, is surrounded by a scenic 135-acre campus in the small town of Front Royal. The Upper School is an accredited prep school in grades 9 through 12, while the Middle School emphasizes a classical education in grades 6 through 8. The school also offers college credits for gifted seniors.

Though the school's structure is nonmilitary, RMA is the only coed boarding school in the country with an Air Force Junior ROTC program. The FAA-certified flight program trains students from ground school to their first solo flight, with the option to become licensed pilots.

RMA's small class size — 10 students to one teacher in the Middle School and 15 to one in the Upper School — creates a good learning atmosphere, and faculty members emphasize the fundamentals and good study habits. In 1997, 96 percent of its graduates went on to college, while two of its graduates signed up for military service and two others volunteered for missionary work.

The campus has an outdoor track, five tennis courts and fields for baseball, field hockey, football, lacrosse and soccer. Other sports facilities include a gymnasium and Nautilus room and indoor swimming pool. Renovations to the main building allowed for Internet and telephone access in each student's room. Total enrollment is about 425 students from 31 states and 27 countries.

INSIDERS' TIP

The cost for a Blue Ridge college education differs widely. Some admissions offices quote a combined cost for tuition and room and board, while others list them separately. When comparing costs, be sure to ask which cost-quoting formula they use.

Wakefield Country Day School
U.S. Hwy. 522, Washington
- **(540) 635-8555**

The late William E. Lynn and his wife, Pamela, were so concerned about the erosion of education standards in public schools that in 1972 they founded Wakefield. Initially, their goal was to provide a good, classical education for their own six children. Since then, scores of students from preschool through the 12th grade have benefited from the school's enriched curriculum. The school enrolls 165 day students from seven surrounding counties and a handful of international students who board at the school.

Studies include two required years of an ancient language as well as two required years of French or Spanish. The school has advanced-placement courses in English, science, math, foreign languages, history and geopolitics. One hundred percent of the graduates have been accepted into their chosen colleges. The school is 10 miles south of Front Royal.

Stuart Hall
235 W. Frederick St., Staunton
- **(540) 885-0356**

The oldest Episcopal girls' boarding school in Virginia, Stuart Hall was founded in 1844 as Virginia Female Institute. It was renamed in 1907 in honor of headmistress Mrs. Flora Cooke Stuart, the widow of Gen. J.E.B. Stuart.

The 8-acre campus has many ties to Civil War history. During the 1860s, Gen. Robert E. Lee served as the president of the school's board of visitors. When the nearby Virginia School for the Deaf and the Blind was turned into a Confederate hospital, Stuart Hall temporarily closed to make room for the VSDB students.

Today, the focal point of the campus is Old Main, a registered historic landmark that dates back to 1846 and houses offices, a $1.1 million library, art studios and an auditorium. Stuart Hall has a rigorous college-preparatory program. By their senior year, students who have completed their high school curriculum may enroll in one or more courses at Mary Baldwin College. The college is just a few blocks down the street. The school also stresses athletic as well as academic training with varsity competition in field hockey, bas-

ketball, tennis, soccer, softball, volleyball and riding.

The faculty consists of 24 full-time members, including 13 with advanced degrees. Classes average 8 to 15 students with a 7 to 1 student-teacher ratio.

The school boards girls in grades 9 through 12 and recently added day classes in grades 6 through 12. Boys are accepted as day students in grades 6 through 8. The total enrollment is 111. The Upper School includes 48 boarding students and 29 day students from 10 states and five countries.

Roanoke Valley

North Cross School
4254 Colonial Ave. S.W., Roanoke
- **(540) 989-6641**

North Cross is a coeducational, college preparatory day school enrolling 540 students from pre-kindergarten through 12th grade. Its goal since its beginning in 1960 has been to prepare students "not just for college or a vocation, but for a full, rewarding life." The school offers a rigorous academic program with many offerings in the fine arts, outdoor education, community service and athletics.

The school's 77-acre campus includes three academic buildings, including an art gallery, theater, library and two computer labs. The Carter Athletic Center offers programs for the whole family, including an outstanding swim program, and the middle school offers a lateral climbing wall. The school teaches respect and responsibility through its Honor Code.

Roanoke Catholic School
621 N. Jefferson St., Roanoke
- **(540) 982-3735**

Roanoke Catholic, founded in 1889, is a coeducational college preparatory school enrolling 489 students ages preschool to grade 12. The school's stated mission is "to develop in students those characteristics and attitudes that will help them achieve full potential in all aspects of their lives." The school focuses on educating the whole child physically, intellectually, emotionally and spiritually.

The school has a strong academic program in a Christian atmosphere. The inclusion of Christian morals and values is an integral part of the entire curriculum. Athletics is also important, with the Athletic Association sponsoring and funding the Upper School sports program and sandlot soccer and basketball teams for the Lower School.

East of the Blue Ridge

Woodberry Forest
Woodberry Forest • (540) 672-3900

This Madison County boarding prep school for boys in grades 9 through 12 sits on 1,000 acres about 30 miles north of Charlottesville and 70 miles south of Washington, D.C. Independent and nondenominational, the school prepares students for successful performance at some of the best colleges and universities in the country.

Woodberry Forest offers a comprehensive advanced-placement program and a curriculum that includes rigorous requirements in English, math, foreign language, history, science, art, music and religion. About 365 boys from 26 states and 12 foreign countries attend the school, with about half coming from Virginia and North Carolina. The school was founded in 1889 by Robert S. Walker, a captain in the Confederate army who wanted a school to educate his six sons. Thomas Jefferson drew the floor plan for the headmaster's residence for his friend, William Madison, brother of James Madison.

The average class is 10 students. The 59 professors — more than two-thirds hold master's degrees and three have doctorates — also live on campus. The campus is beautiful, as one would expect of a school with a $98 million endowment. In 1997, a humanities center was dedicated, featuring a computer network that connects every dorm room, classroom and office on the campus. Fine recreational facilities include an Olympic-size pool and a nine-hole golf course. The school has many teams in every sport, so each student has a chance to compete against other boys of similar athletic ability. One student in three receives tuition assistance.

The Blue Ridge School
Va. Rt. 627 off Va. Rt. 810, Dyke
• (804) 985-2811

The Blue Ridge School maintains an exceptional track record for boys whose grades do not reflect their potential. The school's success formula is based on a solid routine of class work, homework and athletics — all done in a caring, supportive environment. Individual attention and encouragement are the cornerstone of the faculty's philosophy. But boys must keep up their end: hard work in and outside the classroom is expected of them.

About 170 boys attend this scenic school, situated on 1,000 beautiful acres just outside Charlottesville. All students board here, and the proximity to Charlottesville allows the school to take advantage of the town's offerings. Daytrips, for example to movies or to University of Virginia athletic events, are scheduled regularly.

The school's Outdoor Program makes use of the spectacular mountain setting with activities that include canoeing, camping and ropes courses. Athletics range from soccer and football to lacrosse and tennis. The arts programs includes music, drama and studio art as well as a fine arts series that brings a variety of entertainment to the school.

Many boys who enter this preparatory school are not sure they will be able to attend college because of poor past performance in school. But the school boasts a 100 percent college acceptance rate. Graduates in 1996 were accepted at numerous colleges and universities, including Hampden-Sydney, Virginia Tech, James Madison University and Mary Washington College.

The Miller School of Albemarle
Miller School Rd., off U.S. Hwy. 250, Charlottesville • (804) 823-4805

The Miller School is an Albemarle County landmark in education and natural beauty. This college preparatory school sits on 1,600 beautiful acres 14 miles from Charlottesville. The campus covers farmland, orchards, forests, a pond and a 12-acre lake for swimming, fishing and canoeing.

The school's Victorian-style buildings, each a National Historic Landmark, are spectacular with red brick, slate roofs and a gorgeous clock tower. The school's unique architecture caught the eye of Hollywood film scouts, who used the campus as a setting for *Toy Soldiers* starring Louis Gossett Jr.

Opened in 1878, the Miller School combined a state-of-the-art industrial complex and vocational education with a classical academic program, producing graduates who went on to the Ivy League and others who became the artisans for the region and state.

Once known as a prestigious military academy for boys, Miller School began accepting girls in 1992. In 1995, the school returned to its historical roots and became an exploring member of the Coalition of Essential Schools, a group that emphasizes the mastery of information and skills.

The Miller School is coeducational with an enrollment of 120, 80 percent of whom are boarding students in grades 5 through 12. Miller's program is composed of a quality academic college preparatory course of study, required afternoon activities featuring seven major sports and 18 teams, and a weekly service requirement. Service work is done in a three-hour block each week in either Civil Air Patrol, (the school is still an official auxiliary of the U.S. Air Force), community service or environmental studies.

Another innovation at Miller is its January term. The school sets aside this month to allow students to work on specialized projects and course work. Some courses are designed to strengthen student weaknesses, while others are enrichment options that vary from woodworking to Civil War history.

St. Anne's-Belfield School
2132 Ivy Rd., Charlottesville
• (804) 296-5106

Formed in 1970 by the merger of St. Anne's School, a girls' boarding school founded in 1910, with the Belfield School, a coed elementary school established in 1955, St. Anne's-Belfield is in its third decade of educating youngsters. The accredited school is near the University of Virginia on two campuses totaling more than 60 acres.

The school offers a day program for preschool through grade 12, and a five-day boarding program for grades 7 through 12. The school's philosophy stresses personal and educational growth.

The school has a student body of about 800 and limits the boarding program to 40 students in order to maintain a family-like atmosphere. A full range of advanced-placement and honors courses are offered for upper-level students, while younger children study basic subjects as well as French, art, drama, computers and physical education.

A 32,000-foot convocation and athletic center with tennis courts and a new baseball field was unveiled in 1997. St. Anne's has long boasted a strong all-around athletic program. The school has fielded one of the top lacrosse teams in the region for several years, plus it also offers competition in a variety of sports, including squash, golf and football.

Graduates advance to enroll in some of the nation's finest universities every year. Financial aid is available to families who demonstrate need. About 20 percent of the students receive financial assistance.

Index of Advertisers

Index

X

Y

Z

Going Somewhere?

Insiders' Publishing presents these current and upcoming titles to popular destinations all over the country — and we're planning on adding many more. To order a title, go to your local bookstore or call (800) 582-2665 and we'll direct you to one.

Adirondacks

Atlanta, GA

Baltimore, MD

Bend, OR

Bermuda

Boca Raton and the Palm Beaches, FL

Boise, ID

Boulder, CO, and
Rocky Mountain National Park

Bradenton/Sarasota, FL

Branson, MO, and the
Ozark Mountains

California's Wine Country

Cape Cod, Nantucket and
Martha's Vineyard, MA

Charleston, SC

Cincinnati, OH

Civil War Sites in the Eastern Theater

Civil War Sites in the Southern Theater

Colorado's Mountains

Denver, CO

Florida Keys and Key West

Florida's Great Northwest

Golf in the Carolinas

Indianapolis, IN

The Lake Superior Region

Las Vegas, NV

Lexington, KY

Louisville, KY

Madison, WI

Maine's Mid-Coast

Maine's Southern Coast

Michigan's Traverse Bay Region

Minneapolis/St. Paul, MN

Mississippi

Monterey Peninsula

Myrtle Beach, SC

Nashville, TN

New Hampshire

New Orleans, LA

North Carolina's Central Coast
and New Bern

North Carolina's Mountains

Outer Banks of North Carolina

Phoenix, AZ

The Pocono Mountains

Relocation

Richmond, VA

Salt Lake City, UT

San Diego, CA

Santa Barbara, CA

Santa Fe, NM

Savannah, GA

Southwestern Utah

Tampa/St. Petersburg, FL

Texas Coastal Bend

Tucson, AZ

Virginia's Blue Ridge

Virginia's Chesapeake Bay

Washington, D.C.

Wichita, KS

Williamsburg, VA

Wilmington, NC

Yellowstone

THE INSIDERS'® GUIDE

Insiders' Publishing • P.O. Box 1718 • Helena, MT 59624
Phone (406) 443-3021 • Fax (406) 443-3191 • www.insiders.com